PROCEEDINGS

OF THE

GENERAL ASSEMBLIES

OLD AND NEW SCHOOL

PRESBYTERIAN CHURCHES,

CONVENED IN ST. LOUIS, MAY 17, 1866.

ST. LOUIS:
MISSOURI DEMOCRAT BOOK AND JOB PRINTING HOUSE,
Corner Fourth and Pine streets,
1866.

OF THE

GENERAL ASSEMBLIES

OLD AND NEW SCHOOL

PRESBYTERIAN CHURCHES,

CONVENED IN ST. LOUIS, MAY 17, 1866.

ST. LOUIS:
MISSOURI DEMOCRAT BOOK AND JOB PRINTING HOUSE,
Corner Fourth and Pine streets,
1866.

THE CHURCH CONVENTIONS.

PRESBYTERIAN NATIONAL ASSEMBLIES.

THE OPENING EXERCISES.

GENERAL ASSEMBLY OF THE PRESBYTERIAN CHURCH (OLD SCHOOL) OF THE UNITED STATES.

SERMON BY REV. DR. LOWRY.

AN ABLE DISCOURSE IN BEHALF OF THE PURITY OF THE CHURCH: ELECTION OF OFFICERS—REMARKS OF THE MODERATOR.

FIRST DAY—THURSDAY, MAY 17, 1866.

The General Assembly of the Old School Presbyterian Church met at eleven o'clock yesterday in the Church of Rev. Dr. Niccolls, corner of Fifth and Walnut streets. There was a full attendance of delegates and others. After the introductory devotional services, Rev. Dr. Lowry, the Moderator, delivered the opening sermon as follows:

SERMON BY DR. LOWRY.

ACTS I. 8.—"But ye shall receive power, after that the Holy Ghost is come upon you; and ye shall be witnesses unto me, both in Jerusalem, and in all Judea, and in Samaria, and unto the uttermost part of the earth."

We are accustomed to regard the first age of the church as the best. The piety and the evangelical labors of the Apostles and first Christians, are considered an example to the followers of Christ in all subsequent ages; but in so far as the essential things—the things essential to the piety and the usefulness of the Church—are concerned, its members now and its members in the days of the Apostles stand on the same footing. Their circumstances and ours differ in some respects, but both they and we have life and ever live by faith in Jesus Christ; are moved by the same spirit; are called to the same work, and look for the same reward. If, then, the piety and the works of modern Christians are not Apostolic, what shall we say? How shall we account for our falling so far short of their example? And how shall we be enabled to reach their noble standard?

The text will help us to answer such questioning thoughts as these, while it sets before us the power and the work of the followers of Christ in all ages to the end of time.

This verse forms a part of our Lord's words to his disciples just before his ascension. He had corrected their error in looking for an earthly, Jewish kingdom, and he declared to them that they were to receive a divine power and to do a divine work; and then, "when he had spoken these things"—these very words of the text—"while they beheld he was taken up; and a cloud received him out of their sight." They stood, "gazing up into Heaven," trying to look through the cloud to see their friend and Savior as he passed above the skies. And for them his words would ever have the deepest personal interest. But these words have also a general bearing, applicable to all the disciples of Christ. They were spoken at the end of one dispensation and the beginning of another. The Hebrew times were now to cease; the world-wide system of the Gospel was now to be set up. These words declared the speedy manifestation of the Holy Ghost, and this manifestation was to be the power of the disciples, even "the power of the Holy Ghost coming upon them," and then should they go forth to their great work for life and to enter upon their high destiny, as witnesses unto Christ, "both in Jerusalem, and in all Judea and in Samaria and unto the uttermost parts of the earth." The circumstances under which these words were spoken, therefore, their deep import, and their vast range, commend them to our earnest study. I trust, my brethren, we shall find them to be words to quicken and comfort us in our Christian course, and words appropriate to our meeting at present as ministers, elders and members of the Church of Christ, and particularly as office-bearers in the House of God convened in this General Assembly,

I. The first part of the text directs our attention to God, the Holy Ghost, and the power which He would give to the disciples. On this we shall dwell but briefly. No formal statement of the faith of the Church concerning the Holy Ghost need here be made. I need but remind you of His character as God, equal with the Father and the Son, and of His office in the work of salvation—that of applying unto men the benefits of redemption. He is the person of the Trinity through whose agency God puts forth His gracious power on the hearts of men; we are not authorized to expect any saving blessing from God except through His intervention; that the influences of the Spirit of all Grace were obtained for us by and through Jesus Christ; that the Spirit takes of the things of Christ, and shows them unto us; that in all His work the Spirst glorifies Christ, should increase our sense of obligation to our blessed Savior, but shall not diminish our sense of our indebtedness to the Holy Spirit.

It is the power of the Holy Ghost as given to the disciples for a particular purpose—that of their being witnesses unto Christ, that must here chiefly engage our attention. Three things may be specified as included in the exercise of this power and imparted to the disciples. The first is the power of working miracles and of speaking with unknown tongues. The second is the gracious power of the Spirit in their own souls. And the third is the agency of the Spirit in the conversion of the souls of men in connection withe the preaching of the Gospel. By the first, the disciples were accredited divinely attended in their work. By the second, they were qualified for it. And by the third, they were made successful in it. We shall here pass these points over, and proceed to the second part of the text—which sets before us the work to be done by the disciples; they were to be witnesses unto Christ, at home and abroad.

II. A witness is one who is able to speak from personal knowledge, and not from hearsay; and he is one who must speak the truth with fidelity. If either personal knowledge or truth is wanting, his testimony would have no value. Keeping these two things in view, we remark that the disciples must bear witness: 1. To the person and character of Christ. 2. To his doctrines, or the truth revealed by him. And 3. To his truth as the means employed by the Holy Spirit in the conversion of the world, or to his truth as the gospel.

I When the Jews asked our Savior the question, Who art thou? they asked a question of the greatest moment to themselves and to all men. To know the Lord Jesus as the Son of God and the Son of Man—as God over all blessed forever, and as a man having a fellow feeling with our infirmities; this is wonderful knowledge! This is to know the only person in the universe so consituted; this is to know the only person who can stand between a holy God and a race of sinners, and act as a mediator between them; the only one whose exalted dignity, and yet whose place under the law render it possible for him to be the surety of his people in the covenant of grace, to satisfy all the claims of justice in their account by his own obedience, sufferings and death on the cross.

The first disciples were literally eye-witnesses of the life and character of Christ. Some of them were chosen to be Apostles for the distinctive reason, that they had seen the Lord Jesus; and as only those who had actually seen him could be apostles, they can have no successors in that high office. But all the disciples, then and ever since, could be witnesses unto Christ in the sense of their experimental knowledge of his grace. They can speak from their heartfelt conviction of their own sinful, guilty, helpless and perishing situation, until Christ was revealed unto them by the Holy Spirit as the Lamb of God that taketh away the sin of the world, and they were enabled to receive him in his person and his offices as their Redeemer. On this point, we shall dwell no longer here—but proceed to remark concerning the disciples—2. That they are witnesses.

II. They are unto the truth as revealed by Christ. All that he trught and left on record in the Scriptures they receive as of the highest authority, as binding on the conscience, and to be always maintained by them. There are things hard to be understood in the Bible, and there are things of deep mystery far exceeding the limits of human reason, which the disciples do not profess to comprehend; yet to the truth of these things they can bear testimony, because contained in a book divinely attested, because profound mysteries to our feeble intellect may all be plain and clear to the infinite mind of God, and because these deep truths find their echo in their inmost consciences oftentimes. They can bear witness to the truth of the whole inspired record, even if they do not understand some parts of it, just as many a witness in a court of justice gives his testimony to facts of which he is sure, though he may not understand their bearing on the subject, nor see how they are to affect the cause under trial.

Besides giving their testimony as individuals, each in his place and lot, according to his gifts and grace, the disciples of Christ must bear witness unto his truth when associated together as members of the Church. The Old Testament preserves the truth concerning the one living and true God in the midst of a world given to idolatry, The New Testament Church has this also as one of its main designs; it is to be the pillar and ground of the truth; it is to be a witness for all the truth that God has revealed, no matter how it may be opposed or perverted. The creeds and confessions of the Church have the maintaining and preserving of the truth as one of their main purposes.

Subscription and assent to the doctrinal standards of our Church is one way for us, my brethren, of upholding the truth. The venerable Confession of Faith in which we glory is chiefly prized by us for its clear and admirable statement of the truth as contained in Holy Scripture. God will honor the Church that puts honour on its truth. I doubt not that one of the two great reasons of the wonderful prosperity of our Church in the last thirty years is to be found in the fact, that as a Church we were faithful to God's truth; and in whatever is done, or not done, looking in the direction of organic union with other bodies of Christians, the truth and our profession of it must be held sacred by us, and not be in the least degree compromised, if we would continue to enjoy the blessing of the God of Truth.

Our testimony should have reference to the clearness with which divine truths are revealed rather than to any difference that may exist in the importance of these truths. It requires an architect to tell what is essential to a grand edifice and what is not essential; so we are poor judges of the relative importance of the truths of revelation. We shall find it to be a safe and good rule, while we maintain all the truths of the Bible, to give to each that place which it seems to occupy on the sacred page. It is not enough to dwell on a few leading truths. The Bible is our text book, and the world our congregation; to all men, of every nation, class, and condition, to all subjects that have a right or a wrong side in a religious or moral aspect, the testimony of the disciples must have due reverence. We can admit no theory of the province of the pulpit, or of the sphere of a Christian man's duty, which would deprive this testimony of its power as against what is morally wrong. If what is wrong seeks to entrench itself behind public legislation, as in the case of Sabbath mails or lotteries, or behind party political action, as in the case of the oppression of a weaker race, or behind popular movements ending in a riot or rebellion against the powers that be, as in the case of our late conflict, the wrong must not be let alone. The witnessing of the Church should be on the side of truth in these and all other cases, and equally against what is wrong. We have reason to fear that the withholding of this testimony, in too many instances, results in the profaning of God's holy name and day, the denial of justice to the colored races of this country—the Indian, the negro, and of late the Chinese—and the overthrow of those ideas of reverence for law and subjection to authority, which are essential to the welfare both of the Church and the State, especially on one theory of public affairs. For with us the law is maintained more by the power of conscience than by standing military force, and to the right exercise of conscience nothing is more needful than Christian witnessing unto the truth, or at any rate, nothing but the truth itself. Let us dwell on this point a few moments longer:

We plead, then, for no political action by the Church, or by her courts, or her ministers; we plead for no improper meddling with the things of Cæsar by the subjects of Christ's kingdom—for no departure from the themes of the Bible, for no violation of the proprieties of the house of God, for no forsaking of the concerns of eternity. Our Church courts are very properly debarred by our standards—ch. xxxi—from taking any part in the administration of the affairs of the State, except as requested; and this is so ordered for the obvious reason that in this country the Church and the State are not united, and Church courts have here no civil duties such as devolve on the spiritual peers of the British House of Lords and such as ambitious prelates in Scotland would gladly have taken upon them in the age when our confession of faith was reconstructed from the articles of faith which came down from the days of the Apostles. Thankful, indeed, are we for the separation of the Church of this land from the State thereof; but let us guard against the great mistake of thinking that the Church has, therefore, no duty to perform of giving her testimony against iniquity because it may be prevalent in high places.

We are persuaded that in our country our greatest danger is not that of too much interference with public affairs, in the way of testifying against what is wrong, by the church and by Christian people. It is only too easy to let what is wrong alone. It accords too readily with our readiness to avoid the cross; and so the voice of our testimonies is kept back, or lowered down to an insensible whisper. Our greatest danger in this land consists in our not holding forth those revealed truths which best regulate both Governors and people, which assert the supreme authority of God, the sacredness of an oath, the duty of doing that which is just and equal to all men, the need of consideration for their less favored fellow men by the rich, and of contentment and patience on the part of the poor, and, indeed, of both rich and poor, and the solemn interests of the judgment to come and the retributions of eternity; and all these inspired teachings we are to testify not merely in the abstract, but in their application to all such moral wrongs as from time to time seek public acknowledgment. Our testimony should certainly be impersonal—never singling out particular persons in a congregation for public rebuke, and it should also be kept free as far as possible from connection with any political party movements, so that all men should see that it is prompted by fidelity to the truth as contained in the Holy Scriptures. The witnesses unto Christ should exercise their best judgment as to the time and manner of giving their testimony against what is evil. It may even be necessary for them to be silent sometimes, as our blessed Lord was before his unjust judges, but like him his humble disciples will never be unfaithful to their testimony; and when called to do so by Providence, they will declare the whole counsel of God. This must be done in the spirit of Christ, which was eminently loving and meek. He severely censured the hypocrisy of the Scribes and Pharisees, speaking as he only could by authority as the Omniscient Judge, but yet it was in deep compassion even to them. Towards his professed followers, when in error or even in grave faults, he was always considerate and forbearing—not sparing rebuke, yet not putting the worst construction on their misconduct, but always the best and most charitable; and in this we should follow his example.

We must not pass from this part of the subject without considering that there are times when the testimony of the disciples, touching matters of public interest and yet having a religious side, becomes specially important—such times particularly of perplexity, distress and shaking among men as we have lately seen in this country—such as, I fear, may still be seen in two many parts of the land. In giving our testimony through these dreadful years to the duty of rendering obedience to the powers that be—the powers that were over us, whatever political opinions we may entertain of their character—we fulfill a sacred duty. A right understanding of this duty would prevent all civil war in Christian countries. Indeed we cannot but deeply feel that if the people of God in this land had but understood the full meaning of this duty—which has respect to the powers that be in actual existence, whatever may be the theory of their existence, no more countenance would have been given to any efforts to overthrow the Government, so long in the exercise of authority in all parts of the country, than would be given by our missionaries to a rebellion against the Emperor of China or the King of Siam.

We view this whole matter, now, and in this audience, in the light of testimony against what is wrong, and in presenting these views, we but follow the highest examples. We only take such lawful action as was taken by the noble men who settled our church standards, such men as John Witherspoon, Samuel Davies, and many others; and what is far more, we but follow the example of our blessed Lord and the Apostles. How often do our Savior's instructions refer directly to public matters as viewed in their religious or moral aspects, or when in the face of the rulers of the Jews he vindicated the law of marriage, placed the law of divorces on its true ground, asserted the just liberty of his Disciples concerning works of necessity on the Sabbath, taught the duty of obedience even to an oppressive Government by the payment of taxes—all of which were not merely matters of religion, but were also matters of party conflicts or of public law. And so of the Apostles—take the Apostle Paul's noble declaration, that he would know nothing among the Corinthians but Christ and him crucified, and then take up his two Epistles to the Church of Corinth, make out a table of their topics, and you will see how many matters of public interest are discussed by his eloquent pen, how many sided were his lessons, how he referred to matters that had secular bearings, that were subjects of partisan discussion, and even to such as were connected with civil jurisdiction. In all, his great and sole object was to glorify Christ; and, my brethren, let this be our sole aim whenever we feel called to teach or to speak of matters that are connected with the Government, or with party movements, or with secular interests, when, as witnesses unto Christ, we may hope that our testimony will accomplish its proper end and purpose.

3. In still another respect were the disciples to be witnesses unto Christ—in their making his gospel known unto all men. The missionary aspect of their testimony is the one chiefly presented to us in the text. The same view is presented in Luke, (xxiv, 47 | 48,) and it is clearly expressed in the last clause of the verse before us, so that we may regard this verse as a restatement of the duty of going into all the world to preach the gospel to every creature, but doing this with the personal knowledge and fidelity of witnesses. Hence, in the passage just cited in the gospel of Luke, our Lord said to his disciples, "And ye are witnesses of these things;" that is, of the character of Christ, and of repentance for remission of sins to be preached in his name among all nations, beginning at Jerusalem. Their testimony was to be evangelistic. Evidently the first disciples understood the matter just in this sense as soon as their minds were enlightened by the Holy Spirit. And they went forth making known this blessed testimony—the message of love and mercy to lost men.

It was indeed a joyful testimony. Its primary meaning was undoubtedly glad tidings to all people. It was not meant to be chiefly a testimony a against a sinful world. The verse in the Gospel of Matthew, (chap. 24, 14,) which speaks of the gospel being preached "for a witness" to the nations, does not mean a witness against them any more than the same word "witness" in Isaiah (55-4,) when applied to our blessed Lord, is to be understood as a title of severity: on the contrary, it is a title given to our Lord in one of the richest exhibitions of the gospel that is to be found in the writings of the evangelical prophet.

If the gospel is rejected by men, it does indeed become a witness against them, greatly increasing their guilt and misery; but we must keep always in view its primary and chief design as the expression of the infinite love and mercy of God to our lost world. Here is pardon for the guilty; here is peace with God; here is everlasting life; here is all that is needed for the complete salvation of every lost sinner through the atoning death and finished righteousness of Jesus Christ. Here are all these blessings offered to sinful man in every land to the end of the world, and offered on the simplest terms possible—without money and without price. This is the good news which the disciples were to testify unto every creature, speaking from their own personal experience of this precious gospel, and with all fidelity as witnesses to its unspeakable importance.

And so the diciples went forth. They went forth, no doubt, in faith and hope, expecting great results to follow their testimony. They were at first but a mere handful, but a little flock, and their course in their course in the world was to be marked by tribulation and persecution. Our Lord taught them to expect this, but he also taught them to expect a time of triumph for the gospel. Its principles would prevail. Under their preaching, made efficient to salvation by the power of the Holy Ghost, darkness would give way, the idols be overthrown, the Kingdom of Christ be established, and the world for a thousand years be as the garden of the Lord. The disciples went forth to a sacred duty, not as a task, not as sent to condemn their fellow man, but cheered by the hope of the greatest success. They might not live to see it, but it would surely come, and faithful labors would speed its coming.

I know that some good men do not accept these views—do not expect this result. They even venture to teach that it is but an amiable delusion to expect the conversion of the world by the preaching of the gospel: that it was never intended to accomplish any such purpose, but that the Church is always to be small and imperfect until the personal coming of our blessed Lord; and then, but not till then, we shall see the world converted. The whole New Testament record has been appealed to in order to prove that the preaching of the gospel in the present dispensation, as they term it, will not convert the world.

There are weighty, and it seems to me conclusive, objections and arguments against this theory, but they cannot be fully considered in a short sermon. It is a theory based, as I must think, on erroneous interpretations of the Scriptures, in certain respects. These must here be passed over. It is a theory, moreover, which does not consist with other parts of Scripture which we may briefly notice, and which teach a very different doctrine.

Such is the declaration of God's unspeakable love to the world. (John 3, 16—for I will confine my citations to the New Testament.)

This declaration is so comprehensive that we cannot see how the embracing of Christ by a small fraction of the human family can at all correspond with its fullness and freeness. Such also is our Lord's last commandment (Matt. 28, 19-20). We cannot believe that this commandment contemplated preaching the gospel as a witness against men; it was to be good news, the best news to every lost sinner that he can ever hear; nor can we believe that our blessed Lord, clothed as he is with all power in heaven and in earth, would go forth everywhere with his disciples who obey this commandment only to see their labors ending all in vain, and himself almost universally rejected. All this seems to us entirely inconsistent with the great purpose of commandment. Moreover we see the aged Simon (Luke 2, 30—32,) rejoicing in the predicted and now fulfilled salvation, "prepared before the face of all people, a light to lighten the Gentiles." We see John the Baptist proclaiming the fulfillment of a similar prediction—(Luke 3, 4, 6.) We listen with mingled feelings of sorrow, love and hope to our blessed Savior's words, "And I, if I be lifted up, will draw all men unto me."—(John 12, 32.) We see the same precious truth in its easier process of fulfillment embodied in the parables of the grain of mustard seed and the leaven hid in the meal. (Matt. 13, 31—33.) We learn the mere truth in its manifested and regal glory in the numerous texts, which speak of the gracious effects of the gospel, triumphing as a religion in its present administration, under the idea of a kingdom, for whose coming we are taught to pray. (Matt. 6, 10.) We are taught the same view by some of the wonderful things in the book of Revelation—especially the binding of Satan for a thousand years. If we measure these by a common prophetic standard, we may look forward to a period of three hundred and sixty thousand years, during which our Lord's reign of righteousness in the hearts of men shall make this world a paradise, and nobly vindicate the power of the gospel as now preached among men, as the wisdom of God and the power of God unto salvation.

These are New Testament teachings, which show hat the preaching of the gospel is no fruitless means of the conversion of the world; but if the New Testament were silent on the subject, as it is nearly so on some other commonly received parts of Christian faith, we should still find ample warrant for our hopes of the conversion of the world in the numerous predictions of the Old Testament. One such prophecy out of scores that might be cited, "The earth shall be full of the knowledge of the Lord, even as the waters cover the sea," (Isaiah xi 9,) ought to be deemed conclusive.

There are, however, two other considerations which are even more conclusive—one positive, the other negative, and both clearly revealed. Positively, the work of conversion, as we have already seen, is the work of God, the Holy Ghost. We are living under the dispensation of the Spirit. Our Lord himself repeatedly referred to His agency in the work of conversion. We have unlimited promises of His intervention in answer to prayer. I need not pursue this consideration. Let the Church but honor the Spirit as the Father and the Son are honored, let the people of God believe in Him, seek His power, expect His presence, and who shall say that the greatest results shall not be speedily achieved? And let every humble disciple beware of any theory of unfulfilled Scripture that would even seem to lessen or disparage the agency of the Spirit in the conversion of the world.

The negative consideration is not less decisive. The personal coming of our blessed Lord is not revealed to us in Scripture as a means of conversion of men. We humbly trust that our blessed Savior's visible and personal appearing will be a joyful event to us, whenever he shall come; but as we read the Scriptures they furnish no proofs at all that he is ever to take the work of conversion out of the hands of the Holy Ghost. Our Lord's coming is spoken of in three senses, quite distinct, but all worthy of himself (1) by his Providence, as when he came to destroy Jerusalem, (Matt. 24, 34;) and so he comes in the wonderful course of his providence to raise up and cast down kingdoms and nations, and to be ever with his own people, so that they often hear his voice saying, "Fear not, it is I;" and in the hour of their departure from this life they find him present with them to give them all needed grace and an abundant entrance into his everlasting kingdom. (2.) He comes by his spirit into the worshiping assemblies of his people; even though but two or three of them meet together in his name, he will make the third or fourth, (Matt. 18, 20); and so he comes whenever the spirit of grace is carrying on his peculiar and saving work among men. And (3) he will come visibly and personally—his second appearing in visible and personal form, but it will be when he comes as a judge (Matt. 25, 31—46). Our Shorter Catechism well expresses the sense of the Scriptures on this point, when it teaches that Christ will come "to judge the world at the last day." We look for no other coming of our blessed Lord than these.

I will not further dwell on this part of the witnessing of the disciples unto Christ. It is an evangelizing testimony, to be brought to the mind and heart of every creature and to be crowned at last with blessed and glorious results in the conversion of the world unto God.

All this will serve to correct our thoughts with the remaining words of the text—which show that the witnessing of the disciples unto Christ was to be everywhere—"in Jerusalam, and in all Judea, and in Samaria, and unto the uttermost parts of the earth."

The Savior does not seem to recognize our modern distinction of Home and Foreign Missions. Thtre is a certain order marked, however: the witnesses were to begin among those who were nearest to them, going from them to the next nearest, and proceeding onward still to those who dwell in "the regions beyond." This was in fact the course of the Apostles. It is evidently proper to begin with our own people in witnessing unto Christ, but we must beware of restricting our efforts to them. The Gospel is for all men. The Apostles and first Christians so understood the matter; and when at first the deciples were staying too long in Jerusalem, perhaps consulting too much their love of home and of the temple, a persecution was allowed to arise, so that they were scattered abroad, and went everywhere preaching the word—even beyond the boundaries of their native country, though its inhabitants had by no means all become Christians. So it was at Antioch, when the gospel obtained a foothold there, and a church was formed. Some of its leading members and ministers were soon sent forth as missionaries, by divine direction and by the earnest co-operation of the Church, though the people of Antioch and of the province were not then all converted. We need not multiply examples to show how the first disciples understood the extent to which their testimony should be made known. They took their lives in their hand, and went forth into whatever part of the world they could reach. We read of their labors in Africa, in Europe, in Western Asia, and even in the Eastern parts of Asia traces of their presence are found.

We feel sure from the language of the text and from the example of the disciples in the apostolic age that no Christian Church, no member of the Church, much less any office bearer in it, can claim to have fulfilled his duty to Christ in witnessing unto him, who does not keep earnestly before his mind and on his heart this vast range of his calling. There stands the commandment of our Lord: "Preach the gospel to every creature." How can any disciple of Christ neglect this duty? There lies the world perishing in sin. How can any disciple of Him who came to seek and to save sinners be indifferent to the misery of these fellow men? Woe be to any Church that disregards this duty! The presence of Christ will be granted only to the Church that is seeking to bear witness unto Him unto the uttermost parts of the earth. That blessing has rested signally on our beloved Church, since the time when we entered as a Church on the work of sending the gospel abroad. Our foreign missions have been greatly prospered. Churches and Presbyteries are now planted in Africa, Asia, South America, and among some of our Indian tribes. Native communicants, native elders, native ministers, in many foreign parts, now worship God with us in our simple and beautiful order. The work is going on; it is calling for enlargement; it must be extended.

And then as we turn and survey our Church here at home, we see no signs of its being impoverished or weakened by its witnessing work abroad. We do see things that awaken our solicitude—dangers of divided opinions, and especially the danger of being carried away by tides of worldliness; but God has kept us and blest us hitherto. All through the terrible events of the last few years we have had grace given to us and the blessings of Providence, so that we have not fallen away from our noble missionary work abroad; that work has been, like the bow of promise, spanning the dark sky, and pointing to brighter days, when peace should return to bless the land in order that the Church might go on to bless the world.

Whatever may have been our past dangers, whatever present difficulties, they would have been far greater, perhaps even fatal to our churches, if God had not given us grace to bear our evangelistic testimony to the Chippewas, the Bengas, the Hindoos, the Siamese, the Chinese and others, thereby securing the fulfillment of our Savior's promise to us, and thereby enabling many of our Christian people to feel more deeply the preciousness of the gospel to themselves. As we continue our home survey, we see signs of widely spread prosperity in the home interests of our church—in our greatly enlarged number of ministers and members since the year 1832, when the foreign missions of our body were commenced. But, on these and other things we cannot enter.

We bless the Lord for what he hath done for us. We gratefully ascribe all our prosperity, at home and abroad, and all our success to the presence of our blessed Lord with us, as we have endeavored to be witnesses unto him both in our own country and in foreign lands—even unto the uttermost parts of the earth. We see in this the second cause of our prosperity.

Here then we rest in our exposition of the text, and conclude with two other inferences:

1. We see that the duty of Christian witnessing is from God. It is unto Christ, by his last instructions and by his last commandment. It is inspired and made efficacious by the Holy Ghost. In bearing their testimony, the disciples have a divine warrant—they were not unsent; and they may feel assured, therefore, that their witnessing shall not be in vain. Whether many or few accept their testimony, they shall receive a divine reward. Let them seek to be found faithful witnesses, never shunning to declare the whole counsel of God, ever sitting the Lord Himself before them, giving their testimony from love to him, cherishing a sense of their dependence on the Holy Ghost, and then they shall be blessed themselves and a blessing to the world.

2. We see the main elements of success in Apostolic evangelization. Its agents were men impelled by love to Christ and empowered by the Holy Ghost. Their minds were enlightened; their hearts filled with holy affections; their labors abundant beyond measure—all because they were under Divine influence. Their views of their work were clear and well defined; they knew precisely what they were to do and how to do it; they engaged in it at no uncertainty. A noble purpose of consecration to God governed their whole course. As we fix our attention on the life of one of those early disciples, and it matters little which of them, as we consider his faith in Christ, his self-renunciation, his unworldly spirit, his willingness to endure hardship and to practice self-denial, his devotedness to the great object of saving lost souls, and thereby glorifying God, his perseverance in seeking this object in the face of reproach, opposition, persecution, violence and death, even death in the most terrible form, we are filled with admiration of his holy life and his blessed labors. With such a consecration of heart and life, and with the power of the Holy Ghost, at once its cause and its blessing, we do not wonder to see Stephen martyred, and the cause advanced which his death was intended to destroy.

We do not wonder to see the brilliant course of Paul, his abundant labors, his unceasing prayers, his unwearied zeal flaming to the last. These were the missionaries, these were the ministers of the primitive Church. We readily see the secret of their wonderful success. They walked with God, and God was with them, and therefore the gospel won triumphs in the world such as no subsequent age has witnessed. Yes, my brethren, and we may say such as the world will not witness again until our ministers and missionaries become men of Apostolic piety.

3. And this leads to our last remark. We see what is most needed by us as a Church—as a body of Christian people, ministers, elders, deacons and members. It is not purer doctrines; our faith is of God. It is not a better order; our church is at once Scriptural, catholic, beautiful in its worship, and admirable in its government. It is not, perhaps, better plans of promoting the work of evangelization; though these probably might be reduced in number, enlarged in scope in some instances, and simplified in their arrangements; still, it is well to be slow to make changes, and it is well to remember that our plans have worked better than we could have expected; that whatever plans are adopted, we may expect imperfections, and that we must look beyond our methods of benevolent action to their animating principle, and herein it is that we chiefly come short. But it is not in any of these things that we feel our greatest need; it is in the want of Apostolic piety; it is in the want of the power of the Holy Ghost.

Men of the world depend on talent, learning, wealth, station; we undervalue none of these gifts; God has ever used them all. But he also used the weak things of the world to confound the mighty. Thirty years ago a venerable minister said to me, "My young brother, we seem to be living in an age of great events and little men." He said this in a tone of discouragement, and in his unaffected humility he, no doubt, included himself in his remark, though no minister stood higher than he in our Church; but his words embodied a great truth and one that should give us great encouragement. God will so order events that the glory of the world's salvation shall be seen to be of himself and not of men. He will employ great gifts, but he will also employ humble gifts. And if God the Holy Gost be with "little men," they will work wonders. The gift most important, most to be desired by us all, is the outpouring of the Holy Spirit. Let his influences so abound in us, so govern our lives, so animate our prayers, as to make us Christ-like.

Let his gracious power so control us as to consume our worldly aims, our unworthy desires of comfort, our undue regard for the praise of men, and at the same time to raise our conceptions of divine and eternal things, filling our hearts with the love of God, and giving us deep impressions of the power of the world to come; and then shall our course be in some measure like that of the first Christians. The litle company that saw our Lord ascend into Heaven, were soon clothed with power, and then went forth and made their influence felt throughout the world. We serve the same Savior. We have the unlimited promise of the same Almighty Spirit. The same work is set before us as before them, the world stands open to-day, as it did 1,800 years ago, still waiting for missionaries. Oh, let the Spirit of God baptise our ministers, elders and communicants, and how soon would our Church shake this land and shake the world! Oh, that the great ascension gift of our blessed Lord may soon be poured out upon us from on high! Then would our Church go forth like the Church of Jerusalem or the Church of Antioch, and bless the world.

I do not forget, my brethren, that such witnessing unto Christ as we have been considering is no easy matter. Nay, I know that involves oftentimes great and painful sacrifices—of time, property, and life itself in some cases, so that the *word witnesses*, in the original language of the New Testament, is the same word that denotes the *martyrs* of the early church. Stephen was a witness unto Christ, and he was the first martyr. Most of the Apostles, it is believed, suffered death by martyrdom. So did many of the primitive Christians, and many of the people of God in all ages—in the Waldensian Valley, on the hills of Scotland, in England, and in our own day in the Island of Madagascar. If we are now exempted from this extreme sacrifice as the witnesses of Christ, yet are we not sometimes called to sacrifice hardly less severe in the fulfillment of our duty?

I think the modern missionary work of the Church presents examples of this—when parents are called to give up a beloved son or daughter, or when an affectionate son or daughter is called from home and friends, to go far hence to the Gentiles. At such sacrifices, many tears flow, many hearts are bowed down in deep distress—it often seems almost martyrdom. Yet it is for Christ. His grace is sufficient. His presence is with his servants, and they are enabled to go forth with a willing heart to bear glad testimony unto Christ among the heathen. There they are happy and blessed in their work, they who remain, feeling almost bereaved, are comforted.

The Church is but the self-denying lives and examples of her children, and they are blessed reunions in heaven. There shall they and all the faithful witnesses unto Christ rejoice with him forever.

"And one of the Elders answered, saying unto me, 'Which are these which are arrayed in white robes, and whence came they?' "

"And I said unto him, 'Sir, thou knowest.' And he said to me, 'These are they that came out of great tribulation, and have washed their robes, and made them white, in the blood of the Lamb?' "

'Wherefore are they before the throne of God, and serve Him day and night in His temple; and he that sitteth on the throne shall dwell among them.' "

"They shall hunger no more, neither thirst anymore; neither shall the sun light on them, nor any heat"

"For the Lamb which is in the midst of the throne shall feed them, and shall lead them unto living fountains of waters; and God shall wipe away all tears from their eyes."

At the conclusion of the sermon, and after the benediction, the assembly was called to order, Rev. Mr. Lowry, the Moderator, in the chair.

Rev. Mr. Schenck, the Secretary, then read a list of delegates.

[The list not being entirely complete, we omit its publication until our next issue]

The names of several delegates were read whose papers had not been properly made out, and, on motion, they were referred to a committee of three, of whhich Dr. Patterson was chairman.

The Assembly, after prayer, adjourned until four o'clock.

AFTERNOON SESSION.

Prayer by Rev. Dr. Wm. L. Breckinridge.

Rev. Dr. Patterson, Chairman of the Committee on Commissions, reported a list of names whose credentials were not properly made out. The report recommended their admission, and it was adopted.

Nominations for Moderator of the Assembly for the ensuing year being in order,

Mr. Allen of Illinois nominated Dr. P. D. Gurley, of Washington, D. C.

Dr. Krebs nominated Dr. Robert L. Stanton, of Chillicothe.

Rev. Dr. Brookes of St. Louis nominated Dr. Samuel R. Wilson, of Louisville.

Dr. Breckinridge moved that in the election for Moderator and Clerk a majority of all the votes cast be necessary for a choice.

Dr. Humphries moved to amend by providing that in all elections of the Assembly this rule shall prevail.

Amendment accepted and motion agreed to.

Dr. Carter, of Baltimore, nominated Rev. Mr. Loomis, of California.

Rev. Mr. Loomis asked leave to decline, which was granted.

The vote was then taken, and resulted as follows:

Dr. P. D, Gurley	75
Dr. B. L. Stanton	158
Dr. S. R. Wilson	18

Dr. Stanton having been declared duly elected Moderator, the retiring Moderator, Dr. Lowry, appointed Dr. Krebs a committee to inform Dr. Stanton of his election, and conduct him to the Chair.

Dr. Lowry welcomed Dr. Stanton by saying: It gives me pleasure to introduce Dr. Stanton as Moderator, and may God's blessing be with you and guide and direct you in the performance of your duties. You will find in these minutes the rules for the government of the Assembly, and the prayer of the retiring Moderator is that the Divine blessing may rest on you and on this assembly.

Dr. Stanton then said: Fathers and Brethren: I need scarcely say that I am deeply sensible of the honor conferred upon me by being called to preside over your deliberations. This honor, I am well aware, brings with it responsibilities and labors of no ordinary character. While I return you my sincere thanks for this mark of your confidence, I shall endeavor to bring to the discharge of the duties of the chair an honest effort, at least, to advance the wishes of those whose servant only I am. A consciousness of my inability fully to meet the demands of the position you have given me prompts me to throw myself upon your generous indulgence and to ask your assistance in every proper way; while, in order that the business of the Assembly may be properly conducled, it is essential that we should unitedly seek the guidance of that wisdom which is from above.

It has many times been said by members of this body and by others, as well as by the religious journals, that this would be one of the most important General Assemblies of the Presbyterian Church which has ever convened. While we ought not unduly to magnify our office as a Church Court, there may be some truth in the estimate thus put upon what may prove to be the result of our deliberations. Vital questions affecting the integrity of this Assembly, and the purity and peace of the Church at large, will claim from you a prompt and decisive solution. That rebellious defiance of lawful authority which has racked this Nation to its foundations during four years of war, still rages within the precincts where it was born, the Church of God! It is the offspring of heresy, corruption, and all unrighteousness. To meet it promptly, courageously in the fear of God, and with the aid of His grace, is your manifest duty, as well as directly to deal with those who openly deride your most solemn injunctions. To settle all these questions upon principles so clearly right that they shall command the confidence of the Church and give it rest, while they shall advance the Savior's glory and secure his favor, should be the aim of the prayers and the labors of every member. Then, those who have gone out from us upon vain and wicked pretexts may be left to their own chosen way, and if any still remain to revile they may know the cost of setting at defiance the authority which Christ has given to his Church.

The bare mention of these things—to name no others which will claim your attention—shows how greatly we need a wisdom which is above that of man. Let us, then, one and all, seek for our guidance that wisdom and grace which God hath promised; and may he give success to the right!

Nominations for Secretary being in order, the following gentlemen were put for nomination;

Rev. Dr. Hickock, Rev. Mr. Loomis, of the Presbytery of California, Rev. J. P. Davis, of the 2d Presbytery of Philadelphia, Rev. J. G. Rosser, of Leavenworth, Rev. E. Kemphall, of the Presbytery of Elizabethtown, and Rev. Mr. Waller.

Rev. Mr. Loomis, Rev. Mr. Rosser and Rev. Mr. Waller severally declined.

The vote resulted:

Rev. Mr. Hickock	145
Rev. Mr. Kemphall	91
Rev. Mr. Davis	4

Rev. Mr. Hickock was declared duly elected.

Rev. Dr. Lowry, from the committee appointed at the last session, reported that it would be inexpedient to make any change in regard to the manner in which the services of the several Boards shall be conducted.

The report was adopted.

The following order of proceedings was agreed upon: Friday to receive reports of the Boards of the Theological Seminaries and refer to the appropriate committees; for Saturday, to hear the report of the standing committee on the Board of Church Extension; for Monday next, to hear the report of the Board of Publication; for Tuesday, the report of the Board of Foreign Missions; for Wennesday, to hear the report of the Board of Domestic Missions; for Thursday, the report of the Board of Education; for Friday, to hear the report in regard to the disabled ministers' fund; for Saturday, to hear the report of the Freedmen's Committee.

Rev. Dr. McLean offered the following resolution:

Whereas, It is understood that the Presbytery of Louisville has openly defied the General Assembly, and refuses to submit to its orders, in a pamphlet adopted by it of which the following is a specimen, to-wit:

"We will not sustain or execute, or in any manner assist in the execution of the orders passed by the last assemblies on the subject of slavery and loyalty, and with reference to the conducting of missions in the Southern States, and with regard to the ministers, members and churches in the seceded and border States."

And whereas, Said Presbytery has commissioned and sent to this Assembly at least one commissioner who, if the order of the last assembly had been faithfully executed by said Presbytery, there is the strongest ground for believing would have been suspended from the functions of the gospel ministry; therefore,

Resolved, That until the Assembly shall have examined and decided on the conduct of said Presbytery, the commissioners therefrom shall not be entitled to seats in this body.

Rev. Wm. Breckinridge moved that the resolution be laid on the table.

The ayes and noes were demanded.

Rev. Mr. Waller raised a point of order. In order that the question might be understood, he requested the Moderator to state to the Assembly the effect of this motion; if it should be carried in the affirmative, whether it carries this whole subject on the table.

The Moderator. I understand that if this motion is carried to lay this paper on the table, it lays that paper on the table and nothing more. What that paper embraces I cannot distictly call to mind, because I heard it but imperfectly.

Mr. Galloway. I move that the Assembly adjourn until to-morrow morning at 9 o'clock.

A member raised a point of order, whether it was in order to make a motion to adjourn when the ayes and noes were called for.

The Moderator. Yes, sir. The motion is in order, as we have not begun to take the vote.

Rev. Dr. Krebs. Allow me to make a request—not to adjourn until we have had an opportunity of getting a vote.

The Moderator. That is rather in the nature of debate.

Dr. Krebs. It has nothing to do with this business; but for the convenenience of the Assembly I hope they will adjourn.

A Member. The gentleman is making an argument against adjournment.

The Moderator. So I suggested, but the gentleman is a good parliamentarian and he says not. The vote must be taken.

The vote was then taken, and the motion to adjourn was lost.

The Moderator. The question is on calling the ayes and noes on laying this paper of Dr. McLean's on the table.

Rev. Dr. Krebs desired to know, if this motion to lay on the table was carried, whether the resolution could be taken up at any future time, and if it was not laid on the table, whether it would be competent for the House to immediately refer it to an appropriate committee instead of proceeding to the discussion of the matter.

The Moderator. Unquestionably, the House has a right to make any disposition of it they choose.

Rev. Mr. Francis. Permit me to make an inquiry. If it is laid on the table, would it not require a vote of two-thirds to take it up at any time.

The Moderator. I think it requires three-fourths. The Stated Clerk suggests merely a majority. That matter, however, is decided by law, I believe.

Rev. Mr. Francis. I am aware that parliamentary practice requires two-thirds invariably.

Rev. Wm. Breckinridge. If in order I move that hereafter when the Assembly, by vote, lays a paper on the table, it shall have the power to take it up by a majority at its pleasure. I think by referring to the action of former Assemblies on this subject, it will be found almost without exception, if not absolutely, that has been the usual course.

The Moderator. I do not think that motion is in order at the present time. It is equivalent to adding a rule to the standing rules, and may be acted upon hereafter.

Rev. Mr. Breckinridge. I make it as an interpretation of the rule.

Rev. Mr. Carter, of Baltimore, desired to know if the taking of a paper off the table was not in the nature of a reconsideration.

The Moderator decided it was not.

Rev. Dr. Patterson thought the nineteenth rule decided the question, inasmuch as it declared that a question, after it has once been disposed of, shall not be again called up or reconsidered at the same session at which it is decided, unless by a vote of two-thirds of the members present.

The Moderator understood that to refer to a motion that had been considered and decided, the laying of a paper on the table under these circumstances was no decision; therefore, he would not regard this as coming under the 19th rule.

Rev. Mr. Frazier. We discussed that matter not less than a day and a half in the Assembly in 1861, and a resolution laid on the table was taken up by a mere majority. Dr. Hodge and others opposed it, but it was taken up and a new resolution offered by Dr. Spring.

Rev. Mr. Clark. A motion has been made and another motion made to lay that motion on the table. The House has directed the vote shall be taken by ayes and noes. The motion to lay on the table is not debatable. I insist that no debate can be had in the form of questions put the Moderator to decide.

A member. Is not the member putting a question now?

Rev. Mr. Clark. No. I am making a point of order that this whole discussion is out of order.

The Moderator. I am quite well aware that the motion to lay on the table is not debatable, but I have understood these questions to have reference to matters of order. It appears to me there is no specific rule on the subject. My opinion is, that a bare majority may lay on the table, and a bare majority take from the table. As to what the practice has heretofore been, I cannot distinctly call to mind.

The roll was then called.

During the calling of the roll, Rev. Mr. West desired to know whether it was in order for any of the parties to whom the resolution referred to vote.

Rev. Mr. Anderson of St. Louis said: Then all they had to do to put the power of this Assembly in the hands of six men was to charge all the rest of the body with something of this sort. By this means they could put the power of this Assembly in the hands of six men.

Rev. Dr. Wilson. Brother West has stated that the Assembly has made a certain decision. We would like to hear the decision read that refers to this case.

Rev. Mr. West stated that he could not point to the decision just at present.

Mr. Wilson. I only asked for the decision. The Doctor is learned in ecclesiastical law. He says there is a decision that refers to this case. As a party interested in this case I ask for the decision.

Rev. Mr. West. I do not remember the decision sufficiently to give it in detail, but I would like to have time to look it up. I will ask through you, Mr. Moderator, if Brother Wilson denies the existence of such a decision?

Rev. Mr. Wilson. I suppose it is enough for me to call for the decision. As the brother has said there is a decision, I presume he has it.

The Moderator. If it cannot be produced the clerk will proceed.

Rev. Mr. Wilson, when his name was called, said, I shall not vote on this question, but not yielding my right to vote. I simply sit silent. I do not yield my right to vote. I suppose I can do that.

The Moderator. Certainly.

Mr. Wyckliffe, when his name was called. I shall not vote, understanding the language of that resolution, but I do not yield my right to vote.

Rev. Dr. Krebs hoped that the announcement of the vote would be made without reading over the names.

Rev. Mr. Patterson moved that the paper be referred to a committee.

The Moderator said it was usual, after taking a vote, to read over the names, but as Dr. Krebs had made a point that it was manifest the vote had been decided in the negative, they need not wait for the usual course.

The reading of the names was dispensed with.

The vote was then announced as follows: Nays, 212; ayes, 31.

Rev. Mr. McLain asked leave to say a few words.

Rev. Dr. Krebs raised a point or order that after a matter of this kind had been submitted to the house it should be referred to a committee, say of bills and overtures, which was instituted for this very purpose of considering whether it was a proper question to come before the house, and what time it shall come, and in what form. He might be mistaken, and would not urge this proposition with pertinacity; but as it was within five minutes of the hour of adjournment, he would suggest that the whole matter be referred to a committee.

Rev. Mr. McLain. I had no idea I was giving way for a discussion.

The Moderator. Dr. Krebs wished to raise a point of order.

Dr. McLain. What is it?

Dr. Krebs. I cannot state it any more plainly.

The Moderator. With regard to the point of order, I consider Dr. McLain in order; but whether it is policy to detain the house at this late hour, I will leave it to Dr. McLain to determine.

Dr. McLain. When I offered this paper I purposely refrained from saying a word, because I desired to make the motion on my own responsibility, and after consultation with but few of the brethren in the house. I could say a great deal on it, sir, but for the sake of avoiding what might appear to be personalities, I chose rather to sit down. I had a right to go on in all conscience and by parliamentary rule when the motion was seconded. I had a right to speak, but I sat down. Now an attempt is made to lay the whole subject on the table, and that attempt failed by a large majority—and surely the mover has a right to say something if he sees proper; but as the house is impatient, and the hour of adjournment has arrived, I will yield now and claim the floor for to-morrow morning.

Rev. Mr. Monfort desired to offer a resolution in regard to the hour of meeting each day.

Rev. Mr. Brown desired to move to refer this whole subject (in regard to the Kentucky delegation) to the Committee on Elections.

Several motions were made to adjourn.

Rev. Dr. Krebs stated that he desired to make an announcement before the adjournment. The committee appointed at the last meeting, in regard to a new selection of psalms and hymns, had completed their work, and were prepared to report. He requested that the report should be received in regular order for to-day.

The Moderator. With all due respect to Dr. Krebs, who is one of the best parliamentarians, I think this is not in the nature of those notices that are usually offered when a motion of adjournment has been made.

Rev. Dr. Krebs. I am obliged to go away early next week, and hope the house will indulge me by allowing me to lay before it the work which has been done.

The Moderator. I presume it can be done; but we must now take the vote on adjournment.

The vote was then taken and the motion to adjourn was carried.

SECOND DAY—FRIDAY, MAY 19, 1866.

MORNING SESSION.

Half an hour was spent in devotional exercises. After which the minutes of yesterday were read. During the reading of the minutes, Dr. Wilson desired that it should be entered on the records that he declined voting yesterday on the resolution in regard to the Louisville Presbytery, but at the same time reserved his right to vote. This was done by common consent on yesterday.

The Moderator. The gentleman made the request on yesterday and so did Governor Wyckliffe.

Dr. Krebs. It occurs to me there is no need of a motion. Our rule says members ought to vote, and our custom in the interpretation is that any gentleman for any reason declining to vote is permitted so to do. When the ayes and nays are recorded it is recorded that such and such gentlemen do not vote. It is not necessary, I presume, to put on the reason why. This house can always admit that fact; and I presume these gentlemen have a right to have their names recorded as not voting.

A member stated that Dr. Robinson made the same suggestion.

Another member said, we are now correcting the record of our proceedings. Is it not a question of fact that these gentlemen declined to vote? And if so, are they not entitled to have that fact recorded, and will our record be correct unless we do state the fact that they declined to vote?

The Moderator. If there is no objection the Clerk will enter that they declined to vote.

Dr. Schenck, (the permanent Clerk.) I have written that Dr. Wilson, Dr. Robinson and Dr. Wyckliffe of the Presbytery of Louisville decline to vote. We cannot say in general terms that the Presbytery decline to vote, because one or two voted.

A member. Dr. Robinson did not answer to his name.

Another member. That is most emphatically declining to vote.

Moderator. I believe the rule and practice has been heretofore that silent members, unless excused from voting, must be considered as acquiescing with the majority.

Dr. Wilson. We certainly do not wish to be considered as acquiescing with the majority. That, of itself, ought to be a weighty reason.

Dr. Krebs. I move that those gentlemen who decline voting have liberty to be so recor ed.

Dr. Schenck. I suggest that the following should be added to the roll of ayes and nays:

"Dr. Wilson, and Dr. Robinson, ministers, and Governor Wyckliffe, elder, decline to vote."

Dr. McLean moved to amend by declaring that the names of Messrs. Wyckliffe, Robinson and Wilson be recorded as *non liquet*, as Dr. Robinson was not in the house at the time the vote was taken for all they knew. He made no response.

A Member. I think I heard him decline to vote. He was sitting behind me and I heard him decline to vote.

Dr. McLean. I beg pardon. It was so low I could not hear it on this side of the house.

Mr. Harding. If my ears did not deceive me, a gentleman back there objected to the members from the Louisville Presbytery voting, saying they had no right to vote. Some gentleman made that objection. Gov. Wyckliffe when he got up and declined to vote reserved his right to vote.

Rev. Mr. Bracken. It occurs to me it is a very easy matter, or ought to be, to make a record in accordance with the facts in the case. What were the facts in the case? Objection had been made against these brethren voting, and they stated before the Assembly that they declined to vote, though they did not surrender their right. Such are the facts.

The Moderator. That was the statement made by Gov. Wyckliffe and Drs. Robinson and Wilson.

A Member. Is it not universally our custom, when a vote is taken by ayes and noes, that the roll is required to show that such names were aye and such names nay, and if any do not vote, are they are not recorded as *non liquet*. Usually it does not state on the minutes what is the reason they did not vote, unless there is something special, and I think there is nothing in this case so very special as to demand particular reference to them out of the ordinary way.

The Moderator. My opinion is, they are recorded as voting *non liquet* unless they answer.

Rev. Mr. Brown. The case stands something like this: When the Presbytery of Louisville was called, objection was made to those members voting, and pending the decision of that question, certain gentlemen declined to vote; but they waived their right to vote, and that question is not yet settled. As the minutes stand, they do not express the fact in the case. I move to amend so as to present that fact.

The Moderator. That is the amendment that Dr. Schenck offers to Dr. Krebs's motion. Now Dr. Browne offers an amendment to the amendment.

Dr. Brown. This amendment does not cover the ground or state the facts. The amendment that I offer is this: That when the Presbytery of Louisville was called objection was made to its voting because it was interested in the case. Pending the decision of that question Dr. Wilson, Dr. Stuart Robinson and Gov. Wyckliffe declined to vote, but said that they would waive their right to vote. That should be stated.

Dr. Wilson. The only objection to that amendment is that there was no decision at all. A single member of this House arose and said that our right to vote had been decided by the Assembly, and that we had no right to vote. I asked for the authority, but no authority was given, and the Moderator, as I understood, decided when I gave my vote that we had a right to vote. So there was no decision pending before the House, and we did not decline to vote with that understanding.

The Moderator. The gentleman misunderstood me if he supposed that I decided he had a right to vote. I decided that the demand to read the law was a just demand.

Dr. Wilson. There was no question before the house as to our right to vote—no question of order at all. And, therefore, this motion would not be in accordance with the fact. The objection I have to it is, it seems that our declinature turned upon this objection, and that this objection was still pending before the house, when the house had not entertained the objection. That is the state of the case, and it is important, I think, that we should make that clear distinction. The house had not entertained the objection. It was therefore simply the objection of a solitary member, and has no place on your minutes whatever. The reason why I included in my declining to vote the reservation of my right to vote, was because it was essential to do it. It may be in the future, if this business goes on.

I suppose the brother knows what *non liquet* means? And that was not my vote. I declined to vote and reserved my rights. Governor Wyckliffe did the same thing.

Rev. Mr. West. I suppose the General Assembly is competent to understand the significancy of my demand.

I still maintain the proposition that I asserted, that in a judicial case or *quasi* judicial case the ruling of the General Assembly is that persons involved shall not have the right to vote. There are vested rights involved in this paper before us, and that is the ground of my objection.

Mr. Kempshall. It seems to me that we are accumulating amendments to the original motion which are leading the Assembly to some conclusion, and evidently tending to a widening of the debate. I think the original motion will meet with the approbation of the larger portion of the Assembly. I therefore move the previous question in order that we may have a vote.

A member. What is the main question?

The Moderator. The main question is, shall these gentlemen who decline to vote have that fact recorded.

The vote was then taken on the previous question, and it was agreed to. The motion of Dr. Kries was then agreed to.

The reading of the minutes was then concluded.

Dr. Humphreys. I move that in the record of ayes and nays the title of D. D. be omitted on the roll. I see no reason why a collegiate title should be recognized here any more than the title of a physician. There are physicians on this floor, and gentlemen who have held the office of Governor of a commonwealth, and, I suppose, gentlemen who have held military titles. I see no reason why they should not be recognized if the others are. The motion was agreed to, and the minutes were then approved.

The Moderator then stated that he would announce the committees. He said, before announcing the committees, I wish to state that the roll from which I made up the committees came into my hand at a very late hour last evening, but I am able to announce this morning all the committees which are of chief importance, reserving those upon Synodical Record and others to be reported at a future time.

The Moderator announced the following standing committees:

BILLS AND OVERTURES.

Ministers—J. C. Lowrie, D. D., N. West, D. D., J. G. Monfort, D. D., W. L. Breckinridge, D. D., James Alison, T. W Hynes, Alex. Scott, E. C. Sickles.

Elders—Jesse L Williams, Samuel Galloway, Hovey K. Clarke, Barton H. Jenks, Wm. M. Francis, Rober J. McCreary.

The Moderator then said: Before reading the names of the Judicial Committee, I wish to remark it is known to some members of the Assembly, and I wish it known to all, that I am one of the appellants on an important judicial case that comes before the Assembly from the Synod of Kentucky. Dr. Breckinridge and some twenty other gentlemen are appellants in an important case, and that being my relation to the case, it may be deemed, perhaps, improper that I should select the Judicial Committee—although I regard this committee as directing the Assembly in regard to the way in which the business shall be taken up. Of course, when we reach the point of trying that case, if the Judicial Committee report in favor of a trial, then, being one of the appellants, I shall vacate the chair, and some one else will occupy it. I hope the General Assembly will appoint its Judicial Committee in some way.

Rev. Dr. Krebs. I move that the Moderator proceed to appoint the committee.

Rev. Dr. McGill—the Stated Clerk—then put the motion, and it was ageeed to.

The remaining committees were then announced as follows:

JUDICIAL COMMITTTEE.

Ministers—P. D. Gurley, D. D., John M. Krebs, D. D., G. D. Archibald, D. D., Roger Owen, John P. Carter, Joseph Mateer, John H. Bratt, J. G. Reasor.

Elders—Robert McKnight, Lincoln Clarke, Isaac D. Jones, S. D. Sharon.

THEOLOGICAL SEMINARIES.

Ministers—D J. Waller, W. T. Findley, J. D. Mason, John Crozier, T. M. Cunningham, E. P. Raftensperger, R. Irwin, Jr.

Elders—A. E. Chamberlain, James M. Ray, Wm. Thomas, W. P. Van Rennsalaer, Regers Birnie.

DOMESTIC MISSIONS.

Ministers—Thomas E. Thomas, D. D., C. C. Riggs, D. D., F. R. Morton, C. A. Munn, R. G. Thompson, Charles J. Jones.

Elders—Samuel Rea, James Rankin, J. C. Maxwell, Wm. N. Belcher, A. G. Brown.

FOREIGN MISSIONS.

Ministers—A. W. Loomis, D. D., J. E. Spillman, S. R. House, M. D., D. A. Wilson, S. T. Wilson, Jas. Remington.

Elders—Lucien B. Wells, Glass Marshall, John Way, Jr., John Dickson.

BOARD OF EDUCATION.

Ministers—Joseph T. Smith, D D., E. P. Humphrey, D. D., Wm. Bishop, C. W. Finley.

Elders—Wm. Mason, Robert S. Clarke, Ormond Beatty.

BOARD OF PUBLICATION.

Ministers—J. P. Safford, D. D., E. D. Yeomans, D. D., F. J. Collier, W. K. Brice.

Elders—W. L. Orr, John Ogden, Jas. K. Ralph.

CHURCH EXTENSION.

Ministers—D. V. McLean, D. D., J. W. Wightman, James Gardner, Charles L. Thompson.

Elders—James Baylis, H. T. Walker, James Snyder.

ON FREEDMEN.

Ministers—Robert B. Walker, D. D., V. D. Reed, D. D., J. P. Bliss, J. B. Lindsley, D. D., R. F. Patterson, Luther Littell.

Elders—Thomas Buchanan, Valentine C. Glenn, G. S. Ormsby, Wm. S. Caldwell.

SYSTEMATIC BENEFICENCE.

Ministers—J. T. Backus, D. D., W. T. Adams, David Lyon, E. Kemphall.

Elders—John Stewart, Reuben Van Pett.

NARRATIVE.

Ministers—F. T. Brown, D. D., W. A. Hornblower, D. D., S. G. Law.

Elders—Chas. W. Smith, Robert Lyle.

CORRESPONDENCE.

Ministers—H. A. Boardman, D. D., A. O. Patterson, D. D., P. Bixby, J. F. Magill.

Elders—David Wills, S. M. Archer.

FINANCE

Elders—James Blake, Thomas McGeehin, Henry Day.

Rev. Dr. Lowrie presented overtures from the Synod of Northern Indiaan, which were referred to the Committee on Foreign Missions.

Dr. Lowrie then said, after some consultation with members of the house: I have to make a motion which, if it meets with any objection, I will withdraw.

Rev. Dr. McLean insisted on the regular order of business. He said: It is exceedingly embarrassing to entertain these different propositions while you have a matter before the house.

The Moderator. This does not require any discussion.

Dr. McLean. We are continually consuming the time of the Assembly with these outside matters. Adherence to the order of business is the life of success in all proceedings. There are a half dozen others waiting here around me to do the same thing.

The Moderator. It is perhaps courteous to hear what Dr. Lowrie has to offer in the way of business.

Dr. McLean. Here is one and there is one, and you will take up the whole morning.

Rev Dr. Patterson. I wish to fix the hour of adjournment for the accommodation of families in he city.

The Moderator. Will Dr. McLean waive his objection?

Dr. McLean. With great pleasure; but I insist upon it that no more matter shall come in.

Rev. Dr. Patterson then offered a proposition fixing the hours of meeting and adjournment as follows: Meet at 9 A. M.: adjourn at 12:30 P. M. Meet at 3:30 P. M.; and adjourn at 5:30 P. M, and occupy a half hour at the close of each session in devotional exercise.

Dr. Lowrie. I propose an amendment. In order to give time to the standing committees of this body to mature the business entrusted to them, the Assembly will hold but one session on Friday, Saturday and Monday next, ensuing.

Dr. Patterson. I accept the amendment.

Rev. Mr. Ferguson. I think it would be very improper to have devotional exercise at the close of each afternoon session. A great many at that time desire to retire. I hope we will give the Lord the first half hour of our exercises when our minds are fresh, and not under excitement. I make a motion to that effect.

The motion was agreed to.

A member. I have one objection to the amendment, and that is, that the family with which I stay dine at half-past twelve o'clock.

Rev. Mr. Thomas. I desire, with the permission of Dr. McLean who has given way for this purpose, to make a motion. I suppose it will not give rise to discussion, and will pass immediately.

Resolved, That a committee of five—three ministers and two elders—be appointed to confer with a like committee of the Assembly meeting at the First Presbyterian Church, in this city, with reference to joining in devotional exercises during the current session of the General Assembly.

The Moderator. I may be wrong, but I have great doubts whether the member who occupies the floor has the right to give way to introduce entirely new business. It is rather a new question.

Dr. McLean. You will bear me witness, Moderator, that I have yielded very reluctantly to anyone, but on the important suggestion of my friend, I was willing to yield my right to the floor. I do not propose to enter into a discussion of the merits of the paper offered to this body yesterday afternoon, and I shall occupy but a very few moments of the time of this body, only to explain very briefly, as I hope to do, that the members may distinctly understand what the question is before them; and then, sir, I propose to read to you a brief resolution which will put this matter in a shape for the action of this body. I will read the original resolution. (The resolution has already been published.)

I do not propose, as I have already remarked, to touch on the merits of this case. That every deliberative body has a right to judge of the qualifications of its own members is, to me, a self-evident proposition. To deny that would render powerless for good, and utterly useless, and utterly demoralize any public deliberative body; that a public body have a right, where they have been elected, to go back and consider the qualifications of the electors is, to me, equally as plain as the other proposition. If the individual who fills a place in a deliberative body is disqualified by reason of matters connected with himself, even though the electors be entirely competent to elect a delegate, the body may reject the individual proposing to become a member of their body. If any defect exists in the character of the elector, and if there be no fault attached to the individual sent as a member, still the body has a right to reject the member, in consequence of the informality and defect in regard to the elector.

I think these are principles that cannot be obviated. Now, in the present case, the paper assumes that there are rumors and public fame in regard to the electors, and one person, at least, elected, and that ought to be disqualified. In this incipient state of the matter, I have a paper designed, perhaps, to decide this matter, or to prepare a way towards deciding it. It simply asserts that it suspends these persons as members of this house; that they are not entitled to seats in the house, and that the Assembly will proceed with dispatch to investigate these rumors and decide upon them. I propose, therefore, after I have made a motion, to offer this resolution:

Resolved, That a committee of seven be appointed, composed of four ministers and three elders, to examine into the facts connected with the alleged acts and proceedings of the Louisville Presbytery, and whether it is entitled to representation in this General Assembly, and to recommend what action, if any, this General Assembly should take with regard to this said Presbytery.

I now move that the previous question be taken on this paper.

The Moderator. I may not have understood Dr. McLean entirely. Do I understand that the demand for the previous question is upon the motion pending yesterday to adopt the paper originally offered?

Dr. McLean. Precisely.

The Moderator. What has that to do with reference to the committee?

Dr. McLean. Nothing at all.

A member. Dr. McLane had the floor this morning on a question which he debated yesterday. Now I raise a point of order, whether setting aside his right to introduce a new resolution he can demand the previous question, either upon that resolution or upon the whole paper offered by him.

The Moderator. It is certainly his right to move the previous question at any stage. Nothing is more common in parliamentary bodies than for a member to offer a motion, and then demand the previous question. I understand the previous question to be on the paper offered yesterday. That would bring the question to the adoption immediately of his paper. There can be no debate upon this paper. Inquiries for information are in order.

Rev. Mr. West. I will ask for information, through you, Mr. Moderator, of Dr. McLean, whether the paper before this body—which asks of this body to exclude from seats in this house the Commissioners from Louisville till their case is decided—whether the points involved in that resolution are to be determined here and now by the previous question, or whether the Doctor proposes to offer a resolution which will open the whole question for debate?

The Moderator. That is in the nature of debate. Dr. McLean offered a resolution yesterday which I suppose the house understands; if so, they must understand what will be the posture of the case if this is adopted. Shall the question be now put?

Rev. Mr. Anderson. We want to call the ayes and noes on that vote—on the demand for the previous question.

Dr. Krebs. Is it in order to make a point of order, and move a reference of this whole business to a committee? And again, sir, if a motion for a reference is made, is there any need for the previous question?

The Moderator. The motion to refer is not debateable.

Dr. McLean. It is very simple to my mind.

The Moderator. If Dr. McLean will wait a moment, I am looking for a rule which refers to this matter. My impression is, and on reading the rule I am confirmed in it, that the motion of Dr. Krebs is not in order during the pendancy of the previous question.

Mr. Clark. Is this question under discussion.

The Moderator. No sir. There is no question that can be debated before the house. We must proceed to vote for the previous question. A demand for the previous question is made, and Dr. Anderson demands the ayes and noes. In order that that may be tested we must see whether one-third of the house is willing to have the ayes and noes.

Mr. Clark. Did not Dr. McLean have the floor for the purpose of debating the question, and did he not make a motion for the previous question in connection therewith?

Rev. Dr. McLean. I call the gentleman to order. There is no discussion permitted on this question.

Mr. Clark. I am making a point of order and I contend I have the floor. By the 14th rule when a question is under debate no motion shall be received, unless to lay on the table, postpone indefinitely, postpone to a day certain, commit or amend. I contend that this matter is under debate, then, and that I have the right to make one of the motions here specified. If the Moderator sustains my view, then it is regular for me to make a motion to send this resolution to a committee.

The Moderator. I will decide that point of order. I agree with Judge Clark. The question is under debate, but I do not agree with his construction of the rule—that in every case the motions mentioned can be made while a question is under debate, for if that is the case the motion for a previous question could never have been made. Nothing is more common in parliamentary bodies than for the previous question to be moved at any stage of the proceedings. When it is moved, a vote on it must be taken. If the construction of the gentleman is right, then there is no place for the previous question to be made, provided the subject has been once debated. I decide that the previous question must be taken.

Dr. McLean. The Moderator will bear witness with me that my only desire has been—

The Moderator. The gentleman need not state his desire. We must take the vote.

Dr. McLean. No, sir; but the motive and object of making the motion—

The Moderator. That is in the nature of debate, and the gentleman need not state it.

Dr. McLean. Does the Moderator decide that nothing further is to be said?

The Moderator. I decided the gentleman was proceeding to debate the question by stating his desire.

Dr. McLean. No, sir, not at all.

The Moderator. That is my judgment and you must submit or appeal from it.

Rev. Mr. West. I wish merely to say, with all deference to the impatience of the brethren, that I desire to ask for information whether we are not called upon now to vote aye or no on the exclusion of this commission without hearing a word further than what Dr. McLean has said.

The Moderator. The Assembly must be its own judge in this matter.

Rev. Mr. West. I ask as to the effect of the motion.

The Moderator. I presume the Assembly has all the information that I have as to that matter.

Mr. Wyckliffe. I rise for the purpose of inquiring whether the honorable member who moved that resolution can furnish any instances in civilized parliamentary bodies where a duly accredited member to that body had been expelled by resolution and the previous question without being heard.

Dr. McLean. Is that discussion or not?

The Moderator. It is not in order. I hope when members rise they will speak something in regard to the point raised and not debate the question.

Mr. Laws. I rise to inquire if we cannot refuse by this vote to take the previous question. If we refuse then we are prepared to refer it. Under the 16th rule if a motion under debate contain several parts it may be divided. This has the nature of two parts. I think Dr. McLean did not debate it but simply explained it.

The Moderator. I do not understand that the demand for the previous question is at all divisible The demand has been made that in taking the vote the ayes and noes be recorded.

A member I ask as a point of order whether the call for the ayes and noes at this point is in order, inasmuch, sir, as the preliminary question is simply whether house will second the call for the previous question. Whether the call of Dr. Anderson is not properly for the record of the ayes any noes on the previous question, provided it be called by the house.

The Moderator. Certainly, I understand it so, and in order that we may determine whether the previous question is seconded or whether it shall be put.

Mr. Kempshall. May I ask the Moderator to state the effect of this motion. Is it not this, that if the Assembly orders the previous question it brings up the paper offered yesterday and not the resolution? The brethren evidently seem to think they are going to vote on the resolution and not on the paper.

The Moderator. In case one-third of the body shall answer in the affirmative to the question, "Shall the ayes and noes be recorded?"

A voice. A majority is required.

The Moderator. It is a question of recording the ayes and noes, which must be determined by one-third.

A member. There is a question among some of us whether it is in order at all to move the previous question in this way.

The Moderator. I have decided that it is in order.

A member. Allow me to ask Dr. Anderson on what he desires the ayes and noes. Is it on the previous question, or on the main question, after the previous question has been decided?

The Moderator. It is on the first question, which is, shall the main question be put?

Mr. Kempshall. The brethren around me ask you to state the effect of the previous question on the two papers—which of the two will come before them if it is sustained?

The Moderator. If one-third of the body vote affirmatively, that the ayes and noes may be recorded, then the question will come up, Shall the main question be put? If that is decided in the affirmative by a majority, then, if I understand Dr. Anderson's demand, it is upon the main question, which will be the adoption of Dr. McLean's paper, the ayes and noes will be demanded.

Dr. Anderson. No, sir. It is on the previous question. When the other comes up we will be ready for the same motion on that.

The Moderator. Then to answer the question we are brought to a direct vote on the paper offered by Dr. McLean yesterday.

The vote was then taken as to whether one-third of the members desired the ayes and noes on the previous question.

It appeared the ayes and noes were not desired.

The vote was then taken on the previous question, shall the main question now be put? and it was agreed to.

Dr. Wilson. Will the House allow the ayes and noes on the main question?

The Moderator. I had begun to take the vote, but I will give way.

Dr. Anderson. I gave notice in advance that when the question came up I should ask again for the ayes and noes.

The Moderator. I beg pardon, I did not understand it. The question now is, shall Dr. McLean's paper be adopted; no amendments being offered to it.

The vote was then taken as to whether the ayes and noes should be taken, and the ayes and noes were ordered.

The ayes and noes were then called, and the vote resulted ayes 201, nays 50, excused 3; so the paper offered by Dr. McLean yesterday was adopted.

During the calling of the roll several of the committees were called upon to hand in their reports.

Dr. Krebs, from the Committee on New Psalms and Hymns, desired to report but was declared out of order.

Rev. Mr. Forman desired to give notice that he entered a protest.

Dr. Van Dyke. I give notice that I protest.

Dr. Bracken. I give notice that I protest.

Rev. Mr. Smook. I wish to give notice that I protest against the vote on ordering the previous question merely.

Dr. McLean. It is necessary, in order to protest for A B and C to do so individually, or can they not unite in a protest.

The Moderator. Every member may rise and enter his protest individually if he chose to do so.

Mr. Harding stated that he desired to dissent.

Mr. Farquhar. As I understand it is, shall the question be taken by ayes and noes. Twice the Moderator stated distinctly before this last question was taken, Shall the main question now be put? Has the main question been put? We have decided to take the previous question, but I submit that we have not decided on the merits of the question.

The Moderator. The main question has been taken and the vote announced, and the paper is adopted by the votes I have announced.

Dr. McLean. Shall I read the resolution?

The Moderator. Let me explain to the satisfaction of the gentlemen. The form of the adoption was by taking the ayes and noes. I had announced the vote as ayes 201, nays 30, excused 3, therefore the paper is adopted. That is the main question.

Dr. McLean then read his resolution—above given—in regard to the appointment of a committee to whom the resolution in regard to the Louisville Presbytery shall be referred.

Rev. Mr. West. I move to lay the resolution on the table.

Mr. Waller. I desire to offer an amendment to Dr. McLean's motion before it passes—that is, that the case of Rev. P. A. Bracken, Commissioner here from the West Lexington Presbytery, who is affirmed to be a member of that Presbytery, but who is the pastor of a church within the bounds of the Lafayette Presbytery, and has never been dismissed from us, be referred also to the same committee to inquire in regard to the facts.

Rev. Mr. Brookes. I wish to offer the following amendment:

The Moderator. Is that an amendment to an amendment.

Mr. Brookes. Yes, sir.

Resolved, That the committee be also instructed to inquire into the truth of certain rumors charged upon other members of this body, and with the same offenses for which the Presbytery of Louisville has been arraigned before the Assembly, and to report what action should be taken in the premises.

I prefer it should come up at this time, if the Moderator and the Assembly please, and if you will allow me I will make a single remark—not to detain the House. I cannot remain content in my seat seeing that these brethren of the Louisville Presbytery have been excluded from participation in our discussions on account of offensive language contained in that "Declaration and Testimony." They are no more responsible for it, Moderator, than are many of us; and it would be unmanly in me to say that they are any more blamable than I am. If anybody is to be condemned for that paper I am the man. I had more to do with the origination of it—although I did not write it—than either Dr. Wilson or Dr. Stuart Robinson. And inasmuch as these brethren have been excluded from the house because of the use of language that is deemed offensive to this judicatory, I cannot remain silent and see them driven away and retain my place. My object, therefore, is that this committee shall make a thorough investigation of this whole subject, and if we are deemed to be unworthy of a seat in the General Assembly, or a place in the Church of the Fathers, for protesting against what we honestly deemed to be erroneous proceedings on the part of the General Assembly, let us know it, and for one I will cheerfully suffer for what I believe to be God Almighty's truth and Christ's glorious kingdom. [Applause in various parts of the house.]

A Voice. Clear the galleries.

Another Voice. Never mind; they won't hurt you.

The Moderator. I hope all such demonstrations, on either side, will not be manifested in this house.

Rev. Dr. VanDyke obtained the floor.

Rev. Mr. Bracken. I wish to explain before this question is put in regard to my own case, that members may vote intelligently. It is immaterial to me whether they refer my case to a committee or not, but I wish them to simply understand the facts which I will briefly state. The Presbytery to which I belong in Missouri was disorganized during the period of our troubles—that is, for five years no business was done. Three years and a half, if I mistake not, after that Presbytery had ceased to transact business, I presented a letter from the stated clerk of that Presbytery to the West Lexington Presbytery testifying to my standing, and was received by that Presbytery upon your record—as an order was issued by the General Assembly in 1864 in regard to this matter. These are the facts. I think that perhaps about one-half—possibly not so many—but quite a number of the members of the Presbyteries of Western Missouri, were received in other Presbyteries in the same way and during the same period of time. And I presume these Presbyteries thought they were authorized thus to receive them by the action of the General Assembly. I know such was the understanding on the part of the Presbytery of West Lexington, which received me, and of which I have been a member for two years and a half, and have met with them three times, and have twice sat in the Synod of Kentucky as a member.

Rev. Mr. Van Dyke again obtained the floor, and was proceeding to speak, when a point of order was raised in regard to the discussion on the amendment before the House, as to whether it should be confined strictly to the pending amendment.

The Moderator. I shall allow Dr. Van Dyke to go on, and if he gets out of order I will call him to order. I will ask Dr. Brookes to give his motion in writing.

Rev. Mr. Brookes then read the resolution which is given above. He said this is to include all who have signed this Declaration and Testimony to the same committee to inquire how many have signed it, and therefore chargeable with the same offense for which these gentlemen are excluded.

Rev. Wm. Breckinridge. I submit whether that is not the whole question before the Assembly?

The Moderator. I have so decided.

Rev. Wm. Breckinridge. You are right, undoubtedly.

Rev. Mr. West. Can an amendment be discussed before the original motion is discussed?

The Moderator. Certainly.

Rev. Mr. West. Then what do we vote upon when we come to this last amendment?

The Moderator. I can't tell whether we shall ever get to that point. The last amendment is now before the house, and Dr. Vandyke has the floor.

A member. The point is whether either of the amendments is in order.

The Moderator. I regard both in order.

The member. Allow me to suggest a reason why I think they are not in order.

The Moderator. I think when they are decided in order the question is not debateable.

Dr. McLean. It seems to me on taking up a report, the amendment or amendments are only read by the clerk.

The Moderator. What rule is that?

Dr. McLean. Jefferson's manual.

The Moderator. Well, sir, that is not one of our rules. [Laughter.]

Rev. Dr. McLean. I thought you were regulated by parliamentary rules.

The Moderator. We do not recognize Jefferson's Manual as authority on this particular point.

Rev. Dr. McLean. It is authority.

The Moderator. This is all in the nature of debate; Dr. Van Dyke has the floor.

Dr. Van Dyke. I have been waiting patiently all this time, and if I had been allowed to go on I should have concluded by this time. I think, perhaps, it is due to some of the members of this Assembly who have manifested a kind interest in me, and certainly due to myself that I should explain exactly my relation to the business now before it. I have failed many times to receive credit for what I have done, and I have many times received credit for what I have not done. I have been told by several members of this Assembly that I have been accredited with writing the Declaration and Testimony. The brethren do me honor over much. I did not write it. I had no part in the writing of it. I am not responsible for it in any way. If I had either written or approved the putting forth of it at that time I should have signed my name to it. Having said that I am bound to go further, and say that whatever principle is incorporated in the Declaration and Testimony aside from the language—from the practical inference in it—but whatever of principle there is in it I do subscribe to, and practically will ever act upon it so long as God will give me so to do [Applause.] And sir, agreeing with strength those principles, I should do injustice to myself if I were not willing to take my full share of any reproach or any condemnation which might come on those brethren for having advocates these principles, even though they might have erred in the language.

Now, sir, my objection to this whole proceeding is, that it is partial. Why, a stranger coming in here might suppose that these brethren of the Louisville Presbytery are sinners above all men, when it is perfectly notorious that men high in position in the Church, have, from the beginning, protested against the proceedings of the General Assembly in language quite as strong as any of these gentlemen ever used. Sixty-one members of the General Assembly—sixty-one, I think the number is correct—with Dr. Hodge at their head, said the deliverance of the General Assembly was "unconstitutional, a usurpation of Christ's prerogative, cruel and unjust." Is there anything stronger than that in the Declaration and Testimony? It is perfectly notorious that in the Synods of Baltimore and New York—especially in the cities—the orders of the General Assembly have not been attempted to be carried out. I do not know a man in the region of the church from which I come that will consent to carry out these orders; and further, it is well known in the Presbytery to which I belong—and who with the full knowledge of that fact sent me here—that I have not only refused to carry out this order, but have openly said I would not; not out of any rebellious spirit against the Assembly—God knows I have no such feeling—but on the high ground that I owe an allegiance to Jesus Christ, and upon the further ground that according to the Constitution of the Church this General Assembly has no authority to make such an order.

Rev. Mr. West. I rise to a point of order. I desire to know if this whole subject in relation to the principles involved in the Declaration and Testimony is to be gone into.

Rev. Mr. Van Dyke. I am not going into it. I am speaking entirely to the point. I am showing that you have grounds to make your action in this case a great deal broader.

The Moderator. Broader, even, than the action of the last Assembly?

Mr. Van Dyke. No, sir. Our own Confession of Faith says all Synods—

Rev. Mr. West. What is the decision of the Moderator?

The Moderator. I have already decided the point before this talk commenced. I stated if I discovered that the gentleman traveled beyond the bounds of my decision, I would call him to order. I confess I was not paying strict attention to what he was saying at the moment.

Rev. Mr. West. Am I to understand that the merits of the question are to come up.

The Moderator. Just so far as it is necessary to discuss the question, and if he goes beyond that I will call him to order.

Mr. Van Dyke. I will try to confine myself to the question if you will allow me. If the charge alleged against the Louisville Presbytery, in the paper which you have already adopted, and which charge is equally applicable to other brethren, were true, I respectfully submit to you that it involves neither heresy nor crime. When I adopted the Confession of Faith, and affirmed the government of the Presbyterian Church, and solemnly swore allegiance to it, I meant to keep it; but there was a clause there respecting my personal rights in that matter—a right of private judgment.

All Synods and councils since the time of the Apostles, either generally or particularly, may err, and many have erred. They are not to be made the rule of both faith and practice; they may lapse in both. And further: "Before any overtures or regulations, proposed by the General Assembly to be established as constitutional rules, shall be obligatory on the Churches, it shall be necessary to transmit them to all Presbyteries, and to receive the return of at least a majority of them in writing, approved by them." Now, no act of this General Assembly on freedom and loyalty, from 1861 to 1865 (and especially the orders of the last General Assembly) was transmitted to the Presbyteries, and I affirm, according to the language of the book, they are not obligatory on any Church or Assembly, and no binding authority on me whatever. If they had been transmitted to the Presbyteries and adopted by them, then the question would come up fairly as to what is the constitutional rule of the church; but there is no rule that has been violated by the Presbytery of Louisville according to the language of the book. If they could prove all you have said, there then is no violation. The language of the resolution is, they defied the General Assembly. Now, I do not think the facts justify the use of the word "defiance." And what is the proof? The resolution says they have refused to obey the orders of the General Assembly, and said so. That is just what I have done; that is just what three-fourths of the ministers that I am acquainted with in New York and Brooklyn have done. The sessions of my church, immediately after the passage of these orders, moved—one of them on their records—a protest, and refusal to obey, but I objected for the same reason that I did not sign the Declaration and Testimony. I believed, under our confession of faith and terms of membership, and the doctrines of our Church as found in the word of God, that the General Assembly has no authority to make rules in this way that are binding on us, and therefore we have gone forward without reference to what the General Assembly has said, and intend so to do until that action of the Assembly is adopted by the Presbyteries. The only difference between these brethren in Louisville and fifty others, many of whom are on the floor of this Assembly, is, they have openly printed what they intended to do, while the rest have done without openly saying anything. I do not see that, so far as justice is concerned, there is any difference in the case. Now, sir, I do not care to discuss the question further on its merits, because I respect your decision. But there is another remark I must make, and I make it in a spirit of conciliation and kindness, and God knows, with a feeling of grief. The carrying out of the plan indicated by the resolution which you have adopted, whether you make it partial or universal, will defeat its own end, because I take it for granted that the motive in which this paper has originated is a motive that will bear the test of God's word and the light of judgment. I take it for granted it is to promote the peace, purity and unity of the Church. You may rest assured *it will not* promote the peace, purity and unity of the Church. If you sacrifice these brethren of the Louisville Presbytery because they have contended for a principle which some of us hold as firmly as they do, you may make them martyrs for that principle, and you will rally around them an influence numerically, socially and in every other respect which, perhaps, on personal grounds they could not have attained. If this General Assembly, by the force of the previous question, and by papers prepared before the Assembly met—and I do not mean to be disrespectful in this matter, but it is notorious what I allude to—unless the General Assembly mean to cut off the discussion of these great principles that pertain to the kingdom of Jesus Christ, by condemning those who honestly contended for those principles, there are others of us who will be bound by our allegiance to the Church and to God to stand exactly in the same position with them. I have nothing further to say.

Rev. Dr. Anderson. It would be entirely unmanly and unchristian if I should be silent now, though I speak as you perceive, and have done for years with great difficulty. [A voice—"Louder."] I will make the members hear me, if they will wait till I can clear my throat.

I am, sir, the Stated Clerk of the Synod of Missouri, and I wish to say now, in this body, in no spirit of defiance, but that they may know the facts, that by a deliberative body, after a calm and thorough discussion of the principles involved, the main points that are involved in the Declaration and Testimony were adopted by the Synod of Missouri by a vote of three to one. We wish to put ourselves, therefore, in the ranks with our brothers of the Presbytery of Louisville, and others who may fall under the action of the guillotine in holding these sentiments. I wish to say more, sir. I approve of that action of the Synod of Missouri, and voted for it. I wish to say further, sir, and in no spirit of defiance, that at the last meeting of my session but one, we received two members among others, sitting side by side, touching each other, one of whom had ridden in Merrill's horse on the Federal side and the other had bared his breast to the Union bayonets on the Southern side. They were neither of them asked any questions about their opinions with regard to one army or the other, but we received them as Christians, supposing that in their union with Christ there was a bond strong enough to bind them together across that gulf of blood that had for a time separated them. And I wish to say again, sir, in no spirit of defiance, that I should be glad to do that thing at every meeting of my session; and, God helping me, I will never obey an order that makes me determine the political opinions or practices of any man who may come to me to be united in the fellowship of the Church of Christ. I wish to put these facts before the minds of this Assembly and ask them to commission that committee to examine into our acts as well as those that have already been committed to their charge.

Rev. Mr. Forman of St. Joseph, Mo., said owing to physical debility he could not make a speech, but wished to make a few remarks in explanation of his position. He was a member of the Assembly in 1864 and on his way home had consultation with several brethren as to the course best to be pursued in relation to the acts of the Assembly regarded as unscriptural. A conference was suggested. About a year after he received a letter requesting him to attend such a conference. He could not go but wrote a letter counseling prudence and moderation. When the "Declaration and Testimony" appeared he did not and could not sign it, for he regarded it as too harsh in its spirit. But the great principles asserted in that paper he held to be true. The orders of the General Assembly in relation to Southern Christians and ministers he could not execute, because he believed them to be unscriptural. When Southern sympathizers, or those who had been in the rebel army, made application for admission to his Church, he could only ask them whether, as lost and helpless sinners, they were trusting in Jesus as a personal Savior. To go beyond this would be contrary to the teachings of God's word. And now if the Assembly were determined to inquire into the conduct of the Louisville brethren for refusing to execute the orders of the Assembly, he wished the investigation to extend to himself and to all others who cannot observe an act which they hold to be unscriptural. Yea, he would have it extend to Dr. Hodge for his published declarations in opposition to the Assembly acts, and to Dr. R. J. Breckinridge for the paper penned by him and adopted by the Synod of Kentucky in 1861, in such very strong terms condemning the deliverance of the Assembly on the state of the country.

Rev. Mr. Bracken. I will remark, Moderator, that I have never signed the paper known as the Declaration and Testimony. Very many members of the Synod of Kentucky, and indeed many members of the West Lexington Presbytery signed that paper. They did not regard it as wise. The storm of passion was raging all through the land. It had entered the Church and ecclesiastical bodies, and we feared that document would be misapprehended and misinterpreted. We desired to avoid the evils that might result from it. These brethren said in that document that they did not desire a division of the Church. That they stood upon the old platform, and observed the old landmarks, taking the word of God and the constitution of the Church as their guide. But, Mr. Moderator, we feared it might be said that they had other aims in view, and the results have come to pass. No sooner was the document circulated than it was noised abroad over the length and breadth of the land, that here were rebels suspected long of disloyalty to their Church, and now that they had openly avowed that disloyalty, and that alarm was sounded loud and long, and it was prolonged and its echoes may yet be heard. This is what we would have avoided. But I speak with confidence, when I say a large majority of the office bearers of the Synod of Kentucky indorse substantially all that is said in that document; that the majority of the Synod of Kentucky agreed with Dr. Hodge and fifty-seven others, who, in 1661, when the first step was taken—when the seed was planted which has matured and developed and borne its ripened fruit. We believe with Dr. Hodge that that action was unconstitutional in its character—that it instituted new terms of Church membership, and usurped the perogatives of the Divine Master. Furthermore, we believe that when the Synod of Kentucky declared in their report, which was written and introduced by the Brother who would now ask you to exclude those who reassert the same sentiments—we believe with that Synod resolution, adopted without a dissenting voice, that the action of the Assembly was unscriptural and unconstitutional. But changes took place, and new judgments were made to suit those changes. But, Mr. Moderator, it was not the Declaration and Testimony men of the Louisville Presbytery that changed when, in 1865, they repeated the same Testimony of the entire Assembly of 1845. We believe, furthermore, that we could not obey these orders, which we regarded as unscriptural and unconstitutional without violating other deliverances of the General Assembly. We turn back over the record of the Church and we read in the minutes of 1845 the sentiment that Christ did not legislate on these subjects, and the Church could not since the great head of the Church had not. We did not feel like violating the deliverances before given upon the clear teaching of God's word. We felt that we would violate the sentiment of that deliverance if we obeyed the orders of 1865.

A member. I insist that this whole debate comes on the report of the Committeee, and I move to adjourn.

The Moderator. It is not yet time for a recess.

Dr. Bracken. That action of 1845 was taken when the entire Church was bound together by strong cords of brotherly love—delivered at a time when the excitements and confusion of the forum had never been introduced into ecclesiastical bodies. It was delivered when our Church, as the great conservative body of the land, stood forth like a mountain cliff, calm and immovable. There was no disturbance of that kind then. Our Church was then like a firm rock that beat back the muddy waves that dashed against it, and we felt like adhering to that deliverance of the General Assembly. Mr. Moderator, are we understand when acts of the General Assembly contradict each other, that the last act is the one alone which possesses binding force. We felt that this might be very good popery. We had read in the history of the past of Popes who claimed universal dominion, and the argument was that they had received the keys which gave them superior power from Christ, and we had also read that political and civil affairs came under the jurisdiction of the Pope and that when he could not carry out his dictates without military power, the military power was the servant of the spiritual head. We considered it was the same old argument repeated—repeated within the last few years.

And again, Mr. Moderator, every Presbytery almost in the State of Kentucky pronounced that first act as unconstitutional and unscriptural, and since that time almost every Presbytery in Kentucky has taken like action. But that is not all, because, Mr. Moderator, the very brethren who have assumed—

Dr. McLean. Is that the question? What is the question? Is that member in favor or opposed to it?

Rev. Mr. Bracken. Whichever way you choose to have it.

The Moderator. I understand the gentleman that this investigation should take a very wide range. [Laughter.]

A member. I wish to inquire if it is in order for a gentleman to speak more than once to this point without the consent of this body. The gentleman has already spoken upon this subject.

The Moderator. I think that is the first speech the gentleman has made.

Dr. McLean. Let us know what side he is on.

The Moderator. He must tell you that.

Mr. Ferguson. I hope we shall trust the Moderator's judgment; he has said, as soon as the gentleman gets out of order, he will call him to order.

Dr. Bracken, Allow me to say to Dr. McLean, that I am talking now in order to show that there are very many more in a like state. I am speaking on the amendment of Dr. Brookes, and to show that there are many more beside these brethren who stand on common ground, and have given like deliverances. Mr. Moderator, we feel that this would be very partial action, because the very members who differ from us, as has already been remarked, are practically doing the same thing. Where, I might ask, in the Synod of Kentucky, has there ever been an effort made to enforce these orders? I presume that such an attempt has never been made.

Rev. Mr. Thomas. I desire to make a few remarks but as the hour of adjournment is at hand I will move that we adjourn till this afternoon.

The Moderator. The General Assembly will hold no session this afternoon unless they reconsider the decision that they have already made.

A motion to reconsider the vote by which the hours were fixed was lost.

The Assembly then adjourned until Saturday morning at nine A. M.

The following is a complete list of delegates to the Assembly:

SYNOD OF ALBANY.

PRESBYTERIES.

Albany—Ministers, David Lyon, J. T. Backus, D. D.

Londonderry—Minister, Joseph P. Bixby.

Mohawk—Elder, Lucien B. Wells.

Siam—Minister, S. R. House, M. D.
Troy—Minister, Wm. M. Johnson. Elder, G. Fort.

SYNOD OF ALLEGHENY,

PRESBYTERIES.

Allegheny—Minister, Robert B. Walker, D. D. Elder, Valentine C. Glenn.
Allegheny City—Ministers, John M. Smith, Jas. Allison. Elders, Robert McKnight, John Hay, Jr.
Beaver—Minister, C. C. Riggs, D. D. Elder, Wm. M. Francis.
Erie—Minister, George F. Cain. Elder, A. H. Caughiey.

SYNOD OF BALTIMORE.

PRESBYTERIES.

Baltimore—Ministers, Joseph T. Smith, D. D., John Pym Carter. Elders, John Dickson, M. D., Rogers Birnie.
Carlisle—Ministers, J. W, Wightman, S. S. Mitchell. Elders, W. G. Reed. R. G. McCreary.
Lewis—Minister, L. P. Bowen. Elder, Isaac D. Jones.
Potomac—Minister, P. D. Gurley, D. D. Elder, Edward Myers.

SYNOD OF BUFFALO.

PRESBYTERIES.

Buffalo City—Minister, James Remington. Elder, H. Howard.
Genesee River—Minister, Charles Ray. Elder, David McMaster.
Ogdensburg—Minister, James Gardner. Elder, Allen Chaney.
Rochester City—Minister, E. D. Yeomans, D. D.

SYNOD OF CHICAGO.

PRESBYTERIES.

Bureau—Minister, Sam. T. Wilson. Elder Edward Buck.
Chicago—Ministers, R. G. Thompson, Frederick T. Brown, D. D. Elders, Robert Porter, Lincoln Clark.
Rock River—Minister, E. C. Sickles, Elder, James Snyder.
Schuyler—Minister, J. T. Bliss. Elder, Wm. E. Withrow.
Warren—Minister, R. C. Matthews, D. D. Elder, Thomas Muir.

SYNOD OF CINCINNATI.

PRESBYTERIES.

Chillicothe—Minister, R. L. Stanton, D. D. Elder, Wm. Thomas.
Cincinnati—Ministers, J. G, Monfort, D. D., W. W. Colmery. Elders, Thomas McGechin, A. E. Chamberlain.
Miami—Ministers, Thomas E. Thomas, D. D., William T. Findley. Elders, S. D. Sharon, G. S. Ormsby.
Oxford—Minister, A. O. Patterson, D. D. Elder, Wm. Curry.
Sydney—Minister, Wm. Greenough. Elder, Samuel Hover.

SYNOD OF ILLINOIS.

PRESBYTERIES.

Bloomington—Ministers, R. Conover, Wm. T. Adams. Elder, I. B. McKinley.
Kaskaskia—Minister, Thomas W. Hynes. Elder, Hugh Adams.
Palestine—Minister, —— ———. Elder, R. M. Yates.
Peoria—Minister, J. F. Magill, Elder, John C. Grier.
Saline—Minister, John Crozier. Elder, Thomas Buchanan.
Sangamon—Minister, R. W. Allen. Elder, D. C. Brown.

SYNOD OF INDIANA.

PRESBYTERIES.

Indianapolis—Minister, George C. Heckman. Elder, James Blake.
Madison—Minister, G. D. Archibald, D. D. Elder, W. P. Inskepp.
New Albany—Minister, J. P. Safford, D. D. Elder, J. H. McCampbell.
Vincennes—Minister, F. R. Morton. Elder, S. M. Archer.
Whitewater—Minister, R. F. Patterson. Elder, William Blanchard.

SYNOD OF IOWA.

PRESBYTERIES.

Cedar—Minister, James D. Mason. Elder, Thomas Elder.
Dubuque—Minister, ——. Elder, J. K. Duncan.
Toledo—Minister, J. S. Dunning. Elder, Wm. H. Peterson.

SYNOD OF KANSAS.

PRESBYTERIES.

Highland—Minister, Wm. Bishop. Elder, ——.
Leavenworth—Minister, J. G. Reaser. Elder, ——.
Topeka—Minister, I. M. Pryse. Elder, ——.

SYNOD OF KENTUCKY.

PRESBYTERIES.

Ebenezer—Minister, J. E. Spillman. Elder, Charles A. Munhall.
Louisville—Ministers, Stuart Robinson, D. D., Samuel R. Wilson, D. D. Elders, C. A. Wickliffe, Mark Harden.
Muhlenburg—Minister, R. K. Smoot. Elder, ———.
Paducah—Minister, J. T. Hendrick, D. D. Elder, G. W. Garrett.
Transylvania—Ministers, Wm. L. Breckinridge, D. D., Edward P. Humphrey, D. D.. Elders, O. Beatty, J. C. Maxwell.
West Lexington — Minister, T. A. Bracken. Elder, G. Marshall.

SYNOD OF MISSOURI.

PRESBYTERIES.

Lafayette—Minister, J. L. Yantis, D. D. Elder, George W. Buchanan.
Missouri—Minister, John Giffin. Elder, ———.
Palmyra—Minister, J. M. Travis. Elder, J. W. Pryor.
Potosi—Minister, D. A. Wilson. Elder, A. M. McPherson.
St. Louis—Ministers, S. J. P. Anderson, D. D, J. H. Brookes, D. D. Elders, E. Bredell, Joseph Conway.
Upper Missouri—Minister, A. P. Forman. Elder, H. T. Walker.
Wyaconda—Minister, George Van Eman. Elder, ———.

SYNOD OF NASHVILLE.

PRESBYTERY.

Nashville—Minister, J. B. Lindsley, D. D. Elder, Charles H. Smith.

SYNOD OF NEW JERSEY.

PRESBYTERIES.

Burlington—Minister, V. D. Reed, D. D. Elder, Joseph D. Reinboth.
Elizabethtown—Ministers, E. Kempshall, James C. Edwards. Elder, Reuben Van Pelt.
Luzerne—Ministers, Milo J. Hickock, D. D., A. M. Lowry. Elders, ——.
Monmouth—Minister, D. D. McLean, D. D. Elder, Wm. L. Terhune.
Newton—Ministers, Myron Barrett, Aaron H. Hand, D. D. Elder, John C. Labar.
New Brunswick—Ministers, A. Gosman, D. D., Joseph G. Symms. Elders, George S. Green, Wm. Rust.
Passaic—Minister, W. H. Hornblower, D. D. Elder, Albert DeHart
Raritan—Minister, John Barrows. Elder, Hugh E. Warford.
Susquehanna—Minister, Halleck Armstrong. Elder, A. Wickham.
West Jersey—Minister, Charles Wood. Elder, Henry B. Ware.

SYNOD OF NEW YORK.

PRESBYTERIES.

Conneticut—Minister, A. Shiland. Elder, W. P. Van Rensselaer.

Hudson—Ministers, Robert A. Davison, Luther Little. Elders, James Van Keuren, Linden Mulford.
Long Island—Ministers, Augustus T. Dobson, Sidney G. Law. Elder, James R. Rolph.
Nassau—Ministers, Nathaniel West, D. D., Henry J. Van Dyke, D. D. Elder. E. P. Ketchum.
New York—Ministers, Charles J. Jones, John M. Krebs, D. D. Elders, Henry Day, John Stewart, James Bayliss.
New York, 2d—Minister, D. M. Halliday, D. D. Elder, Wm. R. Belcher.
Ningpo—Minister, J. L. Nevins. Elder, ——
North River—Minister, Samuel H. Jagger. Elder, Hugh S. Banks.

SYNOD OF NORTHERN INDIANA.

PRESBYTERIES.

Crawfordsville—Minister, R. Irwin, Jr. Elder, J. G. McMechan, M. D.
Fort Wayne—Minister, C. A. Munn. Elder, Jesse L. Williams.
Lake—Minister, H. L. Vannuys. Elder, H. L. Gillet.
Logansport—Minister, J. C. Irwin. Elder, R. P. Davidson.
Munice—Minister, John A. Campbell. Elder, James M. Ray.

SYNOD OF OHIO.

PRESBYTERIES.

Columbus—Minister, C. W. Finley. Elder, Samuel Galloway.
Hocking—Minister, John H. Pratt. Elder, A. G. Brown.
Marion—Minister, C. H Perkins. Elder, Moses Cole.
Richland—Minister, Alexander Scott. Elder, J. J. Turner
Wooster—Minister, J. C. Gillan. Elder, Jacob Reaser.
Zanesville—Minister, W. M. Ferguson. Elder, Robert Buchanan.

SYNOD OF THE PACIFIC.

California—Minister, A. W. Loomis. Elder, —— ——.
Stockton—Minister, James A. Skinner. Elder. —— ——.

SYNOD OF PHILADELPHIA.

Donegal—Ministers, John Farquhar, Lindley C. Rutter. Elders, David Mitchell, W. W. Watson.
Huntingdon—Minister, John H. Clark. Elder, S. T. Brown.
Newcastle—Ministers, Justus T. Umsted, David W. Moore. Elders, James A. Strawbridge, —— Vanarsdale.
Northumberland—Ministers, C. H. Park, D. J. Waller. Elders, M. C. Grier, James Rankin.
Philadephia—Ministers, William E. Schenck, Henry A. Boardman, D. D. Elders, James Andrews, W. W. Caldwell.
Philadelphia Central—Ministers, J. A. Henry, T. M. Cunningham. Elder, John S. McClellan.
Philadelphia 2d—Ministers, J. B. Davis, Roger Owen. Elder, Barton H. Jencks.

SYNOD OF PITTSBURGH.

PRESBYTERIES.

Blairsville—Minister, B. L. Agnew. Elder, D. W. Shryock.
Clarion—Minister, J. Mateer. Elder, C. Orr.
Ohio—Ministers, Francis J. Collin, J. W. Hazlett. Elders, Samuel McMaster, Samuel Rea.
Redstone—Minister, Joel Stoneroad. Elder, Wm. S. Caldwell.
Saltsburg — Minister, John Caruthers. Elder, John Christy.

SYNOD OF SANDUSKY.

PRESBYTERIES.

Findlay—Minister, W. K. Brice. Elder, John Dobbins.
Maumee—Minister, E. B. Raffensperger. Elder, S. D. Chamberlin.
Michigan—Minister, B. F. Morden. Elder, H. K. Clarke.
Western Reserve — Minister, Solomon Cook. Elder, Robert Lyle.

SYNOD OF SOUTHERN IOWA.

PRESBYTERIES.

Des Moines—Minister, J. P. Bringle. Elder, David Wills.
Fairfield—Minister, D. V. Smock. Elder, Wm. T. Orr.
Iowa—Minister, G. D. Stewart. Elder, Wm. Mason.

SYNOD OF WHEELING.

PRESBYTERIES.

New Lisbon—Minister, Thomas P. Speer. Elder, James Russell.
Steubenville—Ministers, Robert Herron, George Fraser. Elders, Andrew Boyd, H. Hammond.
St. Clairsville—Minister, Wm. M. Grimes. Elder, Robert S. Clark.
Washington—Ministers, Daniel W. Fisher, James Fleming. Elders, Wm. M. Nicoll, Thomas McKean.
West Virginia—Minister, C. P. French. Elder, ——.

SYNOD OF WISCONSIN.

PRESBYTERIES.

Dane—Minister, J. W. Dinsmore. Elder, L. T. Stowell.
Milwaukee—Minister, Chas. T. Thompson. Elder, John Ogden.
Winnebago—Minister, ——. Elder, A. V. Balch.

THIRD DAY—SATURDAY, MAY 19, 1866.

Met at 9 o'clock a.m.
At the conclusion of the devotional exercises the minutes of yesterday were read and approved.
The Moderator announced the remainder of the committees as follows:

DISABLED MINISTERS' FUND.

Ministers, R. C. Matthews, D. D., Wm. Greenough, John Farquhar, R. A. Davidson, D. V. Smock and W. M. Ferguson.
Elders, Charles E. Webster, Hugh S. Banks and Henry Hammond.

MILEAGE.

Elders, David Mitchell, Robt. Buchanan and Wm. Mason.

LEAVE OF ABSENCE.

Ministers, Samuel B. Jagger, B. K. Smoot and Geo. Fraser.
Elders, J. E. Reinboth and Jacob Reasor.

SYNODICAL RECORDS.

Albany—Ministers, Lindley C. Rutter, C. H. Perkins. Elders, John Dobbins, James Russell.
Allegheny—Ministers, J. P. Pringle, Solomon Cook. Elders, Andrew Boyd, Samuel McMaster.
Baltimore—Ministers, John W. Hazlette, Thos. P. Speer. Elders, Samuel D. Chamberlain, John S. McClellan.
Buffalo—Ministers, B. F. Murden, G. D. Stewart. Elders, Wm. M. Nicoll, L. T. Stewell.

Chicago—Ministers, John Carothers, Robert Herron. Elders, A. V. Balch, N. N. Caldwell.
Cincinnati—Ministers, Wm. M. Grimes, J. N. Dinsmore. Elders, Culbertson Orr, James Andrews.
Illinois—Ministers, C. P. French, J. B. Davis. Elders, Wm. S. Caldwell, J. J. Turner.
Indiana--Ministers, Jas. Fleming, C. H. Parks. Elders, John Christy, Moses Cox.
Iowa--Ministers, D. W. Fisher, D. W. Moore. Elders, R. P. Davidson, E. P. Ketchum.
Kansas--Ministers, J. A. Skinner, J C. Gillam. Elders, Thos. McKean, W. W. Watson.
Kentucky--Ministers, W. W. Colmery John H. Clarke. Elders, M. C. Grier, A. G. Brown.
Missouri--Ministers, J. Stoneroad, J. A. Henry. Elders, D. W. Shryock, J. G. McMechan.
Nashville -Ministers, A. Gorman, D. D., J. M. Pryse. Elders, J. F. Vanarsdale, Linden Mulford.
New Jersey—Ministers, J. T. Umstead, John A. Campbell. Elders, J. A. Strawbridge, James Van Keuren.
New York—Ministers, A. H. Hand, D. D., J. T. Hendrick, D. D. Elders, S. T. Brown, T. F. McCoy.
Northern India—Ministers, D. M. Halliday, D. D., J. E Edwards. Elders, Henry B. Ware, C. A. Marshall.
Northern Indiana—Ministers. A. T. Dobson, J. Allen. Elders, A. Wickham, W. P. Inskip.
Ohio—Ministers, R. Conover, G. C. Heckman. Elders, H. E. Walford, J. H. Campbell.
Pacific—Ministers, J. S. Dunning, ——. Elders, A. De Hart, J. K Duncan.
Philadelphia—Ministers, R. T. Patterson, R. W. Allen. Elders, S. M. Archer, Ed. Buck.
Pittsburgh—Ministers, J. Burroughs, W. M. Johnson. Elders, W. Rust, C. W. Campbell.
St. Paul Ministers, C. E Robinson, S. S. Mitchell. Elders, A. H. Caughey, H. Housan.
Sandusky—Ministers, Myron Barret. J. S. Dunning. Elders, Wm. L. Terhune, Thos. Elder.
Southern Iowa—Ministers, A. M. Lowry, Jno. M Smith. Elders, J. K. Duncan, Geo S. Green.
Wheeling—Ministers, H. Armstrong, Geo. F. Cain. Elders, Jno. S. Tabar, Edward Myers.
Wisconsin—Ministers, L. P. Bowen, Charles Ray. Elders, D. McMaster, W. Blanchard.

The Rev. Mr Smook gave notice that he withdrew his notice of protest against the previous question.

The case of Rev. Mr. Giffin, of the North Missouri Presbytery, was referred to the Committee on Elections.

The Moderator announced the following changes in the Standing Committee: Samuel Jagger as Chairman of a committee in place of Rev. Mr. Fraser, who was compelled to decline the position. In the Board of Foreign Missions, Rev. Robert Porter was appointed in the place of George Way.

The Rev. Mr. Safford moved that twelve o'clock be assigned as the hour for recei ing the representative of the First Presbyterian Church, Rev. Dr. Nelson. Agreed to.

The Rev. Mr. McKnight rose to a point of order. The applause in the gallery yesterday was so manifestly a breach of the propriety that ought to obtain in an ecclesiastical body, that he desired the Moderator to make an appeal to the gallery and lobbies, and to those on the floor to refrain from the repetition of such applause hereafter, otherwise he should feel constrained to move that the house take some action on the subject. He hesitated yesterday to make this motion, because the applause seemed to be on the side of those who were in the minority.

The Moderator hoped that a sense of propriety would restrain all such applause in the future.

The Rev. Mr. —— offered the following:

Resolved, That a committee of five be appointed, of which the Rev. Dr. Thomas shall be Chairman, to confer with a similar committee from the Assembly sitting in the Second Presbyterian church in this city with reference to a union in devotional exercises.

The resolution was adopted, and the Moderator stated that the committee would be appointed at the conclusion of the forenoon session.

Rev. Dr. McLean, from the Committee on Church Extension, obtained leave to make the following report:

By the favor of God we are able to report to the General Assembly, that the year recently closed was one of progress in the work of church extension. Though we cannot as in our last annual statement record a noble legacy of $10,000 from one who, in life, honored the Lord with his substance and departing to his regal inheritance blessed the church, through her different boards, with princely gifts; and, though for this reason, we now report legacies of less than $600 instead of nearly $11,000; yet the increased receipts from other sources swelled the income of the year to within $3,000 of its predecessor. In every other particular, advance may be inscribed upon our register. As compared with the preceding twelve months, the applications increased fifty-five per cent; the appropriations forty-one per cent; and the payments more than thirty per cent. The number of contributing churches rose from 751 to 779, while the field open to effort expanded southward over twelve degrees of latitude, enclosing Louisiana no less than Minnesota in its genial lines of aid.

APPLICATIONS.

During the fiscal year ending April 2, 1866, ninety-six churches sought aid to the amount of $65,484 07. This gives an average of $682 12 to each church, an increase of nearly eighteen per cent on the average of the preceding year.

Adding to these the applications on file, and undisposed of April 1, 1865, we find that there were before the Board during the year one hundred and thirty-two applications calling for $100,773 07. Thus it appears that, although the cost of building has not materially diminished, the anticipations of increased applications expressed in our last report have been realized.

In the twelve months under review, thirteen applications calling for $12,800 were for the usual reason stricken from the register. There remained on file April 2, 1866, awaiting the receipt of the requisite information, thirty-seven applications asking for $30,550.

APPROPRIATIONS.

Appropriations were made during the year to sixty-nine churches whose names and localities are given in the appendix. The amount granted to these churches was $34,121 33. This is an average of $494 51 to each, being nearly thirty per cent above the average of last year, and nearly double the advance in the average of applications.

In addition to the above formal appropriations a number of informal pledges of aid were, as in some former years, made under peculiar circumstances. Thus the total liabilities incurred during the year were $8,217 71 in advance of the income.

In every case, allowed by the Assembly, where the necessary information was furnished, a grant was made either of the full amount asked by the Presbytery, or of a sum sufficient to complete the Sanctuary free from debt. Combine this fact with the fact that for four years the average of appropriations has risen more rapidly than the average of applications; and with the further fact that formal grants during that period have been made to thirty-four churches more than the number reported as organized within that time in our connection, and there seems good ground to hope that the people of God will ere long enable the Board to overtake the necessities of the Church Extension work. These facts at least betoken something beyond the dawn of the day when all proper claims of our houseless flocks on the Church at large can be met without the great expense and terrible drudgery of personal indiscriminate appeals for aid by individual solicitors.

Appropriations, amounting to $2,185 25, were during the year withdrawn from five churches for the usual reasons. Two of these, however, were subsequently aided by new grants, though the name of one of them had meanwhile been changed.

Fifty-four churches, between April 1, 1865, and April 2, 1866, drew their appropriations amounting to $25,439 43.

RECEIPTS AND EXPENDITURES.

The balance appropriated and unappropriated on hand April 1, 1865, was $51,521 82. The receipts from April 1, 1865, to April 2, 1866, were $35,870 28. The entire available means of the year were therefore $87,392 10.

The Treasurer's report in the appendix shows expenditures to the amount of $28,390 89. The balance in the treasury April 2, 1866, was consequently $59,001 21. There were, however, unpaid at that date liabilities amounting to $37,628, leaving an unpledged balance of $21,373 21 to meet applications already filed, (and that may at any time be put in proper shape for final action,) amounting to $30,550. Presented in tabular form the financial position of the Board would be properly exhibited thus, viz:

Pledges already made	$37,628 00
Applications filed and that at any time may require final action	30,550 00
Total present demands	$68,178 00
Balance on hand April 2, 1866	59,001 21
Deficit in present means to meet present demands	$9,176 79

THE WORK DONE.

The Board of Church Extension has presented eleven annual reports to successive General Assemblies. A brief summary of these reports would show the sum of $288,237 17 raised for Church Extension; and six hundred and twelve different churches aided to complete their sanctuaries without debt by formal grants amounting to $237,437 80. At a low estimate of cost and capacity, these sanctuaries have furnished comfortable accommodations for 125,000 worshipers, and secured church properties of the value of at least one and three-quarter millions of dollars. Add to these results (which have been obtained without a cent of expense to the Church or to general contributors) the 382 churches aided and the $68,544 06, received during the previous eleven years by the then existing Church Extension Committee of the Board of Missions, and we arrive at the grand fact that our Church, through her organized agencies, has in the last twenty-two years quietly raised for this work $356,781 23. Therewith she has already aided nine hundred and ninety-four of her feeble flocks to provide sanctuaries for over two hundred thousand worshipers; and to secure unincumbered church properties worth over two millions of dollars. Thus at an average cost to the Church at large of less than one dollar and fifty-three cents for each, has room been made in nearly one thousand sanctuaries for over two hundred thousand persons. While these external results may be chrystalized into figures, what arithmetic can express the higher ends to which they have been the means. The Omniscient Eye alone can trace the established relation between this church erection, and the hundreds of revivals and tens of thousands of conversions that have consecrated these "gardens inclosed" and thus lengthened the cords and extended the boundaries of Zion. Only the All Recording Pen has registered the innumerable petitions born in these thousand houses of prayer and noted the blessings with which they have returned fraught to earth. Is it too much to believe that God has seldom honored the labors of the Church in any direction with richer fruit in proportion to the expenditure, and that our fathers did well when looking beyond the mere process, they gave the work a name expressive of its results?

THE FIELD.

While we rejoice in the work already done, let us not forget what remains unaccomplished.

Nearly four hundred houseless churches still need aid from their more favored brethren.

With the return of peace nearly a hundred new and needy organizations will in all probability annually be added to our church roll.

Sanctuaries desolated by war must be rebuilt or repaired. Within a few months we have cheerfully aided in restoring several such, and there yet remain not a few feeble flocks scattered and peeled by intestine strife that must have help in the same good work.

A great field, as yet scarcely touched, opens before the church among the Freedmen, if she proves not recreant to her duty to these millions of semi-heathen at home. Already our brethren of the Freedmen's Committee, oppressed by the responsibilities thrown upon them, have, as they were authorized to do, appealed to us for help in securing houses of worship. Gladly have we responded to every such appeal; and shall continue to do so as long as the means are entrusted to us for distribution.

In view of these varied demands, is it unreasonable to ask the 1,850 churches that neglected this labor of love last year to lend a helping hand for the future, and the 779 churches, with the generous individual donors, who remembered their destitute brethren, not to become weary in well doing.

By order of the Board,

SAM'L J. NICCOLLS, President.

H. I. COE, Secretary.

After the reading of the report, Dr. McLean made a few remarks urging efforts looking towards an increase of the funds of the Board, whereby the ability of the Board to establish new churches would be largely increased.

On motion of Rev. Mr. West, the subject was put upon the docket.

Dr. Krebs, by permission of the Assembly, made report from the Committee of Five, appointed by the General Assembly, on the 19th of May, 1864, to select psalms and hymns from the present books, and from other sources, and publish the same with suitable tunes. The report states that the committee were restricted to forming a small, rather than a large book, to contain about five hundred hymns. A large number of Presbyteries and some individuals had responded to inquiries sought upon the subject, through whom the committee had been enabled to learn what was most likely to meet the wants of the Church. The committee recommend that the book be styled "The Hymnal of the Presbyterian Church ordered by the General Assembly." In consequence of the restrictions imposed, the committee were required to sacrifice personal preferences, sometimes rejecting, sometimes including what others might have reversed. They state that while many persons have regarded with a sacred horror the *mutilation* of old and favorite hymns, they have been found declaiming against the restoration of original forms. The committee had made but few and slight changes, which practically amount to nothing disturbing; and while the changes made may be unpleasant at the first, it is easy to become reconciled to the change, while the children who shall take the place of the present constituents will learn to cherish the present rendering as the former have been cherished by others. As for the name "Hymnal," although not absolutely new, it is desirably distinctive in this day of confusing common titles in the rabble rout of cornets, flutes, harps, psalters, dulcimers, and all kinds of music, borrowed from Nebuchadnezzar's orchestra in the plains of Dura.

Dr. Krebs said the committee was prepared to sustain the report with arguments and examples sufficient to fill a wheelbarrow. Whoever, said he, owns the book will make a fortune, and I had rather this General Assembly should own it than any body else.

The report was received and adopted.

The Moderator then announced that the unfinished business of yesterday would be taken up, and that the Rev. Dr. Thomas had the floor.

REMARKS OF REV. DR. THOMAS.

Moderator: I wish to call the attention of the House to the state of the question before it. Yesterday, by a vote of 254 to 50, this body determined to set aside for the present the representatives of the Presbytery of Louisville until they could investigate the facts connected with their late action, and to decide on a course in connection with this paper. Dr. McLean presented a resolution that was necessary to apply to the action of the house, that a committee be appointed to investigate the facts, and suggest a course of action for the Assembly. While that resolution was before us, a gentleman offered an amendment by way of addition, that an inquiry be made into another case that he suggested, and then a second amendment was offered, by way of addition also, for an investigation into certain rumors floating through the country in regard to other persons that might have sympathized with certain opinions.

Upon this question, sir, we were entertained with four discourses, two from St. Louis, one from Missouri-Kentucky, (for I understand the gentleman holds relations ecclesiastical in both parts of the country,) and another from Brooklyn, and I think there were premonitory symptoms of a fifth from Philadelphia. Hitherto, sir, on the question before the house there has been no reply. You know very well, sir, that it is the nature of debate to kindle that tingling in the blood which Sir John Falstaff declares was symptomatic of apoplexy. He had "read the cause of his effects in Galen." You remember, sir, under the influence of that feeling I arose yesterday to occupy the floor by way of reply to the speeches that had been presented on this question. I rose, sir, very much as the Scottish poet represented the Highlander rising at the call of his country:

"But bring a Scotsman from his hill,
Clap in his cheek a Highland gill,
Say such is royal George's will,
And there's the foe,
He has nae thought but how to kill
Twa at a blow."

Now, sir, the speeches of the gentlemen supplied me with the electric fluid, and I rose forgetting that there was not an afternoon session; forgetting there was an order of the day for ten o'clock this morning; forgetting there was not a full opportunity for entering into the subject; but I am very thankful for the circumstance that prevented me from undertaking a full discussion of the subject—for I concur perfectly with the decision of the Moderator, and with the suggestion of Dr. Breckinridge, that, in point of fact, the business now before this house is the simple amendment of Dr. Brookes, and I call it *simple*, sir, designedly. That is the question before the house.

Shall there be appointed, under the second amendment, a smelling committee to investigate certain disagreeable odors that are said to be floating in the atmosphere. Now, sir, it is very obvious that on that amendment the whole question is not before the house. It is very obvious that very little indeed can be said in reference to that whole question; and I do not desire to imitate, even with the permission of the Moderator and the indulgence of the house, the range that it seemed to me was taken in the remarks made upon the other side of the question.

What I propose, sir, is to open the way to a full and free discussion of this subject. I know very well, sir, that this house understands itself. Several votes have determined its character. A majority of four to one holds the house firmly upon the principles upon which the late Assemblies have acted and they are not to be moved from those principles; but, sir, there is no desire on the part of the majority of this house to prevent full and free discussion. On the contrary, sir, the course that I shall propose this morning is to put the business in such a shape that a full and free discussion from the egg to the apple shall be had; from top to toe; from the deepest roots to the topmost and outermost branches of it. In the word of God and in the Confession of Faith, and in the acts of the General Assembly, and before the church and the country, the majority of this house are prepared to meet and to vindicate the acts of our Assembly. But we cannot do it here, sir. We are hampered by the rules of order, and by the shape in which the business presents itself. I take it for granted, sir, that the majority of the house, and indeed I may say the whole house, I think, are determined to have a decision by ayes and noes. Four to one it has been determined that these representatives shall await an investigation. Does this house intend to let them "hang by the gills?"

Does this house mean to dissolve, leaving this question unsettled? That were unconstitutional—ungentlemanly. Well, sir, after the House proposed an investigation, then the question came up on the motion presented by my friend, Dr. McLean, for the appointment of a committee to conduct it. It is the simple appointment of a committee to investigate the facts, and report a course of procedure for this Assembly. Well, sir, as we want a full and free discussion, the way will be open when that committee shall have made its investigation and presented its report.

What man here can tell the course that they shall propose? It may be a course that will harmonize this whole house. It may be a course that will avoid discussion, and it may be a course that will require extensive discussion; but it will bring the subject before us, and the house can then determine how far and how long they will entertain it. But, sir, when the discussion comes full and free, we want upon this simple, naked question no side issues. We want no amendments, but the simple paper before us.

And what is that?

For five successive years the General Assembly of this Church has discussed the question, and has decided the principles that are at issue in this question. Five years ago, with all the talent that is ever likely to be arrayed on one side of the question, with all the prestige that belongs to the most distinguished leaders of this church in former years, with an influence, the like of which is not soon to be found in this Assembly, and when the destinies of Church and State seemed to hang trembling in the balance, this court entertained the question and discussed it for four or five days, and deliberately, in the sight of God, bore their testimony to the truth as it is in his Holy Word respecting loyalty to the Government.

For five years this church, after a discussion that has reached every hovel in the land—a discussion that has been presented in religious periodicals and political papers, after a full and free debate, has four times repeated the testimony of 1861. Last year, sir, the General Assembly determined that the time had come when these principles should be carried into practical application. And on the minutes of the Assembly you find those specific directions that were given to subordinate courts for the execution of the law of the Church.

Now, sir, what have we here before us? We have a Presbytery of this Church—and let us remember that this is the General Assembly of the Presbyterian Church—that its immediate subjects are Synods and Presbyteries; that it deals with individuals primarily in their relations to Synods and Presbyteries.

Now, sir, we are here as the General Assembly of the Presbyterian Church, and we find one of the Presbyteries of the Church that has adopted a certain paper, in which they say:

1st. That we refuse to give our support to ministers, elders, agents, teachers and those who are in any other capacity engaged in religious instruction who hold to the principles of the General Assembly.

2d. That we refuse to take any part in the discussion or decision by any ecclesiastical court of questions touching the policy and measures which properly pertain to the civil commonwealth.

5th. (Passing over the intermediate points.) That we will extend our sympathy and aid, as we have opportunity, to all who are in subjection to the ecclesiastical court.

6th. That we will not sustain or execute, or in any manner assist in the execution of the orders passed at the two last Assemblies with reference to the conduct of missions in the Southern States, and with regard to the ministers and members of churches in the seceded and border States.

7th. That we withhold our contributions from the Boards of the Church (except the Board of Foreign Missions) and from theological seminaries until those institutions are rescued from the hands of those who are perverting them through their teachings and the promulgation of principles, subversive of the system for which they were founded to uphold and sustain.

This paper, sir, was adopted by the Presbytery of Louisville, at Bardstown, September, 1865; singned by the Moderator and Stated Clerk. It has been published to the world; it has been sent, I suppose, to other ministers of the Church as well as to myself, in order that when we met here as a General Assembly we might distinctly understand their position, and if ever a position was well defined theirs is well defined. Now, sir, what is the position of this thing? You have heard of the hypothetical case in which a body, irresistible in its motion, meets an immovable body. Something, sir, is bound to give way. [Merriment.] The case before us is not precisely the same. It is a subordinate judicatory lifting up its voice in the presence of the highest court of the entire Church, declaring that, in violation of their ordination vows, and of the constitution of the Church, they will not render obedience to this Assembly. Now, sir, I take it, this is a plain case for us to act upon, and what I wish is, that in the disposal the house shall make of this matter, there shall be no diversion from this plain case to side issues. There may be other cases that may demand investigation—there may be other bodies that have acted in this way, and when the testimony shall come before us, let the cases be properly considered.

Moderator, we have in this case the deliberate and intentional defiance of the Presbytery of Louisville to the General Assembly. We have the evidence in the fact that they have sent as representatives, the head and front of this offending. We have it, sir, especially in the fact that they sent one representative, of whom, since he cannot reply to me, I will simply say that his presence here is the most marked affront to the dignity and the loyalty of this house that the Presbytery of Louisville was capable of perpetrating. [Hisses.]

I hope there will be order in the house. I desire to offend no one, but I wish to speak f eely.

Sir, shall we be thrown aside from this plain case? A case that is made up to test the Assembly, and see whether they mean to command obedience. What matters it to us, sir, whether a trio of confederates may have met on a Lee shore somewhere in New York? Gentlemen will understand, perhaps, what I mean. What matters it that they met to devise means towards the dismemberment of the Church? "No weapon formed against zion shall prosper." What matters it that a particular session in Brooklyn moved to record, inadvertently or unwisely, some action on their minutes? Let the Presbytery of Nassau attend to that, and if not, let the Synod of New York take hold of it. What matters it that individuals here or there may have expressed, in writing or in speeches, public or private, their particular views on this subject? Why, sir, that is one thing. I have stood, myself, for twenty years, on grounds which I supposed entirely antagonistic to the position of this General Assembly. I have known this Assembly take action that I believe to be in the face of the word of God; but, sir, I did not set up defiance. I found my place, and I kept it, and did my duty with others.

Twenty years ago there was a solitary couple in this Assembly standing up to testify to what we thought to be the truth, and what the Church now, and the nation, and the world believe.

There is an ecclesiastical way and a Christian way of settling such controversy, and it is not necessary that you should appoint your committees to go and hunt up private journals or public speeches of individuals. Sir, when the National Government finds a State organized in arm d resistance to its authority, does it send its scouts to search the portfolios of boarding school misses to ascertain what namby-pamby treason they may have written to their country cousins? I think not, sir In this case, sir, we have a plain and distinct defiance. The paper of my friend, Dr. McLean, takes the bull by the horns, and, I mean no disrespect, sir, when I say that while we have the bull by the horns we need not trouble ourselves about the bleating of the calves. [Laughter.] It is natural, sir, that they should sympathize in the anguish of their sire. [Renewed laugter.] We have a plain work before us, sir. It is the settlement of this particular question between the Presbytery of Louisville and the General Assembly of the Presbyterian Church of the United States.

There are other reasons, too, sir, not to speak in the spirit of taunting—there are many reasons why we might bear with particular brethren and even with particular churches, and sometimes with larger bodies, too, when in anything like an orderly way, they should express their utter disapproval of the proceedings of the Assembly. Why, sir, there are names on this very Declaration and Testimony, of brethren that I shall love while my heart beats. There is the name of one there, sir, with whom, if I ever reach heaven, I hope to walk arm in arm before God's throne and sing,

"Amazing grace, how sweet the sound,"

as thirty-three years ago we sang it in our boyish days. I have no quarrel with such a man. He may entertain his views, and he may publish them in the Princeton Review, or in any paper he chooses, and if he confines himself to the legitimate work of opposing what he believes to be erroneous, this house will not interfere with his privilege; but if his Presbytery shall, after due deliberation, formally resolve upon open rebellion, and if they shall publish to the world that they will never obey nor execute in any manner the decrees of this General Assembly—dearly as I love him I would part with my right arm, Sir, before I would hesitate for a moment to part with him and let the Master settle it in the great day above.

Now, sir, there is a third aspect of this subject. I confess I felt for a moment a flash of admiration—if that is permissable—when I saw the gallant and almost martial bearing of some gentlemen who presented themselves yesterday for decapitation. [Laughter.] I remember reading, when a boy, sir, the story of Damon and Pythias; and I remember how my young heart was interested in that tender and touching narrative. A thousand times, while I looked upon the pages of that little school book, I pictured to myself those two Greek brothers standing before the tyrant of Syracuse pleading:

"Each that the other,
Might die for his brother."

[Laughter.] I thought of this yesterday, and I thought of many other things.

"The Highland gill was in my cheek." I thought of the Mount of Transfiguration, where James and John met with Moses and Elias, and I thought how beautiful the sight would be to see "Saint James" and "Saint John" grasping in the hand of fraternal affection the dignified "Prophet Samuel." I could not help a certain sympathy in the magnanimity that voluntarily offered itself to the guillotine for his brother, or at least with his brother. And yet, alas sir, age has accomplished for me that which was once given, I think, as a piece of advice to a young minister—it has torn away the plumage from the wings of my imagination and placed them in the tail of my judgment. [Laughter.] When I saw those brethren stepping forth from the galleries, and stretching forth their necks to the ax, I recalled Paul's "earnest expectation"—I believe the Greek word is *apokaradokia*—and it means a stretching forth of the neck. But, then, Paul was a stretching forth of the neck to Heaven, while this is a stretching forth of the neck to a punishment which the Church is not ready to inflict. Let gentlemen bide their time. It will come, possibly. Moderator, the age of martyrdom has passed, I fear, forever. I know, sir, how readily, under the enthusiasm of youth, men are ready to face martyrdom, and I could not but feel as these gentlemen presented themselves that there was something of that old enthusiasm yet, not to say fanaticism, for the crown of martyrdom that affected some men in the early ages. But, then, sir, consider the difference; martyrdom used to mean the sharp ax of Saint Paul; it used to mean the cross of Peter, with his head downward; it used to mean the boiling cauldron of St. John; it used to mean the arrows of St. Sebastian; it used to mean the gridiron of St. Anthony—I think it was, although I must confess very slight acquaintance with these saints. Like the Master, my association has been rather with publicans and sinners. [Laughter.] But, sir, what does this modern martyrdom mean? It means—applause in the galleries. It means a palatial mansion on Brooklyn Heights. It means a trip to Europe. It means the smiles of an "innumerable company of angels" waving their cambric handkerchiefs. [Great merriment and sensation]

Sir, when I want wine, give me the blood of the grape, and not your cider champagne. When the age of martyrdom comes, let it be martyrdom that means something and costs something—a martyrdom that empties a man's church and does not fill it—a martyrdom that drives a man from his pulpit and does not invite sympathizers.

I remember hearing, years ago, the eloquent Tom Corwin addressing an assemblage on a question relating to physiology or geography, whatever it was, connected with his experience, in Butler county, Ohio. This county was the tenth legion of Democracy, and Warren county held about the same position in the old Whig lines; and he mentioned as a curious fact that had been discovered by long experience, that whenever a young lawyer came to settle in Warren county, he was sure to become a Whig; while if he settled in Butler county, he was sure to fall into the Democratic ranks. He attributed it entirely, sir, to the effects of climate and atmosphere [merriment]. Now, sir, our martyrdom takes that shape, and I confess myself indisposed to add to the list of such martyrs as these. If they wish to commit suicide, if they wish to execute the "happy dispatch," there are precedents enough. If they wish to go out of the Church, there is a way to get out, and we say in all kindness, that we don't mean to drive you out if we can help it. If God in his grace will show us how we can maintain his testimony unfalteringly, and yet bear with disorderly and schismatical brethren, we will walk in that way; and we will bide our own time for such action as we may deem proper. But we respectfully say to these brethren, Wait till the General Assembly calls upon you to answer for your action.

But there is one more aspect to this subject, sir. Possibly I ought not to speak of the motives of any man, but we cannot help assigning one motive or another to men in their actions. It may have been in the rapid springing up and utterances of these several brethren in Missouri, and in Kentucky, and in St. Louis, and in Louisville, and in New York—it may have been that there was some intention to show this Assembly that if we are disposed to enter on that kind of work there was a great deal of it to do.

Well, sir, if it was intended to frighten this Assembly from its propriety, I beg leave to remind these gentlemen that they have been asleep these last five years. What, sir! when we met in that Assembly in Philadelphia, when half the nation stood in arms against us; when our friends, and sons and brothers were standing armed in the tented field to meet the enemy, and the heart of the nation was suspended in anguish at the first blood; if, then, when all was uncertainty; when foreign nations hesitated to decide where they should throw their sympathies; when the Throne of Grace was besought by myriads of voices on opposite sides; if, then, in the presence of such foes as this Assembly encountered, opening God's word, it could plant its foot upon the declarations, "be subject to every ordinance of man for the Lord's sake," and "obey your rulers and submit yourselves to the powers that be," if the Assembly, under such circumstances, sir, could adopt this action, they are not likely now to be frightened from their propriety into an abandonment of the principles the nation has sustained, and Heaven has ratified? Have these gentlemen forgotten, sir, that we have poured out three thousand millions of dollars, a sum heretofore in this land undreamed of. Why, I remember hearing very patriotic citizens in their brief talks on this subject, declare that if the war went on for a time it might possibly cost us the enormous sum of five hundred millions of dollars! Do these gentlemen forget that we have poured out three thousand millions of dollars, and all that is nothing, but a drop in the ocean, compared with the three hundred thousand of our best and bravest—our brothers and our sons that offered themselves upon the altar of liberty to maintain the principle of loyalty which this General Assembly has approved? Do they suppose, sir, that when we have met the hydra with his hundred heads, and those hundred heads lie bleeding around us, we are to be frightened from our propriety by the wriggling of his dying tail. [Sensation.] No, Sir! No, Sir! If that be the motive, the influence is lost upon this Assembly. With the Moderator, sir, in his opening sermon, we are prepared to stand firmly upon God's word. We will bear patiently. We will not prevent discussion. It has been discussed, as I have said, for five years; yet the heart of the Church is ready to receive discussion upon the subject; not that we think it needs light, but that we are not willing to gag those who think they may communicate information. Now, sir, when this discussion comes, let it come unincumbered with side issues. Let it be the simple, naked question, whether this Assembly shall command, or the Presbytery of Louisville shall command. Let us settle the principle in that case, and having settled the principle, we can make our application as we may see it is necessary. Moderator, I have done. My whole object in these remarks has been to show the course of action that will open the way, in my judgment, to a simple and full discussion of the whole subject and the settlement of the principle; and, therefore, that we may come to the original question, I now move, sir, the previous question.

Dr. Boardman. The gentleman began and closed with reference to the importance of free debate, and winds up his eloquent and earnest pleading by a motion for the previous question.

Dr. Thomas. I have expressed my views. My object in moving the previous question is to have a free debate.

The Moderator. The posture of affairs is understood, I think.

At the request of several members, the Moderator then stated the effect of the previous question.

Rev. Mr. McKnight. Do I understand the Moderator to decide, if the call for the previous question be sustained, that when the question comes on the main question it will not first be taken on the two amendments.

The Moderator. Yes, sir.

Rev. Mr. McKnight contended that the Moderator erred in his decision.

The Moderator stated that, with all due respect to the gentleman, he understood the matter. The gentleman had been a member of Congress, but he should bear in mind that the rulings of that body were different from the rulings of this Assembly in regard to this particular matter.

The Rev. Mr. Ferguson moved that the ayes and noes be called on this motion for the previous question. He wished it to go to the world who it is that votes this gag-law upon us.

The call for the ayes and noes was subsequently withdrawn, but renewed by another member.

The question was put, and one-third of the members failing to vote, the motion for the ayes and noes on the previous question was lost.

The vote was then taken on the question: Shall the main question be now put?

The motion was agreed to.

The Moderator. The question is now on the adoption of the paper offered by Dr. McLean, for the appointment of a committee.

The question was put, and the paper was adopted.

The regular order of business was then called for, which was the formal reception of the Rev. Dr. Nelson as a representative from the New School General Assembly.

Dr. Nelson then came forward and was introduced by the Moderator, and spoke as follows:

REMARKS OF DR. NELSON.

Mr. Moderator and Brethren of this General Assembly: I am commissioned by the General Assembly which sat in Brooklyn a year ago, and whose successor is sitting at present in the First Presbyterian Church in this city, to bring to you and this body the fraternal salutations of that Assembly, and of the church which it has the honor to represent.

You will permit me to say, sir, on my own behalf, that inasmuch as this is the first occasion on which I was ever honored with so responsible a duty, I feel much diffidence in respect to my own judgment of what is precisely in order and proper to say. I am also so constantly occupied in happy union with my brother, the pastor of the church worshiping here, and chairman of your committee of arrangements in the exceedingly pleasant, and not light duties of making comfortable provision for the entertainment of the members of these bodies, and I am with my brother so happy in the discharge of those duties that I think it quite possible, in shaping the remarks which I will present now, I may inadvertently mix together things which would be most proper officially to say in the character in which I am commissioned, and some things of which my heart is very full connected with these other duties. But I cannot think it will be unpleasantly out of order for me to say that it is with sentiments of unusual satisfaction that I unite with the pastor and people of this Church, and the other Presbyterian pastors, and the people of this city, in welcoming to our city and to our homes these two General Assemblies, *par nobile sororum*, at this interesting time.

It is not my purpose, and I presume it will not be regarded as my duty, to make any reference to any portion of the history which has caused these two bodies to be *two*. I may, without impropriety, I am sure, indulge myself in expressing the satisfaction which I feel that we are now so nearly one that it is difficult for any of us to explain to people outside of us, or to our own communicants, the difference between us. In this respect, I imagine that we are a little like what was said on the platform of Yale College, at an anniversary, by an eloquent speaker, who referred to two of her distinguished alumni, the Rev. Drs. Taylor and Tyler, who were present on the platform, stating that although they had filled Connecticut and the whole land, with the noise of theological controversy, he would defy any man to state the difference between them in terms that either of them would accept.

I may congratulate these Assemblies, as I congratulate my fellow-citizens and fellow-Christians of St. Louis, on the providential circumstances in which you are met, and I think I may, without impropriety, refer, in illustration of what I feel and think in respect to the relations of these two bodies, to the relations to which I can testify as existing between the congregations that customarily occupy the houses of worship in which these two bodies are now sitting. There was a time when it was different. Once I have seen this house crowded more than it is crowded now; I have seen the other crowded more than this is crowded now, within one week by the people of these two congregations, and of the Congregational Church with us, pouring out our tears together amid the dark drapery which sought to express our grief at the Nation's great loss, and for which the Nation's heart is still so sore. We mingled thus here on such an occasion. It is these great griefs, it is this deep experience, it is the conscious sympathy in these great interests, and in these tremendous issues, which have melted down the mountains of division, and they have disappeared at the presence of the God of Hosts.

I take the attitude of these two congregations, and of their pastors—who, in this respect, may claim fairly to represent them—to be an adequate illustration of the present relations of these two great Churches. It cannot be wrong, I think, for me to advert to that great thing in the Providence of God which, more than all things else, has made this state of things possible; and as I ought to condense whatever I have to say here on this occasion, when time is so precious, it is all summed up and all told in these three words: "Slavery is dead."

I sat, sir, in the Convention representing the people of Missouri, not long ago, and listened with intense interest to the sixty ayes against only four noes, which made it forever unlawful for man to hold property in man in the State of Missouri, and I took great satisfaction in remembering that four of those ayes were spoken by four Elders of the Presbyterian church in the city of St. Louis, and I take satisfaction in the belief that it was the calm and steadfast and persistent testimony, which the Presbyterian church, from the beginning, when she was *one*, and recently while she was *two* bodies, has borne, which has resulted in delivering the nation from the enormity of that institution; and I do most devoutly believe that it is not the movement of politicians, that it is not the force of commerce, that it is not any secular force whatever, but that power which God has placed in the bosom of his testifying church, that has wrought this great deliverance; and I believe that when that time shall come, that the last slave on earth shall leap from his broken fetters and toss his free arms out of their shattered manacles, his exulting shout will be "The Truth as it is written in the Bible has made me free."

It is under such circumstances as these that I have the pleasure of bringing to you the fraternal salutation of the sister Assembly. In behalf of that Assembly I may say that it was our great happiness during the whole fearful and bloody struggle through which our nation has passed to have found ourselves on every occasion of the assembling of the General Assembly entirely unanimous in our expressions of determination to stand by the faithful rulers of our land in maintaining the integrity of the Republic, and in carrying forward that fearful work of Jehovah which he entrusted to this nation in those fearful years. I know that to this Assembly the testimony of this absolute unanimity, from the beginning to the end of the war, will be satisfactory, and I wish to be permitted to say that this state of unanimity has been reached—this state of things, which made this unanimity during so trying a time certain—was reached, not by any rash or tyrannical or questionable measures; not by the exercise of ecclesiastical authority in the excommunication of dissentient individuals or factious and dissentient minorities, but by the simple forces of calm, steadfast and fraternal testimony.

The prayers of that Assembly are daily offered for God's grace to be bestowed abundantly upon you. In the midst of these trials through which you are passing, and of which we know something, the prayer of your brethren of the church is that God will keep all your hearts and minds; that he will save you from any action which you will ever regret; that he will prompt you to every action which he requires of you; and without presuming for myself, or those whom I represent, even to suggest any measures for you, we commend you to the guidance of that Divine spirit which evermore dwells with the servants of Christ, earnestly deliberating for the good of His cause, and the glory of His name; and we shall frequently pray, that without tyranny, without violation of any principle of our beloved constitution, without the violation of any command of the holy scriptures, and without shrinking from anything which these scriptures or your present circumstances require of you, God will give you full deliverance from all your troubles.

I know that the hearts of many brethren in both these bodies, and the hearts of thousands of brethren and sisters in the Churches which these bodies represent are full of the question, "Shall we ever be *one* again?"

In this, sir, I am sure that I shall correctly represent the sentiment which prevails in the Church which I have the honor to represent here, by expressing my own personal sentiments. As yet I see not the clear light of God's Providence on that question. To me it appears plain that all things are removed which should prevent our entire union in spirit. It has been with me a solemn question, whether in the Providence of God, He in his holy wisdom saw that inevitably the Presbyterian Church in these United States, made of such stuff as Presbyterian churches in all lands and ages are wont to be made, would not be a greater (and, peradventure) a prouder power than His wisdom would intrust to the administration of fallible men. I reverently wait for His Providence to shed further light on that question. It did happen to me, sir—you will allow me to say—some six years ago on an occasion of considerable local interest in the Presbyterian Church, to observe that whether the Providence of God would ever direct that these two churches should organically be *one* again, I could not devine, but sure I was that the time would come when at least they would pursue their paths, and do their work of evangelization side by side, recognizing each other fraternally as equals in all respects, and having no strife between them. It happened to me confidently to say, "That time will come." I felicitate myself on the opportunity, in such a presence as this, and feel a full sense of my official responsibility here, when I say, "Blessed be God, that time now is."

At the conclusion of Rev. Dr. Nelson's speech, the Moderator said:

REMARKS OF THE MODERATOR.

My Dear Brother: I welcome you, and this whole General Assemby, I am sure, welcomes you as the representative of that other Assembly—a branch of the same Presbyterian Church in these United States. In presenting your fraternal salutations to us, and expressing your congratulations in our behalf for what we are doing in endeavoring to advance the cause in which we are unitedly engaged—the cause of truth and the Gospel in the world—you have referred, and I regret that I cannot refer to it in the same eloquent and fervent words which you have used, to the union of sentiment, which is expressed before the Church and before the world, in regard to those great matters which have so agitated the hearts of this vast people during the years which we have recently passed through.

I can, I think, express the thought that we may felicitate ourselves as an Assembly and as a Church that we have made some progress in regard to those subjects out of which these troubles have grown. There was a time previous to the war when the Old School General Assembly was frequently referred to, and not without reason, as taking such a view of that one great subject which has lain at the foundation of these troubles, and to which you have alluded, as to give occasion to that public sentiment existing North and South which resulted in the rising up of rebellion, and the bringing out of armed forces to put down that rebellion. I allude to the subject of slavery. There was an intense Conservatism, to express it by no worse term, existing in the Old School Presbyterian Church. Doubtless you recognize, as we are happy to recognize, that we have made great progress on this whole subject as a church, and as an Assembly during these more recent years; so that for several years past our Assemblies successively have expressed before the Church and the world what I believe to be the sentiments of the word of God upon that great matter, and directly contrary to what had been entertained as being in accordance with the word of God in the Southern portion of our country. I rejoice in this fact, and I know a vast majority of this body rejoice with me. I am only sorry to say that the entire membership do not.

I believe we may now look on the people of this land, and realize the fact expressed in the beautiful and forcible words of the great Peer of England, Lord Brougham, "that in this land no more shall the sun ever rise upon a master or set upon a slave."

There was a time before the war, and only a short time before the war it was, when a distinguished individual who presented to the General Assembly a munificent donation to endow one of its Theological Semanaries, expressed his view—and I must say it was a view that was entertained very extensively throughout the country—that the two most reliable hoops to bind the Union together were the Democratic party and the Old School P Church.

Well, sir, I have spent almost my entire ministry in the Southern States. I know the sentiments of these brethren, and for many of them I have the most devout and sincere affection.

Some of my most endeared friends do there now abide; and I have all that yearning over their fanaticism, and folly, and wickedness, which any man ought to cherish and ought to express; yet I believe it is the judgment of the Church at large—almost the entire Church at large—that their cause was an unjustifiable one, and the nation has so pronounced in the providence of God, and the word of God sustains both. Now, sir, while we recognize, and you recognize, that we have made some progress in these matters, I congratulate you, sir, and wish you to congratulate the Assembly of which you are the representative, that you stand as a compact body on this subject.

But it is a matter of record, as you must have witnessed by the discussion here this morning, and by the discussions of previous days, that we do not stand unitedly together. We are racked and torn by internal dissensions. It is not improper for me to refer to it, for it is notorious.

I congratulate you that you stand as a compact body. We recognize also that you have made progress in some things upon which we greatly differed at the time of our division. There was then great opposition on the part of those who were embraced in the Synods to the organization of the various agencies of the Church under ecclesiastical boards. Many of your leading men advocated voluntary associations. The progress which you have made, and in which we rejoice, is that during these more recent years you have come, as I think you will allow me to say without offense, substantially to our ground. The Congregational element has been almost entirely purged from your body—and I refer to the Congregational Church with no feeling of disrespect. You now stand as regards these external matters as better Presbyterians, allow me to say, than was the case at the time this division occurred. Therefore, sir, I can respond most heartily, and I think the vast majority of this Assembly can respond also to the sentiment, that we are drawing nearer together than we have been during this generation, or since this division occurred; and I may express on my behalf, and I trust on behalf of a large majority of this Assembly, that we hope the time is not distant when we shall not only be, as I am confident we now are, one in spirit, but one by organic law; and that then these two branches of the great Presbyterian family may stand forth in one solid phalanx against error and corruption.

You have intimated, and undoubtedly it is true, that in the providence of God it is not yet quite clear as to the time and the manner in which this organic union may be brought about. Many have supposed that, from the simple fact that the two Assemblies met in the same city, (the meeting being determined without concert between them,) that the time had come when there should be an organic union; and they have expected that that organic union might now be formed. I hope, before we adjourn, allow me to say, and if it shall meet the views of the body you represent, I hope you, before you adjourn, we may initiate measures (perhaps beginning here, and being responded to by you,) looking to a more close fellowship in all our relations, and ultimately, as soon as the providence of God may open the way, to an organic union. And now, as the time for adjournment has passed, I will close my remarks. I believe I have expressed the sentiments of a vast majority of this Assembly, to show you that we heartily sympathize with you in all your efforts to promote the cause of Christ, and we congratulate you on all the success you have attained.

After the conclusion of the remarks of the Moderator, Dr. Boardman obtained the floor, and claimed the right to it for next Monday morning.

After prayer by the Rev. Dr. Smith, of Baltimore, the Assembly adjourned till nine o'clock on Monday morning next.

FOURTH DAY—MONDAY, MAY 21, 1866.

The Assembly met at nine o'clock, and after the devotional exercises the Moderator announced the following as the committee under the resolution offered by Dr. McLean in regard to the Louisville Presbytery: Ministers, Rev. Dr. McLean, Rev. Dr. Thomas, Rev. Mr. Hines and Rev. Mr. Waller. Elders, Samuel Galloway, H. K. Clark and Judge Davidson.

The report of the Committee on Synodical Records was made the order of the day for twelve o'clock.

The report of the Committee on Church Extension was taken up, and Rev. Mr. Colwell, of Minnesota, made an earnest appeal in behalf of more energetic action among the Churches for the contribution of funds to the Board, whereby churches may be established in desolate sections of the country.

The report of the committee was then adopted.

An invitation was received from Chas. R. Gooding, Recording Secretary of the Mercantile Library Association, extending the privileges of the Library to the members of the Assembly.

On motion of Rev. Dr. Patterson the receipt of the invitation was acknowledged, and a vote of thanks returned.

An invitation was also received from the Directors of the Iron Mountain railroad, extending the privileges of the road for an excursion to Pilot Knob.

The invitation was taken under advisement by a committee, appointed to confer with a committee of the New School Assembly, with reference to fixing a time for the excursion.

Rev. Dr. Safford presented a report from the Board of Publication, of which the following is a brief synopsis.

Total copies of new publications..........	91,500
Re-prints of former publications during the year..........	466,900
Total number of publications......	558,400
Total number of copies of books and tracts issued by the Board since its organization..........	12,707,788

In addition to the above there have been printed during the year—of the

Sabbath School Visitor..........	805,000
Home and Foreign Record..........	129,300
Annual Report of the Board..........	3,500
Report on the Disabled Ministers Fund...	2,500

Dr. Safford, from the committee to whom the report of the Board of Publication was referred, recommended, among other things, that it should be the aim of the Board to reach the children of the street by sprightly publications, and that as soon as the Board can find it financially prudent, to publish the Sabbath School Visitor twice a month instead of once a month, and that the right-arm of the Board in the system of colportage be more directly referred to the churches for a more liberal support.

The report was adopted.

Rev. Mr. Cook, of Pennsylvania, spoke upon the subject of the report. He thought there might be a plan adopted by which the books of the society could be brought more within their reach than they now are. He had been laboring in the Western Reserve of the Presbyterian Church for three years, and he had not been able to secure any books from the Board without sending all the way to Philadelphia, and there paying a catalogue price for the books, and the expressage on the books; and then if he wanted to sell them, he must sell them at catalogue price and be out of pocket himself for expressage. This was too severe a tax on a man who received only four hundred and fifty dollars a year; and he thought that some plan might be adopted by which the books could be put within their reach, either by the establishment of a depository within the bounds of each Presbytery or otherwise.

Rev. Mr. Schenck said that he was satisfied they could meet the real difficulty. The real difficulty was not in the Board, but it was in the brother's Presbytery. They were ready to appoint a colporteur in every Presbytery, wherever the Presbytery might recommend a suitable man. If they would recommend some man of suitable business qualifications to carry their books from church to church and from house to house, the Board were ready to put him to work and to sustain him. If the Presbytery could not find such a man then the Board was ready to appoint some good minister and give him a supply of books as a colporteur, and give him such a remuneration for selling the books that it may be a pleasant addition to the moderate stipend which he gets from his people.

The Moderator then appointed Rev. Dr. Hickock, Dr. Kane and Dr. Wells as a committee in reference to the excursion on the Iron Mountain Railroad.

The Moderator. I have a communication from a convention of ruling elders and ministers, who met in this city on Tuesday evening last, with a request that it should be read before the General Assembly.

The paper was then read as follows:

To the General Assembly of the Presbyterian Church in the United States of America:

The memorial of the undersigned ministers and ruling Elders of the Presbyterian Church in the United States of America, respectfully sheweth:

Your memorialists, the most part of whom are Commissioners, duly appointed to this General Assembly, met in convention on the 15th of May, inst., at St. Louis, in accordance with the recommendations of about three hundred ministers and elders of this church, inviting a Convention of Commissioners, and other ministers and elders, specified in the call as "Persons who instead of reviling the five preceding Assemblies, would *obey* them; for the purpose of prayer, and conference, in view of the approaching meeting of this Assembly; and, in the exercise of their reasonable right to assemble as members of a free, Christian commonwealth, and in seeking Divine guidance, and mutual enlightenment and support, to ascertain, to represent and to propose to the General Assembly, as God should enable them, and with all due reverence, the things which, in our judgment, are needful to the Church, touching its present duties, dangers and necessities.

It is believed that this Assembly will not be free from attempts hostile to some, if not all, of the precious Testimonies the Church has borne for the trust of God and the duty of His children, during the frightful years of sinful insurrection through which we have been led, and to the provisions enacted by the General Assembly for the unity and integrity and peace of the Church, consequent upon the schisms and defections in the very bosom of the Church.

We need only to cast our eyes over the controversies raging even *now* in the Church to understand how wide-spread and how diversified are the evils which threaten her, and how fatal are the principles upon which a counter revolution in her state and action is demanded, and how eager and fierce is the spirit of reaction against her solemn, deliberate and reiterated Testimonies, especially uttered by the preceding five Assemblies, and how vehemently they have been reviled and defied and set at naught.

We believe that the present troubles threatening anarchy and confusion in the Church, and further defection and schism, and are little else than the sinful continuation and working in a religious form of the criminal spirit and designs of the insurrection in temporal affairs; and we are persuaded that neither the country nor Church can have peace or security, until the religious poison is healed or purged out.

In both respect, both of the State and the Church, it is better immeasurably to heal, if it be possible. If that may not be, it is immeasurably better to keep the Church pure and restore it to peace, let it cost what it may.

The Presbyterian Church welcomes to her bosom joyfully all who desire to be as she and her children are. If others will insist on having her blessings, which are neither few nor small, they ought not to be allowed to revile her acts, condemn her authority, waste her inheritance, traduce her character, tear her vitals, and corrupt and destroy her integrity and unity. All such attempts to impair her Testimonies, mar her peace, and hinder her usefulness, *ought to be put an end to*, if God permit, by the General Assembly *firmly adhering to the Testimonies and enactments* hitherto uttered from the highest tribunal of the Church; and by the appropriate exercise of her discipline, effectually dealing with those who may have set themselves persistently to revile her acts, to defy her just authority, to destroy her peace, and to distract and rend her communion.

Thus believing, your memorialists, without presuming to dictate, and without unlawfully combining to carry in this house the measures they propose, do now respectfully and dutifully submit the results of their deliberations to the Church and to this General Assembly.

Your memoralists, therefore, do hereby respectfully represent, in reference to the recent persistent attempts made in various parts of the Church to have the deliverances and injunctions of the General Assembly (produced by the disturbed state of the Church and nation during the past five years) reconsidered and changed; that the General Assembly has nothing in the matter aforesaid to change, nothing to explain, nothing to modify, nothing to take back, nothing to amend in any way, shape or form whatever; it being needful only for any one to correct the misrepresentations published and industriously circulated concerning those deliverances and injunctions, in order clearly to vindicate both the moral and ecclesiastical right of the Assembly to enact the same.

All the more do your memorialists earnestly press upon the Assembly the importance of thus firmly adhering to all that has been said or done, regarding the great moral and religious issues involved in the struggle of the past five years; inasmuch as the spirit of rebellion still rages in some portions of the Church, even to the extent of public official, as well as public personal defiance unto and insult of the authority of the General Assembly, notable instances of which are the adoption, by one of our Presbyteries, and many of our members, of a "Declaration and Testimony" reviling the Assembly, and covering the Church with unmerited reproach, and especially the election of some as Commissioners to the Assembly, whose eminence in open hostility to the loyal deliverances of the Assembly and to the Assembly itself, is unsurpassed in the history of our Church.

Your memorialists, in calling the attention of the Assembly to the opposition thus made by individuals, by Church courts, and by the press, do hereby also invite its attention to the vast multitude of fatal heresies, connected with, and logically growing out of it,—not the least of which is that which denies to the deliverances and injunctions of the Assembly, during the past five years (upon slavery and rebellion) any binding force whatever.

The action of the supreme tribunal of our Church is denounced as contrary to the constitution and immemorial usage of the Presbyterian Church, and disobedience to the same publicly and privately counseled.

The peace and purity of the Church imperatively demand that the General Assembly, whose duty it is to suppress schismatical contentions and disputations, shall adopt efficient measures to put an end to the anarchy and confusion which this course of things is bringing upon the whole Church. They who thus revile the authority and disturb the harmony of the Church, should be required to desist from such revolutionary and schismatical conduct, —and where Church officers or courts persist, in defiance of the order of the Assembly, they should be dealt with as offenders against the peace, purity, and order of the house of God.

Less than this, your memorialists believe will be not only an encouragement of rebellion against the government of the Presbyterian Church, but against the very essence of all lawful government itself, and must inevitably tend to the fearful result of anarchy and irremediable ruin. The General Assembly must be fully aware that even amongst those who cordially approve of its past deliverances and those who will stand by the Church of their fathers, although they may not approve all those deliverances, there is some diversity of judgment as to the course which ought to be pursued by the Church, henceforth, towards the schismatical sect of united Old School and New School Presbyterians which has been organized in the wide region covered by the lately rebellious States; fully aware, also, that to a large extent the Church, in a state of opinion which may be called immature, awaits some clear deliverance of the General Assembly touching the relations which are to exist on our part to that sect. Besidse this, it is notorious that all the past deliverances of the Church condemning the schism in the Church South, and the conduct of those ministers who produced and organized that schism, and used it to sustain the rebellion and the civil war, and now use it, not only to prevent the restoration and spread of our Church in the Southern half of the Nation, but to extend the schism into all parts of the Church have been and continue to be, openly denounced and intentionally disobeyed by all such members and office-bearers of our Church as approve the wicked conduct of the authors of that schism, and repeat its sinful revilings of the Presbyterian Church and its acts. While this Convention has earnestly besought the General Assembly not to take back, nor modify, nor explain away—under rebellious menaces, and heretical expositions and intrigues and conspiracies, in the interest of slavery and disloyalty and schism—any portion of its past deliverances touching the state of the Church and the country, we suppose that a fresh deliverance, founded on the actual condition of affairs, more especially as they affect the Church, and embracing amongst other things the vital subjects contained in this petition and memorial, would be of very high importance at the present time. It needs to be kept in perpetual remembrance that the frightful civil war was encouraged and eagerly supported from the beginning by those who organized this sinful schism as soon as possible after bloodshed began, mainly—as openly avowed by themselves—upon the two atrocious ideas of the perpetuity of negro slavery, and, to that end, the creation of a new nation out of a part of this nation, through its destruction by treason and carnage. It must be further kept in mind that after the lapse of four (4) years, of ceaseless activity in this sinful course, during which all the horrors and miseries of civil war fell upon the land, with a violence seldom exceeded in extent or bitterness, and after the new Nation had expired and the perpetual slavery had perished under an act of sublime National retribution, those same schismatics deliberately resolved to perpetuate the sectarian organization they had created, in such circumstances for such objects, accompanying this last act with formal statements identifying their past conduct and principles with the future career marked out for themselves, and striving, in particular, to make mutual confidence and fraternity, much less mutual fellowship, and least of all, organic unity with the Church, which the great mass of them had betrayed, forsaken and traduced, forever impossible.

The Presbyterian Church has no alternative consistent with safety, with self-respect, with the righteousness of its own past conduct, with fidelity to divine truth or Christian duty, or with obedience to God, but to accept the renunciation of these deluded men, to testify against their sinful acts, and to keep her skirts clear of their miserable doings. Three great duties remain to her, connected with this subject, upon the right performance of which a great reward awaits her, and upon the neglect of which, trouble and confusion! The first is, to purify herself from the widely diffused poison of the times, which (in a form more or less virulent) is diffused through all the Churches; and to do this, as remembering that the discipline of the Church is of God, is an ordinance of mercy to backsliders, and stands related to the threatenings of

God's word in some manner as the sacraments thereof do to the promises of God. The second is to hold out, and wide open, the arms of her love to every child of God in the Southern country who has been a victim—not the willing partaker of the sins against God, against His Church, and against their country, against which Divine Providence has testified by such severe and most righteous judgments. The third is to proceed, at once, and with a zeal proportioned to the urgency of the necessity, to redeem the solemn promise made by the first Assembly, after the schism organized in 1861—that she would wholly disregard its existence, and, as God might enable her, would strive to recover all she might lose by it, and to extend and establish, more and more, throughout the whole South, the precious system of Divine Truth, unto the liberty and power of which God has called her by His grace.

Let the revenge we will ask of God be a double share in the work of saving those who have cast us out as doubly vile.

Adopted unanimously, and ordered to be signed by the officers, in behalf of one hundred and eleven, in Convention assembled at St. Louis, Missouri, May 14th, 1866. W. D. HOWARD,
President.

W. W. Colinery,
J. G. Reason, Clerks.

Several motions were made in regard to the disposal of the memorial, and finally, on motion of Dr. Wm. Breckinridge, it was referred to the Committee on Bills and Overtures.

Rev. Mr. Van Dyke said he had a paper relating to the same subject, which he wished to read and have referred to the same committee.

The paper was read as follows:

This Assembly earnestly deprecates the continuance of the division now existing between the Presbyterian Churches in the Northern and Southern States, together with the strife among ourselves, growing out of this division, as a ruinous and unnecessary schism between brethren who maintain a common faith, tending to perpetuate the evil passions generated by civil war; to prevent the return of the harmony and good will so essential to the prosperity of both Church and State, and to dissipate in futile contentions, the resources and moral influence which the Church ought to employ in common efforts for the defense and propagation of the Gospel.

In the spirit of reconciliation and brotherly kindness, this Assembly desires the restoration of the unity of the Church on the basis of the principles upon which she was originally organized, and upon which, under the Divine blessing, she so long and so abundantly prospered.

Among these principles we regard the following as fundamental:

1. "God alone is Lord of the conscience, and hath left it free from the doctrines and commandments of men, which are in anything contrary to His word, or beside it in matters of faith and worship." (Form of Gov. I. 1.)

2. "All the Church power, whether exercised by the body in general, or in the way of representation by delegated authority, is only ministerial and declarative; that is to say: the Holy Scriptures are the only rule of faith and ministers in the Church judicatory ought to pretend to make laws to bind the conscience in virtue of their own authority, but all their decisions should be founded upon the recorded will of God." (Form of Gov. I. 7.)

3. "Synods and councils are to handle or conclude nothing but that which is ecclesiastical, and are not to intermeddle with civil affairs which concern the commonwealth, unless by way of petition in cases extraordinary, or by way of advice for satisfaction of conscience, if they be thereunto required by the civil magistrate." (Confession of Faith, 31, 4.)

4. "All Synods and councils since the days of the Apostles, whether general or particular, may err, and many have erred; therefore their decisions are not to be made the rule of faith and practice, but to be used as a help in both."—[Confession of Faith, 31, 3.

5. "Since the powers that be are ordained of God, it is the duty of Christians to pray for magistrates, to honor their persons, to pay them tribute and other dues, to obey their lawful commands and to be subject to their authority for conscience sake."—[Confession of Faith, 23, 4.

In accordance with these principles and with a view to promote peace upon the basis therein set forth,

Resolved, That the deliverances of the five preceding Assemblies on the state of the country, including the "orders" of the last Assembly in regard the reception of members from Presbyteries and Churches in the Southern States, not having been transmitted to the Presbyteries for their approbation according to requirements of the Form of Government, chap. 12, sec. 6, are not established for constitutional rules, and are not obligatory upon the Churches. Whatever may be their virtue as a part of the past history of the Church, and as an embodiment of the opinions of the venerable Assemblies from which they emanated, these deliverances form no part of our standards of truth and order, and their adoption cannot be lawfully insisted on as a term of Church membership or of ministerial communion.

Rev. Mr. Brown moved that the paper be laid upon the table.

Mr. Brown, of Huntington, moved that the first five propositions be accepted and the sixth rejected.

The motion was declared out of order.

The motion to lay on the table was lost.

Rev. Dr. McLean. Moderator, I am not in favor of referring this paper, if I correctly understood a sentence in the first portion of it. I think every paper presented decorously and courteously ought to be referred and courteously treated. My doubt, sir, is whether that paper is not in one or two sentences in the first part highly disrespectful to this body. I would like a sentence of the first part of that paper re-read, for I did not quite hear it distinctly. My impression is, if I heard it correctly, that you were asked to stultify yourself; that you were asked to swallow your own words, so to speak; that you are discourteously asked to do what you cannot do with any sort of propriety or respect for your past decisions. If that is not so, I am in favor of reference. If it is, I am not.

Rev. Dr. Van Dyke. I think the gentleman must have heard it very imperfectly.

[The Clerk then read the first portion of the paper.]

Dr. McLean was proceeding to speak when the Moderator informed him that no member could speak more than once on the same subject; that he had already spoken once and the question now was, on referring to Committee on Bills and Overtures.

The question was put and the motion to refer was agreed to.

The Moderator. I have another paper signed by Stuart Robinson and others. I have read the paper and as it refers to a matter which was referred on yesterday to a committee of which Dr. McLean was Chairman, I think it proper that the paper should be read, and either referred to that committee, or take such other direction as the Assembly may deem proper. It is a memorial, and from a hasty reading seems to be respectful. It is signed by three gentlemen, and from the conclusions to which they have come, as regards their status, I think it ought to be read.

The paper was then read, as follows:

To the Moderator of the General Assembly of the Presbyterian Church, now in session in St. Louis:

The undersigned, commissioners from the Presbytery of Louisville, deem it both respectful to the Assembly and demanded by the interests of truth and righteousness, to lay before the body, through you, in this formal and official manner, for record on the minutes, their views and purposes in regard to the resolution passed yesterday, under operation of the previous question, to this effect:

That, Whereas, the Presbytery of Louisville have "openly defied the Assembly" and declared publicly their intention not to enforce the orders of the two last Assemblies, on slaves and loyalty, etc., and have, in act, disregarded them in sending a commissioner here who, by a faithful execution of those acts, would probably have been suspended from the functions of his office, therefore

"*Resolved*, That until the Assembly shall have examined and decided upon the conduct of said Presbytery, the commissioners shall not be entitled to seats in this body."

We respectfully suggest, not indeed as vital to the case, but as illustrating simply the evil of such action, under the operation of the previous question, cutting off all explanation, that both the premises of the Assembly's resolution contain grave mistakes of facts. The Presbytery of Louisville have, indeed, published a Declaration and Testimony against the acts of the five preceding Assemblies, in which many ministers and elders outside the Presbytery formally, and many more in spirit and act, have concurred. But the Presbytery of Louisville have not "openly defied the Assembly," as might have been seen by reference to the whole tenor of the paper, from which a single passage is quoted. Nor has the Presbytery sent any commissioner here, who, even under the act of 1865, in relation to ministers who have gone into the Confederacy or fled, or been banished into foreign countries, could have been suspended from the ministry. Since the only one of their commissioners who has been absent from the country during the past three years, was neither in the Confederacy nor fled, nor was banished; but being absent on a vacation tour, by arrangements made months before, at the inauguration of an unlimited military power under the control of his bitter ecclesiastical enemies, prolonged that absence, with the advice and concurrence of the Church session and of prudent friends of all parties.

Aside, however, from these mistakes of fact in the premises, a far more important matter, in our judgment, is the dangerous error in principle involved in such action, even were the facts as charged. On this view of the case, we beg leave with all respect and deference to suggest:

1. It will be manifest on due reflection, and would have been shown but for the call for the previous question, that the assumption of the right to take such action under the general power of any deliberative body to judge of the qualifications of its own members, arises from a failure to see the want of analogy between the case of the General Assembly and that of legislative and other similar bodies in the secular sphere. The right to appoint commissioners to the General Assembly, and to judge of the qualifications of those commissioners is inherent in the Presbyteries, whose members are a constituent part of the Assembly itself; nor can they be divested of that right save by sentence of deposition from office as Presbyters, reached through the forms so carefully prescribed in the constitution. The claim of any particular Assembly to judge of the qualifications of its own members must be limited in the nature of the case to the question whether the credentials are in accordance with the provisions of the book. But in fact the Assembly in this instance does not pretend to be passing judgment upon the qualifications of its own members at all, but upon the constituency which sent them. This is manifest, not only from the terms of the action, but also from the fact that one of the Commissioners excluded was no party to the "Declaration and Testimony;" neither could he be possibly objected to on the score of disqualification or a defective commission.

2. This, therefore, makes manifest what was confessed on the floor of the Assembly by some who voted for this resolution, that the action was *in its nature judicial*, and it is, therefore, in effect, a judicial sentence, pronounced and executed, not only in disregard of all the provisions for a fair trial, so carefully ordained in our constitution, but, under the operation of the previous question, excluding the parties charged from a word of explanation, defense or protest.

3. And it adds to the aggravation of the wrong done in this action that, even had the Assembly the right thus to act, and were its action according to the forms of law, and the sentence given after a fair hearing, it is a sentence of disgrace, as if inflicted for crime committed; whereas, what was done by the Presbytery could at most be regarded as only the mistaken exercise of the right of protest against what was conceived to be an act of usurpation by the Assembly.

4. A further aggravation of this wrong is the manifest partiality evinced, in thus singling out for condemnation the Presbytery of Louisville, while notoriously a large number, if not a majority, of the Churches in all parts of the country, but also several Presbyteries represented in the Assembly, have *done* precisely the thing which the Louisville Presbytery is condemned for asserting its purpose to do.

5. But a still more important and dangerous principle involved in this action, is, that it takes away from minorities and even individual members of the body, all those safeguards provided for their protection against the violence and partisan feeling of a casual majority of members in all times of excitement and passion. The principle of this action if admitted, would inevitably and speedily change the Assembly from an *ecclesia* organized, restrained and governed by the well established laws of Christ's house, into a mere ecclesiastical gathering under the unlimited control of the majority of members, "the most part knowing not wherefore they have come together."

6. It but evinces more clearly and aggravates the wrong done in this case, that the Assembly resolves not absolutely and finally to exclude us, but only to exclude us until the Assembly "*shall have examined and decided.*" The right to examine and decide under such a resolution; the right to exclude us, even for an hour, pending such examination; the right to exclude us after such examination is had, and the right absolutely and finally to exclude us, are all equally groundless. The injury inflicted on the good name of the Presbytery among the churches from a temporary exclusion, as though *probably* guilty of high crime is *scarcely less* than the injury from a sentence of final exclusion. Besides, even though it was consistent with our proper self respect, and with the honor of the Presbytery for us to await the result of the Assembly's inquisition, thereby recognizing the Assembly's right thus "to examine and decide," we are cut off, by the sentence of exclusion, from the exercise of any right of defense. All of which makes it still more palpably manifest that the action of the Assembly is, in effect, the pronouncing and executing of sentence, and afterward proceeding to examine and decide."

With profound respect for the Assembly as the highest court of the Church, and with unfeigned sorrow that we are constrained, in fidelity to our trust, thus to speak, we feel it our duty to say to the Assembly, that—regarding this action as of the nature of a judgment upon the Presbytery and its commissioners, and this judgment a sentence of exclusion without trial or a hearing in any form in explanation or defense; regarding this action as not only unjust, injurious and cruel, but as subversive of the foundations of all justice, destructive of the constitution of the Church, and revolutionary in its nature; regarding it as setting a precedent for the exercise of a partisan power in the courts of Christ's Kingdom, which leaves all the rights and immunities of his people at the mercy of any faction that may casually be in the ascendency—we should be untrue to the Presbytery, whose commission we bear, faithless to the cause of truth and Christian freedom, false to our Lord and King, should we silently acquiesce in such procedure or in any way recognize its legality. We must regard this action in its effect, so far as relates to us as Commissioners, and to this present Assembly, as final in the case.

With these views and convictions there is but one course left open to us, viz: To take our appeal at once upon the issue as it has been made for us and forced upon us, from this General Assembly to the Presbytery of Louisville in particular, in so far as it concerns ourselves and that body, and to the whole Church in so far as it is an issue involving the great principles of her Constitution, and, indeed, her continued existence as a free Christian Commonwealth in the enjoyment of the franchises and immunities conferred upon her by her adorable Head.

We therefore respectfully inform the Assembly that we shall not attend further upon its sessions.

STUART ROBINSON,
SAM'L R. WILSON,
MARK HARDIN,
C. A. WICKLIFFE.

ST. LOUIS, MO., May 19, 1866.

Rev. Dr. Boardman. I endeavored on Saturday——

The Moderator. I suppose the gentleman understands there is no motion before the House.

Dr. Boardman. I will make a motion in a minute. I endeavored on Saturday to get the floor for the purpose of offering an amendment to the resolution which was adopted, but failing so to do, I will now present the identical resolution which I proposed to offer on Saturday. I will simply connect with that resolution a proposal to refer this paper to the committee already appointed on the case of these Louisville brethren. I offer the following resolution:

Resolved, That the said committee be instructed to inquire and to report with the least practical delay on the expediency of readmitting that delegation to seats in the Assembly until their case and that of their Presbytery, shall have been acted upon.

I have talked with none of these brethren, except with a single one of them, whom I have taken by the hand, either in the aisle of the church or on the front steps. I am not in their councils. I had no intimation that they purposed to come before us with this paper or any other. The resolution which I have just read was prepared entirely on my own motion, under the profound conviction, Mr. Moderator, that as a General Assembly we have placed ourselves, not merely in a most undesirable position, but in a most perilous position. I think we are in a false position. I need not say that the danger of legislating in times of great public excitement, is verg great and imminent. I need not revert to that illustration of it that meets us so perpetually and to which the sessions of the last hour have presented a series of illustrations. Every man is more or less excited, and to that degree, indeed, that the most familiar propositions cannot be presented here and voted upon without drawing in their train the almost unlimited sequences, I liked to have said, of questions of order and rules of order and demands upon the chair for explanations, which, indeed, might well perplex and harass the most able and experienced parliamentary officer.

Sir, the deep forces of society are in motion. The storm of war has subsided. Slavery is dead and rebellion is dead, thank God, and secession is dead, thank God. Take that, brethren! you who have repeated a thousand times over, peradventure, or heard it repeated, that I have more sympathy than you have with secession and rebellion. But I am not here, though, to speak of myself. No man, thank God, has more loyalty than I have. No man rejoices more sincerely than I do that this war is over, that the authority of the Federal Government is re-established and that there is some prospect, however obscure and remote, yet still in the dim distance, that this whole blessed Union is likely once more to be re-established under our glorious Constitution.

But, sir, while the gale is passed, the heavy ground swell is upon us, and it requires but a tyro in the history of navigation or commerce to know that the great peril that besets his ship, or a gallant fleet even, is that of being lifted on the lee shore, amid the heavy ground swell of the ocean after the wind has subsided into a perfect calm; and that, sir, is just the position of our glorious Church today; and there is no hand but One who can rescue us from this peril, unless these sails that are flapping against their yards shall be filled and inflated with the gales of the blessed Spirit and the breath of Heaven, it need not excite surprise here or elsewhere if we shall yet find this glorious bark among the breakers.

I have intimated, at least, that I have no sympathy with the views that have been attributed to some of these Louisville brethren; but, sir, I have some sympathy, I trust, with righteousness and truth and justice, and Christian charity; I have some sympathy with the rights of any man who bears the form of a man, and who carries an immortal spirit in his bosom, and I will not sit here willingly, I will not sit here quietly, and see any man oppressed, though he be the bitterest secessionist in the land. If he is to be arraigned and condemned and beheaded, it shall be done in so far as my voice and my humble influence can accomplish anything—it shall be done under the constitution and laws of the Church. We live, sir, under a government of law. We are not at liberty to take counsel of our feelings or our passions. We are not at liberty to go for our law to precedents to public, judicial or legislative assemblies. We are not at liberty to open our bosoms to all the gales of human passions that may meet and concentrate here. No, sir, we are bound by that Book, and if it were not my deliberate conviction that the teachings of that Book had been infringed upon, I would not trouble you with the remarks that I am now making.

Sir, I regret on Saturday that the gentleman who called for the previous question at the close of an exciting and satirical speech—I regret that he did not waive his right; I regret that on two occasions on the first two days of our session that each of them should have been marked by the inflexible enforcement of the previous question. I will come presently to the alleged reasons for this.

But for a moment let me say, that I do not regret the interruption which occurred subsequently to the enforcement of the previous question on Saturday, and with my brother here, I was willing and happy to give the right hand of fellowship to our respected and honored brother, who came to us from a sister Assembly in this city. I did not regret the interruption afterwards; I do not regret it now; but I think that that interesting Christian colloquy which occurred between the honored representative of that Church and our own honored Moderator may have done something to open the eyes of the fathers and brethren of this body to the actual tendencies of that current into which we are drifting. But what else did we listen to? We listened to an earnest and eloquent harangue—not, as I believe, conceived precisely in that spirit of deep anxiety and solemnity that is reached when a crisis in the affairs of the Church—a speech that was largely embellished with witticisms—a speech, one of the main illustrations in which was drawn from a bachanalian song by Robert Burns, wherein whisky and the shooting of two men at once were duly magnified—a speech in which the majority of this house were triumphantly reminded that we are but a poor handful of fifty to two hundred—that there was a majority of four to one, but considerately apprehending the depth of the wound which that statement might inflict on our sensibilities, the speaker was kind enough instantly to apply the healing balsam by informing us that some years ago the majority against him in the General Assembly was one hundred to one; but that he and one other stood faithful alone among the faithless; that they had stood up and breasted the mighty torrent of delusion which was then sweeping over our General Assembly, and in their judgment bearing our noble Church to destruction.

Sir, history repeats itself. That which has been is that which may be, and if a minority of two may in the course of a few years rise to be a majority of 200, a minority of 50 to 200 may rise to become a majority of 250, and in the Providence of God, sir, the 50 may once more be reinstated with their privileges, and may once more see the desire of their hearts accomplished, and may find their good old Church once more sailing in that dark blue sea, where from her foundation she has been quietly navigating until now. Sir, do not glory in your majority. Truth is stronger than majorities, and in the end truth will triumph.

Well, sir, in respect to the assault that was made upon certain brothren of this city. It is a delicate matter to refer to three or four of those brethren who came forward, as you remember, and who were not arraigned in this indictment with the men of Louisville; but who stood, Mr. Moderator and brethren of the Assembly, in the same condemnation, and who said we hold to the principles of these brethren, and if they are to suffer one wish to suffer with them. To my mind, sir, there was something honorable in it. I thought it was just, and Christian, and manly—just what it became them to say, and just what it became them to do; and I should have supposed that they would at least have won the respect of those members of this Assembly. But yet what do we hear? an attempt to transfix these brethren as would be martyrs, and they were held up to ridicule and their motives were assailed. We were told in effect that they were playing the hypocrite—that they were courting a mere rose-water martyrdom, and that you, sir, in the presence of their own congregation, and of the people whose munificent hospitality we are accepting—even in such a presence as this the brother was not ashamed to pour his ridicule and satire, and exhaust his fertile capacity of invective upon the pastors of these St. Louis churches. Well, sir, whether this is a matter of taste or not, it is a matter of instinct, and although no great amount of care and study may have been given to an analysis of the human mind and its instincts, yet this General Assembly is sufficiently conversant with the human constitution to understand that an "instinct" is something congenital. It is hereditary, and if it is not in a man when he comes into the world, you cannot put it in. With anything else, in any other department of the human mind or the human constitution, you may do something by care and culture with the human intellect. Why, in the suburbs of our city, we have an admirable institution for the training of feeble-minded children, and it is marvellous what results have been attained there under the faithful tutilage of the guardians of that institution, to whom scores of idiotic children have been committed, and by God's blessing they have waked up their slumbering spark of intellect, even in the most stupid of these unhappy creatures. We all know you may do very much to educate the affections; you may do very much towards educating the conscience, but just before I left home, I received a letter from the principal of a well known Accademical institution in our State who had occasion to write me about two boys, and he gave no very attractive portraiture of their characters and tempers, and among other things, he said when they came to him they had no conscience, and he had to inculcate a moral sense into them. Well, sir, you may put a moral sense into a boy, but you cannot put an instinct into him, and therefore when I refer to such demonstrations as we had on Saturday, and in such a presence I simply say, sir, that it is a matter of instinct whether such things are becoming and fitting among a people at whose generous boards we are sitting down and with whom we are daily interchanging the sweet intercourses of friendship.

Well, Mr. Moderator, now for the merits of the case. This Assembly remember the proceedings that were enacted before our eyes upon this platform, and with which our hearts went out with full sympathy between you, Mr. Moderator, and an honored representative of one of our sister churches. We well remember, brethren, that the whole tone of this proceeding on the one side and on the other was bland, refined, courteous, and fraternal. You will remember that there was no harsh word uttered, as there surely was no unkind emotion felt, but that there was a just and mutual attraction—the attraction of a blessed elective affinity, all the more significant, all the more emphatic, because it was the outgoing of a sentiment which has been seeking expression and growing in strength for several years past, and it was altogether a delightful exhibition of a Christian reunion. What fruits may come of it hereafter, I do not know, and this is not the point to discuss that question. But, sir, I will tell you what it was like, coming after that other speech. Have you ever been in a mine, brethren? Have you ever been in one of those lonely, dark, dank mines in the heart of a mountain, with everything black around you, with the water dripping from the sides and from the ceiling, with the air chilling your very frame, compelling you to wrap your overcoat around you; and have you gone out in the sweet month of May into the pure sunshine of heaven, and drawn a long breath, while the fields looked greener than ever and the sun brighter, and have you not felt as Pilgrim felt when his burden fell from his back, as you went forward with accelerated step? Why, sir, it was like getting into another atmosphere on Saturday when we came from the experience of one of these speeches to the experience of that blessed interlocutory. And I could not but ask myself, Why is this? Here is a brother from a sister Church, not one of ours. We love him, we honor him, but he is not one of our household. He comes from another Church, and we open our arms to embrace, we lift our hands in benediction upon him, and we bid him and his God-speed and we sent him home laden with the high expressions and tokens of our Christian affection and good will. But here is another set of brethren —call them the Declaration and Testimony men, call them what you will—I do not approve of their Declaration and Testimony. I think they have gone too far. I think they have been inconsistent, but nevertheless they are brethren. They grew up in our household. They have always sat at our board. They are ours. They are ours. But, sir, while we have spoken with gentleness, tenderness and affection towards our brethern from without, we have turned, Mr. Moderator, to these brethren, of our own household, and instantly our visage has been overshadowed, and we have looked at them with a stern, unrelenting brow, and we have made the very utmost of their errors and their frailties. We have said to our brethren from abroad, we are willing to overlook and forget many a hard thing you have said, and many an unsound doctrine you have cherished, and many a conflict in which we have met; and so, while we are glad to see them sailing down the broad stream of oblivion, we have taken the errors and mistakes of these men: every false step they have made, every unkind sentiment that in their moments of passion may have fallen from their lips, we have taken and visited upon them a rhadamanthine justice. Why is this, sir? Why is this? I will not answer the question. Let me come to these Louisville men. But after all—after all—all that has been said belongs to the concomitants and collaterals of this case, and I have not touched upon the gravamen of the question before us.

Here, sir, on the first day of this question, there came four brethren from the Presbytery of Louisville and presented their credentials to your Committee on Commission—your Committee, not theirs. That Committee passed upon them and found them regular. Their names were enrolled. They took their seats upon the floor by the same authority, Mr. Moderator, with which you and I sit here. There was no question. There was no question as to the accuracy or regularity or validity of this commission. The Presbytery of Louisville was a Presbytery in good standing, as much so as the Presbytery of Chillicothe, or the Presbytery of Miami, or as the Presbytery down in Jersey—I don't know which it is—who sent a brother here to move a previous question. That Presbytery was and is in as good standing as any of these, and these men are here by a right as clear and indisputable as we are—any of us—and what did you do? Well, sir, here is what you did:

Resolved, That a committee of seven be appointed, composed of four ministers and three elders, to examine into the facts connected with the alleged acts and proceedings of the Louisville Presbytery, and whether it is entitled to representation in this General Assembly, and to recommend what action, if any, this General Assembly should take with regard to this said Presbytery.

Well, sir, since the world began, since the institutions of Justinian were organized and established, was it ever heard that a set of men were put upon trial under an indictment like that?

"Alleged acts!" What are they? They are not stated here on this paper under which they are condemned. Certain things are referred to in debate: what has it to do with the action of this house? What explanation is there to be of that resolution as it goes down to your successors? I will not say that a diligent Archæological student in some distant period of the Church may not be able to find out what the first ground of this proceeding was; but surely, sir, it was the equitable right of these brethren to be informed in the paper and resolution by which they were condemned, what they were condemned for; and if they were to be excluded from seats in the house, what they were to be excluded for?

Mr. Davidson. Moderator, I wish to make a point of order. I wish to inquire whether or not, under this discussion, the merits of the original resolution are to be discussed, whether or not the resolution offered by Dr. Boardman is the question before the house?

The Moderator. I think, under the previous resolution for the appointment of this committee, a very wide range was allowed to the debate. From that precedent I think Dr. Boardman is in order. It is impossible for the Moderator, and I think difficult for the members of the Assembly, to point out a course of argument which a person shall take, or the illustrations he shall use,

Mr. Davidson made some further remark which was inaudible.

The Moderator. I cannot hear the remarks of the gentleman. I have already decided the point of order. I think no further debate is allowed.

A member in a distant part of the house also made a remark which was inaudible.

The Moderator. Allow me to say, although I have decided the point of order, that I think four or five gentlemen from St. Louis and other parts of Missouri, from Louisville and New York took a very wide range; Dr. Thomas was allowed to take the same, and I do not think Dr. Boardman is going beyond what was allowed them. I therefore think he is in order. It is only five minutes before we reach the order of the day.

A member. I move that the order of the day be suspended.

The motion was agreed to.

Dr. Boardman. Mr. Moderator, I think I can relieve the mind of the brother over the way, and any other brother who may be similarly exercised in respect to the pertinency of this line of argument to the resolution which I have presented to the Assembly. It is only a further confirmation of what I was just about referring to, namely, the extraordinary state of mind which has been indicated by the remark made fifty times over —if not on the floor, where there is but little opportunity to make it—off the floor, and which I have heard from men of extreme views, and from men not of extreme views—the resolution adopted by the house on Friday in respect to these Louisville brethren was a mere "preliminary" procedure. "Oh, a mere preliminary procedure." "Bide your time, brethren, you will have time to discuss this question."

Now, sir, it is, to my mind, the most striking and significant demonstration that has occurred in this house. That the cloud that has been brought in upon us and overshadowed us—not like that cloud of refulgent light which illuminated the Mount of Transfiguration, but rather, sir, like one of those clouds of midnight blackness which come from yon Western horizon, and enfolds everything within its reach. A "preliminary proceeding," is it, brethren?

Suppose, sir—the case is supposable—that a member should rise in his place on this floor, with a duly prepared paper, and should say: "Mr. Moderator, I am credibly informed there are members on the floor of this Assembly who for years have not given a particle of attention to their appropriate work as Christian ministers—brethren who have brought the tables of the money changers into the house of God; brethren whose walks are associated, far and near, not with the highest spiritual functions of the ministry of reconciliation, but with questions of Wall street, and, sir, I deem it due to the purity of this house that before we can sit together they shall be excluded from the floor, and a committee appointed to investigate their claims to a seat. And now, sir, I move the previous question."

Would that be a "preliminary question?" Would brethren upon whom the ax happened to fall, regard it as a "preliminary proceeding!"

What better right have you or I here to-day than to a seat upon this floor? You deprive me, in wresting that right from me, of all opportunity of explanation—of all opportunity of self-defense, and if I am arraigned and censured, if I am about to be cast out of the Church of my fathers—the Church upon whose bosom I pillowed my head, upon whose bosom I hope to rest, and upon whose bosom I hope to rest in my dying hours, and if there is a tear to be shed by anybody on my humble grave, I hope it may come from that honored mother.

Sir, this Church is dear to me, and all its rights are dear to me, and in striking down these brethren they have struck at me and struck at you, sir, and every man on this floor, and every convenient method of defense. And, sir, rely upon it, it is not the mode of procedure which is recognized in the house of God; it is not the method of dealing with the highest and most sacred rights of Christian men and Christian ministers, which is prescribed in that Constitution; it is an utter invasion of all those rights. You not only find no precedent for it in the history of the Church, and no precedence for it in the history of Christian jurisprudence, I take it.

Sir, did this General Assembly in 1837, when the minute was already prepared by the hand of that revered and illustrious man, Dr. Baxter, of Virginia, (for he wrote it in my house,) a minute which was to lay the foundation for the excluding of those four Synods—sir, did the General Assembly introduce that minute, or the committee who presented it, and say, "Moderator, I move the previous question?" And did the General Assembly sustain the previous question? And did the members from these four Synods get up and go out of the house, or were they allowed the amplest latitude of debate? When the General Assembly dissolved the three Presbyteries of Philadelphia which gave them so much trouble for many years, did they begin, sir, by excluding the members of those Presbyteries from the house, or did they give them plenary opportunity to say what reason they had why they should not be dissolved?

Sir, do you suppose there is a court sitting in that noble edifice over the way—[pointing towards the Court House]—an edifice which would embelish any city in any land—do you suppose there is a court sitting there this morning that would dare to try the veriest outlaw that this miserable jail—the only miserable thing is St. Louis, I believe—that would dare to try the veriest outlaw in this miserable jail for the pettiest offense—for stealing a pocket-handkerchief, if you will, except the man were tried at the bar, and he or his counsel had opportunity to say why he should not go to the penitentiary.

Sir, there is at this time in the jail of Philadelphia a monster—you will have heard of him—a man whose name will go down to posterity as the prince of assassins—a man, who in cold blood deliberately murdered a whole family of eight persons —the father, the mother, the sister, the hired boy, the child, infant upon its mother's breast—this fiend incarnate, a walking devil, if there be one. And, sir, he was tried the other day, and he is now waiting the gallows. But what did they do? Why, sir, they brought him into the court room, and even with the universal conviction on the mind of that community that this man was a monster—not worthy to live even—with the full assurance that the mob would ambush the man on its way to gather aroune the gates of the public square, through which he must pass; that, if it were possible, by strategy and force, to rescue him, they would hang him to the first lamp post. Sir, that Court of Common Pleas would no more have dared to try that wretch without having arraigned him at the bar before them than they would have dared, sir, to have tried you or me—not a bit. Sir, if it required the whole military force of Philadelphia to escort that man safely to the court room and back to his prison, the military force of the city would have been called out to do it.

I tell you, sir, you are traversing here one of the fundamental principles—I will not say of jurisprudence, but of American liberty, and of all liberty. [Applause in the galleries.] I tell you there is no safety from any——

The Moderator. It was suggested the other day, very properly by a member of this body, which I seconded, that there should be no demonstration of applause or disapprobation on either side in the discussion of this exciting question. As I said the other day, I hope our kind friends who honor us with their presence will observe the proprieties belonging to this body.

Dr. Boardman. Well, sir, I say there is no safety for any man if this principle is to be recognized which is embodied here.

My brethren and fathers—I must say it—I believe a mistaken judgment is embodied in the hasty action of this body on Friday last. And I say it was a woful thing for a great assembly, representing one of the greatest Churches on this continent, or of the world—a Church which has gloried alike in holding forth the banner as well of civil as of religious liberty in all lands and wherever yonder sun circuits the earth—it is a woful thing that a General Assembly of this sort should set its hand to a principle which goes to subvert all human rights and all human liberty.

Sir, these men must be heard; and you will not sleep quietly until they are heard. You may have four to one—yes, sir, and you may have four hundred to one, but, sir, you are on trial yourself—we are on trial; and thus far we have made but a very poor showing of it.

The sentiment has gone over this community—among the men that have been faithful Union men during the war—that have poured out their money like water, and that have stood by the old flag with an inflexible fidelity—and among the men whose sympathies have been supposed to be in the other direction—the sentiment has gone forth through this community that you are proceeding beyond the principles of enlightened Christian liberty, or of a government of law or a constitution of freedom, and upon the principles of despotism; and the reputation of the Church is concerned in it. We cannot afford that sort of thing; we cannot afford to have it pleaded by politicians who may have their schemes to accomplish and their purposes to achieve; we cannot afford to have the action of the General Assembly of the Presbyterian Church cited as a venerable precedent as giving sanction to these foul and oppressive measures. No, sir, we must adhere to the great doctrine of human rights, to the principles of our constitution and this great American Republic. I do not refer merely to our respected friends, our fellow citizens, I may say, for the time being, to the comparatively limited assembly which can crowd itself within these doors. We are on trial before the American people, and before all the churches of all lands, before the whole civilized world. And I tell you, sir, that if this action goes forth unmodified, unrecalled, unredressed, by what you are yet to do, it will turn out with you as it turned out in that memorable conflict between Rome and Carthage. "One more such victory will prove your defeat and overthrow." Sir, do you imagine—is any member of this house so simple as to imagine—that these men have been silenced? No, Moderator, there is a silence that speaks louder than seven thunders; there is a sublime allusion to that sort of silence in the opening of the nineteenth psalm, when the Psalmist, lifting up his eyes to the starry heavens, and referring to their perfect symphony, says—for you will omit, as you know very well, brethren, the words that have been interpolated by the translator—"There is no speech, nor language." "Their voice is not heard." "There is no speech, nor language." "Their voice is not heard."

But is it not heard? Do we not know what the music of the spheres is? When you go out on one of these splendid moonlight nights, lift up your eyes to the canopy above—do you not hear music as sweet as that which flowed over the plains of Bethlehem?

I tell you, sir, that the silence of these men who sat along here but the other day, clothed with their sacred right—that the silence—the enforced silence of these men, is a voice which will make itself heard throughout the whole land.

Sir, you cannot suppress it. You might as well attempt to cairn this magnificent river that pours its mighty torrent down to the Ocean—you might as well attempt to impose chains on the blessed atmosphere of God which is diffused over the whole earth. Why, sir, God has not left the weak powerless. In many a condition of affairs—in many a relation in life, is it verified as well as in the personal experiences of Christian believers. "When I am weak, then am I strong."

Sir, you have delegated these men with a power of speech—with a mighty influence which they never could have exercised—a power which they never could have attained here, had you surrendered this platform to them exclusively for a week together.

Let them do their worst, sir, they could not have done for themselves what you have done for them, by sending them forth branded men without the opportunity of making a defense. It has gone over this community, and if the people your are staying with do not delicately hint to you, it will be because their courtesy forbids it.

God has put that feeling in the human bosom—He has lodged it there in the deepest recesses of human nature—He has incorporated it, I might say, in almost every human heart—that sense of sympathy with the wronged, of compassion for the feeble. Why, Moderator, there is every day an example which might occur. Suppose you see a group of boys, and there is a quarrel among them, and half a dozen of them have taken one poor scamp and tied his hands behind him, thrust a gag in his mouth, and are attempting to beat and to pummel him—what would you say? Suppose they told you he is the greatest little rascal in the street; he has done all manner of wicked things, and is likely to do just as many more—what would you say, sir? You would feel like shaking them, and if you had your official gavel in your hand, Mr. Moderator, if the little wretches did not desist, Christian man that you are, and averse to controversy as you are, I almost fear you would strike the little scamps themselves upon the head, as I know you have hit a good many others on the head. [Merriment.]

Now, I tell you, sir, that is what you would have done. You have put these men in a position where every fair minded man who looks at these matters, in any other atmosphere than one which is beclouded as this is—one who looks at these things from a point where these conflicting and surging tides of prejudice and passion and remembered wrong, or anticipated evil, are not met in mighty conflict—you have put these men in a position where the heart of every man, and I am sure of every woman, (who in other circumstances than these) will go forth in sympathy.

I do not want to be in this position. I do not fear the tongues of these men; but I do fear the results of treating with injustice and oppression; I dread their silence. I tell you they have a right to be heard; and I tell you they have a right to be heard, on what these honored brethern call, this "preliminary proceeding." My conscience! A preliminary proceedining which unseats them.

Rev. Mr. Crozier, Moderator. I would like to ask the gentleman if he has read the discipline?

Dr. Boardman. Certainly; I am glad to read anything from the book, and I wish the Assembly would study it more.

Rev. Mr. Crozier. I would just like to point to the Church Discipline, ch. 4, sec. 18.

"As cases may arise in which many days or even weeks may intervene before it is practicable to commence process against an accused church member, the session may, in such cases, and ought, if they think the edification of the church requires it, to prevent the accused from approaching the Lord's table until the charge against him can be examined."

And also to chapter 5, section 11:

"When a member of a church judicatory is under process, it shall be discretionary with the judicatory whether his privileges of deliberating and voting, as a member, in other matters, shall be suspended until the process is finally issued, or not."

Dr. Boardman. I should like to inquire if these brethren are "under process."

Rev. Mr. Crozier. I think they are.

Dr. Boardman. Please read the chapter on process for the benefit of the Assembly.

Rev. Mr. Crozier. I just wished to call your attention to that, sir.

Dr. Boardman. Exactly; but if you are not disposed to read it to the Assembly, please to refer to it for your own illumination.

Rev. Mr. Crozier. Thank you, sir. [Merriment.]

Dr. Boardman. Why, sir, this is the most cheerful thing that has happened to-day. I am delighted to see that one member--I suppose the good brother was one of the two hundred who voted against the poor minority of fifty—I am glad to see this discussion has sent one of these two hundred brethren to the Book of Discipline. My only hope is that this is only a beginning, and that he and all the brethren, in concert, singly, or alone in the silence of their rooms, may take this venerable book and sit down and read it through. There would be no difficulty if the brethren would read it. I think I will not say anything about this quotation; it is too bad.

Now, Moderator, I say that these brethren are just as much entitled to be heard as any member on this floor is entitled to be heard, and if distinctions are to be made, they are more entitled to be heard before you finally dispose of this case, than any man is to be heard either for or against them. It may be a question of life and death with them and their Presbyteries. Sir, by this vote you have for a time disfranchised one of the largest Presbyteries of the Church. I see by the minutes that Presbytery has thirty-three churches. You put them out of the house and entirely ignore them. We have a right to avail ourselves of the accumulated wisdom and experience, and Christian fidelity of every Commissioner appointed to this body, in passing upon every one of the questions which are or may be acted upon. Sir, questions may come up here which the presence or absence of these four men might decide—questions of fundamental importance concerning the policy of the Church; respecting the Theological Seminaries of the Church, and respecting the future interests of our blessed country. And so, therefore, you wrong not only them, but you wrong us all. You wrong our Presbyteries and Churches by excluding them from their seats.

Dr. Thomas said to us that we have one of our Presbyteries before us. I take issue with him. We have not that Presbytery before us. Where is it? It is not before us. You have sent them out of that door. Now, sir, I see that the hour of adjournment is at hand, and I have not gone at all into the general merits of many of the principles and questions involved in this issue. I am thankful I have the opportunity of saying two or three words, and that no brother has seen fit, or claimed the right of thrusting in the previous question upon me. It might be done when I get through. Just do it as soon as you please.

But, sir, in conclusion, no man can look upon this scene without feeling that our Church is reaching a crisis. The Church is in deep waters and there are two policies that meet us. There is a fork in the road, brethren, and you must take one path or the other, and, under God, the whole future of our Church is bound up in the path which you take. On the one hand there is the path of severity and stern, unrelenting justice, and of holding every man accountable for every rash word he has uttered and for every rash sentiment he has written and for every disloyal—I refer to the Church—for every disloyal paragraph he has put forth in sermon or newspaper; you are to hold every man accountable for what has gone forth from him in the season of conflict and excitement which has swept like a hurricane over our land—which has filled it with graves and mourners; and you are to arrign every such man at your bar; you are to visit upon him the full penalty of your jurisprudence for every such offense. But if you do it, sir, your church is divided. The Episcopal Church is gathering up its scattered fragments to unite them once more in blessed fraternity. The Methodist Church, North and South, are clasping their hands together over these lines of blood, and saying one to another we will not see it Let us be brethren Sir, it remains for this Assembly to decide what shall be the policy of our Church, not only for years to come—for a few years to come—but peradventure for a very long period to come.

You may take the other course, in the spirit of Him whose pardoning mercy we are all dependent upon, whose forgiving love we daily pray for daily sins; you may go to these brethren and say, brethren you do wrong, you have fallen in with this torrent of public passion, you have violated the laws of the House of God; you have said things that are discourteous, that are disagreeable and that you ought not to have said, but we will not hold you to a rigorous account; we will bear with you as we have need to be borne with, and we will bear with you; if you will come back to our arms, here they are.

Sirs, on Saturday last I was driving out through the suburbs of this city. It is a beautiful spread of country that reaches far and wide, and as you go out over the crest of the hill, a scene of surpassing beauty and tranquility presents itself. On Saturday last I was driving out with a gentleman of this city, a man loyal to his heart's core, a man whose name is never mentioned in St. Louis by any man, of whatever party, or profession or occupation, but with honor and reverence. He said to me what is the reason that the soldiers—the men who did the fighting—not the holiday soldiers, but the men who did the fighting—are ready to exercise forbearance and forgiveness and peace, while the ministers seem to be in favor of war. Sir, said I, you have propounded a problem to me which I cannot solve. I know the fact, for I have had personal experience of it.

And here again in one of these hospitals during the war. [I see your hour has expired. and I will not trespass. Just give me one minute or two, and I think I can release you.] In one of these hospitals there were two soldiers. They were very badly wounded. Those ministering spirits—those blessed Christian women were in the hospital visiting them. I think it was in the strawberry season, and under the direction of the physician of the establishment one of them was required to go about and mark the couches with chalk, and all the men who could have any strawberries and were in that condition that the fruit would injure them had their couches marked. Well, there were two poor fellows lying side by side. One bed was marked, and the other was not. A lady came along presently, "Well," said she to one of them, "this poor fellow would like some strawberries, I suppose?" She was bearing them with her. "No, the Doctor says they will hurt him; he can't live; he is going to die soon. The Doctor says strawberries will only hasten his death, and he can't have them." She handed the basket of strawberries to his fellow. She had got but a little way off, however, and what do you think she saw? Why, she saw the man with the strawberries, a Union soldier, getting himself out of his couch, and with his crutch he was limping his way over to his fellow's bed, and there he stood resting on his crutch and putting the strawberries into his comrade's mouth. "Why," said she, "you are Union men. I suppose, both of you?" "No, madam," said he; "day before yesterday this man and I fought against each other, but we are brothers now." "We are brothers now." O, brethren, can't you see that? We have fought these men, and we will fight them in time of war. We are here in a State that honors the name of Thomas Jefferson, but you ministers do not honor it much. You never go to Thomas Jefferson for your ethics, I am sure, or to that immortal document—that which came from his pen, and which is an heir-loom in every American habitation, and which every American boy commits to memory substantially, and which is recited every year in your National Legislature. In that immortal document which came from his pen, he said, referring to Great Britain and to the King of England and to his people, "we must regard them as we regard all other nations, as enemies in war in peace, friends." Why, brethren, is it war or is it peace? Shall they who not only profess to sit at the feet of the meek and lowly Savior; shall they whose professed voice and whose hereditary function it is to preach the gospel of peace, to preach forgiveness and forbearance, and universal charity—shall we set our hands to the atrocious doctrine that any class or condition of men in any land shall be regarded by us enemies not only in war, but even in peace? God forbid! God forbid!

I have performed a painful and reluctant duty, Mr. Moderator. If it is the last word I ever say for this beloved and cherished Church, I rejoice to have had the opportunity of making an ample plea for the cause of truth and righteousness, and for the charity of our ever blessed Redeemer.

Mr. Gallaway of Ohio. As the hour of adjournment has arrived, I take this opportunity, merely, to claim the floor at the next session.

Rev. Dr. Gurley, from the Judicial Committee, reported that the committee had agreed for a joint trial in the case of Dr. Breckinridge and others against the Synod of Kentucky, and also on the complaint of Dr. Breckenridge against the Presbytery of Louisville, in the case of J. P. McMillen.

Same committee also reported on the complaint of Rev. J. S. Niccolls and others against the Synod of Missouri, asking that the action of that Synod may be declared null and void.

The committee recommend that the complaint be sustained, the action of the Synod reversed and the Synod censured.

The Assembly then adjourned to 9 o'clock Tuesday morning.

FIFTH DAY—TUESAY, MAY 22, 1866.

The Assembly met at the usual hour, and after devotional exercises, and the reading of the minutes, the Committee appointed to arrange for an excursion on the Iron Mountain Railroad, presented their report, and Saturday next was the day agreed upon.

The presentation of Synodical Records was next in order.

Rev. Dr. Gurley and Lincoln Clark were deputed to represent this Assembly to the First Assembly now in session in this city.

Rev. Dr. Lowrie, from the Committee of Bills and Overtures, presented Overture No. 1, concerning papers relating to the forming of the Presbytery of Shantung, at Tungchow, China, January 29, 1866, by the Rev. Messrs. Charles R. Mill, of the Presbytery of Shanghai; Calvin W. Mateer, of the Presbytery of Marion, and Hunter Corbett, of the Presbytery of Clarion—the said Presbytery to be connected with the Synod of New York.

The Committee find that these brethren followed the order prescribed by the General Assembly of 1848, concerning the forming of Presbyteries in our foreign missionary fields abroad, and recommend that the Presbytery of Shantung be recognized as duly organized, and its name be entered on the roll of the General Assembly. Adopted.

Overture No. 2—A memorial from the Presbytery of Canton, asking the General Assembly to adopt regulations making the Presbytery the last court of appeal in certain cases which will occur in the Foreign Missionary Presbyteries, where there is no local Synod; referring to the difficulty of such Presbyteries being represented in the meetings of the General Assembly, and requesting leave to transmit transcripts of their minutes to the Assembly.

The committee regard the first of these subjects as worthy of continued consideration, but recommend that the Assembly take no action concerning it at present, and also recommend that the Assembly approve of the Missionary Presbyteries sending commissioners to its meetings, as providential circumstances permit, as well as of their sending transcripts of their minutes to the Assembly, and in general recommend that the act of the General Assembly of 1845, concerning Presbyteries in India, be extended to all foreign missionary Presbyteries. Adopted.

Overture No. 3—From the Presbytery of Philadelphia, asking the Assembly to provide a form for the organization of new churches, and also an additional form for the solemniztion of marriage. The committee recommend the following answer: First, that the action of the Assembly of 1834, p. 177, on the subject of organizing churches, is deemed sufficient, and the memorialists are referred to that action as found in Baird's Digest, pp. 54, 55. Second—No further action is deemed necessary on the second point in this overture. Adopted.

Overture No. 4—Being a request of the Presbytery of Passaic to restore the geographical arrangement of Synods and Presbyteries in the printing of the minutes. The committee recommend that no change be made. Adopted.

Overture No. 5—From the Presbytery of Leavenworth asking the General Assembly to place the church of Denver City, Colorado Territory, now reporting to that Presbytery, together with the other churches of that Territory, under the supervision and control of some Presbytery which they in their wisdom think may best promote the interests of the Master in that wide and interesting field.

The committee find that there are but two ministers belonging to our Church within the Territory of Colorado, and although the organization of a Presbytery there is desirable as soon as practicable, yet at present it seems impossible and the committee would, therefore, recommend that this Assembly take no action upon the subject.

Adopted.

Rev. Mr. Farquhar offered a resolution, that the churches be directed not to report under the head of "congregational" any money received for congregational purposes, which is the interest of permanent funds, belonging to churches, nor any appropriations from the Board of Domestic Missions. Also that the Stated Clerks be directed to report as candidates all young men who are studying for the ministry under their care.

The resolution was placed on the docket

Rev. Dr. Loomis presented the following report from the Committee on the Board of Foreign Missions:

REPORT OF THE COMMITTEE ON FOREIGN MISSIONS.

The Committee on the Board of Foreign Missions respectfully report to the General Assembly that they have carefully examined the annual report of this Board, which contains a brief but clear statement of the condition of the missions under its care, together with the report of the Treasurer. We recommend its approval and publication as a document worthy to be studied by all the members of our Church.

From it we learn that our Church sustains missions in nine different countries and at forty-six stations; that we have employed seventy-five ordained missionaries, nine of whom are natives, together with eight native licentiate preachers. We have seventeen lay laborers from this country and seventy-four female assistants; one hundred and forty native teachers, with other native helpers; four hundred and twenty-seven scholars are taught in boarding schools, and six thousand four hundred and thirty-three in day schools. The mission churches have a membership of one thousand one hundred and ninety-three, of which about one hundred and seventy-six have been added during the year. Three deaths of missionaries have occurred during the year. The number of missionaries now employed is three more than were reported a year ago.

From the report it appears that the receipts of the Board from contributions and from legacies is less by more than $46,000 than the receipts from the same sources last year. The total receipts of the Board are $207,526 65; the expenditures $210,376 9[illegible], leaving a balance [illegible] the Treasury of $2,849 93. The whole number of churches contributing is 1.380 against 1,500 last year, being a falling off of 120 in the contributing churches.

The whole number of churches in our communion is 2.629; of these 1,249 appear as having done nothing during the past year towards sending the Gospel to the heathen.

We find that all the missions reported last year have been sustained, but with the exception of a few out stations no new ground has been occupied. While the missionaries in nearly all these fields are calling, as they long have been, for ministers and teachers to be sent to their assistance, as well as to enter into other and needy fields, and in some of the missions new buildings are greatly needed, but which cannot be furnished until the Church increases its contributions.

During the time in which our Board has been in operation the Bible has been translated into many languages and a great amount and variety of religious books have been printed, and thus the way has been prepared for the more rapid diffusion of religious truth in the future than in the past if the men were ready to take these scriptures and religious publications and preach and distribute them amongst the people for whom they were designed.

In all this we find reason both for thankfulness and for sorrow; thankfulness that as a Church we have been able to hold the ground previously acquired, but great grief that our people have not by largely increased contributions enabled the Board both to enlarge its operations in the older missions, and to establish new stations in districts and countries which are accessible, and where they have long desired, as servants of the Church, to plant the standard of the Cross.

In view of these facts, and in view, further, of the claims of the heathen upon us and the command of our Lord to preach His gospel to every creature, we recommend the following action, viz:

Resolved, That this Assembly gratefully recognize the continued prosperity which the Great Head of the Church has vouchsafed to the work of this Board during the past year, which favor has been especially manifested in the goodly number of converts gathered into the mission churches and in the increase of native ministers and assistants.

2. That the members of the Board of Foreign Missions, and especially its Executive Committee, are deserving the thanks of this Assembly for the wisdom, zeal and untiring perseverance with which they have from the beginning conducted its affairs, and particularly during the past years of trial and perplexity.

3 That in view of the lands yet to be evangelized, the many hundreds of millions of people yet in darkness; also in view of the low state of the missionary spirit in our churches, the small number of candidates for the foreign field, and the immediate necessity for a great army of native assistants, we will cry mightily unto God till he revives pure religion in our hearts and amongst our people, and till he so bless the Word preached amongst the Gentiles as to give us our desire in raising up very many from amongst the heathen who shall soon be qualified to preach the Gospel to their countrymen. Nevertheless the Assembly does not mean by this to be understood to say that the Church at home may sit still until such converts are brought into the Church and educated for the ministry; it believes rather that no good reason can be shown for so unequal a division of the ministerial force as exists at present—2,484 ministers remaining here amongst a population of only five or six millions, nearly all of whom already know what they should do to be saved, while we give 83 ministers, 17 of whom are natives, to the many hundreds of millions who have never yet heard of Jesus and his salvation. The Assembly therefore recommends all its young ministers, as well as candidates for the ministry' to give a new hearing to the calls which are coming in for laborers for this wide spread harvest field.

4. That this Assembly regards the whole Church as a missionary society whose main work is to spread the knowledge of salvation; that individual Christians are not merely to enjoy religion themselves, but to be actively engaged in efforts to lead others to Christ; also, that this Assembly recognizes the right as vested in Presbyteries to select and appoint to the foreign as well as to the domestic missionary work any and all such of their number as they believe to be fitted for and to be needed in the foreign field, and that the persons so designated and called may not refuse to obey, unless God by His providence clearly shows that His will is that they remain at home, and that until we come up to this standard we cannot be satisfied that with entire sincerity we can ask, "Lord, what wilt thou have me to do?"

5. That the falling off in the contributions to this Board during the past year, the present indebtedness of the Board, and the fact that so large a portion of the Church has given nothing at all, while the ability to contribute has been greater owing to the return of peace and general prosperity to the land, and the discontinuance of those calls for the gifts of the people which were so numerous during the war, are cause for deep humility and for searching of heart; therefore the General Assembly commends this subject to the prayerful consideration of the churches, and reminds them again of her oft-repeated injunctions that each church shall take up annual collections for the Boards; and where there is a failure to comply with this injunction, Presbyteries are directed to inquire into the cause of such delinquency.

6. That we hold in tender regard those brethren and sisters who, instead of us, have left home and kindred and are now laboring and suffering in unhealthy climes that they may win souls to Christ; and in order that they may be free from anxiety about the future, provision for the support and education of their children, we call the attention of the churches to the statement in the annual report of the Board, that "the fund for the children of missionaries should be largely increased;" and in order that all our members may be brought into closer sympathy with our missionary brethren we urge upon all ministers and church officers the duty of spreading missionary intelligence, maintaining monthly concerts of prayer for missions, accompanying such prayers with contributions for the cause for which they have been praying.

By the report of the Board it appears that an election should be held to fill the vacancies occurring in the Board of Missions. The following names are recommended for the class whose term of office expires in 1866:

MINISTERS.	ELDERS.
William C. Anderson, D. D.,	Alanson Trask,
Charles Hodge, D. D.,	David Olyphant,
Robert J. Breckinridge, D. D.,	Thomas W. Smyth,
John C. Backus, D. D.,	Jonathan Woodruff,
Henry A. Boardman, D. D.,	Robert McKnight,
Job F. Halsey, D. D.,	Walter Lowrie,
David Irving, D. D.,	Jasper Corning,
Samuel Wilson, D. D.,	John D. McCord,
William D. Howard, D. D.,	H. H. Leavitt,
William G. T. Ghedd, D. D.,	James Donaldson,
William M. Paxton, D. D.,	William Baird,
Benjamin F. Stead, D. D.,	Wm. P. Van Rensalaer,
James G. Ralston, D. D.,	Robert McFarlane,
J. E. Rockwell, D. D.,	James Bayles,
Charles C. Beatty, D. D.	David Comfort.

In the class of 1863:

Ministers—Revand K. Rogers, D. D., in place of Geo. W Janvier, D. D., deceased.

Henry R. Wilson, D. D., in place of Robert C. Grundy, D. D., deceased, and Elder Stephen Lockwood, in place of C. C. Lathrop, deceased.

In class of 1869:

Elder David Hotchkiss, in place of Ebenezer Platt, deceased.

Among the papers submitted to this committee was a copy of the records of the annual meeting of the Board of Foreign Missions, in which we find a resolution which was designed for this General Assembly, a copy of which we here present, hoping that the Assembly will entertain it. It is as follows, viz:

On motion of Rev. J. C. Rankin, it was resolved that, inasmuch as a large increase in the funds is demanded for the necessary operations of the Board of Foreign Missions for the ensuing year, it be recommended to the General Assembly to solicit the churches to increase donations to this Board by a sum not less than fifty thousand dollars.

In addition to the foregoing, there were referred to your committee certain overtures from Northern India. No. 1 being an overture respecting the provision to be made for the support of the widows of missionaries, No. 2, an overture touching the subject of inadequate provision for the support and education of the children of foreign missionaries; and No. 3, an overture touching the sustentation and enlargement of the missionary work in India. Respecting these overtures, we recommend that, inasmuch as the Board of Foreign Missions has long had these subjects under consideration, and has already made partial provision to meet the wants specified in overtures one and two, and inasmuch as overture No. 3 refers to matters which belong peculiarly to the Board of Foreign Missions, therefore the General Assembly refer all these papers to said Board, with instructions to give them that attention which, in their judgment, the cases may require

As a part of their report, the committee further recommend that the evening of this day be set apart by the Assembly with a view to the fuller consideration of the interests of this Board.

A. W. LOOMIS, Ch'mn of Com.

Whereas, By the Redeemer's last command to His disciples He has laid the Church under obligation to carry the gospel to every creature; and

Whereas, The difficulties in the way of obedience to that command are so many and so great and the laborers so few as to imperiously demand that every agency adapted to the accomplishment of this work should be employed; and

Whereas, The providence of God, His revealed word and the example of our Lord Jesus Christ, point most emphatically to the employment of the men both of the seas and the rivers in this good work; therefore,

Resolved, That this General Assembly urge upon the pastors and stated supplies of the churches within its bounds the importance of calling the attention of their people to the religious claims of this interesting and useful class of our fellow men and of exhorting them to labor and pray that the abundance of the sea may be converted, in order that the forces of the Gentiles may be brought into the Church.

Rev. Mr. Jones, chaplain of the Sailors' Snug Harbor of New York, said his heart had been thrilled by the reading of this report, and he desired to offer a resolution that the General Assembly urge the pastors and churches within its bounds to more earnest efforts in the work of converting soilors, as a means of carrying the gospel to all lands.

He thought there was a large element in our land out of which they could make up the deficiencies in this Board. We were told by the report that there were but eighty-three ministers sent abroad. He contended that by proper efforts there were vast numbers of men doing business upon the great deep who could be brought into this great work, whose hearts were open for the gospel of Christ, and who would possess an influence all over the world not easily attainable by others.

A motion was made to consider the matter at an evening session.

Rev. Dr. Lowrie concurred with this suggestion. He was exceedingly sorry on yesterday that two of these great home evangelizing agencies were dispatched from the house in five or ten minutes.

Rev Mr. Kempshall rose to say that he made the motion in regard to the adoption of the report on Church extension, but it was made at the request of the Secretary of that Board.

Rev. Dr. Lowrie said that made the matter all the worse. He did not under estimate the importance of the great questions that were monopolizing their time, but he thought there were other matters in the court of Christ that ought to be discussed more thoroughly. He believed also, that this subject should be brought to the attention of this body at this time, because there were a large number of members whose assistance it was desirous to gain who would be unable to be present in the evening. He wished to say that this Board had been constrained for five years to pursue a policy of restriction. It seemed at one time that these Foreign Missions would be broken up, and the Board found it necessary to curtail expenses as much as possible.

Last year the Board issued a special appeal for aid to the churches, and that appeal was responded to. The consequence is there now appears to be a greater falling off in contributions than there really exists. Still, there was a deficiency which it was necessary to make up; and funds were required for the missions at Ningpoo, at Pekin, and in other fields of labor. It seemed to him it was better to call on the people to give as God had prospered them, and he thought there was no doubt that by this means they would have ample funds for this work. Without securing this aid it would be impossible to carry on this instruction further, unless they withdrew some of the missions. It was a matter of regret that they were able to send out so few men. This might partly be accounted for from the state of the public mind in regard to vital questions, but principally because the minds and hearts of God's people have not been turned sufficiently to the power of the grace of God.

The speaker concluded by earnestly recommending renewed zeal in behalf of this great cause.

Rev. Mr. Remington, member of the committee, said it was a matter of regret that there had been a falling off in the contributions, but he hoped that in the coming year they would make up for this deficiency. He urged the importance of this field of labor. He recollected reading not long since, that when the American Board of Foreign Missions, sent a petition to the Legislature of Massachusetts for an act of incorporation, one of the members objected to it on the ground they could not afford to export the influence of religion to other countries. But in reply to this a member said, the more of religious influence that was sent abroad the more they would have at home. He hoped the report would be adoped; and that they would give their efforts, and labor more faithfully to promote this great and important work.

The Rev. Dr. Nevins, of China, said he stood before them to-day as the representative from Ningpoo, China, a representrtive of four millions of our race He had listened with a great deal of interest to the report, and he could not imagine how a good Christian man or woman could read that report without having their hearts thrilled. There were facts there which every Christian man should consider prayerfully. As had been said, the word for the last five years had been retrenchment. They could not imagine how sad that word made them, as it came to them by the overland mail. Last year, it seems, an urgent appeal was made for increaeed contributions, and promises were made to send men and money into these fields; but what had been the result? Forty thousand dollars less had been contributed, and one hundred Churches that contributed year before last, had not contributed a dollar during the last year, for extending the cause in foreign parts.

The resolutions that had been placed on the minutes from time to time have been a dead letter; he feared they had not been read. The business had been mere formality and routine. But he was happy to see that the gentleman who drew the report this year had departed from that routine. He asked every member of the Assembly to take that report and read and digest it. There were subjects there which would furnish many an interesting theme for monthly concerts and family conversation. Before he went to China, thirteen years ago, he remembered that in all the monthly concerts the stereotyped expression of prayer was "that God would open wide the door in every land." And now that the door was open would they not convict themselves of insincerity and hypocricy if they did not enter in and possess the land.

The speaker alluded to the vast population of China and the region of country in which he had labored. He had seen a river in that far off land that in some respects would rival this great Mississippi. He had traveled up that river six hundred miles to the City of Hankaw; which, until within a few years, was the largest city in the world, containing some four or five million of people. This whole region of country had recently been opened to foreign commerce and foreign missionaries, and it was important that this Church should be represented there. All those nations were now open—China, India, Japan—all were on the eve of a new era. Old systems were crumbling. China would soon be the theater of a conflict of ideas, as it had been the theater of a civil conflict for the last fifteen years.

Agencies were at work to create an entire revolution in that country, and it was time for this Church to begin the work of putting forth exertions commensurate to the demands of the cause.

Rev. Mr. Henry said he had listened with a good deal of interest to the report, but he thought a different system should be adopted in the matter of obtaining contributions; he believed in direct appeals to the people of the churches, asking every man to give according to his means. This plan had worked successfully in his own church, and he believed, if generally adopted, would result in increased contributions.

Rev. Dr. Ferguson urged the importance of considering this matter at this time. Other questions of not so much importance to the interests of the Church had been up heretofore, and the papers had been filled with column after column, while only slight reports had been given of such matters as were now before them for consideration. He desired that they should go into this matter now and give it a thorough discussion.

After some further debate the motion to defer the subject to the evening session was agreed to.

On motion of Rev. Mr. Sims, the report of the Committee on Freedmen was made the order of the day for Friday next.

The Moderator announced that he had a protest against the act removing the Commissioners from the Louisville Presbytery, which he desired to lay before the Asssembly.

The protest was then read as follows:

PROTEST.

We, the undersigned, respectfully protest against what we deem to be the mischievous and erroneous judgment of the General Assembly, in suspending the Commissioners from the Presbytery of Louisville from the exercise of their rights and privileges as members of this body, for the following reasons:

1. By this act, the Assembly has violated the fundamental principles of its own organization, and vitiated its own integrity as the highest judicatory of the Presbyterian Church. It is declared in chapter XII of the Form of Government, that the General Assembly "shall represent in one body *all* the particular churches of this denomination;" and again, the General Assembly "shall consist of an equal delegation of bishops and elders from *each* Presbytery." It cannot be denied that at the time their representatives were excluded from the Assembly, the churches composing the Presbytery of Louisville *were and still are an integral part of the Presbyterian Church*. And yet the Assembly, by a simple resolution, adopted under the operation of the previous question, without debate, excluded these churches from all participation in its proceedings at a time when the business under consideration was of vital importance to the said churches. For such a course of action there is no warrant in the constitution, and no precedent in the history of the Church. The attempt to justify it by the usage of legislative and other political assemblies is, in the judgment of the undersigned, utterly futile; because, in the first place, there is no proper analogy between legislative bodies or other secular assemblies, acting under rules of human invention, and the court of Jesus Christ organized under, and bound by the laws of Christ as expounded in its own written constitution; and because, secondly, if such an analogy did exist, it has been violated in this case in the following essential particulars: 1. By the action of its own committee on commissions, and the formal adoption of their report, the Assembly had already decided that the commissioners from the Presbytery of Louisville were entitled to their seats. 2. In legislative and other secular assemblies, when the right of members to the seats they have obtained is contested, they are always allowed to retain their places in the body, and to participate in its proceedings until the case is fully decided.

2. By this act the Assembly has virtually pronounced a judicial condemnation upon the Presbytery of Louisville without observing any of the forms of trial so carefully prescribed by the constitution, and so essential to the due administration of justice. And, in the opinion of the undersigned, this proceeding is rendered the more irregular and unjust in view of the fact that, by the operation of the previous question on the adoption of the resolution excluding them, the commissioners were denied a hearing before the Assembly, either in their own behalf, or in the behalf of the Presbytery they represent. And this disregard of judicial forms is further aggravated by the fact that in the resolution excluding the commissioners from their seats, the Assembly indorsed unsustained public rumors against the ministerial character and standing of one of the said commissioners, and made these rumors thus indorsed without any judicial proof a ground of condemnation against the Presbytery.

3. The facts alleged against the Presbytery of Louisville do not involve any heresy or crime, nor justify the exclusion of the churches comprising said Presbytery from the fellowship of the Church of Christ. Inasmuch as "all Synods or Councils since the days of the apostles"—being composed of uninspired and fallible men—"may err, and many have erred," the right to publicly discuss, dispute and protest against the deliverances of such Synods and councils belongs to every other ecclesiastical body and to every, even the humblest member of the Church. This right has been exercised from the foundation of the Church till the present time and has never been disputed except by the Church of Rome. Moreover, the deliverances and orders of the General Assemblies, against which the Presbytery of Louisville have protested and which they have refused to obey, not having been transmitted to the Presbyteries for their approbation, (according to the requisition of the Form of Government, chap. xii, sec. 6,) are not "established as constitutional rules," neither are they "obligatory upon the Churches." To exclude the churches of the Presbytery of Louisville from representation in this body for refusing to do that which according to express provisions of the constitution was not obligatory on them is, in the judgment of the undersigned, an unwarranted and alarming usurpation of power.

For the foregoing and other reasons, in the name of Jesus Christ, by virtue of the right secured to them in the constitution, and in the discharge of their covenant obligations to study the purity and peace of the Church, the undersigned do solemnly protest against this whole proceeding, as being unconstitutional and revolutionary, as calculated to bring the lawful authority of this Assembly into contempt, to enkindle strife and produce alienation, and to defeat the end for which the Assembly was originally organized, viz: that it might "constitute the bond of Union, peace, correspondence and mutual confidence among all our churches.

Henry J. Van Dyke, R. K. Smoot, J. L. Yantis, A. P. Forman, L. P. Bowen, R. L. McAfee, Isaac D. Jones, G. C. Swallow, S. J. P. Anderson, Glass Marshall, James H. Brookes, John M. Travis, Thos. A. Bracken, J. W. Pryor, Geo. W. Buchanan, J. T. Hendrick, P. Thompson, W. M. Ferguson.

The Moderator then announced that the unfinished business was in order--namely, the resolution offered by Dr. Boardman yesterday, to reinstate the members of the Louisville Presbytery, and that Mr. Galloway had the floor.

Mr. Galloway. Mr. Moderator and brethren of the Assembly, I feel somewhat embarrassed on rising before this Assembly to address them upon this important question, and this embarrassment arises partly from the fact that this is rather a new arena for me. I have been but once before the General Assembly of the Church in the capacity of a representative, and then but briefly addressed the Assembly, and hence I feel a little like the boy who was asked why he didn't spell so well in the new school-house, and he said he "hadn't got the hang of it yet." I feel also embarrassed from the consideration that I am advertised as having been a member of Congress. It is not often that gentlemen of that body appear before ecclesiastical courts, and it is not the best certificate of qualification. [Merriment.] It would scarcely be regarded as *prima facia* evidence of qualification to appear before a deliberative body such as this; and yet, Mr. Moderator, I think I can say in all sincerity that I prefer to sit in an ecclesiastical body of this character—that the interests of the Church are dearer to me than any other interests with which I am connected. I have for many years been an elder in the Presbyterian Church, and as it has become customary to boast of ancestry, I may be permitted to enlarge not a little in regard to that, at least, for I claim to be a descendent from the old Scotch Presbyterian heroes, and I say with Paul, "if others boast, I more." I feel, Mr. Moderator, embarrassed from another consideration, and that is this, that I have been appointed upon the committee to which this matter has been assigned, and it may look like a prejudgment of what may be done for me to express my feelings in regard to matters now under consideration; and yet I can say, Mr. Moderator, that I am as free from prejudice, I think, as any brother in this house. I profess to be a liberal Presbyterian; and although my attachment is specially to the old church of my fathers, yet I can hail, in the bonds of brotherhood, all that love a common Savior. Yet, at this particular juncture, Mr. Moderator, I would desire to disabuse the minds of many brethren of this Assembly as to the feelings and purposes of those of us who represent the majority in this General Assembly.

We are not for engaging in an arbitrary work. We are not disposed to press the brethren who may differ from us, and especially I am indisposed to deal unkindly or unjustly with brethren who have been peculiarly circumstanced during these last days of disaster and of rebellion. Their situation commands my sympathy; and whatever I can do consistently with my obligations to the Church I intend to do. With this declaration, Mr. Moderator, I think I am prepared not only to discuss the question now before the Assembly, and in my capacity as a member of the committee, to discharge the duty as faithfully and impartially as any other brother in this Assembly. I would not at all attempt to address this Assembly, but for the imputations and reproaches that have been cast on the majority of this Assembly.

It has been asserted again and again that the majority here is disposed to usurp and exercise arbitrary power, and to exercise the numerical preponderance which they hold, to oppress those who may be in the minority. I have no feeling of that sort. I have no disposition to suppress free speech or free thought, and indeed it would be very strange that one who had labored so industriously as I and others have done for the past twenty years to secure free speech, and free thought, and liberty and freedom to worship God according to the dictates of our consciences—it would be strange, indeed, if we should exemplify our attachment to these great ideas in the General Assembly by suppressing free speech among our own brethren. It is our commendation to-day, as the majority of this General Assembly, that we have secured free speech for all sections of this country; and that the trumpet of the gospel and the trumpet of liberty can be sounded from the lakes to the gulf. Under the Providence of God, it is our boast to-day that we have labored to secure these high and distinguishing privileges of the freemen af this country; that we have given these testimonies, and have also given the blood of our kindred to seal our faith in those great principles.

Mr. Moderator, with these preliminary remarks, I proceed to the discussion of the question which is before the house, or at least to the views which have been presented by the distinguished brother who has preceded me in this debate. And although I admit that this is not the regular form of presenting this subject—I admit that the brother, by a little ecclesiastical and parliamentary intrigue, has got up this subject for reconsideration, instead of having it put in the usual form—yet I pass that by, for our object is to afford persons here, irrespective of arbitrary rules, a full opportunity to discuss this subject.

The first question that is presented is, whether this body—the General Assembly of the Presbyterian Church—has the right to suspend any Presbytery, or any Commissioner from a Presbytery, from the functions of his office, as a Commissioner. That is the question. It is stated that we have by our actions suspended the functions of these men. It is true, and we done it, Mr. Moderator, as we contend, by a power inherent in this Assembly. Now, the brother who has made this protest just read, says that the General Assembly differs from other bodies —that there is no analogy between this and other legislative bodies of this country.

Permit me to say, Mr. Moderator, that I recollect the remark, and an analogy in respect to this particular course of action. Now, it is well known that in our legislative bodies, although they differ from the General Assembly, they claim and they exercise this power. And I need not go further than to present the action of the Congress of the United States. These men are there with their credentials. They have the prima facie right to a seat and to be enrolled; and although I differ in many respects from the majority now acting on this subject, yet they are exercising that power, and I presume—for it is presumable—that they know what powers they possess as a legislative body. It is within the knowledge of some brethren here, or at least one brother who now meets my eye, that again and again, for many years past, after persons have been enrolled and recognized as representatives of particular localities, they have been removed from the body and their functions as legislators for the time being have been suspended. I now have an instance of that in the somewhat celebrated case of Joshua R. Giddings, who was suspended from the legislative body for language unbecoming that assembly, as it was alleged, and he was again thrown upon the people and was again a candidate and again re-elected. And then, but a few days ago, a resolution of censure was passed on a member of this house, and there is nothing better settled in the legislative courts than that men have the right to control the conduct and actions of those that are sent among them.

Rev. Mr. Ferguson. I desire to know if members under charges in Congress or elsewhere are allowed to vote or act during the pending of a trial, or whether they get the opportunity of voting until the matter is decided?

Mr. Galloway. I presume they get the opportunity of voting.

Rev. Mr. Ferguson. No, sir.

Mr. Galloway. I don't know how that is. I presume brother Ferguson knows more about these bodies than I do. [Laughter.]

Rev. Mr. Ferguson. I confess I do know more about it if he says—— ["order, order."]

Mr. Galloway. I know that brother. He belongs to the same Church with me. [Laughter.]

A member. I suggest that there be no interruption.

Rev. Mr. Ferguson. I understand the courtesy of debate. I know Mr. Galloway well. I know he is a gentleman, and I know he will answer a question as a gentleman should. He said that he did not know; I say they are.

Rev. Mr. Clark. I rise to a point of order. I claim that the gentleman has no right to interrupt debate in this way. The gentleman asked Mr. Galloway a question, and it was answered; and now, sir, he should be permitted to go on. I desire to see it go on, and I insist on my right as a member that it shall go on. I insist that the member has no right to address the Moderator when another member has the floor.

Mr. Galloway. I will waive my privilege in that respect. Brother Ferguson is a little like myself—a little excitable.

Rev. Mr. Ferguson. I insist on my rights. I knew Mr. Galloway would treat me courteously. I asked him a question courteously and he answered it courteously, as a gentleman. I wish the brother to know that I know my rights as well as he does and I will maintain them, excitable or not excitable.

Rev. Mr. Clark. I think we shall get along more smoothly if we stand by our rights. The right for a member to give way to a question is undoubtedly correct. Mr. Galloway did give way to a question. He was answered and the answer, as the gentleman says, was to his satisfaction.

Rev. Mr. Ferguson. Certainly.

Rev. Mr. Clark. And then, I think he should have set down. But then he went on with some remarks which I contend were not in order. Now I insist that he had no right to do this; my point therefore, is that he had no right to go on with his speech.

Rev. Mr. Ferguson. It was not a speech, it was only a word.

Rev. Mr. Clark. It takes words to make a speech generally.

Moderator. I will state the matter as I understand it. Mr. Clark admits that it is the right of every member to give way for an explanation. Mr. Galloway did so. Mr. Ferguson asked the question and it was answered. Mr. Ferguson went on and still Mr. Galloway consented. I think it was in order for him to consent, and for Mr. Ferguson to occupy the floor if he chose. That is my view of the case.

Mr. Galloway. This is a little out of the way of the subject, but nevertheless I am at all times ready to answer any questions that may be propounded. What I propose now, is to read an authority in reference to this subject—an authority which should be regarded, at least by all Presbyterians, as good; an authority connected with the great trial between our brethaen of the New School and the Old School before the Supreme Court of Pennsylvania. That decision is recognized as law. I will read:

"The decisions of every council, to which parties refer a matter for adjudication, IS BINDING, though it be a mere informal reference to a neighbor."

"The decisions of the General Assembly or any other of these general councils, is as binding on all the churches and congregations within its jurisdiction, in spiritual affairs, as the decision of a State tribunal in civil affairs. All are bound to submit to such decisions."

I say, therefore, Mr. Moderator, that this is a right inherent in this body, necessary for its protection, and necessary for it to preserve its self-respect. In the exercise of that power it may do whatever may be necessary for the dignity and self-respect of that body. It is a power exercised by the Congress of the United States. It is a power exercised by our constitutional legislators. It is a power exercised by our courts. This is a Court of the Lord Jesus Christ, and, of course, may differ in many respects from our civil courts; nevertheless in this respect as to its power to preserve its own dignity and self-respect, it does not differ from any other court. Now, in one of our civil courts, if any individual or member of the bar is guilty of contempt, if he insult the dignity of the court he is punished for contempt without any trial he is attached for contempt, and sent to prison for contempt. For example, I, as a member of the bar, after a decision has been made by the court, will say to the court, "You are a tyrant, a usurper: you have transcended your powers." What will the Judge do? He will say, "Mr. Sheriff, take Mr. Galloway to jail. That is done again and again, and would not my f unctions then be suspended.

Dr. Boardman. If you say these things of the court in your office or on the street, will it bring you within the law of contempt without a hearing.

Mr. Galloway. Not unless I bring that paper into court as that Declaration andTestimony has been brought.

Dr. Boardman. It has not been brought here.

Mr. Galloway. Well, sir, the difference between that is the difference between written and verbal slander—between slander and libel. Now, Brother Van Dyke or any other brother, has his own private judgment, and I am willing that he should exercise it. I have exercised it with regard to the last General Assembly for about twenty years, but where that brother puts his private judgment upon paper that which he may properly entertain privately becomes libel, and he renders himself amenable to the law of the land.

Dr. Van Dyke. Fine him.

Mr. Galloway. We have no power to fine, but we have power to do something else; so I say, Mr. Moderator, that it is a power which is exercised by the Courts, and it is necessary for its own dignity and preservation. It is a power which is everywhere exercised. I can not go over to a brother in the Armenian Church and say to him, although I may believe it, that he is in error; that the crowned head of the Church has told me that he is in error, and that I must rebuke him for it. What would he do with me? If he had any respect for the dignity of his body, he would take me by the nape of the neck and turn me out of doors; for it is a power inherent in every body to preserve its self-respect. It won't do for me to stand at the bar and howl about free speech, liberty of conscience and the right to worship God; although I might have felt that I had a special communication from the eternal world to rebuke the errors of that erring brother whom I believe to be delivering false doctrine. I am rather a sociable man in my family, and I certainly shall not entertain a gentleman in my house who comes up and says, "Galloway, you are a tyrant, but I will be glad to take dinner with you to-day." [Merriment.] "You are a scoundrel, but we will hold sweet converse together in the family." Have not I a right to protect my own household? I will do it and so will Brother Boardman and every Christian gentleman. I claim only for this General Assembly the same right. These brethren have gone through the land denouncing us in the bitterest terms. Am I willing to sit with men who regard me as a tyrant, or usurper, or a heretic? Do these brethren themselves wish to sit with a heretic. For my part, I prefer choosing my own company, and whenever I believe this Old School General Assembly is heretical, I will go somewhere else; but with heretics, I never will associate, and they shall never be associated with me by the blessing of God and the government of the Church.

At this point the Moderator announced that the hour for taking up the order of the day had arrived.

A motion was made to suspend the order of the day in order that Mr. Galloway might conclude his remarks.

Mr. Galloway said that he did not desire the motion to prevail, and it was lost.

The order of the day was taken up, which was the formal reception of Dr. Vermilyea, a delegate from the Synod of the Dutch Reformed Church. Dr. V. was introduced to the Assembly by the Moderator, and delivered an eloquent address in regard to the common bond of union which should exist between the Presbyterian Church and the Dutch Reformed Church, and expressing his approbation of the efforts that were being made for the accomplishment of that object, as well on the part of his own Church as on the part of the New School Assembly. He thought the services last evening indicated the early approach of such a union, and the only question was how the marriage settlement should be drawn—how long it should be necessary that the intention of marriage should be published before Prof. Hopkins, of Auburn Theological Seminary, and Prof. Stanton, of the Danville Seminary, shall become man and wife.

The Moderator replied to the address in a happy manner. He alluded to the slight difference between the two organizations and thought from what he had observed that the manner of conducting business in this Dutch Reformed Synod was attended with less confusion than in this Assembly. The brother must have observed that this Assembly was somewhat turbulent at times. In reference to the proposed nuptials, he was ready to respond most heartily with one exception. The brother had placed Dr. Hopkins' name first in order, thereby intimating that he (the Moderator) was the weaker vessel. If he would change the order he was willing the bonds should be approved whenever the parties might agree.

Mr. Vermilyea. Well sir, if the wife is disposed to be turbulent, you had better change the order.

The Moderator hoped by the time the union was consummated the turbulence would have subsided.

At the termination of the reception the Assembly adjourned until half past three o'clock.

AFTERNOON SESSION.

The Assembly met at half-past three o'clock.

Rev. Mr. Stoneroad, chairman of the committee to whom was referred minutes of Synod of Missouri, stated that the committee had only a printed copy of the proceedings of that Synod before them, and that they desired the manuscript record.

After a brief discussion, an order on the Stated Clerk of the Synod of Missouri was issued, calling upon him to produce the manuscript minutes.

The Moderator then stated that the unfinished business would be taken up; namely, the resolution offered by Dr. Boardman yesterday, for the reinstatement of the members of the Louisville Presbytery; and that Mr. Galloway was entitled to the floor.

Mr. Galloway. In the course of my remarks this morning, I referred to the action of the National Legislature, and I quoted it only as a precedent in parliamentary matters. I spoke of the fact that they expelled individuals for an insult to the dignity of the House, or for an insult or an outrage upon any member of the House.

My attention has been called, during the interim, to a case that has occurred within the last three years—the case of a representative from Louisiana—a Mr. Field, who was enrolled as a member of the House, and who voted as a member of the House, and who gave one of the two votes that Gen. Blair got as candidate for Speaker.

This Mr. Field attacked Wm. B. Kelly on the street, and when the intelligence reached the House they caused him to be arrested, brought him to the bar of the House, refused him its privileges and would not restore him until he came in and bowed before the House in a penitential attitude. And, Mr. Moderator, whenever these brethren come before this Assembly, and in the same penitential tones ask forgiveness for what they have done, we will do likewse by them. [Merriment.]

I don't know any better authority than is found in the decisions of the court that settled the suit between our brethren of the other branch and ourselves, and I would read Mr. Hubbell's opinion on that.

"From the decision of this great council there is no appeal; and when the General Assembly declares a doctrine heretical, it must no longer be heard in a Presbyterian Church. Its maintainers must either conform to this decision, or go elsewhere and form new associations: of which they may, at their pleasure, make what are heresies, when compared with our standards. This decision of the General Assembly is the decision of the majority of that Assembly, and hence its results, (however harsh it may seem,) that the construction which the majority put upon the standards is orthodoxy, and that of the minority is heresy. This power is necessary to and inherent in every church establishment, or it ceases to be a church, call it what you please. This decision may be given either in the process of a judicial trial, and be the sentence upon an individual heretic, or it may be an abstract declaration of the Assembly, or 'bearing of testimony' against heretical doctrines.

"In WHATEVER FORM this declaration of the Assembly may be given against a particular opinion, that opinion is heresy, and must be abandoned by the faithful. The malcontents have no alternative but submission or secession."

That, Mr. Moderator, is the doctrine of the Church; it is the doctrine of common sense—it is the doctrine that every parliamentary body is the judge in regard to the qualification of its members. For instance, Sir, if one of the members of this house were to come into this house intoxicated—I do not care what Presbytery sent him here—if he came here intoxicated and disgraced the doctrines of the Savior and the Presbyterian Church, we world turn him out. We have the right to do it; for it is our duty to preserve the dignity of the Court of the Lord Christ. This is a power that is given to the General Assembly, and, sir, I have no right to rebel against this well established doctrine of the Presbyterian Church.

For the last twenty years the deliverances of the Presbyterian church, prior to the war, were against my judgment, but I submitted. I had faith in the doctrines of truth and justice; and I had faith in the progress of truth. I submitted until victory crowned my sentiments by the blessing of God and the power of the people. There is no other way.

Suppose, for example, I am a member of the session, and I am overruled in that session, I must submit. But suppose instead of submitting I become a rebel against the government of the session, and state it as my individual opinion that they are heretics, and perverters of the word of God, will they keep me in the session? Never! They have a right to complain to the Presbytery—they have the right to turn me out of the session if I so behave myself.

The Presbyterian Church is a court, and it must preserve its dignity and do things in order. The greatest indignity that can be perpetrated on any deliberative body is to insult its power and dignity.

Ah! they say, we didn't mean any harm. Why, the men who struck at Fort Sumter did not mean any harm. It was an error of power as sovereigns, and they thought they had the power and the right to be independent of the power of the Government of the United States—not that they had struck at the dignity of the National Government—and they sent representatives, as these men now send representatives to us, to Washington City, ministers plenipotentiary of the State of South Carolina, to confer with the Government of the United States—to ask them whether they would be willing to make terms, and submit to the power of this subordinate State. And these gentlemen of the Southern States profess to derive their power to rebel from the Constitution of the United States. Why, sir, there never was a rebel in the Church or State—heretic or traitor—that did not base his heresy or his treason on the word of God or the Constitution of the United States. [Laughter.] Any one who has had observation and experience knows that to be the fact. One of the most violent arguments I ever heard on an infraction of the Constitution, was made by a man who was defending a grog seller who had violated the law, and the man contended it was not in accordance with the Constitution of Ohio.

I say, then, that it is the necessary and inherent right of every deliberative body to control its own members. We are bound to abide by the decisions of the highest judicatory in the Church, and whenever the Presbyterian Church makes a decision contrary to the word of God, and I shall consider that in so doing they are heretics, I will leave them. Their decisions are the supreme law, and are binding. That is the doctrine of the Church, and the Supreme Court of Pennsylvania has laid down the law upon this subject. Let me read:

"The whole power of the Presbyterian Church is concentrated in the General Assembly. Notwithstanding, that supreme judicatory of the Church has entrusted the exercise of this power, in many cases, to the inferior Church judicatories, the Synods, Presbyteries, and Church sessions, yet, as the General Assembly exercises an appellate jurisdiction over all these inferior judicatories, and is the tribunal of dernier resort, the whole power of those judicatories concentrates in the General Assembly as the primeval fountain of ecclesiastical power. It exercises the same power over the decisions of the inferior judicatories that the Supreme Court in this State exercises over the decisions of the inferior Courts. And you cannot arraign the Supreme Court, on an accusation of abusing its power by reviewing the proceedings of an inferior court; whilst it would undoubtedly be an abuse of power, should the inferior refuse to allow an appeal to be taken from their judgment."

I have had an experience in regard to this matter, and so have many other brethren. For years the Supreme Court sustained the Fugitive Slave Law, and the decisions of that Court in effect were, that a negro had no rights which a white man was bound to respect. We submitted to this. We did not walk up and call those men who delivered this opinion, "You tyrants; you despots; you perverters of the power of the Government." Not at all. If any man had gone in and used that language, he would have been turned out for contempt of Court.

Now, brethren, this is the law, and hence I say to these men, they are rebels against the government of God; and I do not mean it in a political sense. We say to them, take down your standard, haul in your flag, and put up the old banner that has floated over the Presbyterian church, and put upon it the inscriptions that have been put forth in these recent and latter days. Until these brethren retract their errors and become penitent, we cannot take them in.

But, it is said, we can not suspend their functions until they have a trial. I contend that we can turn them out without a trial—on common fame. What is that? Take the declaration and testimony, and you find they become their own accusers. It is a confession of guilt. They say: "We are guilty," and can never be otherwise than guilty; we will fight it out to the last, and we expect the crowned head of the Church to be with us. That is the doctrine, and it is the doctrine of rebels everywhere. But every man who is instructed in the principles of the Government of the United States, and of the government of the Presbyterian Church, which bears a closer resemblance to our institutions than any other governmental organization—knows that it is the duty of these men to submit. But, says a brother, you must serve them with process. Why, sir, they have had process. They have served themselves with process in flaunting their own confession before us—wherein they defy the power of the Church.

And yet these men complain of persecution. Who persecuted them? They persecuted themselves. As the little girl said when her mother left her some work to do, and she preferred standing still to working, and so tied herself to the table. Her mother came home and said, "Mollie, why didn't you sweep the floor?" Said she, "I couldn't, I'm tied." "Why, who tied you?" "I tied myself." So it is with these, brethren. [Laughter.]

They are in an unpleasant predicament, but they digged the pit, and they have fallen into it. They are in the Assembly—their doctrines are here—they have flaunted them in our faces. This Declaration and Testimony—look at it, and see what sort of language is employed by gentlemen who wish to come in and associate with us. Christian gentlemen calling us "heretics," "apostates," and "perverters of the word of God." Why, these are the most serious charges that can be brought against one.

Sir, I have been to some extent a child of the Presbyterian Church. My father was in it, and my grandfather was in it, and somehow, I thought they had found out the best way to Heaven was through the Presbyterian Church. But now, in these latter days, when the war is over, when the Testimony is accomplished and the common glory of the country is consummated, here come in these rebels before the Presbyterian Church.

The good brother over the way talks about a tempest, and the vessel going on to the lee shore. Well, sir, what else could be expected, when there s a mutiny among the land lubbers? [Laughter.] Sir, we have got that old rebel craft to deal with—the Alabama, and it is endeavoring to send that grand old man-of-war, the Kearsarge, to the bottom. Now, brother Boardman, I will take that rule of the Church that you wish to refer to.

Dr. Boardman. You are on another part of the argument now.

Mr. Galloway. I am on that part of the argument that process has been served on them, and I have your own language in reference to this matter in 1838.

Dr. Boardman. If you have any authority for visiting summary punishment upon men without giving them permission to be heard, I should be glad to hear it. Or if you can vindicate in the presence of the learned jurist whom I know to be in the house at this moment, the extraordinary theory of the law of contempt which was presented here to-day, I should be glad to hear it.

Mr. Galloway. I have it on the decisions of the Supreme Court of the State of Pennsylvania.

Dr. Boardman. I heard that quotation this morning.

Mr. Galloway. Well, I have some of your own sentiments on the subject.

Dr. Boardman. As far from the subject as the North is from the South, my good brother. Show me the authority for putting a man out of the house, court or anything else, without giving him permission to open his lips.

Mr. Galloway. The authority is univeral usage.

Dr. Boardman. Will you cite an example.

Mr. Galloway. I cited an example that occurred in Congress a short time since.

The Moderator. I think this colloquy is not in order.

Dr. McLean. Moderator, the speaker would edify the house more if he would not speak to that corner so much, (referring to the corner in which Dr. Boardman sat.)

Mr. Galloway. This is the most interesting corner just now.

Dr. Boardman. This is the only corner where there is any light.

Mr. Galloway. "The light shineth in darkness, but the *darkness* comprehendeth it not. [Great merriment.]

I come now to the language which was used by Brother Boardman in 1838, in reference to the men who were then cut off from the Presbyterian Church without the formality of a trial. It was then he applied, according to McElroy's Report of the Presbyterian Church case to those unfortunate brethren, the Pagan maxim, "Whom the gods wish to destroy they first make mad." So, Mr. Moderator, I contend that these brethern are under protest according to the principles of the decision of this Church case of our General Assembly before the Supreme Court. The difference between Dr. Boardman and myself is, I submit to the Supreme Court, while he yields to the *better* opinion of the Louisville Presbytery.

So, Mr. Moderator, and members of the General Assembly, we condemn these men out of their own mouths. These men are under process by an appeal from the distinguished Father of the Church, Dr. Robt. Breckinridge. They were under process from the day notice was given of the appeal, They are here, and the question is, shall they be allowed to deliberate on other matters? We say they shall not, because of their defiant and reproachful language against the Supreme Court of the Presbyterian Church, constituted by the Head of the Church by the instrumentality of His chosen people. When Brother Boardman wants to overthrow this—

A member. Speak this way, instead of to that corner.

Mr. Galloway, (taking a position on the middle of the platform.) I am so much in habit of addressing one side of a house that it is difficult to accommodate myself to a many-sided audience. [Laughter.] But I do not propose to prolong this argument. I have no unkind feeling toward these erring brethren, only I say they do not belong to the Presbyterian Church at present, having contemptuously repudiated their allegiance to its highest decisions. When they are to be tried we will give them every opportunity that every other criminal has. We intend to give them every right of process, but we have a right to protect our own dignity till the hour of trial arrives. As I said this morning, these brethren cannot, with a proper self-respect, ask to enjoy our intercourse and communion. What! do they wish to be associated with us, whom they have branded heretics and tyrants. Suppose a member would rise in his place in this Assembly and use the defiant and scurrilous language of this Act and Testimony, would he not be rebuked for his gross indecency, and should he persist in his contempt of authority, would he not be ejected without a formal trial from the floor of this Assembly? The House would have the right to vindicate its dignity by its inherant right to protect itself against wilful and deliberate insult.

Mr. Galloway continued to illustrate at length the points assumed by him, and his further remarks will appear in our next issue.

Mr. Reinboth said that, feeling the weighty responsibility which rested upon them as a Church Assembly, and realizing the course this discussion had taken, he had drawn up a paper which after being read might, he thought, be referred to a committee with as much propriety as other papers had been. He then read as follows:

Whereas, The General Assembly for the past five years have greatly erred in their acts and utterances in respect to slavery, rebellion and secession, as well as to all that has been considered subversive of good order and peace in our Church, and contrary to both law and gospel; and

Whereas, The Church is more than threatened not only with schism, but with utter destruction, in consequence of said acts and utterances; and

Whereas, Notwithstanding by large and uniform majorities, the acts and records of the last five years of the Assembly are specially objectionable to many of our Southern brethren, but more especially to those sympathizing Northern brethren, who, unfortunately, have been and still are, in the minority in respect to all the aforesaid acts and records; and,

Whereas, That although the minority should generally acquiesce in the acts and decisions of the majority—inasmuch as the majority of this Assembly, in the spirit of magnanimity, are willing to accord to their brethern of the minority the greater amount of wisdom, patriotism and loyalty—although their record and antecedents are seemingly against them; and,

Whereas, It may be that the said brethren of the minority are right in their views and interpretations of the constitution, order and discipline of our Church; therefore,

Resolved, That the Assembly hereby reconsider, reverse and utterly expunge all and every act and acts, records and deliverances of the several Assemblies for the years 1861, '62, '63, '64, and '65.

Resolved, That it be enjoined upon the members of this Assembly, during its future sessions, to neither think, nor speak of, nor make any reference to, by word or act, the matters thus reversed and expunged.

Resolved, That, in order to secure the Church from schism, division or secession on the part of even one of its members, it be further enjoined upon every member of our Church, young and old, male and female, that hereafter, until the reconstruction of our National Government be fully established, no allusion shall be made to the subject of slavery, or the war growing out of the same, nor to any of the collateral issues and questions arising therefrom; and that no reference shall be made to past political differences; nor shall any of the names or epithets which have commonly prevailed in designation of the respective parties and heir adherents, be used or uttered at any time, nor under any circumstances.

Resolved, That the thanks of the majority of this Assembly are especially due and hereby tendered to their brethren in the minority for the kindly and patient efforts which they have ever righteously and persistently made to convince us of our errors and bring us to a calm and generous acquiesence in and to their views of constitutional law and order.

Resolved, That we sincerely regret and deplore the consequences arising from the acts and records of the Assembly in the years aforesaid, and that now we beg and implore our offended brethren of the South to accept our magnanimity; to excuse our mistaken but well intended zeal, and to receive our extended and fraternal right hand of fellowship.

Resolved, That our aforesaid brethren of the minority be a committee of the whole on the state of the country, and that they be specially instructed to communicate this action to their bretheren of the South.

Without coming to any decision on the question, the Assembly adjourned to meet at 9 o'clock tomorrow morning.

SIXTH DAY—WEDNESDAY, MAY 23, 1866.

The Assembly met at the usual hour, and after devotional exercises the minutes were read and approved.

Rev. Dr. Anderson of St. Louis stated that he was prepared to deliver the minutes of the Synod of Missouri to the chairman of the committee having the matter in charge, as per order of the Assembly on yesterday. He regretted that he had to make the remark that he thought it was unnecessary for the Assembly to take such a course of action as they had, for, had he known that a single member of that committee would have preferred to have had the written rather than the printed record, it would have given him great pleasure to have given it to him. With all respect to the chairman of the committee, he did say he had the written record, but he supposed the printed record would be more convenient. He regretted that any difficulty of this sort should have occurred, for the reason that it might seem to the brethren who knew nothing about them that they were trying to conceal what they had done.

Rev. Mr. Henry wished to explain that the brother had misunderstood the remark that he made on yesterday, or rather a remark made to him a few moments ago, in saying that the minutes were signed by one S. J. P. Anderson; he did not know that that was the brother's name. He hoped that if the gentleman thought there was any reflection cast upon him, he would pardon him. He certainly did not mean any personality at all.

Rev. Mr. Anderson. The explanation of the brother is amply sufficient. I withdraw all that I have felt of unkindness to the remark which was reported to me. I did not think it was courteous for a brother to speak of another brother in the ministry in that way.

Rev. Mr. Gurley presented a report from the Judicial Committee as in order and ready for trial, case No. 3, the appeal of Rev. Samuel Boyd of the Synod of Wheeling. The committee suggest, in connection with this report, owing to the peculiar character of the case and the testimony connected with it, that it be referred, by consent of the parties, to a committee to be appointed by the Moderator—a committee of five ministers and four elders—who shall hear the parties and report to the Assembly.

Rev. Mr. Krebs moved its adoption.

Rev. Mr. Fisher had no objection, but wished to correct one thing; that was in regard to the consent of parties. He did not know that any such consent had been given.

Rev. Mr. Gurley said that this could be done with the consent of parties.

Rev. Mr. Edwards said they had no right to allow this reference to a special committee. He held that the constitution did not give the least countenance to such a thing.

Rev. Mr. Krebs said those familiar with the proceedings of past years must recollect frequent instances in which the course now proposed had been adopted by the General Assembly; to have the case prepared by a committee for the action of the house.

The report was then adopted.

Case No. 4, from the same committee, was then reported—that of B. F. Avery against the Presbytery of Louisville.

Rev. Mr. Krebs moved that this case be referred to the same committee, if it could be done with the consent of parties.

Mr. McKnight moved to place the report on the docket.

Mr. Day moved that the report be referred to a committee to prepare testimony and report the same to this house.

Rev. Mr. Krebs said that was the substance of his motion. He hoped it would not go on the docket, as nobody could tell whether it would be reached before the day of judgment.

The motion to docket the case was lost.

Mr. Fisher said he objected to a reference of this case to that committee because the case from Wheeling would occupy a great deal of their time.

Mr. McKnight said that if it was referred to a committee all the testimony taken before the committee, all the testimony taken before the committee and the arguments would have to be discussed before the house. He did not see that any time would be saved by this course.

Rev. Mr. Humphrey said this was a complaint of Mr. Avery against the Presbytery of Louisville. The commissioners of that Presbytery were not here to answer, and he did not see how it was possible to proceed with the trial of the case, either before the house or before a committee, while the commissioners of that Presbytery were not in the house. He believed it should be put on the docket, and if the commissioners of the Presbytery were admitted to the house, they could proceed to try the case.

Mr. Clarke thought the gentleman was in error. The Presbytery of Louisville were out of the house as judges, but they would certainly come here to the bar as parties.

The Moderator announced that the time for the order of the day had come—namely, the report of the Committee on Domestic Missions.

On motion, the special order was postponed until Monday morning next.

Rev. Mr. Gurley said he understood Mr. Boyd, the appellant in the case of the Wheeling Synod, to consent on yesterday to a reference to a committee. He now states that he is unwilling to have such a reference; therefore they would have to reconsider the vote and put the case on the docket.

The Moderator desired to know if Mr. Boyd had been in the house during all these proceedings?

Mr. Boyd said he had not.

Rev. Mr. Monfort moved that the case of the Louisville Presbytery be docketed.

The vote by which the report in regard to the Wheeling Synod was adopted, was reconsidered, and on motion of Dr. Patterson, placed on the docket.

Rev. Mr. Krebs moved that the second order of the day in the afternoon be the consideration of the appeal from the Louisville Presbytery.

The motion was agreed to.

On motion of Rev. Dr. Patterson, the business of appointing the next place of meeting be taken up.

The motion was agreed to.

Dr. Patterson nominated the Central Church of Cincinnati.

The Moderator suggested that the Board of Trustees of the Danville Theological Seminary had passed resolutions that the Board meet at an early day in Kentucky.

Rev. Mr. Waller said the Committee on Theological Seminaries had agreed to name an early day for a meeting of the Assembly in Kentucky. If they met at Cincinnati they could set apart a day to go into Kentucky and attend to the business of the Danville Seminary.

Rev. Mr. Webster nominated the Central Church of Baltimore.

Rev. Mr. Bently nominated the First Church of New York.

Rev. Mr. Chamberlain said it was by tacit consent last agreed that the Assembly should go to Albany.

Rev. Wm. Breckinridge said he supposed the remark of the brother on his left (Mr. Waller,) was in jest, but it might be serious. It seemed to imply that they would not like to go into Kentucky, for the reason that they would not be kindly received. Having been born in Kentucky and still living there, he felt free to give the Assembly an invitation to meet anywhere in Kentucky, and he would guarantee that the Assembly would be treated with as great hospitality as at any other place in the country.

A member. In what part of Kentucky do you live?

Rev. Mr. Breckinridge. I would be glad to live in every part of it; at present I am in Danville, and if the Assembly will go there, they will be well entertained. I move that they meet at Danville.

Rev. Mr. Remington nominated Buffalo, New York.

Rev. Mr. Humphrey wished to make a remark in regard to the Danville Seminary. The charter provides for eighteen trustees, and the Assembly has power, as often as it meets in Kentucky, to fill vacancies and appoint new trustees. In 1857 the Assembly met in Kentucky and exercised this power, and appointed one-third of the entire Board. He thought that the interests of the institution were safe in the hands of the present Board. His judgment was, that if the General Assembly was not prepared to meet there, that undoubtedly the interests of the Seminary would be safe until the Assembly thinks proper to meet there, and there was no immediate necessity for meeting there.

Rev. Mr. Chamberlain claimed that Cincinnati was as hospitable as any city, not excepting St. Louis, and that was saying a great deal.

Rev. Mr. Scott desired to know whether the Church at Cincinnati was well located, or was it on a noisy street.

Rev. Mr. Chamberlain said it was not.

Rev. Mr. Scott said he would never vote to send the Assembly to such a noisy Church as this.

Rev. Mr. Monfort said it was seventeen years since the Assembly had met in Cincinnati, and he had no doubt the hospitalities of the city would be all that could be desired.

The vote was then taken and resulted as follows:

Cincinnati, 124; Baltimore, 36; New York, 35; Danville, 2; Buffalo, 61.

There being no choice the Rev. Mr. Anderson moved that Cincinnati be chosen.

Rev. Mr. —— moved as an amendment that Buffalo be chosen.

A member objected to holding a meeting so far in the East, and suggested a compromise on Cincinnati.

The amendment was lost, and the vote was then taken on the motion to meet at Cincinnati.

The motion was agreed to.

Rev. Mr. Humphrey moved that the time be fixed upon the third Thursday in May, at eleven o'clock, 1867.

The motion was agreed to.

The Moderator announced that the hour for the order of the day had arrived, namely, the hearing of the report from the Committee on Foreign Correspondence.

Rev. Dr. Boardman, from the Committee of Foreign Correspondence, read a letter introductory of Rev. Dr. McCosh, signed by various eminent members of the Church of Scotland. Dr. B. said the Rev. Dr. McCosh was originally a member of the Established Church of Scotland, but went out of that Church at the time of its disruption, and was for several years and is still connected with the Free Church of Scotland. At present he holds a commission under the Crown as Professor of Logic and Metaphysics of the Queen's College at Belfast, and he was also connected with the Presbyterian Church of Ireland. He need not, in such a presence, refer to those admirable works that had given Dr. McCosh a place in the respect and affection of our whole ministry. We honored him as a profound and able expositor on many of the most abstruse problems in moral philosophy; and he was sure the Assembly would receive him, not only on his own account, but as the representative of churches abroad, and would cordially and gratefully welcome him to this Assembly.

Rev. Dr. McCosh was then introduced by the Moderator.

The Assembly arose to receive Dr. McCosh, after which Dr. McCosh addressed the Assembly at length.

He expressed a deep sense of appreciation for the honor that had been conferred upon him by the invitation. His first feeling, on receiving the invitation was, that he ought to decline it, but again he felt that he must not allow personal considerations to influence him on such an occasion. When he saw this Assembly on Sunday morning, he saw from the very appearance of those who were present that they were men of intellect, who had thought a great deal, and been engaged in great conflicts, personal and public. He came before this Assmbly not exactly as an official delegate. The Presbyterian organization with which he was connected had been sitting since he resolved to come to this country. He felt the need of relaxation in consequence of being engaged in a literary work, which had to be executed speedily to meet a crisis in thought. Longing for relaxation, he was looking toward a visit to this country as a means of refreshing his mind. He wished also to see the great Lakes, the Falls and the great Prairies, and everything of that sort, for he had a passion for natural scenery, and he had all along felt a deep interest in the study of American character. He wished to see the people of this country, and he wished to see the energy of the land. When his Christian friends heard he was about to proceed to the United States, he received various communications, official and private, praying that he might accomplish the desire of the British people, who hold the truth as it is in Jesus, for a more effective union with the Churches in America. The Evangelical Alliance unofficially instructed him wherever he went to call on the ministers and brethren of the various denominations, in order to bring us in closer union. He had come here in fulfillment of this mission as well as to gratify his own personal feelings. He continued: On all previous occasions when it was proposed to bring about a closer re-union there was always an unfortunate topic that came up as a barrier. I am not saying anything as to who was to blame. When there is a fusing of hearts into one, I do not think it is a time to go back and speak of old feuds of the past. When the vile residium is sinking and the waters are purifying it is not for me to stir up the filth. And I am not going now to inquire whether there has been any fault on the part of British Christians or American Christians, but it did so happen unfortunately that whenever we sought to meet with each other, and hold friendly intercourse, there was one subject that inevitably came up and inevitably separated us; and that was the subject of slavery.

The subject always came up somehow or other. British Christians felt that they had a duty to discharge, and alluded to it. You, on the other hand, felt that you were endeavoring, to the best of your ability, to do your duty in the very painful circumstances in which you were placed. You were not very willing sometimes to receive counsel; and the subject always came up between those who sought to bring about a more intimate spiritual relation; but now, God, in his Providence--I give the glory first to God--has removed that great barrier out of the way, and I think--although I do not appear here officially for anybody--I think I can state on the part of the British Churches, who are sound in the faith, and British Christians generally, that they wish now that these obstacles are taken away, that we may rush into each other's arms and live for all future time in very closest intimacy and fellowship. [Applause.]

He was happy to say that there was a very great desire for a closer union in all Evangelical Churches in England and Ireland, and he thought in a few years there would be a substantial union of all the non conformist Presbyterian Churches of Great Britain and Ireland.

He referred to the troubles of the Church in Scotland, and to some facts in his own history, illustrating what the Churches in Great Britain had had to contend with, and passed to the present condition of the Churches. The Free Church of Scotland, though not a numerous body, had contributed for the year ending May 1, 1865, the sum of £350,-000 for the support of the Gospel; had set going a general sustaining fund for poor congregations, a benevolence instituted by Dr. Chalmers, which had been carried on with great vigor and liberality, and to which the church contributed in 1865, £180,000, and for twenty-two years ending May, 1865, the total sum of £6,000,000. The Free Church of Scotland had been instrumental in bringing about a state of things that looked to the union of all the churches of like faith and government not only in the United Kingdom, but in the Colonies, and the speaker took the opportunity to say that the British churches were most anxious to be in some way officially connected with the Presbyterian bodies in this country by having delegates reciprocally accredited to the General Assemblies who might have a voice and a vote on the more important questions of general interest to the church.

There were many reasons why this union should be cousummated. The first was, that as they knew each other better they would love each other better. True, there were many statements in the newspapers concerning us, but when he came here he could not find them verified. But as one of the strong reasons why there should be a closer union, take for instance, the sunken population of the cities, such as London and Liverpool. By a union they might co-operate together to devise some plan for emigration, by which this sunken population might come to these great prairies of the West, where, said he, although not very good citizens with us, they might be very good citizens with you. [Laughter.] True, I have not seen New York, but I am going there to see whether you have any population there as low as ours. You must take care of that population at the beginning, for I tell you if it accumulates to any extent, it is the worst evil that can befall you—worse even than the slavery that has been in your midst.

Then in regard to the contest with Popery. There are four millions and a half of people who are Catholics in my country, and only a million and a half are Protestants. We have not as much success with the Catholics as we would wish, but there is a great emigration going on. In the vessel in which I came over there were over 900, mostly Catholics. When away from the influence of their priests they can be reached. United together as members of one Christian family we may strengthen each other's hands in regard to this matter. Another thing. This union is essential in regard to the missionary field, so that we can see to it that when you have taken up a field Great Britain shall not take up the same field. We could thus confer how we could advance the cause of missions and schools.

Again, we have in our country a great contest of opinion. In the first place, we have a very powerful body, commonly called the Puseyites, or High Churchmen—men, some of whom are possessed with great ability, are devout and are of a high character, and who occupy a high place in the literature and theology of the country. These men, I think, are departing from the simplicity of the faith as it is in Christ, and they must be met by men of equal character. Thus we have Rationalism in our country, and it is that the one promotes the other. We saw that illustrated in our great University at Oxford. In that university, a great many young men went up ten years ago to be trained for the ministry—High Churchmen or Puseyites—but they rebelled and swung back to Rationalism; then they became connected with the literary press of London, and a great many able articles in the literary press of London are written by young men who are Rationalists—who are trained up at Oxford in the manner I have described. During the last few years a greater contest has been going on between Truth and Error, and Infidelity and Christianity, than has been witnessed for the last one hundred and fifty years. One hundred and fifty years ago when this contest began, the Church was in a low state, and there was a determination among men of high thought to put down Christianity. We are now in the thickest of the fight at this moment. These contests are going on, and they will come to your land, and I can conceive of nothing better than for you to send some of your learned Professors to confer frankly with us on these subjects, and to devise means to meet the enemy, and as a united phalanx fight the enemy combined.

Another question connected with this matter was that of universal philanthrophy and Catholic Christianity. I have all along taken a very deep interest in the struggle of your country, and the question arises in this connection, what are you to do with your colored population. You have come through a conflict nobly. It seems to me like that mighty Niagara I saw the other day. You have passed over the rapids and the precipice, and now as you rush along there is nothing left but the foam of the conflict which gradually spreading out into a peaceful expanse.

What were we to do with the colored population? This was a question in which the people of Great Britain feel a deep interest. We have accomplished a great work, but there was a greater work than we had yet had before us. He spoke as a man who had had occasion to study this subject. The great problem was, is the white man ever to improve the black man? He was sorry to say that Great Britain had not settled this problem, although she had attempted it.

Said the speaker, I tell you this frankly. We have had a race of the noblest savages in the world—the New Zealander. I believe we meant to do justly, but we have never been able to do so. We have been at war with them—a most painful war—although I hope it is now terminated. We have not been able to elevate the lowest races. Then we have had our own slaves in Jamaica, and late events there show that we have not been able to settle the question. Now, I say that the people of Great Britain, and the civilized Christians of the world, are looking to you to see how you will settle this question. Are you to go on and prosper yourselves, and let the black man die out? Are you to realize that most awful theory of Darwin, that the higher races must advance and the lower races must be extinguished. That is a dark and gloomy view, and I cannot accept it. I cannot believe that the white man is to prosper and the black man is to fade away little by little until he is extinguished. My hope in God is that you, with the energy that characterizes all your efforts, will settle that question, and that the churches of Christ may meet in harmony and union for that purpose. I am not speaking of politics on this question, but I am speaking of what steps you are to take to train these people to industry, to increase their intelligence and make them, in some measure, equal to you, not merely in civil matters, but equal to you in general advancement. Your State must take such a course; but the State cannot do it alone. It must be done by your churches. And I confess I have been looking to you—to the old Presbyterian Church—as taking the initiative in this matter. You have an influence, and ought to have.

I must say I would like excessively to see the North and the South closely united in this work; for the North to say we have spent all this for the sake of the black man; and let the South say we are friends of the black man. And I would like to see this union consummated between Christian men North and South, for then I believe you would be brought more closely together in the work to which I trust you will devote yourselves, and you will have the best wishes of the best men in Europe.

The Moderator replied briefly to the address of Dr. McCosh He said that he rejoiced that there was a tendency in this country to a like union of which Dr. McCosh had spoken. He believed it foretold great results, not only in this country, but in Europe. He doubted not that the Committee on Foreign Correspondence would arrange it so that members who propose visiting Europe the coming season, might be deputised to the churches, thereby opening a way for the realization of what was so much desired. He had no doubt it would result in great good. It was true that we had just passed through a great war, in which the aristocracy of Europe seemed to sympathize with those who were against us, but all had passed away, and he believed a better state of feeling existed. Now that we were at peace, he hoped it would be a lasting and undisturbed peace, and that in due time they would reach that blue and peaceful expanse where no angry words of passion will be encountered, and where these tendencies to union in all Presbyterian bodies shall have been realized.

Mr. McKnight offered a resolution that the Committee on Foreign Correspondence be instructed to inquire into and report upon the propriety of appointing a committee to open a correspondence with the Churches of Great Britain and Ireland.

Rev. Mr. Kempshall offered the following as a substitute:

Resolved, That the General Assembly has listened, with the deepest interest, to the address of Dr. McCosh, and responds most cordially to the very friendly sentiments and wishes expressed by him for the promotion of a more intimate and direct correspondence between this General Assembly and the Presbyterian Churches of Ireland.

Resolved, That the matter of adopting a plan for carrying into practical effect this correspondence be referred to the Committee on Foreign Correspondence, to report to the General Assembly.

Mr. McKnight accepted the substitute.

Rev. Mr. Smith suggested that some personal recognition of the great services of Dr. McCosh should be made.

The Moderator suggested that it would be more proper to have this referred to a committee.

Rev. Mr. West made a motion to that effect, which was agreed to.

Dr. Boardman moved that Rev. Dr. McCosh be invited to occupy a place at his pleasure beside the Moderator during the session of this Assembly.

The motion was agreed to.

Rev. Mr. Croser moved that in the case which has been before the Assembly for the last two years from Illinois, the parties may appear before the committee which has been appointed and give information on which to make a report.

The motion was agreed to.

The resolution offered yesterday by the Rev. Mr. Farquhar, relative to money received; for congregational purposes and directing stated clerks to report as candidates young men studying for the ministry, was referred to a committee consisting of Rev. Dr. Krebs, Rev. Mr. Farquhar and Elder James Black.

The Assembly then adjourned to 3½ P. M.

AFTERNOON SESSION.

The order of the day being the nomination of officers for the various Boards, Rev. Wm. Wilson and Matthew Howell of Leavenworth, were nominated on the Board for Church Extension.

No action was taken in the matter.

The next order of the day was taken up, namely: the case of Mr. Avery against the Presbytery of Louisville.

Mr. Owens, from the Judicial Committee, said the papers in this case were put in the hands of the Judicial Committee, but the appeal was not found among them.

An application was made to the Stated Clerk of the Louisville Presbytery to attest to the fact that the appeal had been made, and the Stated Clerk said this mornrng that he had prepared the appeal, and, it was properly before the Assembly. This venerable Elder of the Walnut street church of Louisville was duly appointed a delegate from that session to the Presbytery of Louisville. Another who had been appointed by a minority also appeared on the floor of the Presbytery. Mr. Avery presented his case, but the Moderator said he recognized the minutes of the session as the minutes of the Church. The other elder was therefore recognized and Mr. Avery's claims were rejected. Mr. Avery appealed from the decision I have read the proceedings of the case, and it seems remarkable. This Presbytery of Louisville to be an order-loving and constitution-loving and law-abiding Presbytery, but of all the proceedings in the world—

Rev. Mr. Crozier. I rise to a point of order.

Moderator. I think this is not in order. I understand it is your duty to make an explanation, but you seem to be going into the merits of the case.

Mr. Owen. Well, my object was to show that this appeal was in order and that he was the person to sit here.

The Moderator. We take the report of the committee as showing that the appeal is in order.

Rev. Mr. Owen. Have we not a right to show that the appeal is just?

The Moderator. I don't know what you mean by the word just.

Dr. Boardman. I think the court must first inquire whether the parties are present. I wish to make that inquiry.

The Moderator. I suppose that to be inferred from the report of the Judicial Committee, that the case was ready for trial.

Dr. Boardman. I wish the Judicial Committee to answer the question categorically, whether the parties are before us?

Rev. Mr. Owen. I understood that the parties are properly before us.

The Moderator read from the Book of Discipline, and said, the first inquiry was as to whether the parties were here. Do I understand that the written appeal is not before the Committee?

Rev. Mr. Owen. In this case the Stated Clerk of the Louisville Presbytery stated to me that the appeal was properly made, as I have already stated, although he has just now modified his statement somewhat.

The Moderator. Let me explain my view of this case. I had supposed that the Committee had discharged their duty, and I know nothing to the contrary yet. If it is a fact that there is no written document, my judgment is that the rule has not been complied with.

Rev. Dr. Patterson rose to request that the appeal might be read.

The Moderator. I have not yet passed the final step. I have not heard the sentence appealed from read.

Dr. Patterson. I move that the case be postponed to the next General Assembly.

Rev. Dr. Krebs hoped that no hasty action be taken. The committee, in presenting this report, supposed it was properly prepared. He understood that there was an appeal properly made out.

The Moderator said this seemed to be a case that was not properly before them, and it was his suggestion that the matter be recommitted.

The suggestion was agreed to.

The unfinished business was then taken up, namely, the resolution offered by Dr. Boardman to reinstate the Louisville Presbytery.

Mr. Jones, from Maryland, obtained the floor and spoke at length in support of the resolution, and in reply to the remarks of Mr. Galloway and others. He contended that the Commissioners of the Louisville Presbytery had complied with the requirements of the Board; that they had committed no act that could be construed into an offense against the dignity of this body, and this body had no right whatever to punish them either for contempt or anything else. The cases which had been cited by the gentleman from Ohio were not analogous, and it was utterly impossible to find any precedent for the action that had been taken by the Assembly.

To put the most ressonable construction upon the matter, it would appear that these brethren were punished for doing precisely what the gentleman from Ohio, and others, had done when they were in the minority. Then they assailed the decision of the Supreme Court, and continued to make war upon them until, by a popular appeal, they succeeded in overturning them, and abolishing slavery. No attempt was made to turn the gentleman from Ohio out of Congress when he was engaged in this work. The brethren of the Louisville Presbytery stood in precisely the same position in relation to the Church. They had simply uttered their Testimony against the Deliverances of the Assembly, and for so doing they had been expelled from this body.

At the conclusion of Mr. Jones' remarks, Mr. Law of Long Island, obtained the floor, but gave way in order that a vote might be taken.

The Moderator stated the question to be the adoption of the resolution offered by Dr. Boardman.

Mr. Clarke, of Detroit, called for a division of the question.

Agreed to.

The vote was then taken on the motion to refer the matter to a committee, which was agreed to, while so much of the resolution as instructs the committee to report in regard to reinstating the members of the Louisville Presbytery was, on motion of Mr. Clarke, laid on the table.

The resignation of Rev. Dr. Stanton (the Moderator) as Professor in the Danville Seminary, was received and referred to a committee.

The Assembly adjourned.

Conclusion of Mr. Galloway's Remarks.

The following is the conclusion of Mr. Gallaway's speech on Tuesday evening, on the resolution for reinstating the members of Louisville Presbytery, which was crowded out of our last edition. He said:

Take another illustration. Suppose some commissioner of this Assembly should rise in his place in a state of intoxication, and interrupt its proceedings by turbulent and disorderly conduct, would not his indecency be immediately rebuked? And if he pertenaciously adhered to his impropriety, would not the power of this house be exercised even to the extent of ejecting him from the house? Would any one demand that the fact of intoxication should be investigated, and a trial be allowed the offender, when his condition had been manifested to every sober eye, and especially, when he admits himself to be drunk, and insolently defies the authority of the house, can there be any doubt as to the right of this Assembly, for the purpose of preserving its harmony and order, to vacate the seat of one who had thus disgraced himself, and insulted its dignity? Certainly not, and our right is equally unquestionable to rid ourselves of the contamination and insults of those who defame our character and our highest court by the utterance of the vilest libel which can be cast upon a Christian or any Christian organization.

But I pass to the consideration of some other peculiar views of the gentleman. He says that we have not been properly affected by the hospitality of the people, and that we have been deficient in our appreciation of the feelings of that class who sympathize with the members of the Louisville Presbytery. Ah, Mr. Moderator, let me say to that brother and to these dispensers of hospitality with whom he so tenderly sympathizes, that but for the testimonies of the Presbyterian Church, and of loyal Christians of every faith; and for the memorable fact that these testimonies of our Assembly have been sealed with the blood of her sons—the life, liberty and property of the good people of St. Louis would have been sacrificed by the treason and traitors of our land. Yes, it has been the fidelity of the true hearted, who have borne the flag of the country along with the standards of a loyal christianity, which has secured to them and to us the downfall of the rebellion and the triumphs of freedom. [Applause and hisses in various parts of the house.]

The Moderator called upon the audience to preserve order.

Mr. Galloway. Why, Mr. Moderator, I did not expect to please certain ladies and gentlemen of this locality by any allusion to the triumphs of our arms and our testimonies. "Oh ye generation of vipers," it might not have been so well for you, but perhaps a little better for the purity and permanency of our freedom, if our testimonies had received a fuller development by a longer continuance of this war. [Sensation and merriment.] I am acquainted with such specimens of loyalty. Why, sir, in my capacity as commissioner at Camp Chase, I had charge of just such loyal ladies and gentlemen. They had been sent there, as they alleged, by a persecuting government for a conscientious adherence to their views of truth and government. I have fully experienced the perfume of that species of loyalty, and hence can detect its odor here or elsewhere. [Great merriment.] I could not trespass upon the proprieties of this place or occasion by doing or saying anything which might be offensive to the most peculiar sensibilities, and yet I purpose, at all times and in all places, to vindicate the flag of my country and the covenant and testimonies of God's people. I say to all in rebellion against the National Government or the loyal of Christ's Church, seek the communion of those who are your kindred in faith and practice; go your own way; and if that shall end as in the case of Judas—in hanging yourselves—you must take the responsibility. [Renewed merriment.]

You say you are persecuted. The testimony of the word is, "If ye are persecuted for righteousness sake happy are ye, and be not troubled in your minds." But you appear to be very much troubled, and, therefore, I logically conclude that you are persecuted for some other sake. [Merriment.] "*Procul, O, procul este profani.*"

Mr. Moderator, I would not unnecessarily ruffle the sensibilities of any class of people, but I certainly cannot be frightened from propriety or principle by an appeal to my appetites; and hence I am not to be intimidated by the "bread and butter" argument of Bro. Boardman. I am rather disposed to think that those who have survived the disasters and perils of the past few years, will be able to endure a withdrawal of the hospitalities of those who dislike the testimonies of loyal people. This affecting appeal forcibly recalled to my mind an anecdote I once heard of an eccentric but noble champion of truth, Old Father Cravens, (as he was called,) of Virginia. The old preacher was well known for his strong opposition to slavery and intemperance, and was usually accompanied in his travels by a good old man by the name of Fitzgerald, of similar views and feelings. It was the usual custom of Father Cravens to preach on camp meeting occasions, and to address the people, speaking of his favorite topics. On one occasion, in Rockingham county, Virginia, in advance of preaching, he was invited to the house of a slaveholder, and was liberally treated to watermelons. Soon after the feast Father Cravens occupied the pulpit, and whilst discoursing upon his favorite themes, he was less bold than usual in his denunciations of slavery. His brother, Fitzgerald, on his tender treatment of the theme, rose in the Congregation and said, "Brother Cravens, you may as well let all the truth out, for you will get no more watermelons for what you have already said."

As I have not yet been led into the temptation of hospitality by any sympathiser with disloyalty, I cannot appreciate the feelings of those whose principles, whilst in this city, are influenced by what they shall eat and drink. When I am reduced to the necessity of testifying for the church and the country—at the peril of losing an entertainmet of strawberries—or the charms and smiles of those who have not been suspected of a fervent attachment to our views—I will hire a small boat, and take up my boarding and lodging on the other side of the river, and come in between times to the meetings of the General Assembly. [Laughter.]

Bro. Boardman says this is an hour when we ought not to manifest unkind feelings towards these erring brethren. Sir, we are ready to receive repentent rebels, when they come to us washed with the washing of a regeneration, which shall be exemplified by a sincere sorrow for a participation in that terrible crime of treason, which has slain the beloved of many of the households of members of this Assembly.

Mr. Moderator, whilst Brother Boardman was taking his excursion among the surroundings of this city with his hospitable friend, and was surveying the strawberry patches and other attractive scenery, I was visiting and meditating, at Camp Jackson, over the graves of the brave boys from my own and other loyal States, who sacrificed their lives, and saddened the hearts of many homes, that you and I, and the brethren of this Assembly, might enjoy the hospitalities of a home of freedom. [Applause.]

The Moderator. The audience must preserve order.

We are not here, sir, to indulge in strains of sentimentalism or sketches of imagination. We are here to preserve the purity, the patriotism, the doctrines, standard and government of the church of our fathers, and to preserve in all its purity and beauty that glorious temple of spiritual truth which has been the object of our admiration and love. Our testimonies and our works in the great contest which has just been terminated, have been abundantly vindicated and honored by the Providence of God—and the valor of our countrymen. Our mission is one of love for the right, and for all that elevates and adorns humanity. We are ready to welcome all to our fellowship of faith who sympathize with us in the onward and upward movements of the age—of the gospel—and who are ready to co-operate in extending the empire of righteousness and universal freedom.

Mr. Hornblower said they had had too much wit and eloquence—too much sarcasm, vituperation and violence. What was required was calm, clear argument to convince every wavering mind. He had voted with the minority, but those who knew him knew that vote was not intended to oppose any feeble resistance that he could offer to the exercise of justice towards the Presbytery of Louisville. As he understood it, they had excluded from this Assembly not certain persons alone, but a whole Presbytery, by very extraordinary means. And the most extraordinary thing was, that a member of the Synod of New Jersey should be the one to make this motion for expulsion, when that Synod of New Jersey, at its last meeting, and without a dissenting voice, declared the action of the General Assembly of 1865, was to be deplored, and virtually condemned that action.

Mr. Reinboth. It is notorious, I think, that the action of the Synod of New Jersey was not unanimous. They took advantage of the absence of a great number of members. It was not properly the action of the Synod of New Jersey. The action was taken, it is true.

Mr. Hornblower. It was at an evening session after the conclusion of a long and interesting debate, and when nearly all the members of the Synod were in their seats. And at that moment the Synod was as full as it generally is.

Mr. Reinboth. I would like to ask whether a great many of the members of the Synod had not already left; whether it was not late in the evening, and the members anxious to get away?

Mr. Hornblower. According to my recollection, it was a very full meeting of the Synod.

Mr. Kempshall. I am a member of the Synod of New Jersey, and I can bear witness that the gentleman's statement is correct. I saw and read the paper, and it was passed without a word against it, or a single dissenting voice, and I believe the Synod was as largely attended at that time as at any time.

Mr. Hornblower continued. That the next thing that was extraordinary was that the gentleman who presented this paper stated that he had concocted it himself. That a brother should bring in a paper on such a momentous subject—make a speech upon it, and move the previous question, was, to his mind, the most sublime effrontery that he ever witnessed in a deliberative body. It was still more surprising that the previous question should at once be adopted.

They had all come here from the Northern States, at least with a feeling that a wrong had been done, and that it ought in some way to be reached and punished, and it seemed to be a most admirable thing if these brethren who are in the wrong could at once be ousted out of their seats.

The speaker said he was not here to shield them from the execution of justice; but he was here as a member of Christ's Court, to see that the thing was done in accordance with the Constitution and the laws of the Church.

They had been told that the fact of this Declaration and Testimony was that of public rumor. He would like to know how many members of this Assembly had seen that Declaration and Testimony. He presumed it had been sent to many whose names were eminent, but he had not seen it until he came here. And yet these brethren had been excluded. But he contended it was not the men that had been excluded, but the Presbytery of Louisville, and he would like to know where they obtained authority to exclude a Presbytery. They could rebuke it, and compel the expunging from their records of that which was insulting; but he knew of no authority by which they could exclude a whole Presbytery. It had been stated by the brother from Ohio that these gentlemen might be reinstated in their seats, but, judging from that gentleman's speech and others, such a result could hardly be looked for. He beseeched them to consider what they were doing before it was too late.

Rev. Dr. McLean said he was of the opinion that he should survive all that the young brother had said against the little Presbytery, or against himself, for *presuming* to bring an important subject before this house, of which he was a member. The astonishment which Dr. Hornblower manifested perhaps would not be as great if he were a little older, and a little more experienced in regard to men and measures. It was a new doctrine, that because a man happened to belong to a small Presbytery, that therefore it was presumptious in him to make an important motion in the Assembly. He was here as commissioner from one of the Presbyteries of New Jersey, and he held it to be his sacred right to bring any proper subject he chose before this house. No man ought to be surprised at it, and he thought no man except a very young man, like his brother Hornblower, would be surprised. Objection had been made to his motion because it had been made without consultation. What of that? Had not any member the right, on his own responsibility, to make a motion. So far as the action of the Synod of New Jersey was concerned, suppose that body did, at the close of its session, near ten o'clock at night, when many of its members were absent, adopt the paper which had been referred to in reference to this General Assembly, that the action of this Assembly was wrong, that form of discussion availed nothing,

Rev. Mr. West desired to know if the brother would not forego further reference to this matter.

Dr. McLean said he was willing to yield to anything which was properly in order; but he did not think it was courteous, under the circumstances in which he stood before the Assembly, as the mover of the measure, and after the animadversions which had been made upon his course, that it was quite right to prevent him, by entreaties or anything else, from explaining the circumstances of this case.

The Synod of New Jersey did just what the member had stated; and he thought there were but two men in this house, who were members of that Synod, that voted against that paper. What did that indicate? And what did it indicate even if he did make a motion without consultation? Long before he came here he had made up his mind just how he should act on this subject, and he determined that if some one else did not take notice of the matter, he would; he determined that that Presbytery should not be entitled to a seat here until their case was investigated. And when he made the motion which he did, he asserted principles which had not been controverted. The truth was, the tactics pursued had been to annoy, harass and perplex. And these gentlemen, instead of coming forward boldly and facing the matter, had undertaken to delay and protract business. This very motion for reconsideration had this effect. If the committee had been let alone, the probability is that they would have reported by this time, and then they would have had the whole question before them, as it was intended they should, but they had been delayed by side issues; and who was responsible? It was the men who were annoying, perplexing and harassing with vexatious amendments—endeavoring, apparently, to weary the patience of the house.

What did it all mean but to harass the house, and to perplex, and ultimately defeat its action? But there was no danger. They believed they were right in the course they had taken, and it was their purpose to maintain it.

Mr. Jones, of Maryland, obtained the floor, and was proceeding to speak, when the hour of adjournment having arrived, the Assembly adjourned.

SEVENTH DAY—THURSDAY, MAY 24, 1866.

Met at nine o'clock.

After devotional exercises, the minutes of the last session were read and approved.

Mr. Henry Day, of New York, was nominated in the class of sixty six on the Board of Foreign Missions.

Rev. Dr. Lowrie, of the Committee on Bills and Overtures, presented two reports:

First. The Board of Domestic Missions ask that Rev. Andrew Vance, Rev. Wm. Akin, and Rev. Wm. Rankin, connected with certain churches in Tennessee, be constituted a Presbytery under the name of Holstein.

The request was granted.

Second. Overture presented from the Presbytery of Missouri, asking the General Assembly to extend the boundaries of said Presbytery northward, so as to include Woodbury county in Iowa, which is at present included in the former Sioux City territory, and to detach the Presbytery of Missouri from the Synod of Southern Iowa, and unite it with the Synod of Kansas.

Rev. Mr. Stewart said if this Presbytery was taken away, he would ask the General Assembly to arrange it so that there should be but one Synod in Iowa.

Dr. Lowrie suggested that this should come up as a separate proposition.

On motion of Mr. Fisher the report was recommitted.

The order of the day commencing with the report of the Committee on the Board of Education, was taken up. Rev. Dr. Smith, of Baltimore, chairman of the committee, presented the report:

The following summary as to the annual number of candidates, will afford a more satisfactory view of the growth of the Board, and of the periods of its most marked usefulness:

Years.	Average No. of Candidates.	Average Contributions.
1819—24	108	$7,555
1825—29	230	14,026
1830—32	149	9,444
1833—40	501	36,631
1841—45	337	27,238
1846—50	381	34,651
1851—55	368	42,480
1856—61	423	55,007
1862—66	301	47,744

The following is a general view of the pecuniary affairs of the Board during the ecclesiastical year ending the 1st of May, 1866:

	I. CANDIDATES' FUND.	II. SCHOOLS AND COLLEGES.
Receipts	$43,616 53	$3,135 37
Balance, 1865	18,313 53	3,498 56
	$61,930 06	$6,633 93
Payments	41,027 70	3,807 86
Balance, 1866	$20,902 36	$2,826 07

	III. AFRICAN FUND.
Receipts	$.- ......
Balance, 1865	1,039 35
Payments	445 07
Balance, 1866	594 28

Total receipts of the year from all sources, $46,-51 90, $1,913 05 less than last year.

That the above may be understood, it is necessary to explain that the existence of the large balance in our receipts arises from the fact that our collections come in mainly, and should come in almost wholly, in the months of March and April, just previous to our report. This does not indicate that surplus of receipts over payments, but is the reservoir from which the supplies of the remainder of the year must be drawn.

The statistics as to the number of candidates for the past ecclesiastical year are as follows:

Number of new candidates received	83
Whole number on the roll,	
in their Theological course,	168
in their Collegiate course	84
in their Academic course	44
Total	296

Entire number received from the beginning, in 1819 ... 3400

The deaths of two candidates have been reported to us; both spoken of as having been young men of exemplary piety; one of them Mr. P. P. Irwin, having felt it his duty to engage in the defense of his country, died a martyr to her liberties, from the sufferings endured in the Andersonville prison.

The following resolutions were appended to the report:

1. Resolved, That we see reasons for deep concern in the fact that the number of candidates under the care of the Board for the past year, and several preceding years, has been so small (not more than half of the number of some past periods), yet are filled with gratitude and hope for the future in view of the recent wide-spread revivals of religion and the conversion of multitudes of young men.

2. In consideration of these revivals, Presbyteries are requested to be especially careful in the examination of candidates as to their character, motives and general suitableness for the work of the ministry.

3. The attention of the ministry and churches is earnestly called to the great importance of the observance of the day of prayer for such schools and colleges on the last Thursday in February; and to the first Sabbath in March as a period for solemnly addressing parents and children as to their duties, and petitions to God for the outpouring of His spirit upon the several objects; and the Assembly urges a substantial remembrance of the wants of the Board by taking up a collection for its funds in its departments of general and ministerial education.

4. Resolved, That in the present dispersed condition of Presbyteries in some portions of the land, aid may be granted by the Board to instruction of candidates requiring it on satisfactory recommendations from ministers known to it, and that no extra aid be given to any young man unless the same shall be reported to the Presbytery, and to the faculty of the institution in which the candidate is pursuing his duties.

5. Resolved, That the General Assembly desires the Board of Education to give all the encouragement and aid possible towards the permanent endowment of institutions of learning, centrally located, promising in results and under ecclesiastical supervision.

6. Resolved, That copies of the report be sent to the sessions of Churches, with a view to the faith and principles being brought more fully before parents and those interested in the young.

7. Resolved, That the objects of this fundamental Board are commended to the prayers as well as the contributions of the Church, having, as the final end in view, a general revival of religion and the preaching of the gospel to all the world.

On motion of Rev. Dr. Patterson, the report was accepted.

The question being upon the adoption of the resolutions appended to the report, Rev. Wm. Speer, Secretary of the Board, was called upon to address the Assembly. He said that the pastoral letter sent forth by the last General Assembly, that earnest prayer should be made in behalf of the cause of education, had been productive of great results. The prayers of the Churches seemed to have been fully answered. The first object of the report was to show God's purpose in connection with our National chastisements. There were before him some, perhaps, who had been brought into the Church by the great revivals succeeding the Revolutionary war, and there were many facts to show that the revivals at that time were unprecedented. This late war having been much greater, as to the territory involved, the amount of money expended, and the number who had poured out their blood for the country, might it not be hoped that the effusion of the Holy Spirit in revival of religion would be proportionably greater and more powerful, and that result would fill our land with its blessed fruits. He believed that we were entering on a new era—that there were indications that the power of the Holy Spirit was at work in regenerating our nation, and making us a holy people.

Rev. Mr. Stonerode moved that the resolutions be taken up seriatim. Lost.

Rev. Mr. Francis said he should exceedingly regret being compelled to vote against the report. In general it met his hearty approbation, but he had noticed in this Assembly, and in other Assemblies, for many years, that oftentimes in their best reports something dolorous had slipped in. Now, there was one resolution in this series which expressed the sorrow and contrition of this Assembly that so few young men, of late, were applying for aid from the Board of Education. It did not strike him that this was a matter to be complained of. He thought it was a good indication that so many of the young men of the Church were able to help themselves rather than rely upon the charity of others, in order that the Church might be untrammelled, and adapt its means to other causes, equally as sacred as this. If it were true that the candidates for the ministry were decreasing, there would be cause for regret, but the record did not show that. He believed there were great numbers of young men who, having assisted in fighting the battles of their country, and achieved victory and triumph, to-day preparing to meet the great enemy of souls, and fight the battles of the Lord until the sinful world should be subdued.

Rev. Mr. Caldwell moved that the fourth resolution should be amended so as to provide that the recommendations therein contained should be approved by the Presbyteries at their next meetings.

Rev. Dr. Smith explained that the fourth resolution had reference only to that portion of the South in which the Churches were in a dispersed condition.

Mr. Caldwell then withdrew his amendment.

Rev. S. T. Wilson concurred with the remarks of Rev. Mr. Francis, and moved that the first resolution be stricken from the report.

Mr. Bay, of New York, claimed that this Board was established to aid young men who could not aid themselves, and that to thank God that there were no more young men who were in indigent circumstances who would apply to that Board seemed to him an absurdity. It was not understood that this Board aided young men who could aid themselves. They asked God that men of promise might be brought forward who have no reliance upon any other source, who would throw themselves on the Church, and yet the Assembly were asked to thank God that there were no such men, that they have been killed in the war or have gone into the profession of the law, and have been turned out of the Church. As he understood, we asked the Great Head of the Church to bring out these young men who have no time to labor for themselves, and induce them to devote their whole talents to the Church. He believed it was a great mistake to send a half educated man into the ministry, or that he should be placed in a position where he would have to teach school for a portion of the time in order to pursue his studies; that the Board ought to bring up young men so that they would be entirely independent.

The amendment seemed to imply that in certain cases men had been helped who could have elped themselves, and thus threw censure on certain men venerable in this Assembly. Three men were present, who were an honor to the Church who had been sustained by this body. He hoped the original resolutions would pass. He had always felt that it was a contemptible thing to say that a young man had been brought up by charity, when he had been educated by the Church, for it was not so—the Church was begging for men to come forward and give themselves to its work. He affirmed that when he gave his money to assist a young man, he felt that the young man was honoring him in accepting it, and when he heard such a man preach the man always had his thanks. If this idea could be more generally impressed on the minds of the young men who were raised up in the Church, a different state of things would be brought about—a great deal of talent had been lost to the Church for want of it.

Rev. Mr. Heron felt that it was highly proper that the resolutions of the committee should be indorsed. He admired the spirit manifested by the member over the way, who would cultivate a feeling in young men that they should throw themselves on their own resources, but it appeared to him that striking out the part of the resolution proposed would not be proper, and would work disastrously to the interests of the Church. The resolution was predicated on the well understood principle that there always was a proportion between the number of young men entering the ministry and the number who received aid at the hands of the Board of Education, and hence, in proportion as the number of those asking aid diminished, there was a proportionate diminution in the whole number of candidates for the ministry. He therefore thought it inexpedient and unwise to strike out that clause from the report, because in so doing would be stricken out the recognition of a great and well understood fact that there was a great dearth of candidates for the ministry. There was no denying the tendency of the times. Thousands of young men who had returned with military laurels encircling their brows were seeking the various avenues of wealth, and would leave the ministry, because in the ministry they would have nothing to look forward to in their old age, but penury, and perhaps want, while, on the other hand, those who sought other callings did so in order that they might in their old age live in security from want, if not in affluence Under such circumstances it was not remarkable that but few young men came forward and offered themselves, and consecrated their talents to the ministry.

Rev. Mr. Shiland. The remark had been made that there was a great dearth in the ministry, and when there is a dearth what do we want but rain? Why were there so few candidates for the ministry? He stated that it was because of the unwillingness of the churches to support them. He believed that when the Church came up to her obligation in this matter there would be more candidates for the ministry. He questioned whether the Church had performed her duty. Might it not be that the Church had more ministers now than she could well support. When he had seen men in the ministry compelled to leave it for the purpose of supporting their families he could not help thinking that the Church was not performing her duty in this matter. They might call for more candidates for the ministry, but what would it signify? He knew men to-day who were willing to go any where if their families could simply be secured from want, but they were unwilling to labor and see their wives and children suffer for bread. He knew men who had preached the gospel for years, and paid out of their own pockets $500 a year for the privilege of preaching it. He asked "where were the young men who would come into the ministry under such circumstances?"

Rev. Mr. Whitman asked if it was a fact that the number of candidates for the ministry was on the decrease.

Rev. Dr. Smith stated that it was a fact.

Rev. F. R. Wilson said he was unwilling to take the position expressed in the resolution. If it was a fact that the number of candidates for the ministry was decreasing, it was a matter to be mourned over; but if it was only a fact that the number of candidates applying for aid to the Board was decreasing, he did not think it was to be deplored. They might draw a lesson in this respect from the affairs of every day life. In this very city it could be found that the men who had amassed fortunes, and built palatial residences, were the men who came to this city years ago in needy circumstances, and struggled their way into the position which they now occupy; while on the other hand, those who had been provided for in early life, were now the ones who were in needy circumstances.

Rev. Dr. Henry had only one remark to make, and that was in regard to his experience in Philadelphia. There were in his congregation eleven ministers without a church, and he had suggested to the venerable Secretary here to go to Philadelphia and make the number a round dozen. They had become so remarkable in this respect that West Philadelphia was called "Saints' Rest."

Rev. Mr. Ferguson remarked that he did not propose to detain the Assembly, but considered this an interesting question, and would be glad to see the whole day consumed upon it. He had been friendly to this Board. Twelve years ago he went out to look for young men of piety and promise, who could be brought up in the nurture and admonition of the Lord, and be put in the way by which they could reach the ministry. At the place where he resided there was a Presbyterian Academy, and he worked diligently to increase the number of such young men. He succeeded in inducing many to begin the work of educating themselves for the ministry under the auspices of the Board, and thousands of dollars were expended by the Board for that purpose. They grew up and had just enough support from the Board to make them lazy. They did not feel like going out to work in vacation. The Board gave them one wing and told them to fly, and they never put forth any efforts to educate the other. Before three-fourths of the number had reached the period when they should go to the seminary, some had gone to the Methodists—he believed one made now, what might be called a second rate Methodist preacher—another had gone to hack driving, others got married—listening to the calls of Cupid rather than the calls of Christ. Then, of course, their support was drawn off, and they had become farmers, and could not now be persuaded that they ought to refund the money which had been expended upon them. He advised caution in regard to this matter, so that when men are sent out in this way no greenback attractions should be placed before them, otherwise they would be imposed upon. A young man who was not independent enough to work his own way into the pulpit would be a poor and feeble preacher when he was there, and he would say that with all due respect to the dear fathers in the Church at the present time, there was a time when young men had to preach for $13 a month, now they could get $60. He hoped, therefore, no such utterances would come from this Assembly as were put forth twelve years ago.

Rev. Dr. Patterson moved to lay the motion to strike out the first resolution on the table.

The motion was agreed to.

Rev. Mr. Scott thought the fourth resolution was objectionable, inasmuch as it was inconsistent with the second one.

Rev. Mr. Ferguson said he supposed he had been referred to in the remarks of the Secretary. He did not profess to understand the hearts of men, and in soliciting young men to enter the Academy to which he had referred he did so because of the urgency of the Assembly and the need for workers in the ministry.

Rev. Dr. Nevins desired to know if it was in order for a member to speak twice to a question.

Mr. Ferguson said he was sorry that whenever he attempted to speak he had to be called to order.

The Moderator. You are not out of order.

Rev. Dr. Stonerode. I wish to know whether all the young men you have brought into the academy turned out to be scamps.

Rev. Mr. Ferguson said that he had already stated that about one-third of them fell back, but he had not followed the history of every one. He hoped that the amendment offered by Dr. Scott would carry. How did they know but that some terribly disloyal creature in the South might impose upon them under this resolution and draw the funds of the Board?

Rev. Mr. Crozier moved that the motion to strike out the word "candidate" be laid on the table. Agreed to.

Rev. Dr. Smith offered as an amendment that no extra aid be given to any young man unless the same be reported to the Presbytery or the faculty of the Institution.

The motion was agreed to and the report adopted.

On motion of Dr. Gurley, the appeal case from the Synod of Wheeling was made the order of the day for this afternoon.

The Committee on Synodical Records then presented their report in regard to the minutes of the several synods, of which the following is the result:

Found correct and approved—Albany, Alleghany, Baltimore, Chicago, New Jersey, Northern India Ohio, Philadelphia, Pittsburg, Southern Iowa.

No minutes and Committee discharged—Iowa, Kansas, Nashville, Pacific, St. Paul.

Not ready—Kentucky, Missouri, Northern Indiana and Wisconsin; recommitted.

Dr. McLean moved that the order of the day for the afternoon—the appeal case from the Synod of Wheeling—be suspended in order that he might make a report. The motion was lost and the Assembly adjourned.

AFTERNOON SESSION.

On motion of Rev. Dr. Cain, the order of the day (the appeal from the Synod of Wheeling), was laid on the table, in order to allow Dr. McLean, chairman of the committee to whom was referred the case of the Louisville members of the Louisville Presbytery, to make a report.

The following is the report:

Your committee, to whom was referred the papers concerning the Louisville Presbytery, beg leave respectfully to report as follows:

Three subjects were committed to our consideration; viz: 1. To examine and report the acts and proceedings of the said Presbytery.

2. To inquire whether said Presbytery, in view of its action referred to, is entitled to a seat in this General Assembly.

3. To recommend what action, if any, the General Assembly should take in the premises.

As to the first point, your committee remark that the acts of the Presbytery of Louisville come before this court in the way of review and control. We have not, indeed, the original records of that Presbytery. Yet our Book of Discipline provides, [chap. vii. sec. 1. v.] that "if the superior judicatory be well advised, by *common fame*, that irregularities have occurred on the part of the inferior judicatory, it is incumbent on them to take cognizance of the same; and to examine, deliberate and judge in the whole matter, as completely as if it had been recorded, and thus brought up by the review of the records."

We have before us a printed paper, a copy of which is hereunto appended, entitled, "Declaration and Testimony against the erroneous and heretical doctrines and practices which have obtained and been propagated in the Presbyterian Church in the United States during the last five years." It is subscribed by three of the four Commissioners who represent the Presbytery of Louisville; and is farther subscribed as "Adopted by the Presbytery of Louisville, at Bardstown, September 2d, A. D. 1865," with the name of W. W. Duncan, Moderator, and Robert Morrison, Stated Clerk. This paper is widely circulated, and is acknowledged as authentic by the Commissioners referred to. Your committee have no reason to doubt that it is a genuine transcript of the paper adopted by the said Presbytery at the date above mentioned. It will be readily admitted that such a document furnishes far more substantial grounds of proceeding than mere common fame.

This paper, considered as the Declaration and Testimony of the said Presbytery, furnishes the following facts: That Presbytery herein affirms that "for several years past" our "Church has been departing farther and farther from both the spirit and the plain letter of her commission to preach the Gospel, and her charter as a kingdom not of this world."

(p. 3.) It declares that "by the decisions of the Supreme Judicatory of the Church, at its recent meeting in Pittsburg, the consummation seems to have been reached, and the seal finally set upon all previous unconstitutional and unscriptural acts of the body." (p. 4.) It describes these acts of the General Assembly as a "subversion of the Law of Christ's Kingdom and surrender of the Crown Rights of Zion's King, on account of which the name and honor of our Lord are everywhere blasphemed." (p. 4.) It charges an "assumption on the part of the courts of the Church of the right to decide questions of State policy." (p. 5) It characterizes the deliverances of the late Assemblies as a "sanction given by the Church to the perversion of the teachings of Christ and his Apostles upon the subject of the duty of Christians as citizens." (p. 7.) It affirms that the Assemblies of 1864 and 1865 have "laid down a new doctrine upon the subject of slavery, unknown to the apostolic and primitive Church, a doctrine which has its origin in infidelity and fanaticism." (p. 8.) It represents certain language of the Assemblies of 1864 and 1865, as an "unjust and scandalous contradiction of their own recorded testimony and of well known facts." (p. 8.) It teaches that the General Assemblies of 1861 and 1864 "countenanced the doctrine that before a Court of Christ ought to take action on important questions brought before them, it is right and fitting that they should inquire 'what the Cabinet at Washington may wish them to do,' and ascertain what effect their action may be likely to have upon the mind of the President and the army, or upon the price of the Government stocks abroad." (p. 10.) Of the Assembly's reference to the developments of Providence, it says: "A more total abandonment of God's written word for the uncertain light of dark and mysterious and yet undeveloped providences, and these to be expounded by men, it may be, 'having their understandings darkened,' and for not obeying the truth, perchance 'given up to believe a lie,' can scarcely be conceived of." (p. 10.) It proclaims that "the usurpation by the secular and military power, of authority in and over the worship and government of the Church, has been sanctioned by Sessions, Presbyteries, Synods, and the General Assembly, *directly*, by various acts which are fully known to the word;" and adds that the Theological Seminaries of Princeton and Danville have "indorsed in word and act such usurpation." (p. 11.) It testifies that an "alliance has been virtually formed by the Church with the State; by which the State has been encouraged, and even invited, to use the Church as an instrument for giving effect to its various schemes of a political character." (p. 11.) It denounces the last five Assemblies as having practiced "a relentless and malignant persecution," which is sought to be justified by false statements and misrepresentations." (p. 12.) It charges the Assembly of 1865 with "basing an action upon an assertion of what the Assembly had the clearest evidence was not true." (p. 13). It declares that the deliverances of the late Assemblies "are contrary to the word of God and subversive of its inspiration and supreme authority." (p. 15). It assures the world that "our Synods and Assemblies * * have ceased to command even ordinary respect; (p. 19); that the General Assembly * * has become the support of heresy, the abettor of injustice and despotism, the fomenter of discord, and the prime leader in promoting a great and destructive schism in the body of Christ." (p. 21). It charges that "the infallible oracles of God have been abandoned" for "a shallow humanitarian philanthropy; (p. 21);—that "the plainest teachings of the Holy Scriptures respecting the relation and duty of masters and servants have been pronounced cruel and unjust;" (p. 22);—that "the whole mediatorial glory and dignity of the Messiah has thus been tarnished; and all the offices of Prophet, Priest, and King, which he executes for the salvation of his people, are subverted and surrendered." (p. 23). Finally, it sums up these weighty and serious charges with the declaration that "If this be not *an Apostacy*, surely it needs but little to make it so, clearly, unmistakably, fatally." (p. 23).

In view of this alleged position of the Presbyterian Church represented in this Assembly—within a hair's breadth, as they affirm, of utter and final apostacy from Christ—the Presbytery of Louisville adopt ten resolutions, of which the following are a specimen:

"1. That we refuse to give our support to Ministers, Elders, Agents, Editors, Teachers, or to those who are in any other capacity engaged in religious instruction or effort, who hold the preceding or similar heresies"—that is, to all such as agree with our late Assemblies.

"6. That we will not sustain, or execute, or in any manner assist in the execution of, the orders passed at the last two Assemblies on the subject of slavery and loyalty; and with reference to the conducting of missions in the Southern States; and with regard to the ministers, members and churches in the seceded and border States.

"7. That we will withhold our contributions from the Boards of the Church, (with the exception of the Board of Foreign Missions,) and from the theological seminaries, until these institutions are rescued from the hands of those who are perverting them to the teaching and promulgation of principles subversive of the system which they were founded and organized to uphold and disseminate. And we will appropriate the money thus withheld in aid of those instrumentalities which may be employed for maintaining and defending the principles affirmed in this Declaration, against the errors herein rejected; and in assisting the impoverished ministers and churches, anywhere throughout the country, who agree with us in these essential doctrines, in restoring and building up their congregations and houses of worship.

"8. We recommend that all ministers, elders, church sessions, presbyteries and synods, who approve of this Declaration and Testimony, give their public adherence thereto in such manner as they shall prefer, and communicate their names, and when a Church Court, a copy of their adhering act."

To this document are appended *forty-one* names of ministers, and *seventy-eight* names of ruling elders—in all, *one hundred and nineteen;* of whom eleven are ministers belonging to the Presbytery of Louisville.

Such is the tenor and spirit of the act which has been adopted, as we have no room to doubt, by a majority of the said Presbytery, and which has been published and extensively circulated for months. Its character lies upon its surface. It is not simply an expression of disagreement with the vast majority of the Church to which this Presbytery belongs, on the subjects of loyalty and slavery, nor a public protest against what they might regard as seriously erroneous or unconstitutional in the teaching or decisions of the General Assembly. Such a right of protest, public or private, by individuals or ecclesiastical bodies, is the birthright of Presbyterians. It is not even a refusal to sustain the General Assembly and a renunciation of all obligations to support the organizations by which our Church seeks to maintain and extend the gospel among men. Nor is it an act of rebellion simply against the constituted ecclesiastical authorities, to which, in his ordination vow, every Presbyterian minister has solemnly "promised obedience in the Lord." "*It is an organized conspiracy*" against the honor, the peace and the unity of that part of the body of Christ in which they still claim the rights and privileges of membership. It is a violent and studied disruption of the Christian bonds which they claim to be yet unbroken,—a bold denial of mutual obligations by men who demand for themselves the full enjoyment of covenanted engagements, without the poor merit of a rebellion which scorns obedience, proudly defies power, and challenges authority to meet it in the field of deadly conflict; this is the act of men who wear the garb of friends that they may more efficiently do the work of enemies.

While claiming membership in the Presbyterian Church and representation in this Assembly, they denounce that Church as apostate; its highest court as the support of heresy, the abettor of despotism, the fomenter of discord, the prime leader in a destructive schism! Under the form of refusing to support, they set themselves to undermine every living instrumentality of the Church in harmony with the Assembly, from the ministry to the common school teacher. They withhold their contributions from the Boards and Seminaries, that may expend them in advancing the ends of this conspiracy—in sustaining such ministers and churches as will co operate in their conspiracy. Sitting as a court of our Church, in connection with our Assembly, they organize themselves into a head center of treason to the Church, and invite other courts to send in their "adhering acts."

II. The second subject submitted to the consideration of your committee, is the bearing of the action of the Presbytery of Louisville upon its right to representation in this body.

Our constitution prescribes (Dis. chap. v, ix) that when a member of a church judicatory is under process, it shall be discretionary with the judicatory, whether his privileges of deliberating and voting, as a member, in other matters, shall be suspended until the process is finally issued or not." The principle of this rule has been applied by former assemblies to such cases as that before your body. Thus the Assembly of 1837, "Resolved, That agreably to a principle laid down, ch. 5, sec. 9, of the Form of Government, the members of said judicatory be excluded from a seat in the next Assembly until their case shall be decided." (See Baird's Digest, second edition, book vii, title 3, page 726.) A protest against this order was entered on the records as follows: "This Assemby has no power by their vote to deprive commissoners duly elected from a seat in the next Assembly, because that Assembly has the exclusive right of judging of the qualifications of its own members," &c. Even this protest admits the right to exclude in the case in hand. To this protest (with reference to "the next Assembly,") our Supreme Judicatory replied as follows: "The General Assembly, by its very Constitution, is regarded as having a general control of the whole Church, and in its conservative character shall superintend all of its concerns. It is believed that the initiatory steps contemplated by the resolutions authorizing a committee to designate inferior judicatories who may have been guilty of irregularities, to cite them, and report as soon as practicable to this Assembly, do not infringe the spirit or letter of the inherent powers of the General Assembly. And the great principles of analogy would obviously dictate that the members of the inferior judicatories, upon whom these preparatory measures are supposed to operate, should not be permitted to sit in the next General Assembly until their cases should be decided. If there be any sound principle contained in the clause, and the uniform practice which excludes an interested judicatory from voting, that principle and that practice should be applied to the members of such inferior judicatories as may be affected by these resolutions. This view of the subject is exceedingly strengthened by the fact that express power is vested in our judicatories to exclude at will their own members, when on trial before them."

(See Answer to Protest, Baird's Digest, §127, p. 728.)

In all cases of appeal or complaint, it is a common sense principle, as well as a constitutional law of our Church, that none of the members of the judicatory whose act is complained of, or appealed from, can vote in the superior judicatory on any question connected with their own case. (See Disc., c. vii, sec. iii, xii, sec. iv, vii.) In cases at review and control, our book prescribes no rule on this subject. Commonly, perhaps, the question of right is not thought of; the exercise or neglect of it is immaterial. "But it may be," as remarked in ch. vii, sec. 1, "that in the course of review, cases of irregular proceedings may be found so disreputable and injurious as to demand the interference of the superior judicatory." In such circumstances the principle adopted in cases of appeal and complaint must obviously be applied. The gravest questions, involving not merely constitutionality of proceedings, but the doctrinal soundness or the moral character of the body whose records are reviewed, may arise in the course of such review by a superior judicatory. In such cases "it is incumbent on them," as our Discipline declares, "to examine, deliberate and judge in the whole matter." The members of such subordinate judicatory are then "on trial" upon their record, or upon common fame. This judicatory, with its representatives, is "under process" from the moment the superior court has taken a step tending to the exercise of discipline. For what is "process" but that course of action, from beginning to end, which aims to secure the ends of discipline? Where citation is issued, the citation is, as the Assembly has said, "the commencement of a process involving the right of membership" in the superior body. (Digest, Bk. vii, Tet. 3, p. 726.) But there may arise contingencies of such character as to forbid citation. The judicatory alleged to have offended is cited "to *show what it has done or failed to do.*" (Disc., c. vii, sect. 1, vi.) But the records themselves may sufficiently "show what it has done," and the circumstances of the case may require the earliest decision compatible with our Constitution.

As a matter of course, a judicatory under process of trial retains unimpaired its right to be heard, through its representatives or otherwise, in self-defense. Though it cannot, and should not, claim a seat on the bench as an assistant judge, it may, and must, be heard at the bar, in person or by counsel.

III. We are directed "to recommend what course of action, if any, the General Assembly should take with regard to the said Presbytery at Louisville."

Were the case before us one of ordinary character, the proper course of proceeding would be that prescribed in our book of Discipline, chap. vii, sec. 1, vi. "The judicatory next above" that which has offended, (in this instance, the Synod of Kentucky) should have cited the Presbytery to appear and answer, and should have issued the case. But it appears, from an appeal and complaint against that Synod, now in the possession of this House, in reference to the very transactions of the Louisville Presbytery in question, that the Synod of Kentucky refused or declined to take action in the premises; or, at least, that it failed to cite the Presbytery before its bar. There is reason to fear, that besides the injury to the churches in the region in question, resulting from undue delay in the settlement of so grave a question, additional complications might arise and the leaven of rebellion become far more widely diffused. "A little leaven leaveneth the whole lump. Purge out, therefore, the old leaven, that ye may be a new lump, as ye are unleavened."

"To the General Assembly belongs the power," by the express provisions of our constitution (ch. xii, 5.), "at *deciding* in all controversies respecting doctrine and discipline," and "*suppressing* schismatical contentions and disputations." In the General Assembly "the whole church is called to sit in judgment on the acts of a part." (Disc. c. vii. 1.) It possesses, therefore, whatever power belongs to the Church, being the highest instrumentality through which the Church acts. Its methods of action are conditioned only by such express limitations as the Church has imposed on herself in her Constitution. Hence, as our Supreme Court has decided, "any supposed restriction of the right of the General Assembly," (to "cite any other inferior judicatories but synods," for example,) "is explained by the comprehensive character of the fifth part, (ch. vii, lect. 5,) which assigns to the superior judicatory power to examine, deliberate and judge in the whole matter, as completely as if it had been recorded, and thus brought up by review of the records." (Bair's Digest, 2d edit. bk vii, § 127, p. 728.)

The power of the Assembly, then, to act *directly* and *conclusively* in the case before them, is *clear* and *unquestionable*. The necessity for prompt and decisive action is apparent, in view of the position assumed by the Presbytery of Louisville in the paper under consideration, as well as in view of the fact that the Synod of Kentucky has failed to act in the premises. Your committee, therefore, recommend the adoption of the following measures:

Be it resolved by the General Assemby of the Presbyterian Church in the United States of America:

1. That the Presbytery of Louisville be, and hereby is, dissolved, and that the custody of its

records and other papers be transferred as hereafter ordered.

2. That a new Presbytery is hereby constituted, to be known by the same name, occupy the same territory, and have watch and care of the same churches; said Presbytery to be composed of the following ministers, (together with so many elders as may appear,) to-wit: D. T. Stuart, W. W. Hill, S. Williams, W. C. Matthews, R. Valentine, B. H. McCown, J. H. Dinsmore, H. C. Sachse, T. A. Hoyt, J. L. McKee, J. P. McMillan, J. McRae. H. T. Morton and J. C. Young, or so many of them, whether ministers or ruling elders, as shall, before their organization, subscribe the following formula: "I do hereby profess my disapproval of the Declaration and Testimony, adopted by the late Presbytery at Louisville, and my obedience in the Lord to the General Assembly of the Presbyterian Church in the United States;" which formula, together with the subscribers' names, shall be subsequently entered upon their records. The said Presbytery shall meet in the Chesnut street Presbyterian church of Louisville, Ky., on the 20th day of June, 1866; and shall be opened with a sermon by J. P. MacMillan, or in his absence the oldest minister present, who shall preside until a Moderator is elected.

3. That so many ministers belonging to the late Presbytery of Louisville as are not herein named are hereby directed to apply for admission to the Presbytery now constituted as soon after its organization as practicable; and they shall be received only on condition of acknowledging before the Presbytery their error in adopting or signing the Declaration and Testimony, and of subscribing the aforesaid formula, on its records. If, at the expiration of two months from the organization of the new Presbytery, these ministers shall not have made such application, or shall not have been received, their pastoral relations, so far as any may exist with the churches under our care, shall thenceforth be *ipso facto* dissolved. Acknowledgment and promise shall be recorded in the minutes of the Presbytery.

4. That the licentiates and candidates under the care of the dissolved Presbytery are hereby transferred to that now constituted; and the Stated Clerk of the late Presbytery is hereby directed to place the records and other papers of the former in the hands of the Stated Clerk of the latter, so soon as one shall be chosen.

5. That this General Assembly, in thus dealing with a recusant and rebellious Presbytery, by virtue of the plenary authority existing in it for "suppressing schismatical contentions and disputations," has no intention, or disposition, to disturb the existing relations of Churches, ruling elders or private members; but rather to protect them in the enjoyment of their rights and privileges in the Church of their choice, against men who would seduce them into an abandonment of the heritage of their fathers.

D. V. McLEAN, Chairman,
THOS. E. THOMAS,
THOS. W. HYNES,
D. J. WALLER,
HOVEY K. CLARKE,
SAM'L GALLOWAY,
R. P. DAVIDSON.

ST. LOUIS, MO., May 24, 1866.

That in the hearing of the report the committee recommend the following order.

That the Commissioners to the Asssemby from the Presbytery of Louisville be admitted to the floor, to discuss any question coming up on this report, and subject only to the rules of the Assembly.

On motion of Rev. Dr. Waller, it was moved that when the convention adjourn, it adjourn to meet at 8 o'clock in the evening.

Rev. Dr. McLean moved that Rev. Dr. Brookes be requested to inform the members of the Louisville Presbytery in regard to the matter.

Rev. Mr. Brookes said he understood these gentlemen had taken their departure and respectfully bade adieu to the Assembly, to return to their Synod and report the facts. All of these gentlemen, he was aware, had not left the city, and of course he would obey the request and give them the information.

The motion of Dr. McLean was agreed to.

The report of Dr. McLean was then put on the docket for the evening session.

Rev. Dr. Humphries desired to give notice of an amendment which he proposed to offer to the report of the committee, and which he would now read for information. The amendment was read as follows:

"The Declaration and Testimony adopted and published by the Presbytery of Louisville, appears in the terms, spirit and interest thereof, to be derogatory to the just authority of the General Assembly, hostile to the institutions of this Church, destructive to the peace of our people, and fruitful in schismatical contentions and disputations.

"Therefore, the General Assembly expresses its grave disapprobation of this proceeding of the Presbytery, as unbecoming in a low-judicatory of the Church.

"The Assembly also enjoins upon the Presbytery to forbear whatever tends to further disturbances and agitation, to support the institutions of the Church, and especially to take such order at its next stated meeting as will show that it does not intend to defy the authority of the General Assembly, to disparage the institutions of the Church.

"Furthermore, the Assembly does hereby require the Presbytery of Louisville to appear by its Commissioners before the next General Assembly on the second day of its session, to show what it has done or failed to do in these premises, and the Assembly is requested to take up and issue the business. The Commissioners from the Presbytery of Louisville are now readmitted to seats on the floor of this Assembly."

Rev. Mr. Brookes announced that he desired to have an official statement from the Clerk in regard to the action concerning the Louisville Presbytery. He had seen one of the Commissioners who had suggested the propriety of an official statement.

The Clerk was instructed to furnish the required statement.

The appeal case of Rev. Mr. Boyd, from the Synod of Wheeling, was then taken up.

The sentence appealed from was read, and Rev. Mr. Frazier addressed the Assembly in regard to the points involved

It appeared that Mr. Boyd was before the Synod of Wheeling for deserting his wife, but that there was some informality in regard to the charges on which the sentence was made up. Without coming to any decision in the case the Assembly adjourned.

NIGHT SESSION.

Assembly called to order at eight o'clock.

The following communication from the suspended members of the Louisville Presbytery, in response to an invitation to be present, was then read by the Clerk.

The undersigned, Commissioneners from the Presbytery of Louisville, who happen not yet to have left the city, overlooking, in the spirit of Christian forbearance, the insult and seeming mockery of the Presbytery and themselves, in a proposition to appear and be heard before a Court which has already condemned them unheard, in response to the resolution of this afternoon, transmitted to them by the Permanent Clerk of the General Assembly, must respectfully refer the Assembly to their letter of May 19th, as containing very obvious and sufficient reasons why they could not, without further special instructions from their Presbytery, appear before the present Assembly in any capacity.

SAM. R. WILSON,
STUART ROBINSON,
C. A. WICKLIFFE.

ST. LOUIS, MO., May 24, 1866.

The question being on the report in regard to the Louisville Presbytery.

Rev. Dr. Thomas then obtained the floor and spoke for two hours. His argument was able and exhaustive of all the questions involved in the case It will be published in the Democrat in full hereafter.

The argument was not concluded when the Assembly adjourned.

EIGHTH DAY—FRIDAY, MAY 25, 1866.

MORNING SESSION.

After devotional exercises and the approval of the minutes, Rev. Mr. Raffensperger offered a resolution, that in order to avoid the errors and misunderstandings constantly occurring by confounding the Presbytery of Toledo, Iowa, with the Presbytery of Maumee, in Ohio, this General Assembly earnestly request the Synod of Iowa to change the name of the Presbytery of Toledo to that of Jasper.

He considered it was in the power of the Assembly to change the name if they thought proper. He understood, however, that the brethren of Iowa had had a conference, and agreed upon the name of Jasper.

The Moderator suggested that it was in order at the beginning of a session to hear reports, and on motion of Rev. Dr. Schenk the resolution was referred to Committee on Bills and Overtures.

Rev. Dr. Lowrie, from the Committee on Bills and Overtures, presented the following:

Overture No. 7—From the Presbytery of Missouri River asking this General Assembly: first, to extend the boundaries of said Presbytery northward so far as to include Woodbury county, Iowa, which county is at present included in the territory of the former "Sioux City Presbytery," and second, to detach the Presbytery of Missouri River from the Synod of Southern Iowa, and unite it with the Synod of Kansas.

The committee recommended that the request be granted.

Adopted.

Overture No. 8.—Memorials have been presented to the Committee from the Synods of New York and New Jersey, and from the Presbyteries of Lake, Elizabethtown and Logansport, requesting this Assembly to devise measures for the more competent and uniform sustentation of those who are able and willing to engage in the work of the ministry, and also an Overture from the Presbytery of Allegheny City concerning unemployed ministers and vacant churches.

The Committee recommend that in view of the highly important and closely related nature of these subjects, this Assembly appoint a Special Committee consisting of the Rev. Dr. Elliott, D. D., Rev. C. C. Beatty, D. D., Rev. Jas. J. Brownson, D. D., Rev. Loyal Young, D. D., Hon. Wm. M. Francis, Hon. Robert McKnight, and Dr. C. R. Robinson, Esq., to prepare a special report on this subject, which so intimately concerns the growth and prosperity of our Church, to the next General Assembly, and that all the papers now before the Committee on Bills and Overtures, on these subjects, be passed over to this Special Committee. Adopted.

Overture No. 9.—Being a paper from Rev. W. P. Carson on the subject of licensing teachers or catechists. The committee recommend that, inasmuch as the subject is new, and of great importance, and in order to its adoption may require some constitutional legislation; therefore,

Resolved, That the attention of the Presbyteries be called to it, and that a committee consisting of Rev. W. T. Findley, D. D., Rev. F. E. Thomas, Elder Sam Galloway, be appointed to make a report on the whole subject to the next General Assembly.

Adopted.

Rev. Dr. Safford moved that the Assembly request of the Rev. Dr. McCosh a copy of the sermon delivered by him on Sunday morning last for publication in the proceedings of the Assembly. The motion was agreed to.

The order of the day—the report of the Committee on Disabled Ministers—was taken up.

Rev. Dr. Matthews, chairman of the committee, read the report, but as it was subsequently recommitted it will be published hereafter.

Rev. Dr. Matthews wished to call special attention to one of the resolutions, requiring the committee to present to the Board a statement of the receipts and expenditures, and hoped it would be urged by the Assembly.

Rev. Mr. Remington desired to offer the following resolution, in connection with the report:

Resolved, That in the action of the report before us, the Assembly express the desire that the entire ministry may in due time receive adequate support by means of the sustentation fund, similar to that instituted by the Free Presbyterian Church of Scotland.

Rev. Dr. Boardman said that he had been requested by the Rev. Dr Jones, the Secretary, who was absent on account of sickness, to address the Assembly in regard to this subject. This was a case which made its own plea, and he submitted that as the whole principle on which this plan proceeds is one of great delicacy and tenderness towards the brethren who are to be the recipients of the Church's sympathy and care, none of the names of those recipients be given; nobody cared to know who the pastor's widow is who receives aid, or who the orphans were that received aid. They had confidence in the Board of Trustees who have charge of this trust, and he desired to know if the committee would not consent to modify that part of their report requiring the Trustees to give the details as to the receipts and expenditures of the Board. He moved to strike out that part of the resolution which had been reported by the committee. He continued: if I were permitted to select in the whole range of our institutions a case which I would take to the churches with the utmost assurance of its meeting with a prompt, cordial and generous reception, it would be the very case now under consideration. And though up to this time the receipts of the committee have been small comparatively, yet they are small only because their necessities were small, and because the number of individual applications for the benefit of the fund has been very light. Now we have no Suntentation Fund. It is one of the sad things about our churches in this country, and we are constantly reminded by churches abroad that our voluntary plan has failed. But this is a mistake. Our ministers are hard-working men and wear out early. The statistics would probably show that in other countries the Christian ministers live longer than men of any other liberal profession, but in this country the average duration of life in the ministry is less than that of any other learned profession, and it is because the ministry here are hard working men. There is no end to the diversity of the claims and the demands which are made upon them, and the urgency with which these demands are pressed. There are poor men, I have no doubt, who are traveling from twenty to fifty miles from week to week, in order to make a circuit. Sir, such men need the sympathy and aid of the Church. Just look at the ministers' families. Why, the cases are the exception, I take it, in which a minister's widow is not obliged, on the death of her husband, to go to work and support her children. She must open a school or a boarding house, or become a seamstress—publicly or privately she must do something to obtain support for herself and her children. She may be a woman, too, in most cases, who has been reared in the comforts of life, not to say luxuries—a woman of high culture, unused to hard, laborious and exhausting toil; and yet compelled to chose between it and starvation. It is a curious thing, sir, this matter of sympathy with Christian pastors. Now, a congregation, as long as the pastor lives, will gather around him and sustain him, and applaud him, and help him and his family of children. But sir, how long in all ordinary cases does it take after he is laid in the grave for his family to be practically lost sight of, even by that same congregation. Here and there there will be a kind-hearted Christian friend that will remember the children for the father's sake, and the widow will still be beloved for the husband's sake, but we know how it is ordinarily, and therefore I say in behalf of this fund, that you look to it faithfully in its proper distribution.

Mr. Farquhar said he was instrumental in having the objectionable feature introduced in the report, but he was ready to accede to the request of Dr. Boardman, that it shall be left out. The resolution was introduced for the purpose of putting side by side, as far as possible, the contributions of Presbyteries and the amount of aid received, in order that the Presbyteries might be stirred up to more liberality. But he perceived in that direction there might be danger of injustice, because there might be circumstances in which the aid extended to superannuated ministers and the widows and orphans of deceased ministers, might be so great as to exhaust the ability of the Presbytery to give aid.

Dr. Boardman said he would prefer that no details should be entered into in the report of matters connected with the financial arrangements of the Board, as referred to this particular subject.

Rev. Mr. Farquhar said that he understood the amendment was only to strike out so much of the report as required the trustees to report to the General Assembly the amounts disbursed to the several Presbyteries. If it was to strike out the whole he should feel constrained to oppose it.

Rev. Dr. Patterson moved to re-commit the report to the committee.

Mr. Clark of Detroit, desired that some provision might be made by which the trustees of the fund shall be directed to report annually the amount of their permanent fund, and the amount of income received annually from the fund. He would move that resolution as a substitute for the one before the house.

The Moderator said the question was on the motion to re-commit. The motion was agreed to.

Rev. Dr. Gurley, from the Judicial Committee, presented the following:

The Judicial Committee report to the General Assembly case No. 5, being the complaint of Alexander Grey against the Synod of Cincinnati. This case originated in the Presbytery of Oxford and cannot be tried without the records of that Presbytery, or a certified copy of its proceedings in the case; neither of which has been sent to the Assembly. The Committee, therefore, recommend that it be continued and referred to the next Assembly, and that the Synod of Cincinnati be directed to send to that Assembly all the records that we require for a proper adjudication of the case.

No 6. The Judicial Committee to whom was referred the complaint of Messrs. Mack and Crozier against the Synod of Illinois, which was referred by the last Assembly to this Assembly, report that the parties in this case have appeared before the Committee and agreed upon a presentation statement of all the facts which the Committee deem essential to the adjudication of the case, and on these facts they rest the case and ask the decision of the Assembly. The Committee recommend that this statement be read and the case thereon decided.

On motion of Dr. Patterson the report was docketed.

Dr. Gurley moved that the appeal of Dr. R. J. Breckinridge against the Synod of Kentucky be made the first order of the day for Monday morning.

Rev. Mr. Ferguson doubted the propriety of making so many orders. So long as they had express trains on the track they should have the way clear; but if any other orders were made, they would be compelled to switch off.

Dr. Wm. Breckinridge suggested that it be made the order of the day for Monday at eleven o'clock. That would give them an hour to consider the subject of Domestic Missions.

Rev. Dr. Montfort said the report of the Committee on Domestic Missions was very important, and he hoped more time would be given to it than one hour.

The motion of Dr. Breckinridge was lost, and the motion to make the appeal case the order for Monday morning was agreed to.

Rev. Dr. Krebs moved that the order of the day —the report of the Committee on Freedmen—be postponed with the view of resuming the unfinished business.

Rev. Mr. Ferguson hoped the motion would not prevail, as it would look very much like leaving the colored brethren out in the cold.

Rev. Dr. Van Dyke desired to know whether the committee had seen the printed report contained in the correspondence between the Secretary of the Freedmen's Society and Dr. Adger of South Carolina; if not, he desired to move its reference to the committee.

The motion was declared out of order, and the motion to postpone the consideration of the report of the Freedmen's Committee was agreed to.

The unfinished business was then taken up, namely, the case of the Louisville Presbytery.

Dr. Thomas concluded his speech on the subject. He was followed by Dr. Wm. Breckinridge.

The speeches of both these gentlemen will be given in Monday's Democrat.

Adjourned until 3½ P. M.

AFTERNOON SESSION.

Rev. Mr. Sims offered a resolution to resume the appeal case from the Synod of Wheeling.

The Moderator decided the special order of business to be the hearing the address from Rev. Dr. McCosh in regard to the Sustentation Fund in the Free Church of Scotland.

Dr. McCosh proceeded to explain the manner in which this fund originated and the method by which it was carried on. He said that originally five hundred ministers gave up the stipends that had been given them by the State. The people then came to their rescue and made provision for them, feeling that they should be put in a position where they would be free from poverty. It was then that the Sustentation Fund was devised by Dr. Chalmers. Each congregation contributed according to its ability. The collection of the fund devolved upon the Deacon's Court. It was either collected by the Deacons going around in the Districts, or by female agents deputized to call upon the people. The returns in all cases were laid before the Deacons' Court once a month, and if it was found that the contributions from different districts diminished, inquiry was instituted into the cause, and if the evil was not remedied official steps were taken to check it. The fund is distributed equally to all congregations, so that in the last year, each minister was entitled to a dividend of one hundred and forty pounds. The advantages of the system were obvious. Under its workings they were enabled to send into the country districts among the poor people, an able and educated ministry, and each congregation could retain its minister so long as it paid its proper proportion to the fund. It was not for him to say whether the Church in this country should adopt this plan. They were all of one mind that some such measure is essential to the well being of the Church of Scotland. Whether it would be well for the Church here it would be for them to determine, but before proceeding to carry it out they should secure two things. First, the people should be thoroughly prepared for it; the people of Scotland were Providentially prepared for it by the ministers giving up their positions. There they had Dr. Chalmers, who went from town to town and explained it to the people until they understood it. The people should understand that it is not the rich giving to the poor. The main principle is that the rich give and the poor give also, and while the poor receive the rich also receive the benefit of it. He stated in conclusion that if the measure was undertaken it would require all the energy that characterized the American people in order properly to carry it out.

Rev. Dr. Boardman, from the committee to whom the subject of an address to Dr. McCosh was referred, presented the following:

The General Assembly records the high satisfaction it has experienced in receiving the Rev James McCosh, L. L. D., who, although not officially accredited to us by the Free Church of Scotland, bears credentials, having the signatures of many of the prominent and influential ministers of that Church, assuring us that their General Assembly, if in session, would unquestionably, in their judgment, have given him a formal commission to meet this body,

Appreciating the valuable services our distinguished brother has rendered to the cause of revealed religion, by his learned and able disquisitions in moral philosophy and theology, we tender to him personally the tribute of our cordial respect and gratitude.

We welcome Dr. McCosh as the honored representative of the Free Church of Scotland, and heartily reciprocate every sentiment of kindness and sympathy to which he has given utterance, on behalf of that Church and other sister churches abroad.

We share in the hope so eloquently expressed by our esteemed brother, that the various Evangelical Presbyterian bodies of Europe and America may soon be brought into a closer and more beneficent fellowship. Responding to the invitation now presented to us, we are prepared to enter into an arrangement with the General Assembly of the Free Church of Scotland for an annual interchange of delegates. On the assurance of our brother that such a measure will, as he believes, receive the prompt approval of that venerable body, we will send a representative to meet them at their next annual session, as we will welcome any delegate whom they may appoint to the Assembly of our own Church—leaving all matters of detail pertaining to this correspondence to be adjusted hereafter.

This General Assembly again express the pleasure they have derived from the visit of the Rev. Dr. McCosh. We thank him in the fraternal and instructive addresses; and we affectionately commend him to the care of a gracious Providence, that he may be shielded from all peril on the land and on the sea, and that his life may long be spared to the Church of Christ.

Resolved, That a copy of these minutes be presented to the Rev. Dr. McCosh.

The paper was accepted and adopted.

Mr. Clark, from Indiana, called for the special order—the appeal from the Wheeling Synod.

On motion of Dr. Montfort, the special order was postponed.

Dr. Lowrie, from the Committee on Bills and Overtures, to whom was referred the subject of a Union with the New School Assembly, presented the following report:

The Committee on Bills and Overtures report Overture No. 10, on the subject of the re-union of the two branches of the Presbyterian Church, from the Presbyteries of Leavenworth, Muncie, New Lisbon, Madison, Erie and Oxford. These Presbyteries ask the Assembly to take measures at this session to secure at an early day the organic union of the two bodies, whose General Assemblies are now in session in this city.

1. This Assembly expresses its fraternal affection for the other branch of the Presbyterian Church, and its earnest desire for re-union at the earliest time consistent with agreement in doctrine, order and policy on the basis of a common standard and the prevalence of mutual confidence and love, which are so necessary to a happy union and to the permanent peace and prosperity of the united Church.

2. That it be recommended to all Churches and Church courts and to all ministers, ruling elders and communicants to cherish fraternal feelings, to cultivate Christian intercourse in the worship of God and in the promotion of the cause of Christ, and to avoid all needless controversies and contentions.

3. That a committee of nine (9) ministers and six (6) ruling elders be appointed, provided that a similar committee be appointed by the other Assembly now in session in this city, for the purpose of conferring in regard to desirableness and practicability of reunion; and if, after conference and inquiry, such decision shall seem to be desirable and practicable, to suggest suitable measures for its accomplishment and report to the next General Assembly.

Rev. Dr. Van Dyke. I confess I would like to hear an amendment to that report, so that we might include another body of Presbyterians, and consult on their soundness in the Faith. There certainly is as good reason why we should have conference with them as we should have a conference in the soundness in the Faith of the other branch. There are eight hundred and fifty Presbyterian ministers in the Southern States—a body of men as large as the Free Church of Scotland, and a body whose soundness in the Faith this General Assembly has readily indorsed within six years.

Dr. McLean. Has the member a right to speak without a motion?

The Moderator. There is a motion to adopt.

Dr. Van Dyke. I confess it struck my mind painfully that amid all these interchanges of fraternal affection, while we are stretching out our hands across the ocean to those brethren of the Free Church of Scotland, to our brethren in Ireland, and to our brethren of the New School Assembly, and while we are talking about a marriage union with them, there has not been said on this floor a single word of kindness or affection for our own brethren with whom we took sweet counsel and went to the House of God in company until five years ago—not a single word, except those precious words that fell from the lips of a stranger coming among you from a Dutch Church.

Mr. Reinboth. The ministers to whom he calls attention have seceded and declared that they don't wish to have anything to do with us.

Mr. Hines. The brethren to whom he refers in the South are in no way included in the paper before this house, and therefore he is speaking to no point covered by that paper.

Dr. Van Dyke. I move as an amendment that the brethren formerly connected with this General Assembly in the Southern States be included.

Rev. Mr. Heckman. I suggest the gentleman to give the corporate title of that body.

Dr. Van Dyke. The General Assembly of the Southern Presbyterian Church.

Rev. Mr. West. I wish to know if it is competent for a member, in the middle of his speech, to make a motion, if it is not equally competent for any member to move to lay it on the table.

The Moderator. I understand that Dr. Van Dyke proposes to speak to his amendment. As a matter of courtesy I think the house should permit him to do so.

Dr. Van Dyke. Moderator, I did not intend to occupy the attention of this house two minutes when I arose, and I did not intend to intrude the thoughts and feelings which I entertained upon the attention of the Assembly, seeing they are reluctant to receive them, but I cannot discharge my conscience to God and the brethren who sent me here, and what I believe to be the Christian sentiment of the Church, without pursuing the subject which I have mentioned. I am among the number, Moderator, who do not feel so exultant in regard to the present position of the Old School General Assembly. While I should be sorry to indulge in anything that would be esteemed, even by the most fastidious, as disrespectful to this body, the feeling of my heart is expressed in the declaration, "how are the mighty fallen." Eight hundred and fifty—nearly one-third of the ministers of this Church—are to day out of this house, and the General Assembly is occupied with a case in which they propose to cut off another part of the body of this Church, and we have been warned that the General Assembly propose to proceed in this business till it is purged of what some gentlemen seem to consider the old leaven. Now, I believe in the doctrine of the persecution of the Saints. You have on record within ten years, the highest possible indorsement of the orthodoxy of these eight hundred and fifty brethren in the Southern States. In regard to this question of freedmen, a representative from the Church of Scotland has well declared this to be an unsolved question. You have put your indorsement upon the record in regard to the zeal and faith of these Southern brethren in a way which you can never blot out. In that record you give a description of the labors of the brethern in the Southern States in behalf of the negro population of those States. You declare in that Deliverance provision, ample and extraordinary, is made in all their churches that the colored man may hear the pure Gospel. You declare further that men are engaged in preaching to these colored men, not of inferior talents, but the first men in the Church. I do not give exact language, but that is the one that was adopted only twelve years ago, and now when we are here in a grand

Love Feast, and propose to marry ourselves with another branch of the Presbyterian Church—when, in our Christian forbearance, charity and love, we are preparing to swallow or be swallowed by it, and which only a few years ago we pronounced heretical. In the midst of this exercise of Christian charity there is no man to say one word for these 850 men down South, who, in the midst of poverty and suffering, are grappling with this great question; and the only report we have from them in regard to their connection with this great problem, is what you will find in the report of the Committee on Freedmen, on which, if the Assembly enlarge, I shall take the liberty to say something when the question comes up. The only way in which we have recognized their labors for the negro population is by coming in conflict with them under Military Commissions to take possession of one of their Churches, and hold it from those who are acknowledged to be the negro owners. I do not wish to pursue the consideration of the subject, but I cannot sit still and discharge my conscience and the feeling of my heart towards men whom you have taught me to honor, and men that I was brought up to honor, without intimating, at least, that that report ought to be amended.

Rev. Mr. West. I move to lay the amendment on the table.

Rev. Mr. Ferguson. I call for the ayes and noes.

The Moderator. I had begun to take the question.

Rev. Mr. Heckman. I desire to know if the names of these 850 ministers, and the Presbyteries and Synods to which they belong, have been struck from our list.

The Moderator. The gentleman is not in order.

The amendment was laid on the table, and the report was then adopted.

Dr. Van Dyke. I give notice of a protest against the vote that has just been taken.

Rev. Mr. Waller then presented the following report from the Committee on Theological Seminaries:

REPORT OF COMMITTEE ON THEOLOGICAL SEMINARIES.

The Committee on Theological Seminaries respectfully report to the General Assembly that full reports from the Trustees and Boards of Directors of the four Seminaries under the care of the General Assembly have been placed in their hands, and found in order, and are recommended to be read and published in the appendix to the minutes

Miscellaneous papers have also been placed in the hands of the Committee, and received appropriate consideration. The financial affairs of each of these institutions appear to have been carefully administered, and to be in a prosperous condition.

The Danville Seminary has been injuriously affected by the great national convulsion of the last five years to such an extent as to awaken deep solicitude for its continued prosperity and usefulness. The number of students has become so small that three of the four Professors have resigned. The resignation of Rev. Dr. E. P. Humph rey and the Rev. Dr. S. Yorkef have been accepted, and that of the Rev. Dr. R. L. Stanton has been tendered, and your committee recommend its acceptance by the Assembly, while the Rev. Dr. R. J. Breckinridge has signified his readiness and wish to resign. Thus the question of the temporary suspension of the Seminary has become one of serious import. But after mature deliberation, and in view of possible litigation and loss, your committee recommend to the Assembly that Dr. Breckinridge be requested to retain his professorship and look after the intorests of the Seminary, and endeavor to prosecute its more perfect endowment.

He is, also, authorized to confer with the Trustees of the college and with the Synod of Kentucky as to the conditions upon which they will agree to the removal of the Seminary from Danville, and report to the next General Assembly.

In view of the provision in the charter of this institution which empowers the General Assembly to elect Trustees, when sitting within the limits of the State of Kentucky, your committee would call the attention of the Assembly to the importance of holding a session within that State at the earliest practical period.

The following persons are nominated for filling the vacancies in the Board of Directors, which occur by limitation during the present sessions of the Assembly, viz:

Ministers.	Elders.
W. L. Breckinride, D. D.,	B. M. Penick,
J. F. Coons,	O. Beaty,
J. P. Hendricks,	William Prather,
N. C. Burt, D. D.	Glass Marshall,
J. B. Condit,	James Barbor,
H. H. Allen,	A. F. Avery,
R. W. Landis, D. D.,	T. T. Alexander,
R. J. Breckinridge, D. D.,	John G. Barret,
S. D. Crothers,	A. E. Chamberlain.

D. D. Dickey in place of J. A. Lyle, deceased.

E. Anson Moore in place of G. W. Lowes, deceased.

The report of the Board of Directors of the Western Theological Seminary, shows the reception of twenty-nine new students and a total attendance during the year of eighty-four. Nineteen candidates have passed the required examinations and received the diplomas of the institution.

The request of this Board for a revision and reissue of "the plan of the Seminary," "under which all our theological seminaries have been organized," is commended to the consideration of the Assembly The report of the trustees that the sum of thirty thousand dollors has beed added to the endowment fund of the seminary, and two scholarships have been endowed by the gross sum of five thousand dollars, deserves the grateful acknowledgment of the Assembly.

Your committee would respectfully nominate for re election the member of the Board of Directors whose term of service expires during the present session of the Assembly, viz:

Ministers.	Elders.
Samuel Watson, D. D.,	Alexander Laughlin,
George Marshall, D. D.,	Francis G. Bailey,
William D. Howard, D. D.,	B. Rush Bradford.
Elliott E. Swift,	
L. R. McAvoy, D. D.,	
Robert Dickson,	
David H. Riddle, D. D.	

And to supply the vacancy occasioned by the death of Rev. D. D. Clark, D. D., D. J. Waller.

And that occasioned by the resignation of Sam'l McClung, Alexander Donaldson, D. D.

The Trustees of Princeton Seminary report "the net sum of $66,405 15," as raised within the year for payment of debt and endowment. This cheering token of favor to this, the oldest Seminary of our Church, will be hailed with gratitude by the Assembly.

The Board of Directors report fifty-four new students within the year, and an attendance of one hundred and fifty-seven. Of these, fifty-four sustained the usual examinations and received certificates of having completed the three years course.

The Faculty of the Seminary afford the gratifying information that the Seminary has shared with the Colleges and Churches in the town, in a special baptism of the Holy Spirit, while at the same time the regular studies have been prosecuted with increased punctuality and diligence.

Your committee would recommend the re-election of the following members of the Board, whose term expires during this Assembly, viz:

Ministers.	Elders.
Joseph H. James, D. D.	Sebbens B. Ward,
John McLean, D. D.	Ira C. Whitehead,
Wm. B. Sprague, D. D.	James Robinson, in place
John M. Dickey, D. D.	of Ebenezer Piatt, deceased.
N. L. Rice, D. D.	
J. E. Rockwell, D. D.	

W. M. Paxton, in place of Rev. D. Magie, D. D., deceased.

Alexander Reed, in place of G. W. McPhail, D. D., resigned.

The Directors of the Theological Seminary of the Northwest report the reception of fifteen new students during the past session, and the conferring of the usual certificate upon four young gentlemen who have completed their course in the institution.

No return is made of the total number of students owing the Seminary.

The large addition to the library of the institution, through the liberality of the widow of the late Rev. W. B. Phillips, D. D., of New York city, consisting of his library, to the number of 854 volumes, is deserving of the special and grateful notice of this Assembly. The Board of Directors resolved, by a vote of 11 to 9, to request the Assembly to transfer Dr. Lord to Mr. Cyrus H. McCormick, Professorship of Didactic and Polemic Theology, and also to fill the fourth Professorship by an election. The Board, however, inform the Assembly that the opposition to those acts is very firm and weighty.

The friends of the Seminary present in St. Louis from all parts of the Northwest, including a large number of the Directors of the Seminary, have had frequent conferences on this subject, and have arrived at a good degree of unanimity. Their views having been communicated to your committee, it has been our unanimous conclusion that both the comfort and usefulness of Dr. Lord will be best secured by retaining his valuable services in his present department.

Your committee therefore recommend that this Assembly proceed to the election of a Professor of Didactic and Polemic Theology; and we would respectfully ask leave to nominate for this chair the Rev. E. D. McMaster, D. D.

The term of service of ten members of the Board expires during the session of the present Assembly; and your committee would respectfully report the following nominations to fill the vacancies, viz:

Ministers.	Elders.
S. T. Wilson,	Samuel Howe,
F. N. Ewing,	John Woodbridge, Jr.,
J. P. Safford, D. D.,	Henry Phelps,
F. T. Brown, D. D ,	J. McKee Peeples,
J. G. Monfort, D. D.,	J. C. Walker,
J D. Mason, in place of A. A. E. Taylor, res'd.	Jas. M. Ray, in place of Wm. Shuts, resigned.

The subject of an additional year to the course in Princeton Seminary, which has been brought to the notice of your committee, by the reference of the last Assembly, and by a modification of the request from the Faculty, this year, and also by remonstrances from several Presbyteries, has been deliberately considered, and the committee recommend that the Assembly sanction the adoption by any or all of our seminaries, of a course of studies to be pursued, purely at the option of students, during a fourth year (not impairing the three years course as heretofore pursued); provided, no increase of the number of teachers shall be asked on this account. And no distinctive degree or title shall be conferred on those electing to pursue the fourth year's course, save a certificate similar to that now authorized for the three years course.

All of which is most respectfully submitted.

D. J. WALLER, Chairman of Committee.

Rev. Mr. Crozier moved in reference to the 4th resolution that the subject be left to the faculty.

Rev. Mr. Finley thought that the clause in regard to the first course should be struck out.

Rev. Mr. Miller said that this clause had been inserted on the suggestion of the Princeton Seminary.

Rev. Dr. Backus moved to amend the resolution by inserting the words "not impairing the three years' course as heretofore pursued."

Rev. Mr. Riggs said it was the opinion of his Presbytery that the additional year did not accomplish any great good—that if it was necessary to have more than three terms they had better lengthen those terms than add another year.

Dr. Humphrey moved that the whole matter be referred to the next General Assembly.

Dr. McLean thought it would hardly be wise to pass the resolution just now. He concurred with the motion of Dr. Humphrey.

Rev. Dr. Kempshall moved to lay the motion to refer on the table. Agreed to. He then moved to place the report on the docket.

Rev. Mr. Ray moved to lay that motion on the table. Agreed to.

The amendment offered by Dr. Backus was agreed to, and the motion to strike out was lost.

Mr. Clarke thought the action of the committee, in nominating officers, was extra judicial. He hoped it would be remembered that there was no binding efficacy of the report in that regard. The report was then adopted.

Nominations being in order, Mr. McKnight nominated Alexander Donaldson, D. D., for the Board of the Allegheny Seminary.

Rev. Mr Waller desired to state that they had conferred with the members of the Board of Directors of the different seminaries and had their reports and verbal statements before them, and in making these nominations they conceived they were doing precisely what they were authorized to do.

Mr. Galloway nominated Dr. Thomas for the Western Theological Seminary.

Mr. Clark nominated Dr. Willis Lord for the Chair of Theology in the Seminary of the Northwest.

Mr. Day nominated Dr. N. L. Rice, of New York, for the same position.

Dr. Stonerode nominated Dr. McLean for the Board of Directors of the Princeton Seminary.

On motion of Dr. Waller the elections were made the special order for Monday at 12 o'clock.

The Assembly then adjourned till Monday at 9 o'clock.

Speech of Dr. Thomas on the Report Relating to the Louisville Presbytery.

The question being on the report in regard to the Louisville Presbytery.

Rev. Dr. Thomas then obtained the floor, and spoke as follows: Mr. Moderator, allow me to say in introducing the remarks which I have to make this evening in regard to the report before us, that I sympathize very sincerely with the sentiment of our admirable Secretary of Foreign Missions. The sentiment which he expressed yesterday or the day before in reference to spending time in the discussion of questions before us, while the great interests of a dying world seemed to be neglected. I do not wonder, sir, that a brother whose position and opportunities enable him to serve six hundred millions of heathen, should feel oppressed with the thought that in such an Assembly as this, which represents so large and important a body as the Presbyterian Church in the United States, these local interests—these interests of an hour, should engross so much time, employ so much thought, and awaken so much interest, while for the time we seem to forget both Home and Foreign Missions. I sympathize with the sentiment of my friend; and yet while he uttered it, my mind reverted to the first General Assembly of the Church of the Living God that was ever held upon earth. While I thought upon it, this whole scene, as if touched with the wand of an enchanter, was transformed. I was sitting in the upper chamber at Jerusalem, for there, perchance, that council was held of which the record is found in the fifteenth chapter of Acts. You, sir, became St. James, the presiding officer of that council—the Moderator and the Secretary represented the beloved Apostle. The gentleman who is not indeed upon the floor of this house—the time-honored leader of this house, and of this Church, but who comes to present in the way of an appeal, the very question that is now to be discussed, seemed to be St. Paul with his eagle eye and iron will. I will not say who St. Peter was in this Assembly, but I seemed to be sitting in the House at Jerusalem. It was in the upper chamber, I suppose, for they had no Church in Jerusalem, first or second, to worship in. Out of one window we looked on the depths of Gethsemane, and out of the other we beheld Calvary. It was the very chamber in which the Master, now risen, had broken to them the first time that sacramental bread, which we rejoiced to break in his name yesterday. It was in the very chamber where the Holy Spirit descended upon them—coming as the rushing of a mighty wind, and sitting in cloven tongues of fire upon every one of them. Sir, no Assembly on earth was ever gathered under circumstances so solemn, or in a place so sacred as that of the first Council of Jerusalem. There, sir, was the Apostle Paul, and there was Barnabas—a man full of faith and of the Holy Ghost. They had come from Antioch, the first Gentile church in the world. Paul and Barnabas had gone on missionary labors together, and we should naturally suppose, sir, that in such an Assembly, under such circumstances the entire business of the meeting would be that which appertains to a missionary meeting. One would naturally suppose that when Paul rises to speak it is to tell how he has carried the fiery banner of the cross from Antioch round about unto Illyricum. One would suppose he comes to tell how he has laid the corner stones of a hundred churches in the most influential centers of the Gentile world. And yet, sir, it so happens that we possess the minutes of that meeting. In the 15th chapter of Acts we have the record of the proceedings of that first General Assembly. St. Paul has turned aside from his missionary labors St. Paul, with Barnabas, has come from the church of Antioch, to inform the General Assembly that a strife has arisen in the Presbytery of Antioch. I read in the minutes of that proceeding that the question under discussion, having been taken up in the Presbytery of Antioch—for you read of that Presbytery in the 13th chapter of Acts "that there was no small dissentions and disputations among them." And when they came to the Council of Jerusalem, they were not gathered together though the Apostles were there and the elders of the church to consider the questions. They were not gathered together there to discuss that question without signs of much disputing. Yes, sir, when James, the brother of the Lord, was the Moderator; when Paul, with his commission from Heaven was the Representative; when Peter, who had received absolution from the lips of his Master, was one of the speakers; when the beloved disciple was present who had stood at the foot of the cross; in such an Assembly as that, we are told, there was much disputing as to the first case that was ever appealed from a Presbytery to a General Assembly. Mr. Moderator, let us be encouraged. I know how good brethren feel in regard to such matters—I feel so myself—that were it permissible in the Providence of God, they had ten thousand times rather that Brother Lowrie should discuss the claims of a foreign field. And yet, sir, I say let us not be discouraged. Let us remember that in this General Assembly, sitting in this end of the earth, in 1866, we have the very scene, and it may be the identical spirit that was manifested in the first Assembly that was ever gathered together. Why, sir, to look a moment at the nature of the controversy, that then existed; what was it? In the Presbytery of Antioch there had arisen a faction that is commonly denominated in these days, the Judaizing party. Paul was there and Barnabas was there—men inspired, men honored with Apostolic commissions—and yet in the Church where there was an effusion of the Holy Ghost by the laying of the hands of the Apostles, strife and faction and party spirit manifested themselves. And what, sir, was the nature of that party spirit? Why, sir, first and foremost, this Judaizing party was *a party of the past*. They believed in "the Union as it was, and the (Jewish) Constitution as it is." They fought, as Michael and the Devil once fought for the dead body of Moses; just as some among us are fighting for the dead carcass of rebellion and slavery. We may easily infer *who* it was that desired, and for what end, the body of Moses. As a party of the past they were incapable, despite the extraordinary providences of that day, of discerning that a new era had dawned upon the world. They wished to find the world in the old bonds of legalism. They could not understand the liberty wherewith Christ was making his people free, and yet the Master had said to them, "Can ye not discern the signs of the times?"

So, sir, these Declaration and Testimony men, in the plentitude of their wisdom, sneer at the Assembly of 1864, because it undertook to interpret the lessons of God's word in the light of God's providences! Have they forgotten, sir, that a large portion of the Scriptures—the whole prophetic record —can never be interpreted until the providence of God shall throw a flood of light on the pages of Scripture? But this party of the past, despite the Master's instruction and command, were unable to detect the error in which they had been nurtured. More than this sir, they were a small party, numerically insignificant, yet exceedingly active; but, above all, they were possessed with an intense persuasion of a divine commission respecting "Christ's Crown and Covenant." I said just now that Paul was there, sent not of man nor by man, but by the Lord Jesus Christ. He was there with his commission, not only from Heaven, but written *in* the third Heavens, and bearing the broad seal of the ethereal Heavens; bearing the sign manual, the very autograph of the crowned King of Saints, whom all the angels of God worship. In that Presbytery of Antioch there stood Paul and Barnabas, and yet there, sir, could be found a certain sect of the Pharisees—a certain party of the past—certain men that clung to Moses, and that were willing to give up Christ for Moses; certain men that defied the authority of the Church, even where it rested in the hands of the Apostles; certain men that cared nothing for the power of the keys of Heaven, even in the presence of those into whose living hands the living Master had given the keys of his kingdom. Such is human nature, that while Paul, inspired by the power of the Holy Ghost, not one whit less than the very chiefest of the Apostles—when Paul stood in that Assembly and made a motion and Barnabas seconded it, this sect of the Pharisees stood up in the Church and defied the Apostles. They said, sir, as that Declaration and Testimony says to this Church, you are not apostles, but apostates. They claimed that they too had received a commission. What was it? For that glorious Gospel of the blessed God which Paul would have preached to every creature, they would substitute a pair of shears to circumcise the whole Gentile world. Now, sir, it might have been a local question, and it was confined, as far as we know, to the very city of Antioch, and I suppose some good congregational brother would say, "better never to have had a General Assembly, but let the thing die where it was born." Yet the case came up by appeal from the Presbytery of Antioch to the General Assembly at Jerusalem. And now they were gathered there; and if you will read the account in the 15th chapter of Acts, you will see a very singular similitude between that meeting and our meeting. They had in the first place, as we had before opening this Assembly, devotional exercises, for we find in that chapter of Acts how the whole Church met together to welcome Paul and Barnabas. In the next verse we have an account of the next day's meeting; and then came much disputing. Then followed another missionary meeting, such as we have had. The 12th verse tells us that all the people gave audience while Paul and Barnabas declared what great things God had done for them. Brethren, let us not only not be discouraged, but let us learn wisdom. This was God's providence; the beginning of the history of his church; an exhibition of the truthfulness of Him who said, I come not to send peace upon earth, but a sword. It is illustrative of the fidelity of those whom He commissions, not only to preach the Gospel, but to confute and silence gainsayers. There might have been men who thought that an insignificant question. Paul thought differently. He gathered his whole apostolic force, and threw the power of his transcendant mind into that controversy. I suppose if some charitable brother of our day could have looked into that church at Antioch and have seen the Apostle engaged, day after day in his contest with the Pharisees, about this shears question, they would have said, "Paul, let them alone and go preach the Gospel." But Paul knew his commission better. He acted according to the advice the Duke of Wellington gave to a young minister who inquired of him if he thought the world would ever be converted: "Sir, look to your marching orders; go ye into all the world and preach the gospel." The holy spirit of truth set his seal upon the wisdom of the Apostle, if we had reason to question it. In this little volume, how small, and yet how large, how easily perused, and yet how hard to understand in all its hight and depth, length and breadth. In this constitution of the New Testament Church, and guide of a dying world to Heaven, scarcely as large as our form of government and discipline, one whole book, the epistle to the Galatians, written by Paul, is devoted to this shear question, to prove that the doctrine of this Judaizing party was another Gospel which is not a Gospel. I trust that same spirit who indicted that epistle, looks down kindly and benignantly upon us, to guide our discussions in this present controversy.

I pass to another topic. My friend from Philadelphia, Dr. Boardman, was pleased to give me what he thought no donbt a merited castigation; and I feel myself permitted to allude to his remarks simply because I understood them at the time, and still understand them as spoken in a Pickwickian sense. He thought proper to castigate me, however, for my facetiousness, because when some young brethren were pressing forward to seek a crown of martyrdom, I interposed with such remarks as occurred to me to prevent this self-immolation. But my good brother thinks that in such circumstances as these it is not well to indulge in pleasantries; that we ought to be very grave and solemn in such serious concerns. Very good. I will try and be serious to-night; and yet I remember on one of the most solemn occasions in Israel's history, when all the kingdom of Israel were on the top of Carmel, save Jezebel, who took good care not to be there, the question was to be settled whether Baal or the Lord Jehovah was the God of the Covenant people. When that question was raised and the prophets of Baal were cutting themselves with knives, and calling upon their God, that brave old patriarch, that noblest of the Old Testament prophets, who was too good to live, and for whom God sent his chariots of fire, and took him home to glory without death. That old prophet stood up and said in a sneering way, "Cry aloud ye prophets; perhaps he is asleep, or perhaps he is on a journey." That was sharp sarcasm on a very solemn occasion; yet I presume it was right. Yes, sir, there is a place for irony. I will advert to one thing further in this connection: My good brother charged me with being wanting in instincts of a certain character. He frankly admitted, however, that the lack was incapable of being supplied, that it was congenital. You remember how he introduced in that connection the story of the idiot asylum. Does the brother, when he visits that asylum, sneer at its inmates because God has not allowed them a full modicum of sense. If the brother intimates that there is a lack in my composition of some instincts, convenient at least in social intercourse, he ought not to taunt me with the absence of that which it is beyond my power to supply. There was another Philadelphian, born in Boston to be sure, but who lived and died in Philadelphia, and my good brother can walk along the streets of that city and read the inscription upon upon his grave—Benjamin Franklin—who, when he was a bit of a boy, read that passage of Pope, wherein the great master of song says:

> "Indecent words admit of no defense,
> For want of decency is want of sense."

Benjamin Franklin preferred to read it in this way:

> "Indecent words admit but *this* defense,
> That want of decency is want of sense."

I hope my good brother will allow me the benefit of the American amendment.

[The speaker then proceeded to analyze the character and relate the history of the Declaration and Testimony, and to discuss the question of the constitutional power of the Assembly to act in the premises. As the main points of his argument were recapitulated on the following day, when he was permitted to conclude, we omit them in this connection. Owing to the lateness of the hour he gave way to a motion for adjournment, and the next morning resumed and concluded as follows:]

Moderator, I am well aware that I have severely tried, if not already exhausted, the patience of this House; and I wish simply to say in proceeding to the close of my remarks, that I occupy the position in which I stand this morning at the request of the committee whose report we are considering. As I do not expect again to ask the attention of the house upon this subject, let me beg you to consider carefully the closing part of the argument presented last evening. Now, sir, I am persuaded that there is not a member of this House who is not determined to proceed in an orderly and constitutional way in this whole business; that there is not a member who has any disposition to evade the law or to prevent the law even to the accomplishment of the purpose which he feels ought to be accomplished. We are not of those who believe that the end sanctifies the means. It was my purpose, therefore, in the argument presented last evening, to show that we have not only the clear warrant of the constitution, but we have the obligation laid upon us by the constitution of our Church, to preserve the very course that is pursued in this report.

Let me for a moment call your attention to the points that I presented in the course of my argument upon the subject of constitutional law in this matter. I will not dwell upon them, but recapitulate them for the purpose of putting the whole subject distinctly in the possession of this house.

First. Having this case before us, the merits of which I pass over now, because enough has been said upon them for my purpose—having this case before us, I said that it comes in the way of Review and Control.

The *second* point made was that it comes substantially upon the *record*. Review and Control may adopt the method of prosecuting on common fame, or upon the record. In this case we are receiving the case on the record. The *third* point already made is this, that the ordinary course pointed out by our book in cases of this kind is neither advisable nor practicable. The ordinary course, as our book shows, in Review and Control, is that the judicatory next above shall cite the inferior judicatory; but in this case the Synod of Kentucky, as the report states, has either refused or declined, or, at least, has failed to act in the premises. And I ask you, sir, that the 192d page of the records of the Synod of Kentucky shall be read. I will simply state to the house it is the record of the action of members of the Presbytery of Louisville when this case was brought before them.

[The extract was then read.]

Dr. Wm. Breckinridge. I am far from wishing to interrupt the brother, but I think the Assembly would get the impression that it was the voice of the majority of the *Synod* that he is reading. I wish to ask him to read the names of the persons who made that utterance.

Dr. Thomas. Very good, sir. What I want is the facts. The first name is Samuel R. Wilson; then S. P. McPheeters, C. A. Wickliffe, &c.

It is a matter of little consequenee—in fact no consequence at all, as far as the argument is concerned—except as the *argumentum ad hominun*. It is simply to put in possession of this house the judgment of some of those who were concerned in the question before us. Now, sir, if in point of fact the Synod of Kentucky have failed to act in these premises, then I proceed in the fourth place to show that this Assembly has the power to take immediate cognizance of the case. I proved that by showing that in the dissolution of the Third Presbytery of Philadelphia—as recorded in the digest—the Assembly stepped over the Synod and rendered its judgment, and carried it into execution. Now, whatever may be the ground on which they acted, it is of no consequence to us, because we are simply ascertaining the fact that they exercised the power, and that in the exercise of that power the Assembly acted upon what it believed to be its constitutional right.

In the second place the Assembly has the power in this to step over the Synod of Kentucky, from the fact that in another case it cited an offending Presbytery to appear before it, and in that case applying the principle of the rule in chapter five, section nine, they excluded the parties that were cited to appear at the bar of the next Assembly from representation until their case was decided. And here I have simply in mind the fact that the

Assembly has twice exercised this right to pass over the intermediate judicatory and lay hold upon the subordinate judicatories. And I referred on the 723th page of the digest to the answer which the Assembly gave to those who protested against the exercise of the right on the ground that the Assembly could not touch the Presbytery, except through the Synod. That was one of the points. The answer of the Assembly was that any supposed restriction of the right of the Assembly in a case of this kind is explained by the comprehensive nature of that section of Review and Control. Well, sir, I presume this will be admitted, and I pass on. I think I have shown, however, that if it be necessary, the Assembly has the clear right to pass over the Synod of Kentucky, and act on the Presbytery; but, then, I am met here with an objection to which I ask the particular attention of some of the brethren who have spoken to me on the subject. We admit the Assembly has the power to go over to the Presbytery of Louisville, but they say you must first cite them to your bar. I refer to page 720 of the Digest, where the Assembly resolves, first, to cite the Presbytery; and second, that a committee be appointed to investigate the case; and third, that as a citation on the foregoing plan is the commencement of a process involving the right of membership in an Assembly; therefore,

Resolved, That agreeably to a principle laid down in chap. v section ix of our form of government, the members of said judicatory shall be excluded from a seat in the next Assembly till their case is decided.

The whole question lies here in a nutshell. The Assembly says that as citation on the foregoing plan is the commencement of a process, the difficulty on the minds of some brethren is whether a process can begin without citation. They take the meaning of this language to be that in all cases process begins with citation. I direct the attention of the house to the fact that that is very far from being the meaning of the Assembly. First, the Assembly choose a particular plan by which they can prosecute their case. Second, they affirm that on the foregoing plan, in the way which they have have chosen to proceed, citation is the commencement of a process involving the right of membership. The plan they had chosen to pursue was to cite the offending Presbytery before the bar of the next General Assembly; and, of course, in that plan it was the beginning of process. But there are other ways in which to begin a process besides that of citation.

Now let me ask the attention of the house for a moment to the reasons for citations given in the seventh chapter of our Book of Discipline. It is the sixth paragraph.

The assumption of the brethren is that if the judicatory next above must take this as the first step, then a higher judicatory is bound to do the same thing. And what is the reason? They say the Assembly is directed to cite the offending judicatory to show what it has done or failed to do. Now, sir, there are three proofs that, in arguing the case before this house, that rule is inapplicable because the reason of the rule ceases. First, we have before us, as I have said, the record. We are dealing virtually with the record; and the provision of the book expressly is that in a case of record you cannot go beyond that record for information. There is no reason, therefore, for citing a judicatory, because the whole case lies in the compass of this record. There is no need at all of citing a judicatory to show what they have done. The record shows that. And once more, the reason of the rule is inapplicable, because this Louisville Presbytery comes itself and asks an investigation.

Now, sir, the General Assembly of 1837, cited distant Presbyteries to appear at the next Assembly, because it was impossible in the nature of the case that they should appear at that Assembly. They cited them to appear because they were absent and their records also. But what is the use of the rule here? Is our system a system of red tape? When a man comes into the house and says, "Brethren of the Presbytery, here I stand to be tried and I challenge investigation," is it necessary to cite that man to appear? There he is. He brings his record without citation. When he offers it, and distributes it in your seats, and presents it to the country, is it necessary? And if the reason of the rule ceases, then, obviously, the rule is inapplicable.

Now, in the third place, there is no application of the rule in this case, because the Assembly has set aside the rule in a measure of far more questionable character than that recommended to us. The General Assembly of 1837 dissolved the Third Presbytery of Philadelphia. Members of that Assembly protested against the action as unconstitutional, not only because the Assembly had no power to pass over a Synod and act on a Presbytery, but because, as they say, it was condemned "without being accused, cited, or tried—condemned unheard." (See Baird's Digest, p. 758.)

Now, sir, the history of that case is presented, I presume, correctly. I have not here the minutes of the Assembly of 1837, but I presume the protestants against the action of the Assembly were wide awake, understood the facts, and would not state in their protest what was positively false. They protested against this rule because of its unconstitutionality in dissolving a Presbytery without citation.

Well, sir, if that were true, and the Assembly did not deny it, then the General Assembly has expressly decided that in a case of this kind it may step over the Synod, and that in an extreme case it need not be bound by the rule of citation. Whatever may have been the circumstances of that case, I think I have shown in the circumstances of our case the rule for citation ceases, because the reason for it ceases. *Ratione legis, cessante, lex ipsa cessat* is a maxim of law.

Now for the next step in this argument. How does this affect, supposing it be true so far, the rights of the Presbytery of Louisville to a seat in this house? It will be admitted, I presume, on the ground of the action of the Assembly of 1837; that if we should cite the Presbytery of Louisville to appear at the bar of the Assembly we might then exclude them from a seat until their case was disposed of.

Moderator. The same reason and the same rule for exclusion applies in one case as in the other; for when the Assembly of 1837 cited the Presbytery to appear at its bar, and then said this judicatory shall be excluded from representation in the next Assembly, why did they do it? Was it because they were *cited to appear*, or was it because they were *on trial?* No man will contend that the real ground of their exclusion—the ground on which the Assembly had the right to exclude them—was the mere fact that they cited them to appear. No, sir, it was the far more significant fact that, being cited to appear, they were on trial, and being on trial they were under process; and that the principle which applies to an individual minister in his Presbytery applies to the Presbytery in its Synod, or in the General Assembly; that until his case be decided it is at the pleasure of the house, according to the circumstances of the case, to decide whether that body shall retain its seat or not. We must inquire, then, in the next place, whether the Presbytery of Louisville is on trial on its records. Now, I will not repeat the remarks made last night indirectly on this subject, that review and control brings up all sorts of cases, from those of the least significance to those of the very highest moment; but I simply remark here that in any case of review and control upon the record, it will depend upon the magnitude of the offense and the character of the facts on the record whether the body whose records are reviewed be on trial or not. If it is simply a question how they spelled the word Presbytery, or some mere incidental oversight or neglect of a trivial matter, or irregularity of proceeding, we should not say they were on trial and should go out of the house. But if an extreme case comes up—if a case comes up on which, as I supposed last night, the Presbytery has avowed infidelity—has denied the doctrines of the Confession of Faith *in toto* and put it on record—I say, sir, that in view of the magnitude of the offense, when you sit in judgment on their records, they are *on trial.* In such a case as that, review and control brings up everything that an appeal could bring up and accomplish, and it is a question of the most vital character that is decided. Now, when you have them on their records, if it be a case of this magnitude and criminality, it is your duty to say to them, brethren, this is not an ordinary case; stand you on your trial until this case is decided. we do not condemn you unheard, but we do propose to investigate your case; in the course of the investigation to acquit you if you be innocent, and to condemn you if you be guilty; and until that sentence be reached, brethren, you must stand aside as unworthy to share in the duties and responsibilities of this higher court.

We tell these commissioners that they must be removed as incompetent, to use the language of this article, to sit in such a court and pronounce in such a case. If they are on trial, then they are under process from the moment that this Assembly passes the order for investigation.

For what is process? There are lawyers here who can tell what it is, technically, in law courts. It is the writ of the magistrate, perhaps. But a process in our ecclesiastical courts has not that narrow limitation of the statutory law. It is the simple English we are talking now—our mother tongue. Well, the process by which you secure a harvest of wheat, means, fencing in the field, plowing the ground, scattering the seed, gathering the harvest and putting it in your garner—then the process is complete. *Process* is that whole system of means from beginning to end by which a court reaches the ends of discipline. I ask if the first step toward those ends be not the beginning of process? This Assembly might have taken another way. We chose to take this. If we choose to cite that citation it is the commencement of a process. If we choose to appoint a committee to investigate the records of a party, then the appointment of that committee with an order to investigate is the beginning of process.

The constitution has already settled the rule, that when a minister is under process it shall be at the pleasure of the house whether he vote in any other case besides his own till his case is decided or not. (Chap. V. IX) And the Assembly has decided that the principle of that rule applies to such a case as this The Assembly applied the rule in such a case as this. The case is as plain as the light of day, and I do not mean in the use of that expression to allude to my friend, the gentleman from New York.

Now, I have but one word more to say on this point, and that is this: I am not arguing, Mr. Moderator, but simply presenting the naked letter of the *law*. I think I may say that this report can be sustained not only without infringing upon any provision of the constitution, for the very object the law is to guard the rights of the minority. I fully accede to that; the majority can get along without rules. It is the minority that need rules, and I know it is not the temper of this house to infringe upon the privileges of the minority; nor is it the mind of this house to fail to execute the power which God has conferred upon them, and enjoined them to exercise in the government of his house. The course pointed out in the report of this committee is the law of God's house, and the written law of our Church, and above us, not above all, but with all, and added to all, there is this fact, that when in the great Presbyterian Church case of thirty years ago, this question of the validity of the very acts which I have cited as precedents was made the basis of the decision, the Supreme Court of Pennsylvania decided in our favor on the ground that the General Assembly, in these acts, had not transcended its constitutional authority. The question with that court, speaking through Chief Justice Gibson, was not whether the Assembly did right or wrong, in a moral point of view, for that they were answerable to God; but when they appeared to Cæsar, under the laws of the commonwealth, the simple question was, "Has your Assembly, that is charged with having done these acts, the power, by the provision of its constitution, to do what it has done?" Well, sir, the judgment of the Supreme Court affirms the fact; but I will not take time to read it. By virtue of that decision this Assembly is the General Assembly of the Presbyterian Church of the United States. By virtue of that decision we hold our property, and have our records; and brethren familiar with the history of those times will remember how very important and decisive an influence this order to exclude certain bodies from a seat had upon the composition of the next Assembly; how vital that action was in the whole process by which the conclusion was reached. Let me come now to the last part of the report. I have investigated the law of our Church applicable to the case.

I come to consider the method by which the Assembly shall reach the ends of justice. It is indeed a summary method; yet sometimes short roads are the best. It was a very short method by which Pharoah and his hosts were put out of the house, when God moved upon the sea; a very summary process by which the lightning, fire and brimstone came down from Heaven upon Sodom and Gomorrah; and if you think the cases too far-fetched, then it was a very summary process by which, in the presence of a Church Court in Jerusalem, Ananias and Sapphira were sent to the Supreme Court in Heaven, to answer for their crimes. The speediest remedies are commonly the best. But what is this remedy? We propose that the Presbytery of Louisville be dissolved. Can any man question, in view of the decisions I have presented, that this Assembly has a perfect right to dissolve the Presbytery? But brethren will say, though we have the power, it is inexpedient to exercise it. In regard to that I have simply to say that the justice of the rebuke in this case can hardly be questioned. Dr. Humphrey, if I understood the tenor of his brief paper, admits substantially the guilt of the parties, the iniquity of the action and the criminal character of the whole proceeding. Such a paper, such acts, such a pertinacity of rebellion, such systematic organization of conspiracy for the overthrow of the Church of the living God, deserve rebuke, if ever iniquity deserved rebuke from men. There is not only justice in the court proposed, but necessity for it. Mr. Moderator, when mortification ensues in some part of the body, remote from the heart and the vital centers, then, I tell you, a wise surgeon is not long in laying hold of the amputating knife. The apostle Paul, in the Church of Corinth, was not long in purging out the old leaven. He did not give them two months notice, I think, sir, much less refer them to the next General Assembly. When he wrote his sacred epistle he had to bathe his page with tears of sympathy for them, because in the energy of their zeal to do right, they had instantly obeyed his apostolic injunction. They amputated the gangrene limb that they might save the body. I know the impossibility of foreseeing the future. I know in these changing, troublous times, the wisest statesman may fail when he undertakes to predict what sixty or ninety days may bring forth; yet we must act according to the probabilities of the case. What are they? If you leave the Presbytery recognized and defiant, with revenues, with friends, with influence, with a society instituted for the very purpose of congregating friends around this nucleus—if you leave them there in the midst of a Synod which is, to say the least, hesitating, (and I do not impugn their motives; I do not know how I might have acted under the influences they may have felt,) can we hope for a safe issue of events to the Church in Kentucky. Will the interests of Presbyterianism be secured if we leave this Presbytery to the control of a Synod that has seen this evil festering since last September? What may we reasonably expect, what new complications, what aggravated evils, if we leave this matter in this condition? No, Moderator, there is a necessity laid upon us that we shall do justice in this case.

But then, sir, we temper justice with mercy. What do we? We select from this Presbytery the men who have signed this act and testimony, and who have recorded on its books their votes in its favor. There is the overt act of rebellion. Such brethren as were present and voted in the negative, or such brethren as were absent from the Presbytery, or such as have declined for various reasons to put their names to this document, these we gather together and say, brethren, we know some of you do not agree with us in this matter; some of you, it may be, approve of this document, and some of you utterly condemn it; but we say, you have the right to your private opinions. We gather you together who have stood faithful to the Church in this trial, and organize you into a Presbytery. We take you, brethren, "faithful among the faithless found," and we commit to you the watch and care of those Churches, and of those precious souls belonging to this Presbytery. We go further than that, and honor the most faithful. That report appoints a young man, the solitary brother who stood up in that Court, and in the presence of Christ and his enemies in the Presbytery, said: Brethren, No, I cannot vote to adopt this Declaration and Testimony. That "No" stands recorded, and we honor it. We tell him to be the Moderator of that new Presbytery, to preach the sermon, and receive the reward of his fidelity. Then we turn to the other brethren in this report, and say: Brethren, we will see to it that our justice is tempered with mercy. Here is the open door; you may enter if you please. After the organization of this Presbytery, we give you two months for deliberation. We do not touch your pastoral relations for two months. You have seen the act of this house, and you know the temper of this Church. You can review your proceedings and you can come to this Presbytery and say to them, what? Now, I beg brethren to look at that formula prescribed in the report and see if it be not the very mildest thing this house could ask of such offenders. We ask them to say, "I repent of my sin in reviling the Church of Christ and in bidding defiance to her legitimate authority, and promise, henceforth, obedience to my brethren in the Lord."

We do not require them to subscribe to all the decisions of the General Assembly, but we do require each of them to say, "I regret my error in having subscribed to this document. I express my disapproval of the Declaration and Testimony and promise future obedience." Is not that mercy mingled with justice?

Moderator—I will close this argument. I have trespassed too long upon the patience of this Assembly. The great want of our age, sir, is a spirit of obedience to law; of reverence for constituted and legitimate authority; of respect for those who exercise authority, whether in the family, the State, or the Church. Let me illustrate the temper and habits of Young America, sir, by an anecdote respecting the late Hon. B. F. Butler, whose soubriquet of "Sandy Hill" was familiar to politicians of twenty years since. He was invited to a Mission Sunday School in the city of New York. The Superintendent introduced him to the boys as the Attorney General of the United States, one of the most distinguished citizens of their native State, and an active friend of friendless youth; adding, while he pointed to the clock, that Mr. B. would limit his speech to fifteen minutes.

Well, sir, they listened with fixed attention, but they kept an eye on the clock. The orator, warming with his theme, forgot the limitation of his time, and had passed the bound only a few seconds, when a tattered urchin, probably a news-boy, and so familiar with political slang terms, suddenly sprang up, and pointing to the clock, exclaimed, "*Sandy Hill, your time is out!*" That, sir, is an illustration of our respect for those in authority.

Our political papers practice and cherish this pernicious and degrading habit. Our people speak familiarly, contemptuously of the President of the United States of America, the highest dignitary on earth, as "Old Buck," or "Abe Lincoln," or "Brandy Johnson." Is it in the use of such epithets that we "fear God and honor the king"? Is not this the conduct of those that "*despise governments*"? of whom St. Peter says, "presumptuous are they, self willed; they are not afraid to speak evil of dignities."

Sir, the tendency of our times,—perhaps it may be a natural abuse of the nature of our free institutions—is to despise government, to cultivate a spirit of insubordination. Why, sir, if you will pardon me for relating it, I had once a curious exemplification of this Young Americanism in my own household. It has already appeared in the public prints without my consent, and, therefore, it may not be indecorous to allude to it. I had a little son about four years old, whom of course I thought a very bright and promising fellow. During my temporary absence from home for a few days on one occasion, his mother relieved the weary interval with reading him the story of our revolutionary war. The little fellow treasured up the scattered facts and anecdotes, and narratives of battle-fields, until his youthful patriotism was kindled to a flame, and his blood began to boil. I returned home late in the night, when he was wrapt in slumber. He rose later than usual. While we sat at breakfast he came down, and seated himself by my side in silence. He withheld the familiar welcome—the customary kiss. Evidently his mind was engrossed with something. He sat brooding his topic for a few moments, and then, turning to me, he said, "Father, are you British?" "My son," said I, "I had the good or bad fortune to be born in England; but, like the Irishman, I was brought over here so early that I became a native." "Well, sir," said he, his childish face all aglow, and shaking his little fist at me, "*We whipped you once, and we can do it again!*" [Great laughter.] That, sir, is the spirit of Young America.

Mr. Moderator, we may smile at so youthful an exhibition of a free and easy and independent spirit, which forgets the reverence due even to parental dignity. In the heart of a child, the love of country may, for a moment overpower filial affection and obliterate in that flash of patriotism the sense of obligation to a superior. But when that momentary spirit of irreverence becomes the fixed habit of manhood; when self-conceit and self-will systematically trample in disdain the sanctity that surrounds all authority; when insubordination becomes insolent, rampant, defiant; its inevitable result is seen in those sanguinary contests which have desolated in these late years so large a portion of our country. In a hundred bloody battle fields, where some of my dearest friends fill patriot graves, where 300,000 of our best and bravest offered life upon the altar of their country, the civil government has already settled the question of its claims; settled it upon the principles of the Divine word, expounded by the General Assembly of 1861: "Ye must needs be subject, not only for wrath, but also for conscience sake."

The crushing of this infamous rebellion has settled the question of subjection for wroth's sake. And more, when the civil war is ended, when armed resistance yields to the supreme authority of the national will; when every patriot desires to allay the passions engendered by that war, and to bind our whole land in bonds of fraternal fellowship around our common Government and common flag; there springs up this petty rebellion in the Church, this feeble echo of the old war-cry that led the vanquished hosts of treason. Here come these declarations and testimony now, protesting that five years ago we erred when we said, in the Assembly of 1861, that, in the circumstances of the case before us, (and every rebellion must be tried by the circumstances which occasion it,) they who "resisted the power resisted the ordinance of God; and they that resist shall secure to themselves damnation." (Rom. XIII, 2.) Here they come, protesting that the great Presbyterian Church, with all Christendom, sinned, when we gave thanks to God that in His holy and unsearchable providence, he had instantly emancipated four millions of poor slaves. Here comes this Presbytery of Louisville, which has planted itself bodily on this Declaration and Testimony, and tells the General Assembly and the whole Presbyterian Church, in the face of the world, Brethren, we refuse to obey you; we defy your authority; we spurn your "decrees delivered to the Churches to keep;" we have organized a resistance to the supreme ecclesiastical court by which we expect to overturn its influence; and that we may the more efficiently execute our hostile purpose, we demand a seat in your body, a share in your counsels, and the opportunity of thwarting at every turn, whatever measures you may adopt to suppress our schismatical contentions!

Did ever rebellion attain such a sublime audacity of impudence? Sir, in the providence of God this Assembly enjoys the high privilege of forever establishing the fact that government in the Church means something; that it, too, is an ordinance of

Heaven; that it is the delegated authority of Him who holds in his right hand the red-hot thunderbolts of hell. "Whatsoever ye shall bind on earth shall be bound in heaven: and whatsoever ye shall loose on earth, shall be loosed in heaven." (Mat. xviii 18.)

Let this General Assembly, exercising in His name that ministerial and declarative authority entrusted to it; and yet tempering justice with mercy, "for the destruction of the flesh, that the spirit may be saved in the day of the Lord Jesus;" execute this act of most deserved discipline. Let us say to this offending body, your principles are intolerable; your practice unendurable. Some of you we love; all of you we pity; but we must protect the Church, we must purge out the old leaven; we must "even cut off them who trouble you." (Gal. v, 12)

Moderator and brethren, we are called to vindicate ecclesiastical authority, the power of the keys, not only in our own Church, but for all the churches of the land. This thing is not done in a a corner. The eyes of America are upon you. To every city, village and hamlet in the country the news of your decision will be carried on the wings of the lightning. Thousands and tens of thousands who have offered prayers for your guidance by Divine wisdom, are waiting to hear that the Church has sealed the doom of ecclesiastical rebellion Let us meet our responsibility like men, like Christians. The Presbyterian Church expects every man to do his duty. [Applause.]

The Assembly adjourned.

NINTH DAY — MONDAY, MAY 28, 1866.

After devotional exercises and the reading of the minutes

Dr. McLean moved that the report of the committee in the case of the Louisville Presbytery be taken up and finally acted upon, urging as a reason that a large number of the members were leaving for their homes.

Dr. Lowrie hoped that the business would proceed in its regular order.

Mr. Clark, of Indiana, hoped the motion of Dr. McLean would not prevail.

Dr. Krebs said a judicial case had been made the order of the day, and the parties were here ready for trial. In the trial of this case he though a great deal of light might be thrown upon the Louisville Prysbytery.

Rev. Mr Ferguson moved to substitute the judicial case from the Synod of Wheeling, urging as a reason that there was a standing rule that when a judicial case they had already begun the trial of the case, and was taken up it should be prosecuted to its close.

The Moderator decided the motion out of order.

The motion to postpone the order of the day and take up the case of the Louisville Presbytery was lost.

Rev. Dr. Lowrie, from the Committee on Bills and Overtures, presented the following:

The Committee on Bills and Overtures report overture No. 11 from the Synod of New Jersey, viz:

"Is it the intent of chapter 17th, Form of Government, that a minister desiring to resign his pastoral charge shall, in all cases, first make his request known to the Presbytery?"

The committee recommend that it be answered in the negative, for the reason that chapter 16, section 2, provides that when the parties are prepared for the dissolution of a pastoral relation, it may be dissolved at the first meeting of Presbytery. Adopted.

Overture No. 12. Resolved, In order to avoid the errors and misunderstandings constantly occurring by confounding the Presbytery of Toledo, in the Synod of Iowa, with the Presbytery of Maumee, Ohio, this General Assembly, in accordance with the suggestion of the Commissioners from the Synod of Iowa and many others, hereby change the name of Presbytery of Toledo to that of Presbytery of Jasper.

Rev. Mr. —— stated that this subject had been referred to the Synod of Iowa, and that they had refused to act.

The motion to refer to the next General Assembly was agreed to.

The remaining overture was read and adopted, as follows:

Overture No. 13. Being a request of Samuel McCune that the Assembly would answer various questions connected with judicial processes in the lower courts.

The committee recommend the following answer. These questions pertain either to supposed or to actual judicial processes.

In either case it is not deemed proper that the Assembly should give specific answers to them.

Rev. Dr. Matthews, from the Committee on Disabled Ministers' Fund, reported that the Committee had considered the report as recommitted to them, and had made one alteration in the fifth resolution, in accordance with what seemed to be the desire of the Assembly on Friday.

The report of the Committee is as follows:

The committee to whom was referred the report of the Trustees of the General Assembly in relation to the Disabled Ministers' Fund, would respectfully present the following:

Your committee regret very much that the report gives no information in regard to the receipts and disbursements of this fund during the year. or the sources whence their income is derived, but yet from the exhibit that is made of the administration of relief to disabled ministers and their needy families, the committee have reason to believe that there has been a gratifying increase in the fund, and an efficient and judicious management of it.

During the past year somewhat over $22,000 have been distributed upon applications indorsed by Presbyteries, giving timely and much needed aid to forty-nine ministers, sixty six widows and fifty-five families of orphans, comprising among the recipients more than four hundred individuals.

There are no numbers in which can be computed the value of the relief thus afforded to those who, by reason of age, or sickness, or bereavement, have been deprived of the means of support, and compelled to struggle with the cares of poverty when least able to do so.

Your committee think that the claims of our disabled ministers and their widows and orphans cannot be too urgently pressed upon the attention of the Church and they would hope that through the action of the Assembly, the co-operation of the Presbyteries and the liberality of the people, such abundant contributions may be secured to this fund, that this worthy but needy class of persons may be assured of ample provision in their time of need.

The Church owes a debt to its disabled ministers. They have substantially separated themselves from the lucrative employment of life, which ordinarily secure to men not only a subsistence for the present but a provision for the future, and have given their best energies to the service of the Church in the care of souls, and while in that service, and rejoicing to do the works of the Lord, have been incapacitated by reason of age or sickness for further active service in their holy calling.

It is admitted on all hands that the half pay or pension which the State bestows on the faithful soldiers who have been disabled in its service, or upon the families of those who have laid down their lives at its behest, is only just. And certainly like justice requires that the Church should make similar provision for its faithful and devoted ministers who have become disabled in its service, and for the dependent families who have shared their devotion and their lot,

Your committee feel, furthermore, that the provision thus secured to those who, with undivided aim, devote themselves and their all to the service of the Lord Jesus in the ministry, will be an important auxiliary in procuring a supply of ministers. It is an undoubted fact that many are deterred from entering the ministry by the prospect of an insufficient support during the years of toil in the service and the certainty that with such insufficient support nothing can be provided against the time of old age, sickness, or death

The faith of many cannot bear this strain upon it. But by an adequate provision of this invaluable fund these gloomy apprehensions of the future will be banished and one terrible obstacle in the way to entering upon the ministry removed.

It must, also, have a happy effect in producing that cheerfulness and elasticity of spirit with which it is so important that the ministers of the gospel should pursue their work, when they are assured that the Church will care for them in old age and sickness and of the r destitute families after their death.

Your committee would, therefore, hope that the interest already awakened in behalf of this branch of the Church's work may increase to the full measure of the necessity which led to the establishment of this fund.

We recommend to the Assembly the following for adoption, viz:

Resolved, 1. That it is a matter for devout thanksgiving to God that this branch of the beneficence of the Church has found so much favor in the hearts of God's people and that they are thus so truly appreciating the claims of its aged and infirm laborers and their needy families

2. The General Assembly rejoice to contemplate the comfort ministered from this fund to those who by reason of past faithful service have established a righteous claim to a support from the Church when by the act of Divine Providence they are laid aside from active labor: and to all such, to the aged and sick and infirm, and to the widows and orphans of such, the Assembly sends this expression of its sincere sympathy, and prays that God would incline the hearts of his people to devise still more liberal things for their comfort.

3. The General Assembly urge upon all the Churches a continued and increased liberality in their contributions to this fund, not more as a beneficence truly charitable, than as a beneficence truly just, as a debt due for faithful services rendered in caring for the most important interests of men.

4. That the Presbyteries be instructed to adopt such means as will bring the cause to the attention of all the churches, and they are also instructed to take especial pains to discover and present to the attention of the Committee on the Fund, the claims of all who are in need, and for whom the Church designs this provision, not only that there may be no misappropriation of the funds, but also that none who are entitled to aid be neglected and allowed to suffer for want of it.

5. That the Trustees be directed in making their annual reports on this fund, to present a detailed statement of their receipts and expenditures, such as is required from the other Board of the Church, showing specifically what amount of income administered by them is from the funds permanently invested; and what from contributions of the churches during the year, and also what amount is annually invested in permanent funds, and the state of such permanent fund.

6. That the report on this subject by the Trustees be appended to the minutes of the Assembly, and be printed for the use of ministers and churches.

R. C. MATTHEWS, Chairman.
D. U. SMOCK,
WM. GREENOUGH
JOHN FARQUHAR,
H. S. BANKS,
W. M FERGUSON.

Rev C. C. Riggs offered the following preamble and resolutions as amendments to the committee's report, which was read, when, on motion, the subject was docketed:

Whereas, This General Assembly recognizes the principle that the funds, contributed for the relief of disabled ministers, and the widows and children of deceased ministers come to them as a right and not as mere charity; and,

Whereas, It is believed that some, through extreme modesty and backwardness, are unwilling to make their cases known, and therefore suffer in silence from want. In order to meet these cases, and as far as possible to do justice to all; be it

Resolved, That it be and it hereby is made the duty of each Presbytery under our care, whenever any of their members shall, for any cause not inferring crime, cease to discharge the functions of the Gospel ministry, with the consent and approbation of his Presbytery to immediately inquire into the pecuniary circumstances of such minister, so far as to satisfy themselves in regard to the necessity and acceptibility of aid from this fund, and if desirable, to take the necessary steps to procure it for him, and continue it to him from year to year, so long as the necessity exists, without waiting for his personal application And further, upon the death of any minister, in good and regular standing in his Presbytery, the same course shall be pursued by the Presbytery in regard to his surviving family.

Resolved, That this Assembly impressed with the desirableness and importance of increasing, as rapidly as possible, the Permanent Fund for this branch of the Church's benefactions, do hereby renew their earnest solicitation of donations and legacies, small as well as large, to this fund, not only from the wealthy, but also from those in more moderate circumstances And they would urge all our ministers and elders and private members to exert their influence and employ their efforts, by every means in their power, to secure such donations and legacies,

Rev. Mr. Riggs offered the following amendments to the report:

On motion of Rev. Dr. Smith, of Baltimore, the complaint was docketed.

The Moderator announced the order of the day to be the report of the Committee on Domestic Missions.

Rev. Dr. Thomas stated that the Committee were not prepared to report.

Rev Dr. Brown, of Chicago, stated that the Committee on the Narrative were prepared to report.

On motion of Rev. Dr Mason, the report was made the order of the day during a part of the devotional exercises to-morrow morning.

The Moderator announced the appeal and complaint of Dr. Robert Breckinridge, against the Synod of Kentucky, as next in order. He wished before vacating the chair, as it would be his duty to do, to announce the committee on the subject of a reunion with the New School Church. In selecting this committee, he had endeavored to combine all the various shades of opinion, as far as he understood their views on the subject. He had also taken them from all sections of the Church, without taking any two members from the same Synod. Some of the persons named were not members of this Assembly. He believed it was usual, when committess were appointed to consider business after the using of the Assembly, to select persons who were not of the Assembly, as he had done in this case. The committee was then announced as follows:

MINISTERS.

J. M. Krebs, D. D., Synod of New York.
C. C. Beatty, D. D., Synod of Wheeling.
J. T. Backus, D. D., Synod of Albany.
P. D. Gurley, D. D., Synod of Baltimore.
J. G. Monfort, D. D., Synod of Cincinnati.
W. D. Howard, D. D., Synod of Pittsburg.
W. E. Schenck, D. D., Synod of Philadelphia.
Villesvy D. Reed, D. D., Synod of New Jersey.
F. T. Brown, D. D., Synod of Chicago.

ELDERS.

James M. Ray, Synod of Northern Indiana.
Robert McKnight, Synod of Alleghany.
Sam'l Galloway, Synod of Ohio.
H. K. Clarke, Synod of Sandusky.
Geo. P. Strong, Synod of Missouri.
Prof. Ormond Beatty, Synod of Kentucky.

The Moderator then vacated the chair, stating that he had requested Dr. Lowrie, the last Moderator, to fill it, but that gentlemen had declined, and suggested the Rev. Dr. Krebs. Rev. Dr. Krebs was then selected to act as Moderator pro. tem.

The Moderator pro tem. then said: It is my duty to remind the Assembly that they are about to sit in a judicial capacity, and to enjoin members to remember their high character as a Court of Jesus Christ. The first business is to hear the reading of the sentence appealed from.

Rev. Dr. R. J. Breckinridge desired to say as one of the parties interested in this case, that there were preliminary matters which it would be necessary to settle before entering upon a trial of the case. They desired to know first who were the parties to respond, because it would very materially affect their mode of proceeding in opening and continuing the case. The proceedings were in their nature double, and it was as much for the convenience of the court as for the substantial administration of justice that the two cases should be tried together. In the first aspect of the case they complained of a tribunal and the manner in which they conducted business, and he desired to say he intended to press the severe censure of this house upon that tribunal. The Synod of Kentucky was the party complained of. In regard to the signers of the Declaration and Testimony, also complained against, their declinature of further attendance upon this house would not prevent either of them from appearing here during the trial of the case, just as much as though they were members. What he now desired was, to know who of the members of the Synod appear for the Synod. The majority and minority of the Synod were both entitled to be heard, and he desired to know who and how many on each side of the majority and minority were present. He knew of no way of getting at it except the house deciding it.

The Moderator pro tem. stated the question was whether the house would consent to try the several appeals together, according to the recommendation of the Judicial Committee.

Mr. Davidson moved that they be tried together.

Rev. Dr. Breckinridge said there was another party to the case—the parties who signed the Declaration and Testimony. The thing had all through a double aspect—first, leveled against the Synod for its mode of proceeding, and against the parties for their course of conduct. Suggestions had been made to coerce these trials to the alternative of either being appeals or complaints. He resisted it and he would say now, as he had said before, that there were other points that were in doubt. He would say now, for the purpose of disabusing the minds of the brethren, that if he and his colleagues were not allowed to try this case, so as to get substantial justice, and so that it would be final when it was finished, he did not care about trying it all. At his time of life, he had no idea of running about from Kentucky and back again to try fancy cases. If the Assembly should come to the conclusion that it could not be tried in the manner indicated, then it was tantamount to protecting parties who would ruin the Synod of Kentucky, if let alone.

Rev. Dr. Humphreys said he wished to speak for a moment, as to whether these two cases should be tried together. He wished to say—first, that the Synod of Kentucky neglected, by an oversight, he supposed, to appoint a committee to defend them against this complaint; it was therefore left with the majority here to defend the action of the Synod as best they might. Whether they shall be heard as the original parties, or whether they would be heard when the members of the inferior judicatory were called on, was an important question which he desired to submit. They expected to contend, that in the first place the appeal could not lie; in the second case they admitted that these brethren had a right to bring the matter by way of appeal and complaint. There were some of them who were in the majority in the first case in rejecting Dr. Breckinridge's preliminary motion, but were in the minority in the second case. He (the speaker) voted against the resolution of Dr. Breckinridge, and therefore would be bound to answer to this venerable court; but he voted also against the motion of which he complains and was with him in the minority. They would see from this statement, that if these two cases were tried together, he and others would be placed in an anomalous condition.

Dr. Breckinridge obtained the floor.

Rev. Mr. Ferguson raised a point of order. On last Friday, a man by the name of Boyd stood before them in an appeal case, and they would not allow him to speak. To-day, a man named Breckinridge was before them, and he was allowed to speak.

The Moderator, pro tem. The appellant has a right to explain the state of the case.

Rev. Mr. Ferguson. It was not permitted in the other case.

The Moderator, pro tem. The Chair knows nothing of that case.

Rev. Dr. Breckinridge said he had not a word to say that was disagreeable, but he would decline a trial of the case unless it could be tried in a way by which a decision would be a decision when it was reached. This case was before the Synod of Kentucky in three forms, and there he moved in making up the roll that these gentlemen should not be allowed to constitute a part of that body. His object was that when the parties were tried, and convicted in the face of the Synod, it should carry with it a decision that they were no longer either competent or fit to perform any functions in the Presbyterian Church. That was the first appeal, and exactly what this court had to decide, and that was what Dr. Humphrey, with great candor, had acknowledged he had voted against. Then there came up an intermediate case upon the motion of another minister, in reference to the Declaration and Testimony; this the Synod refused to touch. The paper was ruled out but subsequently came up in another way and was passed, condemning in extremely gentle terms, compared with what was deserved, what these gentlemen had done. All who were complainants here voted for that paper, and by reason of this it was passed by a small majority. It was a combination of what were called loyal men and middle men against the extreme Southern sympathizers; and the latter were beaten. When the trial was gone into of McMillan against the Presbytery of Louisville for adopting this thing, the gentlemen who were on trial, drew up, signed and filed, a paper, in which they denied the jurisdiction of the body in that case. From that he (the speaker) made a second appeal and complaint against them, on the ground that they had shown the animus of the acts complained of in the first appeal; whereupon, the Synod, after a little while, broke the trial off in the midst of it, and postponed it for another year. They had gone so far as to begin to be ready to call for the decision of the body by the votes of the members. On that vote Dr. Humphrey now states that he voted against the postponement, and might have been one of the appellants but is not. He did not see that the gentleman's objection altered the case at all, even if it did put him and other gentlemen in an awkward fix. There was no incongruity in the Synod having gentlemen to defend her, in those matters wherein they agree with her, and other gentlemen defend her wherein the first disagree with her. The difficulty, however, would have been more easily removed if Dr. Humphrey had taken the same view with the rest of them. He repeated that the ends of substantial justice could not be reached unless the cases could be tried together. If they were to separate them, and force a trial of one part and then another, it might only end in a decision that the first case is a grave offense but not adequate to the punishment which both offenses committed by the same men before the same body and under the same proceedings would render it necessary to impose upon them. So with the second one; though a very grave offense, it is more grave when it is considered as a part of a premeditated course, and not as an isolated transaction. The whole of this thing was about the Declaration and Testimony, and the gentlemen who issued that paper, and also the action of the Synod on the various parts of it. He contended further that if they separated the cases it would put them in a position where their judgment would be rendered by piecemeal, and no such judgment would cover the questions involved in the sum total. They might say these gentlemen had done nothing more than to deserve simple condemnation; if so, that wes the end. But if they put the whole together, it would amount to a grave offense, requiring grave censure. He did not desire that this Assembly should blow, and then burn and burn and then blow, and keep this thing vacillating from year to year, and never reaching anything definite. He would have nothing to do with any such proceeding as that. For example, it would be plead here that the complaint did not bring the parties to the bar of the house in any form. If they would look at the Digest, under Appeals and Complaints, they would find that a negative decision could be appealed from. After citing various decisions from the Digest, the speaker concluded by saying that if they limited the motion of appeal to purely personal questions, then they would deny that any one had a right to appeal in a personal question except he were a party to the transaction; and if they gave that cast-iron form of interpreiation to this matter, then it would be wholly irregular; but he imagined there was not a decision in the existence of the Church that bore out the principle of the decision in the Metcalf case in 1839, and that hundreds of cases could be found, where appeals had been allowed and tried, where the thing was in no sense personal. He appealed to them again to settle this question decisively, and not begin the business by cutting off the hair of Sampson and then tying him with wythes.

Rev. Dr. Smith desired to know whether it would not be better to refer the matter back to the Judicial Committee, and ask these parties to appear before them, whereby they could agree upon some form by which both cases could be brought before the house.

Rev. Dr. West said he did not understand, that in the trying of these cases together, any violation would be inflicted upon the parties. As he understood Dr. Humphrey's objection, it was simply as to the interpretation of the law, and whether an appeal could come from the Presbytery of Louisville. A motion was made in the Presbytery of Louisville, that certain brethren were unqualified to sit in the house, An appeal was taken therefrom, and it was argued by Dr. Humphrey that this appeal could not lie because it was not judicially tried. In reference to that matter the decision in the Metcalf case had been alluded to, but in the minutes of 1841, and for years afterward, they could find a counter decision of the General Assembly affirming the very opposite what was reported in the Metcalf case, namely, that appeals can lie where there has not been a formal, forensic, judicial trial. As to the original parties in this question, it struck him that one of the original parties was left out; that really the Presbytery of Louisville and Dr. Breckinridge were the original parties.

Dr. Boardman said he had no particular objection to the view of the brother, but if the Presbytery of Louisville was one of the original parties, they were absolutely bound from the adjudication of this case, for they had no right to send one of the original parties out of the house, and then take up and try any issue with which they were concerned.

Rev. Dr. West said the parties were not out of the house in reference to this case. That sophism, if he might be permitted to use the expression, was argued and answered a hundred times in 1837, and what amazed him was, that the brethren who fought in those days for the principles advocated in this conflict, were the brethren who are now turning round and making use, as he would have opportunity to show, of every argument that was made by the opposition in 1837.

Mr. Clark, of Detroit, said that he understood from Dr. Humphrey's objection that these two appeals could not be heard together, because some of the parties would occupy a different attitude in the one from what they would in the other.

Rev. Dr. Humphrey said he was not here as an appellant, but merely to say what his personal relation was to the case appealed.

Mr. Clark said he should be sorry to have this house decide that it cannot do what any court of law can do. In a court of law, when two cases are substantially the same, together with the parties and the questions to be tried, it was a common motion to move that the court consolidate the two cases. His theory of the government of the Church was, that this General Assembly had every power which any court could execise, except so far as it was restrained by the Book of Discipline, and they were not restrained from uniting cases. One of the original parties, it was said, was the Presbytery of Louisville, and they could not try the Presbytery of Louisville, it was said, because they were out of the house. Was the Presbytery of Louisville any more out of the house than Dr. Breckinridge.

Dr. R. J. Breckinridge desired to explain. These gentlemen were arguing the point on the theoretical aspect of the case, derived from the purview of the minutes. If they would carefully examine the complaint, it would be seen that the Presbytery of Louisville never occurs without an explanation. It was distinctly understood at the time that these gentlemen were a minority of the Presbytery of Louisville; but it was alleged that it was a casual minority. That did not prove to be true, but that was his understanding, and in consequence of that it was carefully forborne to assail the Presbytery of Louisville, as believing that it was not involved in the case. They never were, in point of fact, whatever they might be in point of law, on trial.

Mr. Clark said perhaps he would have done better if he had fully understood this part of the question at first.

Dr. Breckinridge said he ought to have made the statement when Dr. Boardman alluded to it, but he felt sheepish about it, and did not do it. [Laughter.]

Mr. Clark. Whether the Presbytery of Louisville should be held as a party or not, their minds ought to be clear on this point; that if that Presbytery should be called before the house for flaunting their declarations before them in a defiant manner, there was no reason why that Presbytery could not come to the bar and answer the same as Dr. Breckinridge or any other party.

Mr. Cain desired to know in reference to the consolidation of cases in Court, whether it was ever done without consent of parties.

Mr. Clark. Often.

Mr. Cain. Suppose the parties state in Court their interests will be prejudiced. Is it a rule for the Court to consolidate?

Mr. Clark said in that case, the Court would hear the arguments, and consolidate or not, as in its judgment it might deem best.

Mr. Cain asked if, upon the affidavit of the party, the Court would not grant a severance.

Mr. Clark said it was often done.

Mr. Cain desired to know what the difference was between carrying a case from the Legislature to the Supreme Court, and the carrying a case from a subordinate Court to the Supreme Court—by what process did they bring a case from a subordinate Court to a superior Court? The simple question in this case, as he apprehended, was whether the Synod of Kentucky was acting in its judicial or legislative capacity. If acting in a legislative capacity, then the maner in which they would bring the action of that body into this Court, would be by complaint; but if they were acting in a judicial capacity, then by appeal, and he apprehended that here the issue between the parties was joined, and that this should have been in the form of a complaint. An appeal clearly implied judicial functions, and how was it possible to carry by an appeal anything to a higher Court, which is not traversed by the Court below? An appeal carries with it an idea of the exercise of judicial functions; therefore, if this was an appeal, they had before them clearly the idea that that Synod had been acting as a Court.

Mr. Clark desired to say that in all the Constitutions of the United States and in the Constitution of the United States itself, the Supreme Court and Legislature are everywhere declared to be co-ordinate powers, and therefore a case could never go from a legislative body to a court. It was not so in this case. Synods, Presbyteries and sessions to some extent have powers that can be allied to legislative powers, but the system of review and control comes in here, and the Presbyterian courts can do that which cannot be done in a court of common law.

Mr. Day doubted much whether the mode under which they were proceeding was a proper and constitutional mode, although he would acknowledge this was a vile thing that was done by the Presbytery of Louisville.

Rev. Mr. Sharon, as one of the Judicial Committee, stated the manner in which the case came up. He did not see anything to prevent the consolidation of the cases and trying them together. The moment they commenced to trace analogies between civil and religious courts they would get into difficulty. All there was to govern a case of appeal and complaint must be regulated by the action and custom of the General Assembly as a court. As to the idea that the Louisville Presbytery was out of the house, if he might be permitted to use the expression, it was an arrant humbug.

Mr. Day offered as an amendment, that the evidence taken shall apply to both cases, but that when the roll is called parties shall have the right to render judgment separately. The amendment was not seconded.

The vote was then taken on the question as to whether the two cases should be tried together, and it was agreed to.

A discussion then arose as to who were properly the defendants in the case, and finally

Rev. Dr. McLean moved that the Synod of Kentucky be regarded as the other party.

At the request of Dr. Gurley the appeals in the cases were then read for information, as follows:

IN SYNOD AT LOUISVILLE, KY., October, 1865.

This appeal and complaint of Robert J. Breckinridge and others, against the several acts of the Synod of Kentucky, in the matters appearing on the records of the Presbytery of Louisville at its recent session, and in matters contained in a certain printed and published paper entitled "Declaration and Testimony" &c, is for the purpose of bringing before the General Assembly of the Church all the acts and doings of the Synod of Kentucky, and the Presbytery of Louisville, and the makers, signers, and publishers of the said Declaration, and Memorial in the premises, in the fullest and most ample manner, that all the subjects, and all the parties be brought before the said General Assembly. And the object of doing this is, that the General Assembly may redress the wrongs done, and the neglects of duty deliberately committed by the said Synod, and by a casual majority of said Presbytery—and that it may censure, as its righteous judgment may deem proper, the sinful acts of the parties brought before the Synod by a minute proposed to it by the said Robert J. Breckinridge, and rejected by the Synod, in part by the votes of the parties engaged. And the reasons of this appeal and complaint, are the same reasons stated in the paper above mentioned of Robert J. Breckinridge offered to Synod, together with the further reasons that the purity, peace and continued prosperous existence of Presbyterianism in the bounds of the Synod of Kentucky demands the early and effective interposition of the General Assembly, in the way of direct action both upon the individual office-bearers, who are in avowed contempt and rebellion against the authority of the Church and against its teachings, and upon Church courts who not only neglect to censure such rebellion, disorder, heresy and schism, but openly connive at the existence thereof; wherefor this appeal and complaint in open Synod.

Signed by ROBERT J. BRECKINRIDGE,
And others.

This appeal and complaint of the undersigned members of the Synod of Kentucky against certain acts of that court, in the matter of the appeal and complaint of J. P. McMillan against the Presbytery of Louisville, then defending before the Synod, is for the purpose of bringing before the General Assembly the said Synod and its said acts of record in the premises, and of bringing likewise before the Assembly the conduct of certain members of the Presbytery of Louisville, acting in Synod in the name of the Presbytery of Louisville, which conduct the Synod, instead of censuring as it deserved, gave efficacy to by allowing it not only to pass without any disapproving notice, but by immediately postponing, till the next annual meeting of the Synod, the case of McMillan against the Presbytery of Louisville, then already advanced to the fourth stage of actual trial prescribed in the standards of the Church. The members of the Presbytery of Louisville designed to be reached by this proceeding, are those twenty individuals whose names are signed to a paper laid before the Synod, when the Presbytery complained of was called on to respond to the complainant of McMillan—which paper is part of the record in this case, and is made part of this appeal and complaint. And the effect, as to those twenty persons, of this proceeding on their part, and the censure, if any, proper to be inflicted on them; therefore, the Assembly is prayed to determine and adjudge. And the nature and deserts of the conduct of the Synod by the Presbytery of Louisville in breaking up the trial in the midst, upon the filing of said written declaration by said twenty persons—thus giving a year's further time for the working of mischief in our Church and all our congregations, by the heretical and rebellious "Declaration and Testimony, &c.," against which McMillan's complaint was being tried, is what the Assembly is also prayed to determine, adjure and correct. The Synod refused, in the first place, to do anything touching the persons of the parties engaged in organized disturbance of the Church and rebellion against its authority; and the appeal and complaint of Robert J. Breckinridge and others was taken from that action, as is placed to be tried by the Assembly, in connection with this appeal and complaint against the third proceeding of the Synod, in refusing, as hereinbefore set forth, to try and adjudge the matters contained in said "Deliverance and Testimony." In the second action of the Synod in the matter of the general disturbance created by that "Deliverance and Testimony," its authors, though it condemned, by the aid of those making this and the former appeal and complaint, acts and proposals of that heretical and rebellious publication and its authors. It refuses to do even this much, unless in connection with such measures of simultaneous action against the acts of the General Assembly for five years past, as was clearly indicative of the views and intentions which controlled the acts of the Synod, which are the special ground of this appeal and complaint, and for the reasons, and with the objects, and to correct the great evils hereinbefore set forth in this appeal and complaint to the General Assembly.

In Synod at Louisville, Ky., Oct. 2[illegible], 1865.

ROBERT J. BRECKINRIDGE and others.

Dr. William Breckinridge said he was a member of the Synod of Kentucky, but he had never been a party to this matter, further than that, as a member of that Synod, he voted against a single resolution. The Book of Discipline declared that they should hear the original parties to an appeal. He had nothing to do with the original parties, and there were none here except the appellants. He hoped the unreasonableness of the motion to make the Synod of Kentucky an original party would be understood.

Without coming to any decision on the motion the Assembly adjourned to three and a half o'clock.

AFTERNOON SESSION.

The Moderator called the Assembly to order.

Rev. Dr. Gurley, from the committee to convey salutations from the Assembly to the New School Assembly, made the following report:

The committee appointed to convey the salutations of this body to the Assembly holding its sessions in the First Presbyterian Church, report that they have discharged the duty assigned them; that their reception by that Assembly was eminently kind and fraternal; and that the response made to the salutations of this Assembly was of a character suited greatly to encourage the hope that at no very distant day these two branches of the great Presbyterian family will become organically one; all which is respectfully submitted. P. D. GURLEY,
LINCOLN CLARK,
Committee.

The Chairman of Committee on Synodical Records reported the following as approved: Illinois, Indiana, Northern Indiana and Wisconsin—save a few pages of the latter, where there is a neglect to state that the Synod adjourned with prayer.

Mr. Galloway moved that the judicial case in regard to the Synod of Kentucky be recommitted to the Judicial Committee, with instructions to report a fuller and clearer statement of its nature and condition, and especially to describe the parties in the case.

Dr. Gurley hoped the motion would not prevail. There were two appeals and complaints. One originated in the Synod of Kentucky; in the other Dr. Breckinridge introduced a paper touching the status of gentlemen who had signed the Declaration and Testimony, which he had urged the Synod to adopt. They refused, and from that decision he appeals. There can be no doubt but that Dr Breckinridge and the Synod of Kentucky are the parties in that case. There is another appeal or complaint. Mr. McMillan appeals from the Presbytery of Louisville, in the Synod of Kentucky, and the matter of that appeal is very much the same as is contained in the paper of Dr. Breckinridge. The Synod towards the close of its session, after they had refused to adopt Dr. Breckingridge's paper, and after they had adopted a paper of their own on the same subject, took up this case and deferred adjudicating it until the next meeting of the Synod. Dr. Breckinridge appealed from that decision. The simple issue in this case is between Dr. Breckinridge and the Synod. The Judicial Committee has thought that the parties in this case are manifestly the Synod of Kentucky and Dr. Breckinridge, and that the Presbytery of Louisville has no connection with the issue now to be tried. Their case is still pending before the Synod of Kentucky.

Mr. Galloway said that was a clear statement, and if it had been made sooner it would have saved much speaking. He thought, however, the case should be referred. The issues involved were substantially the same. The offending party was the Louisville Presbytery. Dr. Breckinridge desired to have the Synod of Kentucky visited with proper condemnation for not acting as they ought to have done. His sympathies were with Dr. B., but they had had about enough of Kentucky before the Assembly and he wanted to dispose of one case before they took up another. He believed, if the report of the committee in reference to the Louisville Presbytery was adopted, the house would be satisfied.

Dr. Boardman said there was another consideration why the report of the Committee on the Louisville Presbytery should first be taken up, viz: That in all deliberate bodies questions pertaining to the personal rights of the members of the house had precedence.

Dr. Breckinridge asked to be permitted to make a personal explanation.

The Moderator decided that he was not in order, not being a member of the Assembly.

Dr. Breckinridge remarked that the Moderator had a singular facility of deciding one way at one time and another way at another time.

Rev. Rr. Anderson. I rise to a point of order.

Dr. Breckinridge. *You* rise to a point of order!

The Moderator stated that he had already decided that Dr. Breckinridge was not entitled to the floor.

Dr. Breckinridge. Well, sir, when I am browbeaten in the Assembly, first by the Moderator, and then by a traitor, I have nothing more to say.

The Moderator. I should have made this decision in respect to any other member.

Mr. Day moved that Dr. Breckinridge be allowed to make his statement. It was due to him on account of his age and reputation that he should be allowed to state his objections at being thus turned out.

The Moderator. There is no disposition to turn him out. The question is simply on instructing the committee on certain points.

Mr. Day. I meant by turning him out, turning him over.

Rev. Dr. West inquired whether or not Dr. Krebs ought to be in the chair.

The Moderator stated that if the Assembly were sitting in a judicial capacity Dr. Krebs would occupy the chair.

Rev. Mr. Grimes said ordinarily he would vote for the motion, but as Dr. Breckinridge had insulted the Moderator and then branded one of the members as a traitor, he should oppose it, believing the dignity of the body required it.

Dr. McLean said no one desired to hear Dr. Breckinridge more than himself, and by referring this to the Judicial Committee they by no means put an end to this matter; it was simply a matter of convenience. They were now in a position to go on with a report of the committee, and when that was disposed of they could take up this case and finish it.

Rev. Mr. Ferguson felt that they should not grant Dr. Breckinridge, with all his dignity, power and greatness, a hearing on this occasion. If brethren were very anxious to hear him, they could hear him from the steps of the church. He made a motion this morning that they should not hear him in the half hour that they did. It was through the courtesy of the house that he spoke, and he thought that he transgressed on their patience.

Rev. Dr. Anderson. I rise to a privileged question. I, sir, when the Moderator was informed by a person not of this body that he had a facility in deciding first on one side and then on the other, rose to a point of order, and the point of order I aimed to make was, that our Moderator could not be insulted, either by a member or by one who was here as an appellant. The answer to that was a repetition of the insult to our presiding officer, and the application to me of an epithet which I will not bear. I was called a traitor. I stand here, sir, to say—and I wish to be heard by every person in this Assembly—that I here pronounce that statement as false and slanderous.

The Moderator. I am requested to state on behalf of Dr. Breckinridge that he wished to make a personal explanation. The vote was taken and the motion to permit Dr. Breckinridge to make a personal explanation was lost.

The Moderator then vacated the Chair. Dr. Krebs took possession of it, and the judicial case in regard to the Synod of Kentucky was taken up.

In response to an inquiry of Dr. Humphrey, the Moderator pro tem. decided that the Synod of Kentucky could be heard as members of an inferior judicatory. After the reading of the papers in the case according to the Book of Dicipline, the Moderator pro tem. said the next stage in the proceedings was to inquire who were the parties. There being no response, Dr. Stanton came forward and said there was an arrangement on the part of the appellant, by which he should speak first. He continued: I have concluded, sir, as there are four persons present as appellants, beside myself, to take no part in the case for reasons which may appear obvious.

Dr. Breckinridge. I have an explanation which I would like to make, if I am at liberty to do so. By an arrangement by three appellants of this case, the work mutually assigned to them was, as it regards Dr. Stanton, that which he now refuses to perform, and says it is for reasons that are obvious. Of that each one may judge for himself. For my part I am not surprised that he does so. I had my doubts always whether he would do it. His having failed to do the part assigned him, renders it impossible for anybody else to do it, because it was the development of the testimony and the settling of the question as to which is the testimony, which is an extremely difficult question. Three days were spent in reading the papers, but there was no part of it that was in a proper sense testimony, except the reading of the Declaration and Testimony. It occurred to me that it would be a very great burden upon the Assembly to spend six or seven hours upon this work; and I therefore personally requested Dr. Stanton, who agreed to it, to make an analysis of it, both as to matters that fall under the head of a general rebellion against the Church, and as to matters that were *ex delictoe*, wrong in themselves, and to lay that paper, as a part of the case, before the Assembly; which paper I think was drawn up, for I know I had a copy of it. It did not occur to me that when a man was tried for the contents of a book, as for example, Mr. Barnes, on which trial I happened to sit, that the whole book had to be read. Some books are very large as well as very empty. I supposed that the order of the court would be, that having the pamphlet before it, any part of it could be read that was demanded, and then having a syllibus of the points relied on the book, it would be like a demurrer. In one respect it would confess they had nothing to allege against the bearings of the paper. If they did not choose to take it in that form, it was their own option, that they have the paper read. We decided that was the best we could do—put them in possession of the things complained of. Dr. Stanton has declined to do his part, and I think for very obvious reasons, but not the reasons that he alludes to. It is obvious to you that, with a perfect understanding of so many signers of that part of the complaint, having had anything to do with it, nobody is prepared to supply this deficiency. Dr. Landis was to do another service in the case as one of its original complainants, and I was to do another, ordering it in such a way, that while we presented the case fully, we might not weary the patience of the body. All the balance that was read as testimony, as far as my memory now serves me, was law—an attempt on our part briefly to lay down the law from the books of the Church. The case, for instance, of the original protest in 1861, in which you will find the seeds of nearly all the arguments that have been brought against the action of the Church from that day to this; and which, as it has been most elaborately and with unprecedented ability discussed, in a series of articles by Dr. West in the Presbyterian, I shall not attempt to analyze here, even if I were going into the case, which I am not. My judgment is, that by reading the sylabus that has been made, and having the paper before as accessible to the house, it is all sufficient for justice to both sides.

I wish to make one slight explanation here, on the action of 1861, and my connection with it. I had made an explanation upon a protest against that action, which was drawn up with great ability, and which contained all the heresy and all the treason that has been preached in the Church on that subject, in its germ. I do not mean to say who are traitors. In regard to my brother who took such high dudgeon in regard to a plain truth, there are some other small matters of much more recent date, which I may take occasion to allude to hereafter. I understand that fighting means death, and therefore I never fight if I can help it, and I never give unnecessaray offense, which everybody will tell you that has quarreled with me, and that aint a few. [Laughter.] Dr. Humphrey and myself and two elders that are here present on this floor, agreed upon a report to the Synod, which was adopted with an amendment, that the Synod did not approve of that act. Neither did I, and I gave my reasons for it in my report to Synod. The reason was this: I attempted to supply a defect in the act of 1862, which I drew up in the Assembly of 1862. My judgment is that the duty of loyalty is a relative duty, and the Government is as much bound to protect the man of whom it requires loyalty, as the man is to be loyal to the Government whose protection he seeks. The act of 1861 indiscriminately laid upon the whole church, the duty of a day of prayer for the Government—a duty of patriotism, but a duty in the performance of which, every man in the seceded States was bound to lay down his life in obedience to the General Assembly. I knew it, and the Assembly might have known it. If they did not do this they were liable to have their property confiscated and their lives forfeited. Well, I thought it was a case which the Assembly ought to have remembered, and therefore, in drawing up the minutes of 1862, I endeavored to see to it that every man had distributed to him things new and old according to his proportion. As for loyalty, if there was any man in this world that was loyal, I reckon I ought to be counted in that category. God knows I have suffered out of the Church and in the Church, and to-day I have the indignity heaped upon me of being refused to make a personal explanation, for that was all I wanted But I was speaking in deference to that minute. I have been charged from that day to this with being disloyal, and two people have done it on this platform since I have been here. I had compassion on their ignorance and said nothing. When it was brought into this house brother Humphrey moved to amend this language, which he said was contrary to reason and the Word of God, I was extremely anxious to preserve that Synod in peace, so that when we were done with war we might go and do our work, no matter which party triumphed I reckon I erred in that respect, for I stood where I ought not to have stood. I found I had finally to perish or fight somewhere; then as far as I could by myself, I commenced this fight which I see is being lost here to-day, and which, if lost, I shall hold this Assembly responsible to the country and God for its being lost—lost by the mismanagement of its friends, and by the betrayal of its cause by the Moderator. Now interrupt me if you like [andressing Dr. Anderson.]

Rev. Dr. Anderson. I do not intend that the dignity of this house shall be insulted.

Dr. Breckinridge. I beg pardon, I would as soon think of boxing the jaws of my venerable mother, after calling her back from the grave, as to insult this Assembly.

The Moderator, *pro tem.* It is the province of the Chair to restrain any member from personal reflections.

Dr. Breckinridge. I have said the worst I intended to say.

Rev. Dr. Anderson. I am prepared for any revelations that may be made here or elsewhere.

Dr. Breckinridge. Well, sir, I think you are prepared for most anything, by what you have done heretofore.

The Moderator. The gentleman must not indulge in personal reflections.

Dr. Breckinridge. Well, sir, I want to go on with what little voice I have left. I am a very bad subject to be browbeaten. I am done, and will now take back as much as possible. I only desire to say that is the history of that act of 1861 in connection with me. Now you will find these papers bearing clear back to the act of 1861. Therefore, on that I have nothing further to say. So far as this case is concerned, as I understand it, it is now in a posture that it cannot be issued. It has been put into the hands of a court which has been sworn. It is not in the possession of the house as a legislative body. It has been made the special order, and was directed to be proceeded with. I suggested to the Moderator that we had better go on with our business. He said it was the habit to do so. Then somebody brought up this other case which had no right to supersede this case. This case had been delivered to the court; the court had been sworn, and there was another presiding officer, and yet the other business was proceeded with, and when I got up, merely to make a personal explanation, I was told I could take no part in the case in that condition of it. I did not recognize it to be before the tribunal in that form. I think clearly and manifestly it was not, and what astonished me, when I rose to say this much, I was ordered to sit down; and what surprised me still more was, that the brother before me should jump up and help the Moderator with a point of order.

Dr. Breckinridge continued at some length in vindication of his course, and at the conclusion of his remarks, the Assembly adjourned.

TENTH DAY—TUESDAY, MAY 29, 1866.

The Assembly met at the usual hour.

The minutes of yesterday were read.

Rev. Dr. West moved to amend the minutes so as to make it appear that under the decision of the House, as to who the original parties were of the judicial case from Kentucky, Dr. Breckinridge declined to plead

Rev. Dr. Nevins moved an amendment to the amendment. He happened to remember the very words with which Dr. Breckinridge closed his speech, which were that on account of the form in which this matter was presented before the Assembly his self-respect would not permit him to argue the merits of the case. He (Dr. N.) moved to insert that he declined to argue the case on account of the form in which it was presented before the Assembly.

Rev. Dr. West desired that this house should not assume the responsibility of driving Dr. Breckinridge from the case, as the minutes would seem to imply.

Mr. Swallow moved that the amendments be laid upon the table. The motion was lost.

Mr Swallow then said he hoped the motion to amend would not prevail. He thought if they assigned all the reasons given by Dr. Breckenridge why he did not prosecute the case, they would have to assign eight or ten which were given in the course of his speech.

During the remarks of Mr. Swallow a demand was made for the question, whereupon a member arose, and said he hoped the speaker would not be interrupted, as he was talking as good sense as any other gentleman.

Mr. Swallow resumed his remarks, saying there were certain gentlemen who took it upon themselves to be the teachers of the Assembly—that he had said all that he desired to say, and he was perfectly willing those gentlemen who were so fond of teaching the Assembly, should go on and instruct them to the end.

Dr. McLean desired to know if it was in order to refer the matter to a committee. He moved to refer the matter to prepare a minute.

Mr. Day thought the clerk was able to keep the minutes properly, and he thought the minute in the case was proper. It did not attempt to assign all the reasons, and the reasons could not be assigned without a reference to the whole speech. It would not be fair to omit one reason and insert others, and it was not proper, he thought, to give all the reasons that Dr. Breckinridge gave. The old gentleman was in some respects under excitement, and they might well pardon him; but he said things which the speaker thought were censurable, and if compelled to do so he should be obliged to vote to that effect.

A motion was made for the previous question, which was agreed to.

The question then being on approving the minutes as read, a vote was taken and the minutes approved.

The following report of the Committee on the Narrative was adopted:

Fathers and Brethren: Your Committee on the Narrative of the state of religion in the Church, made the following report:

We have received narratives of religion, more or less full—some far too extended and diffuse, others much too meagre and unsatisfactory. From 90 of the 130 Presbyteries connected with the General Assembly, including one of the Presbyteries in China, the Presbytery of California, within whose bounds are many thousand Chinese, and the synod of northern India; and. having examined them, feel that the Church has most abundant reason to thank God and take courage. Nowhere does the word of the Lord seem to be going backward, and in many places it is evidently going forward gloriously.

From the reports, and from other sources, we learn that, notwithstanding the embarrassments and increased expenses consequent upon the high price of exchange, the Church has abandoned no work in heathen lands for the want of either men or money, and that detachment of faithful men and women have constantly been going forward to take the places of those who have fallen at their posts, or have been withdrawn because of failing health And there are encouraging indications throughout the heathen world that heathenism is being shaken, and will, ere long, be shaken to pieces and destroyed. What shall then follow we cannot say. There is, therefore, a loud call to the Church to send forward speedily more men to take advantage of these auspicious events for Jesus Christ.

Our frontier Presbyteries report progress. Not indeed such progress as we could wish, for but few of them report revivals, and all of them need much more money and many more men; but progress in the planting of new churches, in the strengthening of those already planted, and in the preaching of the Gospel in many new pioneer settlements in the wilderness

In the older States the older Presbyteries, with scarcely an exception, speak of revivals; many of them of revivals of great power, in which, in the aggregate, thousands of precious souls have been converted to Christ. Of the ninety-one Presbyteries that have sent up narratives seventy-two report revivals, and some of them state that nearly every one of their churches have shared in the blessed work. Your committee believes that outside of our great cities the revival of the past ecclesiastical year exceeds in universality and power that of 1857 and 1858. In the Presbyteries of Donegal, Clarion, Washington, New Brunswick. New Castle. West Jersey. Northumberland, Susquehannah, Red Stone, Chillicothe and St. Clairsvill. the power of the Spirit has been manifested in an especial and extraordinary manner In these, and in some other Presbyteries. the additions to many of the Churches have already been from fifty up to more than a hundred persons, and in a number of them the good work is still going forward In these revivings our schools and colleges and our female seminaries have shared largely. Hundreds of young men and young women in them have been converted, and it is reported that many of these Christian young men have devoted themselves to the work of the gospel ministry; not a few of them, including in their consecration the purpose, God willing, of preaching the Gospel to the heathen. In this connection your committee would call attention to the fact that nearly all of these revivals—certainly nine-tenths of them—began with or originated in the week of prayer at the beginning of the year, or the day of prayer for schools, colleges, etc , on the last Thursday of February.

It was feared by some that our disbanded and returned soldiers would bring with them to their homes and communities so many of the vices of the camp and the army as to make them the polluters of society and the scourges of the Church. But this fear, thank God! has not been realized to any considerable extent Some of the bad have, indeed, returned worse, and some of the good have become corrupted; but to counterbalance this, and far more than counterbalance it, hundreds, aye, thousands, who went into the army sinners, have returned from it Christians, and others have since become Christians. and others, in their increase in manliness and a spirit of obedience, give better promise than before of becoming good soldiers of Jesus Christ.

Another evidence of the presence of the sprit of God in the Church we see in this going forth of the hearts of our people toward visible union with other Christians, especially with those of our own faith and name. There seems to be a growing and strengthening desire with our people to get near to and into closer communion with those of other branches of the Presbyterian Church who hold with us the form of sound words The strong conviction of tens of thousands in the Church seems to be, that in the great fight in which we are engaged, and the greater fight before us with ritualism, rationalism, worldliness and ungodliness, those whose faith is the same, and whose Presbyterian banner is the same, should combine and make common cause for Jesus Christ. And the fact that we do not feel thus toward our aforetime brethren in the South. who. "partly by discipline and partly by their own act, have been removed from us," is not to be interpreted otherwise than in accordance with this conclusion; for our hearts go out warmly toward them, and could we see them cordially abandoning their two darling delusions—(shall we not say sins?)—slavery and rebellion, we would gladly welcome them back as brethren dearly beloved in the Lord.

Other grounds for encouragement and thankfulness we see in the facts that many of our churchss have paid off old Church debts; that many have largely increased the salaries of their pastors: that many are entering with increased zeal in the work of Sabbath school and Bible class instruction; that many are awaking to a duty of a stricter observance of the Sabbrth, and of a more determined resistance to the encroachments of profanity, intemperance, worldliness in professing Christians, and other crying evils of the times.

Of course there are discouragements; but these are patent to the eyes of all.

Upon the whole, in the judgment of your committee, the Church has reason to be devoutly grateful to the great Head of the Church. and to stir up herself to renewed consecration to Him, and to fresh energy and zeal in His blessed work.

So few, comparatively, of the Presbyteries have sent in reports on the subject of moneys, that your committee have nothing to say on the subject, save only as a most important matter to commend it to the consideration of the Church

FREDERICK A. BROWN, Chairman.

Mr. Lowin read the report of the Committee on Bills and Overtures.

Overture No. 14. Being a paper from the Presbyteries of Richland, Marion and Chicago, and the Rev. Messrs. T. D. Harris and L. J. Baird, D. D , relating to the general object of judicial cases.

The committee recommend,

1st. That the General Assembly appoint a committee of three ministers and three elders, to whom shall be intrusted the duty of preparing a new Book of Discipline, to be submitted to the General Assembly at such time as its careful and thorough preparation may require; the reports of former committees of the General Assembly on this subject to be placed in the hands of this committee for their consideration.

2d. That in the meantime, until this new Book of Discipline shall have received the approval of the Presbyteries, provision be made for the adjudication of judicial cases by the General Assembly, by sending to the Presbyteries for their approval or otherwise the following overture, viz:

1. The General Assembly, on the nomination of its standing Judicial Committee, may appoint from the members of the Assembly a judicial commission or judicial commissions as may be required to try during its sessions the judicial cases which may come before the Assembly; their proceedings and decisions to be subject to the approval of the Assembly.

2. These judicial commissions shall in their proceedings be governed by the constitutional provisions respecting judicial processes in so far as these may apply.

3. The change in the method of trying judicial cases heretofore in use which this Overture purposes, if adopted by a sufficient number of the Presbyters, shall govern the General Assembly of 1867 and its successors.

Rev. Dr. Pratt thought there should be appended to the paper the reasons for it, put in clear and forcible light.

Dr. Humphrey offered the amendment that after the words "sent down to the Presbyteries," the words "for their advice," in order to show the Presbyteries that it is not sent down for their approval, so that by their approval it may become a part of the Constitution, but simply for their advice to the next Assembly.

Dr. Lowrie thought Dr. Humphrey's amendment ought rather to be in the form of a substitute, and bad better take that shape. This was intended merely as a provisional system, to be in force only until the new book of discipline is finished.

Dr. Humphrey was pained to differ from Dr. Lowrie, but considered that a provisional amendment to our system was something unnatural It was to be remembered that there was before the Assembly the proposition for a permanent change in the system—the establishment of a Judicial Commission. He objected to any provisional changes.

Dr. Lowrie would defer very much to Dr. Humphrey's views, but it was understood that the proposition of Dr. Craven last year, alluded to by him, has not been adopted by the Church, it having been voted down by a vote more than two to one. He had no objection to sending it down for advice, but he thought it well to adopt it as a provisional measure until the book of discipline was completed.

The report of the Committee on the Overture was adopted.

Dr. Lowrie then read report of the Committee on Overture, No. 15, as follows:

Overture 15. Lake Presbytery to the General Assembly. Extract from the minutes, April, 1866:

Resolved, That this Presbytery do overture the next General Assembly requesting answers to the following questions, viz:

What is the duty of a church session in a case where a member of the Church has married and continues to live with a person who has been divorced from a husband or wife, on grounds other than of adultery or willful desertion.

A true extract. H. L. VANNESS, Stated Clerk.

The Assembly cannot give any other answer to this question than that contained in chapter XXIV, sec. VI, of the Confession of Faith, and chapter XIX, 9, 11, of the Gospel of Matthew. Nor does it think any further answer necessary.

Report adopted.

Dr. Lowrie then read report of Committee on Overture No. 16, as follows:

Overture No. 16. At a meeting of the Committee of Church extension within the bounds of the Presbytery of Potomac, held May 3, 1866, it was, on motion of Rev. A. A. E. Taylor, unanimously

Resolved, That this committee overture the General Assembly to transfer the property of the Metropolitan Church in this city to the Presbytery of Potomac, to be by said Presbytery applied to the purposes of Church extension in this city. LOUIS R FOX,

Secretary *pro tem.*

The committee recommend that this matter be referred to a committee of three members, to report to the next General Assembly. Adopted.

Dr. Gurley stated that property to the amount o $20,000 had been acquired for the purpose of erecting a Metropolitan Church in the city of Washington. When the war came on the subscriptions from the South amounted, as it was supposed, to a sum sufficient to erect the Church, and the first steps were taken in the erection of a lecture room. The war came on, and of course the enterprise was arrested, and all the subscriptions which were expected from the South were lost. The property now laid there useless. There was a loud demand for church extension in the city of Washington. There were three new enterprises on foot; two of these enterprises were greatly in need of larger houses of worship, and what the Committee on Church Erection desire, is, that if it be possible, this money collected for the purpose of erecting a Metropolitan Church may be transferred to the Presbytery of the Potomac, and used for the work of church extension in Washington City. What was desired, was that a committee be appointed to inquire into the whole matter, and report as to the practicability of making such a transfer, and also as to its desirableness, in their estimation, when all the facts were set forth. He hoped the report of the committee would be adopted.

Dr. Smith, of Baltimore, stated that he had taken a great deal of time in soliciting the money that had been collected for this object, and was acquainted with the facts in the case, and hoped that the report of the committee would be adopted.

Dr. Anderson reminded the Assembly that it was touching a matter of great delicacy. The law demanded integrity on the part of trustees. He knew how the money was given, at least some of it, and he thought the Assembly had no right to appropriate that money, even for a better purpose than that for which it was given. The trustees were bound to confine themselves to the purposes for which the trust was created. He desired to call the attention of those who were appointed upon the proposed committee particularly to that point.

The committee's report and recommendation upon this overture was adopted.

Dr. Thomas read the report of the Standing Committee on Domestic Missions. The report was accepted and placed on the docket for consideration, and was as follows:

The committee to whom was referred the annual report of the Board of Domestic Missions, respectfully present to the General Assembly the result of their inquiries into the great interest intrusted to their consideration.

This sixty-fourth report suggests reflections and awakens emotions of a mingled character. On the one hand it occasions gratitude to God that He has given us such an agency for spreading the glorious Gospel throughout our country; that He has permitted it to reach the sixty-fourth year of its operations; that He has allowed us so large a measure of success in the prosecution of our work; and especially that He has graciously revived many of our mission churches.

The Board, its officers and missionaries seem to have discharged their duty according to the standard of former years. To the 338 missionaries in commission in March, 1865, 201 co laborers have been added, making the whole number of home missionaries 539, or 36 more than in the former year. These missionaries supply nearly 800 churches or mission stations, embracing 22,500 communicants; of whom 2,330 were added during the year by letter, and 1,602 on examination. Three hundred and nineteen Sabbath schools are connected with these churches, including 3 240 teachers and 23,000 scholars. The aggregate receipts are:

From church collections........................	$68,034 20
From legacies..	65,263 38
From individual donors	10,993 76
In all..	$144,291 34

Or $20,915 16 above the receipts of any former year.

The facts afford matter of sincere thankfulness; yet, on the other hand, the aspect and results of our home missionary work, when compared with the ability of the Presbyterian Church, and with the singularly inviting and important field which Divine Providence has called her to occupy, cannot but occasion sorrow and humiliation. This sixty-fourth annual report exhibits the sad and shameful fact that our church collections for so noble a cause amount only to the paltry sum of $68,000; that is, to an average contribution of *twenty-nine* cents a member per annum. If we add the almost $11,000 received from individual donors, the average is still but *thirty-four* cents a year for each communicant. Of the 2,630 churches in our connection, 1,208, or nearly *one half*, contributed nothing to this Board during the past year. Well may the report say, in view of such statistics that the resources of our denomination are as yet very imperfectly developed

Another surprising and painful fact is this: that of our 800 Mission Churches or Stations—fewer than half, 379—report the existence of Sabbath-schools; and 45 of these Churches report that they have made no contributions to any of our Boards. We may add, in this connection, that the average increase of our Mission Churchis, notwithstanding reported revivals, is lamentably small. The aggregate additions of the last year were 3,932 communicants; 2,330 on profession, and 1,603 on certificate. Dividing these figures by the 539 home missionaries, we have an average of *seven* persons brought into the Church by a year's labor of each missionary—four on profession, and three by transfer of membership.

This result, indeed, must be modified by another statement of like painful character, viz: that 143 of our missionaries, or considerably more than one-fourth of the whole number, send the Board no report whatever of their yearly labors Surely this is an evil which demands a very prompt and decisive remedy.

The last Assembly directed special efforts to be made in behalf of freedmen, and to secure a footing among our seceded Southern Churches The Board may have done all that was in its power in accordance with this direction, but the result is far from satisfactory Thirteen Missionaries are reported as commissioned during the year to labor in the South; whether among freedmen, the white population, or both, this report does not enable us to say Nine of these are employed in North Carolina, Tennessee and Florida; two in Louisiana; two in Mississippi and Texas. Apparently, the only direct effort to reach our Southern Churches was made in Tennessee; but the attempt was a complete failure.

The suggestion of the last Assembly to substitute the term Home for Domestic, in the title of the Board, seems to have been overlooked or neglected.

This brief survey of the defects connected with our system of Home Missions recalls an inquiry presented in the report itself—"Cannot we attempt some enlarged movement?" (p 21.)

The Assembly of 1865, in considering overtures "asking the removal of the Board of Domestic Missions and the Board of Education to points further West," recommended "that final action be postponed until the next meeting of the General Assembly." (minutes, p. 650] In the opinion of your committee, the time for "an enlarged movement" has fully come, and we respectfully suggest whether a removal of the Board, not to the West, but towards the center of our vast National domain, may not afford a favorable opportunity for such a movement

The old geographic classification and nomenclature of States, still adopted in the report of our Board, which looks from a Philadelphia standpoint, is unnatural and unmeaning. Recent events, and especially the abolition of slavery, have removed former distinctions. The sectional distribution of States, as Northern and Southern, should be obliterated. Our people should be taught to contemplate our vast Empire as one; to be regarded geographically, only in its grand, natural features. The territorial center of these United States is near Topeka, Kansas Why should Ohio, which is a thousand miles east of that center, be styled a Western State? True, it lies west of Pennsylvania, but it also lies east of the eight great States of Indiana, Illinois, Missouri, Kansas, Colorado, Utah, Nevada and California.

Considered in its natural outline, our country comprises three grand groups of States—the Pacific, the Atlantic, and the Central or Valley States. Anticipating some territorial division soon to be made, and overlooking the temporary difference of States and Territories, we have eight Pacific States, sixteen Atlantic, and twenty-four Central—forty-eight in all

The eight Pacific States have one million square miles and half a million of population; the Atlantic States have half a million of square miles and fifteen and a half millions of population; and the twenty-four Central States have one and a half millions of square miles and fifteen and a quarter millions of population.

In general terms, the twenty-four Central States include one half our territory; almost one half of our population, and more than three-fifths of our home missionaries.

The sixteen Atlantic States have one-sixth of our National territory; almost one-half of our population, and over three-tenths of our missionary force.

The eight Pacific States have one-third our territory; one-sixtieth of our population, with one-fortieth of our home missionaries.

Sixty-five years ago (say two generations) these Central States did not contain half a million of white inhabitants. Now their population exceeds fifteen million. Thirty years since Illinois had 100,000 people; now she numbers 1,700,000. The four States of Illinois, Wisconsin, Iowa and Minnesota have risen in the last thirty years from 200,000 to 3,250,000. We have now 40,000,000 of people in the United States. Within the lifetime of the younger members of this Assembly we shall have 100,000,000, of whom, according to past statistics, 10,000,000 will be men of color. And the vast majority of the white population, at least, will occupy these central States This vast and rapidly growing population speaks one language; is everywhere accessible; obeys, and shall obey, our Government, which protects and fosters religious worship and Christian labor. In the midst of such a nation Christ has placed his Church—our Presbyterian element no insignificant part of it—blessed with ample wealth and the highest facilities for co-operative Christian work; is He not gathering here in a fair field from all lands and of all religions a mighty mass of souls to try his Church, whether she will prove worthy of her sublime commission?

Contrast, now, with such a territory, and with such statistics of present and future population, an agency on the Atlantic seaboard raising less than $80,000 from 230 000 living Presbyterians, and ask whether we ought not to attempt an "enlarged movement!"

It is needless to present to such a body as this the many other considerations, derived from the kindred labors of sister churches, the vast and threatening tide of foreign emigration, the wide diffusion of Romanism, and like distinctive errors, the prevalence of infidelity, &c., which present themselves to every intelligent mind as reasons for a great invigoration of our missionary operations.

But the question is raised, Why must the seat of the Board be removed to effect that invigoration? We answer that if one chief agency can supervise and control the Home Missionary work, it would seem rational that its center of operations should be near the center of the wide region upon which it must operate: that the influence of such an agency may be felt alike in every part of the field. The immediate directors, especially the principal executive, must be brought into personal and vital contact with all subordinate instrumentalities The Secretary should have personal and constant intercourse, at least with all the provincial centers of support and co-operation. This indispensable influence can never be exerted while the seat of directors is placed in a remote corner of the land.

It may be said, indeed, whatever be the territorial position of the Board, it is all-important that it occupy the money-center of the Church. Now, it is true that the five Synods of Albany, Baltimore, New York, New Jersey and Philadelphia contributed to our home missions last year almost $45,000, or two-thirds of the whole amount from church collections, while the remaining twenty Synods gave less than $24,000. But let it be considered that of the $45,000 from the five Eastern Synods nearly $15,000, or one-third of the sum, came from four churches in the city of New York. If the money argument is conclusive, then this Board should center in New York City. The proper answer is this: First, that our country and church are one; the aim of our Church is to fill our country with the institutions of a pure Christianity, a pure Presbyterianism Whatever means may most efficiently promote that end should command the resources and energies of our entire body. The center of population is the most natural location of the power which is to reach that population; and that center, at present, lies between Jonesville and Columbus, Ohio. The money, come from where it may, will be most abundantly bestowed upon whatever agency is found to be the most efficient. Besides, as a regard for the interests of civil liberty locates the seat of our National

Government away from the monetary center of the country, so should a wise concern for the welfare of ecclesiastical liberty dissever the power of wealth from the direction of Church affairs

Your committee are further persuaded that the conduct of the work now entrusted to the Freedmen's Committee properly belongs to the Board of Missions. The colored element is but one constituent of our heterogeneous population. We see no more reason for dealing with it through an independent organization than for a similar course toward the foreign elements among us. We have no Irish Board, no German Board; why have a Board for colored Americans? Divine Providence has identified them with us. They will soon compose, as h as been said, one-tenth of our people. We can best secure their sympathies by treating them as we treat other men.

Your committee, therefore, recommend:

1. That the Freedmen's Committee be dissolved, and its work transferred to the Board of Home Missions

2. That the seat of the Board of Home Missions be removed to Cincinnati, as soon after the rising of the Assembly as it can be done without prejudice to vested interests in Philadelphia or elsewhere

3. That the Board, at its first meeting in Cincinnati, be directed to revise our whole system of Home Missions, and devise and adopt such measures as shall redouble the efficiency of our operations.

4. That a committee be appointed by the Assembly to secure a new charter for our Board of Missions from the Legislature of Ohio.

5. We recommend, that during the coming year all the Churches under the care of the General Assembly endeavor to raise for this Board a sum amounting to at least fifty cents for each member; and we most earnestly recommend that each pastor and stated supply shall not only see that an opportunity is afforded every member of his Church to contribute, but that he also urge upon every member the duty of bearing his part.

Dr. Thomas. I beg leave now respectfully to renew a motion that was made yesterday, that the unfinished business of yesterday—

Moderator. It is not open yet, sir. I did not know what you were about to propose Are there any other reports from standing committees?

The records of the Synod of Pittsburg were recommended to be approved. Recommendation adopted.

The records of the Synod of Cincinnati were recommended to be approved with certain exceptions. Adopted.

The Committee on Devotional Exercises recommended that Rev. F. P. Brown be appointed to preach this Tuesday evening at eight o'clock.

Rev. Mr. Shiland moved that the Assembly sit this evening and every evening until the business was completed; it was necessary the Assembly should finish its business and adjourn this week, if possible.

Dr. Thomas. I hope we shall not sit this evening. We are not bound to kill ourselves, and we shall arrive at surer conclusions if we take time. The Church has sent us here and given us time enough to do our work, and let us take the time.

Mr. Herron offered a substitute for the motion of Mr. Shiland which was accepted, and was as follows:

Resolved, That the Assembly reconsider the vote by which the time for closing the afternoon session was fixed at 5½ o'clock, and that 6½ o'clock be fixed as the hour for afternoon adjournment.

An amendment to this substitute was made, that the morning session commence at half past eight instead of nine.

The amendment was objected to for the reason that it would interfere with the elders' prayer meeting which commenced at eight o'clock and continued until nine.

A member thought if they attempted to cheat God out of His part of the proceedings of this Assembly they would fail of His blessing; that if one half of the time of the Assembly was spent in prayer to Almighty God for his guidance, it would but take half as long to do the work as it does now.

Dr. Boardman. I should not have opened my lips on this question if a remark had not been made upon the alleged or assumed necessity of the Assembly adjourning the present week. I hope this Assembly will adjourn when its work is done, and not before. We are here not to look after the interests of our own pastoral charges specifically, much less to attend to any private or personal, or domestic matters. We are here to care for the interests of the whole Presbytery Church, confided under God to our care and administration, and this is no ordinary session of the General Assembly. The consequences of our deliberations and measures here will reach far and wide, and I regret exceedingly to notice indications of impatience on the part of any member of the Assembly, when it must be perfectly apparent to every member who knows anything about it, that we have only this day reached the very threshold of the great questions upon which we are to pass. We have been engrossed—I take no part of the responsibility of that state of things upon myself—we have been engrossed with preliminary matters, with questions of method and order. We have had but one speech as yet, sir, on the merits of the great questions which in several distinct forms are proposed to be submitted to us for the interests of the Presbyterian Church for all time to come, to be passed upon by this General Assembly, and what are our personal affairs, our domestic claims, the interests of our particular congregations, when put into the scales against the mighty issues which are devolved upon this General Assembly.

The lines have fallen to us in pleasant places. I could imagine our being so situated as to afford one great motive for a prompt and early adjournment, but in our present circumstances, enjoying the great—may I not say—the unprecedented hospitality of this community—for I have seen nothing like it—there is everything in our external circumstances to conspire to the paramount obligations we owe to Christ and His Church, to sit here until our business is done; until these great principles have been thoroughly discussed and settled, for in no way can they be satisfactorily reviewed hereafter.

Rev. J. Addison Henry remarked that Dr. Boardman's advice to-day was a little different from that given by him to Mr. Galloway yesterday, when he told him that we could part with his company just as soon as he could leave us; and that given to him, when he, the speaker, in conversation with Dr. B., said that he wished the Assembly would hurry through with its business, as he wished to take a little trip—for Dr. B. then said he could part with him as soon as he saw fit to leave, and he had replied that though anxious to go, he should remain until the business of the Assembly was completed, though he might be induced to go if Dr. B. himself would leave: asserted that he should not leave the Assembly if it continued in session until the 4th of July; it might do some of the Assembly a great good to celebrate the 4th in this city. He did not see how any of the Assembly could go home to their constituents leaving the business of the Assembly incomplete.

Rev. Mr. Ferguson hoped the Assembly would continue here, without change in the times of meeting, and in a calm, dispassionate, and Christian manner, attend to the business before it.

The Assembly then voted to meet half an hour earlier in the morning, and to extend the afternoon session one hour.

The Moderator announced that Dr. Brown would preach in the evening.

Dr. Thomas. I move a postponement of the unfinished business of yesterday in order to take up the consideration of the Committee's report upon the case of the Presbytery of Louisville. My intention is to bring the house to an early decision upon what I consider the vital question of the Assembly. We had been considering that report, and its consideration was arrested, because of the wish of the larger part of the house, to hear an appellant connected with the case which had just been before us, supposing that the discussion of that case would throw some light on the report. It is very obvious to this house, from the proceedings of yesterday, that we are not to look for light from that quarter, and therefore I hope this house will resolve to take up the main question—that question, which, when decided settles all these questions, and the whole principles upon which these matters are to be settled. I hope the house will postpone this interjected matter, and take up the main question.

The motion of Dr. Thomas prevailed.

The Moderator stated that Dr. Wm. Breckinridge was entitled to the floor, his speech having been interrupted by the hour of adjournment.

Dr. Wm. Breckinridge. Mr. Moderator: Allow me to say, if you please, before I proceed to any more serious matter, that I have been taken to task a number of times since I had the privilege of addressing this body on this subject, by persons of various shades of opinion, and especially by those whom I would, without disrespect, call the holders of extreme opinions on this subject. I have been taken very gravely to task for the kindness of feeling I expressed towards my brethren on all sides; the effect of which, in my mind, is to convince me more and more that I am right. One finds very serious fault with me for speaking a single kind and loving word towards my brother Thomas, whom I have known longer probably than the person who rebuked me had lived; and another finds fault with me for speaking a kind or charitable word towards my dear brethren of the Declaration and Testimony wing, many of whom I have known for a long time. I am not in sympathy with either of these parties, but I thank God I can love them all as my brethren, and when I am rebuked for expressing kindness of feeling towards them on both sides, I thank the Lord and take courage, because it convinces me more and more perfectly that the middle ground is the true ground.

If I understand the posture of the business, the report of the committee on the matter of the Presbytery of Louisville is on its passage. The motion before the Assembly is the adoption of the report of the select committee, on the matter of the Louisville Presbytery, the "Declaration and Testimony," and so on—which is a very long document, too long to be read again without necessity, especially as it has been printed in this form, and in the daily papers, which are in the hands of all the members, and, therefore, it need not be repeated. I shall not, therefore, attempt either to read any large portions of it, or go over the whole of it—it is too long.

In what I said in the presence of the Assembly, by year leave some days ago, I attempted to touch but a single point—that was the question of the constitutional power of this Assembly to do the thing proposed by this committee, the sum of which is to dissolve the Louisville Presbytery and immediately organize another: I will not rehearse, sir, all that I said at that time, but with your leave, I will as briefly as possible pursue the line of thought in which I was trying to present the subject. So that if it be of any value in the discussion of this subject, I may put it again fairly before the minds of my brethren, that I may recall it to those who may have forgotten it, or if any may have been absent, that I may state for their information as to the views I expressed, and my reasons for so doing. The ground I took was that the General Assembly does not possess the constitutional power to do this particular ing, and in this way. It will be conceded by all at this body possesses very large power, but this is the point I make that it does not have the constitutional power to do the thing as it is proposed to be done by the report of the committee before you. And now it seems to me, just here, that after conscientious scruples, constitutional scruples are the most sacred with all men who govern each other under Constitutions, as we call them. Under well defined, written Constitutions, there are no scruples that are more worthy of respectful deference and kind treatment from one to another, especially among brethren, than constitutional scruples, except it be conscientious scruples, and in a court of the Lord's house, under the government of the Church, of which our blessed Lord is the head, a constitutional scruple becomes a conscientious scruple, so that the smallest constitutional scruple rises, as it seems to me, to the dignity of a conscientious scruple.

The speaker continued to say that he hesitated to take a single step in the direction of adopting this report, for the lack, as he firmly believes, of the constitutional power on the part of this Assembly to do it. There was a very large minority who held that opinion, who in sincerity and with deference to others, whose intelligence cannot be questioned at all, and whose views were entitled to the most serious and respectful consideration by their brethren. He argued from the general scheme of church government, which consisted of a series of courts, embodied, so to exprsss it, in a series of courts, in a regular gradation, from the session up to the General Assembly. He affirmed that in the chapter granting powers to the General Assembly, not one solitary word could be found about Presbyteries, except as they were the constituency of the Assembly. The chapter stated what the General Assembly had to do with Synods, their proceedings and their records, but not one word about Presbyteries, clearly with the idea that Presbyteries were to be dealt with, and only dealt with, by Synods. It seemed plain that the Constitution of the Church, drawn out of the word of God by wise and goodly men, intended to take all these matters respecting Presbyteries and hand them over to the Synods, declaring that these things were not things that belonged to the General Assembly.

This lack of Constitutional power was confirmed to the mind of the speaker by the fact that there had been no course of standing decisions and precedent to the contrary. Examples of the interference of the General Assembly with Presbyteries may doubtless be found; the Third Presbytery of Philadelphia, for instance, but that Presbytery had been organized by the General Assembly, under the doctrine of elective affinity, which the General Assembly had afterwards utterly repudiated, and this action was afterwards set aside and disowned. There were none but exceptional cases, when, for instance, the Presbytery was not attached to any Synod in which the General Assembly had ever dealt with a Presbytery.

Dr. Krebs called the speaker's attention to the acts of the Assembly in 1846, with regard to the erection of the Presbytery of Wisconsin.

Dr. Breckinridge, in continuing his remarks, claimed that the case of the Presbytery of Wisconsin was one of the exceptional cases; that action was then taken according to the expediency of the case, as the General Assembly erected a Missionary Presbytery, or the other day dealt with the Presbytery in East Tennessee, which was the proper action, for the reason that there was no Synod to deal with it. Hoped this Assembly would connect that Presbytery with the Synod of Kentucky. Claimed that such action had no resemblance to what was proposed to be done by the report of this committee. This question of the lack of constitutional power would not interfere with the plan proposed by Dr. Humphrey. Even if it be granted that the Assembly had the constitutional power to do this, it would certainly not follow that it had the power to take men up in so summary a way, and declare them in Court and proceed to try them. The Presbytery could not be dealt with, without dealing with the men, and the men could not be dealt with except by giving them a trial. But no Court had been organized for their trial; no charge had been pronounced requiring the Assembly to remember their high character as a court of Jesus Christ. If they were tried as a Presbytery they ought to have been cited here as as a Presbytery. (Read from page 104 of the Book of Disciples.) The proper course was to remand the whole matter to the Synod of Kentucky. If the Synod has been negligent, give it to understand that the Assembly regard it as having been negligent, and demanding that it shall do its duty. In that way the General Assembly would set itself right before the Church and the whole world, in that it was proceeding according to law. If, after that the Synod of Kentucky should not do its duty, it could justly be called to account for not doing its duty and settle the question with the Synod. He thought this would be the wisest and best method of dealing with this matter, and would have been from the beginning. Denied the assumption of the report that the Presbytery of Louisville had been cited to this Assembly. The records were not here; the records of the Synod of Kentucky were not here when this report was made. Questioned whether the Synod of Kentucky had been guilty of negligence in this matter. The meeting of the Louisville Presbytery happened in September, and the Synod of Kentucky met towards the middle of October—some five weeks afterwards, and this paper was not made public for sometime after the meeting of the Presbytery of Louisville. He himself never saw the paper until he saw it at the meeting of the Synod. Had this Assembly no charity for men who hesitate what they ought to do—who want to take time to consider what should be done in an extremely difficult case on which very many results hang? The Synod would have acted hastily to have proceeded at that time. Admitting that the Synod was wholly wrong, it should be rebuked, and required to do its duty; but the Assembly ought not to do it in an unconstitutional and irregular way, in order to make up for the neglect of the Synod. Had the proper time come, and the cause a sufficient one the Synod ought to have cited the Presbytery, but that rule applies equally to the Assembly, and it ought not to proceed without citation.

He denied the statement that the Synod of Kentucky had ever "refused" to try these men, but stated that it was impossible to say whether they would neglect or fail to do it if it was required of them by the Assembly. The Synod of Kentucky had never "declined," because to say they had declined, supposes that they had been asked to do something. They had been asked to do something which they wouldn't do, and although it may appear in the judgment of the Assembly and the Church that the Synod did wrong therein, it didn't appear wrong to the speaker yet. The Synod of Kentucky was asked to exclude these men from the Synod, disfranchising them as ministers, to exclude them from the whole Presbyterian body, declare them incompetent, unfit for sitting in that or any other Court of the Presbyterian Church, and to declare all that by a simple resolution on making up the roll, before even the Moderator was chosen. That was what the Synod would not do, and most properly. That was the head and front of the offending of the Synod of Kentucky, and that was what the report of the committee condemned, and asked the Assembly to condemn. It might come out that the Synod of Kentucky would take this matter up for itself, and no man had a right to affirm the opposite, and doubly had no man the right to assume such a thing as that for the purpose of doing anything that was clearly unconstitutional. The Presbyterian Church could stand a great deal. The Synod of Kentucky could stand a great deal; but to stand this, that to the General Assembly belongs the power to do all, everything, because it is the General Assembly, is more than they could stand.

At this point in Dr. Breckenridge's speech, the Assembly adjourned until afternoon.

AFTERNOON SESSION.

Rev. Dr. Van Dyke offered the following protest:

The undersigned respectfully protest against the action of the General Assembly in rejecting a proposal to extend to the Presbyterian ministers and churches in the Southern States, the same expressions of fraternal affection and of desire for organic union, which have been so freely extended to that other branch of the Presbyterian Church commonly known as the New School. Without expressing any opinion as to the practicability of consummating the proposed re union with the last named body "upon the basis of a common standard," the undersigned desire to declare their solemn conviction that the commands of our Divine Master and the exigencies of the times in our country, forbid the continuance of division and strife between brethren who maintain a common faith, and upon whom Providence has imposed a common work for the extension of the Gospel. And we are further persuaded that every consideration which can render Christian union desirable in any case, has a peculiar and pre-eminent force in the relations we sustain to the Presbyterian ministers and churches in the Southern States; we are therefore constrained, by our regard for charity, truth and peace, to protest against the aforesaid action of the Assembly upon the ground of its manifest inconsistency. This inconsistency appears to us the more glaring, in view of the following incontestible facts:

1. The soundness of the Presbyterian ministers and churches in the Southern States in regard to the distinctive doctrines of the Gospel and the fundamental principles of ecclesiastical order, has never been questioned by us, and indeed their title to our confidence and affection on these high grounds, cannot be impugned by this Assembly without denying notorious facts, revoking our own most solemn testimonials in their favor, and involving ourselves in condemnation for having so long and so penitently held communion with them.

2. The questions in regard to civil government and domestic servitude which have separated them from us during the continuance of the late civil war (questions which, in the opinion of the undersigned, ought to be held subordinate and interior to the great doctrines of the Gospel), have been practically decided by the result of the war, in accordance with the views of this Assembly, and to that decision they have unanimously submitted. Slavery has been abolished; and, so far as we have any information of the subject, there is not a man in the Presbyterian Churches at the South who expects, or desires its re-establishment. In regard to the duty of Christians to obey civil magistrates, to submit to the powers that be and to be subject to every ordinance of man, not only for wrath but for "conscience sake," there never has been any fundamental differences of opinion between them and us. The only ground of dispute between them and us in reference to this subject has been the practical and political question, "who are the powers that be, having jurisdiction over the Southern States?" This question, also, has been practically decided by the results of the war in accordance with the views of this Assembly; and to this decision the Presbyterian ministers and Churches in the Southern States have unanimously submitted. Their representatives in General Assembly met, have solemnly declared and published to the world, that "the higher powers now bearing rule over us are confessedly the Government of the United States, and those existing in the States wherein we reside." To these higher powers they solemnly profess their allegiance, and exhort all under their care to submit "with scrupulous fidelity." There is, therefore, no practical difference between them and us, even in regard to the subordinate questions of freedom and loyalty.

3. The inconsistency of the Assembly's action is further apparent when we consider the relation which the Presbyterian ministers and Churches in the Southern States sustained to the great unsolved problem in regard to the evangelization and elevation of the negro population. The fidelity with which they have prosecuted this good work in former years, and the blessed fruits of their labors in this field are fully set forth in the narrative on the state of religion adopted by the Assembly in 1854, an extract from which document may be found on page 818 of Baird's Digest. That the same spirit of love and fidelity to the spiritual welfare of the negro, which, according to the testimony of our Assembly, actuated them in 1854, still animates them, and is greatly increased in view of the peculiar miseries and temptations to which the negro is now exposed, there is abundant and notorious proof. It is the firm conviction of the undersigned that the Presbyterian ministers and Churches in the Southern States have done, and, if they shall be left free to cultivate their own field without interference from strangers, that they will still do more for the conversion and salvation of the negro, than can ever be done by any body of Christians not residing in the Southern States; and for this good work, if for no other reason, they are entitled pre-eminently to the expression of our fraternal confidence and affection.

4. The inconsistency of the Assembly action is further apparent in the opinion of the undersigned, when we consider the influence which it is likely to exert in retarding the permanent pacification of the country and the restoration of good will among all the people; and our apprehensions on this point are rendered stronger by the fact that the representatives of the Southern Churches have "declared concerning other Churches, in the most explicit manner, that we would willingly hold fellowship with all who love our Lord Jesus Christ in sincerity; and especially do we signify to all bodies, ministers and people of the Presbyterian Church, strug-

gling to maintain the true principles of the time-honored confession, our desire is to establish the most intimate relations with them which may be found mutually edifying, and for the glory of God.'' (See pastoral letter of the General Assembly, which met at Macon, Ga., Dec. 14, 1865.

Henry J. Van Dyke, S. J. P. Anderson, R. K. Smoot, W. M. Ferguson, P. Thompson, L. P. Bowen, J. M, Travis, L. J. Yantis, R. L. McAfee, L. A. Braken, Geo. W. Buchanan, R. S. Clark, Glass Marshall, R. Buchanan, G. C. Swallow, A. P. Forman, J. T. Hendrick, Edward Budell, James H. Brookes, G. N. Gantt, Isaac D. James, Aug. T. Dobson, R. W. Allen, D. C. Brown.

After the reading of the protest, the Moderator said, shall a committee be appointed to answer this protest.

Dr. McLean. No answer is required, sir.

Mr. Clark, of Detroit, moved that it be admitted to the record.

Rev. Mr. Ferguson. Do I understand Dr. McLean as saying it shall not be entered.

The Moderator. Wait a moment, if you please. I suppose it is right to admit the protest, unless there is something offensive in it.

The motion to admit the protest to the record was agreed to.

Dr. McLean. My motion was simply that there was no necessity for an answer.

Rev. Dr. West. I move that it be the sense of this Assembly that no answer is required in this case.

Rev. Mr. Ferguson. I move to amend that by saying no answer is possible to be presented. [Laughter.]

The motion of Rev. Dr. West was agreed to.

Mr. Day said he made a motion this morning to lay on the table an amendment to the minutes. He understood that Dr. Breckinridge felt aggrieved at the minutes as they stand, as it puts him in a wrong position before the Assembly. He is in the light of bringing an appeal from Kentucky on an important matter, and he appears now on the record in a childish position. He (Mr. D.) was the last man to do anything to injure the feelings of Dr. Breckinridge. He moved, therefore, to reconsider the vote by which the minutes were adopted. The amendment he desired to offer was as follows:

"The Assembly then called for the original parties in the case, when Dr. Stanton appeared, and declined to proceed with the case; Dr. Breckinridge thereupon declined to proceed, and gave as a further reason for declining to plead, that the Assembly had confined the case to Dr. Breckinridge and others, and the Synod of Kentucky, as the original parties.''

Rev. Dr. Anderson wished to say, that all that was unfortunate in the position of the venerable father was of his own selection, and therefore he thought they were not specially bound to help him out of that difficulty. He had always thought he was able to take care of himself.

Mr. Day. He is not on this floor, and is not able to take care of himself where he is not allowed to speak.

The motion of Mr. Day to reconsider was agreed to, and his amendment to the minutes was adopted.

The following committees were announced:

Revising the Book of Discipline: T. L. McGill, David Elliott and John Krebs, ministers; H. K. Clark, H. H. Leavitt, Geo. Shearsworth, elders.

Metropolitan Church matter at Washington: P. D. Gurley and John Chase, ministers; Edward Myers, elder.

The unfinished business was then taken up—the report of the Committee on the Louisville Presbytery.

Dr. Wm. L. Breckinridge resumed his remarks. He began by saying they had his most profound sympathy in being obliged to listen to him longer, but he would make his remarks as short as he could. At the time of the adjournment, he was speaking of the statement made by the committee that the Synod of Kentucky had refused, declined, or failed to take action of this subject, in the way of the discipline of that Presbytery, and he was showing exactly what the Synod of Kentucky did, namely: That it rebuked and severely censured the Presbytery of Louisville, and if not in terms, yet impliedly, all who signed the Declaration and Testimony. He conceived that under all the circumstances, this Assembly ought not to put a stigma upon the Synod for not having done more than that at that time. If the Assembly requires the Synod to go further, and the Synod will not, then will be the time for the Assembly to lay its hand on that body.

In immediate connection with the report of the committee, he wished to call attention to one remark. The report says, beside the injury to the Churches in the infected regions from the settlement of so grave a question, additional complications may arise, and the leaven of rebellion become more widely diffused. He did not understand what was meant by infected regions. If it meant there were persons who had not stood by the Government, and for which this Assembly should call them to an account, or persons who had not stood by the Church, then he would ask respectfully if there were not such people in all parts of the country. If this stigma was to be put on the Synod of Kentucky, might it not be put on every part of the Presbyterian Church? It was said additional complications might arise. He wished to know what that meant. Did it mean that political affairs might take a sudden turn?—if so, then it should be struck out. But what he wished particularly to refer to, was the point urged that all these evil influences would result from the delay. He did not desire to argue the question, but simply to express an opinion, that this hurrying of matters to a conclusion, as was here proposed, was what involved danger and not delay. If this region was infected, it was far more likely to be infected by the passage of such a proposition as this, than by delay. If it were left to him to say what should be done for the repose of the Church, he would say without hesitation, that the best thing that could be done, was to let this matter alone for the present, because the more it was disturbed, the more attention would be called to it, whereas it would die out if left alone. It was a peculiarity of human nature to sympathize with men in trouble, and who are supposed to be misused, and if they took this proposed action, so as to impress upon the minds of some people that they had been rashly, unjustly and unconstitutionally pursued, it would give them a sympathy which they could not otherwise obtain.

Rev. Dr. Smith, from Baltimore, desired the speaker to give way for a moment, in order that he might say that he had received four letters from Baltimore to-day, which fully confirmed what Dr. Breckinridge had said.

Dr. Breckinridge continued: He next referred to the proposed dissolution of the Presbytery of Louisville. With all respect to the gentleman who proposed it, it appeared to him, not only unconstitutional, but undignified and unworthy. No doubt the design was to exclude certain persons. It was taking what might be called snap-judgment upon them, but even that course did not help the matter, because he knew of nothing to prevent those very men from seeking application in some other Presbytery.

There was another matter to which he wished to allude. The brethren whom they proposed to take in and form a new Presbytery were just as bad as those they proposed to leave out. He submitted whether that was the right way of doing things—making fish of one, fowl of another, and flesh of another. It has been declared that this course would prove inoperative, but no attention had been paid to it, yet he firmly believed it; and in this connection he desired to speak of a subject which was painful to him—that was in reference to the brother selected to preach the opening sermon. He had the utmost respect for him. He was a good, honest man, but he was among the youngest of the Presbytery. The custom of the Church had been, in every part of the country, that in a case of this kind the oldest minister present should preach the opening sermon, and do the work. But in this case, the rule would be violated, and the venerable Dr. Matthews and other worthy brethren would be passed over, and this young brother called upon to preside. The reason assigned was that the brother referred to had stood faithful among the faithless. He defied any man to make it plain that Dr. Mc-

Millan was any truer to the Church, on the views that the Church hold, than was Dr. Matthews. He believed that Dr. McMillan would decline the whole thing and request some one else to take his place. The speaker closed by saying, that one of the most solemn duties encumbered on this Assembly was the exercise of universal pacification. He alluded to the remarks of Rev. Dr. Thomas, and the plea of that gentleman for summary action in this case, and he was exceedingly pained when that gentleman cited as an illustration for their action in this case, with God's method of dealing with Paraoh and his hosts, with Sodom and Gomorrah, and Ananias and Saphira. Did he mean to say that the men who adhere to the Declaration and Testimony were like the people of Sodom and Gomorrah? It was not for him to rebuke any of his brethren, but he did entreat them to disclaim all such sentiments as that kind of figurative speech implied.

At the conclusion of Dr. Breckinridge's remarks, Rev. Dr. Humphrey obtained the floor, and spoke at length in opposition to the report. He was followed by Mr. Clark, of Detroit, in support of the report.

Dr. Humphrey, in the course of his remarks, offered the following amendment, substantially the same as that which he gave notice of on a former occasion:

Strike out the resolutions of the committee, and insert "The Declaration and Testimony adopted by the Presbytery of Louisville, in the terms, spirit and intent thereof, is derogatory to the just authority of the General Assembly, detrimental to the interests of the Church, destructive to the peace of the people, and fruitful in schismatical dissensions and disputations; wherefore, this General Assembly express its grave disapprobation at the action of this Presbytery, as unbecoming a lower Judiciatory of the Church. The Assembly enjoins upon the Presbytery to reconsider whatever it has done tending to a separation from the institutions of the Church, and to take such action at its next meeting as will show that it did not intend to defy the authority of the General Assembly or disparage the institutions of the Church. Furthermore, the General Assembly requires the Presbytery of Louisville to appear by its commissioners before the next General Assembly to show what it has done in these premises, and the next General Assembly is required to take up and issue the business. Furthermore, the Assembly directs all the various Presbyteries to urge upon the brethren who have signed the Declaration and Testimony, to disown the intention of setting the General Assembly at defiance, and these Presbyteries are directed to report at the next Assembly. All this to the end that the whole Church may have quietness and repose."

At the conclusion of the remarks of Mr. Clark the Assembly adjourned.

ELEVENTH DAY — WEDNESDAY, MAY 30, 1866.

MORNING SESSION.

First half hour spent in devotional exercises.

Minutes read and approved.

Dr. Lowrie, of the Committee on Bills and Overtures, reported the following overtures: Overture No. 17. To Presbyterian General Assembly, Old School, in session at St. Louis, Missouri, May 17, 1866:

1. Has any Church, or any part of a Church, in our connection, the Constitutional right to withdraw from a Presbytery, without its consent, and unite with another body?

2. Can any communing member of the Church be rightly debarred from voting in such a case by a vote of the congregation, without some measure of discipline regularly administered by the session of the Church?

R. CONOVER,
Stated Clerk.

The committee recommend that the first of the overtures be answered in the negative.

To the second, that the vote of a congregation of a Presbyterian Church cannot affect the rights of a communing member as such; all such power is vested in the session. Adopted.

Overture No. 18. Put upon the the docket.

Overture No. 19. Request of Rev. F. J. Collier, asking the General Assembly to decide whether it is right for a clerk of a Presbytery, recording the licensure of candidates, to use any other form than that prescribed in the book?

The committee recommend that an answer be made in the affirmative. (See Form of Govt. ch. 14, sec. 8.) And record shall be made of the licensure in the following or like form. Adopted.

Overture No. 20. The Committee of Bills and Overtures, to whom was referred the petition and memorial of Benjamin F. Avery, D. McNoughton, James A. Leich and Thomas J. Harkney, Ruling Elders in the Walnut street Church in Louisville, praying for such redress as in the wisdom of the General Assembly may seem fit and necessary to redress the grievance of said Church as set forth in said memorial and petition,

Report, that they have considered the matter referred, and recommend the adoption of the following:

Whereas, On the second day of January last, D. McNoughton, Benjamin F. Avery and James A. Leich were duly elected Ruling Elders by the congregation of said Church, and on the sixth day of January the said D. McNoughton was installed, and Benjamin F. Avery and James A. Leich were duly ordained and installed Ruling Elders in said Church;

And whereas, the Presbytery of Louisville, after the election of said elders, with the apparent design of discrediting said election, denied to one of this number a seat in said Presbytery, notwithstanding he had been duly elected to represent said Church, at a meeting of said Presbytery.

And whereas, it is evident that the peace of said Church and this congregational rights are in great danger unless this Assembly shall interpose its authority; therefore, this General Assembly, by virtue of its authority and obligation to give advice and instruction in all cases submitted to them, does hereby declare that the said D. McNoughton, Benjamin F. Avery and James A. Leich are to be recognized and acknowledged as Ruling Elders in the said Church, and all Church courts and pastors subject to, or under the care of this Assembly, are solemnly enjoined to respect and maintain their authority as such.

Rev. Mr. Hickman moved to accept the report and place it upon the docket.

Amendment made to adopt the report.

It appeared from the remarks of Drs. Krebs and Lowrie, and Mr. Clark and others, that this matter was before the Assembly in a two-fold aspect.

An appeal from the Presbytery of Louisville, which refused to recognize the elders named in the Overture, and which appeal was referred to the Judicial Committee; and in the form of a memorial on the part of said Elders had been handed to the Committee on Bills and Overtures. The Judicial Committee, as Dr. Gurley stated, could not pass upon the appeal for the reason that the records of the Presbytery of Louisville were not before them. Consequently, the matter came before the Assembly upon the report of the Committee on Bills and Overtures with regard to the memorial.

Dr. Krebs favored the adoption of the recommendation of the Committee. It appeared by the records of the Synod of Kentucky that a committee had been appointed by that body to go to the Walnut street Church in Louisville, to inquire into its affairs, allay differences, and cause Elders to be elected. It was apparent, from an examination of the case, that the Elders mentioned in the memorial had been duly elected and ordained.

Rev. Mr. Hickman hoped the report would be adopted—he had made the motion to docket it in order to prevent discussion at this time.

Rev. Mr. Bracken was not sufficiently acquainted with the history of the case to state all the facts in connection with it; knew that the case was an exceedingly complicated one; that it was still pending before the Presbytery of Louisville; and knew that the Louisville Presbytery, being shut out from this Assembly, could not bring the facts before it.

Dr. Anderson. I was informed by Hon. George Wickliffe that this was a foul wrong attempted to be perpetrated upon this Church in Louisville. I do not know the facts myself, but I say this Assembly is compromising its dignity by proceeding by a process like this, in this case, without hearing the facts. I say that this body cannot afford to settle a question of property and of right, without at least hearing the parties who are adverse to the claim which now appears to be so favorably considered. I say this Assembly is now at the bar of public opinion.

A Member. I rise to a point of order.

Moderator. The gentleman is in order.

Dr. Anderson. Then I proceed, for the benefit of the brother who interrupted me, and all like him—I say the eyes of the country are directed to the decisions of this body, and that we are at the bar of public opinion, and if we want to go before the people of this country with the clean hands and fair reputations we have heretofore had, we must be exceedingly careful what we do. This matter is before the courts of Kentucky. I am informed that at this time the Judge of that District, a very eminent man, has the case in hearing. Are we prepared, when the matter is in his hands, we, a body not knowing the facts, and when the facts are not knowable—are we prepared to take any such action? I protest against it, not knowing the facts myself. I wish to know them before I vote, and I suppose every man in this house wishes to know the facts before he votes.

Dr. Safford stated that living upon the ground he knew the facts, and had known everything about it from the beginning. It was a simple election, and the difficulty had been brought about by those who sympathized with Dr. Robinson and his party.

Rev. Mr. Bracken asserted that it was not a simple question of the election of Elders. These difficulties came up in the Louisville Presbytery, and from them were taken to the Synod of Kentucky, and from the Synod to a committee which met with the Church, and without definite instructions proceeded to elect Elders.

Mr. Kempshall moved to lay the motion upon the table. Lost.

It was then moved to recommit.

Dr. Krebs said there was no reason for recommitting. The whole matter had been investigated. What was to be gained by recommitment? A member upon the floor said it was a very complicated case, but it was very clear. There were documents here from the Synod of Kentucky recording the election. He held a certified copy of the records, and the records themselves were in the house. The committee appointed by that Synod to cause the election had made their report and published it. They had proceeded to cause an election of Elders, an election was made, and the Elders proceeded to the Presbytery of Louisville, but were denied admission on the ground that they were not known there. It was true that a committee had been appointed to pass upon the matter; and that it was before the civil courts; and the man in whose hands it was, desired that the matter should be thrown over until after the decision by this house.

Mr. Bracken called for the reading of the minutes appointing this committee in regard to the election of Elders; affirming it as his belief that there was no such record.

Dr. Krebs read a certified copy of the record—stating that the original record was in the house.

Rev. Mr. Jones claimed that action upon the memorial in this form would be an *ex parte* proceeding, and irregular.

Mr. McKnight stated that not only the records of the Presbytery of Louisville were not here, but the appeal as taken from the decision of that body was not here. Would not say that the records were designedly absent, in order that this case might not be tried and decided—would be sorry to say so—but yet it had somewhat that appearance. Would like to ask if this General Court of the Church hadn't the right, upon any memorial, if they were satisfied with the facts, to take up any overture and send an answer to the question. The facts were that when this committee, appointed by the Synod of Kentucky, after due notice proceeded to the church for the election of the Elders, in accordance with instructions and the notice, they found the church locked. After organizing on the pavement in front of the church, they adjourned to the public school-house in the neighborhood, in order to carry out the very order that was sent to them by the Synod.

Rev. Mr. Smoot. I want to ask Mr. McKnight if this was not the state of the case, that those Elders and other Elders appeared at the meeting of the Presbytery of Louisville, both parties claiming to be Elders; that the Presbytery did not receive or condemn them, but appointed a committee to ascertain which set of Elders were entitled to a seat, and that that committee has not yet reported, and that that committee are to report at the adjourned meeting of the Louisville Presbytery next month.

Mr. McKnight. My recollection is that when they made their appearance on the floor of the Presbytery, the Moderator said "We don't know you, sirs;" instead of having their certificates examined, or allowing them an opportunity of explaining their condition, they were met with "We don't know you," and they were compelled to take their seats.

Mr. Smoot. Does the committee ask the General Assembly to take this action simply upon newspaper statements?—and do they ask the Assembly to decide this question, thus taking it out of the hands of the committee appointed by the Presbytery of Louisville to investigate it, before they have reported?

Dr. Krebs. Does the gentleman deny that the minute I read is authentic?

Mr. Smoot. I didn't deny any statement made by Dr. Krebs.

Mr. Wilson desired that all the papers in the case be read.

Dr. Van Dyke said there were two questions involved in this matter—first, whether the Synod of Kentucky had a right to order an election of Elders, and, second, whether the committee of the Synod had performed their duty. There was no evidence that the committee performed its duty correctly. The committee had never reported to the Synod, nor had the Synod approved of its action. It was affirmed that the committee of the Synod did not hold a lawful election; that the congregation was never called together; that a portion met on the pavement, and adjourned from thence to some other place, with regard to which due notice had not been given; that when they came to claim their seats the Louisville Presbytery declined to admit them without investigation. Under such circumstances what right had the Assembly to decide this matter, when the evidence only of one side was before them?

Dr. Krebs. The committee has reported, and published their report over their signatures.

Dr. Van Dyke. Has the Synod approved of their action?

Dr. Krebs. It needs no approval.

Mr. Clark asked Dr. Van Dyke if an approval was needed to the report of a committee appointed to ordain a minister.

Dr. Van Dyke claimed that they were not analagous cases.

Dr. McLean. I hope there will be no recommitment, but that there will be an immediate adoption of that report. We see here some of the tactics, of some of these Kentucky gentleman, to put off, delay and complicate matters so as to reach their particular aims. Here is a valuable Church at stake.

We ought to find out whether they will *know* men elected in their own city. You are called upon, upon the very best evidence, to say that these men are Elders, and then see whether the brethren of the Louisville Presbytery will know it the next time. The next Synod of Kentucky meets in October; if you tie up things in this way and hold matters in abeyance until next October infinite mischief will be done. The absence of the minutes and appeal looks wonderfully like an effort to force such a result.

A motion was made for the previous question, and withdrawn.

The Moderator stated the original motion to be upon docketing the report, with an amendment to adopt the report, and was proceeding to take the vote when

Rev. Mr. Ferguson rose to a point of order, saying, The state of feeling in this house is such that we are not ready for any question.

Moderator. What is the point of order?

Mr. Ferguson. The point of order is that the gentlemen keep order.

Rev. Mr McAfee. I ask to be excused from voting, for I do not understand enough of this case to cast a vote here satisfactorily to myself.

Mr. Bracken. I will add that we have not only failed to bring out the facts, so as to enable any one to vote intelligently, but that these facts cannot be had without having the records of the Presbytery of Louisville; and as to the insinuations made against that Presbytery, gentlemen can well afford to make them after that Presbytery has been put out of the house.

The amendment to adopt the report prevailed, the motion to docket failing by the adoption of the amendment.

Mr. Bracken gave notice of a protest against the vote just taken.

Dr. Walker then read the following report of the Committee on Freedmen:

"The committee to whom was referred the First Annual Report of the Assembly's Committee on Freedmen, respectfully submit the following report. The minutes of the committee and of the executive committee have been submitted for inspection, and with these certain papers asking for the action of the Asembly. The minutes are full and well kept. The committee have done a good work. They have raised funds to the amount of $25,000—have fifty-five missionaries in commissions; over 3,000 pupils in their schools, and over 2,000 in Sabbath School. Their field of labor is one of paramount importance and of deep interest. The condition of those whom they seek to benefit is one of depression and dependence, and, in many instances, of deep degradation. If they are not to become a disturbing and dangerous element in society they must be educated to take care of themselves. They must have the Bible, the school, and the Gospel with all its purifying and elevating influences. They imploringly appeal to our sympathies as the weaker to the stronger and wiser race. We cannot neglect them without guilt before God. They are immortal beings. We must do what we can to save them or God may require their blood at our hands.

One of the papers referred to, relates to the occupancy of Zion's Presbyterian Church in Charleston. S. C., under the adjudication of the post commander, and asks for the approval, or instructions of the Assembly.

Your committee recommend this answer: The General Assembly regard the avoidance as far as possible on the part of the committee, of all unpleasant collision with the Southern churches, as wise and judicious, and inasmuch as the jurisdiction of the civil authorities has been re-established in South Carolina, the question as to the occupancy of said house in the future is a question of law, and must be left to the adjudication of the civil courts.

Two other papers are Overtures referred to the Committee on Freedmen by the last Assembly, to be reported upon at the present Assembly.

The first of these overtures is from the Synod of Kansas, and has regard to the establishment of a chair of Biblical Instruction for the recognized ministers of the freedmen. The committee, in their report, state that an effort to give such a course of instruction had been made, but entirely failed.

Your committee, therefore, recommend that nothing more be done in the case.

The second Overture relates to the establishment of a "Memorial University," in honor of the fallen President.

Upon this the committee report that, inasmuch as by an act of the Legislature of Pennsylvania, the charter of the Ashman Institute has been enlarged, and its name changed to that of Lincoln University, and as the institution is under the care of one of our own Presbyteries, no effort should be made to forestall it, or hinder its usefulness. In this judgment your committee recommend the concurrence of the Assembly. The committee in their annual report bring to the notice of the Assembly the establishment of the Freedmen's College of North Carolina—intended for the education of freedmen, and for training a Calvinistic ministry for the colored race. By the limitation of the charter, all the members of the Board of Trustees are required to be members of some branch of the Presbyterian Church. Your committee recommend that Rev. Willis L. Miller, of North Carolina, the general agent of this institution, be heard by the Assembly in its behalf.

Upon the memorial referred to your committee by the present Assembly, they report that it consists of a paper from Rev. James St. Clair, of North Carolina, stating his suspension and excommunication on political grounds by the Presbytery of Fayetteville, and asking assistance for the people of color; and also of a petition from some twenty-eight persons of color in North Carolina, declaring their adherence to the Presbyterian Church, setting forth their grievous wrongs and persecutions, and asking ths Assembly to assist them in securing for themselves and their children, schools and the means of grace. Your committee recommend that these papers be referred to the Assembly's Committee on Freedmen.

Your committee respectfully offer for adoption the following resolutions, viz: Resolved

1. That the report be approved and printed for circulation in all our churches.

2. That in the success which has attended the labors of the committee the General Assembly recognize the good hand of God, and the tokens of his favor towards the four millions of human beings from whose necks, He, in His wonder-working providences, has broken the yoke of bondage.

3. That the Assembly commend this blessed cause to the sympathies and prayers and benefactions of all our churches, and asks for their liberal contributions; that thus our people may share in the happiness of that "man that considereth the poor," and that upon them may come "the blessing of Him that was ready to perish."

Your Committee also offer for adoption the following paper, prepared at their request by Rev. Dr. Reed:

Your Committee cordially bear testimony to the fidelity, zeal and efficiency of the Assembly's Committee on Freedmen, and especially to the faithful and successful work of their Secretary during the past year. The thanks of this Assembly are due and are hereby tendered to these brethren for the successful prosecution of the work to the present time.

From no want of confidence in their ability to carry it forward, but on account of the great importance of simplifying as far as possible our benevolent operations, and ultimately reducing the number of appeals to our congregations for pecuniary contributions; and believing that this is a legitimate part of the work of one of our Boards—it being understood, also, that the change contemplated is favored or cordially acquiesced in by those who have heretofore had this matter in charge—the committee recommend the adoption of the following resolutions, viz:

1. That as soon as practicable the work of the Assembly's Committee on Freedmen be transferred to the Board of Domestic Missions, with the special injunction that that Board give immediate and earnest attention to this department of labor, employing such additional executive force as may be necessary to render it efficient and successful.

2. The Committee on Freedmen are earnestly requested to continue their labors until the Board of Domestic Missions are prepared to take up the work and the transfer can be made without derangement to the plans already adopted; and that the teachers and other laborers already employed be continued according to the contracts of the committee until the Board discover satisfactory reasons for a change.

3. That in view of the magnitude and importance of the work among the freedmen, the immediate demand for the expenditure of large sums on their behalf, the Assembly renews the injunction that for the present an annual collection be made for this specific object, and that the first Sabbath in October be designated for such collection.

It was moved to accept and docket the report.

Dr. Van Dyke gave notice of, and read the following amendment, which he desired to have considered when the matter comes up again:

Whereas, The Assembly's Committee on Freedmen, by virtue of authority derived from a military commander of the United States, did take possession of the church edifice belonging to Zion Presbyterian Church, in Charleston, S. C., and hold the same in the name of this Assembly; and,

Whereas, The grounds upon which the claims of said committee to the control of the aforesaid church property were urged and recognized before the military tribunal, were, by the acknowledgment of the Secretary of the Committee, a misapprehension of the facts in the case; therefore,

Resolved, That the Assembly regret the error into which the zeal of the Committee on Freedmen has led them in this instance, and enjoin upon them to do all in their power to rectify said error and prevent the evil consequences it is calculated to produce.

Resolved, That in the prosecution of this great work of evangelizing the negro population of the Southern States, this Assembly has no desire, nor intention, to infringe upon the vested rights of any individual or Church in those States, nor in any wise to disparage the wisdom and zeal of those Christian brethren at the South who are engaged in the same great work, and to whose fidelity and success the General Assembly has borne repeated and explicit testimony.

The report was accepted and docketed.

Several nominations were then made to fill vacancies in Theological Seminaries.

Dr. Safford reported the consent of Dr. McCosh for the publication of his sermon, and asked that an order be drawn on the treasury to the amount of $15 to pay for pamphlet copies of the proceedings of the Assembly to be given to Dr. McCosh. Voted.

A motion was then made to take up the unfinished business of yesterday.

An amendment was proposed that speakers be limited to twenty minutes.

A motion was made to lay the amendment on the table.

A standing vote was taken upon the latter motion, and the Moderator announced that it was carried.

It appearing, however, that some had voted not understanding the question before the house, another standing vote was taken, and the announcement was made that the motion to lay on the table was lost.

The question then recurring upon the amendment of limitation to twenty minutes,

Mr. Neius offered to amend by limiting the time to thirty minutes.

Dr. Boardman reminded the Assembly most respectfully that in the course of the session it had been heard many times over from gentlemen understood to represent the majority of the house, that they were strenuous advocates of free speech, and that absolute liberty of discussion, whenever the Assembly should come to the discussion of the principles involved in the issues now before the house, would be allowed. He protested against any such restrictions upon free discussion as the motion would make, and contended that it was impossible to do justice to the question now before the house in the space of twenty minutes. The vital interests of the Presbyterian Church were involved in the question. The General Assembly did not stand by reason of the action of the first or second day's sessions in a very enviable position before the country in respect to the fundamental liberty of discussion. If he was of the majority on this question he would vote against limiting the time of debate.

Dr. Anderson remarked that not a single argument had been heard from any of the signers of the "Declaration and Testimony." Can say so because he he did not belong to that class. Was the Assembly unwilling to hear these gentlemen, whose heads were at stake, with the loss of all their ecclesiastical rights, longer than twenty, thirty, forty or even sixty minutes. If those gentlemen were allowed to speak the Assembly would hear things they were not prepared for from anything that had heretofore been made. It had been said, and he feared lest the Assembly had and might then act upon the belief, that these men were in favor of a disruption of the Church; that they were maneuvering to rend the Church asunder. But he stood there, though not of them, knowing their counsels, to say that that was an entire misrepresension. It was not their plan when the "Declaration and Testimony" was signed, and was not their plan to-day.

Mr. Clark made an amendment, the precise terms of which we did not understand.

Mr. Nevius asked leave to withdraw his amendment. He was not in favor of any restriction, but desired, if any were made that it should be thirty rather than twenty minutes.

Rev. Mr. Stewart was in favor of free speech; had voted, and probably should vote, with the majority; but was opposed to any restriction.

Mr. Nevius was granted leave to withdraw his amendment.

Dr. Krebs moved to lay all pending amendments on the table, which motion prevailed

The Moderator announced the subject matter before the Assembly to be the report of the Committee upon the case of the Presbytery of Louisville, and that Mr. Clarke was entitled to the floor.

With Dr. Lowrie in the Chair.

Mr. H. K. Clarke proceeded with his argument, stating that he would endeavor to respect the impatience of the house, but was free to say that this matter ought to have a full hearing; that we stood at the bar of public opinion, and by that he meant the bar of the Church; would deprecate nothing more than to have a vote taken and the measure carried through solely by a majority; to have the Church concur with the action of the Assembly, the principles of construction of the Constitution upon which action was taken must be the true principles. It would not do to trust to majorities. If any one wanted to go home, leaving these principles undecided, let him go. He had no sympathy with any man whether agreeing with him or not, unless he was willing to stand by his principles to a vote, particularly upon this most important question of the session.

Rev. Mr. Sharon interrupted the speaker with the question as to what he would do in case of sickness in his family, &c., when the Moderator suggested to Mr. Clark that he was not speaking on the question under discussion.

Mr. Clark proceeded to say that he had felt distracted somewhat by the eloquent oration of Dr. Humphries, when he commenced his speech at the last session, and doubted not that the Assembly had been also, and asked the indulgence of the Assembly while he briefly read the points he had endeavored to make as, follows:

The General Assembly, in the exercise of any of the administrative, legislative or judicial functions with which it is invested, may adopt any method which in its discretion it shall deem expedient, unless some mode is specifically prescribed by the book.

That though a proceeding may be essentially judicial in its nature, that is, may be followed by a decision or a judgment, which parties affected are bound to obey, yet a judicial process by citation and complaint is not necessary, unless required by some positive enactment. Equity requires that the party affected shall have a fair chance to be heard. That secured, the whole subject is fairly before the Court for adjudication—both upon constitutional and equitable grounds.

The first six chapters of the book of discipline relate exclusively to *individual* offenses. There is not one word which prescribes or contemplates proceedings against a Church Court.

The entire absence of any directory enactment leaves this court free to exercise its discretion as to the mode of exercising its jurisdiction.

In this case the commissioners of the Presbytery of Louisville have heard the charge, they have put in a written answer; they have been offered the privileges of members of this Assembly for the purpose of defense, and they have refused to accept the offer.

The duty to examine, deliberate and judge in the whole matter is explicitly declared in ch. vii, sec. 1.

He argued that the simple defiance of the Louisville Presbytery was not the matter before the Assembly; there was something vastly greater and more important than that. The question put in issue by that Presbytery was this: The Church had declared that the rebellion was a sin, it did not declare that all those who participated in it were charged with the guilt of it. The Presbytery of Louisville had denied the first of these propositions and affirmed the second. A member of this body had said it was not their purpose to create a scism in the Church, but they were to be held accountable for the reasonable consequences of their acts.

Rev. Mr. McAfee rose to a point of order, asking if it was in order to take for granted a proposition that had been expressly denied.

Moderator. The member is in order, as the Moderator thinks.

Mr. Clarke cited the acts of the Presbytery in their manner of combination; sending records of their acts broadcast through the land; inviting others thereby to combine with them as evidence of their intent, and proceeded to argue from the action of the Assembly in 1861 and 1865 that the intention of the Church was, as already stated, to declare the rebellion a sin, and only those who had been leaders in fomenting the rebellion, or had voluntarily and without external constraint taken part in it, as guilty of that sin. Affirmed that the Assembly was right in so declaring by the confession of faith and the catechisms of the Church. It had been asserted that the action of the General Assembly last year was unconstitutional because it imposed a new test of communion. It that were true he granted that it could not have been so established; though even then the Presbytery of Louisville would still have deserved censure for their acts. Insisted that it was the duty of every man, and certainly of every Christian, to obey the constituted authorities; that it was the law of the Church that the people should "pray for magistrates, honor their persons, pay them tribute and their dues, obey their lawful commands and be subject to authority for conscience sake." He then read from the 2d section of the chapter on Synods, &c., directing Synods, &c., ministerially to determine controversies of faith and cases of conscience, to set down rules and directions for the better ordering of the public worship of God and the government of His Church, whose decrees and determinations, if consonant to the word of God, were to be received with reverence and submission.

The Assembly of '65 was right, then, in its action, if that action was consonant with the word of God. That was the next question. Asked to know whether there was anybody in the Assembly who denied that the Larger and Shorter Catechism were in accordance with the word of God. Read from the Catechism: "Fifth commandment. Honor thy father and mother. Who are meant? Not only natural parents, but all superiors in age and rights, and especially such as by God's ordinances are over us, in the place of authority, whether in the family, Church or commonwealth." That was an authoritative exposition of the word of God, "What is the honor that inferiors owe to superiors?" &c., (reading from the Catechism.) Could there be any doubt then that if any person set up a rebellion against the Government of the United States in the month of November or December, 1860, that that person was violating not only the law of the State but the law of the Church? If there were no such person or persons, then, perhaps, the Assembly had been taking an unnecessary step in providing for their examination upon their applying for re-admission to the privileges of the Church. He insisted that there were such persons, and, moreover, that they were those who had been the most influential persons in the Church and those that had exerted the greatest influence.

Dr. Palmer, on the 29th day of November, 1860—three weeks before the first overt act had been taken against the Government of the United States by any State Government—three weeks before anybody had any right to say, or any authority or reason to say, that they were constrained by their State Government, ascended the steps of his pulpit in the city of New Orleans, and there exhorted his people in the most violent harangue to rebellion, when he called upon them to strike for their rights, when he likened their position to the position of their fathers, during the reign of George III; when he appealed to them to strike for rights, plainly invited them to maintain their rights by acts of war—when Dr. Palmer did that, I insist that he was a rebel against State authority—a rebel against Federal authority—a rebel against our confession of faith and the catechism, and a rebel against the law of God. The influence of that sermon was immense—it was published and circulated by the thousands and sent broadcast over the land. And this sermon was preached three weeks before the secesssion of the State of South Carolina, and two months before the secession of the State of Louisiana. Now when you bear in mind that that act was committed by a man who had the vows of your Church upon him, who was occupying a position of influence, which the ordination of this Church gave him, can it be possible that this Assembly will do its duty if it does not require that man, should he ever come back to the Church, to come back to it through the door of repentance, and not that of defiance. The speaker contended that the rebellious influence proceeded pre-eminently if not mainly from those who were at the time acting under the authority of the Church, and who should be held in due subjection to its authority, citing further the resolution of the Synod of South Carolina, passed in November, 1860, before the action of the State of South Carolina by which it sought to take itself out of the Union:

"Resolved, The Synod has no hesitation, therefore, in expressing the belief that the people of South Carolina are now solemnly called on to imitate their Revolutionary forefathers, and stand up for their rights. We have an humble and abiding confidence that that God, whose truth we represent in this conflict, will be with us; and, exhorting our churches and people to put their trust in God, and go forward in the solemn path of duty which his Providence opens before them, we, elders and members of the Presbyterian Church, in South Carolina Synod assembled, would give them our benediction, and the assurance that we shall fervently and unceasingly implore for them the care and protection of Almighty God."

Those men were urging forward rebellion, presenting it as a solemn Christian duty to rebel against the powers that be. Upon what authority could the Assembly be held free from guilt if it allowed such enormous wickedness as that to pass uncensured? He supposed that the Synod of South Carolina were among the 800 ministers whom the Assembly was asked to include in the effort of reunion. He had some other authorities to read. That the duty to obey the Government was a doctrine that the Church was bound to obey and enforce had been proclaimed from one of the most influential pulpits in our land; that sermon, too, had been circulated; he did not know to whom he was indebted for his copy. A sermon preached in the First Presbyterian Church in Brooklyn, (Dr. Van-Dyke's,) on Thanksgiving day, November 24, 1859. Would read the doctrines presented in the sermon before he adverted to the circumstances under which it was delivered. He then read as follows:

"Government is a divine ordinance. We do not mean that this or that *form* of government is divine. But it is a divine ordinance that the *magis-*

trate, under whatever form or title, shall bear the sword for the terror of evil doers and the praise of them that do well. And it is a divine command that Christians, wherever their lot may be cast, and under whatever government they may live, shall sustain human law whenever it does not violate Divine law, and *submit to it when it does.* Christianity does not seek to accomplish its benign and glorious ends by seditions and revolutions. It comes to sanctify the individual. Through the individual it will, no doubt, ultimately accomplish the social and political regeneration of the world. But these ends can be most speedily and effectually attained by inculcating a respect for magistrates and a spirit of obedience to law.''

I wish this sermon had been sent to Dr. Palmer.

Dr. Van Dyke. It was sent to him.

Mr. Clarke, after stating that the enormity of the crime of instigating the rebellion was aggravated by the fact that the government against which they had rebelled had been in their hands for sixty years; that at the very time of the rebellion they had a majority in the Senate and the Supreme Court, and that the only occasion for it then, was the fear that in the future they could not maintain the asserted right of secession, and for that cause Dr. Palmer had started the ball from his pulpit in New Orleans. He then read further from Dr. Van Dyke's sermon, as follows:

''It was the policy as well as the *duty* of the Apostles of Christianity to array themselves on the side of law and order, to *inculcate obedience to civil rulers as a Christian duty*, and to cultivate among their disciples a spirit of reverence for magistrates. They felt that even a faulty government was better for their cause than the social upheavings of sedition and revolution; for so long as the preacher might travel from one end of the empire to the other, under the broad protection of the Roman eagle, the leaven of the Gospel would work its quiet way into the hearts and homes of men.'' ''Let every soul be subject unto the higher powers, for there is no power but of God; the powers that be are ordained of God. Whosoever, therefore, resisteth the power, resisteth the ordinance of God; and they that resist shall receive to themselves damnation. Wherefore ye must needs be subject not only for wrath but also for conscience sake. Render, therefore, to all their dues; tribute to whom tribute is due; custom to whom custom; fear to whom fear; honor to whom honor.' '' (Rom. XIII, 1-2-5)

''The law of God inculcates an obedient and submissive spirit in the state as well as in the household. An inspired Apostle gives us a true comment on the fifth commandment, when he says, (I Pet. II, 17.) 'Honor all men, love the brotherhood, fear God, honor the King.' The fierce spirit of independence that chafes under all restraint, and is not willing to pay respect to the person and office of those in authority, does not derive its inspiration from this Holy Book. Its origin and inspiration is earthly, sensual and devilish, and it is doubly wicked, when in a country like ours, where both the law and the ruler can be changed by the popular will legally expressed, it incites to popular violence, plots treason, or threatens revolution.''

In the fall of 1859 resistance against the civil Government was in violation of the law of God. If there were any persons who had been guilty of such violation, had not the General Assembly the right, and must it not maintain the position, that for wickedness so enormous they could not come back into the Church without penitence?

The time for adjournment having arrived, Mr. Clark yielded the floor, and the Assembly adjourned until afternoon.

AFTERNOON SESSION.

Rev. Mr. Brangle moved that so much of the Overture as related to the detaching of the Synod of Southern Iowa, and uniting it with the Synod of Kansas, be reconsidered, and the matter recommitted to the Committee on Bills and Overtures. The motion to reconsider was agreed to, and the matter was recommitted.

Rev. J. D. Wylie, of the Reformed Presbyterian Church, was then formally received by the Assembly. He stated that he had been delegated from the Synod of the Reformed Presbyterian Church to appear before this Assembly, and that it was the desire of his Synod that steps might be taken whereby the whole brotherhood of Presbyterians might stand together more unitedly than they had before. His Church subscribed to the same confession of faith, and used the same catechism, and nearly the same religious books as did the Old School Presbyterian Church; and the Synod of his Church had declared its readiness to respond to any action which might be inaugurated looking to a union. He thought, in reference to a common book of praise, committees could be appointed in all the Churches who would be able to secure a version of the Scripture Psalms which would be acceptable to the Church at large.

The Moderator responded by saying that he felt when they received delegates from the various branches of the Presbyterian Church, they were receiving members belonging to the same household. This Assembly recognized the soundness of the Faith of the Reformed Chusch, and when they spoke of a union of the two branches, he believed there was a sympathetic response on the part of the Assembly. While there was a hesitation as to an organic union with the other Assembly he did not think there was any objection to a full and cordial union with the Reformed Church. He concluded by alluding to a prominent member of the Reformed Church—Rev; George H. Stuart—as a perfect model of a Christian gentleman. He had been told that before the war commenced he sang only psalms; but he had been been at the head of that great philanthropic enterprise, the Christian Commission, and he thought he had made progress, and had sung hymns as well as psalms, not only on the battle field but in the Church. He hoped the time would come when they would all meet on common ground in their devotional exercises.

The Assembly then proceeded to ballot for officers to fill vacancies in the Boards of the several Theological Seminaries.

A committee was appointed to count the ballots, and retired for that purpose.

On motion of Rev. Mr. Raffensperger, the matter of changing the name of the Presbytery of Toledo, of Iowa, was taken up. He stated that the brethren of Iowa had agreed to the name of Vinton for their Presbytery, and if the change were made, it would avoid all further confusion between this Presbytery and others in Ohio.

The motion to change the name was agreed to.

The unfinished business was then taken up—the report of the committee in regard to the Louisville Presbytery.

Rev. Mr. Stewart desired to make a motion that no gentleman representing the affirmative side of question be allowed to speak until two gentlemen whom he underztood wished to obtain the floor on the side of the Declaration and Testimony, were allowed to speak. He had understood that Drs. Van Dyke and Brookes had desired the floor, but could not get a chance as there were so many on the affirmative side who desired to speak. He thought, as Chief Justice Marshall once said to a young lawyer, that he might take it for granted that the court knew some things, and so he thought that the gentlemen in the affirmative might take it for granted, that they did not represent all the eloquence and profundity in this body. He thought no more speeches were required on the affirmative side, and that after they heard the negative side they could finish the business and go home.

Mr. Galloway moved, as an amendment, that then the debate close. Lost.

Dr. Wm. Breckinridge moved to lay the motion on the table.

Mr. Clarke then resumed his argument. He said he would detain the Assembly but a few moments longer. He was fully aware that this Assembly embraced a great amount of the wisdom of the Presbyterian Church, but still it might happen, on certain points, even as humble a member as himself might be able to give information. The only remaining points he desired to discuss, were, what was the power of the Assembly as to the judgment that should be pronounced and what that judgment should be. He referred to the chapter on the power of the Assembly in the Digest and claimed that under that there could be no doubt of the power of this Assembly to dissolve the Louisville Presbytery. In regard to the two measures that had been proposed, he confessed that at first he was favorably inclined toward a plan similar to that proposed by Dr. Humphrey, but upon further examination he had become fully convinced that such a plan would be wholly ineffectual. He had listened with interest to the eloquent tones of Dr. Humphrey, which moved all hearts with emotion, and some to tears, in his earnest plea for mercy. Dr. Humphrey had said that the Kentuckians were a good people. Mr. C. conceded that there were many great and good men in Kentucky, but it is, also, true that if there were mischievous men anywhere they were to be found in Kentucky. And if they left the settlement of this affair in the hands of the Synod of Kentucky, as at present constituted, he felt sure that they would be greatly disappointed. He did not believe the churches of Kentucky would have peace until they were subjected to the administration of the power of the Assembly. It was not the question of loyalty or disloyalty to the Government that was involved in this matter, but loyalty to the Church; and there was every indication that the Church in Kentucky would be ruined by the spirit of contention at present prevailing in it, unless the power of the Assembly was put forth. And he claimed that in the report of the committee, this power had been put forth firmly and yet kindly, and in a manner that would prove to be for the best interests of the Church. He believed that if they withheld the settlement of this question until the next General Assembly the Church of Kentucky would swing from her moorings, and there would be contentions vastly greater than those they were called upon to consider now, and unless they were now arrested the Church would never cease to regret the neglect to seize the present opportunity.

Rev. Dr. West obtained the floor, but gave way for Rev. Dr. Van Dyke, of Brooklyn.

Dr. Van Dyke addressed the Assembly for nearly two hours in opposition to the report. His argument was mostly written. He begged them to lay aside all prejudice which they might have formed against him, and to hear him speak for himself. He was no rebel to the State or to the Church. He thanked the gentleman (Mr. Clark) for reading from his declarations, and he wished he had read more, wherein he spoke of the right of revolution, and concerning the obedience of servants to their masters. He had always obeyed human law, according to the Divine command, and he had never, in thought, word or deed, so far as he was conscious, before God, been guilty of resistance to the lawful authority of the Church; and he had never entered into any plans with men who intended to divide the Church. He claimed the Declaration and Testimony men, whatever might have been their errors, never intended to divide the Church.

At the conclusion of Dr. Van Dyke's remarks, Rev. Dr. Gurley offered the following substitute for the resolutions of the Committee:

Resolved, That this General Assembly does hereby condemn the Declaration and Testimony as a slander against the Church, schismatical in its character and aim, and its adoption by any of our church courts is an act of rebellion against the authority of the General Assembly.

Resolved, That the whole subject contemplated in this report, including the report itself, be referred to the next General Assembly.

Resolved, That the signers of the Declaration and Testimony, and the members of the Presbytery of Louisville who voted to adopt that paper, be summoned and they are hereby summoned to appear before the next General Assembly to answer for what they have done in this matter, and that until their case is decided they shall not be permitted to sit as members of any church court higher than the Session.

Resolved, That if any Presbytery shall disregard this action of the General Assembly, and at any meeting shall enroll as entitled to a seat or seats in the body one or more persons designated in the preceding resolutions and summoned to appear before the next General Assembly, then that Presbytery shall ipso facto be dissolved, and its ministers and elders who adhere to this action of the Assembly are hereby authorized and directed in such cases to take charge of the Presbyterial records and retain the name and exercise all the authority and functions of the original Presbytery until the next meeting of the General Assembly.

Resolved, That Synods, at their next stated meetings, in making up their rules shall be guided and governed by the action of the General Assembly.

Dr. Gurley said this Presbytery had committed a grave offense, which they could not pass by and for which they must be and ought to be called to account, and he was free to say that if this General Assembly should decide to pass by that offense without calling these brethren to account, then, much as he loved the Presbyterian Church, long and faithfully as he had endeavored to serve her, he should feel obliged to seek a home in some other connection. He was not willing to retain his connection with a Church which would suffer brethren to flaunt such insult and abuse in the face of its highest judicatory and then let that offense pass unrebuked. He proposed in his substitute to give these brethren ample time to consider what they had done, and to say whether they will retract. He did not doubt the authority of the Assembly to do just what was proposed in the report of the committee, but he recollected that while all things were lawful, all things were not expedient. He believed it would be better to defer the matter as he had proposed, as there was no extreme necessity for their passing immediately on the case of these brethren.

At the conclusion of Dr. Gurley's remarks the Assembly adjourned.

TWELFTH DAY—THURSDAY, MAY 31, 1866.

MORNING SESSION.

The assembly met at 8½ o'clock.

After devotional exercises and the reading of the minutes,

Mr. Galloway, of Ohio, rose to a privileged question and read from a letter, written, as he alleged, by the Rev. Mr. Ferguson, a member of the Assembly, and published in the Ohio Statesman.

[The extracts contain severe personal strictures upon Mr. Galloway, and also reflect upon the character of the Assembly.]

After reading the extracts Mr. Galloway said he had no remarks to offer, but would leave the matter with the Assembly.

Rev. Dr. Krebs. I wish to move, after making the inquiry, "was that letter written by Rev. Mr. Ferguson—

Rev. Mr. Ferguson. I hope the house will permit me to explain.

Dr. Krebs. I wish to make a motion and then you can have an opportunity to explain.

Rev. Mr. Ferguson. I wish to be permitted—

Dr. Krebs. Does the gentleman acknowledge himself to be the author of that article.

Rev. Mr. Ferguson. I ask the privilege of making an explanation. I do not deny it.

Mr. Galloway. I say he is the author, I know it.

Dr. Krebs. I move that unless he forthwith retracts, and apologizes to this house in the most ample manner, he be forthwith expelled.

Rev. Mr. Crozier. I move that he be referred to his Presbytery as a slanderer, to be tried.

Rev. Mr. Riggs. I think before we pass this motion we ought to give Mr. Ferguson the liberty to make his explanation.

The Moderator. Of course he will be heard.

Mr. Day. I move that Rev. Mr. Ferguson be requested to make any explanation he desires to make, and let us have it now, so that it shall not be understood that he has been shut off.

Dr. Patterson. I move that he be permitted—not requested.

The Moderator. No one has tried to prevent him. I do not think the motion should be to permit. I wish to make this statement. Mr. Ferguson is of course allowed, and it is his privilege and right, to speak without any such motion, and I wish him and every member of the Assembly to understand that he has not been debarred, in a privilege or right to speak I only called him to order, until Dr. Krebs' motion could be heard. It is his right to speak.

Mr. Day. I wish to take away every excuse he may urge that he was not allowed to speak, and to show that he was requested to speak.

The Moderator. My design was to show that no attempt had been made to debar his right.

Rev. Mr. Heckman. I ask that he be permitted, I do not want to request him. Will the gentleman accept that as an amendment?

Mr. Day. I will not accept; I wish to request him, and if he will not respond, let him be forever silent.

Mr. Clarke. Upon Mr. Day's motion I move the previous question.

Dr. Krebs. My motion affords an opportunity of explanation, and demands an explanation. I wish to read it.

Resolved, That unless Mr. Ferguson immediately retract the statements in this offensive publication, and make ample apology to the satisfaction of this house, he be immediately expelled.

Rev. Dr. Stonerode moved that the motion for the previous question be put upon the table in order to give Mr. Ferguson an opportunity to be heard. Motion was agreed to.

The Moderator. Mr. Ferguson can now be heard if he wishes.

Dr. Krebs. I hope Mr. Ferguson will be heard. I am ready to hear anything he may have to say by way of apology or retraction.

Dr. Humphrey. I move that this whole matter be referred to a select committee. [Voices—no, no.] With the agitated condition in which we are, probably some advantage might be gained to ourselves, and we might be able to come to a satisfactory conclusion, if this were referred to a committee. This is a serious and important matter, and I think we should have the advantage of such a committee as could confer with all the parties.

Mr. Willis. That would be more appropriate after the gentleman is heard.

The Moderator. Mr. Ferguson is now requested to make an explanation. [After a pause.] If Mr. Ferguson does not speak I shall put the question.

The question was put, on the motion of Dr. Krebs, and carried by an overwhelming vote.

Dr. Van Dyke was understood to protest.

The Moderator. The motion is adopted, and under it Mr. Ferguson is expelled from the General Assembly. [Applause in the galleries.]

Mr. Ferguson came forward and attempted to speak, but was interrupted by cries of order.

Dr. Krebs. I move to reconsider the vote just taken in order to afford the gentleman an opportunity to be heard.

The Moderator. Before putting the question, I paused in order to afford Mr. Ferguson the opportunity to explain, which he declined to use.

Rev. Mr. Ferguson. I did not understand it so, if you will excuse me from saying so.

The Moderator. I waited long enough, in my judgment, and in the judgment of the Assembly, for him to speak.

Mr. Wilson. I hope, Moderator, that even though the brother had an opportunity and declined, that an opportunity may again be afforded. Our discipline requires that after we have cited a man and he declines or refuses, that we shall cite him again. [Voices. Hear him.]

The question was put, and the motion to reconsider was agreed to with but one dissenting voice.

The Moderator. Mr. Ferguson now has an opportunity to explain.

Rev. Mr. Ferguson. In regard to the article which Mr. Galloway read, I acknowledge that I wrote it. I wrote it under excitement, shortly after Mr. Galloway spoke. My attention was afterwards called to one fact, which was a mistake—that the matter was stated hypothetically in regard to Dr. Boardman; that it was stated "if so and so occurred," &c. The manuscript had gone, and I was sorry I had stated it in that particular. In regard to the other facts, I can state that they are all true; that members on the side of the house to which Mr. Galloway belongs, said those things to me, and that they were very sorry that he had done so; and as for the exhibition he made of himself, in regard to posture, this house is my witness. I had heard Mr. Galloway before, but I had never seen him make such an exhibition of himself; and I confess, under the undue excitement of sorrow that my friend Galloway had acted so, I wrote with a greater strength than perhaps was judicious or proper for a Christian minister, and if I had had the manuscript afterwards, of course it would have been a great deal modified. But the very things referred to in that letter have been spoken of either by citizens of this town or members of this house, in both the street cars and on the steps of the church. I regret exceedingly that these things should have gone forth, to the injury of Mr. Galloway, and under other circumstances, if done over again, I should not write them just in that form. My apology for this is, I expected Mr. Galloway to be a conservative man on this subject. He and I were in discussion last October, in the Synod of Ohio, when a resolution was brought up to cordially indorse the General Assembly, and he arose in his seat and said: "I move 'cordially' be struck out—that I do not cordially indorse the General Assembly in all particulars.'' I respected the brother's conscience and feelings, and hence, when he came out that day in the extreme radicalism of the hour, I mas undoubtedly thrown off my bearings, and wrote these things under the spur of the moment, and hope that if in so doing I have injured the dignity of the house, and the character of that brother whom I greatly respect, I will be excused for this, and that there will be no undue severity or advantage taken. For Mr. Galloway, personally, I have kind feelings towards him, and my heart is right, however my head may have erred. Under the excitement of the hour, and the remarkable excitement of this Assembly, with these nerves of mine that are not entirely stable, I may have penned things derogatory somewhat to the decorum of the house, and hope, so far as I have injured the decorum, I may be excused, and that all the members, individually and conjointly, may be more careful of the dignity of the house than they have been; or if there is a committee appointed, and further explanation necessary, I am willing to meet with them. I have no hard feelings against any man or individual. I repeat again that I wrote under the spur of the moment. It is my first error in this particular, and I ask therefore that you will not visit me with that censure that this house seems willing to vote—or the great majority of them. I will say as far as that statement about Dr. Boardman is concerned, I did not hear Mr. Galloway aright. He did use the language that was there, but it was in a hypothetical sense, and not positively. This is the explanation I have to make, and if a committee is appointed to hear any further explanation, and Brother Galloway wishes it, I am willing to appear before them, and if I have erred I am willing to be forgiven. I will not be so severe hereafter, but will tell the truth in another way.

Mr. McKnight desired to offer an amendment

Mr. Day. I would like to ask Mr. Ferguson if he wrote this letter for publication—expecting it would be published?

Mr. Ferguson. I expected extracts would be published giving an account of the matter. As far as I knew the letter was to be all published.

Mr. Day. I would like to know what the gentleman has to say of his statement in regard to the character of this house.

Mr. Ferguson. That was designed merely as a quotation—that I had heard men make these statements.

Mr. Day. I would ask the gentleman if he intended to state it as his views.

Mr. Ferguson. No more than as a report—that it was the belief of many in this city that this General Assembly under an excited state of feeling, was doing more injury to the cause of religion than the horse races, because of their position, and I have heard many brethren say that here.

Mr. McKnight then offered the following as an amendment:

Resolved, That the Rev. Wm. M. Ferguson, a commissioner to this General Assembly, because of a gross, abusive, and scandalous libel, published in the Ohio Statesman, on members of this body, which he has now qualified in the presence of the Assembly is entitled to, and does hereby receive the grave censure of this Assembly.

Rev. Dr. Brown said he was opposed to the amendment, simply because this was not the first offense of the brother. They had seen statements in the Eastern papers, taken from the Ohio Statesman, extracted from the correspondence of that paper, written by a member of this General Assembly, in which the same—

Mr. Ferguson. I never wrote a letter to the Ohio Statesman before. This is the first communication I ever sent for publication.

Dr. Brown. Are you not the author of that letter describing the manner in which the Moderator was elected?

Mr. Ferguson. No, sir.

Dr. Brown. It has been attributed to you.

Mr. Ferguson. No, sir; I am a new correspondent of that paper.

Dr. Krebs. We have all heard Mr. Ferguson, and I am willing, I repeat, to hear him in full, in way of explanation, apology or retraction—the last being an indispensable requisite. I think this Assembly needs no words from me, or anybody else, to be thoroughly convinced that this is one of the grossest outrages ever offered to a deliberative body. It is a gross insult to this Assembly, and to the whole Presbyterian Church. I am Mr. Ferguson's friend. He has been my guest, and a very pleasant and acceptable one—but I know no man after the flesh. I shall move you, sir, if it be in order, and if not in order now, I shall move it hereafter, that there be a record to this effect—

Rev. Mr. Herron. Is there not now a motion pending before this body?

The Moderator. Yes, sir.

Mr. Herron. Then is it right that we should entertain another motion on the top of that?

The Moderator. I understand the gentleman is reading this for information, as a part of his speech.

Dr. Krebs. My motion is that the records shall state what has occurred as follows, and I offer it as a substitute for Mr. McKnight's motion:

[The paper will be found elsewhere, as subsequently offered by Dr. Krebs, in a more complete form.]

Rev. Dr. West. I rise to ask the house to permit me to read the commission of Rev. Mr. Ferguson to this Assembly and what he says was the object for which he came to this body. It is a public document with some notes and declarations of Mr. Ferguson attached. It is addressed to the chairman of the Committee on Hospitality and Entertainment.

Dr. West then read as follows:

COMMISSIONER TO THE GENERAL ASSEMBLY FROM THE PRESBYTERY OF ZANESVILLE, SYNOD OF OHIO.

WASHINGTON, O., April 26, 1866.

DEAR BRO: I think I know you personally. Did you not once publish the St. Louis Presbyterian? If so, I saw you when on my way to General Assembly in New Orleans some years ago. I also wrote you some articles for your paper against ultraism. Politically, I am the same yet, and am sent by my Presbytery to oppose the radical measures that may come up at our meeting in your city.

Please let my dear Bro. Brookes see this, and to you and him I would say that my wife is to be with me at the Assembly, and I ask as a special favor to furnish her as well as myself a good place to stay. I am to report to two or three papers, (Ohio Statesman, Cincinnati Enquirer and Presbyterian, of Philadelphia,) and any favors shown me or wife shall be thankfully received and faithfully recorded and published to the honor of your great city. Please answer soon on the receipt of this. Address me at Washington, Guernsey county, Ohio.

W. M. FERGUSON.

Rev. Dr. Schenck. I desire to make an explanation. I wish to say in behalf of the editor of the Philadelphia Presbyterian, that I understood from him, before I left there, that Mr. Ferguson was not employed to report for that paper.

Mr. McKnight raised a point of order that this was all extraneous to the question pending.

The Moderator said that he considered the paper was a part of the speech of Dr. West, and it was common for persons to read documents as parts of their speeches on questions pending.

Mr. Day said he had no sympathy with the political feelings or status of Mr. Ferguson, but he sympathised with him in the position in which he was placed. He believed that in a moment of excitement he had committed an act which he would always regret. He was sorry for him that he had committed such a grave act, and he did not stand here to ask that that offense should be passed over. The dignity of the house required that it should vindicate its honor, but he asked the house that their judgment might be tempered with mercy, otherwise this gentleman would go out with a fraud upon him which could never be wiped away—with the mark of Cain, which he would carry to his grave. He was required to retract in a moment of great excitement, and he believed he would make a proper retraction, one that would give satisfaction, if they would give him opportunity.

Mr. Ferguson. If you will allow me to say so I will take it all back now.

Mr. Day said he was glad to see the gentleman was ready to apologize and retract. It was the exercise of a Christian spirit that was commendable. He besought the whole Assembly now to receive the brother back again. He believed he would make an ample apology, one that would be satisfactory not only to the Assembly but to Mr. Galloway. He would ask Brother Ferguson if he was not ready to make a full retraction.

Rev. Mr. Ferguson. I confess I am sorry that under the spur of the moment I wrote so hastily those things I heard from other brethren, and I am willing to meet with Mr. Galloway and other brethren and make such explanation as will be satisfactory to them.

Mr. Day. I move that he be allowed this afternoon to make such retraction as will be satisfactory to this Assembly, in writing. I think it is no more than right that he should do so, and give it to Brother Galloway. It is noble for a man when he has done wrong to confess it.

Mr. Ferguson. What do you want confessed? I confess I am sorry I wrote it, and when I wrote it I had no intention of injuring the dignity of this body. I thought what I said about Mr. Galloway was severe, but just what the people told me, and what they felt on the subject. In regard to any misstatements in it made dogmatically, whether stated by way of hypothesis or otherwise, that was a misunderstanding on my part. You remember what he said—that he would not commune with Brother Boardman till he washed his hands of that.

A Member. Is the brother willing that it shall be published, that he here retracts and apologizes to this house for the insult which he has given it?

Mr. Ferguson. I am willing it shall go to the world in this light; that I am sorry I ever wrote these things on this subject; but so far as there is anything there that is a misstatement, it was altogether from a misunderstanding of the brother's hypothesis. If you will look at the brother's speech, it is there hypothetically.

A member. Will he acknowledge the charge is not true?

Mr. Ferguson. I acknowledge, as far as my presentation of it goes, it is incorrect; but so far as the hypothesis is concerned, it is correct. Bro. Galloway did say, if Bro. Boardman did not do so and so. That was what called my attention to it, and after the latter had gone, I asked about that. "Did you hear Bro. Galloway say so and so," and the reply was, hypothetically, he said so. I was shocked when I understood him at the time. He told us to go away and hang ourselves, like Judas. It filled me with the electricity which the brother spoke of, and afterwards a brother came to me and asked me if Bro. Galloway was addicted to intemperance. I answered, "No, sir; he is a strong temperance man." The brother said he thought he had a "Highland gill" in his cheek. I said I disapproved of all these statements, and that he was a strong temperance man. If I have erred against the brother, I take the error all back.

Mr. Galloway interrupted by saying this charge was false and scandalous.

Mr. Ferguson. What charge?

Mr. Galloway. That I was vulgar.

Mr. Ferguson. I said he acted vulgarly here.

Mr. Galloway. No man has ever charged me with being intemperate or vulgar.

Mr. Ferguson. I have not done it.

Mr. Galloway. I want no recantation except that this charge is false and scandalous; that its publication shall be in the same paper as that in which the charges were made—that it may go before my family and friends as this libel has gone. Sir, I will not sit in the same Assembly wit a man who characterizes me as a buffoon and a blackguard.

Rev. Dr. Laws did not think there was any necessity for precipitate haste in settling this matter, and he desired to offer an amendment that Drs. Krebs and Humphreys be appointed a committee to confer with these two gentlemen and propose terms of agreement.

The Moderator said the amendment was not in order.

Mr. Wilson said that nothing would be lost by taking time to consider this matter. He moved, therefore, that it be postponed until this afternoon with a view of affording Mr. Ferguson an opportunity to present his statement in writing.

Dr. West moved to lay the motion on the table, which was agreed to.

Rev. Mr. Herron thought the longer action was postponed the more likely they would be to act with deliberation and calmness. This brother was evidently of an excitable temperament, and the kind of labor he had performed before he entered the ministry had developed this excitability. He sympathized with him, the more so since he had been informed that by his own unaided efforts he secured an education which enabled him to enter the ministry. He had been the correspondent of a number of papers, and sometimes he had allowed his pen a good deal of liberty. Heretofore he had been arraigned only at the bar of public opinion, as to the correctness of his reports, but to-day he occupied a different position. He was evidently laboring under intense excitement, and this Assembly was not wholly free from it. He supposed that since the Presbyterian Church was founded, no such action had been taken as was here proposed. He hoped, therefore, they would not act rashly or harshly, and thus stand before the world in a false attitude. He had understood the gentleman had retracted.

Mr. Ferguson. I repeat it, so far as I infringed on Mr. Galloway. So far as my intention appears to misrepresent that brother, I am exceedingly sorry my pen run in that dogmatical way, for the whole thing is hypothetical, as you see.

Dr. McLean. Dr., you admit that it is false and slanderous?

Mr. Ferguson. As reported there, but it was not my intention.

Dr. McLean. Did you write it at that table?

Mr. Ferguson. No, Sir. It was written after I went home. Then I was asked whether Mr. Galloway had been drinking. I said no, he was a strong temperance man.

Dr. McLean. After you went home did you believe Mr. Galloway a fool?

Mr. Fisher. I rise to a point of order. Mr. Herron has the floor.

The Moderator. I understand that gentleman gave way.

Mr. Herron continued by saying that he had no sympathy with Mr. Ferguson's political views, but thought in a case of so much importance they should not act hastily.

Rev. Mr. Shiland suggested that Dr. Krebs, Mr. Galloway and Mr. Ferguson, be allowed to retire, to permit Mr. Ferguson to write such an apology as would be satisfactory to Mr. Galloway.

The suggestion was not entertained.

Dr. Boardman. Had not seen the paper referred to in the remarks of the members, had not heard it read, and did not wish to hear it read, but was willing to take the representations made of it by the members he had heard speak. Called upon the Assembly to remember the Master's teachings, and take heed to itself, as well as to Mr. Ferguson. Quoted the passage "If thy brother trespass against thee, &c." Every one had need of forgiveness. Called to mind the action of Christ when denied by Peter, with cursing. He turned and looked on Peter, and he went out weeping bitterly. [A voice—Where are Mr. Ferguson's tears? Does the Bible teach that we are to forgive without repentance?] Would the Assembly refuse this erring brother opportunity to go out? Would it pass this tremendous judgment upon him in the excitement of this hour? Would it exact of him that he should upon the instant exhibit all the fruits of repentance? All he asked of the Assembly was delay. That the members would do as they would be done by. He moved that the whole matter be referred to a committee.

The reading of the resolutions with the amendments was called for, and they were read.

Rev. Mr. Frazer asked of Mr. Ferguson if the communication was written immediately after a certain conversation with a gentleman by the name of Allen.

Mr. Ferguson couldn't state whether it was or not.

Mr. Frazer then went on to say that if it was, he could state from his personal knowledge that at that time Mr. Ferguson was laboring under intense excitement, to that degree that if ever a man of sane mind was not accountable for what he said or did, Mr. F. could not have been then. That he told Mr. Ferguson if he didn't quit talking in the manner in which he was then talking he would utterly ruin himself and that people would think he was crazy. That he utterly condemned the article altogether, but didn't know that he himself was in some degree accountable for the result which followed, by adding, by his remarks to Mr. Ferguson, somewhat to the provocation, but at the same time he did not regard Mr. Ferguson's explanation as satisfactory.

Dr. Lowrie thought the house was nearly ready to come to a vote on the question and wished to make a single suggestion. The offense was a grave one. The offensive article had been written and printed and sent broadcast through the country, and any explanation or retraction should come before the Assembly in somewhat the same form—not printed, perhaps, but written. Thought it would be wise to suspend action until Mr. Ferguson could write down his explanation of the subject, and would say he thought, in coming to a judgment, the Assembly was bound to take into account the characteristics of the brother.

Dr. McLean. There had been a great deal of advice to this house to be calm from a certain quarter, as if the excitement were all on one side. Dr. Boardman had read the Assembly a very pious lecture; but not one word was said to the offenders. Great forbearance must be exercised by the house, but there was no excitement to be allayed on the other side; they were all calm and undisturbed like Dr. Boardman and men on the other side. He asked what sign of repentance had been seen on the part of the offending brother. He characterized the letter as the most monstrous libel on this or any other deliberative body that had ever been issued. Since 1788 there never had been such an outrage perpetrated on the Assembly.

Dr. Montfort rose to a point of order, that Dr. McL. was not speaking to the question, which was upon the motion to refer to a committee.

Dr. McLean being allowed to proceed, said that perhaps the Assembly had not fully appreciated the article in question; he would read it again ; and commenced reading the article.

Mr. Day objected to the paper being read again.

Dr. McLean insisted upon his right to read the article as a part of his speech, and proceeded to do so, commenting as he went along upon the grossness of the libel, and the great indecency of expression.

It was noticeable during the reading of this article, particularly the more gross and scandalous portions of it, that there were persons in the galleries who listened to it with much satisfaction, as a tendency to merriment, almost breaking out into applause, was plainly audible.

Dr. McLean spoke of the wide-spread injury done by this article, both to the Assembly and to Mr. Galloway, whose reputation was injured by such publications, as it would go in the prints, where no retraction or explanation would follow it. Commented upon the insufficiency of the explanation of Mr. Ferguson, who had only said in substance that he wouldn't do it again just in that way, but hadn't said he wouldn't do it again in some other way. Maintained that the resolution offered by Dr. Krebs spoke the truth and ought to be adopted.

Rev. Mr. Reinboth moved to lay all the motions before the house, excepting Dr. Krebs', on the table. Carried.

Dr. Krebs again read his resolutions with some emendations rendered necessary by the further action of the Assembly, as follows :

Resolved, That whereas the Rev. W. M. Ferguson, a commissioner to this General Assembly, is, by his own acknowledgment, guilty of writing and publishing in the Ohio Statesman a gross, abusive, scandalous and slanderous libel against members of this Assembly and against this Assembly itself, and although he has qualified it in the presence of this Assembly this morning, his explanation is not deemed satisfactory.

Resolved, That the Rev. W. M. Ferguson be forthwith expelled as a member of this house,

A motion for the previous question was carried.

Dr. Krebs' resolution then prevailed, with a very light vote in the negative.

Moderator. I NOW ANNOUNCE AGAIN THAT REV. W. M. FERGUSON IS EXPELLED FROM THE GENERAL ASSEMBLY. I wish to state, if I am incorrect, I wish to be informed of it, that this necessarily involves his being expelled from the house, and from the table as a correspondent. [Applause in the galleries.]

Rev. Mr. Shiland. I offer the following resolution:

Resolved, That debate on all propositions now before the Assembly, or that may come before it on the subject matter of the Louisville Presbytery, or on the Declaration and Testimony, be closed at five o'clock this day, and that a vote bethen taken without further debate.

And moved the previous question.

Dr. Breckinridge moved that the motion for the previous question be laid on the table. Carried.

A motion then prevailed to lay Mr. Shiland's motion on the table.

The Moderator then announced that Rev. E. D. McMaster, D. D., had been elected to the Chair of Theology in the Theological Seminary of the Northwest.

The Assembly then voted to take up the unfinished business of the last session, being Dr. Gurley's substitute for the report of the committee in regard to the Louisville Presbytery.

The Moderator announced that Dr. West was entitled to the floor.

Dr. West commented upon the great interest which the public felt in the discussions upon this question. Almost every whisper in the house was reported not only in the religious, but in the secular papers; referred to those in the galleries who honored the Assembly with their presence, and dishonored it during a portion of the sessions with their disorders; affirmed that the unpleasant business by which the Assembly had been delayed at this session (that gross insult to the Assembly) was but a palpable expression of what had been witnessed in the galleries; was sure that no lady and no gentleman, especially no Christian man or woman, [A voice—Are these remarks to the question?] who remembered the fact that they stood before the altar of the Presbyterian Church, would for one moment think of trespassing on the propriety and sanctity of this court.

He characterized the movement of the "Declaration and Testimony" men as the continuation in the Church of God by ministers, elders and the people of the gigantic rebellion which had enveloped the whole land in mourning, lamentation and woe, and affirmed that the aiders and abettors, defenders and apologists of these men are the aiders, abettors, apologists and defenders of that gigantic rebellion through which the Church of God was now passing.

Wished it understood that the speech of his colleague (Dr. Van Dyke) did not represent the principles of any considerable part of the Presbytery of Nassau. Read from a pamphlet entitled "Politics for Christians, by Rev. H. J. Van Dyke," being a sermon preached on Thanksgiving day, 1856, about two weeks after the election of Hon. James Buchanan to the Presidency. What was then Dr. Van Dyke's opinion of the indications of discontent in Massachusetts and other parts of New England, and asked why the same opinion was not applicable to like discontent in the South after the election of Mr. Lincoln. He read from a pubished letter written by Dr. Van Dyke to some one in Georgia, before the secession of South Carolina, and before the Synod of South Carolina had taken its action, clearly counseling rebellion as a religious duty.

Dr. Van Dyke. Will you go on and read the conclusion of that letter?

Dr. West. No, sir, I won't. Every sentence is conclusive.

After reading further extracts from the letter, and commenting upon Dr. Van Dyke's political and Church relations, he said:

He and I personally have no difficulty, but we understand each other most exactly and distinctly on this question." Stated Dr. Van Dyke's arguments to be, that unless the injunctions and orders of the

General Assembly of the Presbyterian Church were obligatory on the inferior courts the Louisville Presbytery was not in rebellion, and the action of the General Assembly against the Louisville Presbytery could not be sustained. The speaker admitted that the whole question was right there, and proceeded to show that the General Assembly had not in 1861 or 1865 decided any political question, but had affirmed a point long before decided; that the action of the Assembly did not infringe unwarrantably upon the behests of conscience; that it had not undertaken to interpret the will of Providence without quoting a text; explained from the report of the Assembly its action with regard to the alleged difference of treatment of Northern and Southern people; claimed that the actions of the General Assembly were binding, as those of an ultimate final tribunal; that the doctrines in support of them were laid down in the confession of faith; held that all the questions raised in this matter had been decided adversely to the "Declaration and Testimony" men in the conflict from 1830 to 1838, between the new measure men and the Assembly, which resulted in the division into Old and New School; that it was then decided that there was no appeal from the decision of the General Assembly; that men must either conform with these decisions or go elsewhere; replied at length to the position taken that the acts of the General Assembly must be submitted to the Presbyteries for their approval before they can become the law of the Church; and asked if any one supposed that the Declaration and Testimony would have been any the more ready to submit if that had been the course taken, and closed by advocating the substitute offered by Dr. Gurley, and expressing his belief that if the Church of God had done her duty we never should have had civil war, and that if she did her duty now it would be the killing of this hydra of rebellion.

Mr. Cunningham obtained the floor, but gave way to Dr. Boardman, who, in turn, allowed Dr. Van Dyke to say that those parts of his letter as read by Dr. West, separately from the context, even if not so intended to do, gave an impression in regard to his views utterly unjust, false and injurious.

Dr. Yantis. I wish to know if it is not intended to let any of us terrible "Declaration and Testimony" men speak.

Moderator. Those who desire to speak must obtain the floor.

Dr. Yantis. We are in no hurry, but we desire to be heard.

Dr. Boardman, after offering to yield the floor to any of the Declaration and Testimony men who desired to speak, which offer no one accepted, proceeded to state that if the Presbytery concerned in this discussion had been that of the Passaic or of St. Lawrence, it never would have come before the Assembly in the aspect in which it is now; that the individual quarrels in Kentucky and Missouri, in which States the war had been one of neighborhoods, had been brought into the Assembly; was gratified that the appealed case had collapsed; reviewed in what seemed to be intended as a facetious vein, the reference of Dr. Thomas to the Assembly at Jerusalem, asking if St. Paul called together a caucus of ministers and elders, the evening before the Synod met.

At which point the Assembly adjourned until afternoon.

AFTERNOON SESSION.

Dr. Hand moved that the debate on the report in regard to the Louisville Presbytery should close at six o'clock; that after Dr. Boardman concluded, all speakers should be limited to fifteen minutes, save those who signed the Declaration and Testimony, who should not be restricted as to time.

He said the silent members of this house were entitled to some consideration. They were weary of this discussion. They felt that they understood the question. They were willing to hear the Declaration and Testimony brethren if they wished to speak, and after they had been heard he thought they would be prepared to vote. They had yet a great deal of business to transact. He thought also some regard should be paid to the people of St. Louis. He thought it would be an imposition on the people of St. Louis to extend their session beyond this week.

The motion of Dr. Hand was agreed to.

Mr. Day gave notice that at the proper time he should offer the following as a substitute for Dr. Gurley's proposition.

Whereas, This General Assembly has had brought to its notice a certain paper called a Declaration and Testimony, which it is alleged was adopted by the Louisville Presbytery, Sept. 2, 1865, and which imports to be signed by ministers and ruling elders belonging to other Presbyteries; and whereas, in the judgment of this General Assembly, the said paper is a most flagrant and unwarranted attack on the dignity and authority of the General Assembly, derogatory to its character, tending to bring odium and disrepute on the highest judicatory of the Church and to increase agitation and alienation in the bosom of the Church, schismatical in effect, contumacious in spirit, unjust and untrue in its statements; now, therefore, this General Assembly, in defence of its authority, in the exercise of its high prerogative to suppress schismatical contentions and disputations, reproving, warning and bearing testimony against error in doctrine and immorality in practice, and in the fulfillment of its sacred duty to secure the union, peace and mutual confidence of all our churches, do resolve,

1. That this General Assembly do consider the alleged action of the Louisville Presbytery and of the ministers and elders who have signed, published and disseminated the said paper called the "Declaration and Testimony," as worthy of the gravest censure of this body, and as an offense against the authority, peace and harmony of the Church, and as a sin against the Lord Jesus Christ, the great head of the Church.

2. That the Synod of Kentucky are hereby required, at their next meeting, to proceed in an orderly manner to try the Louisville Presbytery for the said alleged offense of adopting, publishing and dessemmating the said "Declaration and Testimony," and that they by their records at the next General Assembly do show what they have done in the premises.

3. That this Assembly do hereby require and enjoin on the said Louisville Presbytery to reconsider its action in adopting said "Declaration and Testimony" to cease from disseminating the same and from all agitations and contentions which tend to disturb the peace and harmony of the Church, and to submit themselves to the lawful authority of the Church of Christ as exercised by the General Assembly, and that by their commissioners they report their action in the premises to the next General Assembly.

4. That each and all the Presbyteries with whom any of the subscribers to said Declaration and Testimony are connected, are hereby required at their next meeting to proceed against such subscribers, and try them for said alleged acts in signing and giving publicity to said document, and if it is found that they have been guilty of offense in so doing, that each of said Presbyteries respectively do censure their conduct, and require such members to confess their error, and to cease from their agitations; and such Presbyteries are hereby required by their commissioners to appear at the next General Assembly, and report their action in the premises, while such persons are under process, as aforesaid, to suspend their privilege of deliberating and voting as members, until the process is finally issued; and it is further ordered that the members of said Presbyteries, who have not subscribed said "Declaration and Testimony," shall have the authority of such Presbyteries respectively, shall exercise its proper functions, and shall have charge of the Presbyterial records.

The consideration of the report concerning the Louisville Presbytery was resumed.

Dr. Boardman spoke at great length in opposition to the report; reviewed the past action of the Assembly; considered that its acts for the past three years had been unconstitutional and its requisitions unrighteous and impracticable, and that the Assembly had no power to table the action proposed.

At the conclusion of Dr. B.'s remarks, Mr. Clarke moved that the vote by which it was decided that the debate on the question should close at six o'clock, be reconsidered. Agreed to, and a further motion was adopted extending the time to eleven o'clock to-day.

There being considerable confusion in the house in consequence of a fire in the vicinity, the Assembly at a few minutes past five adjourned to eight o'clock in the evening.

EVENING SESSION.

Rev. Mr. Cunningham obtained the floor, and in reply to Dr. Boardman, said he (Dr. B) represented but a small number of the churches and ministers of Philadelphia, and proceeded to argue the constitutionality of the Assembly's action, when, by request, he gave way to Rev. Dr. Brookes.

Rev. Mr, Smith, of Baltimore, spoke a few moments, urging the Assembly to consider what a division, not only of his own Presbytery, but the whole Church, would be made by the adoption of the committee's report, and was followed by Rev. Dr. Brookes, of this city, in a lengthy, but eloquent and ingenious speech in behalf of the Louisville Presbytery.

Rev. Mr. Yantis then obtained the floor, when the Assembly adjourned.

Speech of Rev. Dr. Humphrey.

The following is a brief abstract of the speech of Rev. Dr. Humphrey on Tuesday:

Rev. Dr. Humphrey, after reading his amendment to the report of the committee, which has been published, said that while other members of the Assembly would return to their various fields of labor and be wholly undisturbed by the questions involved in this controversy, the members of the Assembly from Kentucky, on the contrary, would be more or less affected by it, and, therefore, those who were to bear the brunt of this controversy hoped that the Assembly would bear with them while they expressed their views as to the effect of the measure proposed by the committee. Whatever the action of the Assembly might be, there were some of them who intended to stand by the Church; and they would go home and endeavor to repair the desolation around them. He desired to call the attention of the Assembly to the difference between his amendment and the resolutions of the committee. In the first place, as to the substance of the Declaration and Testimony, and the judgment which they affirmed on that document, the report of the committee and his amendment do not materially differ. Probably the difference between the two in this matter, was more verbal than otherwise. There were three parties in reference to this Declaration and Testimony, namely: those who sustained that document, those who were called the middle-men, and those who were represented by the appeals on yesterday. Between the latter and the middle-men, as they were called, there was no material difference as to the character of the doctrines in this pamphlet. He believed in the principle that all things secular in their nature belong to the State, and all that was spiritual belonged to the Church; but in the great rebellion which they had survived there were moral principles involved which went to the foundation of moral obligation. These questions belonged to the Church, and he thanked God that this great Church in the past five years had declared its Testimony, and attempted to expound the word of God on all those principles. He had not been able to agree with every part of that Testimony, believed that some of it was not in precise accordance with the principles on which these questions should be settled. But the great body of that Testimony as deduced from the word of God, he stood by, and expected to stand by until the end. He supposed, therefore, they were all agreed as to the spirit of this Declaration and Testimony. Until he read that document he was not aware how rich the English language was in terms of objurgation. These terms dance through the whole book, and move to the music of Dixie. So far he proposed in his amendment that the General Assembly should rebuke that spirit. But he contended that the mode proposed by the committee was partial, while his amendment was comprehensive. As had been declared by a gentleman outside of the Presbytery of Louisville, there was no more reason why they should punish the members of that Presbytery than the members of other Presbyteries who were involved in this matter. There was a great deal in the form of judicial proceedings, where either the life, liberty or ecclesiastical relations of the people of God were at stake. The forms embodied the spirit of justice, and they could not trample down the forms of justice without trampling down justice itself. But the plan proposed by the committee was anomalous, unprecedented. The dissolution of the Presbytery of Philadelphia had been cited, but they would observe that the unconstitutionality of the proceedings whereby that Presbytery was established was the ground of its dissolution. It was dissolved because it never had a legal existence. He contended that never before in the history of the Church had a Presbytery been dissolved in the manner in which it was proposed to dissolve the Louisville Presbytery. In the dissolution of the Presbytery of Philadelphia there was a clause in the ordinance which saved the ecclesiastical position of every minister in the bounds of the Presbytery, but here the contrivance was to shut brethren out of the Church, and there was no precedent for it. He wished it to be remembered that these brethren were to be turned out of church without a hearing. It might be said they had a right to come here and be heard. But they were turned out in the beginning and regarded themselves—he would not say justly—as precluded from returning until they received instructions from their Synod. He next referred to the provision in the Book of Discipline in reference to citation, which requires that, although the accused may declare he will not appear on the first citation, yet the second citation must by no means be omitted. These brethren had been cited to appear, but under circumstances which they think they are not authorized to respond to; and the Assembly could not proceed to the extent of administering severe justice in the case which they might do if they had given these brethren a fair chance. He deprecated hasty action in the premises. This Declaration and Testimony was only issued in September last and he hoped no such summary action would be taken as proposed, but that one year more might be allowed, so that these brethren, if they could find it possible, might have an opportunity to return to the allegiance of the Church. He desired also that the matter might be put on such a footing as that a judicial trial of the case could take place. The speaker closed with an eloquent plea in behalf of the Presbyterian Church in Kentucky, in regard to its labors in the past, and he implored the Assembly to delay this question one year more, and then, if that branch of the Church in Kentucky did not bear fruit, they would stand by in silence and see it cut down.

Mr. McKnight desired to know of the speaker whether he had any hope or faith, even as a grain of mustard seed, that if this Assembly should forego the action now proposed, and which, to his mind, was so justly merited by that Presbytery, whether he thought there was any probability whatever that the Synod of Kentucky or the Presbytery of Louisville would review its action and come back to the Church.

Dr. Humphrey said he would answer frankly. He thought the measure he proposed was far more likely to accomplish that object than the measure of the committee, and further, that if they would adopt some such measure as he proposed, coupled with kindness and affection, to their erring Southern brethren—if they would open their hearts to them in some way he believed this agitation would be suppressed, and that they would come together in the unity of spirit and the bonds of peace.

Rev. Dr. West wished to know whether Dr. Humphrey had any faith that if the General Assembly would adopt the amendments which he had offered the Presbytery of Louisville would retract their open rebellion against the injunctions of the last General Assembly.

Dr. Humphrey said he could not answer the question, but thought they were far more likely to do it under a measure of this sort than under the measure proposed by the committee. If they would put this Church in a relation in some degree analagous to the relations which the churches of the South sustained to the Assembly, for the present, he thought, that under such a course the Presbytery of Louisville might be induced to retract. But he could not speak positively, as he did not reside in the bounds of the Presbytery of Louisville, but eighty miles away; and besides he had been in some respects engaged in bitter controversy with those brethren.

Mr. H. K. Clarke, of Detroit, obtained the floor. He began by alluding to the importance of the subject under consideration, and thought the Assembly might never again be called upon to settle principles of such vital importance as were involved in this controversy. He hoped, therefore, the question would be fully discussed. He was amazed, however, a few days ago, when he heard this discussion likened to a fight, and with all due respect to the gentleman from Philadelphia (Dr. Boardman), he was surprised that that gentleman could not find a fitting answer to the remark, "that while the soldiers were for peace, the ministers were for war." Instead of spending his powers in another direction, he wondered why the eloquent Doctor did not reply that war is carried on in the Church because the war is here. The rebellion is at an end against the civil authority. It is crushed, but is it not true that the rebellion against the Church is just as active and venomous as ever. There were two questions they were to meet—the question of the power of the Church, and the question whether this is a fitting occasion for the exercise of that power. There should be the amplest room for free discussion on these points, and no impatience of members should permit them to neglect the present duty of maintaining the deliverances of the Church.

Mr. Clarke proceeded with a discussion of the powers of the General Assembly to hear and determine the case now presented to the Assembly, and continued to the hour of adjournment.

THIRTEENTH DAY—FRIDAY, JUNE 1, 1866.

MORNING SESSION.

First half hour spent in devotional exercises.

Minutes were read and approved.

Dr. Yantis spoke in defense of the Declaration and Testimony men, claiming that the Assembly had no Scriptural right to bring political tests into the Church, nor to arraign men for conscientious protests against such acts of the Assembly. Referred to the Secretary of the Board of Domestic Missions as having attempted to crack his ecclesiastical whip in his race, at a distance of 1,000 miles away, but it didn't frighten him much; but he had been led to inquire on what meat this our Cæsar fed that he had grown so great. Styled the Secretary, in backwoods phrase, as a scavenger, or in more refined phrase, an ecclesiastical detective.

Rev. J. Addison Henry asked if the speaker had a right to attack the venerable Secretary, when he had not an opportunity to defend himself?

The speaker continued to say that he had been attacked at a time when he could not defend himself. Spoke excitedly and defiantly against the acts of the Assembly, asserting that those whom he represented could not, did not dare to undertake the performance of the orders of the Assembly; they did not intend to be attached to the tail of an abolition concern, and be dragged in triumph over this land of theirs; that these things couldn't be forced down the throats of the people; if they took it at all it must be taken in homeopathic doses; as for himself he couldn't do it; it was impossible for him to do it, and if he was to be cut off for that, the sooner it was done the better for the Assembly, and the better for him, for he would be the sooner out of suspense. He supposed it was possible for a man to go to heaven without going from the bosom of the Presbyterian Church; presumed he was talking to a jury whose verdict was already made up, and had thought so all the time; had no choice between the propositions that had been proposed; the only way to treat with the people of Kentucky and Missouri was in love; they were a forgiving people, and loved to forgive their brethren; there was no use to come among them with a sword, for nothing could be accomplished in that way.

Mr. Day had been recognized by the Moderator, and was about to take the stand, when the Moderator declared that Mr. McAfee had the preference as one of the Declaration and Testimony men.

Mr. McAfee referred to the fact that he had once before been a member of the General Assembly, in 1860—was reminded of the language of Job, "Oh! that it were with us as in months past," &c., &c. He had loved the Presbyterian Church; her gracious doctrines, and blessed standards; had labored with the brother who had just taken his seat, to keep their respective Churches in the Old School Presbyterian Church night and day, and had succeeded in doing so. It was not until the session of 1861, that he had met with anything connected with the Assembly that he could not subscribe to. Since that time he thought the Assembly had been gradually getting away from the old paths, and felt there was some degree of apology for the Assembly on account of the great excitement of the times, and the great pressure from without, but honestly believed, before God, that the Assembly had passed measures they had no right to pass; had been almost constrained to feel a gradual departure further from the Assembly. Its deliverances appeared to him to partake of a political character, and he had been taught that the kingdom of our Lord and Savior Jesus Christ, though in the world was not of the world. If the General Assembly would go back to the platform laid down in Kentucky by the venerable father in the Church, who had been here in a different attitude on this occasion, for one he would have met him and said, "Brother, how do you do?" His Presbytery in October had considered the deliverances of the Assembly from '61 and its orders to the lower judicatories prayerfully, and came, he believed, to the unanimous conclusion that they were deliverances which the General Assemely had no right or authority to make. It was not in a spirit of defiance, but because they believed the requirements were unscriptural, and they could not obey them without being guilty of acts repugnant to God's word; had felt, after careful and prayerful examination of the Declaration and Testimony, that he was bound to subscribe to every principle therein laid down; was surprised that the principles laid down in the pamphlet had not been assailed by any speaker here, and asserted that they could not be controverted; declared his loyalty; loved his country, if his country would let him love it; repelled the charge of having engaged in a conspiracy or combination to break up the Church, but stated that he had pledged himself to his brethren of his own Presbytery, and to the men he had joined here to stand with them for weal or for woe. His desire was to bring the Church back to its old standards; had nothing to say in regard to the several papers before the Assembly respecting the matter.

Mr. Day desired that what was done in this matter should be done in a constitutional way; objected to the resolutions of the committee as a matter of practice; might make a bad precedent, and because the judgment would be wrong; it would make trouble and occasion litigation in regard to Church property and funds; objected to Dr. Gurley's proposition because it was intended to bring individuals before the Assembly for trial, and offered a series of resolutions in place of Dr. Gurley's substitute, which were published in our last issue.

The Moderator announced that Mr. Day's resolutions could not be entertained, unless it were voted either to postpone Dr. Gurley's substitute, or lay it on the table

Dr. Gurley said he thought Dr. Brookes had misrepresented him in his speech, when he represented him as saying that he should withdraw from the Church if his proposition was not adopted—what he did say was that if the General Assembly would let such an offense as the "Declaration and Testimony" pass unrebuked, and let the offenders pass without calling them to account, he would feel obliged to seek a home in a Church where Presbyterian government and discipline was something more than a fancy and a form. He then read from manuscript his reasons for desiring that his substitute should be adopted.

Before Dr. Gurley was fairly through, the Moderator announced that the time had arrived for taking the vote.

Dr. Thomas moved to lay on the table the resolutions presented by the special committee, and the substitute of Dr. Humphrey.

The Moderator decided that if Dr. Thomas' motion prevailed, an affirmative vote, if had, would adopt the report of the committee with the substitute of Dr. Gurley in place of the resolutions reported by the committee.

The decision of the Moderator was appealed from and sustained by the house.

The motion of Dr. Thomas prevailed.

Mr. Day moved to postpone Dr. Gurley's substitute, and vote upon the resolutions presented by him. Laid upon the table.

Dr. Boardman moved that Dr. Gurley's paper be postponed and his substituted in its place. Laid upon the table.

The ayes and noes were called for.

Dr. Yantis inquired if he had a right to vote, and the Moderator replied that he had.

The ayes and noes were called. Dr. Brookes declined to vote. Mr. Howard of Buffalo city, changed his vote to aye, having at first voted no.

The Moderator. Before announcing the vote, I wish to say that immediately after its announcement I will entertain a motion that a brother be requested to lead us in prayer. The vote stands, affirmative 196, negative 37.

Dr. Brown moved that Rev. Dr. McGill be requested to lead the Assembly in prayer for God's blessing upon the Church. The motion prevailed, and Dr. McGill offered prayer.

Mr. Forman gave notice of a protest against the vote just taken.

After some little discussion on the part of Mr. Galloway and Drs. Krebs, West and Lowrie, a motion made by Mr. Galloway, that the several papers presented as substitutes by Drs. Humphrey and Boardman and Mr. Day be spread upon the minutes, and that their supporters be allowed to sign them, prevailed.

Dr. Yantis asked what was his position in the house.

The Moderator stated that by the effect of the resolution just adopted the signers of the Declaration and Testimony were no longer members of this Assembly.

J. M. Rice, who was sick and absent when the vote was taken, desired to record his vote and was permitted to do so. He voted aye, making the vote 197 to 37.

The vote, after above mentioned change and additions, stood as follows:

AYES.

David Lyon,
Joseph P. Brixley,
S. R. House,
G. W. Campbell,
Robert B. Walker,
James Allison,
George F. Cain,
Robert McKnight,
Wm. M. Francis,
J. W. Wightman,
P. D. Gurley,
R. G. McCreary,
Charles Ray,
E. D. Yeomans,
Allen Chaney,
Samuel T. Wilson,
F. T. Brown,
J. T. Bliss,
J. G. Montfort,
T. E. Thomas,
A. O. Patterson,
W. Thomas,
A. E. Chamberlin,
Wm. Curry,
W. T. Adams,
J. F. Magill,
J. B. McKinley,
J. C. Grier,
G. C. Heckman,
J. P. Safford,
R. F. Patterson,
W. P. Inskeep,
S. M. Archer,
James D. Mason,
J. S. Dunning,
W. Bishop,
J. W. Scott,
John Giffin,
D. A. Wilson,
A. M. McPherson,
V. D. Reed,
J. D. Reinboth,
E. Kempshall,
J. C. Edwards,
M. J. Hickok,
A. M. Lowry,
C. E. Webster,
D. V. McLean,
Myron Barrett,
A. H. Hand,
J. L. Labar,
W. P. Vail,
J. G. Symmes,
G. S. Green,
W. Rust,
W. H. Hornblower,
Albert DeHart,
John Barrows,
H. E. Warford,
H. Armstrong,
A. Wickham,
C. Wood,
H. B. Ware,
A. Shiland,
W. P. Van Rensselaer,
L. Littell,
L. Mulford,
J. R. Rolph,
N. West,
E. P. Ketchum,
W. P. Hull,
C. J. Jones,
J. M. Krebs,
J. C. Lowrie,
J. Stewart,
J. Bayless,
W. N. Belcher,
J. L. Nevius,
S. H. Jagger,
H. S. Banks,
R. Irwin, Jr.,
C. A. Munn,
H. L. Vannuys,
J. C. Irwin,
J. A. Campbell,
John Newland,
Charles E. Robinson,
Wm. M. Johnson,
G. Fort,
John M. Smith,
C. C. Riggs,
Valentine C. Glenn,
John Way, Jr.,
A. H. Caughey,
S. S. Mitchell,
W. G. Reed,
James Remington,
James Gardner,
H. Howard,
W. T. Cushing,
R. G. Thompson,
E. C. Sickles,
Thomas Muir,
W. W. Colmery,
Wm. T. Findley,
W. Greenough,
Thomas McGechin,
G. S. Ormsby,
Samuel Hover,
Thomas W. Hynes,
John Crozier,
R. M. Tate,
T. Buchanan,
G. D. Archibald,
F. R. Morton,
James Blake.
J. H. McCampbell,
W. Blanchard,
Jerome Allen,
Thomas Elder,
J. G. Reaser,
J. Farquhar,
D. Mitchell,
L. C. Rutter,
W. W. Watson,
T. F. McCoy,
J. A. Strawbridge,
D. W. Moore,
C. H. Park,
M. C. Grier,
D. J. Waller,
James Rankin,
W. E. Schenck,
J. Andrews,
W. W. Caldwell,
J. A. Henry,
T. M. Cunningham,
J. B. Davis,
B. H. Jenks,
R. Owen,
B. L. Agnew,
D. W. Shryock,
J. Mateer,
C. Orr,
F. J. Collier,
S. McMaster,
J. W. Hazelett,
S. Rea,
J. Stoneroad,
W. S. Caldwell,
J. Caruthers,
J. Frothingham,
G. Ainslie,
B. Baldwin, Jr.,
W. K. Brice,
J. Dobbins,
E. B. Raffensperger,
S. D. Chamberlin,
B. F. Murden,
H. K. Clark,
S. Cook,
J. P. Bringle,
D. Wills,
D. V. Smock,
G. D. Stewart,
W. Mason,
R. J. Burtt,
T. P. Speer,
J. Russell,
R. Herron,

J. G. McMechan,	G. Fraser,
H. A. Gillette,	W. M. Grimes,
J. M. Ray,	D. W. Fisher,
C. W. Finley,	W. M. Nicoll,
S. Galloway,	Thomas McKean,
J. H. Pratt,	J. Fleming,
C. H. Perkins,	C. P. French,
A. Scott,	J. W. Dinsmore,
J. C. Gillam,	L. T. Stowell,
J. J. Turner,	C. L. Thompson,
J. Reasor,	J. F. Ogden,
A. W. Loomis,	A. A. Dinsmore—197.
J. A. Skinner,	

NAYS.

J. T. Backus,	J. T. Smith,
John Dickson,	L. P. Bowen,
J. D. Jones,	R. W. Allen,
D. C. Brown,	J. E. Spillman,
C. A. Marshall,	R. K. Smoot,
W. L. Breckinridge,	O. Beatty,
E. P. Humphrey,	T. A. Bracken,
G. Marshall,	J. L. Yantis,
G. W. Buchanan,	R. L. McAfee,
G. C. Swallow,	J. M. Travis,
S. J. P. Anderson,	E. Bredell,
J. Conway,	A. P. Forman,
A. Gosman,	A. T. Dobson,
S. G. Law,	H. J. Van Dyke,
H. Day,	D. M. Halliday,
R. Buchanan,	J. H. Clarke,
J. T. Umsted,	J. F. Vanarsdale,
H. A. Boardman,	J. S. McClellan,
R. S. Clark—37.	

Declined to vote, J. H. Brooks—1.

ABSENT.

L. B. Wells,	G. W. Jarrett,
J. P. Carter,	J. T. Hendricks,
R. Birnie,	J. C. Maxwell,
E. Myers,	J. W. Pryor,
D. McMaster,	H. T. Walker,
R. C. Matthews,	J. B. Lindsley,
E. Buck,	C. W. Smith,
R. Porter,	R. Van Pelt,
L. Clark,	W. L. Terhune,
J. Snyder,	R. A. Davison,
W. E. Withrow,	J. Van Keuren,
S. D. Sharon,	J. L. Williams,
R. Conover,	R. P. Davidson,
R. A. Mitchell,	A. G. Brown,
W. D. Hills,	Moses Coe,
H. Adams,	S. T. Brown,
J. K. Duncan,	J. T. Barnard,
W. H. Peterson,	James Gray,
J. M. Pryse,	John Christy,
S. Robinson,	J. C. Caldwell,
S. R. Wilson,	R. Lyle,
C. A. Wickliffe,	W. L. Orr,
M. Hardin,	A. Boyd,
P. Thompson,	H. Hammond,
J. T. Hendricks.	A. V. Balch—50.

Dr. Montfort moved, in order not to exclude the Declaration and Testimony men from this Assembly, that the resolutions just passed should not take effect until the close of the session. Carried.

A committee was appointed to examine the docket and report at the afternoon session, what business required the attention of the Assembly, and what could be postponed to the next Assembly.

The following resolution of thanks to Dr. Lord was adopted:

The Committee on Theological Seminaries recommend the following resolutions:

Resolved, That the thanks of the General Assembly are due, and are hereby tendered to the Rev. Willis Lord, D. D., for the able and faithful manner in which he has discharged the duties of the chair of Didactic and Polemic Theology in addition to the regular duties of his own department, during the vacancy in that chair in the Theological Seminary of the Northwest.

Resolved, That a copy of this resolution be transmitted to Dr. Lord by the Stated Clerk of the General Assembly. D. J. WALLER, Chairman.

Voted that the report of the Committee on Domestic Missions be first, and that of the Freedmen's Committee be second in the order of business for the afternoon.

Dr. Boardman then read a report from the Committee on Foreign Correspondence.

AFTERNOON SESSION.

Rev. E. Kempshall offered a resolution referring the appealed case of Samuel Boyd to a select committee, for the purpose of hearing the testimony. Adopted.

Rev. Mr. Bracken read a protest against the action of the Assembly with regard to the Elders of the Walnut Street Church of Louisville, as follows:

The undersigned do most respectfully and most earnestly protest against the decision of this Assembly in regard to the Walnut street Church, under the care of the Presbytery of Louisville, for the following reasons:

1. This decision is in its nature and effect, a judicial decision made upon the report of a committee, without the least regard to any of the forms of procedure laid down in the Book of Discipline, and, as appears to us, in violation of every principle and requirement of the form of government of the Church. The case was not before the Assembly either upon the complaint, appeal, reference, or review and control in one or other only of which ways could it be brought under their jurisdiction. The parties were never before the Assembly at all; the Presbytery could not be, because it had been previously excluded from the body. Nothing of the nature of evidence touching the matters involved, was heard by the Assembly. It was therefore impossible for the Assembly to know whether or not the elders were or were not duly elected and ordained.

2. The decision is in our judgment subversive of all the rights of all the lower courts, and of the private members of the Church. It breaks down all the safe-guards of the Constitution, and lays prostrate at the feet of any casual majority of the General Assembly the Christian immunities and liberties, sessions, ministers and people. No one can be safe under a government administered in such a manner. It must have the effect to give a license to the disorderly, and make victims of those who would endeavor to maintain the integrity of the Constitution and enforce in a regular manner the discipline of the Church. It sanctions the principle that the General Assembly *meru motu* may take up a case of discipline pending before a church session, and upon the *ex parte* petition of the party under trial, turn out the members of the court—put the accused in the places of the judges—and practically require the court to submit to the criminal. That when a question of privilege, and that, too, involving the vital question of the legality of an election and ordination to the eldership is pending in a Presbytery, the General Assembly may interfere to decide that question without having the parties whose claims are to be determined before them, and whilst the Presbytery itself is precluded from the possibility of being heard.

That when a Synod has appointed a committee to attend to business brought before it, and report to Synod before that committee have had time to report, and therefore before their action can have become of binding force, or be subject to the review of the Assembly in any constitutional manner, the Assembly may, upon the *ex parte* report and recommendation of an *ex parte* committee, declare the acts and doings of the aforesaid committee of Synod to be final and binding, even to the extent of quashing process of discipline regularly instituted, practically constituting a new session, and setting aside one already existing.

3. The charge against the Louisville Presbytery of having denied to one of these persons, at whose instigation this matter has been pressed upon this Assembly, a "seat in said Presbytery," and "with the apparent design of discrediting" his election and ordination as a ruling elder, contains a most injurious imputation upon the motives of that Presbytery, and based upon an assertion of what we have reason to believe is contrary to fact. It appears from evidence, both printed and oral, that the

Presbytery has not denied any one of these persons a seat in that body. That question is still under consideration by them, upon the report of a committee, to whom the whole matter was referred, at the motion of the party, claiming the right to a seat, and the committee was composed of members of the Presbytery, named by said party. This report was prepared with due diligence and presented at the earliest possible moment, but it being impracticable for the Presbytery to continue longer in session at that time, and they having previously determined to hold an adjourned meeting, said report was laid over to that meeting, then to be fully considered and acted upon. So far, therefore, as the action of the Presbytery is to be taken as evidence of its design, it would seem to be apparent that they designed to do nothing hastily, or to the prejudice of the rights ecclesiastical or civil of any of the parties to this case.

4. The plea of "necessity" under which this decision was pressed to a vote, is dangerous and delusive, no necessity existing for the intervention of the Assembly in this business at this time, but such as the party urging the plea of necessity, had himself created. That necessisty consists, as is apparent from the paper adopted by the Assembly itself, in an anxiety to bring the decision thus obtained to bear upon and control the civil court in a case now pending before that court, in which the said party is the plaintiff. And the Assembly have thus, both by their action and by the very terms of it, rendered it impossible to prevent the injurious impression that this venerable body have gone out of their way, and set aside the fundamental laws of the Church and the essential forms of procedure, in order to reach a decision, with the express purpose of prejudicing the property-rights of one of the parties in a case now under litigation. It is the Assembly, therefore,—not the Presbytery—who, by their action, are imperiling the rights of the members of the congragation of the Walnut street Church. Against the perversion of this high court of the Church to such a use, we do most earnestly and solemly protest.

5. The General Assembly have no power, under the vague pretext of "redressing grievances" or "by virtue of its authority and obligation to give advice and instruction in all cases submitted to them"—upon a mere memorial or petition, to override the Constitutional prerogatives of the lower courts—to confirm or reverse their decisions—to interfere with their proceedings, or to anticipate their action in matters regularly before them, and in which they have primary jurisdiction.

T. A. Bracken, G. J. P. Anderson, J. L. Yantis, A. P. Forman, S. L. McAfee, E. Bredell, G. W. Buchanan, Glass Marshall, J. D. Jones, G. C. Swallow, J. H. Brookes, H. J. Van Dyke.

Dr. Krebs read the following answer:

In answer to the protest of Mr. Bracken and others in the case of the Walnut Street Church of Louisville, the Assembly declare that the election of new elders in that church was ordered by the Synod of Kentucky, on a review of the whole case upon a memorial from the congregation, and was conducted and consummated by the committee appointed by the Synod with plenary powers; all of which is established by the attested records of the Synod of Kentucky and of the committee appointed by that Synod, the premises meeting all the circumstances and requirements of the case.

Both the above papers were admitted to record.

The report of the Finance Committee was then read and accepted.

The week commencing with the first Sabbath and including the following Sabbath were appointed a special session for prayer for the conversion of the world.

A motion to limit debate on all other questions which might come up was earnestly opposed by Dr. Anderson, and finally tabled on motion of Dr. Krebs.

The report of the Standing Committee on Domestic Missions then came under consideration.

Dr. Krebs moved to strike out that part of the report which proposes the removal of the Board to Cincinnati, and all the provisions dependent on such proposed removal, except the requirement to revise the plans of the Board, with view to its greater efficiency.

Dr. Juneway, Secretary of the Board, addressed the Assembly upon the condition and prospects of the Board.

Rev. Mr. Loomis stated the wants of California.

Drs. Brown, Montfort and Thomes, and Messrs. Chamberlain, Scott, Henry, Skinner and Symme, addressed the Assembly upon Dr. Krebs' motion, and upon an amendment made to refer the matter to the next Assembly.

Mr. Symmes moved to lay the amendment to refer the matter to the next Assembly on the table. Carried.

Rev. Mr. Mason thought there should be more confidence in the Board.

Dr. Gurley felt obliged to vote in the affirmative as matters now stood. Suggested referring the matter to a Special Committee to report at the next Assembly, and moved an amendment of a committee of five to report at the next Assembly.

It was moved to postpone the first resolution with regard to the Freedmen's Committee, until the consideration of that committee's report.

Fifth resolution in the report adopted.

Report except those parts referred and postponed adopted.

The Assembly voted to instruct the Board of Domestic Missions to immediately revise its plans of operation.

Voted that it be the first order of the day on Saturday to receive nominations and elect to fill vacancies in the Board of Domestic Missions.

The Rev. S. C. Logan, Secretary of the Freedmen's Committee, by request addressed the Assembly on the importance and greatness of the work entrusted to that Committee. He explained the nature of this tenure by which the Zion Church (colored), of Charleston, South Carolina, was held by the Committee: that it had been claimed by a New School minister, in behalf of an aid society; that the General in command had decided that the Old School Presbyterian Church was entitled to its use; that Mr. Gibbs, our missionary, had taken possession; that the Church might be used for the purposes for which it was originally founded; that the Committee had made no claim upon it as our property; that the whole matter was now before the proper authorities in behalf of the colored congregation by the act of its officers; in short, that the contest is really between the former white trustees and the present colored congregation. In confirmation of this, Mr. Logan read several papers. He then proceeded to explain the difficulties in the way: need of colored laborers, the encouragements, etc.

Adjourned, with prayer.

FOURTEENTH DAY—SATURDAY, JUNE 2, 1866.

MORNING SESSION.

The Assembly met at the usual hour, and after devotional exercises the minutes of Friday were read.

A motion was made to amend the minutes, so as to give those who voted for Dr. Gurley's proposition in reference to the Louisville Presbytery an opportunity to sign the other propositions that were before the Assembly relating to the same subject.

After a lengthy discussion the minutes were amended so as to read, that any person who had *preferred* the papers named be permitted to sign them.

Dr. Lowrie, from the Committee on Bills and Overtures, reported back Overture No. 7, in relation to the Presbytery of Southern Iowa, recommending its attachment to the Synod of Nebraska. The matter was referred tn the next General Assembly.

Dr. Lowrie, from the same committee, reported Overture No. 21, which reads as follows:

The appeal of the Rev. L. R. Lockwood, by his counsel, the Rev. James Remington.

This appeal against the Synod of Iowa, for not sustaining his appeal from the Presbytery of Dubuque, was dismissed by the last Assembly on the ground that no reason accompanied the complaint, and there was no evidence that any notice of complaint was given to the Synod.

Mr. Lockwood now memorializes this Assembly, and alleges that the required notice of appeal was given to the Synod, and that he was then, and still is prevented from attending the Assembly during its last and present session, and he asks that his appeal may be reinstated, and referred to the next Assembly for trial.

The Committee reccommend that his request be granted. He further asks, that the Assembly direct the Presbytery of Dubuque to grant him a new trial on the ground of new testimony.

The Committee recommend that this application be referred to the Presbytery of Dubuque, to the end that if the new testimony be found of sufficient importance to justify that Presbytery, it may afford Mr. Lockwood the relief he asks. But if, in their judgment, a new trial ought not to be granted, that then the appeal shall stand for trial on the record as now existing before the next General Assembly.

The report was received and docketed.

Dr. Lowrie, from same committee, reported Overture No. 22, which was referred to the next General Assembly for trial.

Resolved, That the Trustees of the General Assembly be and they are hereby authorized to release all their interest in lot 3 block No. 26, in the city of Winona of the State of Minnesota, on which is erected a church edifice now or lately occupied by the Presbyterian Church of that city—provided a deed of trust shall be executed by the proper legal parties to the said trustees of the General Assembly, vesting in them an interest in the property on which the new edifice for the use of said Church shall be erected, with the same covenants and considerations expressed in the deed, by which they now hold their interest in said lot No. 3, block 26, in the city of Winona.

The report was received and adopted.

The unfinished business was then taken up, viz: the report of the Committee on Freedmen.

Mr. Logan, the Secretary of the Committee, resumed his remarks.

He said in the efforts to educate the freedmen, it should be borne in mind that they are not more than five generations removed from the most abject heathenism of modern times. Some of them are not two generations removed from the worship of dog's teeth. Whatever plans may be taken, it is necessary that the whole energies of the Church and all Christian people should be bent to the work, so that what is done may be done quickly. The field was ready for harvest. The demand was urgent. The negroes were being brought in contact with influences which must be counteracted, or the result would be deeper degradation. They were anxious to be instructed. Their minds were thirsting for knowledge, and it was very important that their instruction should begin on a right basis. On one occasion he heard a negro pray the Lord to deliver him "from the sin which doth so easily *upset* us," and on asking him what he meant, he replied "that the negroes could smell whisky a great way off." The negroes were now more exposed to the temptations which were being thrown in their way by unscrupulus white men, and these influences must be counteracted. They have a feeling that they wish to be equal to the white race. They discover that it is not altogether education that commands respect among white people, but money, and so there is danger that they will neglect the one for the other. Instead of being thriftless, they as a people, are money making. This is shown in the fact that they are establishing savings banks, and in a bank at Beaufort they already have $400,000. The Freedmen's Bureau was leading them not only to industry but economy, and they are fast getting the idea that in order to be "folks" they must be "rich folks." It was all important therefore that immediate attention should be paid to the salvation of their souls and the elevation of their moral character. In regard to the consolidation of the Freedmen's Committee with the Board of Domestic Missions, the Speaker hoped the Assembly would do what they thought was most advisable. He had made great sacrifices personally and thought the secretaryship of such a committee was about the hardest way to heaven.

Rev. Mr. Miller next addressed the Assembly with reference to the work of educating the colored people of North Carolina, and spoke of a liberal charter which had been granted in that State for an institution in which the education of colored people could be carried forward. He regarded this as one of the most important movements for the evangelization of freedmen that the Church could engage in. If China, Japan, and other foreign fields of labor, exhibited the same spectacle that the colored people in our own land exhibited, the greatest energies of the Church would be put forth to the work of their complete evangelization.

Mr. McKnight considered this work second to none other. Here were heathen brought to our own doors, and it was important that their wants should be attended to. He was opposed to having two separate organizations to this work. He thought the Board of Domestic Missions should attend to the black man as well as the red or the white man. The objections to having separate organizations were numerous, among which were two sets of teachers or missionaries, and the misunderstandings frequently arising among them. If there were but one organization it would save expense and a great deal of correspondence. He thought they could collect just as much money with but one organization. He alluded to the letter of Dr. Adger, of South Carolina, which censures the agents of the Church employed in behalf of the freedmen, on account of having taken possession of a church in that State. The speaker said the Church was not responsible for the retention of that church at the present time. As soon as they ascertained the facts they relinquished all claim. It was then that Mr. Gibbs, a colored preacher of much ability, instituted proceedings for the possession of the church, under the provisions of the civil rights bill. There the matter rests, the colored men contending they are as much entitled to the property as the white men. So far as the Presbyterian Church was concerned, they did nothing more than what was their duty.

On motion of Dr. Patterson, it was agreed to adopt the resolutions seriatim.

Rev. Mr. Skinner desired to know whether the Committee on Domestic Missionaries were prepared to accept this responsibility. He moved, instead of referring this to that committee, that the action of the Assembly be postponed for one year, and that a committee be appointed to consider the matter and report to the next General Assembly what action shall be taken.

Rev. Dr. Gurley hoped the motion would not prevail. The proposed transfer would not be made until the way was manifestly clear. He thought there was no better committee to which the subject could be referred than the one proposed.

On motion of Rev. Mr. Stewart, the motion of Mr. Skinner was laid on the table.

Rev. Mr. Bishop said there was no doubt but that at the time this committee was formed it was intended merely as temporary.

Rev. Dr. Backus hoped the day would soon come when all these boards would be consolidated.

The first three of the resolutions were then adopted.

Rev. Dr. Humphrey said this was a most important matter, and that it required a great deal of prudence and judgment. It was a subject likely to start many difficult problems. He had long been a resident of a slave State, and had given the subject a great deal of study, and he was undecided now as to the best course to pursue. He was opposed, however, to giving up separate organizations. They had common schools and churches to establish among them, and so many difficult matters to attend to, it seemed to him the subject should command the attention of a board composed of some of the wisest men of the Church. He proposed, therefore, to offer the following as an amendment:

Resolved, That this General Assembly, deferring to what appears to be the manifest indications of the will of Providence in the matter, assure the Southern churches and ministers lately in connection with us of our desire to assist and co-operate with them in any judicious measures for the spiritual good of their colored population.

From his knowledge of the people of the South, he thought if it were possible to remove the obstacles that appeared in the way of co-operation with them, that their facilities for instructing the negroes would be greatly increased. He would desire to have the Church in the attitude of co-operation with them rather than in the attitude of competition. He thought this was a good time to put this matter on that footing—by adopting some such resolution as this, which would put them in such relation with their Southern brethren as would prevent the collisions of which they had heard, and which were likely to interfere in the work of that important field of labor. No field of labor now open to the General Assembly was more important—none where the cry came up with such piteous wailings and accents, as from these four millions of people.

A member desired to know whether, under the resolution, the Assembly would not be bound to act according to the principles of the Southern Presbyterian Church.

Rev. Dr. Allison did not know as there was anything specially objectionable in the amendment, but it was likely to convey a wrong impression. The impression seemed to have got abroad that they had come into a collision in this field of labor, but this was altogether a mistake. They had carefully avoided establishing themselves in any place where the Southern Church and Freedman's Aid Societies were operating. He wished to state the facts, also, in regard to Zion church. After the old pastor returned, Mr. Gibbs retired, stating that if the people were willing to take back their old pastor, he would seek another place. The congregation decided that if their former pastor would accept the deliverances of the Assembly, they would have no objection to him. This he declined, and then the Assembly's missionary, Mr. Gibbs, was retained by the choice of the people. But in all cases teachers and missionaries had been instructed to avoid infringing on the labors of others. There was another difficulty in the amendment. The system of instruction in the Southern Church was different. On the whole, he doubted the propriety of adopting this amendment at this time.

Rev. Dr. Heckman was not prepared to vote for the amendment.

Rev. Mr. Frazier said the idea seemed to prevail that the Southern people make use of oral instruction only. This was a mistake, whatever other charges they might have to answer.

Dr. Humphrey concurred in the idea that their object should be to educate the colored people to read the Word of God, and to establish schools. He believed, also, that their efforts should be to instruct them according to the principles of the Church. Whether the Southern brethren would agree to that plan he did not know, but he thought they would; they must, however, carry their work among the freedmen on their own principles, irrespective of any other. And if there was anything in his amendment which committed them to the policy of their Southern brethren, he would cheerfully strike it out. His idea was for co-operation among Christian people.

Rev. Dr. Thomas had no objection to any form of courtesy towards Christian brethren, but felt the time had not come for the adoption of such a paper as this. He had no objections to the Board of Domestic Missions or Freedmen's Committee using any advantages that might be offered them, in the way of co-operation by Christian brethren in the South. But when they adopted a paper of this kind, declaring that they were ready to co-operate with the Southern Presbyterian Church, for the good of the colored people—

Mr. Clarke said he understood that the resolution expressed a desire to co-operate with them on judicious principles.

Dr. Thomas said he understood the resolution to be a recognition of their separate existence as an organization with whom they could co-operate, and the corollary of that was, that being in the possession of that field they ought in all Christian courtesy to leave them undisturbed. He thought that was cutting it rather deep.

Adjourned.

AFTERNOON SESSION.

The appeal case of Rev. Mr. Boyd from the Synod of Wheeling, was taken up and after considerable discussion the report of the Committee sustaining the decision of the Synod of Wheeling was adopted.

Mr. Clarke asked on behalf of himself and others to enter a dissent as follows:

The undersigned dissent from the judgment of the Assembly in the appeal of Rev. Samuel Boyd against the Synod of Wheeling, for the following reasons:

1. The only charge alleged by *common fame* against Mr. Boyd before the Presbytery of St. Clairsville is that he was "living separate from his wife." No specification of the character of this separation whether for sufficient reasons or not, or whether involving immorality or not, appears on the record; nor has any such specification been brought to the notice of this Assembly.

2. No evidence of the charge has been read in the presence of the Assembly. This court was therefore called to pronounce upon the issue of the guilt or innocence of Mr. Boyd in entire ignorance of the testimony by which that guilt or innocence may be determined.

3. The Book of Discipline prescribes the order of proceeding in the trial of appeals in judicial cases, chap. vii., section iii and sections viii and ix. This order confers substantial rights upon parties, and presents specific duties to this court.

It requires the "reading of the whole record of the proceedings of the inferior judicatory in the call, *including all the testimony*"—to hear the original parties—to hear the members of the inferior judicatory—and that the roll of the Court shall be called, that every member may have an opportunity to express his opinion in the case. The record has not been read, the original pleas have not been heard, nor has any opportunity been offered for the purpose. The inferior judicatory has not been called, nor was the roll of this house called as required by the Book of Discipline.

For these reasons the undersigned dissent from the judgment in this case.

HOVEY K. CLARKE,
JOHN OGDEN,
J. W. WIGHTMAN,
R. G. McCREARY,
J. G. REASOR,
CHARLES RAY,
ROBERT S. CLARK,
WM. MASON,
JACOB REASOR.

The Moderator announced the following Committee on the removal of the Board of Domestic Missions: P. D. Gurley, T. E. Thomas and J. Addison Henry, Ministers. Robert McKnight and A. E. Chamberlin, Elders.

The unfinished business was taken up, viz: the report of the Committee on Freedmen.

Rev. Dr. Thomas concluded his remarks. He was opposed to recognizing the Southern Church in any way as a distinct and separate organization, and as illustrating the state of feeling of the brethren of the South, cited a discourse by Rev. Dr. Marshall of New Orleans, which he had recently read in a New Orleans paper, in which Dr. Marshall said the South was right and in the end would have independence; that they should still look for independence, refuse all association with Northern people, and identify themselves with the Southern cause: that in one hundred years spiders would spin webs around the spindles of Lowell, and a Comanche Indian sit on Bunker Hill Monument and sketch the ruins of Boston. Until this element was purged out, and there was evidence that they had returned to the position they once occupied as loyal Presbyterians, he was not willing to meet a direct or indirect proposition to co-operate with them. He moved to lay the resolution of Dr. Humphrey on the table.

The motion was agreed to, and then, on motion of Rev. Dr. Humphrey, the whole question of uniting the Freedman's committee with the Board of Domestic Missions was referred to the next Assembly.

Rev. Dr. Allison then offered the following, which was agreed to.

Resolved further, That six members be added to the committee, and that the committee be empowered to conduct their business by an executive committee.

The committee nominated the following as the additional members: Ministers, E. E. Swift, S. T. Scoval, John Gillespie; Elders, David Robinson, Dr. A. G. McCandless, and Robert C. Totten; and for re-election the following persons whose term of service expires during the sessions of the present Assembly: Ministers, W. M. Paxton, D. D., W. P. Breed, D. D., and J. O. Murray; Elders, Hon. S. Galloway, N. Bakewell, and A. B. Belknap, in the place of James Lenox resigned, and O. B. Lyon in place of R. McKnight, resigned.

Rev. Dr. Patterson, from the Committee on Foreign Correspondence, reported the following as representatives to the different branches of the Presbyterian Churches:

To the General Assembly of the Free Church of Scotland: Rev. E. P. Humphrey, D. D., of the Presbytery of Transylvania; Rev. M. L Hickok, Presbytery of Luzerne; Rev. N. C. Burt, D. D., Presbytery of Cincinnati; Rev. Richard Lea, D. D., Presbytery of Ohio; Elder Alex. Cameron, Presbytery of Allegheny City.

The Assembly also commends these brethren to the Church confidence and fellowship of any other evangelical ecclesiastical bodies whose sessions they may attend.

To the General Assembly of the other branch of the Presbyterian Church; Rev. E. D. Germans, D. D., Presbytery of Rochester City; Rev. Duncan Kennedy, D. D., Presbytery of Troy; Elders W. P. Vanrensalaer, Presbytery of Connecticut; E. A. Raymond, Presbytery of Rochester.

To the General Synod of the Reformed Dutch Church: Rev. John Hall, D. D., Presbytery of New Brunswick; Rev. Joseph Smith, D. D., Presbytery of Baltimore.

To General Assembly of United Presbyterian Church: Rev. R. C. Matthews, D. D., Presbytery of Warren; Rev. W. T. Finley, Presbytery of Miami; Elder George S. Green, Presbytery of New Brunswick.

To General Synod of Reformed Presbyterian Church: Rev. S. J. Wilson, D. D., Presbytery of Washington; Rev. D. R. Campbell, Presbytery of Stubenville; Elder S. D. Sharon, Presbytery of Miami.

To Cumberland Presbyterian Church: Rev. A. O. Patterson, D. D., Presbytery of Oxford; Rev. Jas. Sloan, D. D., Presbytery of Washington; Elder Hon. Josiah Scott, Presbytery of Oxford

To Associate Reform Synod of New York: Rev. E. D. Smith, D. D., Presbytery of New York; Rev. J. E. Rockwell, Presbytery of Nassau; Elder Alexander Cameron, Presbytery of Allegheny City.

Rev. Dr. Farquhar, from the Committee to Revise the Statistical Tables, presented a report recommending certain changes. After a brief discussion the report was, on motion, referred to the next Assembly.

Rev. Dr. Thomas offered the following:

Resolved, That a committee, of which the Moderator shall be chairman, shall be appointed to prepare a pastoral letter to the churches.

He said the object was to give some representation of the action of this Assembly, the measures of the last Assembly and the bearings of the whole. It might serve to conciliate many of the brethren without altering the action of the Assembly.

Mr. Day desired to offer as an amendment, resolutions found substantially in Baird's Digest, page 789, which were adopted in 1837 after the great division. The resolutions are to the effect, that whereas doubts have arisen as to the true construction of the deliverances of the Assembly in reference to slavery and loyalty and the duties of Presbyterians in relation thereto, and whereas the Assembly desire to promote the true spirit of Gospel charity and liberty, and to preserve the consciences of brethren who are laboring to sustain the peace and prosperity of our beloved Church; therefore

Resolved, That we will cordially receive into the fellowship of this Church, all sincere Presbyterians who desire to be united with us, and who are in good and regular standing according to the constitution of our Church, and such members and ministers are invited to seek such union in the mode prescribed in our constitution.

Resolved, That where any Presbytery has reason to believe, by common fame or otherwise, that any person thus applying has been guilty of unholy and wicked conduct in the late rebellion, it will be the duty of said Presbytery to examine into the conduct of all such applicants and deal with them according to the rules and discipline of the Church.

Mr. Day acknowledged that for the peace and purity of the Church those who were charged with heinous crimes should not be allowed to come into the Church. But it seemed to him they were now on vantage ground, and could devise some plan which would overcome all difficulties. He did not ask to have the records of the last five years changed; thought they ought to stand as the record of the great Presbyterian Church on the subject of loyalty, but wished them construed as they ought to be construed—kindly, and in a Christian spirit, with meekness and gentleness.

Dr. Thompson moved to lay the resolutions on the table.

The Moderator said they were not before the house.

Dr. Schenck said he had a paper similar to the above which he thought would harmonize the views of the brethren, and which he desired to read for information. It was read as follows:

Whereas, There is reason to believe that among ministers and members of the Presbyterian Church in the South, there are many who disapproved of the late rebellion against the Government of the United States, and the separation of these churches from this body, and who did not of their own free will consent or lend aid or countenance thereto, but bowed before what they believed to be irresistible necessity; therefore

Resolved, That this Assembly, without expressing an opinion with regard to the propriety of the course adopted by such persons, will still cherish a kindly and friendly regard for them, and whenever any of them desire to return to their former connection with us, we will receive and cordially welcome them; and in regard to those who have countenanced rebellion or separation, this Assembly disclaims all vindictive feelings or a disposition to exercise undue severity, but reiterates its readiness to receive them back whenever they comply with the conditions laid down by the General Assembly, page 563, minutes of 1865.

Dr. Schenck said he had received a great many letters from the South during the past month, and he was persuaded the number of persons here indicated was very considerable. He had received letters from ministers in the South who declared that they were at heart Union during the rebellion, and resisted treason until it was impossible any longer to resist without the risk of their lives or the safety of their families. A clergyman in Mississippi had written to him to the effect that he had been tried by his rebel neighbors; that he had been turned out of the Church, and that it was impossible for him to return. He wished to know how he could get back. All this made it clear to the speaker that the reports current in the South in reference to the posture of the Church were of such a character that some such declaration as he proposed was necessary.

Rev. Dr. Kempshall hoped this paper would pass, as representing the views of the Assembly and the Church at large. There were some who had voted with the majority all through, but who had not had their views fully expressed. He hoped no effort would be made to lay this paper on the table. There were many brethren on this floor and in the Churches North and South, who desired and prayed to God that the day might soon come when a fraternal union should be restored. They might call such men middle men, fence men, or two buckets of water men, or what they pleased, but he hoped their views would be respected.

Rev. Mr. Patterson said there seemed to be an impression in the minds of several members that this Assembly was actuated by a feeling of enmity and revenge towards Southern men, but for himself he could say he had no such feeling in his heart, and never had. When at the head of his regiment he stormed the crest of Mission Ridge, and was wounded by a minie bullet; and when they captured numbers of rebel prisoners, he had no feeling of enmity towards them, and he had none now. All he wanted was the honor of his Church preserved. He liked the expression of this paper, and hoped it would be adopted.

Rev. Dr. Loomis was opposed to Mr. Day's paper because it undertook to interpret the doings of the last Assembly. They were prepared to vote for Dr. Schenck's paper.

Rev. Dr. Nevius regarded this as the most important matter that had yet come before the Assembly. A great many felt that a time had come for mutual concession. We called on our brethren to confess their faults, yet he believed a large majority of the Assembly felt that they were guilty of a fault at the last Assembly. Some of the acts of the Assembly were a dead letter. They could not be executed in churches at the North, and he thought it a gross inconsistency, and a shame for them to call on the brethren of the South to confess their faults, when "we will not confess faults which we acknowledge to be so."

Dr. Krebs saw nothing dishonorable or inconsistent in their explaining themselves; did not know any man who ignored or disobeyed the injunctions of the last Assembly, as some brethern seemed to know them, but believed that they were misunderstood honestly and conscientiously by some. He was therefore in favor of explaining. In 1845 they adopted the last great deliverance on the subject of slavery, except the supplementary paper of 1864, which was largely misunderstood, and in 1846 the Assembly adopted a resolution which explained the deliverance of '45 and set the matter at rest. There was no inconsistency in so doing, and he did not believe when properly understood that there was any real inconsistency between the action of 1864 and 1845 as Dr. Brookes had sought to show.

Mr. Day offered his paper as a substitute for Dr. Schenck's.

Rev. Mr. Forman would like much to vote for anything which looked towards conciliation, but could not vote for anything which indorsed the action of the last Assembly.

Mr. Buchanan thought the paper of Dr. Schenck was no more than reaffirming the deliverances of last year and was opposed to it.

A motion to refer the subject to a special committee was lost.

Dr. Schenck's paper was adopted.

Adjourned with prayer.

FIFTEENTH DAY — MONDAY, JUNE 4, 1866.

MORNING SESSION.

After devotional exercises and the reading of the minutes of Saturday,

Rev. Dr. McLean moved that the forty-nine Synods and Presbyteries in the South have withdrawn their connection with the Presbyterian Church in the United States, and have, as is understood, organized an independent body of their own; therefore,

Resolved, That the names of those Synods and Presbyteries, with their ministers and churches, be stricken from the minutes of this General Assembly.

That this General Assembly will give up no part of the territory embraced within those Synods and Presbyteries, but shall proceed to cultivate it as God shall give us ability. That where any Presbytery, minister or Church, within the bounds of the above named Presbyteries, desires to adhere to this General Assembly and accepts its Deliverances, they shall apply to the nearest Presbytery to be received by them until such time as they can be organized into a Presbytery on their own territory.

Rev. Dr. Smith offered the following as a substitute:

Whereas, The Churches in that portion of our country lately in rebellion, whose names appear upon our roll, have not been represented in this Assembly, and still remain in a state of separation from us; and whereas, the measures adopted by this Assembly, if not carried out by the lower courts in a spirit of great meekness and forbearance, may result in perpetuating and embittering division already existing, and extending them over portions of our Church now at peace. Therefore, be it

Resolved, That this Assembly greatly deplores the continued separation between ourselves and our scattered brethren, so long united in the bonds of Christian love and ecclesiastical fellowship, and expresses the earnest desire that the way be soon opened for a reunion on the basis of our common standards, and on terms consistent with truth and righteousness.

Resolved, That the lower courts who may be called upon to execute the measures of this Assembly, be enjoined to proceed therein with great meekness and forbearance, and in a spirit of kindness and conciliation, to the end that strifes and dissensions be not multiplied and inflamed and extended still more widely, and that the discipline of Christ's house may prove for edification and not for destruction.

Dr. McLean's motion and Dr. Smith's substitute were laid on the table.

Rev. Dr. Stanton, (Dr. Krebs in the chair,) from the committee appointed for the purpose, then presented the following pastoral letter:

PASTORAL LETTER.

The General Assembly of the Presbyterian Church in the United States of America, in session in St. Louis, Missouri, Anno Domini, 1866, *to the churches and people under their care.*

Beloved Brethren: Under a sense of the solemn responsibilities which rest upon us as ministers and elders composing this highest judicatory of the Presbyterian Church, we greet you in the bonds of Christian fellowship. The circumstances under which we are met, the state of the Church at large which we represent, the important business which has come before us, the results which we have reached, and the duty we owe to all the churches and people under our care, as well as to the world without, combine to render it incumbent on us, at the close of an Assembly whose sessions have been unusually protracted, to lay before you our views upon certain matters of great moment to the welfare of Christ's kingdom.

The position of the Presbyterian Church towards our brethren in the South, who were formerly in the same ecclesiastical connection with us, is one of the subjects demanding special attention. That position has been misapprehended by some, and by others perverted.

The General Assembly of 1865 met a few weeks after the last battles of a gigantic civil war, which had continued four years. That war originated in rebellion against the Government of the United States. During its progress, the Church of our fathers became divided, and in December, 1861, some ten Synods and forty-four Presbyteries, with the churches under their care, organized a separate Church under another General Assembly. Four General Assemblies—namely, those of 1861, 1862, 1863 and 1864—had deliberately and solemnly pronounced this rebellion a heinous offense, in the light of both human and divine law, and had enjoined upon the people under their care the duty of upholding the Government against which the rebellion was waged. When, therefore, the Assembly of 1865 convened, recognizing these doctrines upon the rebellion and loyalty as true, and recognizing the well known fact that many persons lately of our ecclesiastical household, some of them ministers and elders, had been prominently concerned in instigating and aiding the rebellion, that body simply designed to apply, as a logical and righteous necessity, the principles laid down by the four preceding Assemblies. As they had successively declared the rebellion to be a sin and gross offense, the last Assembly made provision that those in the Southern Church who had been guilty of willingly aiding the rebellion, should acknowledge their sin and profess repentance as a condition precedent, provided they should wish to return to their former relations with us. It is impossible to see what could have been done less than this, without, on the one hand, totally ignoring the solemn Deliverances of the four previous Assemblies, and in effect treating their doctrines upon rebellion and loyalty as erroneous; or, on the other hand, while admitting these doctrines to be true, allowing the men who had been guilty of setting them at naught to come back into our fellowship without inquiry into their conduct, and thus making us partakers of their sins.

We regard it as completely within the province of the General Assembly to make these provisions. Rebellion against lawful civil authority is a gross sin by the Word of God and is so declared in terms by our standards. These standards, also, make it the duty of the General Assembly to "bear testimony against error in doctrine and immorality in practice in any Church, Presbytery, or Synod." Four Assemblies had borne testimony against the "immorality" of the rebellion; the fifth simply enjoined upon Sessions, Presbyteries and Synods, the duty of requiring repentance of the "immorality" in any who might apply for admission who had willingly aided the rebellion In this, the last Assembly but called the attention of the lower courts to what was their obvious duty without any injunction; but such injunction became necessary for two reasons: first, because some Presbyteries were in doubt as to their duty and had overtured that Assembly for direction; and secondly, because it was feared that in some portions of the Church the lower courts would not act, except under an express injunction of the Assembly. Beyond this, it was manifestly essential that there should be a uniform rule of procedure for all the courts touching the offense of rebellion, applicable to all who should apply for admission from the Southern Church. Such rule the last Assembly provided. In this provision there was nothing new. It was but a direction to deal with gross offenders, should they seek to join the Church from which they had separated. If they should not make application, they would not be disturbed. Not only our standards, but those of every Church in Christendom, deem rebellion against lawful authority an offense cognizable by church courts. The Presbyterian Church of Scotland has many times deposed from the ministry those who have been guilty of rebellion, and it was the unanimous opinion of the members of the General Assembly of our Church in 1864 that disloyalty to "the powers that be," in our civil war, was an ecclesiastical offense. It is thus too clear to admit of doubt, that the Assembly of 1865 was not only fully competent to make the provisions in question, but that, had it failed to do so, it would have fallen short of its duty. The only feature in these provisions which can be called new arises from the fact that the Presbyterian Church in this country had never before been called to deal with such an offense.

While, therefore, the last Assembly but fulfilled its duty in issuing these injunctions, it left their application to the persons concerned, entirely to the lower courts. In its directions to them it showed that it was actuated by conciliation and kindness. It "gave counsel to the several Church courts" that "in discharging the duties enjoined, due regard be paid to the circumstances of the case, and that justice be tempered with mercy." It directed that "tenderness" should be exercised, especially towards the young who had been led astray by "unprincipled and ambitious leaders;" and it expressed the hope that "by kind and faithful instruction and admonition, and by the presence of the Holy Spirit, most of them would be reclaimed from the error of their ways and become loyal citizens and valuable members of the Church."

The injunctions and counsels of the last Assembly were thus kind and fraternal towards those who were guilty of having willingly aided the rebellion. Any concession touching the offenses of such persons would have been the hight of unkindness. It would have been a connivance at their sin, and would have brought down upon them and upon us alike the displeasure of God.

In regard to our brethren throughout the South who did not aid the rebellion, or who aided it from the force of circumstances or under protest of consciene, the General Assembly has ever felt the deepest concern. That of 1862 spake to such as follows: "To those in like circumstances who are not chargeable with the sins which have brought such calamities upon the land, but who have chosen, in the exercise of their Christian liberty, to stand in their lot and suffer, we address words of affectionate sympathy; praying God to bring them off conquerors. To those in like circumstances who have taken their lives in their hands, and risked all for their country and for conscience's sake we say, we love such with all our heart, and bless God such witnesses were found in the time of thick darkness." The Assembly of 1863 thus said to the same class: "We tender our kind sympathies to those who are overtaken by troubles they could not avoid, and who mourn and weep in secret places, not unseen by the Father's eye." The present Assembly, in a paper adopted with entire unanimity, says of the same persons, that we "still cherish a kindly and fraternal regard for them, and whenever any of them shall desire to return to their former connection with us, they will receive a cordial welcome." And the present Assembly further says: "In regard to those who have voluntarily aided and countenanced the said rebellion and separation, this Assembly disclaims all vindictive feelings, and all disposition to exercise an undue severity, and reiterates its readiness to receive them back whenever they shall have complied with the conditions laid down by the last General Assembly on page 563 of its printed minutes."

It thus appears, that six General Assemblies in succession, including the present, have, with remarkable unanimity, maintained the same position concerning the rebellion, and concerning those engaged in it. After carefully reviewing the whole course of these years of strife and alienation, we find nothing to recall or modify in the Deliverances which have been made. We have taken our position upon the clearest principles of the Word of God, as set forth in our standards. We have aimed to reclaim offenders by demanding only what Christ requires of us as rulers in his house. We have repeatedly expressed our solemn judgment regarding their offenses, but we have uniformly done it in faithfulness and kindness only, as our duty required. While to these, our brethren, who have thus offended against the law of Christ, we would reiterate the language of the Assembly of 1862, and "earnestly address words of exhortation and rebuke," we still extend to them the hand of kindness, and desire that our former ecclesiastical fellowship may be restored, whenever it can be done upon those principles which six General Assemblies have announced. To form a union upon any other basis, would only serve to bring together those who could not act in harmony, and to perpetuate strife and alienation.

Another matter embraced in the acts of former Assemblies requires notice. We allude to the Deliverances upon American negro slavery. Much misapprehension exists respecting the action of the last Assembly upon this subject. We may say, in passing, that from the origin of our Church in this country to the present moment, slavery, as it exists in the Southern States, has been, as a system, regarded with disapprobation. The higher judicatories of our Church, embracing many of its General Assemblies and Synods, have repeatedly condemned the system as contrary to the Word of God, and fraught with evil to all classes in the Church and the State. Some of the most severe of these condemnations were expressed in a formal manner by Churh courts and by leading men in the Presbyterian Church, within the States where the system existed; as, for example, in the Synod of Kentucky, as long ago as 1834 and 1835, when the system was not only condemned, but when the Presbyterians of that State were exhorted to seek its termination among them during the generation then commenced. Besides the condemnation of the system by several General Assemblies, many of these Assemblies from the earliest times, earnestly exhorted the people to seek the entire removal of the system at the earliest practicable moment consistent with the interests of all concerned. When, therefore, the Assembly of 1864 met, three years of war had been waged against the United States Government, for the purpose of establishing an independent Government under which Southern slavery should have perpetual protection and unlimited expansion. The Government of the United States was putting forth its energies to maintain its existence, and the issue was trembling in the balance of fearful war. To give greater assurance to its efforts, the Supreme Executive authority had long before decreed the destruction of slavery in the States in rebellion, while some of the loyal slave States were themselves taking measures for the removal of the system; and thus the loyal masses were encouraged to believe that these measures promised success in their aims to maintain the Government and the integrity of the Union, under the great sacrifice of life and treasure which they were expending. What, then, could have been more natural and proper—in view of the frequently expressed desire of the General Assembly that the system of Southern slavery might be removed, and in view of the testimony of the three preceding Assemblies upon the duty of sustaining the Government against the rebellion—than for the General Assembly of 1864, with a unanimity unprecedented, to interpret the signs of the times (which the result has shown that it did correctly), as calling upon the people to pray and labor for the anticipated consummation,

"Which kings and prophets waited for,
And sought, but never found,

and which many of our fathers "desired long,"

"But died without the sight—"

namely, the complete removal of slavery from the country, not only that this withering curse upon the people might cease, but that through its destruction the Government might be maintained! The Assembly of 1864 has not only been vindicated by the providence of God in thus attempting to "discern the signs of the times," but no Deliverance of any General Assembly since the war began has been passed with so great unanimity, or has been more widely approved by the Church.

When the Assembly of 1865 convened, actual war indeed was over, but slavery still existed in some parts of the country; and as nothing but the military power had affected the system in the rebellious States, many persons both North and South believed that its legal existence throughout the South was as secure as ever, and some believed that it would be reinstated in all its power and extent.

This was the hope and prayer, and with many the expectation, among Presbyterians in some of the Border and in the Southern States, while it was well known that the leading men of the Presbyterian Church in the South still cherished the same views under which the people had been led into rebellion—that the system of Southern negro slavery was a "divine institution" as truly as was the Mosaic system of servitude, and was an "ordinance of God" in the "same category with marriage and civil government." Even as late as the year 1865 a person commissioned to this Assembly from the Presbytery of Louisville published a work, which has been extensively circulated and commended both North and South, designed to justify and shelter the system of Southern slavery, "slave codes" and all, under the Scriptural sanctions of the Mosaic system of servitude.

It was under these circumstances that the Assembly of 1865 took its action upon slavery. That action has been greatly misrepresented. It has been frequently asserted in high places that it conflicts with previous Testimonies of the General Assembly, and especially with that of 1845, which declares that slave holding is not a bar to Christian communion. It is a sufficient reply to this, to say, that the action of the last Assembly conflicts with no former Testimony; nor does it make the remotest allusion to slaveholding being, or not being, a bar to Christian communion. The main points of its action upon slavery—indeed the only points referring to those who may apply for reception into our Church from the churches of the South—are, that such applicants shall renounce the errors which assert "that the system of negro slavery in the South is a divine institution," that it is "an ordinance of God" in the sense above stated, and that "it is the peculiar mission of the Southern Church to conserve the institution of slavery" as it was maintained in the South. That these doctrines are not only heresy, but blasphemy, is plainly seen from the Word of God; and if the General Assembly is not competent to declare them so—when "to the General Assembly belongs the power of deciding in all controversies respecting doctrine and discipline, of reproving, warning or bearing testimony against error in doctrine or immorality in any Church, Presbytery or Synod"—then it is not competent to interpret the word of God on any subject whatever.

It is thus evident, that the position of the last Assembly upon slavery is impregnable. It in no way contradicts any former Deliverance. It is indeed admitted that it demands a renunciation of errors on that subject which no former Deliverance required; but this is justified from the consideration that until the late rebellion, these errors were comparatively harmless. They were held as mere opinions with which the Church did not choose to interfere; tenets which excited amazement rather than alarm. But when they had been sown broadcast over the South, and like the fabled dragon's teeth, had brought forth myriads of armed men; and when the question was—how to deal with those who had led the van in publishing opinions whose legitimate consequence was to fill the land with blood, provided they should seek admission into the Church they had left in the interest of these heresies. Then, that Assembly had the right, and it was clearly its duty to require a renunciation of these gross errors, as truly as to demand repentance of the terrible crimes which they had so naturally begotten.

It has been often said, and even reiterated upon the floor of the present Assembly, that it is upon the General Assembly of 1865 rather than upon a small class of men in the Church, that the responsibility rests for reviving this dead issue of slavery. But when that Assembly met, slavery was not a dead issue. As before remarked, it legalty existed in some parts of the country, and its legal extinction in the rebellious States was denied by some of the ablest jurists in all parts of the land. Since then, however, the system has been fully terminated throughout the entire country by an amendment to the Constitution of the United States. Had this been the case when the last Assembly met, it is possible that no action would have been taken upon the subject. But be this as it may, there are manifest reasons why that action should stand. The tenets which that action condemned, and a renunciation of which it demanded, are both heretical and blasphemous. It is essential to the honor of our common Christianity that they should be renounced, in those coming to us from the South, who hold them both for the truth's sake, and for the sake of the evil they have wrought in the land. Their renunciation should also be required by reason of their possible influence hereafter. What that influence may be no mortal can tell. When men embrace and hold such doctrines with the tenacity of religious convictions, and when they illustrate their sincerity in holding them during four years upon a hundred hard fought battle fields, it need surprise no one who is acquainted with human nature and human history, if similar illustrations of sincerity and valor shall be again exhibited upon a fitting opportunity. Those opinions have once enkindled the fires of revolution, to the surprise of all mankind, under the best popular Government of the world. Whether they will ever do it again, none but God can tell. All this is worthy of the more grave consideration, in the light of the Pastoral Letter put forth by the General Assembly of the South Presbyterian Church, sitting in Macon, Ga., in December last. That letter says of the Southern system of slavery, that "the lawfulness of the relation, as a question of social morality, and of Scriptural truth, has lost nothing of its importance;" and that Assembly fervently thanks God, as set forth in this Pastoral, that it had nothing to do with the emancipation of the slaves, saying, "that it may hold up its hands before heaven and earth, washed of the tremendous responsibility involved in this change in the condition of four millions of bond-servants, and for which it has hitherto been generally conceded they were unprepared." When such sentiments are put forth by the General Assembly of the Southern Presbyterian Church, at this time of day, after the tremendous judgments of God have overthrown the system, it is too clear to admit of argument, that we have no occasion at present to abate one jot or tittle of the action of the last General Assembly, touching its demands upon slavery.

Upon both branches of the Deliverances of the last Assembly—loyalty and freedom—we therefore arrive at the same conclusion, that they should be maintained in their integrity.

One other topic demands our consideration. In consequence of the rebellion and slavery, and of the deliverences of the five preceding Assemblies, thereupon, one Presbytery in the Church, and some one hundred or more ministers and elders, have set themselves against these deliverences, by ecclesiastical action, or formal organization, and have published their schismatical doctrines to the world. The disapprobation by ministers and members of the acts of the General Assembly, when expressed in proper terms and spirit, and with due acknowledgment of subordination to its authority, is a right which belongs to every one under its jurisdiction. The General Assembly claims no infallibility; but it posses a clear authority, derived from the Lord Jesus Christ, and its acts resulting from such authority are to be respected. No combination of ministers or members may properly be formed within the bosom of the Presbyterian Church for the purpose of openly resisting the authority of the General Assembly, and of setting at naught and contemning its solemn decisions, while the individuals composing such combination still claim all the rights and privileges of ministers and members; much less may any lower court of the Church thus repudiate the Assembly's authority, and still claim and exercise all the powers of a court in good standing. The principle which would admit this would prove destructive of any government, secular or religious, for it is the essence of anarchy. Notwithstanding this, several Presbyteries have openly declared that they will not regard the Assembly's authority, especially the acts of the last Assembly concerning the terms of receiving ministers and members from the Southern Presbyterian Church. We trust that upon further reflection they will reconsider such action, and again show a proper subordination. One Presbytery, however, that of Louisville, in the Synod of Kentucky, adopted a paper in September last called a "Declaration and Testimony," &c., which arrays itself against all the Deliverances of the five Assemblies from 1861 to 1865, enacted upon slavery and the rebellion. This paper has been signed by certain ministers and elders in other Presbyteries and Synods, chiefly in the Synod of Missouri. The present Assembly felt called upon to take decisive action in the premises. This paper exhibits organized rebellion and schism within the bosom of the Church, whose design is to resist he authority of the General Assembly. It pronounces the last five Assemblies guilty of heresy, schism and virtual apostacy. Such an organization, with such aims, bringing such charges, and animated by such a spirit as the said paper exhibits, the Assembly could not overlook. The simple question presented was, whether a single subordinate court, with such individuals of other Presbyteries as might join it should be allowed to carry on its schismatical and rebellious schemes with impunity, and still claim and exercise all the rights of a court, and the individuals concerned have all the rights of office bearers in the Church accorded to them, while openly defying the General Assembly; or whether the Assembly which represents the whole Church should require due subordination and respect to its authority. The signers of the said paper openly avow their determination to continue agitation against the solemn acts of the last five Assemblies, until they shall bring the Church, through action of the General Assembly, to their views; or, failing in this, they declare that they may feel called upon to abandon the Church.

In this posture of affairs, the Assembly could not hesitate in its duty. It censured all the persons who have signed the "Declaration and Testimony," deprived them of the right to sit in any Church court above the session, and cited them to the bar of the next General Assembly. This measure was clearly justified, and was demanded for the purity, peace, and order of the Church.

We have now, beloved brethren, set before you a few of the important matters which have engaged the attention of the General Assembly at its present sessions. It is cause for lamentation that while the country has passed triumphantly through the war, and the Government and the Union have been preserved, the Church should still be troubled with questions which have grown out of the civil strife. We trust the day is not distant when these dregs of rebellion shall be purged from the Church, and when it shall stand forth as a compact body in purity, righteousness, and peace. To this end we exhort you to labor and pray as God shall give you grace. And may the blessing of God rest upon you, the presence of Christ sustain you, and the Holy Spirit richly dwell within you.

Unanimously adopted in Committee, Henry Day, Esq., being absent.

R. L. STANTON, Chairman.
P. D. GURLEY, JOHN M. KREBS, THOMAS E. THOMAS, } Ministers.
GEO. S. GREEN, JAMES M. RAY, } Elders.

After the reading of the letter, Rev. Dr. Smith said this was a question which touched the very life of the Church and threatened its existence in the border States. He asked this Assembly to pause, after the summary judgments that had been already inflicted, and to speak some word of kindness to those churches that are now agitated and trembling with such unspeakable anxiety.

Mr. Charles Wood thought the pastoral letter contained the very words of kindness which Dr. Smith desired.

Rev. Mr. Wilson thought the word "blasphemy," which occurred twice in the letter, was too strong; and that some other word should be substituted.

The ayes and noes were demanded on the adoption of the pastoral letter.

Rev. Dr. Backus desired to offer the following as an amendment to the pastoral letter: "At the same time this Assembly distinctly recognizes that individuals or judicatories of the Church may, without contumacy and with entire loyalty to our Church, disapprove of and reject the Deliverances alluded to, and may consistently discriminate between the absolute obligation to constitutional rules and the respectful regard which is due the injunctions and orders of the General Assembly that are not of the nature of constitutional principles.

Laid on the table.

DR. KREBS' REPORT.

In regard to the Deliverances of the last and the five preceding assemblies, as well as this, and especially the requisitions to examine applicants from the South touching their views of slavery and rebellion, the Assembly would observe that although the war is over, secession effectively quashed, and slavery abolished, yet in view of the spirit of these dead issues, which, it must be admitted, still survives, rampant and rebellious, perhaps more virulently in the religious form than elsewhere, it was necessary to guard the Church from being disturbed by this element which has asserted itself so rebelliously, and continues to be so vehemently proclaimed, and therefore to require satisfactory evidence of the practical repudiation of these heresies.

Nor does the Assembly deem it needless to observe that while manifestly the views put forth by these Deliverances, and the views which it was proposed to elicit from applicants for admission to our Churches and Presbyteries, have regard only to those more recent opinions concerning the system of Southern slavery, out of which secession and the war grew, for its perpetuation and extension. The Assembly considers that there is no contradiction between these latest expressions of the Assembly needed by a new state of case and the whole current of consistent Deliverances on the subject of slavery, which the Church has from the beginning and all along uttered, especially from 1818 to 1846.

The Assembly in those things has desired to impose no new terms of communion, it has but pointed out the appropriate treatment of the rebellious and disobedient; and, in the language of no less an authority than the illustrious Calvin, it did but make "a genuine and simple application of the *lex dei* to the times and manners for which it was designed." In this special application it has only, in the still further language of the great Reformer, "guarded against offenses which are most expressly forbidden by the Lord," without "taking away one *punctum* of Christian liberty." (Instit. Lib. IV, chap. X, § IV, 21 22.) And in regard to our Deliverances on these subjects, the Assembly here contents itself as sufficient, with declaring that it has but exercised the constitutional right and duty of the Assembly, which has been constantly exercised from the time of the fathers who made the constitution of our Church, to utter its sentiments, warnings and exhortations on all points and questions, which, while we are properly restrained from invading the jurisdiction of civil tribunals, do, nevertheless, belong to that class of things which we may handle, viz: those moral and religious questions which, even although they may embrace points in which politics, whether in their larger or lesser sense, are involved; because while relating to civil and political affairs they are also questions of religious duty, and cannot be thrown out of the religious jurisdiction.

Dr. Krebs, in reply to a question by Dr. Riggs, said his paper was designed to affirm the views set forth in the pastoral letter.

The paper was adopted.

Dr. Gurley presented the following paper:

It having come to the knowledge of this body that some of the ministers under our care, not able to subscribe to the recent Testimonies of the General Assembly on the subjects of Loyalty and Freedom, and that some who have not signed or formally approved the Declaration and Testimony, do, nevertheless, hesitate to comply with the requirements of the last Assembly, touching the reception of members from the South, known, or supposed to have been in sympathy with the rebellion; therefore,

Resolved, That while we would treat such ministers with kindness and forbearance, and would by no means interfere with the full and free discussion on their part of the Testimonies and requirements referred to, we deem it a solemn duty which we owe to them and to the Church to guard them against giving countenance in any way to declarations and movements which are defiant of the Assembly's authority, and schismatical in their tendency and aim; and we do earnestly exhort them, in the name and for the sake of our common Lord and Master, to study and pursue the things which make for peace.

On motion of Dr. Thomas, the paper was adopted.

Mr. Collier moved that the pastoral letter, and the additional papers, be published in pamphlet form by the Board of Publication. Agreed to.

Dr. Krebs, from Committee on Unfinished Business, reported the following yet remaining to be disposed of:

1. The appeal of Rev. Dr. Breckinridge against the Synod of Kentucky. This case was referred to the next General Assembly.

Judicial case No. 2 being the complaint of S. J. Niccols and others against the action of the Synod of Missouri passed at its session in October, 1865, whereby it declared the previous meeting of its own body "not a free Court of Christ, and its entire acts null and void and of no binding force." As the last General Assembly did recognize the Synod referred to as a free Court of Christ, and its acts as valid and of binding force, the Committee recommend that the complaint be sustained, the action of the Synod complained of reversed, and that the Synod itself be censured for not showing due submission to the action of the last Assembly.

Dr. Anderson raised a point of order, that the case was not properly before the Asssembly, on the ground that the Committee in recommending the above action, exceeded its power as prescribed by the rules.

Dr. Gurley said that the Committee had been governed in their action by the fact that all the principles involved in the case were severly decided by the last Assembly. The last Synod of Missouri declared that previous meeting was not a free Court of Christ, and that its actions were not binding. Last year the records of that Synod were before the Assembly, and the Assembly approved the minutes of that very meeting which the Synod of Missouri at its last meeting declared was not a free Court of Christ. Then in the second place there was a case of complaint coming from Reverend Mr. Farris and Watson, which complaint was dismissed by the Assembly. There was a protest against that action of the Assembly for dismissing the case, and in that protest the whole question was argued. The Assembly adopted an answer to that protest, which answer, it seemed to him, made it plain that this whole case was decided by the last Assembly.

Dr. Anderson said the approval of the minutes of the meeting before the last was the approval of a record that had not in it a word about military intervention, the administration of an oath, and the exclusion of members for not taking it. That meeting of Synod deliberately avoided a record of the facts, in order that they might not be embroiled with the Assembly.

Efforts were made to have the facts put on record,

but failed in every instance. He hoped the Assembly would not be held accountable for all the enormities of that infamous meeting. He spoke intelligently. The highest legal authority in the United States had said to him when he saw the record of that transaction, that he never blushed for his Church before. The meeting of that Synod wherever it was known would send a thrill of horror through the breasts of Presbyterians. It was a false record that went up to the General Assembly, and he was responsible for what he said. A man in that Assembly without a beard on his face decided who should sit in that Synod and who should not. Call that a free court of Christ. Why just about as they were to commit an enormity that he was afraid would stamp the Church of his fathers with infamy, he said to a brother: "If you have any regard for the Church and your own reputation, go out of this court and dissolve it;" for his going out would have dissolved it. And what did he say? Looking the speaker in the eye he said, "I would not be here if I dared to be away." The speaker contended that if this question was determined by the General Assembly, without hearing one word of the facts, without ever having the means of knowing what they were, they would fill the heart of every Presbyterian with sorrow and shame. He said that body not only excluded its own members, but a minister was arrested and put on parole and the facts suppressed. Messrs. Farris and Watson were recorded as having been received on Wednesday morning, but they were rejected on Wednesday evening, and their names were not put on again until Thursday morning. He knew of one minister who was arrested for quoting from the Confession of Faith. He appealed to the Assembly not to affix this stain on the Church which he loved. He had loved this Church from his youth up. He had said to members all around him, "do not leave the Church." So far as his own Church was concerned they could leave, because the property was not subject to the Assembly, but he had sought to prevent a separation on account of the love he bore to the Church.

Rev. Mr. Forman said that he was not present at the meeting of the Synod last Fall, and as he had not read the proceedings carefully, he was not prepared to say whether he could indorse everything that was done. It was a matter of surprise to him, however, that any man could declare the Synod of 1864 a free Synod. He thought, in after years, the proceedings of such bodies would be printed in small type in the Digest, as the Church of Scotland had done in similar instances, to show that they were unlawful.

Dr. Krebs desired to know whether these things were matters of record in the Synod of Missouri?

Dr. Anderson said there was no record until the last meeting of the Synod, when the facts were drawn up and sworn testimony taken of members and persons who were spectators, and the facts were as he had stated.

Dr. Van Dyke moved a reference of the case to the next General Assembly.

Rev. Dr. Nicolls, one of the complainants, was invited to address the Assembly, and in response said if it was the desire of the Assembly to postpone action until the facts in the case could be fully investigated, he had no objection.

Thereupon the motion of Dr. Van Dyke to postpone to the next Assembly was agreed to.

Dr. Krebs, from the Committee on Unfinished Business, reported in favor of the adoption of the report on the Hymnal, which provides for an authorized version of Hymns and Psalms.

Dr. Riggs offered a substitute which was laid on the table.

Dr. McLean offered a substitute disapproving the action of the Committee on the Hymnal, and instructing the Board of Publication to cease printing the same.

Also, that the committee prepare a different book and report to the next Assembly.

On motion of Rev. Mr. Hines the substitute of Dr. McLean was laid on the table.

Rev. Dr. Montfort moved to refer the matter to the next Assembly.

A motion was made as a substitute, that the Board of Publication cease printing until the next Assembly.

Dr. Krebs addressed the Assembly at length in support of the report of the Committee on the Hymnal.

Pending the discussion, adjourned.

AFTERNOON SESSION.

Rev. Dr. West presented the following answer to the protest of Rev. Dr. Vandyke:

Answer to protest in case of excluding commissioners from Louisville Presbytery:

The paper upon which the Assembly acted in the exclusion of the Commissioners of the Louisville Presbytery from their seats in this body until their case should be decided, indicates sufficiently the true ground of that action. It is no other than the constitutional right of the General Assembly to protect its own dignity and vindicate its own authority, as a supreme tribunal of the Church, in view of open insult to that dignity and open defiance of that authority, by an inferor court subject to its jurisdiction.

1. The argument of the Protestants that the Assembly has, by this action, violated the fundamental law of its organization, in this respect, that no Assembly can be constitutionally valid unless *all* the particular Churches and Presbyteries are actually represented in the body, is an utter misinterpretation of the constitution, and the assertion of a principle that would vitiate the validity of nearly every meeting of the Assembly and render the organization of any Assembly almost an impossibility. So conspicuous a fallacy as that of confounding the fundamental law and right of representation with the actual presence of the whole company of the representatives themselves needs only the statement of the fallacy in order to furnish its refutation, not to mention the various clauses of the fundamental law which evince its glaring absurdity. Form of Gov. chap. XIII.

2. In reply to the Protestants asserting that there is no warrant in the Constitution, no precedent in the history of the Church, and no sufficient analogy for such exclusion, to be found in any secular Assemblies whatever, the Assembly simply utter the counter assertion. The Protestants, moreover, err greatly in supposing that the Assembly is organized by any "formal adoption" of the report of the Committee on Commissions, or that the *ex officio* organization of the Assembly, by the Clerks of the House, as the ministerial officers of the Assembly, renders impossible any subsequent action of the Assembly in reference either to the Commissioners themselves or to the Presbyteries which are the electors of those commissioners.

3. The Protestants moreover utterly misrepresent the action of the Assembly in the exclusion of the Commissioners of Louisville Presbytery, by denouncing it as a "judicial condemnation" of the Presbytery without a regular trial. So far from this being the case, the truth is this, that the action of the Assembly was only the suspension of the functions of the Commissioners, interdicting their participation in the deliberations of this body until their case should be decided, in the consideration of which case the Commissioners themselves were not only allowed but particularly invited, by formal vote to appear, discuss the case, and defend the action of their Presbytery to the fullest extent. The allegation that the Assembly decided the case of the Louisville Presbytery merely upon public rumors without proof, is entirely untrue.

4. It is unnecessary to enter upon any detailed denial of the protestation that the Louisville Presbytery has done nothing that can by any possibility justify the Assembly in the suppression of the privileges of the Commissioners. The Presbytery, according to its own "Declaration and Testimony" is in admitted, open and persistent defiance of the authority of the Assembly, the lifting up of a standard of revolt in the Church, and the call upon all Presbyterians to engage in rebellious, heretical and schismatical conduct, and so the Assembly has judged. In reference also to the doctrine that no decrees and determination of the General Assembly are of binding force upon the inferior judicatories, unless

previously submitted to the Presbyteries and approved by a majority of the same, the Assembly declares that this is simply a violent wresting of chapter XII, section 6, Form of Government, from its historical connection and design, and in opposition, not only to the usage of the Church in past days, but also to the careful decision of the whole matter as it emerged in the early controversies of the Church, (Digest), p. 49, 50.

5. As to the right of protest by any individual or court in the Presbyterian Church, the Assembly fully recognize the same. But it is utterly unendurable, as it is utterly unconstitutional, to prostitute or pervert the right of decent and respectful protest to the ends intended by the Louisville Presbytery, to-wit: to open rebellion against the authority of this body, to the propagation of a vast brood of fatal heresies, to bitter misrepresentation of the acts of the Assembly, and to the organization of conspiracies against the very existence of the Church itself.

6. The declaration of the protestants that, by the Assembly's action the churches under the care of the Louisville Presbytery have been excluded "from the fellowship of the Church of Christ," is illegitimate, illogical and gratuitous. There is not a particle of evidence to justify the implication that the Assembly deals with the Churches under its care in precisely the same way in which it has dealt with the Louisville Presbytery. Should every minister of the Presbytery be not only suspended from his ecclesiastical functions, but deposed from the Gospel ministry, the churches of the Presbytery would still remain in connection with and under the care of the Assembly, until, by their own act of insubordination, they had rendered themselves obnoxious to the censures and judicial or legislative discipline of this supreme tribunal, and thereby been lawfully excluded from our connection.

N. WEST,
W. T. FINDLEY,
F. T. BROWN.

Rev. Mr. Stonerode offered the following report of Committee on Synod of Missouri, which was docketed:

That the proceedings of the Synod seem to be recorded with unusual correctness, the orthography, chirography and punctuation being worthy of all commendation.

The committee, moreover, feel constrained to make a different report as to the constitutionality, the regularity, the wisdom and the equity of at least a part of their proceedings, resulting not as it should, in the edification of the Church, but in distractions and divisions.

While, therefore, the committee recommend the approval of the records from page 345 to 381, they report the following exceptions:

First. On page 357, where the Synod declares that "said body (that is, the Synod of 1864) was not a free court of our Church, duly constituted according to our form of government, and that the acts of said body are null and void and of no binding force."

The committee except to this part of the record, for the reason that this action of the Synod is in direct contradiction to the action of the Assembly of 1865, which Assembly, by their approval of the minutes, recognized the constitutionality and validity of the court.

Second—On page 365, where the Synod reaffirms their testimony of November, 1861, with regard to the action of the Assembly of the same year, known as the Spring Resolutions; which testimony declares the action of that Assembly on the state of the country to be "unscriptural, unconstitutional, unwise and unjust, and of no binding force whatever on this Synod, or upon the members of the Presbyterian Church within our bounds."

The committee also recommend that besides excepting to the record as above stated, the repeated exhibition of such a rebellious spirit on the part of any inferior Court towards the supreme judicatory of the Church, should not pass without censure.

Dr. Krebs concluded his remarks in support of the Committee on the Hymnal.

Rev. Dr. Schenck said—having had a large correspondence with Churches—he was satisfied that it would give universal satisfaction.

Rev. Mr. Agnew spoke in favor of it with a corrected index.

Rev. Dr. Gurley thought nearly three hundred old and favorite pieces should be added to the appendix without music.

Rev. Dr. Backus reviewed at length the difficulties overcome by the committee, and the completeness of the work offered.

Two or three gentlemen endeavored to gain the floor opposing it, when Rev. Mr. Skinner moved the previous question, which was sustained by the house.

Rev. Dr. Krebs then read the following report of Committee on the Hymnal, which was adopted:

1. Resolved, That the report be adopted and printed in the appendix.

2. Resolved, That the Board of Publication be directed to publish, also, a cheaper edition of the book.

3. Resolved, That this General Assembly approve the Hymnal as published and allow the same to be used in all our churches; but it is not required that it shall supersede the books in present use.

4. Resolved, That the Board be authorized, at their discretion to suit purchasers, to append the Shorter Catechism, the Form of Government, the Directory, Book of Discipline and the Rules of the General Assembly.

6. Resolved, That the Board of Publication keep on hand and publish sufficient copies of the existing Book of Psalms and Hymns for those who prefer to use it, or need it with the Hymnal.

Rev. Dr. Krebs of Committee on Unfinished Business, moved that the case of Slack, against the Presbytery of Cincinnati, and the case of Guy against the Synod of Cincinnati, be referred to the next General Assembly. Adopted.

A majority and minority report of the Synod of Kentucky, was presented by Committee on Record of Synod of Kentucky, which was referred to next Assembly.

Rev. Dr. Krebs moved that a note of the language used by the Ohio Statesman, in the case of Mr. Galloway, be appended to the minutes for reference in future cases.

Rev. Dr. Thomas thought it would not be agreeable to Mr. Galloway's feelings as that gentleman had suppressed the only copy which had been in the Assembly, containing the offensive correspondence.

Rev. Dr. Schenck moved to amend by filing it. Agreed to.

The Committee on Unfinished Business reported a resolution to pay expenses of Committee on Re union from the funds of Board of Publication, which after discussion was adopted. Also, a request in Overture No. 4, from the Presbytery of Passaic that the geographical boundaries of Presbyteries be restored, which was laid on the table.

Rev. Mr. Frazier read the report of the Committee on Systematic Benevolence. Adopted.

The report of the Committee on Synod of Missouri was then taken up, and after sharp discussion, Mr. H. K. Clark offered the following:

Resolved, That this Assembly does not approve the records of the Synod of Missouri; that so much of such records as attempts to declare void the previous action of the Synod, which had been formally approved by the Assembly, is an act of insubordination to the authority of the Church, which said Synod is required to reconsider and reverse, and that they report to the next Assembly what they have done, or failed to do in the premises, and that, until then, the usual certificate of the Moderator be withheld.

It being near the hour of adjournment, the Assembly adjourned until eight o'clock, P. M.

EVENING SESSION.

The Assembly met and was opened with prayer by Rev. J. T. Backus.

The unfinished business was then taken up, being the amendment of Mr. Clarke, which, by motion, was temporarily postponed to take up other business.

Rev. J. Allison offered the following:

Resolved, That the papers in the case of the Rev.

James Sinclair, referred to the Committee on Freedmen, be transferred to the Board of Domestic Missions. Adopted.

Dr. Gurley offered the following amendment to the action of the Assembly concerning the Hymnal:

Resolved, That the Committee on the Hymnal be requested to prepare and the Board of Publication be requested to publish, if possible, in the next edition of that book, a supplement of not more than three hundred additional hymns and psalms, to the end that many hymns long dear to the Church but not found in the Hymnal in the present form may be supplied and the book made more complete and permanently satisfactory to our people.

Resolved, That the Board of Publication be requested to publish a smaller and more portable edition of the Hymnal, suited to the wants of the prayer meeting and lecture room.

A motion was made and carried that the amendment be referred to the Committee on the Hymnal and that Dr. Gurley be added to that committee.

The case of the Synod of Missouri was then taken up and an amendment offered to Mr. Clark's motion by Rev. Dr. Backus, as follows:

Resolved, That all after the words "an act of insubordination" be stricken out, and instead the resolution read, "and that the Synod be directed to purge itself before the next General Assembly of all intentional insubordination."

After discussion, a motion was made that Dr. Backus' amendment be laid on the table. Carried.

A motion was then made that Mr. Clarke's paper be adopted, which was carried.

The Moderator raised the question as to who the records should be delivered to, as he understood that there were two Stated Clerks.

It was moved to refer to the Committee on Records. Laid on the table.

H. K. Clarke moved that the records be deposited with the Stated Clerk of the Assembly until the question be decided.

On motion of Rev. Mr. Wilson, it was laid on the table.

The judicial case of Rev. Mr. Crozler and Rev. Mr. Mack vs. the Synod of Illinois was taken up and, on motion, referred to next Assembly.

Overture No. 18, being an application from the Presbytery of Palmyra, asking the General Assembly to convey certain property to Branch Hatcher and wife, in trust, to enable Palmyra Presbytery to establish an academy for the education of youth, to be forever after the property of the Old School Presbyterian Church.

The committee recommend the application be made to the Board of Education of the General Assembly. Adopted.

The amendments heretofore published of Rev. Dr. Riggs and Rev. Dr. Smith were then taken up and adopted with the report.

Protests from Messrs. Jones, of Maryland, Hines, Dr. Boardman and A. P. Frorman, against actions of the Assembly were presented and received except Dr Boardman's, which was referred back on account of being disrespectful.

The following vote of thanks was adopted:

Resolved, That the thanks of this General Assembly are hereby tendered to the Second Presbyterian Church for the use of its house of worship; to the families and hotels of St. Louis for their generous hospitality to the members during these sessions; to the Mercantile Library Association for its courtesies; to the Iron Mountain Railroad Company for the pleasant excursion to Pilot Knob; to H. C. Crevlin and officers of the Transfer Company for the free use of its coaches in going and returning from the cars on that occasion; to the Rev. S. J. Nicolls and the Committee of Arrangements for the complete provision made for our entertainment; to the secular press of this city for its full and accurate reports; to George D. Hall, Esq., and the other members of the Committee on Railroads for their successful efforts to secure a reduction of fare; also, to the following railroads, viz: Pennsylvania Central railroad; Pittsburg, Columbus & Cincinnati, (Pan Handle;) Columbus & Central Indiana; Indianapolis, Terre Haute & St. Louis; Northern Central; Baltimore & Ohio; Central Ohio; Little Miami; Columbus & Xenia; Indianapolis & Cincinnati; New York & Erie; Atlantic & Great Western; Bellefontaine, Dayton & Western; all the railroads in Missouri; the Chicago, Alton & St. Louis railroad; the Ohio & Mississippi railroad, and also to the steam packet on the Mississippi and Illinois rivers for reduction of fare.

Mr. Clarke moved that the Committee on Revision of Book of Discipline also revise Rules of Order. Adopted.

The minutes were read and approved.

On motion, the Assembly was dissolved and another was ordered to meet at Central Church, Cincinnati, the third Thursday in May, 1867, at eleven o'clock, A. M.

The Assembly was then closed by prayer and Apostolic benediction by the Moderator.

The following was omitted in our report of Saturday's proceedings—afternoon session:

Dr Thomas, from the Committee to nominate candidates for Directors of the Board of Domestic Missions, reported the following: Ministers—W. C. Anderson, D. D., J. Addison Henry, W. F. Finley, R. L. Stanton, D. D., A. Hills, J. E. Rockwell, D. D., V. D. Reed, D. D., P. O. Studdiford, A. Donaldson, G. C. Heckman, S. M. Irwin, S. A. Muchmore, M. A. Hoge, D. D., S. B. Spottswood, D. D., Charles W. Shields. Elders—S. Galloway, J. L. Williams, James M. Ray, James Bateman, M. Newkirk, John M. Harper, H. D. Gregory, C. Falconer, Thomas McMechan.

The nominations of the committee were confirmed.

Dr. Krebs offered a resolution adopting the reasons of Dr. Gurley, presented on the adoption of his substitute adopted on yesterday in the case of the Louisville Presbytery, and ordering the same to be printed with the minutes of the Assembly. Agreed to.

Dr. Lowrie, from the Committee on Bills and Overtures, reported Overture No. 23, as follows:

Memorials from the Presbyteries of Washington, Donegal, New Lisbon, Redstone and Southern Minnesota, and Mrs. S. E. Parsons, concerning the new book of chants, psalms and hymns with music, called "The Hymnal," mostly expressing opinions adverse to its adoption by the General Assembly, and some of them making valuable suggestions for its improvement.

The committee make no recommendations concerning these memorials, inasmuch as the subject to which they refer has come before the General Assembly in another way.

The report of the committee was adopted.

Dr. Lowrie, from the same committee, reported Overture No. 24, an inquiry concerning Synodical correspondence from Rev. S. C. Jennings, D. D., by the Rev. J. F. Collier:

In view of our Form of Government (chap. 12, sec. 5), which says: "To the General Assembly belongs the power of corresponding with foreign churches, on such terms as may be agreed upon by the Assembly and the corresponding body," and in view of the exception taken by the Assembly to the records of the Synod of Tennessee in 1827, p. 13, and as found recorded in full in (Baird's) the Assembly's Digest, p. 506—has any Synod a right to institute a correspondence by delegation with the Synod of another denomination or branch of the Church?

Respectfully submitted, at the request of Rev. Dr. S. C. Jennings, by

FRANCIS J. COLLIER.
Commissioner.

The committee recommend as an answer to the particular question contained in this overture, that no legislation is necessary on the subject.

The report of the committee was adopted.

Dr. Lowrie, from the same committee, reported Overture No. 25, memorials and papers from the Synods of New Jersey and Philadelphia, from the Presbyteries of Newton, Lewes, Northumberland, Oxford, Toledo and Palmyra, from a Convention of Ministers and Ruling Elders, which met in this city on the second evening previous to the meeting of the General Assembly, and from the Rev. Dr. F. S. Janeway and H. J. Van Dyke, all having reference to the Deliverances of the General Assembly for the last five years, on the rebellion and slavery," and to the relations of our Church with the ministers and churches in the Southern States, formerly under the care of the General Assembly.

The committee recommended the following minute:

That the memorial of the Convention be approved, and printed in the Appendix to the Minutes of the General Assembly, as the General Assembly has considered substantially the matters embraced in said memorial, and expressed, by its action, the judgment, it is deemed unnecessary to suggest any additional measure for rebuking the spirit of rebellion against the authority of our highest court, in a few sections, of our Church. The dissatisfaction and discontent consequent upon the Deliverances of the Assembly of 1865 are abating with increased knowledge of the design and propriety of these decisions, and it is confidently believed that maturer reflection will produce a fuller acquiescence in the authority of the Church. It is alike the past and present purpose of our Church to preserve within its fold all who sincerely and earnestly love its orders and doctrines, and to fan into life and energy every lingering spark of genuine attachment to our faith and order which may exist in those portions of our country, where the spirit and unrelenting power of the rebellion drove many true and loyal Presbyterians into a hostile attitude toward the Church and country. With this enlarged and Christian view it is appropriate to declare that whilst the testimony and authority of our Church are to be obeyed, the fullest Christian liberty of opinion is tolerated and protected, and no enforcement of the deliverances of our Church is expected or demanded, except that which will debar from our communion and Church courts all those who refuse to submit to "the powers that be," and remain in willful antagonism to the manifestations of God's providence and the authoritative decisions of our Church.

The report of the committee was accepted and adopted.

Dr. Lowrie, from the same committee, reported Overture No. 26, as follows:

Overtures have been presented from the Synods of northern Indiana, Wheeling and the Presbyteries of Madison, Lewes, Lake and Monmouth, respecting the removal of the Board of Domestic Missions. The committee recommend that inasmuch as a committee has been appointed to report to the next Assembly on this subject, no further action is necessary.

The report of the committee was adopted.

Dr. Lowrie, from the same committee, reported Overture No. 27—a request from the Board of Church Extension, that the Trustees of the General Assembly take charge of certain deeds, mortgages, &c.

The committee recommend that the Assembly adopt the following resolution, viz:

Resolved, That the Trustees of the General Assembly of the Presbyterian Church of the United States of America are hereby authorized and required to receive and take charge of any estete, real or personal, which may be granted or conveyed to said Trustees, at the request of the Board of Church Extension of this Church; and whenever the said Board of Church Extension shall request the said Trustees to grant, convey or release any right, title or interest in any estate, real or personal, which has been or may hereafter be vested in said Trustees, by reason of or in consideration of any grant or appropriation of said Board, in aid of the erection of any church edifice, then the said Trustees shall make such grant, conveyance, and release to such parties and upon such consideration or condition as the said Board of Church Extension shall by resolution direct, provided that the contracts contained in any such grant, conveyance or release so executed by said Trustees shall be such only as said Trustees shall approve.

The report of the committee was adopted.

After prayer the Assembly adjourned.

ARGUMENT OF REV. J. H. BROOKES, D.D.,

Delivered before the General Assembly of the Presbyterian Church of the United States, on the 31st of May, 1866, in defense of the Louisville Presbytery.

Mr. Moderator: It is with unfeigned reluctance that I appear before you and this venerable Assembly to-night. Had I consulted my own wishes rather than a sense of obligation to the little band which I am here to represent and to defend, I would have remained silent during the exciting discussion that has been going on in this house for the last two weeks. But, sir, continued silence on our part would be wrong in the circumstances that surround us. Among all the speeches with which we have been favored through our protracted session, not one word has been uttered in behalf of the small party that signed their names to the hated "Declaration and Testimony." From nearly every quarter we have listened to the sternest denunciations uttered against that now famous protest, and it seemed impossible for any one to obtain a hearing in the Assembly without washing his hands of all complicity in the guilt of those who dared to publish it to the world. Some have boldly avowed their sympathy with the principles there set forth, but even these have been careful to inform you that they cannot indorse its language and that they are in no wise responsible for its appearance.

First, we had the fierce onset of the gentleman from Ohio, (Dr. Thomas,) who borrowed his glowing imagery from the most terrific judgments of God, in order to express his abhorrence of our crime in sending forth a document which has fallen like a firebrand in this house. In the heat of his passion he likened us to the guilty inhabitants of Sodom and Gomorrah, consumed by flaming brimstone, and then to Ananias and Sapphira, suddenly smitten by the unseen hand of the angry Jehovah, and at last invoked the red-hot thunderbolts of hell to fall upon our devoted heads.

The gentleman from Kentucky (Dr. Humphrey) followed with an amendment to the motion of the Chairman, and accompanied the amendment with a speech, in which he used, if possible, still harsher and more cruel terms than those employed by the gentleman from Ohio. He declared in the presence of this venerable Assembly, and in the presence of God, that he had never known the exceeding richness of the English language in vituperation until he read the "Declaration and Testimony." He pretended to see metaphors, burning metaphors, dancing through its pages to the tune of Dixie, and could not find words to convey his righteous indignation against the rebels and traitors who, according to his excited imagination, are proudly defying the authority of the Church and despising her sacred institutions.

So the gentleman from Washington City (Dr. Gurley) in presenting a second amendment, or rather, a substitute for the original motion, pronounced us slanderers, worthy of condign punishment, and solemnly avowed his purpose to leave his beloved Church unless the punishment should be speedily inflicted. He could not commune with such sinners, and would be compelled to seek an ecclesiastical home elsewhere if this hated Declaration and Testimony party were allowed to remain among the saints.

Even the brother from Philadelphia (Dr. Boardman), whom I have long revered for his high Christian character, and whom I have learned to love for his noble Christian heart, took occasion to express his disapproval of our course, and to say in the paper which he read that we deserved censure for carrying our sound and invulnerable principles to extremes. And finally, my brother from Brooklyn, whom I also love for his manly defense of the truth, was unable to say anything for the document which has stirred this wild commotion, because he had not signed it, and could not be answerable for its language. Thus, sir, we stand alone in this great assemblage, and hence my position this evening is one of immense disadvantage, Still, as I did not come here to struggle for victory, but only to contend earnestly for the faith once delivered to the saints, and to battle for the truth as it is in Jesus, I shall proceed with firmness, and I trust with respect for this high court, to express the views entertained by those who have been haled to your bar. The opprobious epithets which have been heaped upon us without stint will not be returned upon their authors, but until you can show us by an appeal to the Holy Scriptures and to the Constitution of the Church that we are in the wrong, we must stand where we are, undaunted by threats and violence. Let gentlemen cease from their wholesale abuse and prove that we are in error; or, sir, we will maintain our position unmoved, so help us God. Amen. [Great applause in the galleries, which Dr. Brookes promptly checked; begging those present to abstain from all such demonstrations, and to remember that they were in the house of God. With this remark the Moderator concurred, asking the excited crowd to repress their feelings.

Mr. Moderator: It has been asserted again and again on the floor of this house that the Declaration and Testimony party are laboring in the interest of secession, and are trying to vitalize the dead body of slavery. If this be true—if this is our motive and aim, we richly merit the severe punishment which it is the manifest purpose of the majority to inflict upon us. Nay, I cheerfully admit that we are utterly incompetent, unfit and disqualified in every respect to sit in a Court of Jesus Christ, or even to exercise the humblest functions of the Gospel ministry. But let me ask, are gentlemen sure that we are responsible for the agitation of these subjects in the Church? Did we begin the conflict which has raged in the Assembly for two weeks, and which threatens to end in complete separation? Sir, we had supposed that secession was ended by the war. We had supposed that slavery was done away with by the war, and what evidence have you that we refused to acquiesce in the stern decisions of the sword? What evidence is there that we were so dissatisfied with the result of the dreadful contest, that we were determined to try the issue again even at the expense of rending our Church asunder? None, none whatever. Do you desire to know who dragged these questions from the dead past to agitate our people with useless contentions? Do you desire to learn who has thrown secession into our midst as the apple of discord? Do you desire to know who has gone about to vitalize the mangled body of slavery and make it a source of endless dispute and division? Sir, I believe before God it was the General Assembly. [Suppressed applause.]

Boldly do I affirm that it was not the Declaration and Testimony party, it was not the Louisville Presbytery which began this unhappy strife, but it was the fell and fanatical spirit that would not be content to let the dead past bury its dead, but insisted on making the dead past the test of our present standing in the Church and the controller of our future destiny. We have acted entirely on the defensive, and have only striven to bring back our beloved Church to her forsaken standards and to equip her for her glorious mission of saving souls.

It only remains, therefore, to discuss three propositions which I now submit to the candid consideration of this venerable court:

1st. Was there sufficient ground for the protest which the Louisville Presbytery and others have made in the "Declaration and Testimony" against the proceedings of the Assembly during the past five years?

2d. Had we the right to protest? And

3d. Was the protest made in a spirit and form justified by the exigencies of the case, and by the perilous condition of the Church?

If these three questions can be answered in the affirmative, then, sir, we expect an honorable acquittal at your bar, instead of condemnation. Nay, we demand, as we deserve, not your censure, but your grateful plaudit, "Well done, good and faithful servants."

To investigate the first of these questions intelligently let us consider the action taken by the General Assembly in 1861, which was, to the action of 1865, but like the cooing of a dove compared with the angry screams of a vulture; or lest this may seem disrespectful to the body, I will say it was the faint and feeble moaning of the gathering storm compared with the roar and rage of the tempest, sweeping with resistless fury over the fair heritage we received from our fathers. To determine whether we had sufficient ground of protest against this first and fatal action of 1861, which required the Presbyterian Church of the whole country to uphold and perpetuate the Government at Washington city, I will cite a few witnesses whose high standing will not be questioned by any here.

The first of these witnesses is Rev. Chas. Hodge, D. D., of Princeton, New Jersey, the true Nestor of the Presbyterian Church, whose reputation, extending far beyond the Atlantic, has gained him a host of admirers wherever learning can be respected or piety revered. Dr. Hodge, speaking of the action of '61, in his own behalf and in behalf of about sixty other members of that Assembly, published to the world the following judgment: "It pronounces or assumes a particular interpretation of the Constitution. This is a matter clearly beyond the jurisdiction of the Assembly. * * * The General Assembly, in thus deciding a political question, and in making that decision practically a condition of membership to the Church, has, in our judgment, violated the Constitution of the Church, and usurped the prerogative of its divine Master."

Mark it, and ponder it well, fathers and brethren, the highest authority, in some respects, in our communion affirms that the Assembly violated the Constitution of the Church and usurped the prerogative of its Divine Master. Think you the Declaration and Testimony men had a sufficient ground of protest? But, again, Dr. Hodge goes on to say, "We protest, because we regard the action of the Assembly as *unjust* and *cruel* in its bearing on our Southern brethren." Unjust and cruel? Why this sounds as if it might be found in our Declaration and Testimony. Can you discover there any stronger language—any more disrespectful terms? "And finally," says Dr. Hodge, "we protest because we believe the act of the Assembly will not only diminish the resources of the Church, but greatly weaken its power for good, and expose it to the danger of being carried away more and more from its true principles by a worldly or fanatical spirit." Ah, Mr. Moderator, if that venerable man of God had possessed prophetic vision he could not have foretold with more unerring accuracy the certain results of the assembly's first departure from the established principles of our Church government.

The next witnesses I wish to cite in a body to testify whether the Declaration party had sufficient cause to protest, are Rev. R. J. Breckinridge, D. D.; Rev. W. C. Matthews, D. D., and Rev. R. W. Landis, D. D., all thoroughly loyal men. These gentlemen introduced a paper into the Synod of Kentucky, in the fall of '61, which affirms: "In the judgment of a large minority of the Assembly, and of multitudes in the Church, the subject matter of the action of the Assembly in the premises, being purely political, was incompetent to a spiritual court. Undoubtedly it was incompetent to the Assembly, as a spiritual court, to require or to advise acts of disobedience to actual governments, in the manner and under the circumstances which existed; and still further, it was neither wise nor discreet for the Assembly of the whole Church to disregard, in its action, the difficulties and dangers which rendered it impossible for large portions of the Church to obey its order without being liable to the highest penalties. The action of the Assembly being exhausted by the occurrence of the day of prayer recommended, and no ulterior proceedings under the order of the Assembly being contemplated, this Synod contents itself with this expression of its grave disapprobation of the action of the General Assembly." But the testimony of these loyal gentlemen, emphatic as it is, was not strong enough to satisfy Rev. E. P. Humphrey, D. D., who stepped forward and offered the following amendment, which was unanimously adopted: "Which (action of the Assembly) the Synod judges to be repugnant to the word of God, as that word is interpreted in our Confession of Faith." Mr. Moderator, my surprise is almost unutterable when I compare this strong language with the boast of the gentleman on the floor of this house that he was loyal to all the deliverances of the Assembly, and intended to stand by them. What! Stand by action which he deliberately and solemnly affirmed to be repugnant to the word of God. What! Talk about the amazing vituperation to be found in the Declaration and Testimony, and watch the dance of metaphors along its pages to the tune of Dixie, when he himself pronounces the act of the Assembly unscriptural and unconstitutional! It is vain, sir, to reply that he and the other loyal gentlemen who voted for this amendment did not refuse to obey the Assembly. I will not insult them by even hinting at the possibility of their obedience to that which they loudly proclaim to be repugnant to the word of God, and therefore we find them occupying precisely the ground on which the Declaration and Testimony men so firmly stand.

But I must proceed to notice briefly the acts and deliverances of subsequent Assemblies, to see whether we had sufficient reason for issuing our solemn protest. It would be ungracious in me to weary your patience by noticing minutely the action of '62, which was certainly taken without the slightest authority either from the word of God or from the constitution of the Church; or by examining at length the action of '63, which exhibited the frenzy of that state of mind which led a venerable court of Jesus Christ to occupy two or three days in discussing the question whether a flag should be raised above the building in which the Assembly convened. I hasten on to consider the action of '64 touching slavery, affirming it to be an "evil" and "guilt" and "sin," "the root of rebellion, and bloodshed, and a long list of horrors," and in short adopting in effect the familiar saying of the old abolitionists that it is "the sum of all villanies." And so, sir, on the floor of this Assembly have we heard again and again that slaveholding is sinful, but not one word of proof has been alleged either here or by the Assembly of 1864 to make good this confident assertion. "Sin is the transgression of the law of God;" but it is a remarkable fact that an ecclesiastical council, assembled in the name and by the authority of Jesus Christ, adopted a long paper on the subject of slavery without even referring to the Bible, according to my recollection. They *said* it is sinful, but did not *show* it by appealing to the law, which is the only standard of righteousness. To form an opinion concerning the sinfulness of an act or relation I want a higher authority than man's prejudices and passions; I want the authority of God's holy word; and no Assembly has the right to bind the conscience or to demand obedience without this authority.

Especially does such a right entirely disappear when we find the actions of 1864 to be in direct and glaring conflict with the action of 1845. The former was passed at a time of tremendous excitement—in the midst of a bloody war—under the sway of an extravagant loyalty, and seemed to be an expression of the wild delirium which prevailed throughout the nation, while the latter was passed after mature deliberation, and was precisely the one act which expressed the calm and settled conviction of the Assembly in its best days in relation to this vexed and vexing question. Let us see what that Assembly said, when entirely free from the control of passion and from the pressure of public sentiment. I read, sir, from the Digest:

"The Church of Christ is a spiritual body,

whose jurisdiction extends to the religious faith and moral conduct of her members. She cannot legislate where Christ has not legislated, nor make terms of membership which He has not made. The question, therefore, which the Assembly is called to decide, is this: Do the Scriptures teach that the holding of slaves, without regard to circumstances, is a sin, the renunciation of which should be made a condition of membership in the Church of Christ?

"It is impossible to answer this question in the affirmative without contradicting some of the plainest declarations of the Word of God. That slavery existed in the days of Christ and his Apostles is an admitted fact. That they did not denounce the relation itself as sinful, as inconsistent with Christianity; that slaveholders were admitted to membership in the Churches organized by the Apostles; that whilst they were required to treat their slaves with kindness, and as rational, accountable, immortal beings, and if Christians, as brethren in the Lord, they were not commanded to emancipate them; that slaves were required to be "obedient to their masters according to the flesh, with fear and trembling, with singleness of heart as to Christ," are facts which meet the eye of every reader of the New Testament. This Assembly cannot, therefore, denounce the holding of slaves as necessarily a heinous and scandalous sin, calculated to bring upon the Church the curse of God, without charging the Apostles of Christ with conniving at sin, introducing into the Church sinners, and thus bringing upon them the curse of the Almighty.

* * * * * * * * *

"The Assembly intend simply to say that since Christ and His inspired Apostles did not make the holding of slaves a bar to communion, we, as a Court of Christ, have no authority to do so; since they did not attempt to remove it from the Church by legislation, we have no authority to legislate on the subject."

Here, sir, we have a position carefully taken and thoroughly fortified by the word of God, and yet in the face of this deliberate testimony we are required to believe slavery an "evil" and "guilt" and "sin," and the fruitful source of rebellion, bloodshed and all manner of crimes. Mr. Moderator, I cannot and will not so believe. I care not for slavery, but I do care for the authority of the sacred Scriptures, and according to the light I now have, the action of 1864 was contrary to these Scriptures, and tended directly to infidelity. "The grass withereth, and the flowers thereof falleth away, but the word of the Lord endureth forever," and it endureth unchanged and unchangeable amid the rudest conflicts of earth. To the divine authority of that word we must all bow with implicit submission; and since in the opinion of the declaration and testimony men there was a direct conflict between the action of '64 and the plain statements of the Bible—nay, between the hot and hasty action of '64 and the calm and collected judgment expressed in '45—we feel that there was abundant ground for an earnest and vigorous protest if we would save the Church from a still more grievous departure from the faith. Why, then, should we be arraigned at the bar of this high court as the chief of sinners, when it is apparent on the very face of the testimony I have just adduced that we could not adopt both actions of the Assembly without being guilty of gross absurdity and childish inconsistency? Tell us, sir, which of these two actions we are bound, as loyal Presbyterians, to accept. The action of '45 remains unrepealed, and was, indeed, unassailed down to '64, when it was quietly ignored, not even receiving the honor of being mentioned in the long paper adopted by the Assembly. We insist that there was sufficient reason to protest against such conduct.

But, Mr. Moderator, when we come to consider the proceedings of the Assembly which convened in Pittsburg in 1865, the reason for protest becomes manifold and imperative. That Assembly, as we have heard on the floor of this house, simply reduced to practice the principles and doctrines affirmed through the preceding four years, and, consequently, a great struggle must ensue, or the liberty of God's children and the crown rights of Jesus Christ as King in Zion must be tamely and basely surrendered.

Why, sir, we find an ecclesiastical body enjoined by their own ecclesiastical constitution "to handle or conclude nothing but that which is ecclesiastical, and not to interfere with civil affairs which concern the commonwealth," gravely pronouncing against the erroneous interpretations of the doctrine of State rights," thanking God that the rebellion was suppressed without the National honor being tarnished by deeds of outrage and cruelty," directing the Board of Domestic Missions to employ none to preach the Gospel unless "they are in cordial sympathy with the various deliverances of the General Assembly in the United States of America, touching doctrine, loyalty and freedom," and requiring all Synods, Presbyteries and Church sessions to examine everybody coming from the South; "whether he has in any way directly or indirectly, of his own free will and consent, or without external constraint, been concerned at any time in aiding or countenancing the rebellion and the war which has been waged against the United States;" and "whether he believes slavery to be a divine institution which it is the mission of the Southern Church to conserve and perpetuate." If it be found by his own confession or by sufficient evidence that he has in any way voluntarily aided the rebellion, or that he believes in slavery, every such person is required to repent and foresake these sins, on pain of exclusion from the Church and from fellowship with his bretheru in the courts of the Lord's house.

Whether this action furnishes a sufficient reason for protest, let every man judge. I have yet to hear of the first minister or elder who has obeyed these orders and enforced these injunctions. But, on the other hand, several brethren have come to me during our present sessions, and without hesitation declared they would not give heed to the voice of the Assembly touching the requirements just mentioned. So the Declaration and Testimony men have declared both privately and publicly, and this is the head and front of our offending. We have proclaimed openly and above-board, on the house-tops, what others all over the land have said in the ear and in the closet, and for this we are arraigned, and are about to be cut off from the Church of our choice and of our fathers. Well, be it so. But those who apply the knife of excision must testify in the very act of punishment that we had good reason to complain of proceedings which they themselves set at naught. Especially did the cause of complaint become urgent and inexorable in its demands upon the attention of those who lived in Missouri. One of our ministers, well known to many of us as a laborious and faithful preacher of the Gospel, applied to the Board of Missions to furnish him pecuniary aid in the work of saving souls. In due time he received a reply from the Secretary of the Board in the following words:

DEAR SIR: The General Assembly have enjoined the Board to commission no one except of loyal submission to the Government, and to the deliverances of the Church on the subject of slavery. We are informed your record is not fair, and we decline sending you a commission.
Yours, truly, THOS. L. JANEWAY,
Cor. Secretary, &c.

I have seen, sir, a copy of the answer to this astounding communication, which the worthy brother of whom I have spoken forwarded to the Secretary, and in that answer he solemnly declares that he is and always has been a loyal man. He preached constantly during the war in a part of the State where suspicion was almost certain death, and though officers and soldiers frequently attended his ministry, he suffered no disturbance at their hands. And yet this consistent man of God was cruelly denied the assistance he so much needed, and was driven to hard manual labor to obtain a support for his wife and little ones.

Another brother, whose loyalty I have never heard questioned, made application to the Board for aid, and received the unanimous indorsement of his Presbytery—a Presbytery, too, enrolling among its members some who are loyal to the highest possible degree, and according to the highest possible standard—but after awhile the decree came forth from the Secretary's office in Philadelphia:

"Mr. Forman will hardly come up to the requisitions of the last General Assembly. His is *quasi* loyalty, and he is hardly in accord with the Presbyterian Church in its declaims on freedom. It may be hard for him, but he reaps as he sowed. Such men have well nigh ruined the Chuch; and it is hardly expected that loyal men will contribute to support one in affiliation with rebellion. Yours, truly.
"T. L. JANEWAY."

What, Mr. Moderator, was to be done under these circumstances? We were either to place ourselves in an attitude of resistance to the injunctions of the Assembly, or to see brethren whom we knew and loved crushed by the operations of an order that seemed to us most cruel and unrighteous. I leave it to every generous heart to determine what was the path of honor and the path of duty. The Declaration and Testimony party disobeyed, and hence we are here to answer for our sin; but here on grounds that justify our emphatic protest in the sight of God and angels and men.

I need not occupy your time in a discussion of the second inquiry concerning our right to protest, for every Presbyterian in the world recognizes the right, and enjoys this right when he sees fit to employ it in the expression of his views, or in the protection of his sacred privileges. Perhaps there has scarcely ever been an Assembly without a protest being entered on its records, and every year the proceedings of this venerable body pass in review before the Synods and Presbyteries to call forth an expression of their views, and to receive their intelligent sanction or their respectful dissent. It would be idle, therefore, for me to establish a proposition which is self-evident to every member of this Assembly.

I pass, then, to a consideration of the last question: Is the protest contained in the Declaration and Testimony, and adopted by the Presbytery of Louisville, presented in a spirit and form justified by the necessities of the case? Mr. Moderator, in answer to this inquiry, it might be sufficient to state that we all listened attentively to the lengthy report of the committee on this villified document. That committee had it long under consideration, and doubtless searched it carefully and anxiously to discover every objectionable expression which it might contain. And what did they find? Nothing, nothing, sir, after their laborious research, that can be fairly construed into disrespect to this venerable Assembly. It may be owing to my ignorance ot the "fatal imposture and force of words," or my want of a refined and cultivated literary taste, but I confess I cannot see any reason for all this uproar about the violent language employed in the paper was before the house. Gentlemen may rave and rage as they denounce its fierce and vituperative style, and invoke the hot thunderbolts of hell to strike us dumb and to strike us dead, but they will come much nearer to something that is tangible when they are kind enough to point out the expressions that are so disrespectful as to justify our expulsion from the Church.

It is a remarkable fact that in a debate extending through two weeks not even one speaker from the majority has touched the merits of the question before the house, either by attempting to expose the unsoundness of the principles contained in the Declaration and Testimony, or the impropriety of the language in which these principles are embodied. We have had denunciation without measure, but not a word of argument or proof. I submit, sir, that the accusers of the Louisville Presbytery have utterly failed to make out their case, even on the ground of disrespectful terms employed in the paper for which they have been arraigned at your bar.

But there is another way of determining the question which I am now discussing. It is by way of comparison. We will take other protests from other parties, and see whether the Assembly has been in the habit of judging harshly of those who assail their action, or whether the present Assembly is disposed to deal out an even-handed justice to all, without respect of persons, who are involved in the same condemnation. The gentleman from Ohio (Dr. Thomas) tried to draw a distinction between what he was pleased to call the organized rebellion of the Presbytery of Louisville, in formally adopting the Declaration and Testimony, and the individual action of others in various parts of the country who signed that immortal document. But I shall show you that it is a distinction without a difference. I shall show you that numerous judicatories have taken practically the same ground occupied by the Presbytery of Louisville, and hence even for consistency's sake, should receive precisely the same treatment at your hands.

I will not occupy your time by citing in proof of this assertion the action of a large number of Church sessions in view of the unconstitutional proceedings of the General Assembly, but call your attention first to the action of Transylvania Presbytery, prepared by Rev. W. L. Breckinridge, D. D.

"The Presbytery of Transylvania, having maturely considered the proceedings of the last General Assembly (1865), find in them several acts touching the troubles in the Church, which, in our judgment, exceed the powers of the Assembly, and are unwise and inexpedient if they were otherwise; which we also judge to be impossible of execution where they were intended to be enforced, therefore nugatory as to their design." The Presbytery of Ebenezer, at its last fall session, declare, "1st. We find neither in the Word of God, nor in the Confession of Faith of the Presbyterian Church, the least authority to interrogate the minister or the private member on the subject of loyalty to the General Government; and while this Presbytery recognizes the right of every Presbytery to examine ministers asking admission into their body as to soundness in the faith as revealed in the Word of God, yet this Presbytery does most unhesitatingly deny that the questions involved in the matter in hand are a part of the "faith" of the Presbyterian Church, inasmuch as they relate solely to the policy of civil government. We believe that the introduction of such questions into our Church courts is fraught with mischief, as it assumes the decision of civil questions by an ecclesiastical body, and tends to destroy the peace and harmony of the Church as a kingdom not of this world. This Presbytery, therefore, expresses its firm determination not to investigate the civil relations of ministers and private Christians; assured that its jurisdiction as a court of Christ's Church is limited to things spiritual and ecclesiastical.

"2d. That this Presbytery will neither accede to nor enforce any new terms of Christian or ministerial communion on the subject of slavery; ncr will they allow 'cordial sympathy' with the Assembly's action touching this matter to control the reception or good standing of ministers and members."

The third resolution, after announcing that the Presbytery had ceased its connection with Dr. Janeway's Board in the work of Domestic Missions, declares that the action of the Assembly concerning this subject embraces, in our opinion, an unwarranted assumption of power, as well as a perversion of the objects of the Church, claiming that, in addition to the fact that the qualifications above specified are thoroughly unscriptural, this whole matter of ministerial qualifications belongs solely to the Presbytery."

Is there anything stronger than this in the Declaration and Testimony?

The Presbytery of Sangamon (Ill.), a loyal Presbytery in a loyal State, unanimously adopted the following resolutions with regard to the Assembly's acts of 1865:

Resolved, That we, as a Presbytery, in the examination of persons seeking admission to our body, will adhere strictly to the form specified in our standards, believing that there is nothing in the existing state of affairs to justify us in departing therefrom, and that we recommend the pastors and sessions of the churches under our care, to stand in the ways, and see and ask for the old paths where is the good way, and walk therein.

2. That we regard the Board of Domestic Missions as the mere servant of the Presbyteries—the executor of the Presbyteries' will—and we cannot consent that it should be clothed with power to sit in judgment upon a Presbyterial recommendation. We cannot tamely submit to have this or any other Board thus set up as lords over God's heritage.

3. That if the Board of Domestic Missions should presume to exercise the power thus unwisely granted, we will feel ourselves called upon to withhold our contributions from said Board, and to seek some other avenue of contributing to this most worthy cause.

This, Moderator, seems to me to be right decided language for a loyal Presbytery, and places it in the same condemnation with the Louisville Presbytery.

So, too, we find the Presbytery of Lewes, (Md.,) which met May 3, 1865, declaring "that we sincerely deplore the action of the General Assemblies of our Church during the past five years upon the political questions which have convulsed the country with strife and war; that in our judgment such action was not authorized by the constitution of our Church, &c."

If time permitted, I would read in your hearing the resolutions adopted by several other Presbyteries, and by the Synods of New Jersey, Missouri and Kentucky. The first of these dissents unanimously from the action of the Assembly mainly on constitutional grounds, and because it will necessarily aggravate and perpetuate, instead of healing the breaches between the Northern and Southern Church. The Synod of Missouri adopted by a vote of three to one a paper which condemns the action of 1865 in terms as emphatic and explicit as those found in the Declaration and Testimony; and the Synod of Kentucky last fall passed a series of resolutions, the first of which, on a motion to adopt the whole, received the vote of Rev. R. J. Breckinridge, D. D., on a call of the ayes and noes. I will give the resolution that the Assembly may perceive the amazing inconsistency for those who have dragged the Louisville Presbytery to your bar: "The acts of the last General Assembly on overtures Nos. 6 and 7, and resolution 4, on the report of the Board of Domestic Missions, in the judgment of this Synod are unwise, as tending to destroy the peace and harmony of the Church, and in some of their provisions unconstitutional and unscriptural; and we indulge the hope and belief that the General Assembly in calmer times will review and correct these Deliverances." And yet, Mr. Moderator, these same gentlemen have hurried the Louisville Presbytery before you, and demand their instant expulsion from the Church for saying precisely what they have said, to-wit: That the action of the Assembly was unwise, unconstitutional and unscriptural, and hence of no binding force. Consisteney is indeed a jewel, but I cannot find it in the prosecution or in the majority of this house, if either of the papers before us is finally passed.

But let me go to older records to show you how the Assembly was in the habit of dealing with judicatories and ministers who defied its authority and despised its institutions. It is a noteworthy fact, Mr. Moderator, that the Presbytery of Chillicothe, which has the honor of having furnished this Assembly its presiding officer, refused to send Commissioners to the General Assembly on account of the exscinding acts of 1837, and afterwards because the Assembly declined to make slaveholding a term of membership. It is a noteworthy fact that the same Presbytery so prominently represented here passed the following resolution:

"Resolved, That this Presbytery cannot hold fellowship with any Presbytery, Synod or other ecclesiastical body while it tolerates under its jurisdiction either the sin of slaveholding or the justification of the sin of slaveholding; and especially the justification of it by appeal to the Scriptures, which, in the judgment of this Presbytery, is blasphemy of Almighty God, and a shocking prostitution of His word."

I have never heard that the General Assembly, and particularly the gentleman from Ohio (Mr. Thomas) summoned the red-not thunderbolts of hell to smite the Presbytery of Chillicothe for pronouncing the action of our venerable Court blasphemy of Almighty God, and a shocking prostitution of His word; but then we must remember that circumstances alter cases, and it is the Presbytery of Louisville arraigned here for the use of terms which all must admit are far less reprehensible than those employed and never retracted, according to the best of my knowledge and belief, by the Presbytery of Chillicothe.

But, I find still stronger language, if this were possible, in regard to the action of 1845, and I comment it to the attention of the Assembly. It is extracted from the leading article of the Christian Monthly Magazine, Vol. I., No. 6, Sept. 1845, and edited by one Thomas E. Thomas, who at that time resided in Hamilton, Ohio. If he did not write it, he at least gave it his hearty approval, and I trust the brethren who are so sensitive about the dignity of the Assembly will listen to it: "That homely maxim—he that steals will lie—is sound Bible theology. The amount of it is, that the man who willfully violates one of God's commands will not hesitate to defend himself by the violation of some other command; and frequently he will do it un disturbed by the consciousness that he is add ing sin to sin. A richer document, in both *proof* and illustration of this, we have rarely seen than the report on the subject of slavery adopted by the last General Assembly. It clearly proves the declaration of the advocates of universal liberty many years ago, that the united wisdom of the highest judiciary of the Presbyterian Church cannot defend slaveholding or any gross violation of God's law without uttering nonsense, or falsehood, or heresy, or blasphemy. Is it true that the highest court of the Presbyterian Church stands on the concession that slaveholders are not to be disciplined? Our object in this inquiry is not to convict the last Assembly of a breach of the ninth commandment. But we do wish to expose a slander, * * and to call particular attention to the falsehood, absurdity and moral filth, always and necessarily embodied in an apology for the sin of slavery, even when it is carefully prepared by a body composed of chosen delegates from every section of a large denomination." "A little stealing makes a Presbyterian a thief —but stealing largely makes him a saint."

There, sir, to borrow the gentleman's own chaste and classical language, let him stick this feather in the tail of his judgment and appear again on the platform to the gaze of his admiring friends. This man could call the Assembly of 1845 a thief and a liar, could charge it with uttering nonsense, falsehood, heresy and blasphemy, could pronounce its action full of absurdity and moral filth, and as his reward is exalted to be the recognized champion and leader of the Assembly of 1865, while the Declaration and Testimony party, for trying by a firm but temperate course to bring back the Church to her forsaken and dishonored standards, are to be driven from the visible fold of Christ. Admitting that our protest contains expressions offensive to the Assembly, they cannot be worse than the epithets just quoted, and why this great distinction between the offenders?

"Strange all this difference should be
'Twixt tweedledum and tweedledee"

But perhaps the difference may be accounted for by a principle embodied in another familiar compact which leads certain men to

"Compound for sins they are inclined to,
By damning those they have no mind to."

So it may be in this instance, and the Presbytery of Louisville will probably be stricken down for doing precisely what others have been permitted to do with impunity. Nay, to put the case in a still clearer light, they will be sacrificed for openly saying what others over the entire land are secretly saying—for boldly taking the position which others are everywhere clandestinely assuming. Our brother from Philadelpha (Dr. Boardman) pointedly declared this afternoon, that he did not believe there were five men in the Assembly who would refuse to indorse the principles set forth in the Declaration and Testimony, and is the Presbytery of Louisville to be dissolved for expressing these principles in language that may seem to some a little to strong? If this is to be, sir, then I am free to say that all who signed the protest which they adopted are bound by the tender claims of friendship, by the high demands of honor, and by the sacred obligations of duty, to fall with them.

If this is the fixed purpose of the "solid majority of four to one" in the Assembly, then, in my judgment, the adoption of the paper presented by the committee will be the wisest course that can be pursued. This will end the conflict at once; but mark my prediction, the acceptance of the amendment offered by the gentleman from Kentucky (Dr. Humphrey) or of the substitute offered by the gentleman from Washington City (Dr. Gurley) will not bring peace to the agitated bosom of the Church.

And yet, Mr. Moderator, strange as it may appear to the Assembly, peace is what I most earnestly desire. To purchase that peace, although the remark will no doubt call forth another sneer, I would cheerfully offer myself a victim to appease the insulted dignity of the body. I was taught at my mother's knee to venerate the General Assembly of the Presbyterian Church next to my God, and it was certainly far from my design or wish to use unbecoming and disrespectful language towards this high Court of Jesus Christ. Show us that we are in the wrong, and most gladly and promptly will we retract our Declaration and villify our Testimony, but depend upon it, injustice and needless severity will not quiet the disturbed elements that threaten the stability of our Zion. We may fall, but others will take up our cause and carry it forward to victory, if not speedily, then surely at the appearing of our Lord. We bide our time, and standing unmoved in the consciousness of right, are not here to ask for mercy, but to ask that you, too, may do that which is right in view of the account we must all so soon render in the day of judgment.

Brethren, in arriving at your verdict concerning the Louisville Presbytery, bear in mind that I am chiefly responsible for the Declaration and Testimony. I did not write it, but I inaugurated the movement which led to its preparation and publication, and if, in so doing, I have disturbed the peace or retarded the prosperity of my beloved Church, withhold not, I pray you, the blow which shall lay me prostrate at your feet.

When I read the acts of the Assembly of 1865, for the first time in my life I was obliged to assume an attitude of resistance to the authority of this venerable body. Although dissatisfied with the acts of the four preceding Assemblies, I looked upon them as plague-spots that had appeared only on the walls, and fondly hoped that the dire infection would not reach the deep foundations. But, sir, when the Assembly of Pittsburg had closed its sessions, nothing was left for me to do, except to withdraw from all connection with our ecclesiastical courts, or to gird myself for the conflict. The former course I much preferred, and was on the point of pursuing it when letters began to reach me from various quarters urging co-operation in the attempt to reclaim the Assembly from its wanderings.

This attempt, so far, has signally failed, and nothing has come of it save excitement, wrangling, and in all probability division. We made the effort with downright earnestness, and perhaps with too much rudeness, but we thought that we were justified by the pressing necessity of the case, and hence were not over careful in the choice of the means to accomplish our ends. We might have been more particular in our selection of nice words, but we really felt that there was no time to parley about delicate shades of meaning and courtly phraseology.

Mr. Moderator, while listening, just before the close of the afternoon session, to the earnest and eloquent tones of the brother from Philadelphia, (Dr. Boardman,) my attention was called away by the sudden darkening of the windows. I looked up and saw a black volume of smoke roll heavily toward the sky and the next moment heard the sharp, quick cry of fire, and the hurried tramping of feet, and the rattling of the swift engines, as those who are set to guard our city against the destructive element rushed forward to quench the angry flames. They went hastily, and, I suppose, rudely, for they could not be very ceremonious while the fire was darting its red tongue above the roof that sheltered us. Thus, sir, it was with the Declaration and Testimony men. They saw the beautiful temple in which our fathers worshipped on fire, and with a loud shout they dashed into the midst of the curling flames to save our holy place from utter destruction. Even granting that the danger was not so great as they apprehended, must they be deemed worthy of severe punishment for a mere excess of zeal in a righteous cause? If so, they will receive the stroke not in anger, but in unutterable sadness, having, as their last consolation, the sweet thought that Christ sits enthroned in undisturbed composure above all these tumultuous passions of earth, and will surely vindicate His faithful followers at His coming. What, meantime, is to be the result of all this strife, none can predict. We only know that there is One in heaven who will bring order out of confusion, making the wrath of man to praise Him, and the remainder of wrath restraining by His almighty hand.

A song which once stirred the heart of a nation and changed the destiny of an empire owed its origin to a storm. A poet went forth to gaze upon the face of nature, after a tempest had held high carnival in one of her most lovely retreats, and while musing upon the desolations around him he heard the bewitching melody of a bird ascending in praise to God. The bird sang so gratefully because refreshed by the water which it had just been drinking from the upturned cup of an acorn lying on the ground. And the acorn had been dislodged from its lofty bough by the violence of the storm which, though casting it down, also filled its dissevered cup with the rain. After all, then, the storm gave to the world a mighty and immortal song, and I can only pray that the tempest which is now beating upon our beloved Church may suggest truths to some chosen servant of God which will impart to the anthems of the redeemed who are to come after us a loftier and sweeter rapture.

"Behold, we know not anything,
I can but trust that good shall fall
At last—far off—at last to all
And every winter change to spring."

Mr. Moderator, I thank you for the courtesy which you have shown during these discussions, to me and to the little minority which I represent.

Fathers and brethren, I thank you for the patience and the kind attention with which you have listened to one defending a cause so unpopular.

May the blessing of God rest upon this venerable Assembly.

THE BROAD AND THE NARROW CHURCH.

A DISCOURSE BY REV. JAMES McCOSH, L.L.D.,

Delivered before the General Assembly (Old School) Presbyterian Church, May 20, 1866.

Philippians, iv, 8.—"Finally, brethren, whatsoever things are true, whatsoever things are honest, whatsoever things are just, whatsoever things are pure, whatsoever things are lovely, whatsoever things are of good report; if there be any virtue, and if there be any praise, think on these things."

FATHERS, BRETHREN AND CHRISTIAN FRIENDS: Though I have been deeply interested in the struggle in which your country has been engaged, and look upon it as specially the great event in our world's history in this century, yet it will not be expected of a stranger who has come to seek for rather than to give information about your national affairs, that he should speak of American questions. I believe that those who have done me the honor and allowed me the privilege of addressing this venerable Assembly will be more gratified if I give an account of some of the conflicts of Great Britain, which, though they have not been like yours, with "garments rolled in blood," will notwithstanding issue in important practical results—possibly reaching beyond my country into yours.

In Great Britain we hear much about the BROAD CHURCH. It is marked by certain features, so that we can distinguish the person who belongs to it, whether he professes to do so or not. It appeared first in one particular branch of the Christian Church, but it has spread over other bodies, showing that there is a pre-disposition in our time to catch its peculiar spirit. It is found in Scotland as well as England. As yet we have not much of it in Ireland, but with the influence exercised by the centralizing London press, and the close intercourse between the three kingdoms, whatever prevails in the larger country will be sure to find its way to the others. In these circumstances, thinking minds in every land would do well to consider the principles, temper and operations of this influential, if not numerous, religious party.

In looking to any system recommended to our favorable consideration, we should of course inquire whether there be any evil in it, with the view of avoiding it, but also whether there be any good in it, in order to accept and adopt it.

I certainly would not reckon it an evil in the Broad Church, were it seeking, as its name might seem to imply, to bring the various sections of the Church of Christ to a clearer understanding and to a closer union. One of the most hopeful signs of our day is the breathing on the part of so many praying and loving Christians after a more intimate communion among the different branches of the one Church. I am convinced, that sooner or later, these earnest desires and fervent prayers will realize the end they contemplate, and be consummated in a happy, if not incorporation, at least co-operation, which will greatly strengthen the cause of pure religion by combining energies which are at present scattered, and exhibiting before the world the visible unity of the Kingdom of Christ. But I am not aware that the Broad Church is specially striving after a union of the evangelical churches in the three kingdoms, on the continent of Europe, in America, or throughout the world. I rather think, that in this respect, it is a Narrow Church, aiming to combine only those who have imbibed its peculiar spirit; rejecting what may seem to the Greeks as "foolishness;" relishing only what is elegant or academic; having little or no sympathy with the less refined, though it may be more zealous bodies whose speech "bewrayeth" them as showing that they come from the provincial Galilee, and are not natives of the churchly Judea.

But a heavier charge can be brought against this new system, or rather spirit. Its avowed aim is to blunt the sharpness of some of the doctrines and precepts proclaimed in the Churches of the three kingdoms. But in carrying out its purposes, it has deprived these of their point and edge, so that they are no longer "quick and powerful and sharper than any two-edged sword, piercing even to the dividing asunder of the soul and spirit."

As to the Bible itself, its language is always hesitating, often doubtful. It acknowledges that the Bible is in some sense the word of God, but it does not profess to yield obedience to it as a rule of faith and morals; it would receive only so much as is verified by reason and human sentiment, and if it does not reject, it at least sets aside, or overlooks other doctrines or precepts. It is to be admitted in its behalf, that it allots a high place to certain truths of Scripture. It delights to exhibit the purity, the elevation, and the love of the Divine Being. It acknowledges fully the Deity of Jesus Christ,—though sometimes it seems to found it on doubtful philosophical speculations, rather than on the written word—and it dwells with rapture on the lovelier features of his character. But on the other hand it seeks to lower and to modify the doctrine of the atonement made by Jesus Christ for transgression. Indeed the view which it accepts and presents of sin seems to me to be superficial in the extreme. Acknowledging it to be unlovely, it does not contemplate its exceeding sinfulness, as a violation of that law of God. which is holy, just and good. The consequence is that it scarcely sees the need of an atonement, and it does not appreciate the depth of meaning in the Old Testament sacrifices, and in the strong language of the New Testament, as to Jesus suffering in our room and stead. We have here a doctrine imbedded both in the old dispensation and in the new. It may at times have been put in an offensive form, by vulgar minds. The transaction has been represented as a commercial one, in which the Father exacts a payment in a forbiddingly rigid manner, and the Son, of a gentler nature, gives the exacted payment; whereas it is a deed of love throughout, of love on the part of the Father and the Spirit, as well as the Son; the whole originating in the love of Father, Son and Holy Ghost, and the Father giving the highest proof of his regard in giving the Son freely to the death, and the Spirit consenting to enter these polluted hearts of ours. But the gross representations often given must not tempt us to set aside or in any way to change the all important truth, that it is through the propitiation made for our sins by One who suffered what we should have endured, that we have liberty of access to God, and receive pardon and peace and grace, and an answer to our prayers, and a meetness for glory. The preachers to whom I refer are all right in representing the gift of Christ as an evidence of love, of supreme, unmatched, unspeakable love, but then, why did this love require one of the persons of the ever existing and everblessed Godhead, to bear such sorrow, shame and suffering, including a hiding of God's countenance and an awful forsaking on the part of the Father towards his own Son? We cannot understand this unless we realize the full meaning of the declarations of Scripture—"who his own self bare our sins in his own body in the tree;"—"for Christ also hath once suffered for our sins, the just for the unjust, that he might bring us to God." This doctrine is not, as has often been said, a speculation of Anselm (who has undoubtedly given a beautiful exposition of it) but has a place in the Church of God, since Abel offered in sacrifice in type of the coming Lamb of God. This doctrine, though it is to be accepted on the authority of Scripture, had all along had a response, as our great ethical writers have shown, in the natural conscience, which declares that sin is of evil desert and demands punishment, and is pacified only when it hears of Him who "was wounded for our transgressions, who was bruised for our iniquities." This aspect has drawn the eyes of thousands toward the Cross in all ages and should never be concealed or disguised.

The Broad Church acknowledges the existence and the operation of the Spirit of God, making him work everywhere, in the heavens and in the earth, producing all that is grand, all that is lovely in inanimate nature, and in human character. In this respect, it has the advantage of certain sects of Christianity which have narrowed the work of this blessed Agent, the Beautifier, the Purifier, the Comforter, so as to make Him the author of mere ecstatic impulse, and shrieking terrors, and depressing fears, which can serve no good purpose except as a mean to a higher end, a mean of rousing us from our complacency, and making us seek something higher. But on the other hand, those to whom I refer do not sufficiently perceive and avow that beside what our old divines called the common operations of the Spirit of God on all things, and on all men, there is need of a special work to awaken the sinner from his habitual lethargy, to convince him of sin, and to produce a radical change in the heart, so as to bring it out of a state of alienation into a state of reconciliation, out of a state of darkness into a state of marvellous light.

In regard to the precepts of the Divine Word, the tendency of the system is to soften whatever may seem harsh and unpleasant. It would not do away with the Sabbath, but it would lessen some of its obligations, and lower its peculiar sacredness. Now it may be that in former times, and even by some few in these times, the Sabbath has been imposed and observed in a Pharisaic temper and spirit, and made a day of oppressive formal ceremonies instead of a day of rest and cheerful service—a day of gloom when it was meant to be a day of liveliness and holy joy. But on the other hand, it should ever be resolutely maintained that the Sabbath is sanctioned in the law of God; that it has a place among the ten moral commandments; and that if we give up its divine obligations or detract from its sacredness, we shall have a greater difficulty in preserving its acknowledged advantages; and if we begin to turn it into a day of amusement we are losing sight of its original and holy intention; and the working classes will find in giving up the ground of principle that they have an ever increasing difficulty in defending it even as a day of rest against the encroachments of avaricious masters.

The system does not require nor recommend any of those graces and virtues which imply self-denial or self-sacrifice, such as parting with all for Christ's sake, parting with self and self-righteousness. It would endeavor so to dress up religion as to remove the offence of the cross. But the attempt is vain, and must ever terminate in open failure. No doubt, when there is so much in our hearts and in the world to oppose spiritual religion we are not to add to all this by raising up further offences. But as long as our nature is what it is, and our religion is what it is, as long as there is a carnal nature to resist the entrance of a purifying spirit, we can never do away with the offence of the cross. Sin has polluted our souls, and the defilement cannot be covered except by blood. And that blood spot must remain to remind us of our sin and the way of salvation. In the Old Testament almost all things were purified by blood, to remind the worshippers that "without shedding of blood there is no remission." In the New Testament, the grand object presented is Jesus Christ suspended on the cross. It is never to be forgotten that we are followers of a crucified redeemer, and that if any man would follow Christ, he must take up his cross and follow him. In heaven itself the saint beholds a "lamb as it had been slain" in the very midst of the throne of God. With such a view before him, no sinner need despair, for that lamb was slain for sinners; and with such a view no saint dare be proud or presumptuous, for it is through the sufferings of that Lamb of God that the saint has attained his privileges. The object is represented as in the very midst of the throne of God, that man may never look up to heaven without seeing it; and that the saint on earth may join the saint in heaven, in ascribing the glory of their salvation to Him that sitteth on the throne, and to the Lamb that was slain.

Opposed to the Broad Church is what we may call the Narrow Church. These two repel each other, and each drives the other away farther from the centre. The Broad Church becomes broader and lighter as it is blown away from the Narrow Church, and the Narrow Church becomes more shrunk and shrivelled out of a terror of being caught in the folds of the Broad Church. The fault of the Narrow Church consists essentially in its being incapable of comprehending the great breadth, or appreciating the full love of the religion of Jesus Christ. This may sometimes arise merely from its partizans having received little or no liberal education to expand their minds; and at other times from their being beset with a narrowness of intellect; in such cases we can excuse the persons—unless, indeed, they become what they are often tempted to do, censorious of others who can take a wider and a more loving view than they. But it springs most commonly not from mere unfavorable circumstances, or a defect of natural gift, but from the culpable narrowness of heart, which will not allow itself to be enlarged by the full influence of christian love.

It may display itself in a variety of ways. First, so far as the Scriptures are concerned, it may look upon them as a mere charm. I knew a person who was required by her office to engage in what she believed to be sinful work; but in order, as she told me, to ward off the displeasure of God, she always carried a Bible with her when so employed; as if the Bible she carried had not condemned her. There are some who would not go so far as this, who yet look upon the Bible as having some virtue to do them good, apart altogether from their catching the spirit of its truths. There are some, I fear who read their passage of a morning merely as a perfunctory duty, but who never think of doing with it, as they do with their breakfast, that is feeding upon it and digesting it for nourishment. We have been accused of worshipping the Bible; but we worship not the Bible, but the God who has revealed himself in the Bible.

There are some who expect from the Bible what it does not profess to furnish. I suppose there is no one who expects the Scriptures to teach men their trades or professions. They convey a far more important and at the same time difficult lesson. They show us the temper in which we should engage in our daily toil, a spirit of endurance, a spirit of thankfulness, a spirit of cheerfulness. They show us how to buy and sell and get gain, and suffer loss; not with the mere design of promoting our personal and family aggrandizement, but in order thereby to promote the glory of God and do good. But just as the Bible does not instruct us in the outward offices of the business of life, which we may learn otherwise by the faculties which God has given us, so there are other branches of knowledge which it does not profess to teach us, such as the arts and sciences, and the general history of nations, which are to be learned in the proper exercise of our natural powers, and by observation and industry. It has indeed a special lesson to give in regard to such pursuits; but it is to conduct them in a truth-loving spirit, accepting the facts whatever they are, and in a devout temper, giving to God the glory of his works.

Science must be allowed to prosecute its own ends, that is the discovery of the laws according to which God carries on his works, in its own way—that is by observation and experiment. When it does so, it can discover nothing but truth, and the truth will always glorify God. True, there will be professedly scientific men rising up from time to time, who will inflate their theories far beyond their facts; these must be met, not by religious denunciations, but by a better, that is a more accurate science. What a host of rash speculations as to the origin of new species of plants and animals have been put to flight by the extensive and careful observations of M. Pasteur, of Paris. It is now admitted on all hands that there is no such thing in the present operations of nature as spontaneous generation, that is the generation of animate beings out of inanimate. But then it was maintained by some who pleaded observation in their favor, that out of putrescent matter of our pools, filled with decayed organic matter, you could produce animals or plants without a seed or germ or a parent after their kind. But it has been shown within the last year or two, by the great naturalist whom I have named, that if you allow him to take the proper steps for securing that there be no germs, or to destroy them if they exist, no living creature will appear. I adduce this as an example of the way in which science, proceeding on a sure method, ever rectifies its own errors, or rather the errors of its adherents. Some of its truths may seem, at first sight, opposed to the Scriptures, but in the end it will turn out that we have misread the Word or misread the facts. There may be times when it is impossible to effect a reconciliation; but then it is equally true, that there are times when one part of true science cannot be reconciled with another. The Church of Rome thought that the doctrine of Galileo as to the earth's moving, endangered the authority of revelation; but every one is now convinced that this truth, while it has widened our views of God's works, has left the word of God where it found it. So will it be, I venture to say, with those geological discoveries which are alarming timid believers, and are acclaimed with shouts of triumph by infidels. There are points of difficulty in Scripture, on which science has thrown some light. It used to be an objection to the record in the first chapter of Genesis, that it represented light as being created at an early date before there were days; and the sun and moon as being created on the fourth day. What can be more absurd, it was urged, than to make light, and even day and night before the appearance of sun or moon. But now we find Sir John Herschell declaring that light is intimately connected with the essential nature of matter. It now appears too, according to the highest scientific authorities on this particular subject, that our earth must have had days and nights, and been covered with plants and supplied with heat before our sun existed in his present state or fulfilled his present functions. In adducing this case, I do by no means assert that this reconciliation may be the ultimate one. I advance it as a possible one, and as showing how difficulties which at first seem formidable, may be removed by the progress of knowledge. In some points we see a curious correspondence between the first book of Genesis and geology. They agree in this that God did not fashion the earth, as it now exists, at once, and that there were stages in the Divine workmanship. They both tell us that there was an orderly progression from the lower to the higher, from the inanimate to the animate, from the plant to the animal, from the inferior animal to the superior. Both agree in this that man appeared on the Earth only at a comparatively late period. So far the two correspond, and we are encouraged to cherish the hope that when the truths of science are finally adjusted --which they are far from being at this present time—they may help us to understand that first chapter of Genesis more clearly than the narrow theologians of former times did, when they prematurely drew from it a complete cosmogony.

To turn to a different topic. That man belongs to the Narrow Church, and deserves to be called an exclusive churchman to whatever sect he may be attached, who looks upon the Church as consisting only of those who bear office in it, such as ministers and presbyters, members of ecclesiastical courts, ministers, elders and deacons. The Church invisible consists of all who believe in Christ and are united to him. The Church visible consists of all who profess their faith in Christ and live consistently with their professions, in the use of the sacraments and the other ordinances of God's appointment. All of these have high privileges secured to them, and have important duties to discharge. It certainly does not prove any one to belong to the Narrow Church that he loves his own denomination, that he strives to advance its interests by his own contributions, his exertions and his prayers, and to have its sphere of influence widened for good. But he is a member of the Narrow Church, with whatever sect, large or small, he may be connected, when he looks on his own denomination as constituting the Church of God; when he unchurches all other churches; nay, when he refuses to acknowledge that there are other sheep who are not of his fold; when he shuts himself up within the narrow precincts of his own communion and declines to look on the things of others to see if there be anything good or imitable in them; when he prays for no other body of Christians than his own; nay, when he neglects to read about the misssionary exertions at home and abroad, of other religious organizations seeking to Christianize the world. 'I believe in the Holy Catholic Church' in a nobler sense than the adherents of the Church of Rome do. 'I believe in the communion of saints,' in the universal communion of saints on earth, as well as of saints in heaven. A Christian cut off from the communion (I mean here outward communion) of the Church is not, as every one knows, in a favorable position for advancing in the Christian life, for growing in love. I believe that in like manner, a Church cut off from the communion of the Churches of Christ, is in an equally unfavorable position. It is like a pool cut off from living streams; apt to become dead and stagnant, mantled all over with green envy and black prejudice. The Christian Church, like the Christian man, should be like a lake receiving fresh streams from above, and giving them out from beneath, to mingle with other streams and to foster fertility as they flow far and wide.

There is a narrowness and a partiality exhibited by many in the manner in which they treat the truths revealed in the Word. Some seize on a clause of Scripture, and without viewing it in its connections, or comparing it with other parts, they hasten to apply it to their immediate purpose. I need scarcely refer to those who accept a part of what is revealed, and decline the rest. Thus there are some who will attend to nothing but the precepts of the Word. They relish, they say, the high morality of the Bible, especially of the New Testament, and they often quote its wise maxims, and its elevated sentiments. But I ask such, have you kept these precepts which you profess so to admire? If they acknowledge that they have not, which they will at once do, if they at all deal faithfully with themselves, then I ask how pardon and peace are to be had except in the blood of atonement, which is revealed as one of the doctrines of the Word? I ask them farther, what hope have they of being able to keep that law of God in time to come? Through their own strength or how? The answer to this, if they give it honestly, will be that this can be secured only in one way, the way pointed out in the doctrines of God's Word, that is by the washing of regeneration, and renewing of the Holy Ghost.

Again, there are some who fondly fix on a few favorite doctrines, and pay no regard to any others. Perhaps these doctrines are in themselves all important such as the depravity of man, justification by faith, and the necessity of conversion. These certainly are about the most momentous truths contained in God's word. He who abandons them will find that he has left another gospel which is not the Gospel. But there are other truths besides these to be attended to, and to be received in faith. Otherwise what can we make of large portions of Scripture? Of those, for instance, which speak of the works of God and call on us to admire them? Of those which illustrate Divine providence by the history of God's dealings towards his ancient Church? If we fail to catch the lesson which these narratives, and which the songs and parables teach us, the loss will assuredly be ours. For "all Scripture is given by inspiration of God, and is profitable for doctrine, for reproof, for correction, for instruction in righteousness, that the man of God may be perfect, thoroughly furnished unto all works."

At the other extreme there are those who value doctrine and nothing else, and very much overlook the precepts, or at least certain of the precepts. I ask these persons how they account for the important place allotted the ten commandments in the Books of Moses, and the continually increasing prominence given to moral precepts in the writings of the prophets? I ask them what they make of the Sermon on the Mount, the longest recorded discourse of our Lord, or those earnest injunctions to duty enjoined by the Apostles in all their epistles?

Let us look for a minute or two at the stars in that constellation of graces, recommended in the passage I have chosen as a text. "Whatsoever things are true": where we have a truth-seeking, truth-loving, truth-confessing and truth-speaking spirit enjoined. "Whatsoever things are honest": meaning that which is worthy of esteem and veneration by God and by man. "Whatsoever things are just": referring to transactions between man and man. "Whatsoever things are pure": as opposed to unchastity of every kind. "Whatsoever things are lovely": that is, worthy of love, fitted to call forth love. Alas, that there should be professing Christians, that there should be real Christians, who do not seem lovely. There can indeed be no Christian without love, love to God, and love to man; but, alas, there are Christians who are without those amiabilities in temper, in conversation and in act which are fitted to diffuse happiness, and to draw the affections of others toward us. "Whatsoever things are of good report": by which is not meant that we should do whatever is favored and recommended by the world, but we are to cultivate whatever is deservedly well reported of. "If there be any virtue." The word *virtue* occurs only three times in Scripture. It is rather a heathen phrase, but it is baptised into Christ, and thus made pure, denoting whatever is worthy of moral approval and commendation. "If there be any praise": that is, deserving of praise. Combining these in one, we see how rich the cluster, how fitted to attract the eye. We see how best the Christian may recommend religion to those around him. He who gives a cup of cold water to a fellow disciple, is exercising a virtue and will by no means lose his reward. He who from the heart offers a genuine word of sympathy to one who suffers, to one who sorrows, is doing that which is lovely. He who in all humility, as knowing that he himself is a sinner, is striving to restrain prevailing vices, or to make the world, or that, it may be, small portion of it with which he is connected, better than he found it, is fulfilling these injunctions, and if he does secure the favor of men he at least deserves it. He who acts faithfully and benevolently as a master or as a magistrate, is falling in with the spirit of these precepts, provided in doing so he is swayed by love to men and love to God. He who favors and supports a good society as a good institution, fitted to advance Christianity or to relieve suffering, and spread happiness, or to elevate the morals, or the very intelligence and tastes of the community, is doing that which is worthy of praises. We see how extensive and varied the means by which Christians may adorn and recommend the doctrine of God our Savior.

Such graces and virtues as these are gems worn by the Christian, more precious and more dazzling than the stones on the breastplate of the high priest, and by their beauty and brilliancy they draw towards him the eyes of others. It is the prominence given by the Broad Church to such precepts which constitutes its only excellence. It is the neglect of them by the Narrow Church which constitutes its weakness; in attending very possibly to small matters of form as insignificant as the payment of tythe, anise and cummin, they "have omitted the weightier matters of the law, judgment, mercy and faith." It is no reason for neglecting these excellencies that heathens have so far exhibited them and that some of them may be practiced by persons who make no special profession of religion. On the contrary, this is rather a reason why Christians should pay a special regard to them, that the men of the world will not respect our religion unless we present it to them with this ornament. In respect of the virtues which the world respects, the Christian should see that he is at least equal to them. If we neglect them it is certain that the men of the world will some time or other turn round upon us, as the heathen King of Egypt did upon Abraham, and rebuke us for our inconsistencies. Nay, the very heathen at the day of judgment may rise up against us and say, "Were not we when on earth better than you with all your knowledge, and all your privileges and your profession?"

It has been felt by many that there is a courage, an openness, and a manliness possessed or valued by other bodies of Christians, but not practiced or valued in the Evangelical Churches of a certain type. I believe it is a duty we owe to God to cultivate as far as our position admits, every natural gift with which God has endowed us. I do not like the phrase "muscular Christianity"; (I find Professor Kingsley disowns it;) but I have no objection to the commendation of muscular exercise, provided the end be, not to expend a useless energy on levity, or worldly amusements, but to strengthen the body to make it the fit minister of the active soul. I know that "bodily exercise profiteth little" in the worship of God, but it may profit much in promoting the health of that bodily frame which God has given us, in keeping it from falling under the influence of sour and depressing humors, and securing that we have *mens sana in corpore sano.*

These graces and virtues constitute the flowers and the fruit of the Christian character. A professing Christian without them is like a plant that never yields a blossom, that never comes to the seed to germinate other life; that is he is an abortion, he has failed of the very end of his life. Some theologians recommend these graces as being simply a manifestation or exhibition (as they call it) of Christian faith. But this is a low and altogether an inadequate view. They are to be cultivated not as a mere exhibition and proof of something else, but as in themselves excellent and worthy, as being in fact, at least some of them, among the highest perfections of the Christian character. What is it that makes Jesus Christ so dear to the believer, which so wins our hearts and draws our regard towards him? Is it not the possession of these and such like qualities? This it is that raises him so much above our world, which makes us feel that he has come down from a higher region, that he walks our earth with the halo of a heavenly radiance. And is not the highest glory of the Christian, not simply that he believes on Christ—this is necessary as a mean in order to a higher end accomplished by the mean—but that he resembles Christ, being formed anew after his image, and living as he lived, and walking as he walked, having the same mind that was also in Christ Jesus?

Not that in our admiration and approbation of these graces we are to forget that they need to be sustained and supported. First, the plants on which they grow as flowers and fruits, must be rooted and grounded in Christ, must in fact be grafted on him before they will live, flourish and bear such products. Without such a soil to feed them, and stock on which to grow, we should look in vain for the higher graces in these corrupt hearts of ours. Nor must we forget that these virtues are not independent of other graces. The plant must have humility for its root, and faith as its stem, and be watered by the tears of penitence, before we can expect such a cluster and crown of flowers to adorn and recommend it.

The conclusion we reach, is, that we are to hold by the old truths which have been from the beginning. These appear in the oldest books of the Bible, and in nearly every page of it from the commencement to the close. The readers of the Word have seen them there all along, and believers in every age have gratefully received them and fed upon them, and been quickened and nourished by them. We are certainly not to defend any position which we believe to be indefensible; the sooner we abandon the traditions which have been added to the pure truth of God the better. But on the other hand it is foolish to expect that we are the least likely to gain the enemy by surrendering any portion of the truth. We already see that those who give up "Moses in the law," will immediately, after they have done so, be asked to give up the "Prophets," and in the end, all that is supernatural in the New Testament. Those who abandon the Atonement will soon be tempted to part with the proper Deity of Jesus Christ, there being no very obvious reason, why one equal with the Father should assume our nature and die such a death, except that which is to be found in the infinite evil of sin. Those who think they can preserve and defend the Sabbath while they allow that it is not of Divine command, will soon be made to see that in these times, it will not continue to be respected, merely because it has the authority of the Church's command, and that in fact the portions snatched from the harsh demands of such taskmasters as trade, commerce, and labor, will be devoted to pleasures which do not elevate the soul in this life, or prepare it for a better. Those who think they can improve the ethics of the New Testament will soon find that they are in the fetters of a legal and self-righteous system, which brings no pardon for the past, and furnishes no sufficient motives for regeneration in the future.

But on the other hand let us labor to exhibit religion in all its loveliness, as Jesus himself presented it in the flesh. By all means, let us defend the truth, the Bible and its characteristic doctrines, by such learning and logic as we can command. Let us pray that God would raise up in the Church, and more especially in the Schools of the Prophets, able and erudite men, fit to wrestle with those who are assailing Divine truth. But in the days when Jesus was on the earth, it was by his character, more than even the "signs and wonders" which he wrought, that men's hearts were drawn towards him. And we may depend upon it, it is by receiving fully and embodying the spirit of Jesus that the Christian can most effectually recommend the religion of Jesus to those prejudiced against it, and to the world in general. He who has attained this spirit in any measure is like the typal Moses when he came down from the Mount, after conversing with God; he may not know it (it is all the better that he does not know it, that he does not think about himself at all) but his face shines with the reflection of the light of God's countenance. It is thus that he is able to recommend religion to others—not so much because he may be consciously striving to do so, and thus put himself in forced and affected attitudes, if not saying, at least looking as if he might say "Stand by, for I am holier than thou;" but unconsciously, because the light has been shining upon him, and is reflected from off his character, and wherever he goes, men take knowledge of him that he has been with Jesus.

GENERAL ASSEMBLY

OF THE

PRESBYTERIAN CHURCH OF THE UNITED STATES.

(NEW SCHOOL.)

SERMON BY REV. JAMES B. SHAW, OF ROCHESTER, N. Y.

FIRST DAY—THURSDAY, MAY 17, 1866.

The General Assembly of the Presbyterian Church in the United States, commonly known as the New School Presbyterian Church, met, agreeable to appointment, in the First Presbyterian Church of this city (Mr. Nelson's), corner of Fourteenth and Lucas Place, and was called to order by the Rev. James B. Shaw, D. D., of Rochester, N. Y., Moderater of the last General Assembly.

The present General Assembly of that branch of the Presbyterian Church is well attended by ministers and elders, and the session bids fair to be a harmonious one.

The first order of exercises was an opening anthem by the choir and organ of Dr. Nelson's church. A full choir was in attendance, and the singing was good on the opening voluntary, which was an appropriate selection from Mozart's twelfth Mass, entitled "Glory be to God in the highest."

The Assembly then joined in prayer with Rev. Dr. Hopkins, D. D. After which a portion of scripture was read, and the choir sang the anthem entitled, "How beau tiful upon the mountains are the feet of him that bringeth good tidings."

After prayer, the congregation joined in singing the 103d psalm, first part.

"Bless, O! my soul, the living God,
Call home thy thoughts that roam abroad;
Let all the powers within me join
In work and worship divine."

The opening sermon was then delivered by Rev. James B. Shaw, D. D., of Rochester, N. Y.

SERMON OF THE REV. JAMES B. SHAW, MODERATOR OF THE LAST GENERAL ASSEMBLY.

"O, thou that hearest prayer."—Psalm lxv: 2.

There are some philosophical objections to prayer, but the same objections are as good against work. That which would drive a man from his closet would drive him from his field. It were easy to show, after the manner of some, that the weakest thing any man can do is to draw nigh unto God. "He is of one mind, and who can turn Him? and what His soul desireth, even that He doeth." And that is what your own book says. Turn Him, and turn Him by any considerations which we may present—the man who approaches the Most High with any such expectations insults Him to begin with. Now, I can take the same arguments by which the suppliant is convicted of folly, and show that the weakest thing any man can do is to go into the field and put his hand to the plough. God has already determined whether the man shall have a harvest; and "He is of one mind, and who can turn Him?" Can ploughing and sowing and harrowing, and all this careful toil avail, if he has decreed that the earth this year shall bring forth no fruit? An attempt to raise a harvest is only an affront to the Infinite Majesty, as if the Creator in any way could be circumvented by the creature.

But some will say, it is not to prayer in the abstract, but prayer as represented in the Scriptures, to which we object. Now we cannot deny that there are some strange things revealed in the Bible concerning prayer, and things which ought, if possible, to be explained. It is strange that we should have to ask anything of God. He knows our wants; He is abundantly able to supply them, and has represented himself as more willing to give than any other father. Why, then, is the blessing withheld until we come and ask for it? But there is a stranger thing than this. In some cases we must keep coming, keep asking, press our request, become importunate, stand at God's door as the sturdy beggar does at ours, determined not to be sent empty away. And even this will not always suffice. We must wrestle with the Lord, take hold of him, not let him go, detain him until the day break, constrain him to give the blessing which we seek. Now we would remind any of God's dear children who have been troubled about these things, that our Heavenly Father has other gracious ends to secure by prayer besides supplying our wants. He who has done a great work for us has also a great work to do in us, and this work is wrought chiefly through prayer—through communion with the Father of our spirits and his son, Jesus Christ. This is the reason why we must ask, and keep asking, and sometimes wrestle before the blessing comes. There is something beside the blessing, something behind the blessing, and in God's estimation far more important. Will He give only what we ask? Are our desires the measure of His mercies? Do we go to Him as the poor man in Judea goes to the oven, and get just as many coals as our potsherd, our broken bit of earthenware, will hold? One of old testified, saying: "He is able to do, exceedingly, abundantly, above all that we can ask or think." And this statement is verified by the experience of every man who bows his knees to the God and Father of our Lord Jesus Christ. But I have not come hither this morning to remove the objections which have been urged against this Christian duty. No one in this house doubts the efficacy of prayer. Many here would cease to breathe sooner than cease to pray. This is a congregation of suppliants—a company of intercessors—men and women who can tell what great things the Lord hath done for them in answer to their imperfect petitions. As such believers I address you at the present time, and I am quite confident that I need not solicit your attention while I dwell for a few moments on the thoughts suggested by the text. It is a subject in which every one of us has a heart interest: "Oh, thou that hearest prayer."

GOD DOES HEAR PRAYER. This is the first thing to show. Now prayer is much oftener answered than many disciples of the Lord Jesus are willing to believe. There is sometimes a lurking suspicion in the heart of the believer that, after all, God is not so ready to hear—not so willing to give. Have you never felt, in some dark day when you went to the mercy-seat, again and again that it is really harder to get anything from God than from a kind and generous-hearted fellow-creature? We hear much about the conditions of prayer—it must be this, and it must be that, and it must be the other thing, or it cannot prevail—and I am afraid we may have heard too much about the conditions of prayer. There seems to be an impression that, while we have a throne of grace, the Most High has put a tight fence around it, as he did around the Mount where he descended of old. Now, the fact is, that no place on earth is so accessable as the mercy-seat, and no being so approachable as Him who sits thereon. Any one can come, at any hour of the day or night, and never find the door closed, or the One whom he seeks away. How can I doubt that God is willing to give, when there are so many things for which He does not wait to be asked. "He presents us with the blessings of his goodness." He is beforehand with us. How can I doubt that God is willing to give, when he leaves so many blessings at the doors which have never yet been opened to Him—He the only one suffered to stand and knock? How can I doubt that God is willing to give, when he paid such a price for some of the blessings He bestows? Remember Bethlehem, remember Gethsemane, remember Calvary, and never again doubt that he is willing to give.

God, then, does hear His children when they call. "He does regard the prayer of the destitute." The unanswered prayer is the exception. When Otho opened the tomb of Charlemagne, he found the once mighty monarch seated on a throne, arrayed in a royal robe, a sceptre in his hand, and none to break the silence or share the solitude. But no dead king sits on the throne which you and I daily approach; and if this King on the mercy seat does not speak it is because we could not hear the sound; if He does not shine forth in His glory, it is because we could not endure the sight. No dead king sits on that throne. In the dark ages, when the Pope took umbrage at the treatment of any monarch, he laid his kingdom under what was called an interdict. At midnight each priest, holding a torch in his right hand, chaunted the *miserere*, and when the dirge was ended the torches were thrown down and extinguished and the kingdom left in darkness—and darkness it was. No church might be opened while the interdict lasted; no child might be baptized; no grave might be dug in holy ground; no religious rite might be performed. The consecrated bread was taken from the altar; the cross on which the Savior hung was covered with crape; the bells hung silent in the towers. The women and children stood aghast as if Heaven itself had been shut and they left out.

But even then one throne might be approached—the throne of heavenly grace. Even then one ear was open, that ear in which you and I have so ofen poured our complaints. No dead king sitteth on the throne which we daily approach. God does hear prayer.

But while God does hear prayer, yet he oftentimes answers His children in an unexpected way. This is the next thing to show. When we pray, if I may be allowed to say it. we necessarily leave much to the divine discretion of our Heavenly Father. Such is our blindness, that we do not know what may be a good thing for us, much less do we know in what way the blessing should come. The manner in which the mercy is bestowed, sometimes, is far more important than the mercy itself. And yet this must be left with Him, who knows us so better than we know ourselves. My brother, you have often asked God to subdue your pride, to lay it dead at your feet. You know how He hates it, how hard it is for Him to bear with it, and especially to have any thing so odious in the heart of his child, and you have oft besought him, with tears, to cast it out. Did you ever dare to tell him how it should be done? No doubt, if you ventured a suggestion, you would have him deal tenderly with it; cast it out in a gentle way; not resort to any severe methods. See that lad rolling on the ground, foaming at the mouth, biting his tongue until the blood starts. What a pitiable sight. But it is over now. It has been too much for the poor boy. Is he not dead? There is no sign of life which any one can discover but the Son of God. Ah! that certainly is not your way of casting ont a devil. But it is the Lord's way. Oftentimes nothing short of this will suffice. Brother, before the pride which possesses your heart and mine has been cast out, we may have ot go through as much as that lunatic child did. This may be one of the causes where mild methods will only make things worse. A devil is a devil, and pride is something more; the leader of the gang, the chief of the banditti. Have you not heard that this is the wretch which dares in Heaven to strike at God? And can you bind this Sampson with a tow-string, or a green withe, or his own gory locks twisted into a cord? I have seen more than one man try to tame pride, teach it to speak softly, and walk humbly, and put on sackcloth, and take the lowest seat. I have known more than one man to bring pride into the sanctuary, to the table of the Lord, and try to make it a good church-member. I have looked on as pride stood up in the broad aisle to enter into covenant with God and his people, and I heard it say: You thought that I was lifted up, that I carried a high head, and moved with a lofty step—that I felt above coming into the church and identifying myself with the followers of the despised Nazerene. Now, confess that, for once, you were mistaken See how meek I am. I would wash the feet of Judas if he were here. Yes, and wear the towel with which I did it, as a badge, all the remainder of my days, and have printed on it in large letters, This is the towel with which I, Pride, washed the feet of the traitor. Beloved in the Lord, we cannot tame pride. Pride can never forget that it was once in Heaven, and there dared to confront the Almighty on His throne. Pride must have the breath beaten out of it, and it will take perhaps many a hard fall to do it. But this must be left to our Heavenly Father. And how much beside this must we commit to His divine direction! Who would presume to tell Him how the blessing which he seeks shall be brought to his door? A creature of yesterday, who knows nothing—a worm of the dust, on his way from the cradle to the tomb, stopping before the throne to tell his Maker what is the wisest thing for Him to do. It makes us shudder to think of it. "Who hath directed the spirit of the Lord, or being His counselor, hath taught Him? With whom took he counsel, and who instructed him and taught him in the path of judgment, and taught him knowledge and showed him the way of understanding?"

But I pass to say, in the third place, that sometimes the answer comes in an unwelcome way. Now God's people, for the most part, look for answers to prayer only in the line of their mercies. There are many here who can bear witness to this; many here ready to charge themselves with this mistake. I never thought that a trial, a sore affliction, the blow which broke my heart, could be an answer to prayer, and, because so severe and so hard for a father to inflict, the strongest possible proof that the One whom I approach doe hear, that the One to whom I have committed all is faithful, is mindful of the covenant and will send what I need, no matter how much it may cost Him. When the prophet stood before the king with that dread alternative, seven months of famine or three years of war, or three days of pestilence, did the king suspect that the messenger might have come in answer to his prayer? If the offer had been three great mercies—seven months of plenty, three years of peace, or three days and not a death in the land—the son of Jesus might have said: "Now know I that it is not a vain thing to draw nigh unto God; I waited patiently for the Lord, and He inclined His ear unto me and heard my cry." And here the prophet comes with the answer.

One whom the Lord loveth is sick; you are standing by his side, and what does he say? My dear pastor, I needed this; I deserved it: I have felt for a long time that something of this kind was necessary. There he stops. Let us begin where he leaves of. Brother, this sickness has come in answer to your prayer You would never have been here had you not besought the Lord so earnestly that you might not fall away from him. Can you not recall the hour when you entered your closet and fell on your face, and with tears that almost drowned your words, besought the Lord to keep you—keep you if he must build a wall of fire round about you? He thought that you were in earnest; that you meant what you said; He took you at your own word, and therefore you are here. How faithful He is! With what care He watches over you. Alas! that is something of which we seldom think. In numbering our answers to prayer, we begin and end with our mercies.

Jacob, at Bethel, besought the Lord that He would be his God, and the answer came, you say, in his prosperity, in his wealth, in his great triumph at Peniel, when he won the name of Israel; and I contend that the answer came also in the many afflictions which were sent to his door, in the anger of Esau, in the perfidy of Laban, in the loss of Joseph, in the famine which brought him into such straits, in the parting with Benjamin, whom he never expected to see again. David knelt before the Lord and said, "Create in me a clean heart, O, God, and renew a right spirit within me." And the answer came in the rain of Tamar, in the death of Ammon, in the treason of Absalom, in that rebellion which drove him a fugitive from his throne. I see the aged King going up the sides of Olivet, barefooted, weeping as he goes. I see troubles gathering thick and fast, like thunder-clounds, around his head, and it is all in answer to prayer. Peter, I have no doubt, as every good man does, had often asked the Lord to show him his dependence; make him feel that he was nothing; and the answer came in that desertion—that denial—that swearing and cursing, which the stones of the pavement must have trembled to hear, and that look of wounded love which broke his heart. When Saint Paul returned from Paradise, he came back praying—have you any doubt that he did: Lord, let me not be exalted above measure; let me not be lifted up by those glorious things which I have seen and heard—let me toil as earnestly and suffer as patiently—do my work as cheerfully and as well as if I had never been to Heaven. The Lord heard his cry, and the answer came in that thorn in the flesh, so sharp, so ragged, so imbedded in the muscles, as not to be extracted by any human skill. "For this thing I besought the Lord thrice, that it might depart from me;" and that, O man of God, was thrice too often.

Has it not come in answer to your prayer? Did you not beseech the Lord that you might not be exalted above measure through the abundance of the revelation? And this uncomfortable and humiliating thing is the witness that God has heard thee and will not suffer that heavenly vision to prove thy ruin. Would the Lord, to whom thou art so dear, who loved thee so that he could not wait for thee to die before he took thee to Heaven, would He have sent this thorn, if anything but this could have kept thee down? And so I have thought when Paul and Silas were cast into prison, where they were treated with every possible indignity and cruelty; where they were scourged, their bleeding backs washed in brine, their feet made fast in the stocks, and they were so happy that they cou'd not sleep, could not do anything but sing—I have thought that perhaps all this again was in answer to prayer. It may be that the Apostle had besought the Lord to give him one more soul in Phillippi; and all that befell him that night, and the jailer, with his drawn sword and lighted candle, and face whiter than the wall, trembling before the men fast in the stocks, is the answer to the prayer. Oh! that earthquake not only shook the prison—it wrenched the door from the jailor's heart. Beloved the Lord, let us be wiser for the days coming and no longer look for answers to prayer only in the line of our mercies. It is a great mistake, and one which has robbed your soul of many a comfort, and in the dark day when you needed it so much.

But I haste to say once more that many a prayer, if answered at all, must be answered by an afflictive dispensation—by a terrible thing, as the Psalmist calls it. We are sometimes to choose between the terrible thing and an unanswered prayer. Blesεed be God, he dees not leave us to make the choice. He chooses for his people, and sends the sore affliction, the terrible thing; sends it, yes, because He knows that He can sustain us under it; because He knows that He can carry us through, and make this trial from which we so shrink do more for us than any blessing His bountiful hand ever bestowed. This is the thing we overlook when we sit in judgment, and we do sit in judgment on our Maker. Many a man has said, "I would not do as God does. If this were my world, do you think that I would suffer it be to filled with mourning and lamentation and woe? If man were my creature, would I suffer him to shed so many tears, endure so much pain, passing from one disaster to another? And when he had been worn out by misfortune, would I wrap him in a shroud and lay him under the clods, as if I were glad to have him off my hands?" Thomas Guthrie once found a woman in deepest poverty; he besought her, as she seemed near her end, to think of her soul. Her reply was, "I am cold and hungry." He sent for bread, and while the messenger was gone besought her again to think of her soul, and her reply still was, "If you were as cold and hungry as I am, you could think of nothing else." Now you say, if that woman were my child, if my hand had made her, I would not suffer her to be cold and hungry. Now bear with me while I say if that woman were your child, and you were as great as God, had His resources, could see as He sees, and do as He does, and your heart, like His, were set on some blessed result which could be brought about in no other way, you would suffer her to be cold and hungry. You would suffer your child to be thrown into the den of wild beasts, if you, like God, could stop the mouths of the lions. You would suffer your child to be cast into the fiery furnace if you, like God, could quench the violence of the fire; if you, like God, could make it sure that the flames wonld burn nothing but the bones of your child, and consume nothing but the dross; if you were as confident as God is that your child would come forth from that furnace everything that your loving heart could desire. When shall you and I learn that God's ways are not our ways, nor His thoughts as our thoughts, and that it may be lawful for Him to do what it would be madness, and more, for a worm of the dust to attempt. And when shall we learn that these terrible things are answers to prayer, and sent in love, as our mercies are, and furnish the highest possible proof that He who sitteth on the throne doth hear. Why are we so sure that God heard Elijah? Because in answer to his prayer he did that which it must have been so hard for him to do. "Elijah was a man subject to like passions as we are, and he prayed earnestly that it might not rain; and it rained not on the earth for the space of three years and six months." There is the wonderful thing, that the Most High, in answer to any one's prayer would have sent such a thing as a drought—such a thing as famine; that He, so full of tenderness and love, for three years and six months would have withheld the rain and the dew because the Prophet asked him to do it. Who doubts now that He hears prayer? Oh! it is not that God in answer to the cries of the Prophet would open the windows of Heaven, but that He would shut them and keep them shut. And here again is something which we would not do. We would not send a drought or a famine. Yes, we would, if we could gain as much from these terrible things as the Lord God of Elijah did.

The text suggests one thought more. Prayer is the same thing now that it was in the earlier days of the Christian Church. Many doubt it. Many take issue with me here. The age of miracles is past. Have you forgotten it? Those were wonderful times when the blind saw, the deaf heard, the lame leaped, the dumb spake, the dead came forth from the grave as one leaves his bed in the morning. There was some encouragement to pray then. Beloved in the Lord, there is just as much enconragement to pray now. God now can give anything which you and I may lawfully ask, and do it without a miracle, without setting aside the laws which he has ordained, without a direct interposition of His almighty power. Anything, we say, which the Christian may lawfully ask; this is the only limitation. It would not be lawful, for instance, te kneel down by the side of that dead child and ask the Lord to restore him to life. There is no reason to believe that any one offered such a prayer in the days gone, unless moved to do it by some special divine impulse. Did David ask the Lord to quicken again that little child in which his heart was so much bound up? He fasted and wept, and besought God for the child, while it was alive; but his last prayer went up with the last breath of the one so dear. And when that heavier blow came, when Absalom was laid in the neglected grave, where the sinner sleeps, did David ask God to bring him forth? He did not venture to offer such a prayer, any more than you or I would dare to do it. Everything, however, which his child may lawfully ask, God can give, and give without any direct interposition of His almighty power. How often it is said such a thing cannot be brought about without a miracle! Now, that is the ground which the unbelieving lord took—the man who paid so dear for his unbelief. The prophet predicted that before another day had gone food would be plenty in famine-stricken Samaria. "Then a lord, on whose hand the King loaned, answered the man of God and said: Behold, if the Lord should make windows in Heaven. might this thing be." But the prediction was fulfilled. as the scoffing man learned to his cost. and no window made in Heaven. The prediction was accomplished, through natural causes, by the same kind Providence, and which gives every one here his daily bread. Now this was left on record, that no one from that hour forth might distrust the power of him who sitteth on the throne—that no one might approach him with hesitating step, and ask in faltering accents, as if he did not know, whether the All-bountiful one could do it or not. Oh! child of God, is it not time that there were a stop put to this thing—an end to this shameful unbelief? Shall we limit the Holy One of Israel? Shall we set bounds to infinite love? Shall we hold down the hand which feeds us and clothes us and gives us everything good? How many of God's dear people dare not open their mouths wide; dare not stretch out both their hands; dare not borrow all the vessels in their neighbor's houses: dare not ask great things, because they are not sure that the Lord can bring it to pass without a miracle? We return to those words already quoted: "Elijah was a man subject to like passions as we are, and he prayed earnestly that it might not rain, and it rained not on the earth for the space of three years and six months. And he prayed again, and the heavens gave rain, and the earth brought forth her fruit." And it was such a rain as had not fallen since the flood. Ahab had to hasten down to his palace, drive as Jehu did, or he would have been intercepted by the swollen stream. Every window in Heaven must be opened. How it pours! God goes on as if he repented of having withheld the blessing so long. But what have we here? An Israelite coming out from the houses with a pitcher, or a bowl, or a cup, to catch the shower, as if that cup could hold all that God can afford to give. A rain that was to replenish the tanks, fill the pools, make the fountains flow, set the silent streams to surging again, and this Israelite coming with his cup to catch it! Now, so is it with us. We go to God, the God who keeps the sea full and never lets the rivers run dry, in the same spirit when the times of refreshing come—"when there are signs of abundance of rain." When the whole heavens are covered with clouds, and "the skies pour down righteousness," we reach out our little vessel, as if that would hold all that God could afford to give. Beloved in the Lord, had we not better settle the question whether our God is the living and true God; whether He is any stronger, or richer, or more bountiful than those who are marching with us to the grave; whether he did stretch out the heavens; whether he did make all these worlds and hang them upon nothing; whether he did speak, only speak, and it was done; whether he did command, only command, and it stood fast; whether he is the one who said, "Let there be light," and there was light; the Lord God of Noah, who sent the flood; the Lord God of Elijah, who answered by fire; the Lord God of Peter, who bowed the heavens and came down?

Beloved in the Lord, we, as a Church, in our own case, have an interesting illustration of the fact that God does hear prayer. During the last Assembly, and especially during the morning hour set apart for devotional services, the burden of every prayer was for the outpouring of the spirit. We felt our need of a baptism of the Holy Ghost, and besought the Lord not to withhold it. So it began and so it ended. And when we parted at Brooklyn, it was with the expectation that God, during the year, would do great things for us. Nor have we been disappointed. "They shall not be ashamed that wait for me." "In the wilderness did waters break out and streams in the desert; the parched ground became a pool, and the thirsty land springs of water," and throughout all our borders there was scarcely an arid spot or a dry place. "This is the Lord's doing, it is marvelous in our eyes." And surely it is worthy of record, that no Church in our land has received such a blessing as that in which the Assembly met, and that no brother has been so highly favored as the beloved pastor of the Lafayette Avenue Church at Brooklyn, whose Christian kindness and courtesy some of us will never forget, so long as we can remember the One who put it into his heart.

"Holy brethren, partakers of the heavenly calling," we have met at an auspicious time for our beloved Zion. This Church, dearer to us than "the ruddy drops which warm our hearts," has seen dark days, has encountered hard storms, and sometimes has had to shorten sail, more than once has been caught in the place where two seas met. There was a time when it was thought that she must go down, and some took to the boats and left her, as they predicted, to her fate. But there is One who never left her, because He is in the ship, she still floats; never so staunch; never so well equipped; never so thoroughly manned; never so richly freighted: never such harmony among the crew; never making such progress; never so near the harbor, and sure to make it; moving majestically on, guided by Him who guided the ark; and all this in answer to prayer. But for the supplications of God's praying people, this good ship might have foundered, or might have been so crippled, that all the pumps could scarcely keep her afloat. Let us, then, encouraged by our own experience of the divine faithfulness, continue to call on God; let us keep the censers smoking through the year, remembering that which Satan, above all other things, would have us forget, that the hands which do no work can never prevail with God. Importunate prayer, earnest work, and that faith which takes the obstacles thrown in her way and makes them the steps by which she reaches the top of the pyramid, are the three things essential to success. Pray, work, toil, and God will make "our walls salvation and our gates praise," and we, as a church, shall bear our part in bringing about the blessed day, "when the light of the moon shall be as the light of the sun, and the light of the sun shall be sevenfold, as the light of seven days."

We have heard that the Lord is in this place; that he is pouring on His people here a spirit of grace and supplications; that some have come to the Savior; that others are on the way; and would it not be a shame to us and a reproach to Zion—might it not even compromise the glory of the Master, if we, while here, should hinder the work—if we should come and go and leave no blessing? May this be known as the PRAYING Assembly; may the good people of St. Louis hold this meeting in grateful remembrance, because by us so many were led to Christ. And when we part, may each one go away with a lighted brand, prepared to kindle anew the flame on that altar where he is appointed to minister.

Prayer was then offered by Rev. W. S. Curtis, D. D., of Knox College, and the opening services closed by singing the 549th hymn, and benediction was pronounced by the Moderator.

After prayer by the Moderator, Bro. Dr. Nelson, of St. Louis, of Committee on arrangements, reported the hours of meeting to the Assembly as follows, viz: the daily sessions to commence at one-half past eight o'clock in the morning, at three o'clock in the afternoon; the morning services to close at twelve noon, and the afternoon services at one-half past five; that the evening services commence at one-quarter before eight; and that the daily morning prayer meeting commence after the calling of the roll and reading of the minutes, at nine o'clock, to continue until ten o'clock A. M.

The report of the committee was accepted and adopted.

After prayer, the Assembly adjourned until 3 o'clock P. T.

AFTERNOON SESSION.

Three o'clock, P. M.

Prayer by Rev. Dr. Campbell, of New York city.

Minutes read by Secretary and approved.

Roll of commissioners called and corrections made.

Revs. Z. M. Humphrey, DD., of Chicago; S. M. Hopkins, DD., of Auburn; L. D. Hatfield, DD., of New York city, and Wm. Hogarth, DD., of Detroit, were nominated for Moderator of this Assembly.

Rev. Dr. Hogarth desired to withdraw his name.

The first ballot showed a plurality only for Dr. Hopkins. The second ballot resulted in the election of Rev. S. M. Hopkins, DD., as Moderator for the ensuing year.

Rev. John W. Bailey, of the Presbytery of Bloomington, Ill.. and Rev. Charles P. Bush, of the Presbytery of Albany, were chosen temporary clerks.

On motion of Rev. Mr. Cornwall the rules as printed in the "Appendix" were adopted by the Assembly.

The roll was ordered to be printed.

It was made the order of the day, for to-day (Friday) at 10 o'clock, to receive the Synodical records and reports.

The Treasurer's report was read, and referred to an auditing committee. The report is simply that of the Assembly in account with the Treasurer, and shows the income and expenditure (incidental) to be some six thousond dollars, each, leaving a balance of $37 43 due the Assembly.

Docket read by the Stated Clerk, Rev. E. F. Hatfield, D. D.

Ordered that the report of the Trustee of the Church Erection Fund be the first in order of receiving reports from the permanent committee to-day, (Friday,) and that the report of the standing committee on the report of the Trustees be the first in order on the 4th day of the session, in the course of receiving the reports of the standing committees.

Ordered that it be a standing rule of this Assembly, that a standing committee be appointed to whom shall be referred the whole subject of Sabbath schools, and to whom the permanent committee, when there is one, shall report, and that the nomination of a permanent committee be referred to this committee.

After prayer by the Moderator, the Assembly adjourned its business session until eight and a half o'clock, A. M. to day.

The roll of the Assembly yesterday was incomplete, but it will appear in full in our paper to-morrow.

The New School Assembly held prayer and conference meetings last night, at the First and the North Presbyterian Churches. That at Dr. Nelson's church was very largely attended—of the other, in a remote quarter, we do not hear. During the war, the Assembly, at its anniversary, has devoted the first evening after convening to a prayer meeting in behalf of the Nation in its struggle with treason.

The present occasion was one of thanksgiving for the National triumph, and the sentiments uttered were of grateful patriotism. Dr. Nelson presided. Some of the speakers dwelt impressively upon the duty of the country to establish justice as the sole hope of National safety, and deplored the prevalence of a disposition to fail in the exaction of this righteous security.

SECOND DAY—FRIDAY, MAY 18, 1866.

MORNING SESSION.

The Assembly met, and opened with prayer.

The first hour was occupied with devotional exercises.

The roll was called, and the minutes of the last session were read and approved.

The Moderator announced the following

STANDING COMMITTEES:

Judicial Committee—Ministers, Edwin F. Hatfield, DD., J. Jermain Porter, DD., Henry Calhoun, Thomas S. Milligan, Johnathan H. Noble, Levi P. Crawford. Elders: Hon. Wm. I. Cornwell, Alex. Milne, Hon. Wilmer Worthington, Alex. Shelby, Mavor Brigham.

Place of meeting, S. S. room, 3d story.

Bills and Overtures—Ministers, James B. Shaw, DD., Thomas J. Sheppard, DD., Benjamin B. Parsons, DD., Philip S. Cleland, Thomas T. Bradford, John W. Cunningham. Elders, Andrew Flesher, Ira I. Fern, Samuel C. West, Homer H. Winchell, Beaumont S. Holmes.

Place of meeting, Chapel, second story.

Polity of the Church—Ministers, Henry B. Smith, DD., Wm. Hogarth, DD., Ebenezer Bushnell, Peter S. Van Nest, Horatio Pettingill, Geo. P. Tindall. Elders, Edward Wells, Joseph H. Plumb, Albert M. Brown, J. Marshall Paul, M. D., Theodore W. Collins.

Place of meeting, Chapel, second story.

Home Missions—Ministers, Wm. E. Knox, DD., Martin M. Post, DD., James W. Stark, Alexander M. Heizer, J. Addison Whitaker, Frederick H. Adams. Elders, John Hill, Luther H. Trask, Russell Scarritt, Horatio Newhall, M. D., Edward E. Wilson, Jeremiah P. E. Kumler.

Place of meeting, Church Parlor, first story.

Foreign Missions—Ministers, Walter Clark, D.D., George W. Wood, D.D., Alfred E. Campbell, D. D., Milton Bradley, John Montieth, Jr. Elders, Octavius Knight, Joseph W. Edwards, David C. Anderson, Manley Rogers, Ephraim G. Stitt.

Place of meeting, Infant Sabbath School Room, second story.

Education—Ministers, Wm. S. Curtis, D. D., Beriah B. Hotchkin, Calvin Waterbury, John F. Kendall, George D. A. Hebard, Alexander Duncan. Elders, Wm. A. Booth, Joseph R. Dixon, Asa D. Lord, M. D., Brackley Shaw, James H. Sayre.

Place of meeting, Sabbath School Room, third story.

Publication—Ministers, Samuel D. Burchard, D. D., George C. Noyes, Samuel W. Pratt, Levi B. Wilson, James R. Gibson, Samuel Ward. Elders, Edward A. Durant, Timothy R. Porter, Robert Russell, Lewis G. Hewling, Luther Edgerton.

Place of meeting, Choir Gallery, east stairs.

Church Erection—Ministers, Zepheniah M. Humphrey, D. D., William A. Niles, William E. Moore, Joseph Chester, Thomas H. Tatlow, Joseph A. Ranney. Elders, Hon. Henry W. Williams, Hon. Truman P. Handy, Hon. Joseph Allison, Wm. S. Webb, Wm. M. Gregory.

Place of meeting, church parlor, 1st story.

Sabbath Schools—Ministers, Henry Fowler, Charles E. Knox, William Hart, Asahel S. Books, Thomas H. Robinson. Elders, Hon. Edward A. Lambert, William H. Christie, Albert W. Allen, Oramel Rugg.

Place of meeting, chapel, 2d story.

Ministerial Relief—Ministers, Chas. P. Bush, Nelson Millard, Aratus Kent, Whitney C. Burchard, Samuel F. Bacon. Elders, William Newton, Jonathan A. Marsh, M. D., Columbus Crane, Samuel M. Thatcher.

Place of meeting, choir gallery, east stairs.

Narrative of Religion—Ministers, Cornelius H. Taylor, D. D., John N. Combs, Peter S. Davis, William C. Turner, Albert True. Elders, Thos. Hamilton, John H. Carson, Philo Merrill.

Place of meeting, choir gallery, west stairs.

Mileage of Commissioners—Elders, Truman P. Handy, Silas K. Stowe, Stephen M. Clement.

Place of meeting, Sunday School room, third story.

Devotional Exercises—Ministers, George F. Wiswell, Charles N. Mattoon, D. D., Livingston Willard, John L. French. Elders, John C. Hines, Thomas Stillwell, M. D., Samuel Bond.

Place of meeting, Pastor's study, first story.

Leave of Absence—Ministers, Robert R. Kellogg, Lucius I. Root, Wm. S. Page, James A. Giffes. Elders, Wm. A. Eldridge, Elijah Churchill, David Compton.

Place of meeting, chapel, second story.

COMMITTEES ON SYNODICAL RECORDS.

Synod of Albany—Ministers, Isaac G. Ogden, James Boggs, Henry V. Warren. Elders, Elijah Churchill, Simon Harwood.

Synod of Utica—Ministers, Oliver Crane, Geo. O. Little, Edmund B. Miner. Elders, Edwin S. Wells, Samuel Wade.

Synod of Onondaga—Ministers, Charles T. Berry, Ebenezer Bushnell, Ezra Jones. Elders, Wm. Newton, Nelson Noble.

Synod of Geneva—Ministers, John L. Jones, A. E. Ernest, Allen Traver. Elders, Stuart T. Terry, Samuel Barr.

Synod of Susquehanna—Ministers, John C. Moses, Thomas Harries, Thomas A. Steel. Elders, Gilbert M. Gifford, Alfred Lockhart.

Synod of Geneva—Ministers, Ebenezer Buckingham, Joseph L. Morton, William L. Tarbet. Elders, James R. Curry, Benjamin A. Hunt.

Synod of New York and New Jersey—Ministers, George Spaulding, William L. Page, Giles M. Smith. Elders, Luther Edgerton, J. S. Metcalf.

Synod of Pennsylvania—Ministers, O. H. Perry Deyo, Richard M. Sanford, Leonard E. Richards. Elders, James M. Reeder, Robert Russell.

Synod of West Pennsylvania—Ministers, Levi G. Marsh, Lewis Thompson, George Ransom. Elders, Martin Allen, Solon Massey.

Synod of Michigan—Ministers, James R. Gibson, Geo. O. Phelps, James E. Vance. Elders, Silas Moore, William Storer.

Synod of Western Reserve—Ministers, Donald B. Campbell, John Gibson, Thomas Brown. Elders, Proctor C. Samson, Solomon Beckley.

Synod of Ohio—Ministers, Edward C. Johnston, Joseph B. Little, Horatio Pattengill. Elders, Alex. H. Holden, Joshua Moore.

Synod of Cincinnati—Ministers, Beriah B. Hotchkiss, Alexander Duncan, Henry Calhoun. Elders, Levi Walker, Jonathan Hoyt.

Synod of Indiana—Ministers, Thomas T. Bradford, Nelson Willard, George P. Tindall. Elders, David Ewing, Samuel C. West.

Synod of Wabash—Ministers, Livingston, Willard, E. S. Davis, John L. French. Elders, Ira I. Fenn, Samuel N. Thatcher.

Synod of Illinois—Ministers, William E. Moore, Charles C. Hart, John W. Cunningham. Elders, Thomas Hamilton, John Otto.

Synod of Peoria—Ministers, Charles N. Mattoon, D. D., Jeremiah P. E. Kumler, George C. Noyes. Elders, John Hill, Joseph R. Dixon.

Synod of Wisconsin—Ministers, Lucius I. Root, John N. Coombs, Wm. C. Turner. Elders, Lorenzo Russell, Jonathan A. Marsh, M. D.

Synod of Iowa—Ministers, Jonathan H. Noble, Samuel W. Pratt, Charles E. Knox. Elders, Philo Merrill, Theodore W. Collins.

Synod of Minnesota—Ministers, James B. Fisher, Whiting C. Birchard, Alexander M. Heizer. Elders, Beaumont S. Holmes, Joshua Moore.

Synod of Missouri—Ministers, William A. Niles, Samuel F. Bacon, James A. Griffes. Elders, Luther H. Trask, Octavius Knight.

Synod of Tennessee—Ministers, William Hogarth, D. D., Levi B. Wilson, Gamaliel C. Beaman. Elders, William A. Booth, Hon. Wilmer Worthington.

Synod of Alta California—Ministers, ——. Elders, ——.

The order of the day was then taken up, and the report of the Trustees of the Church Erection Fund was then read by Jesse W. Benedict Esq., Secretary and Treasurer, of which the following is an abstract.

LOANS AND DONATIONS.

During the year there have been received twenty applications for aid, amounting to $7,525; thirteen of which were for Loans, amounting to $6,075, and seven for Donations, amounting to $1,450. Ten of the applications for Loans were granted, amounting to $4,675; three amounting to $1,400 were refused; one of these required the loan to be made in gold; by the other two it appeared that after obtaining the Loan the congregation would not have the amount necessary to complete their building; they were informed that as soon as the deficiency should be provided for, their application would be granted. Four of the applications for Donations, amounting to $750, were granted; three amounting to $700 were refused; one of these absolutely for the reason that the aid required was for the purpose of paying a debt which had been contracted in 1858; one as premature, it appearing from the application that, after obtaining the required donation, the congregation would not have the amount requisite to complete their building. They were informed that as soon as this deficiency should be provided for their application would be granted. The other application for a donation was refused for the reason that it was not in due form, and the amount ($300) asked for exceeded the amount limited by the plan for d nations. In one case, after the application for a donation had been granted, the congregation refused to execute the bond and mortgage required by the plan, and have not availed themselves of the grant.

These applications were from eleven synods, five from the synod of Missouri, three from the synod of Minnesota, two from each of the synods of New York and New Jersey, Illinois and Wisconsin, and one from each of the synods of Genesee, Pennsylvania, Indiana, Wabash, Peoria, and Alta California.

RECEIPTS FROM CHURCHES.

There have been received during the year from 40 churches on account of loans, $5,394 22; from 65 churches on account of donations, $839 07, and from 13 churches for interest, $986 58, making a total of $7,219 87.

LEGAL OPINIONS.

The last General Assembly directed this Board to procure the written opinion of eminent legal counsel as to the powers of the Assembly in respect to the Church Erection Fund, especially in reference to the question whether having received this fund, "as a special trust," and in 1854 committed the custody thereof to a Board of Trustees, incorporated by a special statute of the State of New York, the Assembly has the power so to alter the Church Erection Plan as to make an absolute gift of the increase of the fund beyond the sum of $100,000, for the purpose named in the first article of the plan. The Board were directed to report such opinions to this Assembly, with the addition of any recommendations which they might deem expedient.

In compliance with this direction of the Assembly, the Board have obtained from three eminent counsel written opinions, which are herewith submitted. None of these gentlemen had any knowledge of the opinions of the others; in fact, neither was aware that any other opinion excepting his own had been or would be obtained. It will be seen that they differ in their views of the power of the Assembly over the fund, all agreeing, however, in this: that the fund can never be used excepting for the objects set forth in the first article of the plan.

The Board have carefully considered these diverse opinions, and will only add that they trust that the time will never come when, for the purpose of judicially settling the powers of the General Assembly over the fund, a resort shall be had to law, the proverbial uncertainty of which has received a new illustration in the opinions herewith submitted to the Assembly.

It is certain that the donors of the fund intended to inaugurate just such a scheme of benevolence as this, and thus far in its management the Board have not in any particular violated any of the principles contended for in these opinions; and it certainly will be safe to continue to administer the fund substantially upon the same principles which have heretofore obtained, enlarging or diminishing the amount of loans and donations, and their terms, as the exigencies of the congregations to be aided from time to time may require.

AMENDMENTS TO THE PLAN.

In their report to the last Assembly the Board recommended amendments to the plan, increasing the amount of the loans to $750, and of the donations to $300. It was greatly regretted by the Board that when these amendments came before the Assembly for their final action, it was found that the requisite number (two-thirds of the enrolled members) were not present.

By the present plan loans are limited to $500 for three years without interest (and in no case can exceed one-third of the amount contributed for the house and lot). Then the principal is required to be refunded in four equal annual installments, interest attaching, in case of default, on the whole amount during default.

The Board now recommend that the plan be so altered that loans to the amount of $750 (not exceeding, however, one third of the amount contributed for the house and lot) may be made for five years, without interest, to be then repaid in six equal annual installments; interest to attach as heretofore on defaut. Should this amendment be adopted, the Board believe that increased activity will be given to the fund, and that the object for which it was raised will be greatly advanced. The Board, therefore, recommend that Article XIV of the plan be so amended as to read as follows:

ARTICLE XIV.

"The Board shall not in any case loan or donate any portion of the fund to any congregation, unless such congregation own, in fee simple and free from all legal incumbrance, the lot on which their house of worship is situated, or on which they propose to build; nor shall any loan or donation be made for the payment of any debt, except that which may have been contracted within one year previous in erecting a house of worship.

The amount loaned to any congregation shall never be more than one-third of the amount contributed for the house and lot, nor exceed the sum of $750, nor shall the amount given to any congregation as a donation be in any case more than $300, or exceed one-fourth of the amount contributed for their house and lot: *nor* shall a loan and a donation be made to the same congregation. The donations within the boundaries of any Synod shall never be more than one-fourth of the amount appropriated to that Synod.

All loans shall be made on the following conditions:

1. The principal shall be paid in six equal annual installments, the first installment becoming due in five years from the date of the loan.

2. If all the installments are punctually paid, no interest will be required on any part of the loan.

3. In default of the payment of any installment, interest shall be required on the whole loan unpaid from the time of such default until such installment, with all the interest that may thus accrue, shall be paid.

The conditions of all donations from this fund shall be, that, in case the church or congregation shall cease to be connected with the General Assembly, or their corporate existence shall cease, or their house of worship be alienated except for the building or purchase of a better house of worship, they shall refund to the Board the amount which they have so received with interest from the time of receiving it; and further, that every congregation receiving a donation shall annually make a collection in aid of the fund, transmitting the same to the Treasurer, until the amount so collected and paid over shall equal the sum received as a donation.

The fulfillment of the above conditions, in respect to both loans and donations, shall, in all cases, be secured by the bond of the trustees of the congregation, and a mortgage on their house and lot, made in favor of the Board; which bond and mortgage, duly executed and recorded, shall always be placed in the possession of the Board, before any money is paid over to the congregation."

The Board also recommend that in Article XIII, in the 12th and 13th lines, the words, "A copy of" be stricken out, so that the sentence will read, "This certificate, together with the application made to the Committee of the Synod, shall be transmitted to the Board."

This last amendment merely conforms the plan to its practical working. The original application, and not a copy, is invariably forwarded to the Board. The Board, therefore, recommend the plan to be amended accordingly.

ELECTION OF TRUSTEES.

The term of office of the Rev. J. Few Smith, D. D.. Rev. Samuel D. Burchard, D. D., and Wm. A. Booth, Esq., is soon to expire; it will be necessary for the Assembly to fill their places.

The Church Erection Fund; in account with Jesse W. Benedict, Treasurer, from May 1, 1865, *to May* 1, 1866.

DR.

To Cash, Loans to Churches..............	$2,775 00
" Donations to Churches..........	400 00
" Call Loans and Temporary Investments......................	221,331 45
" Expenses, being salary of Secretary and Treasurer, rent of Office, Stationery, Printing, Postage, &c..................	1,845 07
" Miscellaneous	68 11
To Balance in Bank........................	1.942 17
	$228,361 80

CR.

By Balance from former account..........	$17,228 32
By Cash, from Call Loans and Temporary Investments	198,951 00
By Cash, Interest on ditto.................	4,835 21
" Installments from various Churches on account of their Bonds and Mortgages..........	5,394 22
" Interest on ditto.................	986 58
" Annual collections received from Churches on account of donation..............................	839 07
" Miscellaneous....................	126 40
	$228,361 80

By Balance in Bank........ $1,942 17

This certifies that we have examined the vouchers in the hands of the Treasurer, and find the above account correct. EDWARD A. LAMBERT, JOHN P. CROSBY.

NEW YORK, May 2, 1866.

CONDITION OF THE CHURCH ERECTION FUND, MAY 1, 1866.

Amount of loans to churches secured by bonds and mortgages..................	$32,046 70
Amount of donations to churches secured by bonds and mortgages.................	15,013 18
Amount of call loans and temporary investments	77,425 45
Interest earned thereon to date............	1,072 02
Cash in bank...............................	1,942 17
Total.................................	$127,499 52

This certifies that we have examined the securities in the hands of the Treasurer, and find the above statement to be correct.

EDWARD A. LAMBERT,
JOHN P. CROSBY.

NEW YORK, May 2d, 1866.

The report was accepted and referred to the appropriate committee.

In the absence of the Secretary, Walter S. Griffith, Edward A. Lambert, of Brooklyn, read the report ot the permanent committee on Foreign Missions. Report adopted and referred to the appropriate standing committees.

Ordered that the places of meeting of the several committees be printed, in connection with the roll of commissioners, and standing committees.

After prayer by Rev. Mr. Tyndall, the Assembly adjourned until three o'clock P. M.

AFTERNOON SESSION—THREE O'CLOCK P. M.

Rev. Dr. H. B. Smith in the chair.

Jessee W. Benedict, Esq., read the annual report of the permanent Committee on Education, which report was referred to the appropriate standing committee.

Rev. Thornton A. Mills, D. D., with regard to the Union Theological Seminary of New York, stated that its faculty was full, and full of able men.

The fifth annual report of the permanent Committee on Home Missions was read by Rev. Walter Clarke, D. D., of Buffalo, New York. The report discussed the rapid increase of the population at the West, the laws which regulate its movements, making particular mention of the rapid extension of railroads at the West, of the Pacific Railroad and the vast mineral regions at the West, and the great influx of foreigners into the country, prairies, forests, mineral tracts, and where railroads are built, there the people go.

The report claims that never before have railroads been so rapidly built as now, and never so full a tide of travel flowing into the Western States, and the gold and silver bearing regions of the Rocky Mountain division.

The tending to the centralization of population was also noticed. Never did the great cities of the world grow so rapidly as now. Great centers open at the West, and for a brief time must have missionary aid. This depletes and drains the East, and makes a demand for aid to the feeble and decaying churches there,

An encouraging view of religious progress and reconstruction in East Tennessee and Missouri was given. About forty missionaries have been employed in these two States, who have labored, on the whole, with encouragement and success.

Elsewhere at the South but little has been done, but some efforts among the freedmen have succeeded well.

The obstacles to the work were said to be as follows:

1. The task of ministers. The ministers are too few to meet the demand of the people. More men could be located in one month than all the theological seminaries have turned out in a year. There is no limit to the work, if the ministers were plenty.

2. Lack of church edifices. The report insists that the Church is not awake to the importance of this matter, and it shows how much the Baptists, Congregationalists, Methodists, Unitarians, Universalists, and Episcopalians are doing in the cause, and urges the Assembly to devise some method to build churches, especially for all the feeble but promising congregations in the West.

3. Lack of funds. The Treasurer's report shows that less than $92,000 have been contributed, but $106,000 expended during the year. Such a state of things cannot last, The report shows that the church is able to contribute much more, and calls on the ministry and people to redouble their energies to meet the demand, Only about 800 churches out of a total of 1,500 in the body had contributed anything during the year.

The whole working force in the missionary field has been 385 men—58 more then last year. Six of these have died.

The statistics of the year are very encouraging. About 50 churches have been formed, 5,500 souls converted, and 3,250 have united with the church.

Mr. Lambert read the Treasurer's report, and the two reports were accepted and referred to the appropriate standing committee.

Rev. John W. Dulles of Philadelphia, read the report of the permanent Committee on Publication.

This report showed a balance in treasury of $465.

Report accepted and referred to the appropriete Standing Committee.

Rev. T. J. Shepherd, D. D., of Philadelphia, read report of the Committee on Presbyterian House. Accepted and referred.

The Rev. Geo. F. Wiswell, of the Committee on Devotional Exercises, read the following list of exercises in different churches of the city and vicinity for to-morrow, (Sunday.)

EXERCISES FOR SUNDAY, MAY 20.

First Presbyterian Church, 10½ A. M., Moderator, Rev. S. M. Hopkins. 4 P. M. Z. M. Humphrey, D. D.

Union Methodist, corner Eleventh and Locust, Rev. J. J. Porter, 10½ A. M. Rev. C. N. Mattoon, D. D., 7¾, P. M.

Clark Avenue Baptist Church, Fourteenth and Clark avenue, Rev. A. E. Campbell, D. D., N. Y., 7½ P. M.

Second Union Methodist Church, west side Sixth between Franklin avenue and Wash, Rev. W. E. Knox, D. D., 10½ A. M. Rev. W. Hogarth, D. D., 7½ P. M.

Simpson Chapel, Tenth and North Market streets, Rev. J. L. Morton, 10½ A. M. Rev. J. N. Coombs, 7¾ P. M.

Pratte Avenue Mission, between Clark avenue and Gamble avenue, Rev. J. F. Kendall, 10½ A. M. Rev. Charles E. Knox, 7¾ P. M.

City Hospital, St. Ange street and Lafayette avenue, Rev. W. E. Moore, 2½ P. M.

City Jail, corner Sixth and Chesnut streets, Rev. Hannibal L. Stanley, 4 P. M.

Mt. Vernon Band of Hope, corner St. Charles and Sixth, Rev. W. L. Page, 3½ P. M.

Colored Church, corner Twelfth street and Cass avenue, Rev. A. M. Heiser, 10½ A. M.

Rock Hill Church, Rev. Walter Clark, D. D.

North Presbytery Church, corner Chambers and Eleventh streets, Rev. S. D. Burchard, D. D., 10½ A. M. W. A. Niles, 7½ P. M.

First Congregational, Tenth and Locust streets, Rev. E. F. Hatfield, D. D., 7½ P. M.

Jefferson City, Rev. H. Kendall, D. D.

Monticello, Ills.—Rev. John Monteith.

Alton—Rev. Dr. Shaw, 10½ A. M. Rev. C. Bushnell, 7½ P. M.

Upper Alton—Rev. W. C. Turner.

Allenton—Rev. L. Wilson.

Mr. Wiswell further stated that there would be preaching in Dr. Wilson's Church in the evening, services commencing at 7 3-4 P. M.

The Assembly then adjourned.

We publish below, the roll of the present General Assembly:

OFFICERS.

Rev. Samuel M. Hopkins, D. D., Moderator; Rev. Edwin F. Hatfield, D. D., Stated Clerk; Rev. J. Glentworth Butler, D. D., Permanent Clerk; John W. Bailey and Stephen Bush, Temporary Clerks; Mr. William A. Booth, Treasurer.

2

Commissioners.

SYNOD OF ALBANY.

PRESBYTERIES.

Champlain—Minister, Asa E. Everest.

Troy—Ministers, N. S. S. Beman, D. D., Jonathan H. Noble. Elder, Silas K. Stowe.

Albany—Minister, Stephen Bush. Elder, Edward A. Durant.

Columbia—Minister, Charles T. Berry.

Catskill—Minister, William Hart.

SYNOD OF UTICA.

PRESBYTERIES.

St. Lawrence—Minister, Samuel W. Fratt. Elder, William A. Eldridge.

Watertown—Minister, J. Jermain Porter. Elder, Samuel Bond.

Oswego.

Utica—Ministers—William E. Knox, D. D., James B. Fisher. Elder, Gilbert M. Gifford.

SYNOD OF ONONDAGA.

PRESBYTERIES.

Onondaga—Minister, John F. Kendall. Elder, Timothy R. Porter.

Cayuga—Ministers, Samuel M. Hopkins, DD., and Henry Fowler. Elders, Albert W. Allen, Hon. Wm. I. Cornwell.

Cortland—Minister, Giles M. Smith. Elder, Joseph R. Dixon.

Tioga—Minister, Samuel F. Bacon.

SYNOD OF GENEVA.

PRESBYTERIES.

Geneva—Ministers, Ezra Jones and John C. Moses.

Steuben—Minister Wm. A. Niles.

Chemung—Minister, Isaac Clark. Elder, Jas. M. Reeder.

Ithaca—Minister, George Spaulding. Elder, Nelson Noble,

Wellsboro—

Lyons—Minister, William L. Page. Elder Columbus Crone.

SYNOD OF SUSQUEHANNA.

PRESBYTERIES.

Otsego—Minister, Geo. O. Phelps. Elder, Robert Russell.

Chenango—Minister, John L. Jones. Elder, Wm. Newton.

Delaware—Minister, Leonard E. Richards. Elder, Elijah Churchill.

SYNOD OF GENESEE.

PRESBYTERIES.

Buffalo—Ministers, Walter Clarke, D. D., Richard M. Sandford. Elders, Stephen M. Clement, Joseph H. Plumb.

Ontario—Minister, Levi G. Marsh.

Rochester—Ministers, James B. Shaw, D. D., Charles P. Bush. Elder, Simon Harwood.

Genesee—Minister, Allen Teaver. Elder, Phineas Stanton.

Niagara—Minister, Lucius I. Root. Elder, Myron P. Hopkins.

Genesee Valley—Minister, Isaac G. Ogden. Elder, Alfred Lockhart.

SYNOD OF NEW YORK AND NEW JERSEY

PRESBYTERIES.

Hudson—Minister, Robert R. Kellogg. Elder, William S. Webb.

North River—Minister, O. H. Perry Deyo. Elder, Edward Wells.

Long Island—Minister, Thomas Harries. Elder, Stuart T. Terry.

New York, 3d—Ministers, Alfred E. Campbell, D. D., Edwin F. Hatfield, D. D., Samuel D. Burchard, D. D. Elders, William A. Booth, William H. Christie, Alexander Milne.

New York, 4th—Ministers, Henry B. Smith, D. D., George W. Wood, D. D. Elder, Albert N. Brown.

Brooklyn—Minister, William S. Karr. Elder, Hon. Edw. A. Lambert.

Newark—Ministers, Charles E. Knox, Nelson, Millard, Joel Parker, D. D. Elders, James Reeve Sayre, John C. Hines, Hon. A. H. Holden.

Rockaway—Minister, Lewis Thompson. Elder, John Hill.

Montrose—Ministers, Oliver Crane, Horatio Pattengill. Elder, Samuel N. Thatcher.

SYNOD OF PENNSYLVANIA.

PRESBYTERIES.

Wilmington—Minister, George F. Wiswell. Elder, Samuel Barr.

Philadelphia, 3d—Ministers, Beriah B. Hotchkin, William E. Moore. Elders, Hon. Wil'r Worthington, Hon. Joseph Allison.

Philadelphia, 4th—Ministers, Thomas J. Shepherd, D. D., James Boggs. Elder, J. Marshall Paul, M. D.

Harrisburg—Minister, Thomas H, Robinson. Elder, Lewis G. Huling.

District of Columbia—Minister, John N. Coombs. Elder, Octavius Knight.

SYNOD OF WEST PENNSYLVANIA.

PRESBYTERIES.

Erie—Minister, Thomas T. Bradford. Elder, Jonathan A. Marsh, M. D.

Meadville—Minister, Whiting C. Birchard. Elder, David Compton.

Pittsburgh—Minister, Peter S. Davies. Elder Hon. Henry W. Williams.

SYNOD OF MICHIGAN.

PRESBYTERIES.

Detroit—Minister, William Hogarth' D. D. Elder, Alanson Sheley.

Monroe—Minister, Charles N. Mattoon, D. D. Elder, Brackley Shaw.

Marshall—Minister, Livingston Willard. Elder, Philo Merrill.

Washtenaw—Minister, George P. Tindall. Elder, William M. Gregory.

Kalamazoo—Minister, Milton Bradley. Elder, Luther H. Trask.

Coldwater—Minister, Joseph A. Ranney.

Saginaw—Minister, Donald R. Campbell.

Grand River Valley—Minister, George Ransom. Elder, Jonathan Hoyt.

Lake Superior—Minister, Frederic H. Adams, Elder, Joseph W. Edwards.

SYNOD OF WESTERN RESERVE.

PRESBYTERIES.

Grand River—

Huron—Ministers, Ebenezer Bushnell. Elder, Thomas Stilwell M. D.

Trumbull—Minister, Levi B. Wilson. Elder, Martin Allen.

Cleveland and Portage—Ministers, William C. Turner, John Monteith, Jr. Elders, Truman P. Handy, Hon. John A. Foote.

Elyria—Minister, James E. Vance. Elder, Isaac S. Metcalf.

Maumee—Minister, ——. Elder, Mayor Brigham.

SYNOD OF OHIO.

PRESBYTERIES.

Athens—Minister, Charles C. Hart. Elder, Luther Edgerton.

Pataskala—Minister, Ebenezer Buckingham.

Franklin—Minister, Henry Calhoun. Elder, Asa D. Lord, M. D.

Sciota—Minister, James R. Gibson. Elder, David C. Anderson.

SYNOD OF CINCINNATI.

PRESBYTERIES.

Cincinnati—Ministers, Joseph Chester, John L. French. Elders, Franklin V. Chamberlain, Andrew Flesher.

Dayton—Minister, Joseph B. Little. Elder, Solon Massey.

Hamilton—Minister, J. P. E. Kumler. Elder, Benjamin A. Hunt.

Ripley—Minister, Henry V. Warren. Elder, Theodore W. Collins.

SYNOD OF INDIANA.

PRESBYTERIES.

Salem—Minister, Thomas A. Steele. Elder, Silas Moore.

Madison—Minister, Amzi W. Freeman. Elder, Edwin C. Whitney.

Indianpolis—Minister, Philip S. Cleland. Elder, Thomas Hamilton.

Green Castle—Minister, Thomas S. Milligan. Elder, John Ott.

SYNOD OF WABASH.

PRESBYTERIES.

Crawfordsville—Minister, Edward C. Johnston. Elder, Edmund G. Wilson.

St. Joseph—Minister, George C. Noyes.

Logansport—Minister, Martin M. Post, D. D. Elder, Lewis Martin.

Fort Wayne—Minister, Geo. O. Little. Elder, George W. Rhodes.

SYNOD OF ILLINOIS.

Illinois—Minister, William L. Tarbet. Elder, Joshua Moore.

Schuyler—Minister, Alexander Duncan. Elder, James R. Curry.

Wabash—Minister, Sam'l Ward. Elder, David Ewing.

Alton—Ministers, Cornelius H. Taylor, D. D., John Gibson. Elder, Samuel Wade.

SYNOD OF PEORIA.

PRESBYTERY.

Ottawa—Minister, Levi P. Crawford. Elder, J. R. McLain.

Knox—Minister, William S. Curtis, D. D. Elder, Ira I. Fenn.

Galena and Belvidere—Ministers, Aratus Kent, John W. Cunningham. Elders, H. Newhall, M. D., Manley Rogers.

Chicago—Ministers, Zeph. M. Humphrey, D. D., J. Lyman Morton. Elders, Stillman R. Bingham, Edwin S. Wells.

Bloomington—Ministers, John W. Bailey. Elder, Oramel Rugg.

SYNOD OF WISCONSIN.

PRESBYTERY.

Milwaukee—Minister, Peter S. Van Nest. Elder, Samuel C. West.

Fox River—Minister, James W. Stark.

Columbus—Minister, Edmund B. Miner. Elder, Ephraim G. Stitt.

SYNOD OF IOWA.

PRESBYTERY.

Des Moines—Minister, Alexander M. Heizer.
Keokuk—Minister, Gamaliel C. Beaman. Elder, Solomon Beckley.
Iowa City—Minister, George D. .A. Hebard. Elder, Beaumont S. Holmes.
Dubuque—Minister, Albert True. Elder, Proctor C. Samson.
Chariton—
Cedar Rapids—Minister, Hannibal L. Stanley.

SYNOD OF MINNESOTA.

PRESBYTERIES.

Dakota—Minister, John P. Williamson.
Minnesota—Elder, Daniel W. Ingersoll.
Winona.

SYNOD OF MISSOURI.

PRESBYTERIES.

St. Louis—Minister, J. Addison Whitaker. Elder, Russell Scarritt.
Lexington—Minister, Benjamin B. Parsons, D. D. Elder, John H. Carson.
Northern Missouri—Minister, Thomas H. Tatlow. Elder, Homa H. Winchell.
Kansas.

SYNOD OF TENNESSEE.

PRESBYTERIES.

Union—Minister, James A. Griffes.
Kingston—Minister, Thomas Brown.
Holston—Minister, Calvin Waterbury. Elder, John Lynn.

SYNOD OF ALTA CALIFORNIA.

PRESBYTERIES.

San Francisco.
Sierra Nevada.
San Jose.
Washoe.

CORRESPONDING BODIES.

1. General Assembly that met at Pittsburg, in 1865.
2. General Assembly of the Cumberland Presbyterian Church.
3. General Assembly of the United Presbyterian Church of North America.
4. General Synod of the Reformed Protestant Dutch Church in North America.
5. General Synod of the Reformed Presbyterian Church in North America.
6. General Synod of the German Reformed Church in the United States.
7. General Synod of the Evangelical Lutheran Church in the United States.
8. General Conference of Maine.
9. General Association of New Hampshire.
10. General Convention of Vermont. [Rev. Benjamin F. Ray.]
11. General Association of Massachusetts.
12. General Association of Connecticut.
13. Presbyterian and Congregational Convention of Wisconsin.
14. Union of Evangelical Churches of France.

THIRD DAY—SATURDAY, MAY 19, 1866.

Moderator in the Chair.

First hour spent in devotional exercises.

Rev. Walter Clarke, DD., read a communication from Hon. S. D. Barlow, President of the St. Louis and Iron Mountain Railroad, tendering to the members of the Assembly a train of cars for an excursion to Iron Mountain and Pilot Knob, on any day next week which the Assembly might select.

The Moderator requested Dr. Clarke to make a motion in regard to the matter.

Dr. Clarke stated that he was sorry the request had been made of him, as he was hardly in favor of doing more than accepting the courtesy, and respectfully declining the invitation; there were 500 delegates here from both Assemblies enjoying the great hospitality of the people, to whom hospitality must be a care, and if continued too long, a burden; that we have so much to do, that while we thank this company for their courtesy, we must decline the pleasure of seeing Iron Mountain.

Mr. Kellogg was sorry to differ from Dr. Clarke and hoped that the invitation would be accepted.

Dr. Hotchkins favored accepting the invitation, and moved that the matter be referred to a committee.

After some further discussion the Assembly respectfully acknowledged the courtesy of the invitation, and referred the matter to the following special committee:

Rev. B. B. Hotchkins, Rev. R. R. Kellogg, Elder Horatio Newhall, M. D.

Rev. A. E. Knox. I have been requested by a member of the Assembly of the Old School (not officially) that a committee of conference with reference to joint religious services be appointed by this Assembly to meet a similar committee to be appointed by that Assembly.

Dr. Booth objected to this Assembly taking the initiative step in the matter. We had done so once and nothing came of it.

Rev. Mr. Knox stated that it was desired that the committee should be appointed this morning that a joint meeting might be held tomorrow.

The Moderator. I have just been informed that the other Assembly has just appointed such a committee.

Mr. Booth. Let us wait until there is some official notice given to us from that body.

Mr. Knox's motion was withdrawn by consent of the Assembly.

Rev. J. Glenworth Butler, DD., read the report of the Executive Committee of Ministerial Relief, showing a balance in the Treasury of $1,606.

Report accepted and referred to appropriate standing committee.

Hon. John A. Foote expressed a desire that every minister would see to it that the recommendations contained in the last report were carried out.

Dr. Hatfield stated that Dr. Thomas had informed him that a committee had been appointed on the part of the Old School Assembly to meet a similar committee appointed by this Assembly to make arrangements for joint devotional exercises during the next week.

Dr. Knox renewed his motion for the appointment of a committee of conference.

The motion prevailed, and the following committee was appointed:

Rev. W. E. Knox, DD., Rev. W. T. Curtis, DD., and Hon. John A. Foote.

Rev. Joel Parker, DD., remarked that the Presbytery of Newark, enjoined upon the commissioners to present papers embodying a request that the General Assembly would take into consideration the expediency of furnishing some publications in the German language for the use of our German Presbyterian Churches. I propose that the matter be givrn into the hands of the standing Committee on Publications.

Dr. Parker's proposition was accepted, and the commissioners of the Presbytery of Newark were instructed to meet with the Committee on Publications.

Hon. Joseph Allison, of special committee, to whom was referred overture No. 14, which is as follows:

To the General Assembly of the Presbyterian Church, now in session in the city of Brooklyn, N. Y.

The undersigned respectfully submit to the General Assembly the following overture, viz:

When the judicatory have proceeded, in accordance with chapter IV section 13 of the Book of Discipline, to take the testimony in the case of an accused person, may they proceed to *pass judgment* thereon as if he were present, or shall he be left simply under censure for contumacy?

H. W. WILLIAMS,
E. C. ADAMS,
DANIEL MARCH,

Read a report of which the following is an abstract:

"The question thus presented is exclusively one of power. It is not whether, in all cases, it is advisable that a Church judiciary should proceed to a final determination of the case, nor is it what has been the usage in some of the tribunals of the Church, but it is strictly what does the Book of Discipline authorize? It is freely admitted that a long course of usage under a statute is no inconsiderable evidence of the meaning of the statute, but it must be a usage growing out of the enactment itself, and claimed to have been authorized by it. Mere neglect to exercise powers conferred is no proof that they were not granted."

* * * * * * *

"Undoubtedly there have been differences of opinion, and, possibly, it may have been decided in some judicatory, that jurisdiction over an offense charged is necessarily suspended whenever an accused person disobeys the citations, but this is of little value in determining what the framers of the Book of Discipline meant by its directions respecting process, trial and judgment. It is much more important that, in certain cases, where the proof is clear, as where the accused has confessed his guilt, or where he has been convicted of violating the civil laws and has absconded, Church sessions have been accustomed to proceed to trial and judgment, nothwithstanding a refusal of the accused to appear in answer to citations. Such cases are judicial assertions of power; never denied, so far as we are informed."

* * * * * * *

"The ends of discipline are clearly defined. They are declared by the second section of the first chapter to be "the removal of the officers, the vindication of the honor of Christ, the promotion of the purity and the general edification of the Church, and, also the benefit of the offender himself."

* * * * * * *

"Contumacious disobedience of citations is another distinct offense, punishment for which is entirely collateral to discipline for the cause that induced the commencement of the process. It is contempt of the lawful authority of the church, and suspension for it is summary punishment for the collateral offense alone. Neither directly nor indirectly is it an expression of opinion respecting the delinquent's guilt or innocence of the charge preferred originally against him. Suspension for contumacy would be proper, without regard to anything beyond it. It is quite conceivable that an accused person may willfully disobey citations, and yet be innocent of the charges made against him. It certainly would be an anomaly in any judicial proceeding to hold that a penalty inflicted for a collateral offense vindicates the law against another and possibly much greater crime.

"If, therefore, the defined ends of discipline are to be secured, a Church session must have power to proceed to trial and judgment, though the accused person refuse to obey the citations duly served upon him, and it is not to be concluded without clear evidence that means given to secure those ends are inadequate. When the meaning of the language used in the fourth chapter is sought, the best guide to it will be found in the paramount intention the language was designed to subserve. The directions given must be construed consistently, with that intention, to further, rather than to defeat it. Looking then to the sections of the fourth chapter, and regarding them as part of a system designed for the purposes above mentioned, to be interpreted so as to harmonize with those purposes as well as with each other, the conclusion seems inevitable that whenever an accusation has been made against a church member, and a church judicatory has entered judicially upon its consideration, and obtained jurisdiction by service or citations upon him, it may go on to final judgment, though he refused to obey the citations."

* * * * * * *

"Judgment in all ecclesiastical courts must be founded upon evidence. As a judgment for default of appearance is not authorized, it is proper that the accused should have special notice of taking the testimony, though he may refuse to appear in answer to the citation. In fact, however, notice that the testimony will be taken is notice that the judicatory will go on with the trial, for taking testimony is a part of trial, its first stage. Undue influences are therefore drawn from the form of the notice; it is supposed to indicate that the proceedings are to stay, when the testimony shall have been taken. At most, it raises but a very feeble implication that, because notice of one thing is required,(a thing very peculiar in itself,and always demanding a special notice,) therefore nothing else can be done. A similar mode of reasoning would render a trial in any case impossible."

* * * * * *

"Taking all these sections into consideration, and regarding them as parts of one system, as having reference to the same subject matter, and designed to secure the ends avowed, the committee are constrained to regard them as applicable to the course of proceeding through all the stages of trial, alike in cases where the accused does not appear in obedience to the citations as when he does. In both the judicatory is empowered to proceed to trial and to final judgment.

"To this conclusion an objection has sometimes been urged that, at first mention, seems to have some plausibility. It is, that trial of a person in his absence, and the rendition of judgment against him, are in conflict with common right and justice; that even criminal courts in State governments do not try offenders in their absence, and that ecclesiastical courts ought to avoid *ex parte* proceedings. The objection aims less at the power of a judicatory. as recognized by the book of discipline, than it does at the policy of exercising it. But it misapprehends what are acknowledged common right and justice, what are the proceedings of courts of law and equity in analogous cases, and what are *ex parte* proceedings. Nowhere is it held that a man may not deny himself his plainest rights. While he may not be tried for an alleged offense without having an opportunity to be heard, he has no just cause to complain of a trial to which he has been summoned by a tribunal having jurisdiction, and which he has persistently refused to attend. In such a case, it is he who has thrown away his own rights. They are not taken from him. This is a principle universally recognized in courts of civil law and of equity, and such courts go further. They construe a refusal to obey process requiring an appearance as a substantial confession of the complaint, and they render judgment accordingly. It is true State courts, having criminal jurisdiction, do not try persons for crimes and misdemeanors in their absence. This is for two reasons. They have power to compel attendance, which ecclesiastical courts have not, and the punishments they inflict affect the life, the liberty or the property of the convicted criminal. In fact they concern the life or the liberty of the accused, for even if the penalty be only a fine, its payment is usually enforced by detention in custody until satisfaction be made. But ecclesiastical tribunals can pronounce no judgment that touches either the life, the liberty or the property of the accused. Their sentences are peculiar. Indeed it is asserting a false analogy to assimilate a trial before a church session to an indictment and trial in a criminal court. It bears a much stronger resemblance to proceedings very common in courts of law, in which members of associations or corporations are called upon to respond for some alleged breach of corporate duty, for which they are liable to be punished by the imposition of penalties, or by a motion from membership. In such cases, when the person summoned refuses to obey the mandate of the writ, courts proceed at once to dispose of his case and render final judgment. No one ever supposed that by so doing injustice was done, or that any right of the accused was invaded. Much less can he complain who has been cited to answer an accusation taken into judicial cognizance by a church judicatory, and who has contumaciously refused to obey the citation. if the tribunal proceed to try the case, presuming nothing against him but contumacy from his refusal, but founding its judgment solely upon the testimony of witnesses. This objection, therefore, when examined, seems to be without substance.

"In conclusion, it remains only to recommend, as the opinion of the committee, that the overture be answered by a declaration of the Assembly, that in the case proposed, the judicatory may proceed to trial and final judgment, as if the accused were present.

SAMUEL W. FISHER,
W. STROUPE,
JOSEPH ALLISON,
THOMAS BRAINARD."

The report was accepted and ordered to be put upon the docket.

Dr. H. B. Smith, of the Special Committee in regard to the formation of a National Protestant League, stated that there bad been no action taken, the committee therefore had no report to make, and asked that the committee be discharged.

Dr. Hatfield moved that the first business in order on Tuesday morning be to receive reports of delegates of corresponding bodies, which motion prevailed.

Dr. H. B. Smith. There is one subject upon which the Assembly has always appointed a committee of late years, and that is, "On the State of the Country." We have passed through the state of war, and come to the state of peace, but are still in the midst of difficult questions which seem to demand some expression of opinion from ecclesiastical bodies. I have been expecting a motion to this effect from some other member of the Assembly, but none having been made, I now move that a Special Committee be appointed On the State of the Country. I make the suggestion that the oldest and most venerated member of the Assembly, Dr. Beeman, be appointed chairman of this committee.

A member, whose precise words we could not hear, objected to the motion, on the ground that it would make a great outcry for a ministerial body to discuss such questions at this time; that it would be imprudent to say a single word in regard to the state of the country.

Hon. John A. Foote. If I heard correctly, I understood the gentleman to oppose the motion. I take an entirely different view. It seems to me, sir, that a body so large, so respectable as this, and representing so large and respectable a constituency, cannot but have weight. It seems to me, sir, that the motion of Dr. Smith is eminently a proper one. We all know that there is a great kiversity of opinion, and many feel that the present is a time as full of dangers and difficulties as any through which we have passed. A distinguished man when addressing the country said that, using the expression made by some of the ancients, he felt that it would be more appropriate to pray than to speak.

The country expects that we will, after prayer, give our views upon a question that interests everybody. We have to-day heard most eloquently of the importance of work as well as of prayer. Now then we certainly ought not to shrink from giving the opinions that we may have upon these great questions. If we say nothing more to our constituency than that it behooves them all to pray to God in this exigency, it will do a great deal of good. If we say to them that we call upon all our rulers to approach this question without selfishness, asking God to aid them, and putting aside everything like hatred, malice, ill-will, and everything of that kind, it will do good. And if we say that looking upon him whom we have for President, and seeing that at the original inception of the rebellion he stood up alone from the Southern States and denounced treason as a crime, we feel under obligations to him for that; it seems to me something that would allay prejudice; and, if we should further say that we cannot conceive that he should make the great mistake that an Executive was going to be the Judiciary, the Legislature, and all the other departments of the Government—to use the language of the sailor—that he was Captain, mate and all hands.

Now, it seems to me it is eminently proper that we should express our opinions. I spoke to one of the gentlemen this morning who is on the Committee of Bills and Overtures, and I asked him if they were not going to report on the subject. He said "No, they had already reported with reference to this particular crisis." Now, a man might have an excellent coat made a certain number of years ago it might be an excellent coat, but it might not be in fashion now.

Very many things have taken place since the last meeting. Now, it seems to me that it is eminently proper that we should utter our opinions on the subject and give no uncertain sound, and when we speak on the subject we should speak of a number of questions that are near our hearts; and permit me to say, it will come with great effect and with great weight, for I remember I never before was a member of a General Assembly except in 1863. That Assembly passed a resolution; we commenced on a particular point; it was precisely the point between loyalty and disloyalty, and we discussed it almost all day. I felt willing to go for it because Dr. Barnes proposed it. I study Barnes' notes a great deal. When the resolution was read to the President, he said: "Gentlemen, I thank you for the point you have made (it was precisely that point); it strengthens me to feel that I have all the denominations now sustaining me. I don't pretend that I have every one of all, but I have all the denominations, and it strengthens me to feel that I have praying men to sustain me."

The utterance of this body will have a very great effect. I have not had a political office for more than ten years, don't expect and don't want one. I have just the feeling I ought to have as a Christian and as a man, in regard to these questions, and old as I am, feel that my interests are bound up with this country, and old as I am I fear that I may still see confusion and every evil work in our land if we don't take the right stand.

It seems to me that we should honestly, judiciously and intelligently give our views.

Our friend here (referring to the last speaker) is undoubtedly a very excellent man. I esteem him very much, but when he gave his views in regard to another matter he didn't agree with me entirely, and objected to the report, which was most exhaustive and was necessary, because the question that came up would not have been satisfsctorily answered without going through with that thorough report. It now has come to the conclusion which I would be perfectly willing to rely upon.

As I said with reference to the President, I feel under great obligations to him, but I must say that I have not unlimited confidence in him. He evidently is a man, and no more than a man. I read in the last speech he made that he was sometimes a whole day without thinking he was President. When I read that I could not help thinking that his position had elevated him so much that he was not exactly the man he would be, if he was in the position that I am in. I remember in a town, over near where I live, was an old woman, whose husband was Justice of the Peace. Her husband had the house painted green, and she once said that she sat sometimes a whole day without once thinking that her house was green and her husband a Justice of the Peace. [Laughter.] Now the trouble with her was the same as the trouble with the President. It wasn't strange that he shouldn't think of his being President for a whole day, or that the old lady should forget about the green house, but the unfortunate thing was that he should have mentioned it, and that there should have been a correspondent *of the London Times green enough to have reported it.*

The motion prevailed, and the Moderator announced the Committee on the State of the Country as follows:

Rev. N. S. S. Beaman, D. D., Rev. H. B. Smith, D. D., Rev. W. H. Hogarth, Rev. Henry Fowler, Hon. Geo. Allison, Hon. F. V. Chamberlin, Hon. F. P. Handy.

Dr. T. J. Shepherd, of the Committee on Bills and Overtures, reported back certain papers, with recommendation that they be referred to the appropriate committees, which action was accordingly taken.

The following changes in religious services of Sunday were reported from the Committee on Devotional Exercises.

Rock Hill, Dr. William Hogarth, 10 1-2 A. M.

Webster Grove, Dr. William Hogarth, 7 1-2 in the evening.

Rev. Walter Clarke, D. D., First Presbyterian Church, St. Louis, 10 1-2 A. M.

Rev. G. F, Wiswell, Second Union Methodist Church, St. Louis, 7 1-2 o'clock.

The hours for the meeting of various committees were announced, and the Assembly adjourned until 8 1-2 o'clock A. M., Monday, May 21st.

FOURTH DAY — MONDAY, MAY 21, 1866.

Rev. Lucius D. Root moved that the reports from the Committees on Synodical Records be made the first in order for the afternoon. The motion prevailed.

The report of the Committee on the Excursion to Iron Mountain was presented by Rev. Mr. Kellogg, recommending Thursday as a day appropriate for the trip.

Jas. W. Edwards, Esq., offered an amendment that the day fixed be Saturday—the day after adjournment.

Hon. Jas. A. Foot expressed a desire that the report would be accepted, and Thursday the day appointed.

The determination of the matter was deferred until after the usual devotional exercises, which then took place.

After the devotional exercises, the matter of the excursion again came up. The invitation was accepted, and after some discussion between the days, Saturday, Friday, and Thursday, Thursday was fixed upon as the day for the excursion.

The members of the Assembly who proposed to go upon the excursion were requested to enter their names and the names of their hosts, that the President of the road might know for how many excursionists accommodations would have to be provided.

On motion of Professor Smith, it was voted that the communication from Rev. Dr. McCosley, representing the Free Church of Scotland, be received by us, and that the Assembly appoint to-morrow morning, at eleven o'clock, to hear the communication.

On motion of Rev. Dr. Shaw, Rev. Dr. Harper, representing the United Presbyterian Church of North America, was invited to address the Assembly.

Rev. Dr. Harper. Mr. Moderator and Brethren of the Assembly: It is my privilege to present to you the fraternal regards of the United Presbyterian Church of North America. I am not aware that I am acquainted with a single individual in this Assembly, and yet I do not feel as though I were entirely a stranger among strangers. There is a bond of Christian sympathy and union among all the followers of our Savior, which makes us feel that we belong to a common Christian brotherhood. There may be shades of difference in matters of form and government, and faith even, as there are shades of difference in the family groupe, yet, after all, I feel that we are children of the same parent, and brethren of the same household, and heirs to the same glorious inheritance, and therefore I come to you to-day, to speak to you as brethren in Christ.

Perhaps it may be proper for me, at the outset, to read to you some statistics which I have prepared, that you may thereby gain some information in regard to the church which I represent, This church had its existence from the Union of the ———— and the Associated Reform Church, in 1858. In all matters of faith, and government, and practice, we are closely identified with the larger bodies of Presbyterians in this country. We have fifty-one Presbyteries, seven Synods, one General Assembly—constituted like your own, of delegates from the Presbyteries. We have a Presbytery in Oregon, India and Egypt; missionaries in Syria, India, China, Egypt and——— We have 80 foreign missionaries, 120 home missionaries, 40 to 50 laborers among the freedmen, chiefly in Tennessee and Mississippi; 4 theological seminaries; 2 colleges; 516 ministers; 70 licentiates; 91 students of theology; 659 congregations; 6 permanent boards, viz: Home Missions, Foreign Missions, Pnblication, Church Extension, Education, and Freedmen. We publish three weekly religious papers, one monthly periodical, and have a printing press in the city of Alexandria in Egypt. We raised for all the boards last year $180,000.

It may be proper for me to state to the Assembly that that portion of the Church which I represent, feels that the great work of the Church of God in this age is the work of missions. Time was when it was necessary that the Church should secure an orthodox Creed, but those days are passed. The age of Creed making is gone, and now it seems to us that the great work of the Church of God is to disseminate those principles which we have secured, and scatter them far and wide. This we regard as pre-eminently the age of missions. Never was the world so accessible before, never were there so many facilities of doing God's work, never did the Great Head of the Church call us by His Providence so loudly as he is now doing to engage in His work. So feeling, we are devoting all our energies and powers to this great work of evangelizing the world, in this country, and in foreign lands.

We feel as though, for the accomplishment of this great work, there should be increased unity and co-operation among all the followers of Christ. We desire, therefore, the increased unity of the Church of the Living God. It seems to us especially desirable from the fact that our own existence is the result of union; we know, by our own experience, how pleasant it is for brethren to dwell together in unity, and realizing this blessed feeling among ourselves we hail with feelings of joy the efforts made in Great Britain, and in this country of the different parts of the Church of God, towards a closer union.

Let me speak to you on this subject freely—it lies very near my own heart. It is admitted generally that the Church is in an unnatural and divided state, and that these divisions are sinful and wicked. These things are generally admitted, but after all, how little do we feel it—how little do we feel in our very souls that these divisions are shameful and wicked, dishonoring to God, and retarding the progress of the conversion of the world. If we realized and felt it, we would labor more for it, and pray more for it.

I apprehend, after all, the great difficulty in the way of perfect union, is not a matter of doctrine, but it is in the selfishness of our hearts —in the natural selfishness of our hearts. I have often noticed in the army that when regiments were to be consolidated, the trouble was not with the private soldiers, but the difficulty was to find places for the colonel, the major and the captains. So I think it is to a great very extent in the church.

Another fact. We are disposed to look too

much at the points about which we differ, and not enough at the points about which we are agreed.

Let me ask you to think of these things. If our beloved Savior prayed that the Church of God might be one, should this not be our prayer and our effort? May I not ask you to think of these things, and may God speed the day when we shall look forth like an army with banners, when "Ephraim shall not envy Juda, and Juda shall not vex Ephraim."

We desire to cultivate the most fraternal relations with this body, and to be colaborers with you in the great work of preaching Christ. We desire to congratulate you on the noble and manly position you have taken as a church on the great question of human freedom. [Applause.] Your voice has been clearly marked, and well understood in this land, and in the hour of our nation's conflict, when others have been unfaithful, I have thanked God that you have stood up as a church under the banner which adorns your church here to-day. Though that banner has been consecrated with the blood of hundreds of thousands of patriots, the conflict is not yet over. There is yet a great battle to be fought by the pulpit and the press of this land. You have been faithful thus far, and I trust you will fight it out on this line, if it should take you until the millenium. God grant that your church may never recede from the noble position you have taken.

The Moderator responded, that the Assembly received with great satisfaction the fraternal greetings of the church represented by the speaker; congratulated that church upon its loyalty, missionary activity and success, and the noble example of unity which it had set to the Christian world, and invoked God's grace, mercy and peace upon the church, and good speed in all its efforts.

Voted, that the reception of salutation messages from corresponding bodies be made the second order of the day to-morrow (Tuesday) morning.

A communication was read from the Mercantile Library Association, tendering to the Assembly the courtesy of the library and reading room of that association during the session of the Assembly.

Voted, on motion of Dr. Hatfield that the tender be accepted, with thanks.

Rev. Dr. Knox, from the special Committee of Conference, reported a recommendation that there be a joint devotional meeting of the two Assemblies in the Second Presbyterian Church, at a quarter before eight o'clock this evening, (Monday), the two Moderators to preside, and make the opening addresses; that Rev. Dr. Joel Parker and H. B. Smith from this Assembly, and two to be chosen by the other Assembly, also address the meeting; also, that there be in this, (the First Presbyterian Church), a joint sacramental service on Wednesday evening, at a quarter before eight, and that the address on that occasion, on the part of this Assembly, be made by the Rev. Dr. Humphrey.

Voted that the report be accepted and adopted.

Rev. Dr. Clarke then read the report of the Standing Committee on Foreign Missions, of which the following is an abstract:

The committee to whom was referred the report of the Permanent Committee on Foreign Missions, respectfully represent to the General Assembly that that report invites attention especially to the following points, to wit:

To an altogether satisfactory relation with the A. B. C. F. M.; the alarming decrease in the number of our missionaries in the service of the Board; the continued neglect on the part of many of our churches and church members to make annual contributions to the cause of missions; the importance of even a larger co-operation on the part of our Western churches; the need of a more efficient use of an ecclesiastical apparatus, and the fitness of this present period of our national ministry, for a broader, mightier and more successful assault upon that empire of darkness for whose conquest and illumination the Church aspires and exists.

That the number of our missionaries should have been reduced one-sixth in three years, so that whereas in 1863 we had fifty six in the field, we have now only forty-seven, is a fact which the world will contemplate with surprise, the Assembly with sorrow, and to which we can make no other honorable answer, than in the voice of our sons and daughters, saying in scores, "Here are we, send us."

It is matter of much congratulation that under the many burdens and exactions of the time our congregation gave to the cause of missions last year not less, but more than in any previous year. Nevertheless the Assembly ought not to pass lightly over the humiliating revelations of the committee's report touching the continued neglect of a portion of our churches and church members to contribute their just quota to the cause of Christian missions.

Your committee recommend that some morning be set apart by the Assembly to prayer, especially for this object, that our ascended Redeemer may hear our united cry and inspire in all our congregations with these sessions, supplies and pastors, that sentiment of expansive zeal, which we need to make us to the full extent of our ability a Missionary Church.

The Churches in our Western Synods, have a vast home field, which they cannot dutifully or safely neglect. And all our Churches, whether in the newer or older States, have in charge the magnificent enterprise of establishing upon this great continent the seat of power, the home of liberty, the goal of the ages past, the starting point of the ages to come; that glorious sunshine of Christ, for which the continent was created, for which the republic stands. We must not try to abate, but rather to increase the instinctive ardor which fires the hearts of our people in the East and West in behalf of Home Missions. But to do this home work well, we must do our work in other lands well also; for we are of least use to ourselves when we are most selfish, and shall do most and most successfully for Christ's cause at home, when we do most and most willingly for his kingdom abroad. May God, by whose favor alone we can be made strong in this or other lands, keep our Churches from the fatal mistake of doing little for missions among the heathen, under the impression that thereby they can do more for Christianity at their own doors.

The committee learns with great satisfaction, that ten of our Presbyters are employed in missionary labor, and two others are under appointment in the service of the American and Foreign Christian Mission. The Rev. Ranor Mentsalvatage, of the Presbytery of Brooklyn, and Rev. A. J. McKim, of the Presbytery of Athens, are successfully at work, in not the least inviting of the many fields now opening to that efficient and worthy society; that is to say, in Brazil, South America.

The committee recommend to the Assembly the adoption of the following order, to wit:

That it be earnestly enjoined upon all the Synods, Presbyteries, sessions and congregations connected with this Assembly, that by the appointment of Synodical and Presbyterical committees, the faithful presentation of the cause to the people for their annual contributions, the diffusion of intelligence through the Presbyterian Monthly, Missionary Herald, Christian World and the religious newspapers, regular observance of the monthly concert, report to the permanant committee, and every other appropriate method of instruction and appeal, they endeavor from this time to make our entire Church what it ought to be, and can be: the joy of the Redeemer, the glory of the age, the light of the world.

In behalf of the committee.

W. CLARKE, Chairman.

Dr. Clarke. I am sorry that the committee have compelled me to add a word of exhortation to this report, for my bodily health is such that I can hardly stand upon my feet, but I must discharge what I can of my duty.

It seems to me that God is speaking in a voice never before so audible, to His Church, especially on this continent. It seems to me that our Church is the Church in the best possible attitude at this time to hear and respond to the call of the Great Head of the Church. Nobody who has been skeptical hitherto in regard to the supremacy of Christianity in the world, can doubt so since these last five years of American history have inscribed their lesson on the page of public memory, that this land belongs to Christianity; that it belongs to Christ for His Church; that His Church is to be erected on this continent as a tower of light for all the nations; that this part of the globe exists especially for that, none of us, it seems to me, can for a moment doubt, and if these things be so, it must be true that the Common Head of the Hosts of Zion is looking upon His Church upon this Continent to discern which of them is most ready to enter into the fore front of the great work which is to be accomplished here and abroad in the coming half century. That Church in America which is prepared to receive most Christian spirit, to enter most perfectly into Christ's great work, to contribute most for the consummation of his kingdom in the whole world: into that Church our blessed Redeemer will most certainly enter, and make that the Juda among the tribes of Israel in this land. By His Providence and spirit he has been dealing with our Church in a most remarkable manner, and in a manner of preparation. An aggressive army must have few *impediments*, and slavery was an impediment, which hanging upon any Church, unfits that Church for the great aggressive work which Christ has to do in this world. From that impediment, by the good providence of our ascended Lord, this Church has been delivered, and from every intestine conflict. Then by the good providence of God our Church has been planted on just the spot where it can have the easiest access to every part of this continent and the world. Christ, if we do not reject him by a bad spirit, must enter into our Church, and fill it with His temper, and what is the temper of Christ, but just the temper of missions? What is the temper of Christ, but just the largeness of benevolence which this work calls for?

It seems to me that the day has come when every Presbytery in our Church, when every member in our Church, ought to feel, "I am a Presbyterian to carry Christ's kingdom wherever I can carry that blessed light, here, at home and abroad." And not only this—we ought to feel that we are called to act, and that we do not deserve the name of Presbyterians in this day; that we deserve to be cast out unless through all our ranks we engage in spreading the kingdom of our Lord, not only at home, but abroad.

God give us the joy of hearing it reported at the next General Assembly that not a Church in our connection has come short of its duty in this good work.

Dr. A. E. Campbell suggested an omission in the report respecting missionary publications, which Dr. Clark stated should be embodied in the report.

On motion, the morning hour of Tuesday was set apart as a special occasion for prayer for foreign missions.

Rev. G. W. Wood, Sec. A. B. C. F. M., spoke in substance as follows: I am here by request of the Prudential Committee, in accordance with a resolution of the Assembly which met at Wilmington in 1859, asking that thereafter that the Prudential Committee would depute one of their or secretaries to attend the General Assembly and present the interests of the cause of foreign missions.

The Prudential Committee desire, through me, to present their greeting to this body, and their congratulation of the special circumstances under which you are assembled, and especially on account of the prosperity of your beneficent enterprises. The committee, though they so deeply regret that so large a part of the churches have as yet failed to come up to that interest in the cause of foreign missions which seems so indispensable to their spiritual life, yet are gratified at the progress which has been made within the limits of this branch of the Church during the last few years. The amount of contributions during the last year is very considerably in advance of that of any preceding year. I am desired especially to impress on the members of the Assembly the desirableness of a still further advance. It is a matter for devouter thanksgiving that during this period of our civil conflict, when the demands made upon the benevolence of the Church have been so unprecedented, the demand has been so fully met, and the board was enabled to close the war with a surplus of $1,148 in the treasury, though it entered on the period of the war with a deficit of $28,000. Yet there is great danger that now that the war is passed and the cost of exchange is somewhat declining, the feeling will go abroad among the contributors to the cause, that there is not a demand for so much exertion in this behalf, and that contributions will fall off.

The missions require an enlarged support, and the cut is increasing from year to year, the rise of prices is universal throughout the world. Urgent as is the need of funds, the want most deeply felt at the present time is that of men, and I am desired to speak as strongly as I may be able in this regard. It is incumbent on me to say that unless we can get reinforcements to our missions they must sustain the greatest damages.

Dr. Hatfield announced that on Friday evening at 8 1-4 o'clock in this house the Presbyterion Historical Society propose to hold a public meeting and they invite the General Assembly to be present on that occasion. Rev. Dr. McLean of the Old School Assembly is expected to deliver a discourse on the life and character of Rev. Wm. Kenneth.

Dr. Smith, of Committee on Church Polity, reported a recommendation of that committee that the Presbytery of Superior be transferred from the Synod of Michigan to that of Wisconsin.

On motion the recommendation was accepted and adopted.

Dr. Smith further reported a recommendation that the time of meeting of the Presbyteries of Chemung and Geneva, designated for the last Tuesday of September, be changed to the third Tuesday of the same month.

Recommendation adopted.

Dr. Smith further reported a recommendation of recognizing the Presbytery of Osage, and that it be attached to the Synod of Missouri, according to their request.

Recommendation adopted.

After some little discussion, during which Detroit and Rochester were named as the next places of meeting, the time and place of meeting were referred to a committee consisting of Drs. Shaw, Hogan and Rev. H. W. Williams.

The first week of January, 1867, beginning with the Sabbath and running through the week, was appointed as a concert for prayer.

After prayer, the Assembly adjourned until 3 P. M.

AFTERNOON SESSION—3 P. M.

Opened with prayer. Dr. Shaw in the Chair.

The Chair announced that Truman P. Handy was excused from serving on the Committee on the State of the Country, and the names of Rev. Thomas Brown, Hon. John A. Foot and Mr. Russell Scarrett be added thereto.

The several committees on Synodical Records then made their reports.

The standing Committee on the Ministerial Relief Fund reported, to the effect that this subject has never yet been presented before our churches as it should be, as is shown from the fact that only 130 out of 1,479 churches have contributed to this fund.

Report received and adopted.

Dr. Humphrey, of the Committee on Church Erection, read the following report:

REPORT OF THE STANDING COMMITTEE OF THE GENERAL ASSEMBLY, OF 1866, ON CHURCH ERECTION.

By the twelfth annual report of the Trustees of the Assembly's Church Erection Fund, it is painfully apparent that this fund is but imperfectly accomplishing its original design. The amount of the fund in 1856 was $100,000. Now, after ten years' use, it has increased to over $127,000, $80,000 of which, at least, remain in the hands of the Board, subject to the call of the churches. Year by year the applications for aid become fewer. But $2,755 were taken from the treasury last year, in the form of loans, and but $400 in the form of donations. Meanwhile the receipts from the churches, on account of loans, donations and interest, have been over $7,000, which added to the interest accruing on the fund itself—nearly $5,000—constitute an actual increase of the unemployed fund, after deducting expenses, &c., of about $7,000.

The reason of this is not that the aid which might be afforded by this fund is undesired. The more wealthy churches in all our large centers have been besieged with applications for assistance in church building as pertinaciously as if there were no fund for that purpose in existence. Large amounts have been given in answer to such appeals by the very churches which originally contributed to the now neglected treasury from which it was expected all feeble churches would draw. So pressing, in fact, have been the applications that it is manifest that the whole fund, if accessible on terms favorable to the churches, would soon be completely absorbed.

The reason of such neglect must be looked for in the practical working of the plan on which the fund has been administered. That plan was most carefully devised. It embodied the wisdom of some of the most eminent men in our Church. For the period when it was adopted it was most excellent. But since its adoption a great change has taken place in our position and circumstances. The last ten years have been revolutionary. The Nation has trembled under the shock of war. We have passed through financial embarrassments and borne the brunt of a struggle which has cost our churches some of their choicest blood. Debts incurred for the erection of houses of worship have become burdensome. The churches have in many instances been depressed by the very means through which they sought to gain strength. Obligations to the General Assembly have often been borne under the disadvantage of contrasts drawn between the policy upon which our plan of church erection and that of some of our sister denominations is based. The result has been that the fund has fallen into disfavor. Churches needing assistance have been advised, in some cases by Synodical or Presbyterical action, not to encumber themselves with loans such as others had found it so unpleasant to bear, and so difficult to pay.

At the same time the cost of building has so enormously increased that $200 form but a comparatively insignificant item in the expense of constructing an ordinary house of worship—worth applying for, indeed, but not desired under the conditions upon which it was to be obtained.

There is, therefore, an imperative call for a modification of the plan of administering our church erection fund, and this call becomes the more imperative when we consider that the rapid extension of the lines of traffic has made cities of villages, and villages of hamlets. Where ten years since it was supposed a few hundred dollars would suffice for the wants of the people, as many thousand dollars are now found to be insufficient. An almost unanticipated necessity has arisen to establish churches at key-points, and to provide them with commodious and attractive sanctuaries. The spirit of the times has changed. A new impulse, felt by all denominations, has been given to domestic missions. Looking towards the glowing future of our country, we are incited to new exertions for its evangelization. Among the ruling ideas of the day this is prominent—that to provide a church edifice is almost as important as to provide a missionary, and that the work of church erection must be carried forward upon the same enlarged and liberal scale, which is adopted for the support of ministers of the gospel. Were the idea a false one, to resist it would be like stemming the currents of the Mississippi in a flood; but your committee believe it to involve a true principle, though it, like all other ruling ideas, is liable to unnatural freshet.

This Assembly has assumed the work of domestic missions, as it had not when its church erection fund was established. Then that work was committed to the American Home Missionary Society.

Now that we have entered this field side by side with our sister denominations, we must carry on our work with an energy and a liberality like theirs.

In view of these considerations, your committee believe that could the whole fund be immediately scattered among our feeble churches, in the form of donations, without interest or return of any kind, while the churches aided should remain in our connection, the effect would be most happy. This we believe to be desired by many on the floor of this Assembly. Were such a course possible we should favor it. But a careful examination of the whole case, has brought your committee to the stubborn conclusion, so often reached by others who have surveyed the same ground, that such a disposition of the fund was rendered impossible by the very terms on which it was collected. It was to be a *permanent* fund. To destroy its permanency would be a breach of trust which might and which ought to be legally resisted. The legal opinions submitted to the Assembly by the Board of Trustees, place this position beyond reasonable dispute.

The question therefore is, how the mode of administering the fund shall be so changed as to make it most useful to the churches. After mature deliberations your committee recommend the abandonment of the system of loans and the adoption of that of donations upon the following plan, viz:

1. That the whole of the fund now in the hands of the Board, together with such receipts as may return in fulfillment of pledges from the churches already aided by loans and donations, and together with whatever may be hereafter contributed to the fund, be securely and permanently invested.

2. That the accruing interest be annually distributed by the Board on proper conditions and in proper proportions, to churches applying therefor, in the form of donations without interest and without pledge of return, except in case the church or congregation thus assisted shall cease to be connected with the General Assembly, or their cor-

porate existence shall cease or their house of worship be alienated, except for the building or purchase of a better house of worship.

As supplementary to this, your committee recommend that a collection be taken annually by all our churches, to be forwarded to the Treasurer of the Board, to be used by them in the same manner as the accruing interest of the fund.

The necessary amendments of the Assembly's plan, together with all essential details, are submitted herewith. It is believed that in these changes no legal principle is sacrificed and that the utmost practical efficiency in the use of the fund is secured.

Your committee cannot but regard it as a providential indication of the wisdom of these proposed changes that they have been suggested to several different minds without concert and that they have been regarded with favor before this by those high in position in our Church, as will be seen by reference to the report of the special committee to whom this whole subject was referred by the Assembly of 1863.

Your committee would, also, recommend to the Assembly to consider the expediency of appointing a General Secretary of the Board, whose duty it shall be to discharge the functions in this Board which are discharged in the Committee of Home Missions by its Secretary.

It becomes our duty to nominate three Trustees to fill the places of Rev. J. Fen. Smith, D. D., Rev. Samuel D. Burchard, D. D., and William A. Booth, Esq., whose term of office is soon to expire. We cordially recommend that the same gentlemen be reappointed.

A few overtures have been referred to the committee upon the consideration of which we ask further time.

All of which is respectfully submitted.

Z. M. HUMPHREY, Chairman.

St. Louis, May 21, 1866.

The Assembly ordered that the above report be printed in the Democrat in full.

The committee on church erection recommended that the same gentlemen whose term of service expire with the Assembly as trustees of the church erection fund be reappointed. Adopted.

The standing committee on foreign missions nominated Rev. Joseph A. Tuttle, Rev. W. E. Dodge and —— —— to fill vacancies. Adopted.

The standing committee on mileage was granted another day to make up their report.

It having been announced that it would probably be impossible to print in full the report of the committee on church erection, in Tuesday's edition of the Democrat, that vote was reconsidered, and the question of the adoption or rejection of the report called up, when it appeared that the chairman of the committee had taken the original report and gone to make arrangements for carrying out the resolution of the assembly, and after a lively debate, in which much interest was displayed, not so much as to merits or demerits of the report, as to the desirableness of immediate and early action, action upon the report was made first in order for this [Tuesday] morning.

Dr. Shaw of the special committee on next meeting reported a recommendation that the Assembly should meet with the Brick church in Rochester, N. Y., and extended a cordial invitation to the Assembly.

The recommendation was adopted.

On motion time of meeting this (Tuesday) morning was changed from 8 1-2 to 9 o'clock.

After prayer, the assembly adjourned.

The report contemplates the following amendments of the "plan for the management of the church erection fund."

The preamble together with the articles I., II., III., IV. and V. are unaltered.

SUBSTITUTE FOR ARTICLE VI.

The board is directed to invest and to keep at interest on sufficient security the fund as now established, as the same shall hereafter be increased, by gift, bequest, or otherwise.

ARTICLE VII.

The accruing interest of the fund thus established shall be apportioned by the board among the synods as their exigencies may require, and be distributed by said board at their discretion to such congregations as make application therefor, on the conditions and subject to the limitations hereinafter prescribed.

ARTICLE VIII.

No amendment except by substituting the words "accruing interest" for "this fund", and by cutting out the words "loan or."

ARTICLE IX.

No change except by the substitution of "accruing interest" for "fund."

ARTICLE X.

No change.

ARTICLE XI.

Amendments in *brackets*.

If the Committee of the Synod, to whom application for aid has been made as above provided, shall, after a careful examination into the condition and prospects of the congregation so applying, be satisfied that such congregation have done all that should reasonably be expected of them, and that, with the aid which can be afforded from this fund, [the accruing interest and the voluntary contributions hereinafter mentioned,] they can build or possesss a house of worship adapted to their wants, and be free from indebtedness, then the Committee shall sign a certificate addressed to the Board, stating the application, and that they have examined and approve of it; and also stating the amount which it is proper to donate to the congregation. This certificate, together with the application made to the Committee of the Synod, shall be transmitted to the Board. On the receipt [thereof, in due form,] the Board shall, as soon as practicable, if the application is [granted,] forward the necessary papers, to be executed by the trustees of the congregation, and to be approved by their legal adviser, or some other attorney proposed by the congregation and accepted by the Board. When the papers, so executed, approved and properly recorded, are returned to the Board, they shall authorize the Treasurer of the trustees of the congregation, or any other person duly appointed by them for this purpose, to draw on the Treasurer of the Board for the amount thus [applied for and donated].

ARTICLE XII.

No change except to accomodate the article in phraseology to the new plan.

ARTICLE XIII.

No change.

SUPPLEMENTARY ARTICLE.

As supplementary to this plan and in order to enable the board fully to meet all the reasonable demands of feeble congregations for aid in erecting houses of public worship the general assembly earnestly recommends to all the congregations within its bounds to take up annual collections and transmit them to the Treasurer of the board, to be appropriated by said board and distributed by gift for the objects contemplated in the plan, and on the conditions and limitations prescribed therein.

And the better to secure this end, it shall be the duty of the board to present with their annual report, an estimate of the amount probably needed for the ensuing year, together with the facts and reasons upon which such estimate is based, in order that the assembly may determine the amount it will recommend the churches to raise by voluntary contribution.

FIFTH DAY — TUESDAY, MAY 22, 1866.

First hour spent in devotional exercises.

Minutes of last session read and approved.

Reports were then called for from the delegates to corresponding bodies, and were read from the delegates, to G. S. of the Cumberland Presbyt. church; to Gen. Con. Congregational church, Maine; the General Association of N. H.; to the Gen. Association of Mass.; and Presbyt. and Congregational Con. of Wisconsin.

These reports all testified to the fraternal cordiality and Christian love with which the delegates had been received by the several religious bodies to which they had been accredited.

Dr. Hatfield stated that there was an informal report by letter to a member, from the delegate to the General Association of Connecticut, to the same purport as the other reports which had been read.

Delegates from corresponding bodies were then invited to adress the Assembly.

Dr. Hatfield read a letter from B. T. Howard of the General Conference of Maine, in which, after stating that it was an unexpected and grievous disappointment to him that he was unable to visit St. Louis during the session of the Assembly, he assured the Assembly that the Conference of Maine felt strengthened by the harmony which existed between the two Churches in Christian doctrine and anti-slavery and loyal principles; that they were disposed more than formerly to test the question which of the Church polities is better calculated to win the world to Christ; that the membership of the Conference numbered a little less than 20,000; that its increase was hindered by the large numbers who annually pour into the great West; there were 251 Churches, 192 ministers; that Bowdoin college at Brunswick, graduated about 30 students annually, and the theological seminary at Bangor 15; that the Churches were at present blessed with a quickening influence of the Divine Spirit; that the Conference would cordially welcome a delegate from this body at the meeting in Bath.

Rev. Henry F. Ray was introduced to the Assembly as a delegate from the General Convention of Vermont, and spoke substantially as follows:

"It is my pleasure on this occasion to bring the cordial salutation of the members of the Congregational Churches of the state of Vermont. We claim to be your brothers in Christ, and though we feel that you look upon us as a small body in an unimportant State in this great confederacy, yet we feel that you will not hardly despise our greeting, or contemn our prayers, or the interest we feel in your prosperity. We number nearly 200 Churches, and somewhat over 17,000 members.

"We are of a great Calvanistic family. The orthodoxy of New England has been sometimes suspected west of the Hudson, but it has been my pleasure to read to my people an article of our creed, we believe the Western Association shorter catechism to be a good compendium of religious doctrine. Now I think you will not consider us very far gone in heresy so long as we retain that in our creed. And in this regard we do not claim to be an exception to the Churches of New England."

The Rev. gentleman then adverted to the missionary spirit which had been rife in the Churches of Vermont, and New England generally; and to the pleasure it gave him to meet with so many in his travels at the West, who were in some way or other connected with his native State, and named among the many sons of Vermont who had become eminent in the Church, William G. T. Shedd of Union Theological Seminary; referred to Congregationalism as having unfolded individuality and a sense of personal responsibility in the little farmer boys of New England and thus brought many of them into the foremost ranks of other Church organizations, and concluded his remarks as follows:

"There is one more bond between us which I believe must ever unite us, and that is represented by the symbol above your own seat. We love you, bretheren, because you have set forth unmistakably your spirit as the spirit of liberty, as the spirit of freedom, as a law abiding and government loving Church, and could we of the free Green Mountain air do else than love the body planting itself on the Declaration which we have heard from you for the last few years? We must love you. We hope to claim your regard in the future. We bid you as a Church reforming intelligent body "go forth, occupy as Providence shall open to you—we never will envy—we never will try to supplant you; if we can only labor with you, we will almost be content to follow after you, if God will speed you in the great work which devolves upon you."

The Moderator in response assured the delegate that it gave the Assembly the greatest pleasure to receive the Christian salutation of his constituents in words so fitly spoken, and that the Assembly was very far from contemplating with disrespect or want of cordial affection the Church he represented; that New England was dear to all of this Assembly, who could almost all of them trace by a very short descent their origin in New England; alluded to Prof. Shedd in terms of great appreciation and friendly regard; expressed the thought that the two Churches loved each other the better because they had drawn a little apart, and requested the delegate to return to the bretheren he represented the very kind Christian salutation of the Assembly, and its desire for their utmost Christian prosperity.

Dr. Hatfield then stated the contents of a letter from Rev. Frederick Monod, with regard to the union of the Evangelical Churches of France, from which it appeared that the time of meeting had been changed to October 25th, 1866; a new and important step had been taken towards the separation between the Evangelistic and the liberal parties in the established Protestant Churches. The meetings had lost their pastoral and Christian character, and had changed into exciting and unprofitable discussions. They had pronounced their own dissolution by a vote of 162 to 50, after which a new conference was immediately organized. The letter, after reference to national affairs, closed with the following sentiment:

"God grant to you all, beginning with the President and Congress, the wisdom which is first pure, then peaceful, justice to all, charity to all, and malice to none, as your glorious Lincoln did."

Dr. Hatfield then read the report of Dr. Nelson, delegate to the General Assembly now in session in the Second Presbyterian Church, as follows:

ST. LOUIS, May 22, 1866.

To the General Assembly of the Presbyterian Church, sitting in the First Presbyterian Church, St. Louis:

BELOVED BRETHREN: I have the honor and pleasure to report that I have presented to the General Assembly sitting in the Second Church the commission with which I was honored by our General Assembly of last year, to convey to that body the fraternal salutations of our own.

I was received by the Moderator of that body, Rev. Dr. Stanton, with a degree of fraternal kindness quite remarkable, both personally and officially. I was abundantly satisfied by the reception accorded to me, and I am sure that the published report of Dr. Stanton's address will abundantly satisfy all my constituents.

I need not speak ot the delightful meeting of the two Assemblies, on a subsequent evening, to the members of this Assembly who were present, but may be permitted most thankfully to say that it seemed to me that the clock of Presbyterian history then struck, ringing in a new era of peace and love.

Most respectfully, H. A. NELSON.

Dr. Hatfield next read a letter, received after the last session of the General Assembly, accompanying a communication from the General Assembly of the Free Church of Scotland, and also the communication, as follows:

To the General Assembly of the Presbyterian Church in the United States, N. S.

DEAR CHRISTIAN BRETHREN: We take advantage of the meeting of our General Assembly at present convened, to greet you cordially in the name of the Lord. We feel constrained to do so in consequence of the singularly momentous character of recent events in your country, and of their mighty influence on your respective churches. It may be premature to say much, as the echoes of war have scarce yet died away, and the future may be, in other ways, as eventful as these four years of conflict; but, without anticipating Providence, we have a plain Christian duty to discharge, in consequence of what falls already within the province of history.

"God has assuredly been speaking to your country by terrible things in righteousness. The plowshare of war has gone deep into the soul of your people. You have been long familiar with scenes of bloodshed, such as the world never saw before, and we pray God, if consistent with his holy will, it may never witness again. But, even in this respect, good has come out of evil; for the agony and ruin of war have opened up to you many new fields of Christian philanthropy. We refer in particular to the work of your 'Christian Commission,' with its rich provision for the temporal and spiritual wants of your soldiers and sailors; and we hope that all churches shall profit by this noble exhibition of Christian love in a singularly arduous and self sacrificing sphere of labor.

"We have special pleasure in referring to the sympathy lately awakened on behalf of America among all classes in Britain, by the assassination of your great and good President; and we adore the Most High, who has thus turned one of the blackest crimes of our age into a means of softening down asperities of feeling, of correcting grave misunderstandings, of fusing the hearts of nations in love, above all, of calling forth in full measure the prayers of Christ's people on this side of the Atlantic on behalf of your sorely-stricken land. We rejoice that your country is to have rest from war, and that the restoration of peace is to be followed by the abolition of slavery. No words could better express our views than those of your lamented President, written in April, 1864: 'I claim not to have controlled events, but confess plainly that events have controlled me. Now, at the end of three years' struggle, the nation's condition is not what either party, or any man devised or expected. God alone can claim it. Whither it is tending seems plain. If God now wills the removal of a great wrong, and wills also that we of the North, as well as you of the South, shall pay fairly for our complicity in that wrong, impartial history will find therein new causes to attest and revere the justice and goodness of God.' The divergence of sentiment and action formerly existing between you and us as to this question thus ceases, and we give the glory to Him, who is righteous in all His ways and holy in all His works. As there is really nothing now to prevent a complete and cordial understanding between the British and the American Churches, we take the earliest possible opportunity of giving utterance to this conviction and desire of our hearts. Our prayers shall rise with yours to the throne of grace in asking for your rulers and your people all heavenly wisdom in dealing with one of the weightiest social problems ever presented to any country for solution. We shall watch with the liveliest interest the future history of the negro race within your borders; and you have our best wishes for the success of every scheme bearing on their temporal or spiritual welfare. We are by no means forgetful of our former share of National guilt as to negro slavery, and it would ill become us to judge you harshly or unadvisedly. But, it is right and proper that we should encourage you by our British experience—for the abolition of slavery in our West India Islands removed a great stumbling block out of our path—it led to a marked quickening of the public conscience—it gave our country a far higher Christian place among the nations, and it enabled all the churches to proclaim with fullness and sincerity the gospel of salvation through Him, who came to undo the heavy burdens and to break every yoke. We have no doubt that your churches will be ready to follow where Providence now points the way.

"As the General Assembly of the Free Church

of Scotland, we have every cause to reciprocate sentiments of brotherly kindness and charity towards members of the same Presbyterian family with ourselves. We must all feel the necessity for closer fellowship between churches that have a common language, a common ancestry, a common faith. Presbyterianism would thereby become vastly more influential for good. It would bulk more largely in the eye of Christendom and every section of our ecclesiastical commonwealth would get enlargement of heart by partaking of the heritage of truth and grace common to all. We beg to add that the greatest advantage would follow from the occasional visits of accredited deputies from your churches to us, and from us to you. We have much to learn from your varied schemes of Christian usefulness in dealing with a state of society so different from ours; and we know from the testimony of Dr. Duff and many others, that in the field of heathenism there are no missionaries of more truly apostolic spirit than those sent forth by the churches of America. You on your part might also find it not unprofitable to study the working of Presbyterianism in Scotland, fragrant as our beloved country is with the memories of the martyrs, and earnestly contending, as it still does, for the faith once delivered to the Saints. We must not forget, however, that there are other churches beyond the circle of Presbyterianism, with which we desire to cultivate a spirit of concord, and from the field of whose experience we seek to gather like precious fruit. Let us provoke one another to love and to good works. Let us strive, as in the fire, to prevent at any subsequent time the possibility of estrangement between our respective nations. Let us pray that the same blessed spirit, poured down so largely on your land during the period of your revival, may become the living bond of unity and peace between us. And let us ever realize the solemn fact that, humanly speaking, the Christian interests of the world hang mainly on the efforts put forth by Christ's people in Great Britain and America.

"And now, dear brethren, we beseech the God of all grace to overrule these shakings of the nations for the up building of that kingdom which cannot be moved; and we affectionately commend you to Him who will give strength to His people, and who will bless His people with peace. For of Him, and through Him, and to Him, are all things—to whom be glory forever and ever. Amen.

"Signed in name and by authority of the Free Church of Scotland, at Edinburg, the thirtieth day of May, in the year one thousand eight hundred and ixty-five, by James Begg, D. D., Moderator of the General Assembly of the Free Church of Scotland."

Dr. Hatfield. I have the honor to move that this communication be accepted, and that a response be prepared by a committee appointed by the Moderator, to be sent to the Free Church of Scotland, and that this communication be printed in the appendix to the minutes of this Assembly. Adopted.

Dr. Hatfield then read a communication from several members of the Free church of Scotland, introducing to American Christians Rev. Dr. McCosh, of Belfast, Ireland. Dr. Hatfield stated that James McCosh, L. L. D., was present, and called upon him to address the Assembly.

The Assembly rose to receive Dr. McCosh as he ascended the platform. His address was marked with deep feeling and earnestness, and was listened to with profound attention and respect, and greeted with frequent applause. He explained that he did not come officially as a delegate from any church, but, wearied with his writing and his classes, having visited repeatedly the Continent, and not feeling inclined there again, he felt a longing to spend his vacation in visiting some new country, that he might have a glimpse of the future that is before the world. He had taken part with this great nation in its great struggle. In his little field of influence, both as an author and speaker, he had declared his attachment to the cause, and had never for a moment doubted of our success. He was anxious to see the country engaged in the great work of reconstruction. Such were the motives which induced him to come to this country; but when it became known among his friends that he was about to proceed to the United States, he received communication after communication, asking that he might accomplish another end. The Evangelical Alliance had a meeting for the special purpose, and enjoined upon him to say to American Christians how much it was desired, on account of that Alliance, that the American and British churches should be brought into a more thorough understanding and unity. His friends forwarded to him the letter which had been read. He had been received by the two bodies that have met in this place in a way altogether disproportionate to his position as an individual, but nevertheless accepted it all because he knew it proceeded from genuine and loving hearts, and because he regarded it as a declaration of respectful feeling towards the British churches. He would take care to repeat this to the British Churches, and he knew the general body of them will receive it with joy. Declared that America and Great Britain were bound together by strong bands—were one in race, one in liberty, and one in the love of education, and especially and above all, one in believing in one God and one Savior; that the Presbyterians in both countries were one in faith, discipline, and polity generally. He referred to the troubles of the Church in Scotland, and to some facts in his own history, illustrating what the Churches in Great Britain had had to contend with, and passed to the present condition of the Churches. The Free Church of Scotland, though not a numerous body, had contributed for the year ending May 1st, 1865, the sum of £350,000 for the support of the gospel; had set going a general sustaining fund for poor congregations, a benevolence instituted by Dr. Chalmers, which had been carried on with great vigor and liberality, and to which the church contributed in 1865, £180,000, and for 22 years ending May, 1865, the total sum of £6,000,000. The Free Church of Scotland had been instrumental in bringing about a state of things that looked to the union of all the churches of like faith and government not only in the United Kingdom, but in the Colonies, and the speaker took the opportunity to say that the British churches were most anxious to be in some way officially connected with the Presbyterian bodies in this country, by having delegates reciprocally accredited to the General Assemblies who might have a voice and a vote on the more important questions of general interest to the church.

Dr. Hatfield moved that the suggestion of Dr.

McCosh be referred to the committee about to be appointed, to answer the letter received from the Free Church of Scotland. Carried.

The Moderator announced that action upon the report of the Committee on Church Erections was in order.

Russell Scarrett, Esq., moved to reconsider the action of the Assembly whereby it voted to accept the report of the committee, and to go into its consideration article by article, and stated that he did so for the purpose of moving the adoption of the following plan:

1. To repeal, as to the guidance and control of the future operations of the committee, all present laws or instructions of the Assembly.

2. That this committee be the channel through which our denomination may do its work of church erection as fully and finally as it does its home missionary work through its Home Missionary committee.

3. That this committee may freely loan and donate its funds for the erection of churches according to its ability, and the need of the churches, making its own rules, only limited as follows:

First. It shall execute its duties, both in respect to its present and future funds, in conformity with the spirit of its trust and the obligations of its charter.

Second. It shall not reduce the fund by donations to a less amount than $100,000,

Third. It shall not loan or donate to any one church an aggregate sum of more than $3,000

Fourth. That it shall not charge interest on loans until from and after the maturity of the debt.

Fifth. That loans shall not be for a longer term than five years, reasonably secured on real estate.

4. That this Assembly appoint a Secretary, or agent, who shall be to this work what Dr. Kendall is to the Home Missionary work.

Dr. Humphrey, chairman of the Committee on Church Erection, rose to explain how it happened that the report of the committee appeared in the Democrat this morning, though the Assembly had recconsidered its vote to publish it. He said he found on consultation with the reporter of the Democrat, the reporter was unwilling to pledge himself that it should appear in the paper of Tuesday morning, unless the report of the remainder of the proceedings were omitted, but nevertheless thought that it might be done, though he was unwilling to take the responsibility of saying so; that he (Dr. H.) immediately took the papers and went to the office of the Demscrat, and while he was gone the resolution to reconsider was passed.

The result was that the report in full, and a condensed form of the plan wsa published in the morning papers, notwithstanding the decision of the Assembly. Dr. H. further stated that any change in the existing plan would require a two-thirds vote. in number about 150.

After prayer, the Assembly adjonrned until afternoon.

AFTERNOON SESSION.

Opened with prayer.

Mr. Scarritt's motion of the morning to reconsider prevailed, and after some discussion as to what was before the Assembly, the Moderator decided that the question was upon the adoption or rejection of the report of the Committee on Church Erections.

Mr. Scarritt addressed the Assembly at length in regard to the management of the fund, claiming that the existing plan looked more to the continuance and reservation of the fund than to the building of churches, and illustrating the need of a change in the plan of administering the fund by reference to the congregation of Webster Grove. Was opposed to the adoption of the report of the Committee because it wouldn't build the churches.

Dr. Humphrey stated that the Committee in framing the report and recommendation, was in full sympathy with the last speaker in the desire to make the utmost amount of money available for the erection of churches, and claimed that those who were in the cities could understand the state of the case as well as those in the country, for they were continually receiving applications for assistance which press upon them the necessity which he has urged to-day, and it certainly is their desire to relieve the people from these incessant calls, though they would be willing that they should give more than they have been accustomed to give in a desultory way. It had been the desire of the committee throughout to propose and bring forward to the Assembly such a plan as would secure the largest possible amount for the churches, and on such terms as would be most favorable to them. He stated that the plan placed no restriction upon the trustees in loaning any amount whatever to any Church, if they considered in their judgments as business men that the Church could afford to give good security for the money. He explained at length the difficulties that arose from churches contracting loans, both as it regarded the churches hemselves and the fund.

Dr. Clarke opposed the plan as recommended by the Committee. He claimed that this $100,000 should, in the shortest possible time, be put into the form of churches, and not continued in the form of a fund; that the churches of the East would respond to all calls when once this amount was exhausted; that of the $5,000 proposed to be expended each year, Missouri would receive two and a half per cent, and asked what kind of a provision that was for church erection in this great State? Proposed that the whole amount should be loaned out to churches in average sums of $1,000 for ten years, which would build at least eighty ohurches within the next year, and, as the yearly installments became due and were paid, would build eight churches each year thereafter.

Judge Williams, of Pittsburg, advocated the adoption of the report, which he stated had been drawn up in accordance with the legal opinions as reported by the Permanent Committee.

The discussion was further continued by Messrs. Hebard, Tyndall and Foot, when the hour of adjournment arrived.

Mr. Starr, at the request of R. R. Kellogg, gave the following notice in regard to the excursion on Thursday:

The depot of the Iron Mountain railroad is on Plum street and Main about half a mile below the termination of Olive Street. Persons who desire to go must be present at the depot by 6.30 in the morning. The street cars do not generally run so early as that in the morning and they will have to start earlier on foot from the north and west parts of the city.

All persons must be punctual as the cars will start at the minute specified.

There are no accomodations except a well of water at the mountain, and a spring at Pilot Knob. All persons must bring their own provisions, as the company does nothing but furnish transportation. It is hoped that the train will reach the city on its return by 6 o'clock in the evening. The committee have sent special invitations to such of the hosts as can be conveyed in the train.

After prayer by the Moderator the Assembly adjourned.

[The following report, read in Monday's session of the New School Presbyterian Assembly, but crowded out of yesterday's issue, is published to-day by special request.]

The standing committee to whom was referred the Second Annual Report of the Executive Committee of the Ministerial Relief Fund, respectfully report:

That they have had the same under careful consideration, and find in it much cause for gratitude to Almighty God for the success which has already crowned our efforts in this matter, and much also for serious thought in view of that which remains to be done.

The report of the Executive Committee shows that the General Assembly did not move one moment too soon to provide for the wants of her disabled ministers and their families—we now wonder that it was a subject neglected so long—and shows also how ready the Church as are to respond to this just appeal when once it is brought before them. It is no small thing that, with so little effort, the contributions to this cause should have doubled in the past year.

And yet it is manifest that we have but just made a reasonable beginning in the work thus committed to our hands. There must be many clergymen and families of deceased ministers in want, whose cases are not yet reached. Many cannot yet know that such relief is provided for their need, or how to obtain it; and many of the Churches manifestly do not seem to know that such a fund has been projected, and needs their generous contributions, for only 180 out of the 1,479 Churches connected with this Assembly have remembered this cause in the past year.

Your Committee are confident that if all our Churches could have heard the reading of the report of the Executive Committee, as it was presented to this body, or could look in upon some of the families of dear and honored ministers of the gospel whose wants were presented, there woald hardly be a church in all our connection which would fail to remember this cause by a generous contribution.

Your Committee are sure that this subject is not yet before our Churches as it should be, and has not that consideration which its great importance demands.

To express the sense of the Assembly on this subject, your Committee propose the following resolutions:

Resolved, That the ministers of our Churches be requested, at an early day, to preach upon the subject of the Ministerial Relief Fund, calling the attention of their people to these peculiar wants, for which this fund aims to provide.

Resolved, That it be considered the duty of every Church to take an annual collection for this cause.

Resolved, That the attention of the Presbyteries be again called to this subject, and that they be earnestly requested each year to appoint one of their own number specially to look after this matter, and to see, if possible, that collections be taken in all the Churches within their bounds.

Resolved, That the Executive Committee be instructed to publish their annual report, or an abstract thereof, in the religious newspapers, for the information of the Churches.

All which is respectfully submitted,

In behalf of the Committee

CHAS. P. BUSH, Chairman.

SIXTH DAY—WEDNESDAY, MAY 23, 1866.

Minutes of last session read and approved.

The unfinished business of yesterday was taken up.

Rev. W. A. Niles spoke in support of the Church Erection Committee's report. He deprecated any slighting allusions to the Church Erection Fund, as if it had not cost sacrifices and great labor, and was not the result of large benevolence; and deprecated very much the position that some have taken, that it was better this fund were drowned in the depths of the sea. This fund had done too much for the Presbyterian Church—was a noble fund in its origin, and had been nobly administered, whatever may be said about it, because it had been administered strictly on the principles on which it had been established. He referred to the history of this fund, the disposition of the donors of the fund towards the Western Churches; to his own experience with regard to its early workings and to the good it had done; to the fact that all the Church Erection Funds in the land are but the result of this present fund, which was secured at great sacrifice, and had aided so many churches. He asked that this fund of $100,000 should not be regarded as a small thing; could not see why a Church should object to a permanent fund; claimed that circumstances had changed, and it was desirable that there should be a great deal more money expended by the Presbyterian Church for building sanctuaries.

The speaker next adverted to the objections which come up year by year to the administrations of this fund; that the great objection was to the loaning system; that loaning had the effect of estranging the Churches; the dunning letters of the Secretary became so distasteful that he failed to get answers to them, and had to resort to writing to the postmasters as to the existence of the churches assisted and their conditions. Another objection was to the smallness of the amount either as a donation or a loan.

There were three distinct propositions before the Committee. The first proposition gave the whole fund away. It was said that Daniel Lord had given it as his opinion that the money could be given away; other lawyers said you could not give it away, that the trustees could not give it away upon the order of the General Assembly without rendering themselves liable as such trustees, and it was understood that if such course were attempted, there would be applications in the courts for injunctions, and consequently that plan was laid aside as impracticable. The next plan presented was the enlarged old plan—the recommendation of the Board of Trustees and of the standing committee of last year—but this plan was a system of loans. and the cry from all sides was don't touch it at all. The Committee were urged to make a radical change in the plan. Other denominations were *giving* money to build churches, and to maintain its position this Church must do so too. The loaning system had proved a failure, and the next proposition, the one adopted by the Committee, was to *give*. And *giving*, to give how much? All the law would allow. It was thought that the increase of the fund was not a part of the fund, and that the increase could legally be given.

Dr. Humphrey interrupted the speaker to say that the amount of money uncollected already, it was thought, would not be legally construed as a part of the fund, but subject to gift.

A member rose to ask information. I wish to ask if in the old plan the entire fund may not be loaned to the churches in sums of $500? and is not that Committee competent, according to their understanding of the term donation, to give the whole sum to the churches in sums of $200?

Moderator. If I understand the questions, I answer the first in the affirmative, an the second in the negative.

Mr. Niles, continued to say that if the Church would go to work earnestly in the matter they could raise a sufficiently large sum of money in addition to the proceeds of the fund to accomplish the desired ends. If the secretary of the trustees have an opportunity to present his claims before the Churches, $40,000, $50,000 or $60,000, could annually be raised for this object.

Here John A. Foot moved that a vote be taken upon this report of the committee at half past 11 o'clock, and by an amendement to the motion speeches were limited to five minutes. Carried.

Rev. P. S. Van Nest offered a resolution as a substitute to the motion before the Assembly, to the effect that this Assembly enjoins upon the presbyteries under its care or within its jurisdiction, that at their first meetings, respectively, after this injunction shall reach them, they shall take action upon the question, shall the General Assembly make application to the Legislature of the State of New York for the repeal of the charter in such a manner that the fund can be donated to the feeble Churches belonging to it; that the General Assembly at this session appoint a committee whose duty it shall be to make such application to the Legislature of New York after three fourths of the presbyteries shall, have voted affirmatively upon, the proposition and that said committee report action to the next General Assembly.

Hon. J. Allison stated that the resolution was wholly impracticable; that neither the General Assembly, nor the Presbyterian, nor the State of New York, through its Legislature, have a right to touch that fund in the manner proposed, for any such action would be impairing the integrity of a trust.

Mr. Benedict explained that the trust was created by the resolutions of this Assembly, passed in 1863, and that the Assembly having accepted the trust by those resolutions, no power on earth could alter it; that the difficulty was not in altering the charter or altering the plan, but in impairing the obligation of the trust which imposed the necessity of retaining this as a permanent fund; that the difficulties experienced by the churches who had sought and received assistance from the fund arose not so much from the plan as from their disobedience of the regulations of the Assembly with regard to this fund; that the churches which had strictly followed the regulations had always been thankful for the assistance rendered, and those churches only were in trouble who had incurred large indebtedness in addition to their indebtedness to this plan.

At the request of the Assembly, Mr. Benedict read the resolutions referred to in his remarks. The question was put upon the substitute of Mr. Van Nest, and it was rejected. Rev. Henry Fowler thought that Western men were mistaken in following the lead of Dr. Clarke of Buffalo, and deserted their representative on this floor, Dr. Humphrey of Chicago; that the Committee on Church Erection had been constituted with special reference to the interests of the West; that the plan proposed by the committee was the best thing that could be done; that not $50,000, but $100,000, ought to be raised this year in the Churches for Church erection: called to mind the objection of Dr. Clarke that the Churches would not give as long as this fund was unexpended, and asked if the permanent fund of the A. B. C. F. M., the Bible and Tract Societies were obstacles in the way of collections for these objects; was sure that Dr. Clarke could take $10,000 or $100,000out of the pockets of his people in Buffalo for this object, and if he would raise $10,000 in Buffalo, pledged another $10,000 from Auburn, and was confident of another $10,000 from Rochester.

Mr. Hebard asked if the proposition made by the Committee was understood by the trustees to be in harmony with the resolutions just read by Mr. Benedict?

Mr. Benedict replied that there had been a difference of opinion among the trustees on that point, but the legal opinion that had been given declared the plan proposed to be in accordance with the resolutions.

Dr. Clarke, after reference to the *poetic* remarks of Mr. Fowler, and to the experiment of raising a Church Erection Supplemental Fund last year, proposed, as an amendment to the Committee's report, the adoption of the recommendations of the Permanent Committee, made in its annual report, upon the tenth page of that report, with this modification, striking out from Article XIV, (already published,) the words "nor exceed the sum of $750, nor shall the amount given to any congregation as a donation be in any case more than $300."

Mr. Allison reiterated the evils of the loan sytem of administering the fund: stated the object of the committee to have been, while observing the resolutions of 1863, to get rid of this loan system, which has been the cause of all this discontent which has come up to this Assembly, and which is the only demon which it is necessary for us to cast out. When this is done, and by means of the proper machinery this matter is laid before the Churches, a supplemental fund can be raised.

In the course of his remarks the speaker spoke feelingly against repudiation, and the violation of the trusts under which this fund exists, and warned the Assembly against following the suggestions to that end, at the same time looking and gesticulating towards Dr. Clarke.

Dr. Clarke called the gentleman to order, and desired him to retract the charge that he (Dr. C.) had advocated repudiation or violation of any trust.

Mr. Allison stated that he did not mean to impugn the motives of Dr. Clarke or intimate that he intended any such result to his suggestions, but simply to say that the suggestions made by him would have that effect.

The hour of half after eleven having arrived, it was voted that the vote be further postponed until twelve o'clock, and that the speakers be confined to three minutes each.

Dr. Knox thought it the duty of the Assembly to attend to its character as regards the permanency of the fund; and that the East and the West could join together in this good work of putting into the hands of the Committee funds for church erection just as far as their necessities shall demand.

Rev. E. B. Miner declared the whole system of loans a perfect failure; was from a Presbytery which had not a self-supporting Church, and there was not a Church in the Presbytery of Columbus that would ever derive any benefit from this fund from loans.

A Member. We do not want loans. If we refuse to follow the example of the Congregational and Old School Church in giving our money, we shall be compelled to give it through another channel. I am one of a Church which is saddled with one of these debts, but for which, and with a very small donation a year ago, it would have been self-supporting, and not obliged to rely upon the Home Missionary Society.

Another member lived in a neighborhood where most of the children had never seen a church, but the congregation met in schoolhouses. He was opposed to the system of loans, and favored the report of the Committee; thought that the cause of his Presbytery was being decided to-day.

Mr. Bailey made a proposal that the money should be loaned to the churches without limitation of amount or time, with the expectation of having it returned again when the church is able to do so.

Mr. Whittaker heartily endorsed the amendment as proposed by Dr. Clarke.

Judge Williams opposed the amendment of Dr. Clarke.

The question was about to be put by the Moderator upon the amendment, when it was suggested that the time had arrived for voting upon the adoption of the Committee's report, and the Moderator decided that the question should be taken upon the motion to adopt the report.

On an appeal from the decision of the Moderator, the Moderator was sustained.

The Assembly having adopted the report by a majority vote, it was suggested that as the report involved a change in the plan a two-thirds vote was necessary. The roll was then called and the vote was announced 180 ayes, 9 noes, absent or not voting 26.

It was voted to take up the amendements in the plan proposed by the committee at half past three in the afternoon and vote upon them at half after four.

An additional annoncement in regard to the excursion was made, and after prayer, the Assembly adjourned until afternoon.

AFTERNOON SESSION.

Opened with prayer by Dr. Campbell.
Minutes were read and approved.

The report of the special committee on manses and ministers' libraries was then read by Dr. J. G. Butler, as follows:

Rev. J. Glentworth, D. D., Chairman of Special Committee on Manses and Ministerial Libraries, made the following report:

The Special Committee on Manses and Ministerial Libraries, respectfully report:

That in the autumn of last year a circular of inquiry was forwarded and sent to 700 pastors, and stated supplies, and also published in our religious journals. To these circulars 100 replies have been received. From these replies, it appears that one-fifth of the churches have manses, and one-tenth have libraries for the use of ministers.

These replies convey a strong impression of the great importance of the subject matter of the circular, and express the hope that the General Assembly will use every means in its power to bring the subject before, and urge it upon the attention and practical regard of the churches. They also suggest the idea of creating a general fund for the erection of manses.

Without expressing any opinion upon the expediency of the latter suggestion, your committee deem it both advisable and practicable to bring the matter definitely before the churches through the action of the Presbyteries.

They therefore recommend the adoption of the following resolutions:

Resolved, 1. That this General Assemely direct its Presbyteries to send to the churches under their care a pastoral letter of inquiry, and suggestions with reference to the provision of a manse and a library for the use of the member in charge of each congregation.

2. That the Presbyteries be requested to embody in a report to the next General Assembly any information that may be obtained in the answers to the proposed inquiry, with their judgment concerning the creation of a manse fund, and also any practical suggestions appertaining to the subject matter of manses and ministerial libraries.

All of which is respectfully submitted.

J. GLENTWORTH BUTLER,
Z. M. HUMPHREY.

The report of the committee was adopted.

Dr. Butler. I move that J. M. Wilson, who has labored in this matter at his own cost for many years out of a simple interest in this great matter, be invited to address the Assembly for a few minutes. Carried.

Joseph M. Wilson thanked the Assembly for the privilege of speaking in behalf of manses and ministers' libraries. Having introduced the subject to the Assembly of 1862, he had been identified with the prosecution of the enterprise ever since. The proper support of the ministry is involved in the question, as well as the liberal sustentation of the various objects of benevolence which characterize the Church. The large amount paid by the ministry for rent is equal to the whole amount contributed by the Churches to the various objects of benevolence, and it is to be hoped that thoughtful and earnest men in the Church would take up this interesting subject. In connection with manses will be found libraries in the manse. He spoke of forming periodical associations, formed of members of Bible classes and Sabbath school teachers, and set forth clearly how there is work for every one in a well ordered congregation.

The report of the Committee was then adopted, and the Committee continued.

Mr. Fowler, of the standing Committee on Sabbath Schools, read the report of that Committee, as follows:

The Standing Committee on Sabbath Schools respectfully submit the following report:

This Committee is now constituted for the first time in the history of our Church, in consequence of overtures from Presbyteries, in accordance with the desire of many members of the Churches, and by order of the General Assembly of 1864.

The Committee do not hesitate to assume that the Assembly appreciates the value and discerns the scope of the sabbath school as the auxiliary of the pulpit in the salvation of souls, as oftentimes its forerunner in the providing of churches, and at all times its best substitute when the strength of Christ's collected followers may not be sufficient to sustain the stated preaching of the Word.

We believe that the Sabbath School is the nursery of the Christian Church, one bulwark of Christian doctrine, a promoter of Christian union, and the organizer of Christian labor. In other words, it saves the young, it secures the faith, it settles differences, and it develops power.

The first proposition is made manifest by the fact that of 5,086 members belonging to 311 churches (which have the last year reported to the Committee of Inquiry, appointed by the Eldership), 2,387 were added from the Sabbath School.

The second proposition is evidenced by comparison of the lapsed convictions of churches without Sabbath Schools with the sound faith of those which sustain them. Sabbath School work is the healthy outgrowth of a grounded faith; the branches, leaves and fruit return vitality to the root.

The third proposition is seen in the happy union existing between the members of different and of the same denominations who join in Sabbath School enterprises. Diversities are ignored; agreements multiply; they sing the same Zion-songs; they meet at the same mercy seat; they speak from the same platform; they fraternize at the union convention; there is one book, the Bible; one Lord, who said "Suffer the children;" one Savior, who is the way, the truth, and the life.

The fourth proposition is demonstrated from individual experience as well as church experience. The young Christian who lays hold of mission school work grows in knowledge and grace, with no stinted increase, sometimes the sad sequel of a vigorous germination. The older Christian, becoming a Sabbath School teacher, exchanges spiritual sluggishness for an inspiriting vitality. The Church with a good Sabbath School, even though in the present small, is master of the situation.

In view of these considerations, the Assembly has ordered the appointment of a permanent Committee on Sabbath Schools. It is recommended that their duties (subject to future modification or enlargement) shall be:

1. To supervise the Sabbath School literature of the Church, in co-operation with the Permanent Committee on Publication. Their recommendation will promote the circulation of the many good books; their disapproval will eliminate the few not good books; their suggestions will open new classes of subjects upon which books may be written; and even their silence will discourage the use of weak and wordy trash,

2. To issue circulars which may help the cause, and use other appropriate methods of the press.

3. To collect data, and from facts to work out practical theses, which may assist pastors, superintendents and teachers in the Sabbath School work.

4. To promote the establishment of Sabbath Schools in localities needing them, within the bounds of the Assembly, among the freedmen of the South and the Germans of the West, in co-operation with the Permanent Committee on Home Missions.

5. To promote the Sabbath School cause in heathen lands in co-operation with the American Board of Commissioners for Foreign Missions.

6. To promote the establishment of Sabbath Schools in Mexico, Central America, France, Italy and Germany, in co-operation with the American and Foreign Christian Union.

7. To promote the increase of the Ministry through influence brought to bear upon the Sabbath Schools, and thus prove an auxiliary of the Education Committee.

Your committee further recommend that the Presbyteries be instructed by General Assembly to appoint a Presbyterial Committee on Sabbath Schools, whose duty it shall be to attend to the interests of the Sabbath School cause within the bounds of Presbytery, and that such committee report itself for instructions to the Permanent Committee.

Your committee pass over to the Permanent Committee the consideration of two propositions suggested by members of the Assembly. 1st—The devising of a plan to be presented to the next General Assembly by which the students of our Theological Seminaries may receive special instruction in the relations of the Pastor to the Sabbath School, in the best modes of conducting Sabbath Schools and in the approved methods of Sabbath School work. 2d—The devising of a plan to be presented to the next General Assembly for the establishment of Normal Schools for the instruction of Sabbath School teachers.

It is also recommended that the Publication Committee be authorized to send the publications of our Church to the Sabbath School Committee, in response to their address.

Your Committee, in the selection of names for the Permanent Committee, have been coutrolled by the considerations, 1st, that a majority of the Committee should be within easy call from a favorable center. 2d, that the members of the Committee shall not be preoccupied on other permanent committees.

The following nomination is submitted: James B. Shaw, D. D., Grosvenor W. Heacock, D. D., Charles Hawley, D. D., William E. Knox, D. D., Samuel M. Campbell, D. D., Rev. Charles P. Bush, Rev. William A. Niles, Rev. Marvin R. Vincent, Rev. Charles E. Knox, Ralph Wells, E. F. Huntington, George W. Parsons, Josiah P. Bailey, Truman P. Handy, Samuel Field.

In conclusion it is recommended that the Permanent Committee hold its first meeting at Rochester, New York. at the call of the stated Clerk of the Assembly; that it be guided in its action by the practice and rules of the other Permanent Committees, and that its expenses for the first year be met by individual subscriptions from residents of Western and Central New York.

All of which is veey respectfully submitted in behalf of the Committee.

HENRY FOWLER, Chairman.

Mr. Edward Winans invited the members of the Assembly to attend the devotional exercises held at the City University, commencing at half past eight o'clock in the morning.

Mr. Kendall moved a reconsideration of the vote by which Thursday was appointed as the day for the excursion to Pilot Knob, and stated as his reason that he thought it was going to rain, which would interfere very much with the health of the Assembly; and more particularly because there was so much business still to be attended to, and that by Friday a large number of the members expect to leave, particularly the elders, upon whom so much dependence is made to take hold of the home missionary cause which is yet to be considered by the Assembly. He thought the matter could be set before the kind friends who had projected this excursion in such a manner as to prevent any ill feeling or suspicion of discourtesy.

After considerable discussion regarding the amount of business still to be done by the Assembly on the one hand, and the impropriety of reconsidering the vote at this time, when all the preparation had been made, both by the railroad company and the hosts of the Assembly the motion to reconsider was rejected by a large majority.

The recommended changes in the "plan" of church erection, as made by the standing committee on that subject, (published in our issue of Tuesday,) were then considered, article by article, and after much discussion and close questioning of the committee, and of Mr. Benedict, Secretary of the Trustees, as to the intent and effect of the proposed changes, the recommendation of the Committee was adopted by a vote of 172 to 20, with one amendment, viz: the striking out of the words "of its members" from the article providing for the appointment of a committee.

Voted that the Trustees be instructed to appoint a suitable person as Secretary, as required by the amended plan.

Voted that the first order of the day for Friday morning be to hear the report of the Committee on Educatioh.

Voted that the amended plan for church erection take effect on the first of August next.

Dr. Nelson gave notice, with explanations of the arrangements which had been made for the conveyance by railroad and boat of the members of the Assembly, free of charge, on their return, upon certificates of their having been in attendance upon the Assembly, and having paid full fare on the same road or boat in coming to St. Louis.

After prayer, the Assembly adjourned until Friday morning at 9 o'clock.

The following appointment was inadvertently ommitted in our report of the proceedings of Tuesday afternoon:

The Moderator appointed the following as the Committee of Arrangements for the next General Assembly:

Rev. J. B. Shaw, DD., Rev. J. W. Campbell, Rev. C. P. Bush and Louis Chapin.

SEVENTH DAY—FRIDAY, MAY 25, 1866.

MORNING SESSION.

Met at 9 o'clock.

First hour spent in devotional exercises.

Minutes were read and approved.

Rev. Dr. Curtis read the report of the standing Committee on Education.

REPORT OF THE STANDING COMMITTEE ON EDUCATION.

The Standing Committee on Education for the Gospel Ministry report that they have given their attention to the annual report of the Permanent Committee on Education, which was placed in their hands.

They find gratifying evidence of enlargement in both directions—that of means and that of candidates for the ministry. The amount of funds is about the same as last year. The increase in young men is 35 per cent. Though the amount paid to each young man is considerably in advance of former years, as ordered by the last General Assembly, the Permanent Committee have been enabled to fulfill their engagements. No suitable applicant for aid has been turned away empty. It is believed the importance of the educational cause in successfully carrying forward the Kingdom of Christ is being more generally realized, and a deeper and more permanent state of feeling is being awakened on the subject.

Nevertheless, notwithstanding all that is calculated to cheer our hearts, and encourage the Permanent Committee to go forward in their chosen work, the pressing demands of the Church in this direction have not been met. All our efforts are disproportionate to the calls of Providence. At the present rate of bringing forward young men into the ministry, the vacancies made by the superannuated and the dead only are filled. When it is considered how many are taken from the active duties of the ministry to become presidents and professors in our colleges, instructors in our theological seminaries, and secretaries and agents in our benevolent operations (and there seems to be no better way), and the number who turn aside through failure of health, it is not surprising that the demand should outrun the supply, not to mention the wants of the slave States.

When we consider the fields that are constantly opening before us in the newer portions of the country, the case is truly alarming. Our excellent Secretary of Home Missions tells us in his report that we have no missionary in Idaho, Utah, Arizona, Washington and the State of Oregon—not because there are not calls for men, but because the men cannot be found. The report also on Foreign Missions speaks of an equal want of men for the missionary work abroad. They cry for men, almost frantic, from East Tennessee uttered on this floor still rings in our ears. The claims of the freedmen, also, for a preached Gospel cannot be ignored.

Standing, as we do, at the confluence of the Mississippi and Missouri, pouring their flood-tide of waters at our feet to the ocean; turning the eye from this central position to the North, the West and the South; viewing the present population and the long lines of emigration, both home and foreign, passing up these mighty rivers and their numerous tributaries; marking the moral forces already at work on this field, the man of sin, as in this city, strongly intrenched with churches, schools and institutions for charitable purposes, and commanding millions of money, the old fanaticism of the early Church revived on the banks of the Rhine in the form of Rationalism and Pantheism now transplanted and made to flourish on American soil, and the motley crew of materialism and infidelity of indigenous origin—contemplating all this, the educational course in preparing men for the ministry becomes of vital importance, because in its related aspects, and in the interests dependent upon an educated ministry, the educational course should receive far more of the prayers and contributions of the Church. Pious parents should dedicate their sons to the ministry. The elders should seek out promising young men, and confer with them on the subject. Pastors should confer with young men recently converted to God, and roll the burden of preaching the Gospel upon their hearts. Presbyterian committees on this subject should be more faithful. Scholarships to the amount of $2,500 each should be secured, the interest of which will yield the annual appropriation to one young man.

The day of fasting and prayer for colleges, seminaries and other institutions of learning should be more generally observed. Collections not in a few but in all the churches should be statedly taken up. The plan of the General Assembly is a good one and has worked well. It is only needful that Presbyteries, and pastors, and churches be more faithful in putting it into operation.

The committee would recommend the adoption of the following resolutions:

Resolved, 1. That the demand for educated ministers in our country was never greater than at the present time.

Resolved, 2. That the educational cause should occupy a higher place in the estimation of pastors and the Church.

Resolved, 3. That the day of fasting and prayer for colleges and other institutions of learning be faithfully observed; that pious parents consecrate their sons to the work of the ministry; that this subject be annually presented from the pulpit; and that continual prayer be offered to the Lord of the harvest, that he will send forth many more laborers into his harvest.

Resolved, 4. That the appropriation to young men for the past year be the same, namely: 33 per cent above what the rule requires; $160 to a theological; $130 to a collegiate, and $100 to a preparatory student.

The names of the following persons are presented to fill the vacancy occurring by the expiration of the term of office in the class elected in 1863: Rev. John J. Owen, Jonathan F. Stearns, Jesse W. Benedict, Wm. W. Wicks and Chas. Taylor.

As supplementary to their report, the committee report that they have examined the "Memorial of Union Presbytery to the General Assembly in relation to Maryville College," and also have listened to remarks from brethren in relation to other institutions of learning in East Tennessee.

The committee are gratified to see so much interest manifested in the subject of education, and express the hope that all these institutions may be retained in the service of the Church.

Resolved, That the general subject of education, in connection with our Church in East Tennessee, be favorably received by our churches, and that what funds may be raised shall be expended under the direction of the Presbyteries of East Tennessee, until the Synod of East Tennessee shall have taken the whole subject under its care.

Resolved, That this Assembly recommend the Rev. Lucius J. Root as an agent to raise funds for this object, according to the above resolution.

Rev. Dr. Mills, Secretary of the Permanent Committee on Education, addressed the Assembly, stating that there never was a greater want of ministers in the Presbyterian Church than at the present time; that thirty-two years ago he happened to preach in this city, and found here the Stated Clerk of this Assembly laboring as a missionary pastor, and any one who could contrast the present condition of the country with what it was then would have some idea of what there was to be accomplished; he called to mind the utterances of Rev. James Gallaher, who finished his earthly career in St. Charles, of this State, at an anniversary in Cincinnati. He had been called upon to make a home missionary speech, and closed his speech somewhat in this style: It occurred to me lately to stand at the confluence of the Mississippi and Missouri rivers. As I stood there I thought of the 3,000 miles that the Missouri had come, from the Rocky Mountains, to that meeting of the waters. I thought of the 1,800 miles that the Mississippi had come from the North to mingle its clearer waters with the more turbid stream of the Missouri. I thought of the 1,000 miles that the Ohio had come from the slopes of the Alleghanies to join this great meeting of waters, and the question came to my mind, "Shall this land be given up to Satan?" and raising his giant form he said, "I raised my hands to heaven and said, Lord Jesus, all this land shall be thine. The Church will never give up a foot of it, until every foot of it owns thy sway."

This work must be done by the ministry. Preachers are needed, until we have enough to evangelize the land.

The Lord has favored us with revivals, but the question comes, what will be the result of these revivals? will they increase the ministry largely? Fewer ministers came out of the revival of '57 than we hoped for. The report mentions that prayer was necessary. The Savior gave but one direction about the increase of the ministry, and that was, "when you need the ministry, go to God for it." A ministry is needed that shall be ready, in the strength of God, to undergo any and every sacrifice.

The congregation should be taught to pray for this object. There is rarely a prayer for this object offered at a General Assembly, until the matter has been brought forward and urged upon it. When he commenced his work as Secretary, he was advised to confer with Dr. Van Rensalaer, of the Old School Board, and he said the first thing to be done was to get the people to pray.

Thought that Satan had produced an extraordinary blindness of mind and hardness of heart in their matter. No good cause had ever prevailed in the Church and received its prayers and confidence, which had not first received the confidence and labors of the ministry. Out of 1200 churches but 334 had contributed during the last year. Some churches had begun to work well, and fallen away, thus denying the Calvanistic doctrine of the "perseverance of the saints."

Desired to call attention to the importance of giving due attention to the circulation of the Presbyterian Monthly; it had as yet but 3000 subscribers—ought to have 20,000. The Educational Manual ought to be widely distributed. It contained the whole plan of ministerial education.

There were some subjects that needed special preaching; one of them was the duty of a Christian people to educate their sons. Young men were now a days tempted away from the schools and colleges by business; another was the principles upon which young men should choose their professions for life! Related the instance of a minister in the State of New York, asking a wealthy merchant and Church member to educate his son for the ministry; the merchant replied, "There is a pen and ink and a check; you may sit down and fill up that check with any amount you think proper under $10,000, and you may have it for the cause, but you must not ask me for my son; I want to send him into finance."

A young man came into his office, last winter, and handed him a recommendation from one of the Presbyteries, stating that he had just received a note from his father, in which he refused to furnish him any more funds, though a member of the Church, and a man of abundant means, because the son had written him that it was his intention to go abroad and preach the Gospel to the heathen. There was a growing tendency in this direction, and ministers must preach on these matters.

Rev. J. F. Kendall remarked that the Home and Foreign Missionary Committees both complained of the want of men. They must be got from the Education Committee, and the Education Committee make the same complaint. The men must come from the churches. Ministers and elders must take an interest in this matter. He was rejoiced when the requests came in from Christian parents for the prayers of the Assembly that their sons might be raised up to the Christian ministry. Another want was money. Though there might be money enough for the present number of men, there wasn't enough to educate the number of men needed; was surprised to hear a brother say that he had never taken a contribution for this cause in his pulpit. Enjoined upon the ministers and elders to go home with this cause in their hearts, and ask that their churches might give to this cause.

The third want was a baptism of the Holy Ghost. It required the Holy Spirit in a young man's heart to turn him into the ministry, when there were so many avenues open before him to make money.

Mr. Scarritt thought that the idea that the young minister must sacrifice so much, was brought too prominently before young men and their fathers. He told his boys it was safer for their maintenance and comfort in life, and respectability of position, to devote themselves to God's ministry than as if their father was able to leave them a large fortune.

Rev. Mr. Smith of Kansas, stated that he had for 18 years been laboring on the border; alluded to the troubles and difficulties to be met with and which he had encountered, particularly during the war; that he only received a salary of $600—while laborers in the same community were receiving $2.50 or $3.00 a day. Did not wonder that young men were discouraged in view of such a life, yet for himself he preferred to labor in the West, in this great valley rather than in the East; affirmed that half a dozen men were now needed in Kansas, and as many churches might be built in that State during the next year, with a little assistance from this Assembly. Dr. Smith, regarded this as an important subject. We were entering upon a new era, which should be characterized essentially by the spread of education, intelligence and religious spirit and character of the nation. There must be educators in sufficient numbers, and of sufficient zeal to go wherever there were men to be educated in morals, and in religion. The great need of the Church was to raise up men for this emergency, to carry on this work. That was *the* great thing to be accomplished. There was money enough—the money would come, just as soon as the channels were prepared for it. Did not believe in extemporized educators—there was need of the best and wisest, the best trained men precisely in the van of the advance of the civilization of our land. Believed that the ministry was and alwas would be a self sacrificing body of men—would not have it otherwise. It was better for the Church and better for the land that those who engage in this work should give up something of the riches and comforts of this life. Young men who are willing to enter upon the ministry should be carried through their studies so as not to be saddled with a debt when peradventure they enter upon the work of preaching to a feeble Church and to be able to do that, the Theological Seminaries must be strengthened.

Mr. Edwards adverted to the fact that there were many churches from which there were never any contributions received. The reason was because the pastors neglected to bring the matter before them; cited his own Church, which had had a pastor for seven years who never asked them for a contribution towards any object whatever, alleging as a reason that the Church was too feeble to do more than support itself. The result was that the pastor's salary, about two years out of three, came out short, and the trustees had to make up the balance. At last he was induced to make the attempt, and the first year presented two objects of benevolence to the attention of the Church. He came in one morning, and without any previous announcement presented the subject of foreign missions, and collecied $91, and a few months after that presented the cause of home missions, in the same way, and collected about $50. At the end of that year the minister's salary was paid in full and the Church fairly reorganized. For the last year the minister was paid $1200 for his services, which was supplemented with a cash donation of $300, and contributions taken for four of the boards, averaging from $40 to $75. He thought the brother who got but $600 a year had never presented these objects of Christian benevolence to the Church to which he ministered, and imagined that that was the reason he was so poorly paid himself. His Church had found that the more they did for these great objects the more they were able to do for themselves, and he believed that would be found true always and everywhere. One-third of the ministers were afraid to touch upon these subjects, for fear that it would touch on their own salaries, but the fact was that was the best way to raise their own salaries.

Dr. Mattoon was in favor of adopting this report. Desired to go back a little further in this matter, lest when they left this Assembly, where they had been sitting together in heavenly places in Christ Jesus, they forget the vital points. Money would not buy the men, if there were no additions of converted young men to the churches. He called upon the ministers and elders of the churches to go about among the families and prayerfully and earnestly seek out young men and bring them into the Church and ministry. In his opinion this was the beginning of the education cause; that there would be no need of money when the men are ready.

Mr. Tindall believed in all that had been said, but did not believe that any man ought to be in the ministry who couldn't get a living by preaching. The ministry was a heroic calling, was captivating by reason of the influence it exerted; he regarded that it was infinitely higher than any other in the world.

Dr. Paul stated that he had had considerable experience with young men, and knew the power a man could exert over a young man in turning his course in life. God had honored him in turning many a young man to Christ and the ministry, and at so little trouble that he had been perfectly astonished. Whenever we had a right motive and a right desire to work for Christ, Christ worked with us and met us half way. If the two hundred and thirteen elders and ministers would only solemnly promise God that they, when they go home, would endeavor to turn some young man to Christ and the ministry, he thought they would have in a few months two hundred and thirteen young men ready to enter into the ministry, and if they continued their prayers and efforts, they could have two hundred and thirteen more over and over again.

Mr. Watterbury asked that there might be a division of the subjects embraced in the report, that the resolution in regard to East Tennessee might be considered by itself.

Mr. Tindall moved that the vote upon the adoption of the report be preceded by prayer. Carried.

Dr. Mills offered prayer, after which the report was adopted, except the East Tennessee resolution.

Dr. Curtis then read the resolution in regard to East Tennessee.

Rev. Mr. Brown, of East Tennessee, addressed the Assembly at length in regard to the situation and prospects of his State, educationally and religiously; stating that before the war there were forty-three or forty-four ministers in the Synod of Tennessee, and at one time all the ministers were educated at Marysville College. During the war that institution had been broken up. The loyalty of East Tennessee was owing, in no small degree, to the influence of that institution. The ministers educated at that institution had generally been loyal men, and had exerted an influence for good during this rebellion. He had ministered to two churches since 1828, alternately, and with the exception of perhaps one individual in each church, there had been no sympathy with rebellion. [Applause.] They had been loyal men and loyal women, while other congregations in the vicinity, under the influence and pastoral care of disloyal men, had been almost to a man disloyal. He remarked that the negroes were all anxious to obtain an education, not only for themselves, but for the children, and commented upon the conscientious piety of the negro race.

The time for adjournment being near at hand, it was voted that the report of the Committee on the State of the Country be received at four o'clock this afternoon.

After prayer the Assembly adjourned until afternoon.

AFTERNOON SESSION.

Three o'clock, P. M.

Opened with prayer by Moderator.

Minutes read and approved.

Mr. L. I. Root addressed the Assembly upon the present state of East Tennessee, the subject under consideration being the supplementary resolutions proposed by the Committee on Education. He spoke at length of the desolation of the country, owing to the war, of the injury done to the institutions of learning, of the fact that several seminaries, whose former owners had been rebels, were about to be sold under the hammer, and urged the propriety of their being secured to the interests of the Presbyterian Church. The institutions to which he particularly referred are situated at Jonesborough, Marysville and Greenville.

Rev. Mr. Waterbury stated that the utter desolation of East Tennessee could not be described. When the rebels got the mastery in East Tennessee they swept away everything into their treasury—the college fund, the educational fund were utterly gone forever, annihilated—libraries were used to kindle fires with, and the leather covers of the books for making shoes. The church denomination which laid the broadest foundations for educational institutions in East Tennessee would be predominant there.

Dr. Clark moved that this part of the report be recommitted, with a view of having the committee recommend some permanent committee or special committee, whose business it should be to supervise this matter.

Mr. Waterbury objected.

Mr. Griffis didn't see the advantage of such a motion.

After some further discussion Dr. Clark withdrew his motion.

Rev. Mr. Griffis, of East Tennessee, added a few words on the subject of his native State; said there were from 50 to 60 in his own congregation who desired to avail themselves of educational advantages, most of them with the purpose of entering the ministry.

The resolution was adopted.

Mr. Griffis moved a resolution to the effect that the Assembly recommend Rev. L. I. Root as agent to raise funds for this object, according to the resolution. Carried.

The Committee on Church Erection submitted a resolution to the effect that $85,000 being needed for the aid of feeble churches during the coming year, the third Sabbath of December next be fixed as the day for raising said sum. Adopted.

The Committee was discharged.

Rev. Mr. Miller addressed the Assembly upon the condition of the freedmen in North Carolina, soliciting aid in the establishment of a manual labor college for freedmen.

A committee was appointed, of which Dr. Clark was chairman, to confer with Mr. Miller in reference to his project.

Rev. Dr. Smith read the report of the Committee on the State of the Country, as follows:

The Committee on the State of the Country propose to the Assembly the following Declarations:

This assembly records its devout gratitude to Almighty God, that he has delivered us from the calamities and horrors of civil war, and restored peace throughout our borders.

That He has so far quelled the spirit of secession that the supreme and rightful authority of our beneficent National Government is now restored in all our States and Territories, and we remain, as we were intended to be, one Nation, with one Constitution and one destiny.

That He has so overruled the progress and results of this unparalleled conflict as to make it manifest that our republican institutions are as well fitted to bear the stress and shock of war as to give prosperity and increase in times of peace.

That, by his wise and constraining Providence, guiding us in ways we knew not He has caused the passions and wrath of man to enure to the welfare of humanity, so that a whole race has been emancipated from an unjust and cruel system of bondage and advanced to the rights and dignity of freemen; so that now involuntary servitude, except for crime, is illegal and unconstitutional wherever our National authority extends.

That He gave to our people such a spoeousntan, impassioned, and unbought loyalty—a loyalty that can neither be forced nor feigned—such resolute and abiding faith, and such a supreme consciousness of our National unity, that we were able in the darkest hours to bear with cheerful patriotism our heavy burdens and our costly sacrifices, so that our very sacrifices have knit us more closely together and made us love our country more.

That He has purged and enlightened our National conscience in respect to our National sins, especially the sin of slavery; and has also made us recognize more fully than before the reality of Divine Providence, the sureness and justice of retribution for National guilt, and the grand fact that a nation can be exalted and safe only as it yields obedience to His righteous laws.

That He bestowed such grace upon our churches and ministry, that with singular unanimity and zeal they upheld our rightful Government by their unwavering testimony and effectual supplications, identifying the success of the nation with the welfare of the Church.

That above all these things, He has, according to His gracious promise, watched over his Church and kept it safe during these troublous times; so that not only has our American Christianity been vindicated, our faith and order maintained intact, and our Christian benevolence enhanced, but our purpose and plans for the future have been also enlarged in some proportion to the needs and growth of our country; while, to crown all these favors with his special benediction, He has also, in these latter days, rained down spiritual blessings in abundant measure upon so many churches all over the land.

This Assembly, while humbly recognizing these judgments and mercies in the past and the present, also bears testimony in respect to our urgent needs and duties as a nation in view of the new era upon which we are now entering, as follows, viz:

1. Our most solemn National trust concerns that patient race, so long held in unrighteous bondage. Only as we are just to them can we live in peace and safety. Freed by the National army they must be protected in all their civil rights by the National power. And, as promoting this end, which far transcends any mere political or party object, we rejoice that the active functions of the Freedmen's Bureau are still continued, and especially that the Civil Rights' rill has become the law of the land. In respect to the concession of the right of suffrage to the colored race, this Assembly adheres to the resolution passed by our Assembly of 1865 (Minutes, p 42): "That the colored man should in this country enjoy the right of suffrage, in connection with all other men, is but a simple dictate of justice. The Assembly cannot perceive any good reason why he should be deprived of this right on the ground of his color or his race." Even if suffrage may not be universal, let it at least be impartial.

2. In case such impartial suffrage is not conceded, that we may still reap the legitimate fruits of our National victory over secession and slavery, and that treason and rebellion may not enure to the direct political advantage of the guilty, we judge it to be a simple act of justice, that the constitutional basis of representation in Congress should be so far altered as to meet the exigencies growing out of the abolition of slavery; and we likewise hold it to be the solemn duty of our National Executive and Congress to adopt only such methods of reconstruction as shall effectually protect all loyal persons in the States lately in revolt.

3. As loyalty is the highest civic virtue, and treason the highest civil crime, so it is necessary for the due vindication and satisfaction of National justice, that the chief fomenters and representatives of the rebellion should, by due course and process of law, be visited with condign punishment.

4. The Christian religion being the underlying source of all our power, prosperity, freedom and National unity, we earnestly exhort all our ministers and churches to constant and earnest prayer for the President of the United States and his constitutional counsellors; for the Senate and House of Representatives in Congress assembled; for the Judges in our National Courts; for those that bear rule in our army and navy, and for all persons en-

trusted with authority; that they may be endowed with heavenly wisdom, and rule in the fear of the Lord, and so administer their high trusts, without self-seeking or partiality, that this great Republic, being delivered from its enemies, may renew its youth, and put forth all its strength in the ways of truth and righteousness, for the good of our own land and the welfare of mankind.

5 And we further exhort and admonish the members of our churches to diligent and personal efforts for the safety and prosperity of the Nation, to set aside all partisan and sectional aims and low ambitions, and to do their full duty as Christian freemen; to the end that our Christian and Protestant civilization may maintain its legitimate ascendancy, and that we become not the prey of any form of infidelity, or subject to any foreign priestly domination; that the sacred interests of civil and religious freedom, of human rights and justice to all, of National loyalty and National unity, may be enlarged and perpetuated, making our Christian Commonwealth a praise among the nations of the earth, exemplifying and speeding the progress of the Kingdom of our Lord and Saviour, Jesus Christ.

N. S. S. BEMAN,
HENRY B. SMITH,
WILLIAM HOGARTH,
THOMAS BROWN,
HENRY FOWLER,
JOSEPH ALLISON,
F. V. CHAMBERLAIN,
J. A. FOOTE,
R. SCARRETT.

Rev. Mr. Fowler moved that the consideration of that report be made the special order for Monday evening. Lost

Rev. Mr. Gibson, of Illinois, moved that the article that condemned the leaders of the rebellion, to punishment be stricken out, because it was not becoming for the Assembly to say a single word about it.

Mr. Gibson's amendment was lost and the report adopted without a dissenting vote.

Voted that a copy of these resolutions be forwarded to the President of the United States, through the Secretary of State, and to the President of the Senate and Chairman of the House.

Rev. Dr. Knox read report of Committee on Home Missions.

Dr. Kendall called the attention of the Assembly to the fact that more money was needed; that they were bankrupt in six months unless more money was provided than had been coming in in the last six months. There had been $15,000 more money spent the last year than had been collected. There was need of about $10,000 a month. Would have to borrow $30,000 before the middle of September.

After remarks by Messrs. Scarrit and Van Nest, the further consideration of the report was deferred.

On motion,

Resolved, That the General Assembly pledges the Church to furnish the Home Missionary Society $120,000 for the ensuing year, and instructs the committee to go forward on that basis.

The following appointments for Saturday evening and Sunday were then read:

First Presbyterian Church, corner Fourteenth street and Lucas Place—Rev. W. Hogarth, D. D., 10½ A. M. Service for children by Rev. Joseph Chester, 4 P. M.

North Presbyterian Church, corner Eleventh and Chambers streets—Rev. W. S. Karr. 10½ A. M.; Rev. D. L. Kiehle, 7½ P. M.

Union Methodist Church, corner of Eleventh and Locust streets—Rev. J. T. Kindau, 10½ A. M.; Rev. Isaac Clark, 7¾ P. M.

Second Union Methodist Episcopal Church, Sixth street, between Franklin avenue and Wash street—Rev. G. P. Tindall, 10½ A. M.; Rev. John Monteith, Jr., 7¾ P. M.

Simpson Chapel, corner Tenth and North Market streets—Rev. H. L. Stanley, 10½ A. M.

Pratt Avenue Mission, Pratt avenue, between Clark avenue and Gamble avenue—Rev. Stephen Bush, 10½ A. M.; Rev. Geo. O. Phelps, 7½ P. M.

First Congregational Church, corner Tenth and Locust streets—Rev. Walter Clarke, D. D., 7½ P.M.

Fourth Baptist Church, corner Benton and Twelfth streets—Rev. W. A. Niles, 10½ A. M.

Colored Church, at Freedmen's Orphan Asylum, Twelfth street, near Cass avenue—Rev. L. P. Crawford, 10½ A. M.; Rev. F. H Adams, 3 P. M.

City Hospital, corner St. Ange and Lafayette avenues—Rev. J. A. Griffes.

City Jail, corner Sixth and Chesnut streets—Rev. J. A. Renney, 2½ P. M.

Rock Hill—Rev. B. B. Parsons, D. D.
Bunker Hill—Rev. Thos. Harries.
Monticello—Rev. J. L. Morton.
Rolla—Rev. L. B. Wilson.
Alton—Rev. E. F. Hatfield, D. D.
Warsaw—Rev. G. D. A. Hebard.
Jerseyville, Ill.—Rev. Isaac G. Ogden.
Upper Alton—Rev. W. E. Knox, D. D.
Baptist Church, Alton—Rev. H. Fowler.

A meeting for children and young persons at four o'clock P. M., in the First Presbyterian Church.

Addresses by Rev. Dr. J. Parker, Rev. A. L. Brookse, and Messrs. E. S. Wells and D. H. Ingersoll.

Notice was also given of a meeting of the Elders of the two Assemblies, to be held in the Second Presbyterian Church, on Saturday evening.

After prayer the Assembly adjourned until half after 8 o'clock—the business session to commence at 9 o'clock.

EIGHTH DAY—SATURDAY, MAY 26, 1866.

MORNING SESSION.

Met at 8 1-2 o'clock.

First half hour spent in devotional exercises.

Rev. Dr. Campbell, Secretary of the American Christian Union, addressed the Assembly at length upon the interests and condition of the Union. Stated that it had a fund of at least $30,000 or $40,000, secured from the Old and New School Presbyterian Churches, and from these two branches and the Congregationalists it had received about $40,000, and but little from any other denomination. There were a great many things connected with the work which it was not proper to publish, or even speak of, before this Assembly. There were many things which gave a great deal of trouble. Two years ago, at an anniversary in Italy, there were some Catholic priests present, who, eight weeks afterwards, published a pamphlet which came back to us bearing bad reports in regard to the missionary work, throwing prejudice upon that work until it was ascertained from whom the pamphlet emanated. A great work has been done in Italy during the past five years; had sent thorough-going Americans and Yankees to that field, who understood the value of money and our mode of doing things. About ten years ago there was no such thing as toleration in Italy; the priests had it all their own way. We now had our American Chapel there, the Scotch Church, and Waldenses have a seminary there, and during the past year, with the agency of the American Bible Society, we have been able to print and circulate 10,000 copies of the New Testament. There were three colporteurs there and several bible readers who were laboring for the distribution of the word of God. Altogether there were forty-seven laborers in Italy. Among other things the government had declared marriage a civil contract, so that the Protestant ministers could marry members of the Protestant Churches and the Waldenses, without the intervention of the priests. During the past year there had been 70,000 who professed Romanism come to the missionaries and left the faith. That was the work in Italy. They were a noble band of missionaries, who had been able to convert even some of the priests. Gave an account of Mr. Constantine, of Italy, who came to this country for an education and was now laboring in Italy. Described the work that had been accomplished in South America, at Valparaiso, by Mr. Trumbull, who first went there seventeen years ago, in the service of the American Seamen's Aid Society, and had been fighting the battles for toleration; was first obliged to labor on shipboard, where he could be protected by the American flag. Also gave a brief history of the labors and success of Mrs. Rankin, who from Brownsville had penetrated to Monterey, in Mexico, and was now in this country in order to procure the sum of $15,000, with which to build a seminary at Monterey.

The order of the day was taken up, the first thing in order being the adoption of the report of the standing Committee on Home Missions, which was read to the Assembly yesterday by Dr. Knox, and was as follows:

HOME MISSIONS.

The Standing Committee on Home Missions in making their report would suggest that there are three things in which the Assembly is agreed, viz: That the work before us is great beyond conception and competition, that the Church is the proper agency for doing it, and *now* the favoring time, admitting no postponement.

Love of adventure, lust of gain, the march of enterprise, the great tidal movement westward of the nations, and, finally, but not less providentially, sedition and war have been busy clearing and widening the home field for the Church's occupancy. Within the months just past the Holy Spirit has anew and most earnestly invited to the cultivation of the ground, and in many instances to the gathering of already rich harvests. The Church could not be heedless of these signs without ignoring her manifest mission and destiny in this land. She has heeded them, and hence the marvels that have accompanied her way, as in the ancient journeying from Goshen to Canaan. "God has been in the midst of her; he has helped her, and that right early." Is her mission therefore fulfilled? Do we not know, on the contrary that the land to be possessed is more than the territory already subdued?

From Maine to Mexico, from the Atlantic to the Pacific wave, from the great lakes to the Southern Gulf, how wide the field stretches out; its needs even in the older States, East, Middle and South how numerous; in the States and Territories West and Northwest how immense and stupendous.

The question of opportunity and duty being settled by Divine Providence, that of the way and means of fulfilling both press heavily on our hearts. We can hope, on this point, to do little more than emphasize the suggestions of the report already submitted.

We need, of course, to this end, a great increase of the Christian ministry. We say increase, because its actually effective portion is already employed up to the full measure of its capability. It the West has not an adequate supply of ministers, it is because the East cannot spare them. Those whom she can spare as well as not, are such as the West do not want, and those she knows not how to spare have already been drawn upon beyond her means. The weakening of an Eastern church by withdrawing an efficient pastor is simply at the cost of the Western by cutting off the supplies of men and money necessary to its sustenance, and it is allowable only under the plea of some peculiar and dominant necessity. We can, therefore, meet the demand for ministers only by an increase of candidates for the ministry. And to accomplish this, the piety of the Church must be deepened, and its channels opened and widened in this direction. The attention of our youth must be summoned to this claim on their talents, as a reason why they should anew, or for the first time, consecrate them to Christ. Parents must be made to feel the duty of training and yielding their children to a work so inviting and remunerating.

Ministers and elders must take this matter into their special charge; seeking to gain our young men, not by worldly considerations, whether of a literary or pecuniary sort, but by pointing them to the grand opportunities here offered of usefulness to God and their country through the same earnest consecration and cheerful self-denial so conspicuously illustrated in the examples of Christ and his apostles.

Next to the provision of preachers is that of preaching places. By this is not meant congregations which already exist in greater numbers than we can supply, but houses of worship for these congregations. We have come to understand that there can be no progressive and permanent church edification without a church edifice. It is as much needed for ministers and people as houses to live in are needed for them. The attention of the Assembly has been so thoroughly called to this subject the present session that we need not enlarge upon it.

What we have most required is a settled policy, that should not be constantly discussed and revised, but that should be put into instant and persistent operation. It is to be hoped, from action just taken by the Assembly, that we have now reached that point. We know better than heretofore what we have need to do and what we are able to do; that which remains is *to do it*. The chief discouraging hindrance of a debated plan being removed, let us arise and build. Let the gift fund be swelled as the loan fund never was. The wants of the Great West have become measurably appreciated by this convocation on the right bank of the Mississippi, and let us return to our congregations to report what our eyes have seen and our ears heard, and thus prepare our people for new and more liberal benefactions to this object, at some not remote day to be agreed upon for a united effort. In this way we shall best silence the voice of complaint issuing from so many promising missionary centers, and telling how the work of God is stayed for lack of houses of worship. The next report at our General Assembly will be that of gratitude for the unhindered upbuilding of Zion's waste places.

The money question, however, does not pertain to the Church erection fund only, but to all departments of the missionary work. That it demands new discussion is evident from the treasurers statistics. One of these discloses the average contribution on the part of our membership of barely 63 cts., which is 5 3-5 cents per month, or a cent and a quarter per week. If we have made advances in the latter over former years, it is clear there is still wide room for improvement. It needs but a glance at the greatness of our work to reveal the inadequacy of our efforts. It needs but another glance at the vastness of our resources to expose an exceeding parsimony in their disposal.

One important suggestion the committee would offer in this connection. It relates to christian giving as a duty to be enforced on every church not only, but on every individual. It is not enough that contributions should be taken in the Sabbath congregation; but in addition to this, or instead of it, by collectors passing through the congregation, and calling upon each family and person. A general observance of this plan would, it is believed, immediately increase our total receipts 75 or 100 per cent. The committee recommend that an effort be made to realize an average contribution of at least one dollar per member the present year. This would insure a total collection of $120,000, and would require a marked advance in our wealthy as well as feeble churches.

Meanwhile the home missionary work enlarges upon our hands, and calls for an immediate increase of faith, labor and prayer. There is no real source of discouragement but in the narrowness of our own hearts. There is no department of effort into which we have entered with any vigor upon which God has not shed his approving and inspiring favor. Witness to this the blessing attending our special effort in behalf of East Tennessee, in a discouraged and distracted church reinspirited, dispersed congregations regathered, in pastors settled over long vacant parishes, and the revival of religion experienced in unprecedented power. Witness the story told by delegates from all parts of the land of the descending and quickening Spirit. Even the labors employed on behalf of our foreign population, usually regarded as far from hopeful access, have not been without significant results. The Presbytery of Newark, after a sixteen years experiment among the Germans, have now as its fruits, six churches organized on a Presbyterian basis; all but one provided with houses of worship, with settled pastors, good congregations, a vigorous, prospective growth and an healthful, positive influence going out upon the surrounding population in behalf of Sabbath observance, temperance, social order and every moral and spiritual interest. The example thus set us by Newark Presbytery, and already emulated by Philadelphia and Cincinnati, should rebuke the prevailing skepticism on this subject. There is a grave responsibility laid upon us here, and we may not shirk it. Let us remember that while the Irish immigration is fed by a home supply of six and a half millions, the German springs from a fountain head of forty millions. Not to care for this industrious, enterprising and accessible people is to take very poor care of our own interests.

Our labors for the native freedman, so far as we have prosecuted them, have been reasonably successful. Here again it is our straightened faith that produced our limited efficiency. If the millions of China and Caffraria are to be evangelized, how much more those multitudes at our own doors. While slavery has depressed the adult negro population too low for even Christianity easily to elevate them, it is to be noted that 1,150,000 of this race are between the ages of five and fifteen, and thus as impressible as any class of our white population by educating and evangelizing influences. This, with the almost equally needed work to be done for the poorer whites of the South is a labor sufficient of itself to tax our utmost energies.

Truly God has everywhere set before us an open door throughout this broad and free land, and that which we need is the strength of Christian faith, love and patience to pass in and accept the goodly heritage.

The following persons are recommended for reelection in the place of those members of the present committee, whose term of service expires with this Assembly, viz: Jonathan F. Stearns, D. D., Rev. Charles S. Robinson, Howard Crosby, D. D., A. C. Post M. D., and George Lockwood, Esq.

All of which is respectfully submitted.

W. E. KNOX, Chairman.

Dr. Campbell. Thought that the simple recommendation that $150,000 should be raised would not meet the case; that there ought to be a co-operating Secretary at the West, instead of at Philadelphia; that more collecting agents should be put into the field, the best men in the Church, to go among the churches. Explained what Rev. Mr. Winis had accomplished in the establishment of German Presbyterian Churches in Newark, and insisted upon the need of Presbyterian publications in the German language.

Dr. Parsons. Believed that the General Assemblies did not feel the importance of this subject of Home Missions as they should feel it. The time was when we could preach the Gospel in this country to every creature, but we neglected to do the work then as we should have done it, caring more for the roods and acres of these prairie farms than for the souls of men. It was now again possible for us to preach the gospel to every creature. There were some ministers on the frontier who felt the importance of this matter sufficiently to convince them that they must work and induce others to work. We had given to this object of our abundance and not of our penury. It was not enough for us to say that we recommend that $120,000 be raised for this object during the current year. It was necessary something should be done here which would reach individual members of the churches. Last year they had besought the General Assembly to care for and assist them in Northwest Missouri. The General Secretary and those associated with him had done what they could, but the work had not been done. There were churches to be occupied—numbers of men were wanted. Should they who are placed at the outposts of Zion go home from this Assembly and say that they had an able report on Home Missions, which was received with marked interest; that many elaborate speeches were made, and the recommendations of the committee passed without a dissenting voice to raise $120,000 this year, and be compelled to stop there? Should they be permitted to go home and say to those who look up to them from the right and left and ask them couldn't they find a man to send into their country who will visit thirteen or fourteen counties in that section and only say they hoped and trusted, but couldn't say anything definite about it. It seemed to him that the time had come when they should not only feel deeply the obligations resting upon them, but should also do something commensurate with the demand—when the giving must be not only from their abundance but from our penury. An utterance from this Assembly was needed that should reach the Church which should say that this work of Home Missions must be prosecuted as the work of Foreign Missions is.

The report was adopted.

Mr. Foote introduced the following resolution:

Resolved by this Assembly, that the deliverance on the state of the country be read in the several churches on the first Sabbath of the month of July, and advocated the adoption of the same in a few remarks, to the effect that the restoration of peace to the country was in a great measure due to the clergy, and that the clergy might now exert a large influence towards settling the matter, now in controversy upon a proper basis.

Resolution adopted.

Dr. Parsons, of the Committee on Bills and Overtures, made report as follows:

"Overture. A church member comes before the session, makes a voluntary confession of heretical sentiments, acknowledges a breach of covenant and waives the formality of a trial, in view of, and in order to excommunication from the Church: can such church member be excommunicated on such confession and declaration without the actual process prescribed by the book?"

The committee find that the question thus raised was answered substantially by the last Assembly, [see minutes, page 12,] and whilst they recommend that the party asking, be referred to that response, also recommend that the Assembly affirm the impropriety of a Church court reaching and recording such a grave result of discipline as excommunication from the Church without a strict adherence to these forms of fair, impartial trial, by which alone the result may be justified. If an accused person confess judgment the actual process may be shortened, but should not be dispensed with.

Rev. Mr. Kendall, thought there was no necessity for a trial when a person pleaded guilty, and asserted his readiness to be excommunicated.

Mr. Fowler said the Assembly should be very careful how it nullifies the decisions of a previous Assembly; advocated following the example of civil courts in this matter, stating that trial was never dispensed with in the civil courts by reason of a plea of guilty, though the testimony might be; that both in the civil and religious courts a fair and impartial trial, in cases of confession had its advantages, which ought not to be overlooked.

Report adopted.

Dr. Parsons reported another

"Overture. From certain members of Madison Presbytery, who desire to make the following inquiries:—

"A person is under suspension in one of our own churches. He removes and unites on examination with another of our churches, the session of the latter one being wholly ignorant of his former membership, and, of course, of his suspension. The facts are however afterwards discovered. Would this discovery of itself vitiate his second membership and leave him simply a suspended member of the former church?

"Would unworthiness for church membership, clearly manifested while in the latter church, and before said discovery, rightfully add efficacy towards producing these results?"

To the first of the above questions the committee recommend an answer in the affirmative.

To the second, if the question means whether the session of the second church has jurisdiction in the case of unworthiness manifested in the second relation, the committee recommend an answer in the negative; but if the question means whether the unworthiness manifested in the second relation be proper ground of separate process by the session of the first church, the committee recommend an answer in the affirmative.

In respect to the whole matter, the committee agree in the statement following:

The person uniting with the second church an examination, unites deceptively. As soon as the facts are ascertained by the session of this second church, the proper order of procedure is for that session after conference with the accused person, to strike his name from their roll of church members, as not under their jurisdiction; to communicate their action to the session suspending him, with the reasons for it, and to request the said session to proceed against him on separate process, for duplicity and disorder.

Recommendation adopted.

Rev. John W. Chickering, Jr., delegate from the General Association of Congregational Churches in New Hampshire, was invited to address the Assembly.

He tendered to the Assembly the Christian salutations and congratulations of the Congregational Churches of New Hampshire. Of those who joined the Presbyterian Church it might be said *nulla vestigia retrorsum*, through the Congregationalists had received from that church the Rev. Dr. Smith, who was now engaged in reconstructing 'Old Dartmouth,' and was succeeding most gloriosly. There were 188 churches in this association, 6 of them presbyterian, with a membership of over 20,000 and 177 ministers. He referred to the large accessions to the Presbyterian Church from the Congregationalists in of New England to the revivals of the past year; to the reliance of Congrugationalists upon the teachings of the Bible, rather than upon the decisions of any church organization, and the readiness of his constituents to unite with any and all denominations who held to the truth as laid down in the Bible, in efforts to Christianize the world. He concluded by expressing his joy that he was where he could see the old flag over the pulpit; that among this Assembly there had been not even the taint of treason, and that the Assembly had seen fit to utter the noble sentiments of yesterday's session on the state of the country.

The Moderator responded in fitting terms, affirming that a converted Congregationalist, if only thoroughly converted, made a pretty good Presbyterian; that the Assembly were all lovers and friends of New England; that there never was a more senseless babble or disgraceful outcry of insignificant politicians, than that which was raised in some parts of the West, that New England should be left out in the cold; that that cry of senseless party hacks deserved to be hooted with contempt; that New England had a cold place geographically, but had a warm place in the hearts of all this great people.

Dr. Samuel D. Burchard then read the report of the Standing Committee on Publication, as follows:

REPORT ON PUBLICATION.

The committee having carefully examined the documents placed in their hands, would respectfully submit the following:

That from the time the General Assembly resolved to issue a distinctive literature, bearing its own *imprimatur*, setting forth and defending its own doctrines, there has been a gradual and growing interest in the work. Doubt and distrust have given way to confidence; funds and facilities of usefulness have steadily increased; so that now there is an open field, hearty co operation and the universal conviction that the publication cause is one of the mightiest instrumentalities committed to the Church for her vindication, her spiritual vitality, and her promised and permanent victory. Books issued by her own press are both the source and the indication of ecclesiastical and spiritual life, a power and a blessing which it is our privilege to wield and to enjoy.

Your Committee rejoice, therefore, that the cause has passed the period of the doubtful experiment and is now to be pushed and prosecuted with a vigor equal to its importance and to the increasing wants of the field we occupy.

The past year is a prophecy of what is to be. The receipts have been greatly in advance of any previous year, and there has been a consequent increase in the number and value of the tracts and books issued and circulated. Still the field is widening; the calls are becoming more imperative and universal; the entire South and West are open; the cry comes up from the missionary, in his open yet half occupied field, for books and tracts authorized by the Church wherewith to suppliment his labors, and this is met by a whole chorus of voices from the Sabbath schools of the land pleading for a life giving and heaven-inspiring literature.

God's voice to the Church in this department of service is evidently "Go Forward!" We cannot afford to pause; we must go up and possess the land.

It is the judgment of your committee that some system of *colportage* should be inaugurated, under the supervision of the Synods or Presbyteries, securing a more extended circulation to the publications of the committee. The plan suggested is this: Let each Synod or Presbytery employ a colporteur, whose work shall be two-fold—the disposal or sale of books, receiving his salary largely from commissions allowed, and co operation with pastors in attending upon social meetings and aiming to extend a deep religious interest throughout the bounds of the Presbytery or Synod. This would help many a deserving young man in his preparatory course, give a wide circulation to our literature, and encourage and facilitate the pastors in their work.

As this arrangement is designed to be only occasional and temporary, your committee suggests that a place of sale be designated in every principal town throughout the land, where the publications of the committee can be obtained after the retiring colporteur shall have sown the seed, awakened an interest and done his work.

Your committee beg leave to call special attention to the Hymn and Tune Book as in their judgment well adapted to the devotional exercises of the lecture room, the prayer meeting, and even to congregational singing on the Sabbath. The book everywhere will be found a grand aid to worship.

The Presbyterian Monthly is hailed as a benediction wherever it is taken, and the only regret is that it should not be taken by every Presbyterian within our bounds. The information it contains is needed by every pastor and session, while every family would be greatly enriched by its monthly advent. A large circulation which, by a little effort on the part of pastors and elders might be realized, would make it self-suspporting at the low price of fifty cents a year. Your committee would recommend that a copy be sent to every pastor, *sine sumptu*, in the hope that his Church will take a collection during the year for each of the objects represented in this monthly.

While your committee have suggested measures by which the remunerative circulation or sale of the committee's publications may be vastly increased, they are not unmindful of the purely benevolent character of the work. Thousands of pages must be gratuitously circulated in the hope not of pecuniary but of moral returns in the actual good done, and a full reward on the great pay day of the world, when every man shall receive according to his works. With this view collections are recommended in all our churches.

There is one more item to which your committee would call the attention of the assembly—the wants of the rapidly increasing German immigration.

The numbers landed monthly on our shores are immense. These are the most inquiring, the most given to reading, of all the people that come to us from abroad. Though many of them are skeptical in their tendencies, yet the Protestant portion, in their ecclesiastical affinites are with us. True, on their arrival they are ignorant of us, and skepticism would misrepresent us and mislead them; but properly instructed by means of our Presbyterian publications, they affiliate most naturally with us in doctrine and polity, and become an element of strength. They may be easily turned to infidelity, or to a Protestant, and vital christianity, according to the influences first brought to bear. It is the opinion of your committee that no more hopeful field is now open for the circulation of our religious literature.

In conclusion and in a review, the committee would respectfully propose the following resolutions:

1. That we gratefully acknowledge the favor of God to this cause during the past and previous years.

2. That the Synods or Presbyteries be recommended to appoint students, unemployed ministers or earnest Christian laymen, as colporteurs, to circulate the books of the Publication Committee, and to co-operate with pastors in every good word and work.

3. That a place of sale be designated in every town, where it shall be known that the committee's publications may be obtained, and at the lowest retail price.

4. That the "Social Hymn and Tune Book," recently published by the Committee, be commended as pre-eminently adapted to social and congregational worship.

5. That more vigorous efforts be put forth to introduce the Presbyterian Monthly to all our congregations.

6 That it is recommended that collections be taken to aid in the gratuitous circulation of the committee's publications.

7. That a special committee of five be appointed, who shall prepare fresh tracts and books, or, if thought desirable, translations, *to be published in the German language*, in co-operation with the Assembly's Publication Committee, and who shall take into consideration the expediency of publishing a German religious newspaper adapted to the wants of the German population of the country. The following persons are nominated for that committee, viz.: D. W. Poor, D. D., Geo. L. Prentiss, D. D., Rev. Johann U. Guenther, Rev. J. J. F. Brunow, and Rev. Nelson Millard.

The committee recommed that Rev. Daniel Marsh, D. D., Rev. J. G. Butler, D. D., Wm. F. Judson, Esq., Samuel C. Perkins, Esq,, Hon. William Strong, whose term of service now expire, be re-elected for the ensuing three years.

The committee would also recommend that John A. Brown, Esq., W. A. Balkwin, Esq., Samuel H. Perkins, Esq., Rev. Thos. Brainer, D. D , Rev. Ezra Adams, D. D., whose terms of service now expire, be re-elected Trustees of the Presbyterian House for the ensuing three years.

Rev. J. W. Dulles, Secretary of the Permanent Committee on Publications, addressed the Assembly upon the subject of the report—alluded to the addition that had been made to the publishing house, an establishment which did not belong to the committee, but to the Church. Called the attention of the Assembly to the publications of the committee, which were to be disposed of by donations and sale; that every one might become a preacher by being instrumental in distributing the tracts of the committee. Collections were needed to defray the expenses of donations and the publication of German books and papers. The circulation of the Presbyterian Monthly ought to be extended until it was to be found in every family.

Rev. Mr. G. O. Little believed the way to have books read was to circulate them by means of colporteurs. They had employed a colporteur in the Wabash Synod, guaranteeing him $500, and thinking that they would have to contribute $250 of that amount. He commenced on the first of January, and has now more than paid all his expenses.

Dr. Hatfield informed the Assembly that Dr. Gurley and Judge Clark were present with the Assembly as Commissioners from the Assembly in session in the Second Presbyterian Church, and moved that they be received at one quarter after eleven o'clock. Carried.

Rev. Mr. Bradford considered the Presbyterian Monthly the most valuable of all the publications, and urged its extensive circulation. Stated that all the publications of the committee could be obtained at No. 9 North Sixth street, in this city, at Mr. McIntire's.

Dr. Parsons bore witness to the avidity with which these books were read in his congregation, and to the manifestly good results growing out of their circulation.

Dr. Clarke stated that having found in Buffalo that the books of the committee were too far off they had already raised $1,200 towards a fund to found a depository among themselves. Thought if this were done generally in the Presbyteries these books would be more within the reach of the people.

Rev. Mr. Griffes. They had commenced the work in Tennessee; had an experienced colporteur in the field there.

Rev. Mr. Ransom, of Mich., spoke of the great need existing in the Home Missionary Churches for these publications; the Congregations on the border were mixed congregations of different denominations, and several denominations were striving to get a foothold among them. Many of the preachers with whom they were brought in contact were without education, or without that education which Presbyterians consider necessary; they come and go, and many of them present their views and doctrines with a degree of plausibility which is attractive, and often gain very much by misrepresenting the views and doctrines of the Presbyterians. Could they have a full supply of tracts and publications of the committee they would be a great help in the work. The influence of the Presbyterian Monthly was very much needed there. Attributed the difficulty in getting contributions from the people to a lack of intelligence among them in regard to these great interests.

Dr. Parker alluded to a publication of the committee, "Bowen's Daily Meditations," as being the best book for family devotions that he was acquainted with, and urged the necessity of religious German papers and periodicals; considered the use of tracts very advantageous in meeting points of doctrine raised from time to time by other denominations.

Mr. Rhodes, had been very successful as a colporteur, though he had entered upon the work feeling himself unfitted for it; heard a great many inquiries for German books from those who said their children could read English but they could not.

The report of the committee was adopted.

The Rev. Dr. P. D. Gurley and Hon. —— Clark, Commissioners from the Old School Assembly then appeared upon the platform, and Dr. Gurley addressed the Assembly as follows:

SPEECH OF DR. GURLEY.

Mr. Moderator, and Members of the General Assembly: The Hon. Mr. Clark and myself are here by appointment of the Assembly which holds its session in the Second Presbyterian Church in this city to convey to you the fraternal salutations of that body; and this we do with all earnestness and sincerity. It is not a mere matter of courtesy and form. I think I can say it is an utterance of the heart. We recognize you as our brethern in the Lord—bought with the same blood—renewed by the same spirit—servants of the same Master—engaged in the same work, and going with us to the same Heavenly Home, and therefore, with all our hearts, we can say, "The Lord bless you and keep you. The Lord make his face to shine upon you and be gracious unto you. The Lord lift up his countenance upon you and give you peace."

We have heard of yourgrowth—of your steady advancement in strength and influence—of your fidelity to Christ, and all the interests connected with His glory, and especially of recent and copious outpourings of the holy spirit upon your Churches; and as we have heard these things we have been ready to say with blended joy and gratitude "The Lord hath done great things with them, whereof we are glad." May He continue to revive, and strengthen, and enlarge, and bless you, and make you a blessing to the world—is the steady and earnest prayer of our heart.

I am glad and grateful to be able to say that during the past year the Lord has not left us without some tokens of His favor. Many of our congregations, schools, academies and colleges have been blessed with His holy spirit which has been shed down upon them like rain upon the mown grass, and as showers that water the earth, and the result is that hundreds of our dear youth, and others, who a year ago were dead in trespasses and in sin, are now alive unto God, and engaged in his service.

It is the Lord's doings, and marvelous in our eyes. But as you have been similarly blessed in this regard, and perhaps more largely, we may well exclaim as we stand before you, "O magnify the Lord with us, and let us exalt His name together."

It has been a great pleasure for us to meet you as brethren in this city, to mingle with you in conference and prayer, and to sit down with you at the sacramental table; and when on last Wednesday evening—an evening never to be forgotten—the two Assemblies filled this house, and partook together of the symbols of our Redeemer's death, doubtless we all felt that it was good to be here, and that our little denominational differences and distinctions were all swallowed up and lost in that greatest and best distinction that "One is our Master, even Christ and we all are brethren."

Yes, we are brethren. We have one Lord, one faith, one baptism, one God and Father of us all, who is above all, and through all, and in us all; and why then should we not love one another with a pure heart, and fervently? And why should we not bear one another's burdens, and so fulfil the law of Christ? We should, and I believe we do—

"We share our mutual woes,
Our mutual burdens bear,
And often for each other flows
The sympathizing tear."

Much has been said of late on the subject of our becoming organically one; and why may we not become so at no very distant day? We are both thoroughly Presbyterian in doctrine, in government and discipline. Our forms of worship are the same. The means, methods and agencies by which we seek to promote the cause of our Redeemer and advance His kingdom in the world, are now substantially the same; and though, since we became two bands, we have been called by different names, you being designated as New School and we as Old School, yet it is manifest enough that we have both been educated in the same school—a school where the Westminster Confession of faith, and the longer and shorter catechisms are the prominent and venerated text books, the teachings of which we adhere to now as setting forth most clearly and ably what we are to believe concerning God, and what duties God requires of us.

Moreover, recent events have brought us into a closer alliance and fellowship, than we have ever felt before. In the years of our country's peril we have rallied together round the dear old flag, and while the conflict was going on, we have sung and prayed together:

"The Star Spangled Banner—Oh, long may it wave,
O'er the land of the free, and the home of the brave."

[Applause.] And when, at last, the rebel flag went down, and with it slavery, Oh! then we lifted our hands and hearts together unto God, and said: "Not unto us, oh Lord, not unto us, but unto Thy name give glory, for Thy mercy and Thy truths' sake. Thy right hand and Thy holy arm have gotten Thee the victory."

These are recent events, and they have brought us into the bonds of a nearer and a heartfelt fellowship.

We know not how you may feel on the subject, but as for ourselves, we feel that the time perhaps has now come when some practical step should be taken looking to the securing of an organic unity, and accordingly the General Assembly which I represent, on yesterday, by an almost unanimous vote, adopted the following resolutions, which, with your permission, sir, I will read, and then will leave them, as I am directed to do, upon your table.

[Dr. Gurley then read the resolutions of the Old School General Assembly,as published in our issue of Saturday in the report of Fridays proceedings,which were received with applause,and concluded as follows:]

And now, sir, having expressed to you our whole mind on this subject, as well as our feelings of fraternal affection towards you, and the Church you represent, it only remains for me to thank you for your courtesy, and to ask, if you please. that you will extend a similar courtesy to my associate, Judge Clark, who is here with me.

SPEECH OF HON. W. CLARK.

Moderator and Brethren: In the discharge of the humble part which devolves upon me touching the mission with which we are charged to you, what better words or sentiments could I utter, than those which pertain to the reunion of our branches of the Church, and the establishment of fellowship between us? In doing this I shall not subject myself to the charge of arrogance in speaking of the ways and means by which this can be done, nor in saying that this is the time when it can be done. All this will be done by concerted means, at a proper time, but I surely may speak of the desirableness of the consummation, and if the cloud is tinged with light to cheer, I may look at it, and I may ask you to look at it also. And I think I see the light there.

Mr. Moderator, if tnere is any blame which lies anywhere respecting the divisions which have pervaded us, I have to say that the blame is by no means all yours. But if there is fault let us see wherin it consists. If there are obstacles in the way let us endeavor to ascertain what they are, and to study the means by which they can be removed.

I may speak of facts, I trust, without disturbing harmony of feeling in the heart. It has occurred to me that if St. Paul were to write another letter to the churches, especially to ours—and when I say ours, I mean your branch, and that to which I am attached also—he would say, "I hear that there are divisions among you," and I believe it fully.

My friends, there is such a thing as the unity of the Spirit, and the bond of peace, and this means something. It should not be regarded as merely theoretical, for if we should so regard it, we should dishonor a high precept. My friends, I remember that a worthy puritan pastor once said in his parting injunction to a portion of his beloved flock, that he was persuaded there was more truth yet to be broken out of the word of God. This certainly was a clear declaration that there was more for them to learn, and it clearly implied another thing—that there was more of grace to be imbibed, and shall we not heed the injunction?

My friends, it has been said by some tha divisions in the house of God were advantageous. For myself, I could never see the force of it. I have to say here now to you that I do not believe it. It is a poor commentary on the precepts of the Gospel, if the family of Christ is to be divided into segments in order that one portion may watch over the other—constitute itself the guardian of the other, so that it do not go astray—to keep it in what it would consider the proper road. I say that this is assuming—it is wrong—it is derogatory to the Gospel and to the Savior. It is clear to me that divisions in the house of God are not desirable, but prejudicial, and in many important respects. The very name, where one title is set against another, is disadvantageous, as well as to the condition of society. When one is called by the name of Apollos and the other by the name of Cephas, it implies antagonism, and as a matter of fact, antagonism has been the fruitful result. I do not suppose that members of the Church are in all respects unlike other men. Wherever there are divisions there are, at least to some extent, criticisms, jealousies, and a failure to accomplish that which union would accomplish. Does it not result in the divisions respecting churches and the ministry that one minister might discharge all the work of a single field in many cases where there are two? Does it not work prejudice, these church divisions, as regards our literary and thelogical institutions? Does it not divide the resources of the Church, and consequently weaken the cause? To my mind all this is clear, and we ought, if we possibly can, to remove this objection out of the way; and it seems to me that some concession, and something of an increase of the spirit of charity might effect this thing. My friends, how long shall it be said that "They eat each other's hearts, Ephraim Manasseh, and Manasseh Ephraim, and both Judah?" It is time this religious misanthropy should be done away.

My friends, the angles have heretofore been acute; can we not render them obtuse—can we not swell the obtuse angles into something like a circle? This would certainly, as it appears to me, be most desirable.

My friends, my ministerial brother, who is charged with the chief portion of this mission has alluded to the difficulties, the troubles which have prevailed in our land for the last four or five years, and they have been of a degree never before equalled in this country. They have created division, they have caused separations by deep and dark lines—they have divided the church. Whether these lines shall ever be obliterated, whether the chasm shall close up, whether they shall come together again, and be as afore time, it is not for me to say; but if the agitations which have divided society have wrought such results, why should they not come with some healing results too? If they have wrought divisions, why should they not bring segments t gether? It seems to me that this is reasonable, and that it may be reasonably expected.

My friends, united we have a glorious mission before us, and united we can accomplish vastly more than we can by being separated as we are now. It is said that large things move slow. I do not believe that this is always the case; but even if they do, they move with increased momentum, and with surer results. If then, with a broad gauge, and a grand trunk, we can assume that gauge, and travel upon that trunk, what may we not expect to do in scattering abroad the blessings of evangelism, in attacking the strongholds of spiritual wickedness in high places, in all their forms, and in all places on earth, whether liberalism, rationalism, deism, or infidelity, and all the various forms of heathenism all over the world? To me it is clear, Moderator and friends, that we shall accomplish vastly more being united, than we can do being separated. My friends, can we not here set up a standard, inscribe on it "Truth and Righteousness," add display on all its ample folds the ensign of the "Lion of the tribe of Judah?" Christ is our great teacher; we must go forth under his instruction. He is the great Captain; we must go forth under his lead, and fight these moral battles, and then in the accomplishment,

"When that illustrious day shall rise
And all these armies shine,
In robes of victory through the skies,
The glory shall be thine."

[Applause.]

The Moderator. My dear brothers, Dr. Gurley and Judge Clark: It is with very great, and unaffected feeling that I now attempt to reply to the salutations and addresses which you have brought us—on the part of this Assembly. I count it one of the very principal happinesses of my life, that I should be the organ, in the providence of God, for communicating such suggestions as you have made to this Assembly, and to the Church which it represents. You will permit me to say that we regard it as an especial happiness that not only our honored brother, who has just addessed us, but that you yourself, (addressing Dr. Gurley), who have become known to us in connection with the conspicuous and honored position you lately held in the Capitol of this country, and more especially with the place you occupied during the closing hours of our dear and martyred President, should have been made the commissioners on the part of our brethren of the other Assembly to bring to us these salutations.

All that you have said, dear brethren, in regard to our existing, substantial unity, in respect to doctrine and order, and the desirableness or closer union, resulting in a true and proper organic union between these bodies, finds a response, as you already perceive, in the hearts of this Assembly. We know that it is true, as you yourselves will be pleased to acknowledge, that this body is Presbyterian, and thoroughly so in all respects, both as to its doctrine and order. I can answer for a very large number of the churches represented in this Assembly—those which are congregated so numerously in Central and Western New York, and I know those churches love the doctrines and polity of the Presbyterian Church. These two bodies, thus being Presbyterian, have been, in the providence of God, approaching each other during all these past years. We have come to feel more and more that we have great interests and great sympathies that bound us together, and in accordance with the demands laid upon us by the providence of God, and the influences, as we believe, of the spirit of God, which is calling for greater unity on the part of Christ's disciples, we have felt that we are called upon to meet all these kind advances which you are pleased to make, and to throw no obstacle in the way of such a union.

Our dear and honored brother from Ireland has told us, and we were rejoiced to hear, how they were there drawing new unification, and how those various minor details of difference were disappearing and melting away.

This is the tendency of the times—the mandate of Providence to us that the churches of Christ should be brought nearer to each other.

You have referred to the precious revivals of religion, with which your churches have been favored, and with which ours have been favored during the past year. In the portion of country from which I came, in carrying on these most precious revivals of religion, we have found it most fitting and proper to work with brethren of other denominations. Our Baptist and Methodist brethren have come in most kindly, and worked with us. They believed with us in the alienation of the natural heart from God, in the total depravity of human nature, and the necessity of the application of the atoning blood of Christ, and in justification by faith in his atoning sacrifice alone, and this has furnished ground enough for us to work together in promoting the interests of Christ's Kingdom. Now, if we can work together in this way, we of different denominations, it would certainly be a shame if we who are members of one family, and one household, should not be prepared to work together also.

I have regarded it for years as a foregone conclusion that these bodies were to be reunited, but as a Church, we had not hoped for the happiness of seeing this consummation, so much to be desired, brought so near to us, as it appears to be at the present time.

We accept, with the most hearty satisfaction, the sentiments you have expressed in regard to that substantial unity which exists between us, and the desirableness of a closer organic unity. There may be difficulties in arranging details for such a unity, but those difficulties can be obviated. You will permit me to say that it will be very desirable that neither you on your side, nor we on ours, should be discouraged, if there should be some want of sympathy with this tendency in individual cases in both Churches. We should be prepared to extend indulgence in such cases. We should not think it hard if there were some, indeed many of our own brethren who were not prepared for this unification. There may also be found some in the other branch of the Presbyterian Church, who are not yet prepared for such a union, but let us have indulgence towards these brethren.

Be pleased, dear brethren, to bear back to the venerable Assembly which you represent, the sentiments which you perceive upon the countenances and in the actions of these brethren, the sentiments of affection, confidence and friendship, and our earnest desire for the closest possible unity with you at the earliest possible day. [Applause.]

Rev. H. B. Smith, D. D., read the report of the Standing Committee on Church Polity in relation to overtures Nos. 5 to 15, on the subject of reunion of the two branches of the Presbyterian Church, from the Presbyteries of New York. 3d and 4th Dubuque, Greencastle, Athens, Steuben, Alton, Monroe, Keokuk, Long Island and Trumbull. All these Presbyteries, with different degrees of urgency, recommend to this Assembly to initiate or to respond to proposals looking to an entire reunion of the Churches represented by the two General Assemblies now in session in the city of St. Louis.

The General Assembly now in session in the Second Presbyterian Church of this city have also adopted resolutions appointing a committee to confer with a similar committee of our own Church in regard to the desirableness and practicability of such a reunion.

Your committee recommend to this Assembly the adoption of the following resolutions:

Resolved, That this Assembly tender to the Assembly representing the other branch of the Presbyterian Church its cordial Christian salutation and fellowship and the expression of its earnest wish for a reunion on the basis of our common standards received in a common spirit.

Resolved, That a committee of fifteen, nine of whom shall be ministers of the Gospel and six elders, be appointed to confer on this subject in the recess of the Assembly with the committee to be appointed by the other General Assembly, and to report the result at our next General Assembly.

Resolved, That we enjoin upon the committee, upon all our ministry and Church members, to abstain from whatever may hinder a true Christian fellowship, to cherish and cultivate this feeling and purpose, which looks to the peace and prosperity of Zion, the edification of the body of Christ and the complete union of all believers, especially of those living in the same land, having the same history and the same standards of doctrine and polity.

Resolved, That a copy of these resolutions, with the names of our committee, be sent to the other General Assembly, now in session in this city.

The report of the committee was unanimously adopted amid applause and demonstrations of great satisfaction.

Dr. Knox moved that a committee of five be appointed, whose duty it should be to nominate the committee of fifteen as proposed by the Committee on Church Prolity. Carried.

The Moderator appointed the following members of the Assembly on that committee.

Rev. Drs. Knox, Hatfield, Hotckins, Hon. John A. Foote and Judge Williams.

An invitation was announced to the members to visit the Public School Library.

The Chairman of the Committee on Devotional Exercises gave notice that there would be a farewell service in Dr. Nelson's Church this (Monday) evening, at one quarter before eight o'clock, in case the Assembly finished its business to-day.

Adjourned until Monday, May 28th, at 8 1-2 A. M.

Closed with prayer.

NINTH DAY—MONDAY, MAY 28, 1866.

MORNING SESSION.

Met at eight and a half o'clock.

First half hour spent in devotional exercises.

Minutes of last session read and approved.

Motion made in regard to $120,000.

On motion, Resolved, That the Assembly pledge the churches the largest possible amount of contribution for Home Missions, and that the Committee be authorized to go forward, relying upon the churches for all it needs.

Judge Allison presented the certificate of Rev. David Herron, of the Presbytery of Sharumpon, of the Synod of Northern India, as delegate from the Reformed Presbyterian Church of North America. Rev. David Herron was invited to address the Assembly, and did so, excusing the lateness of his appearance in the session, by the fact that his attendance seemed imperatively demanded at the Assembly of his own Church; presented the fraternal greetings of the Church he represented; adverted to the Synod with which he was connected in Northern India; they had 5 ordained ministers, 1 native, 3 licenciates, 10 students of theology, all ordained as Bible readers, and teachers, 200 native Christian communicants, old and young, and about 1,000 native youths under their instructions; expressed the pleasure of his own Church in view of the prospect of an early union between the two branches of the Presbyterian Church, whose Assemblies are now in session in this city, and its hope that the union would be upon such a basis that all the churches of the Presbyterian family, itself among the rest, could be joined therein.

The Moderator made fitting response.

The following resolutions were proposed by P. L. Davis:

Resolved, In view of the general prevalence and great increase of intemperance in this country, this General Assembly bear the following testimony, viz:

1st. We rejoice in the renewed diligence shown by the Church in correcting this great evil.

2d. That total abstinence from all intoxicating drinks as a beverage is demanded by every Christian, by the condition of society, the purity of the Church and the word of God.

3d. We recommend that on the last Sabbath of June next, ministers in our connection preach on the subject of Temperance.

A member proposed an amendment to the effect that the words "and the word of God" be stricken out, asserting that God required temperance but not total abstinence.

Amendment lost; resolutions adopted.

The standing committee on mileage reported, and their report was accepted and adopted, with the thanks of the Assembly to the Committee for their continued and arduous labors.

The report of the standing Committee on Sabbath Schools was then adopted, with the following amendment, viz:

That part of the report styling the Sabbath School the nursery of the Church, was changed so as to read a nursery of the Church.

The following gentlemen were then elected as Trustees of the Church Erection Fund for three years:

Dr. J. Fen. Smith, Dr. S. D. Burchard, W. A. Booth, Esq.

The following resolution was adopted:

Resolved, That a sum not less than $120,000 is necessary for the work of Home Missions during the coming year, and that the Assembly pledge the churches to all faithfulness and diligence in collecting that amount.

The following resolution was presented by Rev. Henry Fowler, and adopted:

Whereas, This Assembly, in its Deliverance on the state of the country, has affirmed the truth that "Our most solemn National trust concerns that patient race so long held in unrighteous bondage," and

Whereas, The education of the freedmen is essential to their endowment with all the rights and privileges of American citizens, and is promotive of a safe and permanent reconstruction; therefore,

Resolved, That the Churches be recommended to take up collections in behalf of the freedmen, supplementary to the regular collections sor Home Missions, said collections to be forwarded to such association, in behalf the freedmen, as, by the wisdom and integrity of its management shall best commend itself to the confidence of the congregations.

Dr. Knox of the special committee to nominate a committee of conference with the Old School Assembly reported the following names:

MINISTERS.

Rev. Thomas Brainard, D. D.
" Wm. Adams, D. D.
" E. F. Hatfield, D. D.
" J. F. Stearns, D. D.
" P. H. Fowler, D. D.
" J. B. Shaw, D. D.
" H. L. Hitchcock, D. D.
" R. W. Patterson, D. D.
" H. A. Nelson, D. D.

ELDERS.

Hon. Joseph Allison.
" E. A. Lambert.
" H. W. Williams.
T. P. Handy, Esq.
R. W. Steele, Esq.
W. H. Brown, Esq.

Report adopted.

A resolution was then adopted recommending the use of the Westminster Assembly Catechism in all Sabbath Schools where it was not already in use.

The following gentlemen were then elected as Trustees of the Presbyterian House for three years.

John A. Brown, Esq.; M. W. Baldwin, Esq.; S. H. Perkins, Esq.; Thomas Brainard, D. D.; E. E. Adams, D. D.

Dr. Smith, of the committee appointed to prepare a letter to the Free Church of Scotland, reported the following resolutions and letter:

The General Assembly of the Free Church of Scotland, in a letter bearing date May 30th, 1865, having proposed to us a closer fellowship by "occasional visits of accedited deputies" from our respective Churches, and the same proposal having been confirmed in the address of Rev. James McCosh, LL. D., therefore,

Resolved, That this Assembly accede to this proposal for an interchange of deputies on such specific terms as may hereafter be designated, and that two deputies be appointed to represent our Church at the next General Assembly of the Free Church of Scotland, in Edinburgh, May, 1867.

Resolved, That the committee having in charge the correspondence with the Free Church of Scotland be authorized to make this appointment in the name of the General Assembly.

Resolved, That we tender to the Rev. James McCosh, LL. D., our sincere thanks for the able and eloquent manner in which he has discharged his office as virtual, if not technical, representative of the Free Church of Scotland; that we offer him the assurance of our personal honor and regard; and that we pray for his continued and unceasing success and influence in the great and useful labors to which his life is devoted.

The committee to answer the letter addressed to our Church by the Free Church of Scotland, propose to the Assembly the following reply:

The General Assembly of the Presbyterian Church in the United States, (N. S.) in session in the First Presbyterian Church in the city of St. Louis, Missouri, May 28th, 1866, to the General Assembly of the Free Church of Scotland, greeting:

Dear Brethren: The most welcome letter of your venerable Assembly bearing date Edinburgh, May 30th, 1865, and subscribed by your Moderator, the Rev. James Begg, D. D., has been received by our Assembly with heart felt gratitude and approval. We warmly reciprocate your affectionate Christian salutations, and respond with lively emotions to your expression of sympathy and confidence, and to your proposals for a closer fellowship. Though separated by a broad ocean, we are bound together by no ordinary ties. No Church of another land has a stronger hold than yours upon our love and honor. The one reformed faith is our common heritage. We express that faith in the same symbols; we have, in essence, the same Presbyterian polity; and we are equally engaged in kindred Evangelical labors at home and abroad. There are also between us many ties of a common ancestry, and we venerate the names of your early reformers; our ministry are still instructed by the reading of your great divines; our faith is strengthened by the bright example of your heroic martyrs, who fought a good fight for religious and civil liberty; and in your special conflicts and sacrifices for a free Church, you have had, these twenty years, our constant and warmest sympathy. We honor the high wisdom and extraordinary liberality which have made you prosperous and strong and the new testimony you have given to the self-sustaining power of the Christian Church, when contending for its righteous liberties. It is a good thing that the sacred fire kindled by the old covenanters is still burning in the heart of Scotland, and that their flaming torches have been handed down from sire to son. In all these things, dear brethren, we rejoice and will rejoice.

It is then, with no ordinary satisfaction that we have received your proposal for an interchange of accredited deputies between our Churches, as occasion may serve. As you will see by an accompanying minute, this Assembly has unanimously resolved to appoint two such deputies to represent us before your venerable Assembly in May, 1867. They will, in due time, be named and commissioned, and we bespeak for them a fraternal welcome. We also invite you to send deputies to our own Church, at its next session in the city of Rochester, in the State of New York, May, 1867, assuring them a most cordial reception.

We have this year been favored with an address made in your behalf by the Rev. James McCosh, L.L. D., of Belfast, Ireland, who came to us with ample testimonials from several of the honored ministers of your Church. Already known to us by his elaborate and thoughtful works, so important in relation to the great conflict between Christianity and some of the modern infidelity, he hardly needed any external recommendation to insure him an attentive hearing. His eloquent and sympathetic words have drawn us to you by the cords of a common faith and love.

The sympathy you express in the calamities and sufferings brought upon us by our recent war, in the assassination of our beloved and venerated President Lincoln, a martyr to the cause of human freedom, and your fervent congratulations upon the abolition of slavery throughout our States, as well as your wise suggestions, derived in part from your British experience in respect to the future condition of the negro race, call for our grateful recognition. These things have weighed, and still weigh upon the mind and the conscience of this Nation. God has guided us by his wonder working Providence, bringing good out of evil. He has sorely chastised us for our National sins, and we bow in penitence, yet in trust, beneath His mighty hand. He has indeed caused the wrath of man to promote His own high purposes of grace and wisdom, and in the difficulties and perplexities that still beset our path, in the vast social and political, as well as religious problems, that we are called upon to solve, we humbly invoke, and rely upon His wisdom and grace. Here, too, we feel assured that your prayers will mingle with ours.

You say that "the divergence of sentiment and action formerly between us, on the question of slavery, has now ceased," and "as there is really nothing now to prevent a complete and cordial understanding between the British and the American Churches, we take the earliest possible opportunity of giving utterance to this conviction and desire of our hearts." We thank you for these words; we unite with you in the petition for the removal of all estrangement and the establishment, not only of our old, but even of a better and nearer friendship. And because of this our common wish and purpose, we are emboldened to say to you, with the utmost Christian frankness, as well as affection, that during the progress of our recent and terrible struggle for the very life of our nation, involving as it did by a vital necessity the emancipation of the slaves, we have at times been deeply pained and grieved by the apparent indifference of the British Churches to the great principles and the manifest moral issues that were here at stake. From the beginning of the great rebellion, our American Churches, as with one voice, proclaimed the real nature of the contest.

Our own Assembly never faltered or wavered in the declarations, that it was essentially a conflict between freedom and slavery, and that national unity was necessary to national freedom. And we shall ever more regret that in our darkest days, when we were in travail in the throes of a new birth, and when sympathy would most have cheered our hearts, we had, with few exceptions, such light encouragement from those so nearly allied to us in faith and in the fundamental principles of civil and religious liberty. But those dark hours are past, nevermore, we trust, to return, and we are glad that the clouds are dispersing, and the mists vanishing away, and that we are coming to see eye to eye, and to know better each others' hearts and minds.

You allude to the interest with which you "shall watch the future history of the negro race within our borders." The views of this Assembly on some of the points herein involved are set forth in a declaration just adopted on the state of the country, a copy of which will be sent to you. The freedom of that unhappy and long-suffering race has been bought at a great price of blood and treasure. Slavery is now prohibited by an amendment to the Constitution. The civil rights of the freedmen have been secured by law. Other guarantees will doubtless follow in due time. This nation is under the most solemn responsibility as to the future destiny of this class of its citizens. Meanwhile, our chief reliance must be on those social, moral and religious influences which alone can make men fit for freedom and truly free—and which alone can fully retain the Union of the States, and bind us to together in a common brotherhood.

In these troubled times, even when the horrors of war were upon us, the Great Head of the Church has given us fresh occasion to magnify his faithfulness. Our American Churches, no less than our Republic, have emerged from this conflict still strong in their faith and order. The principles of our American Christianity have received a new vindication. Our benevolent institutions have been constantly increasing. And we are now girding ourselves for the great task that is laid upon us, especially in our Southern and Western States, among our freedmen and our emigrant population, and against the progress of Romanism, of materialism, and of a false rationalism, in humble reliance, as we trust, upon the grace and wisdom of Him who will not leave us if we lean upon His mighty arm and follow the guidance of His all-wise Providence. An increased desire for Christian union, too, has been kindled throughout our land. Many of our Churches, also, have been visited with fresh outpourings of the spirit of grace, showing that the Law is at work amongst us as of old.

We, too, desire with you in a special manner a closer fellowship between the Presbyterian Churches in our own and other lands. We are glad to see the movements in this direction in England and Scotland, and in your colonial dependencies. The same spirit is at work among ourselves. The two great branches of the Presbyterian Church in this country are drawing nearer together; this year they have touched each other, and each of our Assemblies has appointed a Committee of Conference and Reunion. Our Deputies will inform you of the progress of this desirable object. And we fervently hope that here, as never before, all Christian Churches may forget their lesser differences and unite together, so far as possible, in the great work of the Lord.

Dear brethren, beloved in the Lord, we send to you these our Christian salutations, beseeching you to pray for us. We commend you unto God, and to the word of His grace. May the one Great Head of the Church bless you with all spiritual blessings. May our Churches and our lands live in amity and unity. May we all live for the Glory of God in the kingdom of His Son, our Lord, two whom be praise forever. Amen.

The resolutions and draft of the letter were adopted by the Assembly.

Judge Allison, called up the report of the special committee, (an abstract of which has been published) on Overture (of the last Assembly) No. 14, and pending an argument in favor of the adoption of the report, the Assembly took a recess until afternoon. Closed with prayer.

AFTERNOON SESSION.

Opened with prayer.

Judge Allison concluded his argument.

Dr. Hogarth opposed the adoption of the report.

Judge Williams addressed the Assembly in favor of the report.

Hon. W. J. Cornwall opposed the report.

The report was adopted.

Dr. Clarke, of the special committee, appointed to confer with Rev. Mr. Miller in regard to the establishment of a manual labor college for freedmen in North Carolina, reported that after an ample conference that they had agreed that the matter had not sufficiently matured to come before this body, and asked that the committee be discharged.

Voted that the committee be discharged.

Dr. Knox moved that the Committee of Conference have power to fill such vacancies as may occur during the recess of the Assembly. Carried.

Dr. Hatfield offered the following resolution:

WHEREAS, Mr. Joseph M. Wilson, of Philladelphia, has for some time been engaged in collecting information regarding the histories of Presbyterian Churches, to be published in his Presbyterian Historical Almanac, therefore,

Resolved, That the Ministers and Elders of the Churches under the care of the General Assembly be earnestly requested to co-operate with Mr. Wilson in his valuable labors in behalf of the Church.

Dr. H. remarked as follows:

I scarcely need say a word in regard to our friend and brother, who has distinguished himself in his love for the Presbyterian Church, not only in his valuable labors for years past, but also in the expenditure which he has so freely subjected himself to, in publishing his Presbyterian Historical Almanac, and various other matters pertaining to the welfare of the Church, and I propose we hear Mr. Wilson in regard to these propositions which he has to make to the Assembly, and what he proposes to accomplish by his labors.

Mr. Wilson, after thanking the Assembly, stated that he had issued a circular making inquiries to obtain the history of the Presbyterian Churches throughout the world. These circulars would reach every Church, and from the magnitude of the work he needed the active co-operation of the ministers, the elders and the people, as it must be evident that, in order to place upon record a full, reliable and well arranged history of every Presbyterian Church, reduced to one general plan, classified by Presbyteries and Synods, replete with statistics suggestive and interesting. All intelligent Presbyterians must feel and manifest to a certain extent a personal interest in its success. But this effort, to obtain those histories upon such a large scale, is only a further development of the idea that prompted me to begin the Presbyterian Historical Almanac, which I did a number of years ago. That work, comprehending within the limits of a large volume the annual operations of the Presbyterian Church throughout the world, commends itself to the earnest attention of the Church. I began it because I felt that much of the difference of opinion existing in the Presbyterian Church arose from the want of information about each other, and this annual volume proves that however they may differ outwardly, in the Almanac they are a unit. In practice they may "be distinct as the billows;" in the Almanac they are "one as the sea." As my observation and experience increased, I enlarged the plan of the work and introduced my Biographical Department, in which is recorded the memories of all the Presbyterian ministers who die during the year. It has been a melancholy reflection upon the Church to think that at times it did seem as if the righteous died and no man took it to heart. I felt that it was wrong to let the grave rob us of all we hold most dear, and by placing upon the pages of the Almanac a full, impartial and faithful record of the lives of those whom God had called to enter upon the saints' everlasting rest, we could profit by their example, and it would be a source of gratification to those who come after us. In a further expansion of the Almanac I included tables, entitled "The Clerical Record of the Brethren," then the histories of the various Boards and Seminaries, and to render it still more effective as an element of power in the Church I introduced the *Manse* question and the Almanac is committed to the great plan of inducing the Churches to erect Manses, so that Presbyterian ministers will have comfortable homes for their families free of rent. As the work grew upon me I felt that the time had come when the histories of each Presbyterian Church ought to be recorded, and this labor, in which I am engaged as a servant of the Churh, I hope will meet with favor. If there are any persons in the Church who have any suggestions to make by which the objects of the Almanac can be fully carried out, they will have their views carefully considered; and I hope that Presbyterians, especially those in my native land, will join and sustain the Almanac, which has a reputation in Scotland and Ireland. Apart from the labor, the expense attending such a work can only be met by a generous support, such as I have, up to this time, only been able to hope for, surely a work which places in the hands of its friends a yearly photograph of every branch of the great Presbyterian family should be sought for, especially in these days of union. If we would unite *wisely*, our zeal must be in accordance with our knowledge. The Almanac meets all the requirements of the occasion. When replies are received to the circular referred to in the resolution, I intend publishing them in the Almanac, arranged by Presbyteries and Synods. These Synodical Histories will be accompanied by ecclesiastical maps, showing the location of each Church, the boundary of each Presbytery and the extent of the Synod.

Mr. Wilson concluded by hoping that these efforts would awaken that active co-operation so necessary to carry out the object contemplated, and if this appeal would meet with that result, then would he feel that his visit to St. Louis had not been in vain.

Rev. Dr. Niles followed in an earnest appeal to his brethren, not only of the ministry, but the eldership. He had supposed that from the known value of the work that it had been as successful as it was meritorious. And he finds that such is not the case, and is ashamed to own it. This ought not to be so, and Presbyteries owed to themselves to sustain an enterprize so worthy and so useful.

The Moderator, on putting the motion, asked the privilege of urging upon his brethren the absolute necessity of giving such a circulation to the Almanac as to place it above the fear of failure. He was somewhat familiar with Mr. Wilson's plans and details and he has been amazed at the extent of his knowledge on subjects pertaining to the Presbyterian Church; not only does his Almanac put into the hands of its friends all that relates to the current history of the Church, but the histories of the seminaries, the memories of our deceased brethren, the accounts of our missions, and every thing having any direct or remote tendency to develop a love for the Presbyterian Church—and then the thoroughness of his efforts comprehending every conceivable item of interest and value, necessary for a developement of his plans. He is one of the most remarkable men of the times, and an honor to the Presbyterian Church, and he ought, as he must be sustained.

The report was adopted.

A letter was read from Dr. Porter, of Brooklyn, who had been appointed by the Synod of the Reformed Dutch Church, at their meeting last year, to attend this Assembly, in which, after expressing his regret that circumstances prevented his presence in person, he presented to the Assembly the salutation of fraternity in Christ.

The report of the Delegate to the Presbyterian Assembly that met at Pittsburg last year, was then read.

The report was adopted.

Dr. Knox stated that he was not present when the resolutions on the subject of temperance were passed, or he would then have submitted a resolution he would now propose; made a few remarks in regard to a National Temperance Society organized in New York, by which Drs. Hatfield, Humphrey and himself had been appointed commissioners to this Assembly, and then offered the following resolution:

Resolved, That we regard the New National Temperance Society with favor, as well adapted in the form, vigor and scope of its organization, to grapple with the great national sin of intemperance, and as such commend it to the faithful prayers, liberal support and earnest co-operation of our Churches.

Adopted.

The report of the Committee to nominate delegates to corresponding bodies was read and adopted, as follows:

Old School General Assembly—Principal, Rev. E. D. Morris, DD.; E. D. Mansfield, LLD. Alternate, Rev. E. P. Pratt, DD., and F. V. Chamberlain, Esq.

Cumberland General Assembly — Principal, Rev. Henry Little. Alternate, Rev. Joseph Chester.

United Presbyterian General Assembly—Principal, Rev. H. L. Hitchcock, DD. Alternate, Rev. Richard Craighead.

General Synod Reformed Dutch Church—Principal, Rev. Joel Parker, DD. Alternate, Rev. A. E. Campbell, DD.

General Synod Ref. Presbyterian Church—Principal, Rev. E. J. Richards. Alternate, Rev. T. J. Shepherd, DD.

Maine General Convention Congregational Churches—Principal, Rev. Stephen Bush. Alternate, Rev. A. B. Lambert, DD.

Vermont General Association — Principal, Rev. J. H. Noble. Alternate, Rev. E. A. Buckley.

New Hampshire General Association—Principal, Rev. D. H. Allen, DD. Alternate, Rev. A. E. Kittridge.

Massachusetts General Association—Principal, Rev. F. S. McCabe. Alternate, Rev. Henry M. Field, DD.

Connecticut General Association—Principal, Rev. Conway E. Wing, DD. Alternate, Rev. F. Ralston Smith.

Wisconsin Presbyterian and Congregational Association—Principal, Rev. George J. King. DD. Alternate, Rev. E. A. Pierce.

Union of Evangelical Church of France—Rev. A. Eldridge, DD.

Mr. Wiswell stated that Rev. E. B. Walsworth, of the Presbytery of San Jose, California, met with an accident in New York, on his way to the Assembly. His commission was duly forwarded.

Dr. Taylor read the report of the standing Committee on the Narrative, of which the following is an abstract:

Eighty-nine out of the 110 Presbyteries on the roll had forwarded their annual reports for examination. 113 churches were reported to have enjoyed revivals of religion during the previous year, and in response to the prayers of the Churches, 214 revivals were specially mentioned this year. The subjects of the work had been mainly youth between twelve and twenty. Many of them had commenced in, but they had rarely been confined to the Sabbath Schools. The chief agencies of the work had been "the ordinary means of grace." One Evangelist is mentioned in the narratives—Rev. E. P. Hammond—whose labors are spoken of with gratitude as very abundant and faithful. The revivals had been most fruitful in churches under the care of settled pastors. The ingathering is still going forward. Six Presbyteries give an aggregate of 1,048 additions by profession. A number of Churches had doubled their membership, several had received over two hundred on profession of faith, since their revivals began. The eye of faith could see many promising omens of the continuance of the work. Three thousand five hundred conversions were reported by our home missionaries; fifty Churches have been organized, and many old churches resuscitated. Noticeable in the narratives is a strong desire for reunion with the other branch. In some places, where the Spirit of God has been poured out the most abundantly, the work of revival begun in an open and bold attack of all the most prominent vices of society. The Sabbath schools were mentioned as being in a very flourishing condition. Churches had generously contributed in the efforts for religious education among the freedmen.

The benevolence of the Church is shown to be somewhat on the increase; aggregate of its contributions larger than during any previous year, yet the standard of giving was below the ability of the Church as a whole. The lack of means to build churches is the great drawback in the frontier States. Looking at the condition of the Church from either a worldly or a religious standpoint, its prosperity appears greater than at any previous period.

The following ministers have died during the year:

Rev. Milton Kimball, of the Presbytery of Schuyler.

Rev. O. P. Hoyt, D. D., of the Presbytery of Kalamazoo.

Rev. Samuel Lee, of the Presbytery of Cleveland and Portage.

Rev. Truman Baldwin, of the Presbytery of Onondaga.

Rev. Abraham Luce, of the Presbytery of Long Island.

Rev. Horner B. Morgan, of the Presbytery of Watertown.

Rev. Joseph L. Riggs, of the Presbytery of Wellsborough.

Rev. Jacob Tuttle, of the Presbytery of Pataskala.

Rev. Edmund D. Holt, of the Presbytery of Winona.

Rev. J. Holmes Agnew, D. D., of the 4th Presbytery of New York.

Rev. Daniel A. Abbey, of the Presbytery of Tioga.

Rev. A. D. Hollister, of the Presbytery of the District of Columbia.

The report was adopted, and the Assembly adjourned to meet in the evening for farewell services.

EVENING SESSION.

Was devoted to religious exercises. Rev. T. H. Robinson, of Harrisburg, Pennsylvania, made the opening address, in which he set forth the beauty of Christian love, and foreshadowed the grand union of Christians of all names, but who hold the common faith of the evangelical world.

Rev. Dr. Hogarth, of Detroit, Mich., spoke of the strong social feelings created by the intercourse with the people of this city, and the kindly associations awakened by meeting so many of the brethren whom he had only known by reputation. He spoke of the early labors of the pioneers of our Christianity, who preached and planted the Gospel in this Western country long years ago.

Rev. Dr. Knox, of Rome, New York, took a general view of the peculiar relations existing between the Assembly and the good people of St. Louis. Referred to the influence of Hamilton College, New York, and his early recollections of the pastor of the church, Dr. Nelson, and the noble stand taken by him, sustained as he was by his people. He spoke of the hospitality of the citizens of St. Louis, and of their great kindness.

Rev. Dr. Wiswell, of Wilmington, Delaware, offered the following resolutions, which were adopted unanimously:

Resolved, That this General Assembly take peculiar pleasure in here publicly recording their warmest gratitude for the large and generous provision made for their comfort and enjoyment by the people of St. Louis, in circumstances of great difficulty, owing to the unexpected pressure of so many delegates from other religious bodies as their guests.

Resolved, That we specially tender sincere thanks to the Committee of Arrangements, the Honored Pastors of the First and North Presbyterian Churches and their excellent people, for their thoughtful regard and provident arrangements for all our sessions, and their kind and persistent efforts to make their homes our own during our stay; to the choir of the First Church for their valuable services; also to the President of the Iron Mountain Railroad Company for the pleasant excursion to Pilot Knob and his personal attention on that occasion; to the Mercantile Library Association, to the President of the City University, to the Board of Directors of the Girls' Industrial Schools, for invitations to visit these respective institutions; to the Superintendent of Public Schools for copies of the last report; to the St. Louis Transfer Company for the generous offer of their omnibusses; to the four steamboat companies who have furnished dinners from day to day to many of our members from a distance; to the several railroad companies who have granted commissioners a reduced fare over their roads; to the press of this city, and especially to the Missouri Daily Democrat, for faithful reports and a full report of our proceedings in pamphlet; to our beloved and excellent Moderator for the promptness with which he has so cheerfully, ably and impartially presided over our deliberations, and as we say farewell to the people with whom it has been our delightful privilege to mingle in heavenly places in Christ Jesus,

Resolved, That it is in all our hearts to pray constantly that grace, mercy and peace from our common Lord and Saviour may ever remain with them.

Rev. Dr. Nelson addressed the Assembly in behalf of the people of St. Louis, of the members of the congregations, of the interest manifested by the pastor and members of the North Presbyterian Church to carry out the known hospitality of the people; he spoke of the important events now transpiring in our Church, of the prospective union of the two branches of the Church.

Dr. Hatfield, of New York, spoke of his early ministerial career, which began thirty-three years ago in this city of St. Louis, where there was only one Presbyterian Church in the city, and but 7,000 inhabitants within the corporate limits of this great and beautiful city of the West; that when he sat in the General Assembly of 1835, it was as a Commissioner from the Presbytery of St. Louis, the only Presbytery between the Mississippi and the Pacific ocean, and recollecting these early scenes, his heart is filled with the tenderest emotions, and now to see that in this city there are two General Assemblies of the Presbyterian Church, he could not fail to exclaim, "what hath God wrought."

The Moderator, Dr. Hopkins, addressed the Assembly in a few pertinent remarks, the minutes were read and approved, the roll called, and, on motion, it was

Resolved, That this Assembly be dissolved, and that another General Assembly, convened in like manner, meet in the Presbyterian Church, Rochester, New York, on the third Thursday of May, 1867.

Closed with prayer and singing the Doxology, and the benediction by the Moderator.

Thus closed the interesting session of the General Assembly of the Presbyterian Church, (New School.)

We are requested to correct our report of Dr. Campbell's remarks, as published on Monday, as follows:

On the fifth line it is said "it had a fund of $30,000." It should be "we have received during the past year $30,000 from New and Old Schools, and $40,000 from Congregationalists."

On line fifteen from top an anniversary in "New York," not "Italy." The Catholic priests in Sienna, Italy, published the pamphlet and sent it to this country.

About forty, fifth line 70,000 less as reported by the Bishop of Milan came to mass and confessional than the year previous.

Line fifty, Mr. Constantine of Athens, Greece.

Mr. Trumbull went out under the Seamen's Friends Society.

ADDRESS BY REV. Z. M. HUMPHREY, D.D.,

Delivered at an Evening Meeting of the New School Presbyterian Church.

Of the ideal representations of our blessed Lord, one of the most impressive has been given us by that commentator of the pencil, Aug Scheffer, and is known by the title *Christus Consolator.* It represents the Savior as seated in the center of a group of men and women, all of whom have been drawn about him, apparently, by some irresistible attraction. Each face is marked by a strong individuality. Each heart revealing itself through the features has its peculiar want; all turn for satisfaction to the same Being. On one side are representative figures of the Jew, Greek and Barbarian; on the other are figures representing men of different occupations. The three Marys are there; the penitent thief holds his dagger in hands folded over a contrite heart; a woman, perhaps the Magdalin, leans her head upon his arm as if bathing it with tears; at his feet bows a mother over the dead body of her babe; the slave kneeling stretches out his manacled hands; the warrior with broken blade beside him sinks back in death, while the chains of mortality fall from him at the touch of Jesus. One only is turned from Christ. It is a poet, his head crowned with the laurels which did not assuage his great sorrow, and who, mourning, refused to be comforted. The scripture beneath the picture is, "He hath sent me to bind up the broken hearted, and to proclaim liberty to the captives." It might have, perhaps, better been, "There is neither Jew nor Greek; there is neither bond nor free; but ye are all one in Christ Jesus."

This picture is, indeed, a vivid interpretation of the latter scripture. The union of believers with Christ is perfect, notwithstanding all outward diversities—notwithstanding all inward peculiarities of nature. It is common to represent this union by the figure of a circle, from whose circumference all lines converge to a common center. The figure does not accurately answer to the fact, for the unity thus presented is mechanical rather than organic. Our Savior himself represents this union as vital. His figure is that of living branches joined to a living vine. Christ is equally *the* Savior of all, and affords to each the strength and sympathy he needs. His nature is so broad and full that in Him all are satisfied. He is divine, and has all the perception of Omniscience to enable him to appreciate our wants. He is human, and has all that quickness of sympathy which is needful, that he may completely identify himself with us, "being made in all points like as we are," having tasted of experiences like ours, that he might succor us in every extremity. Christ was not in his human nature a perfect man, simply. He was a representative of all men. He was more than "many sided;" he had in himself all that is peculiar to man in all his conditions. In him there is "neither Jew nor Greek," but both. Men differ in constitutional peculiarities, in habits of thought and of feeling. There is that in Christ which fits him to be the most helpful friend of each. In him was the sum of all temperaments, in him were the qualities of all forms of manhood. This was indeed a matter of necessity that he might be the Savior of all. He must be able to understand all our peculiar temptations to sin, that he might be our sacrifice, our advocate, our friend. The record of his life shows that he was capable of occupying any position. We are constituted with peculiar aptitudes. One is an orator, one a poet, one a mechanic by natural gift. He would have excelled in anything which the best of us can do but poorly. He had all the fervor of the poet, all the graces of the orator, all the taste of the artist, all the sagacity of the statesman, all the capacity of the artisan. This is abundantly evident from his words, his counsels and his habits. He could suit himself to all whatever their peculiarities. In him was "neither bond nor free." He had liberty for the one and sympathy for the other. In him was "neither male nor female." The peculiarities of both sexes were blended in him. He had all the qualities which make man most manly, all that make woman most womanly. He was loved by Mary and Martha as if he had been a sister. Lazarus could ask for no more in a brother. He had the stuff in him from which warriors are made, yet there was that gentleness in him which induced women to bring their children to him as if He himself were a mother. He provided with a woman's thoughtfulness for the wants of the hungry multitudes on the shore of Genessaret, and then, when a woman would have entreated him to seek shelter and rest, he went away into the mountains to spend the hours of darkness amid the rocks in prayer. Men and women loved him with an equal devotion. The sisters of Bethany turned to him for comfort in their affliction, and the impulsive but manly Peter was ready to die in his defense.

Thus in him is all that any might wish. I have thought it providential that there is no authentic portrait of Christ in existence. It seems strange at first that no artist should have ever reproduced the likeness of so remarkable a Being, but there is no reliable portrait. That said to have been copied from the handkerchief of the "holy Beronica" is spurious; the story of Beronica is but a legend. The intaglio preserved as a likeness has no valid authority. The very description of the Savior ascribed to Publius Lentulus is a forgery. Why have we nothing to make the features of Christ familiar to us, as are those of the great men of history? Because we are to form our own ideas of this our personal Savior and should only be confused by any traditional representation of him. Now, every man may shape for himself a conception of Jesus, answering in every line and feature to his own ideal. Each is his own artist and may paint in colors and after forms which are borrowed from his own heart. Nay! better than any portrait. Each of us may have his personal, living Savior, in whose face is just what is noblest or sweetest to us all, a perpetual guest in his heart.

Such being the nature of the union of the disciple with Christ, we have next to consider the union of the disciples in him with each other. Such a union logically follows from that which has already been described, for if all are one *in* Christ, all are one *with* him. Each of us joined to Christ partakes of his nature, and thus all are one. When the magnet is presented to the filaments of iron, all the particles cling by a natural affinity to the attracting pole. Each of the filaments is imbued with the magic virtue of the magnet. All together are imbued with the same subtle principle. So all believers in Christ are one *in* him and one *with* him.

By such a union, my brethren, are we united to Christ and to each other as we gather about this table to-day. He is here, and it is as if we could see him and hear from his blessed lips, as he extends his hands in benediction over us all, "Ye are all one in me." Not even the imaginary line of denomination separates us. We are one. And here we may commune with each other without restraint—as we also commune with Christ. At this table all difference of speech are forgotten. When persons of different nations come together at a table with sharpened appetites for food they do not remember that in the language of each there is a peculiar word for *bread*. They eat and are satisfied, without discussing whether the French, the English or the Asiatic word is the most expressive. So, as we gather here with true hunger of heart, we do not think of our peculiar forms of statement, if we have any, respecting this bread of heaven; we eat and are filled.

Families widely scattered gather about the thanksgiving board in some New England home, to which with true migratory instinct they turn when the season of the annual festival returns, and forget all their varied tastes and habits. One has come with face browned by the sun upon the tropical wave. Another has been breathed upon by the frosts of the Pole. Another has driven his plough along the hill-side. Another has come from the dusty counting-house of the city. All sit down together as one. All bend as one to receive the blessing of a common parent. This is our thanksgiving table to-day. We have been separated as a family. The common Father looks down upon us in love. Some of us are kindred by blood. I cannot forget that you, sir, (turning to Dr. E. P. Humphrey,) are my brother in the flesh. When we sit down together at the table of our mother, or stand at the grave of our sire, do we ever think of any possible differences which may have separated us in our ecclesiastical relations? Why then should we here? We will not. We do not. We will all come to this our thanksgiving table—our table of communion—to-day, and rejoice that in Christ there is neither Jew nor Greek, there is neither bond nor free, there is neither male nor female, but we are all *one*.

LETTER FOR WHICH REV. MR. W. M. FERGUSON WAS EXPELLED FROM THE OLD SCHOOL PRESBYTERIAN ASSEMBLY.

The following is the letter to the Columbus (Ohio) Statesman, for writing which Rev. Mr. Ferguson was expelled from the General Assembly of the Old School Presbyterian Assembly:

The debate in the Assembly ran higher to-day, or rather *lower*, than ever. It was reserved for Mr. Galloway, of Ohio, to cap the climax of vulgarity and demagogueism. He certainly outdid himself in low allusions, false assumptions, bitter invective, personal abuse, and in every other mean thing that could characterize an orator who appeared to be at the same time both a fool and a fiend!

I grant this is strong language, but not a whit more so than the truth will warrant. His manner was monstrous! A dancing monkey's motions were graceful to it. Indeed it was awful! Sublimely ridiculous. His twistings and bodily contortions, could they have been photographed, would have furnished comic almanac-makers with an almost limitless number of grotesque samples for all time to come. Besides his disgusting egotism—his self-righteous laudations—his canting use of Scripture—his boasting, dirty insinuations—in a word, his scurrility and blackguardism exceeded anything of the kind it was ever my painful misfortune to hear.

The fact is, he disgraced himself—his Presbytery—his Church—this Assembly, and religion generally, by his long, vile, illogical and most wickedly impassioned harangue. It brought a tinge of shame on the cheek of his best friends. Some who had no personal acquaintance with him thought he had a "Highland gill" in his cheek. But it is declared that he is a radical temperance man. This most unfortunate exhibition of vulgarity and malignity was called forth by a resolution of Dr. Boardman on yesterday, on the unwarranted and wicked course being pursued by the majority of the Assembly in regard to Gov. Wickliffe, Jr., Stewart Robinson and Dr. Wilson, Delegates from the Presbytery of Louisville, because said Presbytery did publish to the world a strong statement on the illegal procedure of the General Assembly of last year in Pittsburgh. Mr. G. boldly affirmed that "a word spoken against the Assembly was treason, and the speaker a traitor;" that "Dr. Boardman was a traitor, and his speech yesterday treason, and till he washed his hands of the blood of this hellish crime, he (Mr. G.) would never sit down with him at the Lord's table." These were his words. His speech, as published in the Democrat, may be bad enough: but as that sheet is exceedingly radical, and the only one that pretends to give verbatim reports phonographically taken, and as Mr. G.'s friends were shocked at the outlandish indecencies and fallacies of this unfortunate affair, some of the more vulgar and blasphemous parts may be omitted.

But I weary you. Mr. Galloway surely forgot himself to-day. He has disgraced himself forever in the estimation not only of Christian gentlemen, but in the opinion of the ungodly world. Why he did so no one can tell. It was unprovoked and unexpected. He was not called to order by either member or Moderator, as the latter requested the Assembly to permit "great latitude" of discussion. It was as good as a monkey show to the populace—some of them hissed, others cheered!

Thus we go—*go to pieces* as a Church of Christ. It is alarming to witness how rapidly and superficially the legitimate business of the Assembly is passed over, and how eager many are to "take up the unfinished business" relating to Louisville Presbytery, &c. It is painful to say it, but many think and say that this Assembly has done far more against the interest of true religion in this city since it convened last week than the big horse races that have been in progress here for some time. What a curse Radicalism is!

But I weary you. So, for the present, I close, sorry that the great State of Ohio has been disgraced by the only two really unsufferably Radical and disgustingly vulgar speeches in this Assembly so far.

PROTEST.

The undersigned, for themselves and others, respectfully protest against the entire proceedings of the General Assembly concerning the Louisville Presbytery and the signers of the "Declaration and Testimony,"

1. The summary exclusion from this house of the Commissioners of the Louisville Presbytery, under the operation of the previous question, without allowing them or their friends one word of defense or explanation, was, in our judgment, a usurpation of powers not belonging to the General Assembly, a gross invasion of the rights of the Presbytery, an act of oppression towards the Commissioners themselves, and a violation of those principles of justice and equity which every deliberative assembly, and especially a Court of Jesus Christ, is bound to hold inviolate. For a proper analysis of this procedure we refer to a protest of certain members of this body, to be found in the minutes of the 22d ult., and in most of the reasons for which the undersigned concur.

We lay the utmost stress upon this point, because everything that followed pertaining to this business must be judged in the light of the fact that the Assembly was passing upon the conduct of men who, by its act, not their own, were not present to defend themselves. The allegation that the Assembly offered to hear them when a report was introduced proposing to visit upon them the severest penalties, can be of no avail; for in the resolution of expulsion it was their Presbytery which was arraigned, and they could not properly return to their seats without consulting their Presbytery. Nor is it believed that there was a single member of the Assembly who expected them to plead at the bar of a court which had opened their case by ejecting them from their seats unheard, and three days after, voted down a resolution to readmit them to their seats until their case should be disposed of.

2. Throughout the entire course of these proceedings, and pervading the elaborate arguments of the majority, it was maintained that this was a "judicial case," and that these brethren were "on trial" before the Assembly. Whereas the notorious fact is that they had never been arraigned and tried; that neither in Presbytery nor Synod had there been any mention of formal charges, of citations, witnesses, or any of the steps essential under our Constitution, to a judicial process. The Form of Government and the Digest show that it is not competent to a judicatory to take up a case *judicially* on "Review and Control." And this plea is further barred by the fact that the records of the Presbytery of Louisville were not before the Assembly. As the General Assembly has no original jurisdiction in cases of offense, the whole proceeding, in so far as the case was treated judicially, was, in our judment, irregular and unconstitutional.

3. The case was biased by the action of a Convention called together to consider these very matters on the eve of the Assembly's meeting, and sitting, it was currently reported, with closed doors. The inflammatory memorial sent to the Assembly by this Convention (some of them members of the Assembly) discloses a state of mind on the part of the authors ill suited to calm and impartial deliberation upon such questions as were involved in this case.

4. The severity of the judgment visited upon these brethren was greatly disproportioned to their offense No one had charged them with heresy, or with immorality. The principles affirmed in their pamphlet are substantially the principles incorporated in our Confession of Faith and held by our whole Church. They believed that General Assemblies had violated the principles, and especially that the Assembly of 1865 had undertaken to impose certain laws upon the Church in derogation of the plain provisions of our constitution. In this belief they are sustained by the Synods of New Jersey and Philadelphia, by several Presbyteries, and by numerous ministers and laymen of the Church. Their error lay in the measures by which they sought to redress these evils. We do not justify them in these measures. We condemn them. But we insist that they should have been allowed to plead their own cause without its being prejudged, as it was by their instant exclusion from their seats on the second day of our session. We insist that they should have been allowed time to review their proceedings, and cancel (if so disposed) the offensive terms they had applied to the General Assemblies of the Church. We do not object to their being required to do this, and to answer to their Presbyteries and Synods, and to the next Assembly as to what they may have done in the premises; but we regard the spirit and terms of their exclusion from all the church judicatories, (the Session excepted,) until the next Assembly, and the contingent dissolution of Presbyteries, as needlessly harsh measures, pregnant with evil to the Church. And we fortify this conclusion by the fact, fully established in debate and controverted by no one, that one of the Presbyteries now represented in this house, and even one or more of the members of this very Assembly, had used language and performed acts quite as pregnant with rebellion towards the Assembly, without being subjected to the slightest censure.

5. We protest against these measures because they will inevitably tend, as we believe, to foment strife and alienation. The Church needs repose. Rent asunder by the war and agitated with conflicting passions, it requires to be soothed and cemented and comforted. The final action of the Assembly, as connected with the previous measures and debates, (for the whole must be taken together,) can hardly fail to bring about another secession or separation, to divide congregations, to instigate lawsuits, to diffuse and prolong a bitter but hitherto local controversy, to create wide-spread dissatisfaction with the deliverances of the Assembly and to alienate many of the best friends of our institutions. With one accord, our several Boards have appeared before us deploring the falling off in their receipts and the decay of sympathy in their operations. We greatly fear that the measures against which we protest will aggravate these evils.

6. We believe that the interests of the Church and of the country are identified. And thus believing, we protest against these proceedings as adapted to impair the capacity of the Church for its legitimate and beneficent work, and to increase and perpetuate the jealousies and animosities which still vex the land.

7. And finally, we protest against these ordinances, because they are likely to defer, if not prevent, that Christian co-operation between the Presbyterian Churches, North and South, which is so needful to the evangelizing of our people, and especially to the religious instruction of four millions of freedmen, most of them now as sheep without a shepherd.

In General Assembly at St. Louis, Mo., June 2, 1866.

HENRY A. BOARDMAN,
J. S. McCLELLAN,
J. E. SPILMAN,
CHAS. A. MARSHALL.

www.ingramcontent.com/pod-product-compliance
Lightning Source LLC
LaVergne TN
LVHW011238110826
845150LV00006B/1673
9781425513825